KĀ TAOKA HĀKENA

TREASURES FROM THE HOCKEN COLLECTIONS

Kā Taoka Hākena

Treasures from the Hocken Collections

Edited by Stuart Strachan & Linda Tyler

OTAGO UNIVERSITY PRESS

Treasures photography by Bill Nichol

Book design by Jenny Cooper

DONORS

The following have contributed to the cost of producing this book:

Alexander McMillan Trust, R.J. Anderson, Colin Ashby, Brent Southgate and Mary Atwool, Rex and Miriam Austin, Bill and Natalie Baylis, Gary and Margery Blackman, R.H. Booth, Lindsay and Eleanor Brown, Lois Burleigh, George Chance, Peter Chin, Ian Church, Les Cleveland, William Cockerill, Chris Collins, Community Trust of Otago, Doreen Cowan, Mayford Dawson, Dunedin City Council, Eion and Jan Edgar, Annette Facer, Ian Farquhar, Friends of the Hocken Collections, Sylvia Girvan, Joy Green, George Griffiths, Professor Jocelyn Harris, Shirley Hay, Holcim (NZ) Ltd, Professor Peter Holland, Rosemary Hudson, Mark Hughes, Lorraine Isaacs, David Kitchingman, Professor Helen Leach, Frank Leckie, Russell Lund, E.E. MacFadyen, Graeme and Eunice Marsh, E.J. McCoy, Jock McEldowney, John McIndoe, Stuart McLauchlan, J.M. Neuman, Val Parata, Gordon Parsonson, Perpetual Trust Ltd, Thomas K.S. Sidey, Dr Mark Stocker, Professor Ray Stone, Stuart and Jean Strachan, Ruth Taylor, The Wayland Trust, Trustees Executors Ltd, V.E. van der Hurk, Jan Warburton

Otago University Press
PO Box 56 / Level 1, 398 Cumberland Street, Dunedin, New Zealand
Fax: 64 3 479 8385. Email: university.press@otago.ac.nz
Website: www.otago.ac.nz/press

First published 2007

ISBN 978 1 877372 40 7

Printed through Condor Production Ltd, Hong Kong

Contents

Preface

A distinctive feature of some great universities is their possession of important research libraries donated by private collectors. One thinks of examples such as Thomas Bodley's gifts to Oxford, the Parker Library at Cambridge, or the John Carter Brown Library in the USA. The University of Otago has been fortunate in this respect. Thomas Morland Hocken's munificent gift formed the nucleus of research collections that are unmatched at any other university in Australia or New Zealand.

This publication marks the centenary of the Deed of Trust signed by Dr Hocken in 1907. He wanted the University to maintain his collection for the benefit of the people of New Zealand. Today the Hocken contains not only books and manuscripts, but also newspapers and journals, maps and plans, paintings and drawings, photographs, and music. The unifying themes are the history and culture of New Zealand, the Pacific and Antarctica, with a particular emphasis on southern New Zealand.

For many years following Hocken's death, the University was small and strapped for cash. Nevertheless, the commitment to maintain the Hocken Library was honoured and its contents grew more than a hundred-fold during its first century. The expansion and enrichment of the collections are due not only to purchases but more especially to the generosity of numerous benefactors who have followed Hocken's example. The collections outgrew their first two homes and are now housed in a superb building opened in 1998 as the University's main project to celebrate the 150th anniversary of the Otago Settlement.

Unlike most research libraries, that new building has the words 'Open to the Public' proudly emblazoned on its walls. Yet while scholars and researchers come from afar to use the Hocken, I suspect that many people do not realise what treasures it contains. For example, few New Zealanders would know that the Hocken has one of the most important collections of New Zealand art in existence anywhere – including modernist paintings. It contains over 220 works by Colin McCahon.

I hope that this delightful publication will whet people's appetites and illustrate the breadth and richness of the Hocken Collections today. The editors and contributors, as well as the Otago University Press, should be congratulated. Documentary heritage collections form an essential basis for much research and education in the humanities. This book shows that they can also be a source of fascination and pleasure.

David Skegg

University of Otago, Dunedin, 2007

A Labour of Love: Dr Hocken and His Collection

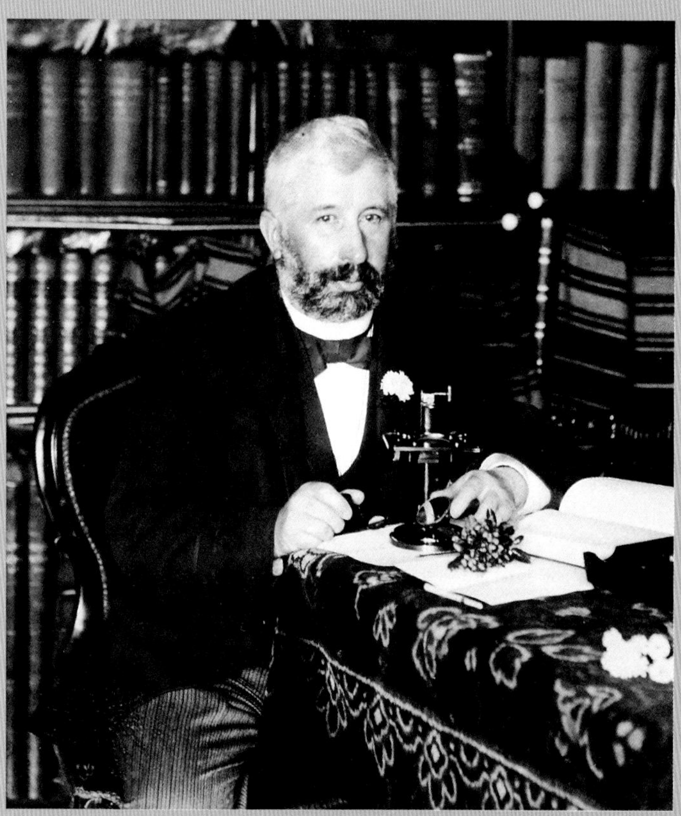

Dr Hocken in his library at home, 'Atahapara', studying a botanical specimen, 1893. This photograph was almost certainly taken by his wife Bessie, a skilled photographer. Album 43. Original Collection.

Rachel Barrowman

Thomas Morland Hocken arrived in Dunedin in February 1862, eight months after Gabriel Read discovered gold at Tuapeka. Hocken was not a prospector of gold, but he was to become a prospector of another kind – for the written traces of New Zealand's history, which would in time form a library that he was not unjustified in claiming to be 'without doubt the best in the world in N.Z. literature'.[1]

Hocken was born on 14 January 1836 in Rutlandshire, England, the son of Joshua Hocken, a Cornishman and Wesleyan minister, and his Yorkshire-born wife, Anne Richardson. Initially 'Tom' to his family, by the time he was in his teens he had chosen to be known as Morland; in New Zealand he would be universally known as 'Dr Hocken'. He was educated at Woodhouse Grove School, a Methodist school near Leeds, before undertaking medical training, a not unusual choice of profession for the younger son of a clergyman. He was first indentured to an apothecary in St Helen's, Leeds; attended the Newcastle upon Tyne College of Practical Science in 1854–56, and was then apprenticed to a surgeon; and studied for a session at the quite prestigious Ledwich School of Surgery and Medicine in Dublin. It was a revolutionary time in medical science and practice – of advances in areas including microscopy, clinical chemistry, the use of the stethoscope and diagnosis by physical examination, anaesthetics and antiseptic surgery – and in medical education. He gained his MRCS and LSA (certifying him as a Member of the Royal College of Surgeons and a Licentiate of the Society of Apothecaries) in 1859.

Despite the prospect of a partnership with his Newcastle master, Septimus Rayne (so he recorded), in October 1859 Hocken signed on as a ship's surgeon, possibly for health reasons.[2] He made two return voyages to Melbourne, on the clipper *White Star* and the steamship *Great Britain*. On his third trip out he obtained his discharge in Melbourne in January 1862, inspired to seek his fortune in New Zealand, he later said, by the thousands of miners heading for the Otago goldfields. He arrived in Dunedin on 22 February, at the age of 26.

Within a few days of his arrival Hocken had set himself up in general practice in Princes Street, moving three years later to premises in Rattray Street, above the El Dorado Tea Rooms. His practice quickly thrived. There was no lack of need for doctors in 1860s Dunedin. The usual evils of the nineteenth-century new colonial town – disease and drunkenness, dirt, disorder and decay – were multiplied and magnified by the influx of miners and other fortune seekers. Between December 1861 and December 1864, Dunedin's population swelled from nearly 6000 – double what it had been six months earlier, when Read made his find – to approaching 16,000. There were a dozen doctors in the town in late 1862; twenty-seven a year later.[3] Throughout the 1860s Hocken regularly earned at least £10 a day, his fees often paid in gold dust or nuggets. In 1864 he gave evidence before the Sanitary Commission, established in response to alarm at the town's rapidly deteriorating state of health. At a time when the nature of disease was being much debated, his evidence, in which he stressed the dangers of inadequate drainage and sewerage and insanitary water supplies, while indicating that he adhered to the long-accepted miasmic theory of the cause and spread of disease was also consistent with the newer, and not yet widely accepted, germ, or contagion, theory.

Over his forty years in practice in Dunedin, Hocken became a prominent and successful member of the town's medical profession, respected for his integrity and appreciated for his geniality. He was by nature gregarious, generous, industrious and kind. He was family physician to many of Dunedin's élite, showing particular skill in treating women and children. He held a number of honorary positions, such as honorary surgeon to the Dunedin Hospital Board, the Otago Benevolent Institution (which he helped to found in the 1860s), the Dunedin Naval Brigade and the Artillery Volunteers; he was founding president and a long-serving executive member of the Otago Medical Association, and inaugural president of the New Zealand Medical Association when the provincial organisations amalgamated in 1896. In 1876–77 he was briefly appointed lecturer in clinical surgery at the University of Otago (despite having been one of the dissenters on the committee that recommended that the university establish a medical school), although it appears that he never actually took up the position.[4] He was also a long-serving member of the university council.

Not shy of self-promotion, in December 1862 Hocken had put himself forward for, and the following month was appointed to, the position of Dunedin coroner. He was to perform this role for twenty-two years, and enjoyed the growth in his public profile and power, as well as associated controversy, that it brought him. His two most celebrated cases came in the 1860s, within just a few years of his appointment: the sinking of the *Pride of Yarra* off Blanket Bay in 1863, with the loss of twelve lives; and the murder by poisoning of Mrs Jarvey by her husband, ferry master Andrew Jarvey in 1865, a case which involved the exhumation of the body and the execution of the accused. Alongside such famous instances, there was the routine and regular occurrence of accidental and suspicious death by suicide (strychnine was the preferred method), alcohol, drowning and fire. In the decade from 1864 Hocken presided over 274 inquests (which were usually held in the nearest hotel, there being no public morgue).

Controversy also attended Hocken's appointment generally. Lawyers criticised his lack of legal training. (Although it was a few years after he had relinquished the office, it is tempting to see Hocken's costuming himself as a member of the judiciary for a fancy dress ball at Government House in January 1890 as evidence of his sense of irony.)[5] Conversely, there was the question of a potential conflict of interest and opportunity for self-advancement. In 1885 he was removed as coroner, to his great chagrin, after legislation was passed preventing physicians from holding the office while engaged in private practice. This was the result of a long campaign – which Hocken believed was a personal vendetta – by the Otago politician and labour law reformer J.B. Bradshaw, who had first introduced a bill into Parliament in 1876, supported (or, it has been argued, led behind the scenes) by Millen Coughtrey, Dunedin medical practitioner and the founding professor of anatomy and physiology at the university. There had always been animosity between Hocken and Coughtrey. Hocken was not the only coroner who refused the governor's request for resignation and was consequently dismissed. But the episode illustrates a less attractive element of his personality: a tendency to self-righteous obduracy, deriving from a combination of professional pride, self-assurance and a prickly sensitivity (the latter, it might be thought, a product of his diminutive height: he was just five feet two).

Hocken's public associations also included the Anglican church: he became a pew holder at St Paul's in 1862, contributed building funds towards the cathedral and was later a churchwarden and lay canon. Why he abandoned the evangelical Methodism of his upbringing is not known, but there may have been an element of strategic thinking. In England, Anglicanism was the religion of the establishment. In Dunedin, Hocken found his circle among the Anglican middle and upper classes, in a predominantly Scottish and Presbyterian settlement. He quickly rose socially in the town, becoming a member of the Dunedin Club in 1863, putting himself on committees and joining campaigns.

The streak of opportunism in his character that had brought him to Otago also saw him engage in property speculation, with the purchase of thirty-four sections in the paper town of Mansford, in the West Harbour area, for example, and other properties as far as Blueskin Bay and Balclutha, and business investments. At his death his estate was valued at some £26,000, and included shares in more than a dozen companies. He was also a founding director of the Otago Daily Times and Witness Newspapers Company. By 1870, within a decade of his arrival, he had established himself well enough to commission the design and building of a handsome, two-storeyed house on a prime section in Moray Place – across the road from First Church – which he named 'Atahapara'.

•

'[S]mall in stature, rotund, bustling, purposeful', E.H. McCormick neatly described the doctor.[6] The opportunism, energy and ambition that Hocken displayed in his professional and social life he also applied to his collecting.

Despite his relative material success, Hocken did not acquire the wealth to support the habit of a nineteenth-century gentleman collector. Among the wealthy British middle classes of his time, book collecting was a well-enough established cultural tradition to support its own literature of guidebooks and manuals, and one which certainly could be, and was, indulged in – or rather from – the distant colonies by those with the inclination and means, such as the Wellington merchant Alexander Turnbull and the governor George Grey. Together with Hocken, these form the pre-eminent three of New Zealand's nineteenth- and early twentieth-century collectors. Hocken, however, did not acquire the rare Milton editions of Turnbull, nor the medieval manuscripts and incunabula that distinguished the library of George Grey. He was not a connoisseur collector. Nor was this his interest. Rather, Hocken's collection was a working collection, accumulated to support his passionate interest in New Zealand history.

Where that interest came from, apart from an inquisitive

mind, a collector's instinct and a romantic imagination, is not known, but from the 1870s it became an enduring one. In 1869 he was a founding member (or at least was a member within the year) of the Otago Institute, which thereafter regularly and conveniently held its meetings, soirées and conversaziones at 'Atahapara'. He gave many lectures to the Institute, including a chronological series of fourteen lectures between 1880 and 1896 which were collected and published posthumously as *The Early History of New Zealand* (1914); others were printed in the Dunedin newspapers and the *Transactions of the New Zealand Institute*. His one monograph, *Contributions to the Early History of New Zealand* (settlement of Otago), was published in 1898. As both an historian and a collector Hocken was essentially an annalist, enthusiastically engaged upon what his friend Justice Chapman described as 'the assemblage and assimilation of accurate facts'.[7] Yet it was not the dry record but the 'romance' and 'singular charm' of the colony's early story that inspired his quest.[8]

Hocken built his collection through tireless fieldwork. He corresponded and travelled widely, meeting and comparing notes, and soliciting historical material, information and stories from participants and fellow recorders. He also visited the places where history had occurred. '[I]t was scarcely possible,' Chapman remarked after his death, 'to mention any person connected with the history of New Zealand or the literature relating to New Zealand without his disclosing that he had a minute knowledge of the family and affairs, and character and disposition referred to' (a somewhat frightening proposition).[9] His surviving travel diaries record eight major journeys in the North Island between 1879 and 1905, and he had certainly travelled north earlier: an 1877 lecture described two trips to the Hot Lakes district. In 1881 he first visited George Grey at his home on Kawau Island, after correspondence with him about his lecture – and a treatment for Grey's constipation – and he continued to visit and correspond with the ageing politician on both historical and medical matters over the remainder of the decade. (Grey was not the only person with whom Hocken traded medical advice for information and items for his collection.) But Otago and the southern provinces were his immediate stamping ground; 'He had, one feels,' wrote McCormick, 'walked over and identified every spot connected with the founding of Otago.'[10]

The collection Hocken amassed eventually numbered 4300 printed volumes,[11] along with copious manuscript and other material; far fewer than the 55,000 volumes in Alexander Turnbull's library, but yet, as he himself estimated it, one 'of great value – monetarily worth many thousands, intrinsically unique and inestimable as far as connected with New Zealand history'.[12] It comprised books, pamphlets, newspapers, manuscripts 'and other litera scripta',[13] official documents, maps, plans, drawings and pictures, collected for their documentary rather than their artistic value. Hocken was not the completist Turnbull was, but there were notable areas of strength in voyage literature, the journals and accounts of the seventeenth- and eighteenth-century explorers and scientists, especially Tasman (including eighteen accounts of the first voyage); missionary records, especially those of the Church Missionary Society and

Samuel Marsden; and Otago history. The newspapers – 200-odd bound volumes – and pamphlets included a significant number relating to early New South Wales and Tasmania.

Hocken first met Alexander Turnbull on one of his northern excursions in 1894 (when Turnbull found the doctor 'an entertaining little man')[14] and they maintained a relationship of friendly rivalry; Hocken was, Turnbull observed, rather stingy with his duplicates, always seeming to have some stashed away to trade. It was a year earlier that Turnbull had declared his intention to collect '[a]nything whatever relating to this colony …', a classic statement of the colonial collector's mission; and it is true that, in differing ways, Turnbull's collecting was a personal response to the colonial experience. Like Hocken he corresponded widely, personally soliciting material and debating its provenance. But he remained a gentleman collector, and an armchair collector, continuing to buy his books principally through his London agents. He sought first editions and rare specimens, where Hocken would be content with copies. He bound his books in elegant morocco or calf-skin, while Hocken's bindings were sturdy, plain and serviceable. Hocken's collection was notably stronger than his in manuscript material. Turnbull's motivation remained that of the bibliophile; Hocken's, the historian.

In common with Turnbull, Hocken also acquired a rich collection of Māori and Pacific artefacts: cloaks, carvings, tiki and mere. As early as 1865 he had exhibited Pacific Island costumes, along with moa bones, at the New Zealand Exhibition in Dunedin. Among the prizes of his artefact collection were the carved Tu Moana house panels exhibited at and purchased after the 1890 New Zealand and South Seas Exhibition, for which Hocken was secretary of the Early History, Māori and South Seas committee and lent many of the items displayed. His Pacific interests saw him make a visit to Fiji and Samoa in 1898, the fruits of which included a paper on Fijian fire walkers and some volumes from Robert Louis Stevenson's Vailima library in Apia.

It might seem curious that, despite the active intellectual interest that underlay his collecting, and although among his most regular correspondents were those stalwarts of the Polynesian Society, S.P. Smith, Elsdon Best, and Alexander Shand on the Chatham Islands, Hocken did not (as Turnbull did) join the society, which, after it was founded in 1892, quickly became a centre of the country's developing indigenous intellectual life. Perhaps it was just that, as an historian, his interest lay more in the enterprise of colonisation, in the exploits of missionaries and surveyors and government and New Zealand Company officials, than the ethnographic purpose of the Polynesian Society. Or it may have been that he saw the Polynesian Society as primarily a Wellington group, whose meetings he would find difficult to attend. (Or perhaps he was not asked to join, and was too proud to request membership.)

An earlier interest was botany and natural history. He had been awarded a silver medal for botany at the Newcastle College of Practical Science, and collected botanical specimens on his travels around New Zealand. The glasshouses and garden were one of his joys at 'Atahapara'. In 1882 he made a trip to Britain, one result, and possibly one purpose, of which was his election as a Fellow of the

Linnean Society later that year. He was to take no active involvement in the affairs of the society, however. Hocken enjoyed and sought the signs of public distinction, such as becoming a member of such a society.

•

It was possibly on this trip that Hocken met Elizabeth Mary – Bessie – Buckland, whom he married in July 1883. This was not his first marriage. In July 1867 at Waikouaiti he had married Julia Simpson, the daughter of an Edinburgh lace maker. How they had first met is not certain, though Hocken had been in Waikouaiti in 1866 investigating a scarlet fever outbreak. For Hocken it was not a happy marriage. Julia is believed to have been an alcoholic, and died of liver failure in 1881.

Bessie, in contrast, was the daughter of a prominent Auckland merchant family. She had had a European education, and was a talented artist and photographer; her album of sketches of Hocken's Māori artefacts is one of the small delights of the Hocken collections. She was also a talented linguist: it was Bessie who, on a summer holiday at Kinloch on Lake Wakatipu in 1894, translated from the old Dutch Tasman's 1642 journal relating to New Zealand, which Hocken published in the *Transactions of the New Zealand Institute* in 1895 – a contribution he acknowledged coyly, when at all. (His own knowledge of foreign languages

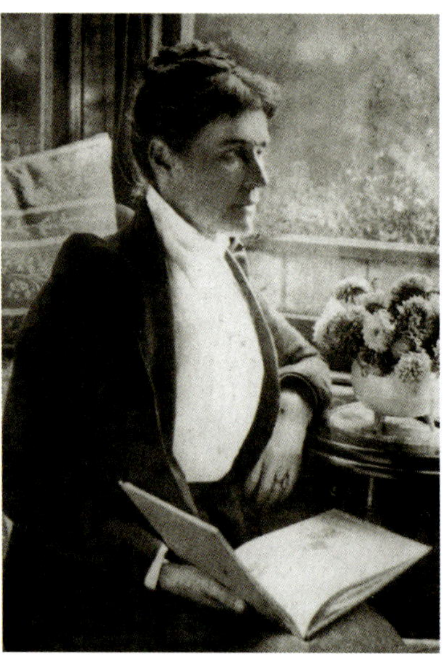

Elizabeth (Bessie) Mary Hocken (1848–1933), in every way TMH's helpmeet, was a fine photographer, artist, and important benefactor in her own right. Photographer unknown. Hocken Collections (S07-122).

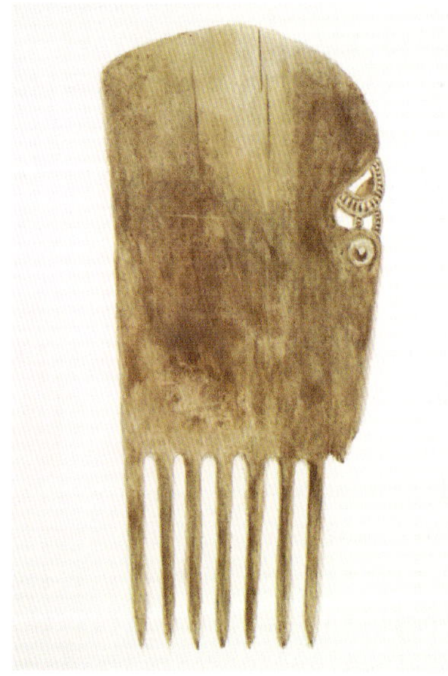

Painting of an unattributed comb by Bessie Hocken. *Mrs Hocken's Sketchbook*. Hocken Collections (GH685).

apparently did not even extend to everyday French.) But he was devoted to Bessie, 'to whose counsel and help I owe so much', as he did acknowledge in the dedication to *Contributions* ...; as he was – perhaps excessively, in the way of the middle-aged first-time father – to their daughter Gladys, who was born in 1884.

In August 1901 Hocken, Bessie and seventeen-year-old Gladys left for an extended visit to Britain and the Continent. They were away for three years (which was rather longer than Bessie and Gladys may have wished) on what was primarily a foraging expedition for Hocken, to hunt down 'all the records of New Zealand's early [pre-1840] days of which I have been able to discover any trace'.[15] They sailed via Japan, where Hocken wanted to test a theory (derived from a statement in Tasman's journal) about the common origins of the Japanese and Polynesian races (it was, he decided, without foundation);[16] and Egypt, where he did two stints as a medical officer on a houseboat on the Nile (and Bessie sent home photographs for publication in the *Otago Witness*). In Britain Hocken sought out surviving members of the families of missionaries and officials – the ninety-four-year-old widow of Bishop Selwyn in Lichfield, for example, the widow of Edward Shortland, the daughters of Captain Hobson – retrieving, or if that was not possible copying, any records in their possession. Back in London he attended lectures, dined at the Reform Club and socialised energetically (the Bucklands were well connected).

But Hocken's major labours in England were in the Public Record Office, sorting, straightening and copying the records of the New Zealand Company, the whereabouts of which he had first inquired after in 1882 (through Francis Dillon Bell, New Zealand's attorney general in London, whom he knew personally: Hocken was the family doctor). He spent some two months in 1903 reading and taking notes on 'every document' with 'the exception of vouchers and accounts etc',[17] having offered his archival services in the hope of securing their patriation to New Zealand – and any duplicates for his own collection. In this he was disappointed. The Colonial Office and Public Record Office declined to hand over the records, but did eventually agree to give away the duplicates. This material, selected by Hocken at the request of the New Zealand government, was finally despatched to New Zealand in 1909. It went not into Hocken's library, however, but was kept by the government to be the foundation of a proposed national archive collection. Hocken was doubly piqued, learning also of the papers' arrival in the country through the press.

For his own collection Hocken did secure the papers of the Canterbury Association (which he had also been chasing for many years), from Lord Cobham, the son of Lord Lyttelton. At some stage he also acquired from William Cargill's son all of Cargill's Otago Association papers. But the greatest prize of his British prospecting tour were the missionary records he rescued, by his own account, from neglect and decay in the basement of the Church Missionary Society offices in Salisbury Square (some money was paid), including, most significantly, the letters and journals of Samuel Marsden. On the way back home he spent several more months on the trail of Marsden in New South Wales, where he uncovered further material that had been 'crumpled and thrust into an old cornsack, a bottle of red ink having apparently been then broken over them, and were then thrown into a coal or wood house, where hens, mice, spiders, and fungus abounded', he told a reporter for the *Otago Witness* – imbuing his researches with the same romance and heroism he found in the tales of the colony's past.[18]

•

Hocken's 1901–04 expedition effectively marked his retirement from doctoring, and from most of his public activities, aside from the Institute and the university council. His remaining years were devoted to history and his collection. Projects that would remain uncompleted were the 'one or two' volumes of provincial history that he had always intended would follow the Otago one; a new edition of H.G. Robley's *Moko* (for which he secured the publishing rights and purchased the original plates and additional notes in 1908); and – his first priority – an edition of the letters and journals of Marsden. In the autumn of 1905, at the age of sixty-nine, he went on an 'historical ramble' around the far North 'in the footsteps of' Marsden, visiting the old mission stations, the 'very spot' where Marsden had first preached the Gospel and that where the Treaty of Waitangi was signed, the battle sites of the northern wars and the scene of the burning of the *Boyd*. He lamented that the missions had fallen into ruin and decay and 'indeed, the halo of the past, the ancient attractions, the old landmarks of history had almost vanished'.[19] But the work evidently did not proceed very far.[20]

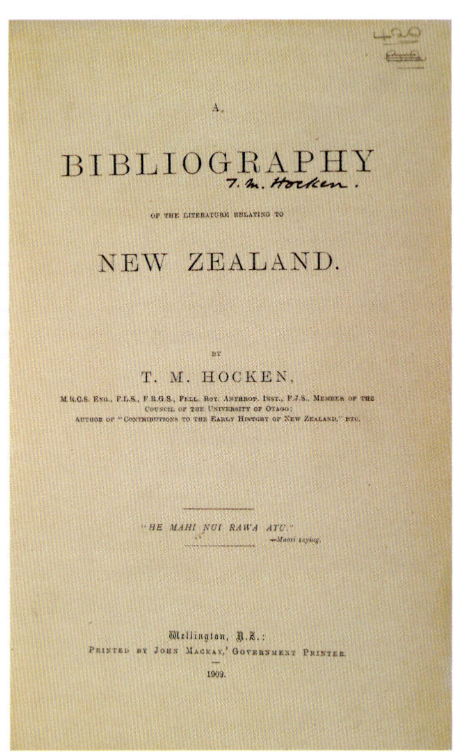

A

BIBLIOGRAPHY

T. M. Hocken.

OF THE LITERATURE RELATING TO

NEW ZEALAND.

BY

T. M. HOCKEN,

M.R.C.S. Eng., F.L.S., F.R.G.S., Fell. Roy. Anthrop. Inst., F.J.S., Member of the Council of the University of Otago;
Author of "Contributions to the Early History of New Zealand," etc.

"HE MAHI NUI RAWA ATU."
—Maori saying.

Wellington, N.Z.:
Printed by John Mackay, Government Printer.

1909.

Dr Hocken's major scholarly achievement was his *Bibliography* published in 1909. It remained the standard reference for sixty years. This copy was presented to him by John Mackay, the Government Printer, on 15 July 1909. Original Collection.

On his return from Britain, Hocken also busied himself with putting the finishing touches to the bibliography that he had been working on since at least the 1880s, and which, along with his library, constitutes his major contribution to New Zealand scholarship and history. He approached the government about publication in 1906. After a personal inspection of his collection by the Parliamentary librarian, Charles Wilson, who declared it 'far and away the most comprehensive collection of works dealing with the early history and literature of this colony' (and hoped the government might in due course purchase it for the General Assembly Library), and his equally enthusiastic report on the bibliography ('There is nothing like this work in print that in any way approaches it for practical value'),[21] Hocken's

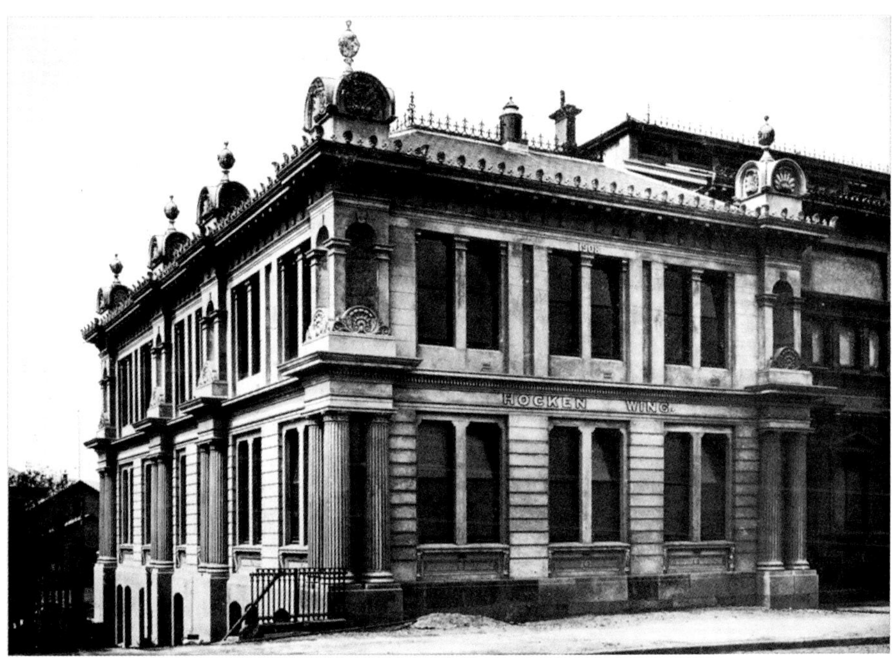

Designed by Dunedin architect John Burnside, this handsome addition to the Otago University Museum was built to house Dr Hocken's gift. Opened on 31 March 1910, it remained the main premises of the Hocken Library until 1979. Photographer unknown. From *Otago Witness*, 6 April 1910 (507–119c).

Bibliography of the Literature Relating to New Zealand was published by the Government Printer in 1909. It would remain the standard reference for more than sixty years.

Along with its comprehensiveness (which included, for the first time, attention to literature in Māori, of which he had 'taken infinite pains' to collect a significant amount), Hocken's bibliography is also distinguished by its annotations: the 'many little sidelights, biographical references, dates, and other special points' and 'attempt … made to run throughout a thread of historical interest'.[22] His satisfaction at its appearance was marred only by what he perceived as 'jealous' and 'curious' criticism in a review by James Collier, a former government librarian, whose own bibliography, *The Literature Relating to New Zealand* (1889), Hocken's surpassed and superseded. With some justification, Collier complained that Hocken had incorporated notes from his own work without acknowledgement.

Hocken first made public mention of his intention to gift his library to the people of New Zealand in 1897, in an apparently off-the-cuff remark: Bessie did not learn of it until she read a report of a meeting called to discuss the establishment of a public holiday to mark the anniversary of the Otago settlement in the paper the next day. During the meeting Hocken had expressed his admiration for the handsome Auckland Public Library (opened ten years earlier) to which Grey had given his collection, and suggested that if a similar building were to be erected in Dunedin he would do the same. The matter was not followed up for some years, however – nor had he intended it to be; he was still making much use of his library himself – although he did inquire in 1899 about the conditions under which the Australian collector David Scott Mitchell was bequeathing his collection to the Public Library of New South Wales.

He reiterated the offer in 1904 on his return from abroad. It was another two years before a campaign to raise public subscriptions for a suitable building got under way, in 1906: plans were then afoot for a new public library, and in response to a suggestion that Hocken's collection be incorporated into it (which he rejected on the grounds that the proposed building was too small, unsuited and on the wrong site), he advised that if his offer was not taken up seriously within eighteen months he would be compelled to

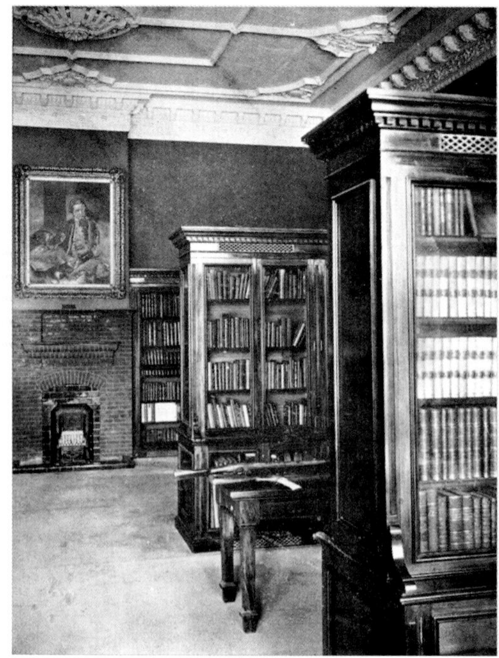

Interior of the Hocken Library at the University Museum. Captain Cook's portrait is above the fireplace. *Otago Witness*, 6 April 1910. Hocken Collections (S07-119d).

withdraw it.[23] A sum of £2800 was raised by subscription, and matched by a pound-for-pound subsidy from the government, and an architect commissioned to design a new wing for the Otago University Museum to house Hocken's collection in the manner he felt it deserved.[24] The deed of gift was signed on 2 September 1907. The bequest included all of the printed volumes and manuscripts, maps, plans, drawings and pictures; but not the bulk of the artefacts. These had been acquired by the museum by gift and purchase progressively since 1891.

The Hocken Wing of the museum was formally opened by the governor, Lord Plunket, on 31 March 1910. Hocken himself, however, was too ill to be there. He had been suffering from cancer (of the oesophagus) for the last few years, and died three weeks later, on 17 May at 'Atahapara'. In a letter read out at the occasion, in which he outlined the contents of the collection, and his expectation of its proper maintenance, he explained his creation of it in terms of loyalty, patriotism and public-spiritedness (as befitting such an occasion); but more simply, and perhaps honestly, as 'a labour of love'.[25]

NOTES

1 Hocken to J. Hall-Jones, 20 Feb. 1906, quoted in Bagnall, 'The rival bibliographers', pp. 23–4.

2 A comment he later made left it unclear whether he had gone to sea following two or three years of poor health, or left sea for this reason. He would also once remark that he could not stand the cold European winters.

3 Wood, *Dirt*, p. 226, n. 16; A.G. Hocken, 'Dr Hocken of Dunedin', ch. 7, p. 11.

4 The appointment was terminated apparently after he failed to obtain the appropriate (university) recognition from Britain of his qualifications; though his quibbling over his salary may also not have pleased the university council.

5 *Otago Witness*, 23 Jan. 1890, p. 41.

6 McCormick, *The Fascinating Folly*, p. 33.

7 *Otago Witness*, 25 May 1910, p. 65.

8 T.M. Hocken, *Bibliography of the Literature Relating to New Zealand*, p. iii; *Otago Witness*, 27 Dec 1905, p. 54; Hocken to George Grey, 24 Jan 1881, quoted in McCormick, *The Fascinating Folly*, p. 37.

9 Ibid.

10 McCormick, *The Fascinating Folly*, p. 365.

11 In fact about 6000 items, when one allows for those bound in the pamphlet volumes.

[12] Hocken to Mark Cohen, 2 July 1906, printed in *Otago Witness*, 18 July 1906, p. 63.

[13] Ibid.

[14] Alexander Turnbull to Robert Turnbull, 22 Feb. 1894, quoted in Barrowman, *The Turnbull*, p. 17.

[15] *Otago Witness*, 6 Jan 1904, p. 26.

[16] Hocken had a fascination with Japan, as did many of his contemporaries, and on his visit purchased books and prints.

[17] Hocken to Colonial Office, 22 Oct. 1903, quoted in Strachan, 'Not quite half a loaf', p. 5.

[18] *Otago Witness*, 27 Dec. 1905, p. 54.

[19] *Otago Witness*, 5 April 1905, p. 15.

[20] A five-part series of lectures on Marsden's life was, however, published in the *Otago Witness* in December 1905–January 1906.

[21] C.O. Wilson to J. Hall-Jones, 22 Feb 1906, quoted in Bagnall, 'The rival bibliographers', p. 25.

[22] T.M. Hocken, *Bibliography of the Literature relating to New Zealand*, p. v.

[23] Hocken to Mark Cohen, 2 July 1906, *Otago Witness*, 18 July 1906, p. 63.

[24] He also stipulated that a 'proper librarian' be appointed: 'an archivist – a man of culture, a man with some predilections for historical research; in short, a man who would be more than a librarian in the ordinary sense of the word' (*Otago Witness*, 6 April 1910, p. 15).

[25] *Otago Witness*, 6 April 1910, p. 15.

REFERENCES

Bagnall, A.G., 'The rival bibliographers: James Collier and T.M. Hocken', *Turnbull Library Record*, 1 (2), November 1967, pp. 22–31

Barrowman, R., *The Turnbull: a library and its world*, Auckland: Auckland University Press, 1995

Dr Hocken's Collection, 75th anniversary exhibition catalogue, Dunedin: Hocken Library, University of Otago, 1985

Hocken, A.G., 'Dr Hocken of Dunedin: a life', unpublished manuscript

Hocken, A.G., *Dr T.M. Hocken 1836–1910: a gentleman of his time*, Dunedin: Hocken Library, University of Otago, 1986

Hocken, T.M., *Bibliography of the Literature Relating to New Zealand*, Wellington: Government Printer, 1909

Hocken, T.M., *Contributions to the Early History of New Zealand (settlement of Otago)*, London: Sampson Low, Marston and Company, 1898

Hocken, T.M., *The Early History of New Zealand*, Wellington: Government Printer, 1914

McCormick, E.H., *The Fascinating Folly: Dr. Hocken and his fellow collectors*, Dunedin: University of Otago Press, 1961

Rodda, L., 'Calendar of Dr T.M. Hocken's personal letters and documents preserved in the Hocken Library, University of Otago', 1948

Ross, J.C., 'Thomas Morland Hocken', in W. Baker and K. Womack (eds), *Nineteenth-century British Book-Collectors and Bibliographers*, Gale Dictionary of Literary Biography, vol. 184, Detroit, Washington; London: 1997

Strachan, S., 'Hocken, Thomas Morland 1836–1910', in *Dictionary of New Zealand Biography*, updated 7 April 2006, http://www.dnzb.govt.nz

Strachan, S., 'Not quite half a loaf: Dr Hocken and the "patriation" of the New Zealand Company archives', unpublished paper given to the Australian Society of Archives/ARANZ conference, October 2005

Traue, J.E., '"For the ultimate good of the nation": the contribution of New Zealand's first book collectors', in *Committed to Print: selected essays in praise of the common culture of the book*, Wellington: Victoria University Press, 1991

Wood, P., *Dirt: filth and decay in a new world arcadia*, Auckland: Auckland University Press, 2005

The Hocken Collections 1910 to 2007

Stuart Strachan

When Lord Plunket, Governor of New Zealand, opened the Hocken Library (as it became known) on 31 March 1910 to great and justified acclaim, the expectation was that the collections would grow. It might not have been anticipated, however, that over the next seventy years its fine, new, and seemingly commodious quarters, on the first floor of the Otago University Museum, would become quite so crammed with fresh additions, including not a few new treasures.

The appointed Trustees continued to be responsible for management and funding. Their first task was to employ a librarian to organise the collection and publish a catalogue, so that its content could be widely known. They chose W.H. Trimble, a noted Walt Whitman scholar, and two years later the *Catalogue of the Hocken Library, Dunedin* appeared in two parts: an index to authors, and a subject catalogue according to Trimble's own classification. Distributed to libraries around the world free of charge, it was to have a long and useful life. Scholars refer to it still.

The second, less easy, task was to provide for a permanent librarian, building maintenance, and new additions to the collections. These required a substantial capital sum. A separate public appeal had enjoyed only very moderate success, so that when the Trustees handed their responsibilities to the University in 1913 just £1495 was in hand. A newly formed Hocken Library Committee, which included W.J. Morrell, Chancellor of the University, *Otago Daily Times* manager George Fenwick, and Alexander Bathgate, lawyer and writer, took up the reins. A full-time librarian being out of the question, the University had appointed Beatrice Howes part-time University Librarian and part-time Hocken Librarian. She was succeeded by H.D. Skinner (1919–26), Assistant Curator at the University Museum. This arrangement, with the Library effectively managed as part of the Museum, lasted almost twenty years with minor changes. Membership of the Committee did change, however, and notable amongst later members were Professor Benham, W. Downie Stewart, J.R. Elder, J.T. Paul, and from 1928 especially H.D. Skinner, who served until 1955 and was responsible for most pictures acquisitions. Many on the Committee had known Hocken personally.

The main business of the Committee was to approve new acquisitions, by purchase and by donation. Only £50 for purchases and £5 for binding was available per annum for new acquisitions. Little additional assistance could be expected from the University, itself notably under-funded. Book-sellers in all the main provincial centres were approached for advice on local publications and Miss Alice Evans in London agreed to act as agent there.[1] In 1919 shortage of funds led the Committee to restrict new acquisitions to the period before 1901, with particular emphasis on filling gaps identified from Dr Hocken's published *Bibliography*, leaving the McNab Collection at the Dunedin Public Library to acquire post-1900 items.

These financial limitations were offset by some important gifts: the John Kinder collection of photographs and paintings (1922); Louis le Breton watercolour of Otago Harbour and a Lindauer portrait (1924); John Buchanan watercolours (1920s); letters from the Rev. Pratt to Marsden, J.A. Gilfillan sketches, and Walter Buller letters (1934); and the very beautiful George Bayly voyaging journal (1935). Most significant of all was the bequest in 1936 by Sir Frederick Chapman of his own and his father's collections of New Zealand books and pamphlets, 'the most important single benefaction since Dr Hocken's foundation gift.'[2] Some unaffordable opportunities were reluctantly declined, such as the offer of manuscripts of C.R. Thatcher songs from Victoria, Charles Kettle's diary (eventually to go to the Turnbull Library), and the Burton Brothers photographs collection which later found a home in the Dominion Museum.

The twenties and early thirties, with Mrs R.W. Macdonald as part-time librarian (1926–35), were constantly penurious, funds for purchases being temporarily exhausted in 1922 and 1929. Use of the collections, though growing, was small and unsteady, partly due to the short opening hours – Tuesday, Wednesday and Friday afternoons, and Saturday mornings – well adrift of Dr Hocken's stipulation that they be the same as those of the Museum. In 1919, Dr Skinner had reported that 'the library has been used for special research by one student from Gisborne, one from Wellington, six from Christchurch, one from Oamaru, six from Dunedin, and one from Invercargill.'[3] By 1926, it could be stated that 'upwards of eighty people, three-fourths of whom were students, have made use of the Library for periods ranging from a day to seven months.'[4]

There were other changes. In 1930 the opening hours were extended to include all day Wednesday and Saturday afternoons. Three years later, electric heating was introduced and in 1936 a telephone was installed. Electric lighting

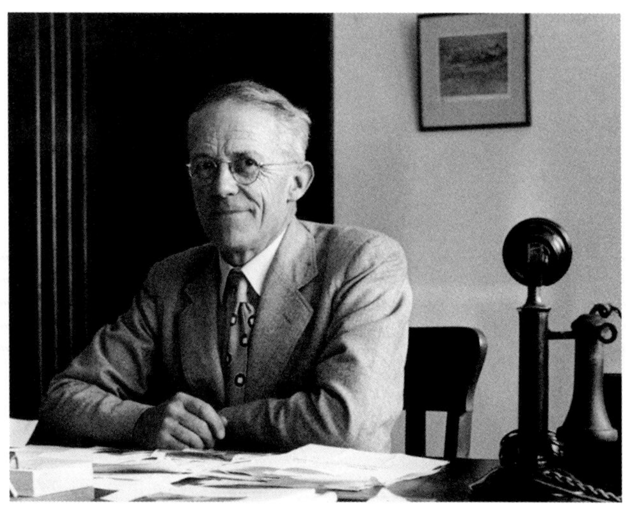

Henry Devenish Skinner (1886–1978), ethnologist and Otago Museum director, maintained an active interest in the Hocken Library from 1919 until his death and was its single most influential figure until he retired from the Hocken Library Committee in 1955. D.S. Marshall, photographer. c. 1951. Hocken Collections (S07-119a).

replaced gas the following year. Some augmentation of funds came with a gift from Lindsay Buick and additional interest from the estate of Dr Hocken following the death of Mrs Hocken in 1933. But the undoubted high point of this period was the publication in 1932 of Samuel Marsden's letters and journals, amongst the Library's very greatest treasures, edited by J.R. Elder, professor of history at the University.

The year 1936 proved to be a major turning point, when E.H. McCormick, a rising literary star, was appointed Hocken Librarian. He rapidly produced an influential report on the state and future direction of the Library, making recommendations on scope, co-operation with other libraries, staffing, publication, cataloguing, display, and indexing, among other matters. He suggested revisiting the earlier decision made to restrict new acquisitions very largely to pre-1901 material, pointing out that it had 'drastically reduced' the scope of the collection and, in any case, had not been fully adhered to by the McNab or Hocken libraries. He noted that under this agreement no twentieth-century periodicals and very little creative literature had been acquired, and that foreign language writing had been almost completely ignored. On staffing, McCormick advocated closer support by the University Library.[5]

The issue of collection scope was not formally addressed for another twenty years, but that of support was speedily resolved by Hocken's incorporation that same year into the University Library, bringing to an end the period of Museum control. The University Librarian responsible, the able, dynamic, well-intentioned John Harris, was greatly hampered by lack of resources. McCormick quickly departed for greater things in Wellington, and Harris struggled to provide staffing and funds for purchases. The war years were especially grim. In 1941, as a precaution, staff removed the manuscripts, pictures and rarer printed works to the security of basements and strong rooms, and the library was closed to casual readers. That year only forty-four works were added and two pictures. But even in these times good things continued to arrive. In 1945 two early O'Brien watercolours of Otago Harbour were purchased. Post-war, use of the Library began to recover, particularly in anticipation of the 1948 Otago centenary. In 1946 there were forty-one readers, but a paltry £53 allowed only 111 items to be added. Two years later, the number of readers rose to 132, but by then Harris, frustrated, had left for a distinguished university career in Nigeria.

Harris's successor, Frank Rogers, also an archivist and historian, took up the cause of the Hocken collections, but with the advantage of increased resourcing. In 1950 he secured the appointment of the Hocken Library as an approved repository for Justice Department records of local interest, so beginning its development as a modern archives repository. Shortly after he began to gather in local authority records, including those of the Otago Education Board. Equally significant was the appointment in February 1952 of the first full-time professional librarian, Gloria van der Poots (later Strathern). Opening hours became full-time, and that year 450 books were accessioned. The first reel of microfilm was also acquired, appropriately of forty Church Missionary Society letters relating to the New Zealand Mission. The following year a remodelling of the first floor provided more space for readers, books, and manuscripts, relieving the overcrowding, though at the expense of gallery space. A new era had begun.

By 1955 the Hocken was much more established within the University and had gained wider recognition nationally. To foster interest, a regular bulletin of activities had been started during the year before, as had a group of Associate Members, to whom desiderata lists of books and artists were circulated. The Hocken Library Committee's membership now included Charles Brasch, editor of *Landfall* and later chair of a newly established Pictures Subcommittee. With increased publicity, more exhibitions and the active interest of associate members, donations increased markedly, and in this period the Library received some of the most important items in the collections – ten Hoyte watercolours, Colonel Williams's Taranaki war sketchbook, Herries Beattie papers, and George Craig Thomson papers, including those of Octavius Harwood. A great boost was the Sargood Trust's gift of £500 for the purchase of paintings, which was put to good use. Other

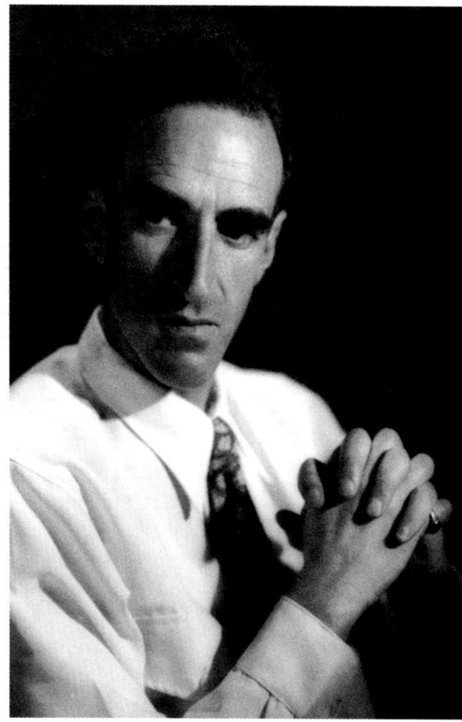

Charles Orwell Brasch (1909–73), poet and editor, gave new direction to the Hocken Library's pictures collection and after Dr Hocken was, by far, the Library's most important benefactor. Photographer unknown. c. 1960. Brasch Papers (996-12/683), Hocken Collections (S07-119f).

signs of better times were the appointment in 1956 of a second full-time staff member and a part-time pictures assistant. By 1959, income from endowments had risen to £350 and non-recurring grants totalled a further £165. From this time, though a policy of co-operation with other libraries had been reaffirmed in 1955, acquisitions expanded to include post-1900 publications generally. In 1964 the Committee considered amalgamation with the McNab Collection to create a single enlarged research collection; although the idea was welcomed in principle, the practical difficulties proved too great.

The Pictures Collection, guided by Charles Brasch and his close friend Rodney Kennedy, changed from one of historical representation and early twentieth-century expressionism into a fully representative museum of New Zealand art, embracing modernism. It began with Rodney Kennedy's gift of twenty-three Colin McCahon drawings in 1956, the first of many acts of generosity. His example was followed by Charles Brasch, who began giving works in 1958 that later included McCahon's very famous 'Virgin and Child Compared', and by Charlton Edgar, who from 1961 donated the Mona Edgar Collection of 400 modernist works, justifying the appointment in 1963 of a full-time Curator of Pictures. A third major gift, of Colin McCahon pictures, came in 1973 from the estate of his parents, which with further gifts from the artist himself established Hocken as a leading repository of his work.

The 1960s and 1970s were years of steadily improved funding and staffing. The two University Librarians who succeeded Rogers, Peter Havard-Williams (1957–60) and Jock McEldowney (1962–87), were committed to developing the Hocken as a major research library, as was Michael Hitchings, Hocken Librarian (1965–85). Perhaps the most striking development was the very rapid growth of the archives and manuscript collections. As early as 1956 the collection of business archives, for which Dunedin was a happy hunting ground, got under way, ultimately leading to my appointment as the first Curator of Manuscripts in 1970. Other areas were developed: maps and photographs began to be acquired systematically from the mid-1960s, and in 1977 a recorded New Zealand music collection was established. All are now major collections with their share of treasures, as illustrated in this volume.

Further major contributions came indirectly through

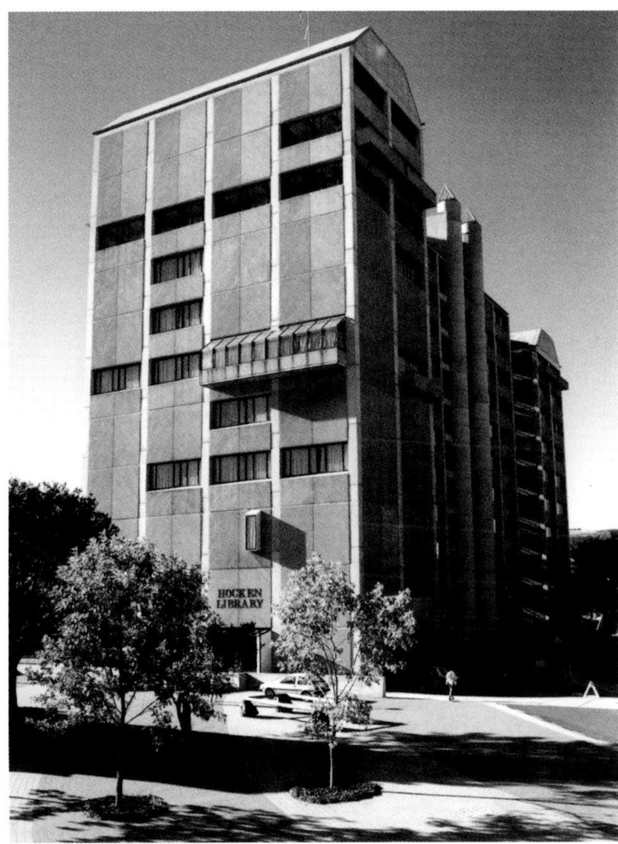

The south end of the Hocken Building, strikingly designed by Ted McCoy, was the Hocken Library's home from 1979 to 1998. G. Brook, photographer. March 1985. Hocken Collections (S07-118e).

the establishment of the Robert Burns and Frances Hodgkins Fellowships in 1958 and 1962 respectively. The first led, in time, to the very generous gifting of literary papers, including those of Janet Frame, R.A.K. Mason, and James K. Baxter, which now are amongst the chief glories of the Hocken Collections; and the second to the donation of many fine works by contemporary artists, such as Ralph Hotere and Jeffrey Harris. In 1973 Charles Brasch bequeathed to the Library not only his own very comprehensive collection of literary papers, including those of *Landfall*, and remaining paintings, but also half of his considerable residual estate. This, together with two other major bequests, Molly Morpeth Canaday and C.E.R. Webber, laid the foundation for a good-sized trust fund that would at last allow the purchase of manuscripts, paintings, and rare books as originally envisaged.

The 1970s are remembered by the writer as the heyday of traditional research at the Hocken without benefit of computerised systems, when a good part of New Zealand's literary and scholarly world came through its doors, whether it was James K. Baxter, dropping off his papers by instalment in plastic bags, Keith Sinclair discussing his forthcoming biography of Walter Nash, or W.B. Sutch, researching Coates and instructing staff on how best to make his lapsang tea. Staff and readers crowded cosily together at tea breaks in a smoke-filled workroom, after which slop buckets would be disposed of by staff in the men's toilet, where a large stuffed rhinoceros resided. That most courteous of researchers, Robert Pinney, was kind enough to write of the time: 'Though I have enjoyed study at Gothenburg, the lovely Karmeliterhuset at Elsinore, the Bodleian Library, and many English record offices, I like the Hocken Library best of all.'[6] Some of this was certainly due to David McDonald, who in 1970 had begun his long and distinguished career as reference librarian before his untimely death in 2000.

Apart from massive growth in all collections, the chief developments since the 1980s have been computerisation, which from 1985 has revolutionised control of and access to collections, and improved accommodation. In 1979, the collections were moved from their grossly overcrowded quarters in the Museum to purpose-built premises in the Hocken Building on campus. Further rapid growth rendered these in turn insufficient, and from 1989 supplementary quarters were occupied in the old Leith Street vehicle testing station. The only other relief was the transfer in 1993 of all central government archives to the newly established Dunedin Office of National Archives.

Still the gifts continued. Two of the most notable came from Southland: the Bruce Godward collection of early antipodean books, maps and prints (1991–2); and, from the Hall-Jones family, watercolours and oils of J.T. Thomson, the pioneer surveyor (1992). A number of Kai Tahu bodies and local Māori have also entrusted their own taoka to Hocken's stewardship, a relationship well symbolised in the southern dialect name given it by local rūnaka, Uare Taoka o Hākena, drawing on Dr Hocken's own Māori name for himself. Considerable support has also come from the Friends of the Hocken Collections, founded in 1991, who have given funds annually for the purchase of primary sources to support regional research and worked hard to make the collections better known.

In 1998, as the University's major Otago sesquicentennial project, the collections were handsomely consolidated, with considerable financial support from the government and community, in a specially converted dairy factory building in Anzac Avenue, where they were reopened by the Governor-General, Sir Michael Hardie Boys, on 2 December. Today, in spacious, well-equipped and climate-controlled accommodation, the Hocken Collections are vastly larger and more varied than the original gift of 1907, and better cared for. They now comprise more than 240,000 published volumes, 8500 linear metres of archives, 13,500 sound recordings, 11,500 maps, over 1 million photographs, and 14,000 pictures. Annually, the Collections now receive an average of 12,000 visits. It is a remarkable testament to the University of Otago, which, over the last fifty years at least, has fulfilled its obligations to the Hocken Collections extraordinarily well, so that not only is Hocken the largest institution of its kind outside Crown ownership in New Zealand but is also unparalleled by any university within Australasia and remarkable anywhere. Dr Hocken would surely be astounded, and pleased, that what he had begun as a 'labour of love' now stands as one of the nation's greatest heritage repositories, a place of many treasures, of which a selection is shown in the pages that follow.

NOTES

1. Committee minutes, 29 September 1913.
2. Annual Report, 1936, p. 8.
3. Annual Report, 1919, p. 12.
4. Annual Report, 1926, p. 12.
5. Report presented to the Hocken Library books committee, 20 March 1936.
6. Robert Pinney, p. 3.

REFERENCES

Hocken Library. Associate membership bulletins and annual reports, 1954–

Hocken Library Committee. Minutes, 1913–55.

Hocken Trustees. Minutes, 1906–13.

Otago University Museum. Annual reports, 1902-36.

R.B. Pinney. *Early northern Otago runs.* Auckland: Collins, 1981.

[E.J. Robinson]. 'The control and administration of the Hocken Library: a survey'. Unpublished report. 1961.

University of Otago Library. Annual Reports, 1936–

Contributors

AB	Anna Blackman, Curator of Archives and Manuscripts, Hocken Collections
ACC	Amy Coleman, Arrangement and Description Archivist, Hocken Collections
AJ	Anne Jackman, Reference Librarian, Hocken Collections
AJC	Ali Clarke, Assistant Archivist, Hocken Collections
AP	Anna Petersen, Assistant Curator (Photographs), Hocken Collections
AR	Alexander Ritchie, Technical Services Assistant, Hocken Collections
DJM	John Milnes, Ab Epistulis, Knox College
DK	Donald Kerr, Special Collections Librarian, University of Otago Library
DM	David Murray, Assistant Archivist, Hocken Collections
IF	Ian Farquhar, Shipping Historian, Dunedin
JB	John Broughton, Associate Professor, Department of Preventive and Social Medicine, University of Otago
JH	Judith Holloway, Periodicals Assistant, Hocken Collections
JW	Jim Williams, Lecturer, Te Tumu, University of Otago
KC	Karen Craw, Senior Maps Assistant, Hocken Collections
KM	Katherine Milburn, Senior Reference Assistant, Hocken Collections
LE	Laura Elliott, Postgraduate Student, Department of History, University of Otago
LT	Linda Tyler, Director, Centre for New Zealand Art Research and Discovery, University of Auckland
MD	Malcolm Deans, formerly Reference Assistant, Hocken Collections
MH	Mark Hughes, Technical Services Librarian, Hocken Collections
NP	Natalie Poland, Curator of Pictorial Collections, Hocken Collections
NW	Noel Waite, Lecturer, Design Studies, University of Otago
PH	Pennie Hunt, formerly Assistant Curator (Pictures), Hocken Collections
PM	Paulette Milnes, Music Assistant, Hocken Collections
SI	Susan Irvine, Supervising Project Archivist, Hocken Collections
SRS	Stuart Strachan, Hocken Librarian
TH	Terry Hearn, Historian, Dunedin

Archives and Manuscripts

Anna Blackman and Stuart Strachan

At the heart of the Hocken Collections' rich assortment of archives and manuscripts are those gathered by Dr Hocken himself. The doctor devoted much time and energy to seeking out manuscripts related to New Zealand's early colonial history, particularly the mission period and the earliest years of organised European settlement, 1810–60, prior to his own arrival at Otago in 1862.

The letters and journals of Samuel Marsden and other Anglican missionaries, including William Colenso, Thomas Kendall, George Clarke, James Kemp and James Hamlin, are of first importance. Hocken obtained these by delicate negotiation with the Church Missionary Society during a visit to England in 1903. Collectively, they are the most significant holding of their kind anywhere.

The correspondence and other records relating to planned settlement are equally notable. These include the journal of William Fox, records of the Nelson surveyors Frederick Tuckett and John Barnicoat (who together selected the site for the Otago settlement), and the papers of Charles Kettle (who surveyed the town of Dunedin), the papers of Captain William Cargill (lay leader of the Otago Settlement), and the minutes and related records of the Canterbury Association, including the correspondence of Henry Selfe Selfe, its secretary. This original group of records also includes the crucially significant journals and observations of Dr Edward Shortland, the first European to record systematically Māori legends and traditions, during his travels through New Zealand in the 1840s and 1850s.

Hocken gathered original documents wherever possible, but some could only be borrowed and copied (usually by his wife Bessie), assuring survival when the originals were later lost. Curiously, Hocken collected very little from his contemporaries, even when he had the opportunity. Probably because of his preoccupation with origins, there are no papers of nineteenth-century politicians in the founding collection.

Of equal renown are the literary papers, mostly of writers who have had a close association with Otago and the University, particularly its Robert Burns Fellowship established in 1958 by Charles Brasch, a keen supporter of the Hocken Collections. Brasch's own papers contain his diaries and letters, a major source for New Zealand literary history from the 1940s to the 1970s, and the records of *Landfall,* which he founded and edited from 1947 to 1966. Other major writers represented are Janet Frame, James K. Baxter, R.A.K Mason, Ruth Dallas, Noel Hilliard, Robert Lord, Roger Hall, Hone Tuwhare, and others. Artists' papers, though less numerous, include those of Colin McCahon, New Zealand's foremost modernist, and of RKS Art, a leading Auckland dealer gallery.

From the 1960s, what was to become the country's largest collection of business archives steadily built up. As Dunedin was New Zealand's major centre of business for much of the nineteenth century, the archives of many significant firms of the time are now found in the Hocken Collections: the NMA Company of New Zealand, the Union Steamship Company (until 1912), Hallenstein Bros, Ross and Glendining, Mosgiel Woollen Mills, Donaghy's Industries, Milburn Lime and Cement, Taieri and Peninsula Milk Supply Co., New Zealand's first co-operative dairy company, as well as those of a large number of legal firms and closely associated gold mining companies. Pastoral station records held include those of Kawarau Falls, Moa Flat, Ida Valley, Longlands, Lauder, Te Anau Downs and Puketoi. The business records of Octavius Harwood, 1838–45, which relate to shore whaling in Otago, are New Zealand's earliest.

Given Dunedin's long history as a centre of education, health and religion, it is not surprising that there should be many allied archives. The headquarters records of the Royal New Zealand Plunket Society, founded in Dunedin in 1907 by Frederick Truby King, are particularly important, as are those of Otago Medical School, New Zealand's first. The records of the University of Otago are reasonably complete from its foundation in 1869. Complementing them are the Otago Education Board archives, including its first minute book, 1856–62, discovered and purchased in England. The records of over 200 schools, public and private, are heavily used. Church records are especially rich. The Hocken is the official repository for the Anglican diocese of Dunedin, and has major Otago holdings of the Baptist, Methodist and Congregational churches as well as of the Jewish synagogue. Clergy papers include those of the Rev. James McNeur, Presbyterian missionary in China, the Rev. William Johnstone of Port Chalmers, Henry Jenner, first Anglican bishop of Dunedin, Anglican Canon Hoani Parata, the Rev. J.F. Wohlers, Lutheran missionary at Ruapuke, and the Rev. Robert Ward, pioneer of Primitive Methodism in New Zealand.

Other national organisations held are the New Zealand Alpine Club and Bowls New Zealand. Numerous smaller bodies represented range from large provincial organisations, such as the Otago/Southland Division of the New Zealand National Party and of the Otago Provincial District of Federated Farmers, sporting bodies such as the Otago Racing Club, to very small societies, such as the Toko Collie Club and the Haeremai Club, 1929–68, membership of which was limited to twenty Dunedin women.

There are many records of Kai Tahu interest. Amongst the most important are the Rev. James Watkin vocabulary of southern dialect Māori compiled at Waikouaiti in the 1840s and accounts of traditions gathered by Herries Beattie in the 1920s and 1930s. Some rūnaka have deposited archives, and a complete set of the major Ngāi Tahu Waitangi claim records is held for the Ngāi Tahu Development Corporation.

The papers of individuals are especially diverse. Politicians include J.T. Paul, W. Downie Stewart, E.J. and Mabel Howard, Ethel McMillan, and Michael Cullen. Amongst prominent women are Ethel Benjamin, first female lawyer, and Emily Siedeberg, first female medical graduate, as well as Lady Stout, the influential suffragist. Scientists include the geologist and explorer Sir James Hector, nutritionist Dr Muriel Bell, albatross researcher Lance Richdale, and G.M. Thomson, Otago naturalist and science reformer. Conscientious objection is well represented by the letters of Ron Malcolm, but these are outnumbered by soldiers' letters and diaries, particularly of the First World War.

English recipes for New Zealand • 1739–40

This recipe book is part of a collection relating to Frederick Locke and his wife, Elizabeth, who originally lived near Durham, England where Elizabeth is believed to have been a cook at Castle Eden, near Stockton-on-Tees. The couple emigrated to New Zealand in 1872, and settled in Riverton where they ran the Aparima Hotel and later the Commercial Hotel.

It seems likely that Elizabeth acquired this recipe book when at Castle Eden and brought it with her, along with four other similar recipe books from the early nineteenth century. Several styles of handwriting are evident, showing use by many people. This book includes recipes for obviously English delicacies, with titles such as 'To Stew Soals', 'To Jugg a Hare', 'The Best Orange Pudding that Ever Was Eat', 'Pigeons in Lettice', and some recipes with an eastern or Indian influence: 'Pickled Lemmons', 'To make a Pilau' and 'To Make Curry'. The most unusual recipe is a cure for 'fitts' which involved drying earth moles (blood, guts, bones and hair) in the oven until they could be powdered. The powder was then taken three times a day.

The books are an interesting example of how women passed on useful household information to successors and relatives, and of how British cookery practice was transferred to New Zealand. AB

New Zealand mission proposed • 1808

Samuel Marsden arrived in New South Wales in 1794 as assistant chaplain to the colony. His first foray into missions came in 1804, when he was appointed local agent for the London Missionary Society. After meeting visiting Māori, particularly the chiefs Te Pahi and Ruatara, Marsden's mission focus gradually turned to New Zealand. In November 1807 he returned to London to secure support. In this letter, dated 24 March 1808, Marsden brought the proposed mission to the attention of the Church Missionary Society. He writes of his 'ardent wish' that Māori 'may enjoy the Sweets of Civilization' and the 'inestimable blessings of Divine Revelation'. New Zealand's closeness to New South Wales would enable the safety and success of missionaries, while ministers already established there, 'if they were men of piety', would provide practical support.

After further correspondence, the Society agreed to a mission under Marsden's supervision. So began a long and fruitful relationship between the Society and the chaplain. Establishment was delayed, however, and it was not until 23 December 1814 that Marsden arrived in the Bay of Islands. He held the first Christian service in New Zealand on Christmas Day. On 24 February 1815, Marsden purchased land at Rangihoua, on which New Zealand's first missionary settlement was built. SI

Rev. Samuel Marsden. *Letter to Rev. Josiah Pratt, Secretary of the Church Missionary Society, 24 March 1808*. MS-0498/001/001. Donated by D.K. Webster, 1973.

Ivy Lane, March 24th 1808

Rev. Sir/

With great diffidence I respectfully submit the following Observations relative to New Zealand to the Consideration of the Society for Missions to Africa and the East, as that Island may lie within the limits of the Society's Designs towards the Heathen— From the different Reports we have had of the natives of New Zealand, and the late Communication with one of their Chiefs, who visited Port Jackson, and who appeared a very extraordinary man, possest of the greatest natural Abilities, and express'd the most ardent Desire to improve his Subjects, according to human Estimate this Island seems to afford some Prospect for missionary labors. New Zealand & its natural Productions are little known to the civilized world— no Commerce has been carried on there further–

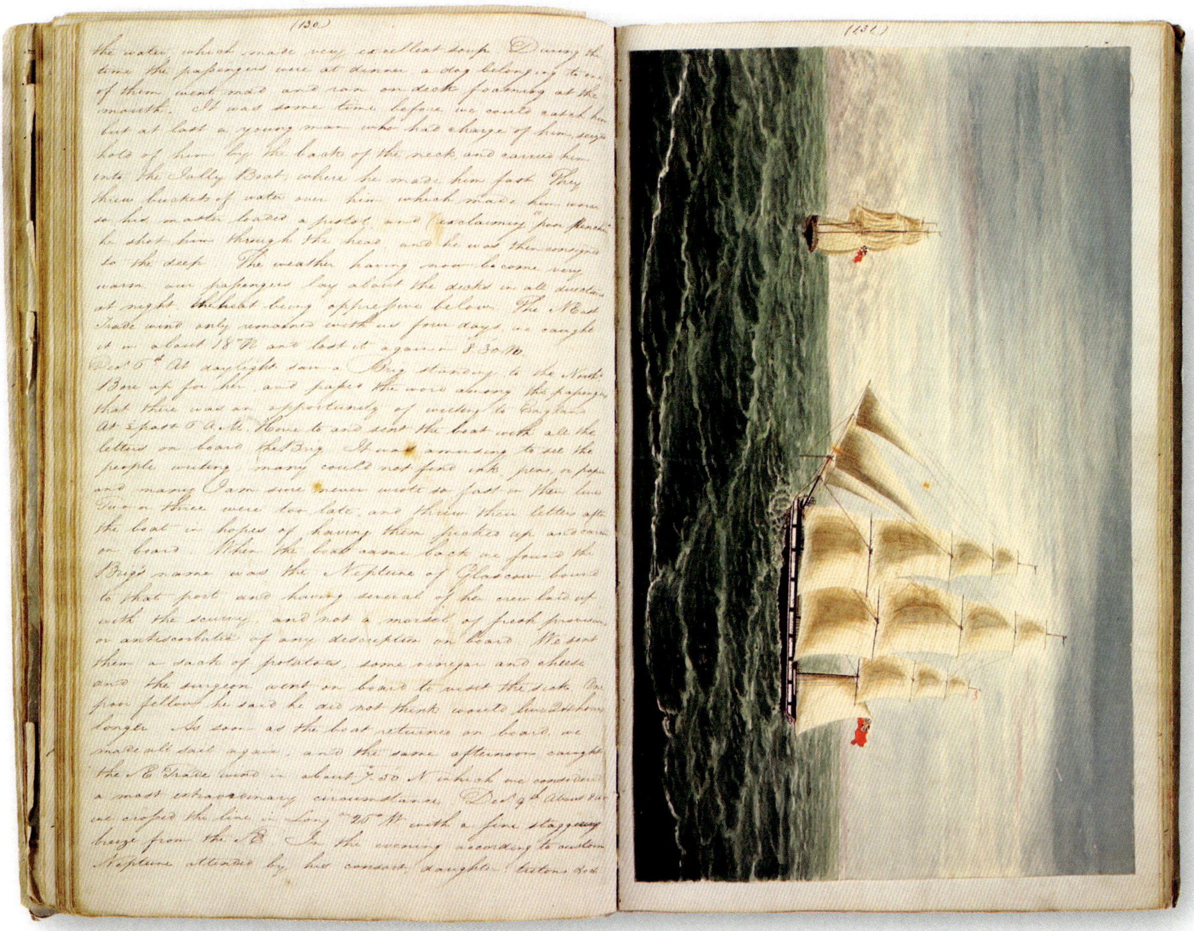

Journal of a life at sea • 1824–38

George Bayly. *'Journal of Voyages to various parts of the World written by George Bayly for the amusement of such of his Friends as feel themselves disposed to read it, Vol. 1st' 1824–38.* MS-0145. Donated by the Misses Saunders, 1934.

George Bayly was born in 1808 at Rotherhithe by the River Thames in England. He came from a seafaring family and, at the age of sixteen, accompanied his uncle on a voyage to Jamaica, the first of many he was to make. Bayly kept a detailed record of his travels. This, the first of two volumes of his journals held at the Hocken, describes nine voyages between 1824 and 1838. In this time Bayly progressed through the shipboard ranks, beginning as an apprentice in 1824 and reaching the rank of captain and part-owner by 1838. He eventually became commander and sole owner of the *Hooghly*, the ship on which most of these voyages took place.

The voyages (transporting convicts and immigrants, and trading) took Bayly around the world, to Australia, South America, New Zealand, the Pacific Islands, India, and back to England. Sailing methods and routes are described in detail, but it is his accounts of shipboard life – passengers and crew, their behaviour and habits – and of incidents on land that are of most interest. They throw light on seagoing lives at a time when the world relied on ships for transportation and communication. Thirteen watercolour illustrations, mostly of ships, embellish the journal. ACC

Three months before Ngāi Tahu paramount chief, Tuhawaiki, signed the Treaty of Waitangi at Ruapuke, this declaration was drafted in another hand for Tuhawaiki, presumably at the chief's request. He signed it with both his moko and his signature, which ends with four, neat, circular flourishes, superimposed over the letters, surely evidence that he fully understood the significance of writing his name as a signature. The document asserts that 'John Touwaick' (this is also the spelling he uses in his signature) is 'principle [sic] chief of the middle Island and its dependencies' and names, in order of precedence, ten parties with a share in the ownership of Ruapuke Island. All rangatira names in the document are spelt phonetically, with appropriate capitals and sometimes using an English word of similar sound, for example 'Cabbage'.

Not only a valuable antiquity in itself, but also a unique window into the politics of chiefly precedence in the south and a clear indicator of Tuhawaiki's grasp of the European notions of land tenure and legal documents. By signing with his moko and his signature, the document would be seen to have standing in both the Māori and European worlds. JW

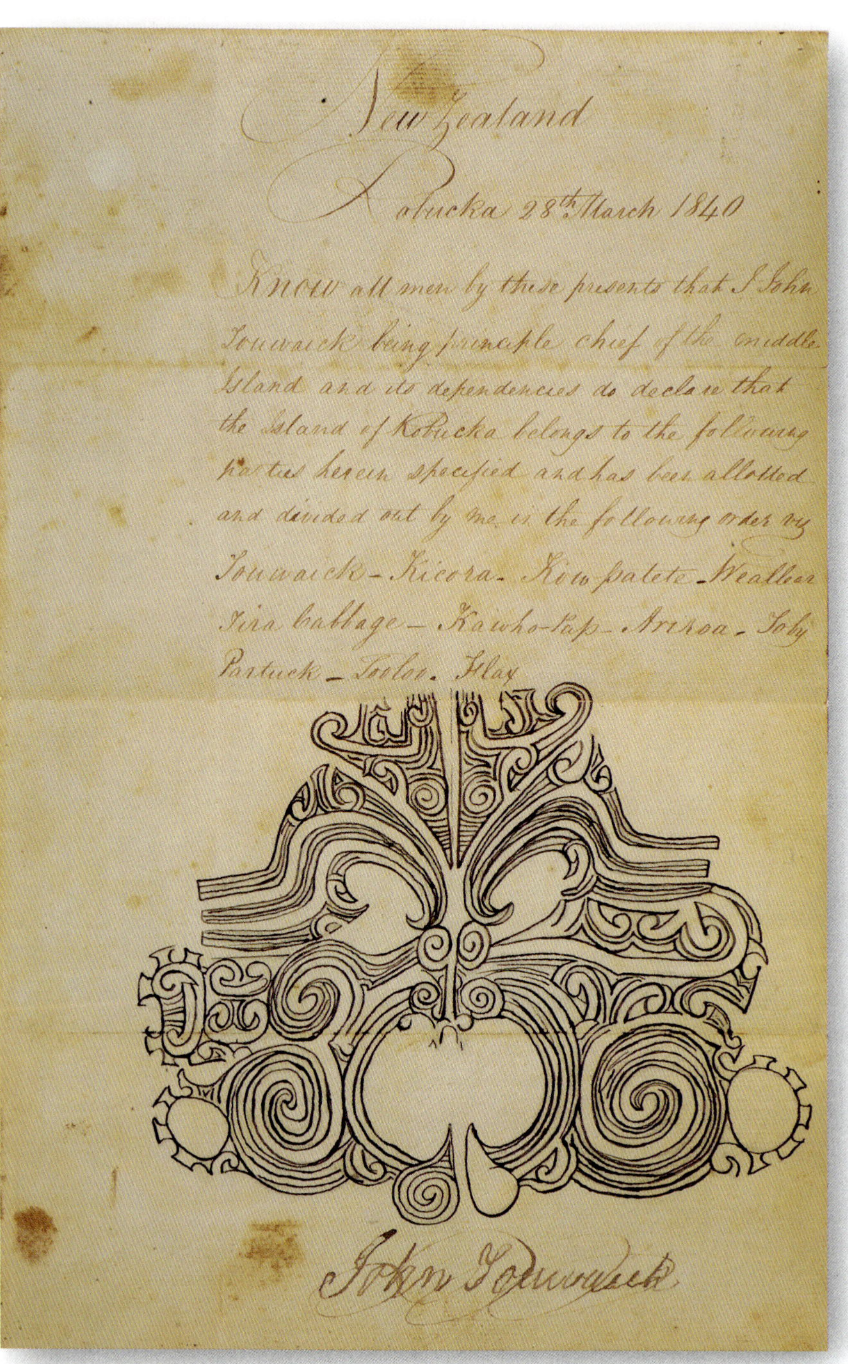

New Zealand
Robucka 28th March 1840

Know all men by these presents that I John Touwaick being principle chief of the middle Island and its dependencies do declare that the Island of Robucka belongs to the following parties herein specified and has been allotted and divided out by me in the following order viz Touwaick – Kicora – Kowpatete – Weallear Tira Cabbage – Kawho-tap – Arikoa – Toby Partuck – Toolor. Flay

John Touwaick

Hone Tuhawaiki. *Declaration of ownership of Robucka* [sic] *Island, 28 March 1840*. MS-0808/B. Original Collection.

South Island Māori word-list • 1840–44

Rev. James Watkin. *Vocabulary of Maori words compiled at Waikouaiti, 1840–44*. MS-0031. Original Collection.

The Rev. James Watkin was Wesleyan missionary at Waikouaiti from May 1840 to June 1844. He had previously been a missionary for six and a half years in Tonga, where he had become fluent in the language. Within a month Watkin had collected 400 words and phrases that he needed to communicate with local Kai Tahu and to preach the word of God. He wrote in his journal on 14 June, 'I pick up words and phrases with considerable facility, but should do so much more rapidly if the language spoken here were the same with that spoken in the Northern Island', which he had studied in preparation for his South Island mission.

Watkin was clearly aware of the merging of *ng* into *k*. Other differences, however, are less consciously reflected, such as the less full pronunciation of short final vowels. Some forms recorded are not found elsewhere in Māori. Whatever other differences may be inferred from Watkin's list, it supports the view of South Island Māori as a distinct dialect rather than as a separate language, and confirms that it is the most important single written source of the time for its vocabulary. The word list was presented by Watkin's son, the Rev. Edwin Watkin of Melbourne, to Dr Hocken in March 1893. SRS

Whaling at Otago • 1838–40

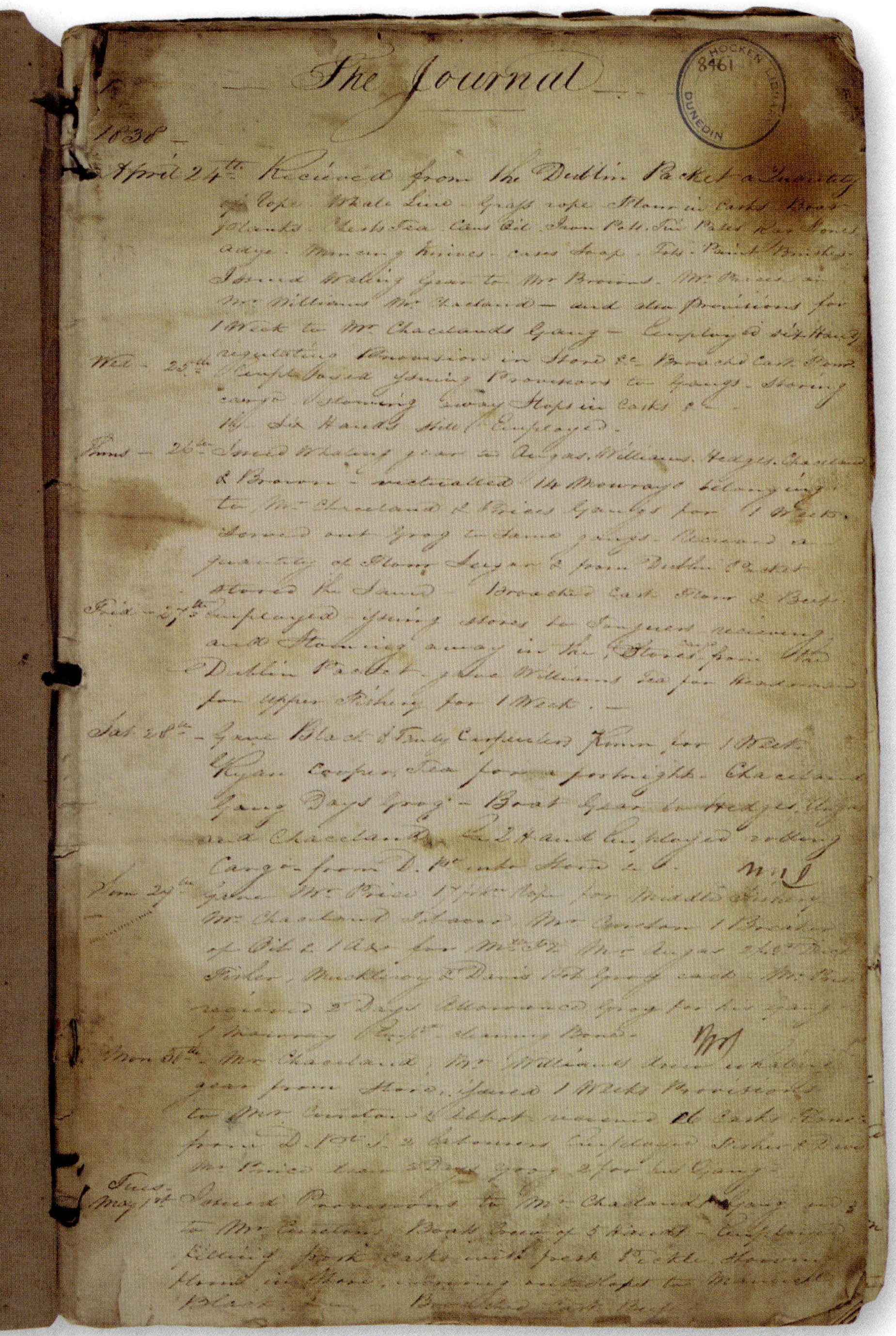
The Journal

1838 —

April 24th Received from the Dublin Packet a Quantity

This is the first page of Octavius Harwood's journal from his arrival in April 1838 at Otakou, near present-day Dunedin. Harwood was employed by the Weller Brothers of Sydney (George, Joseph and Edward) as a clerk to assist with the running of their whaling and sealing business established at Otakou in 1832–33. Hand-bound, perhaps by Harwood himself, in rough brown paper, the journal records the daily business of the store at the whaling station and forms part of a collection of journals, notebooks, letters and financial papers which are amongst the earliest business records in New Zealand.

Harwood was primarily employed running the store: he issued equipment, provisions, 'slops' – cheap ready-made clothing – and grog to the whalers; liaised with visiting ships and whalers from other stations; and organised work, such as cleaning bone and maintenance of the boats. He also won the confidence of the local Māori, and wrote letters, did medical work, drew up agreements, and witnessed marriages and conducted funerals for Māori and Europeans. As Harwood also recorded the names of all who visited, his journal is a crucial record of life in Otago before organised European settlement. AB

Octavius Harwood. *Journal, 1838–40.*
MS-438/001. Purchased, 1951.

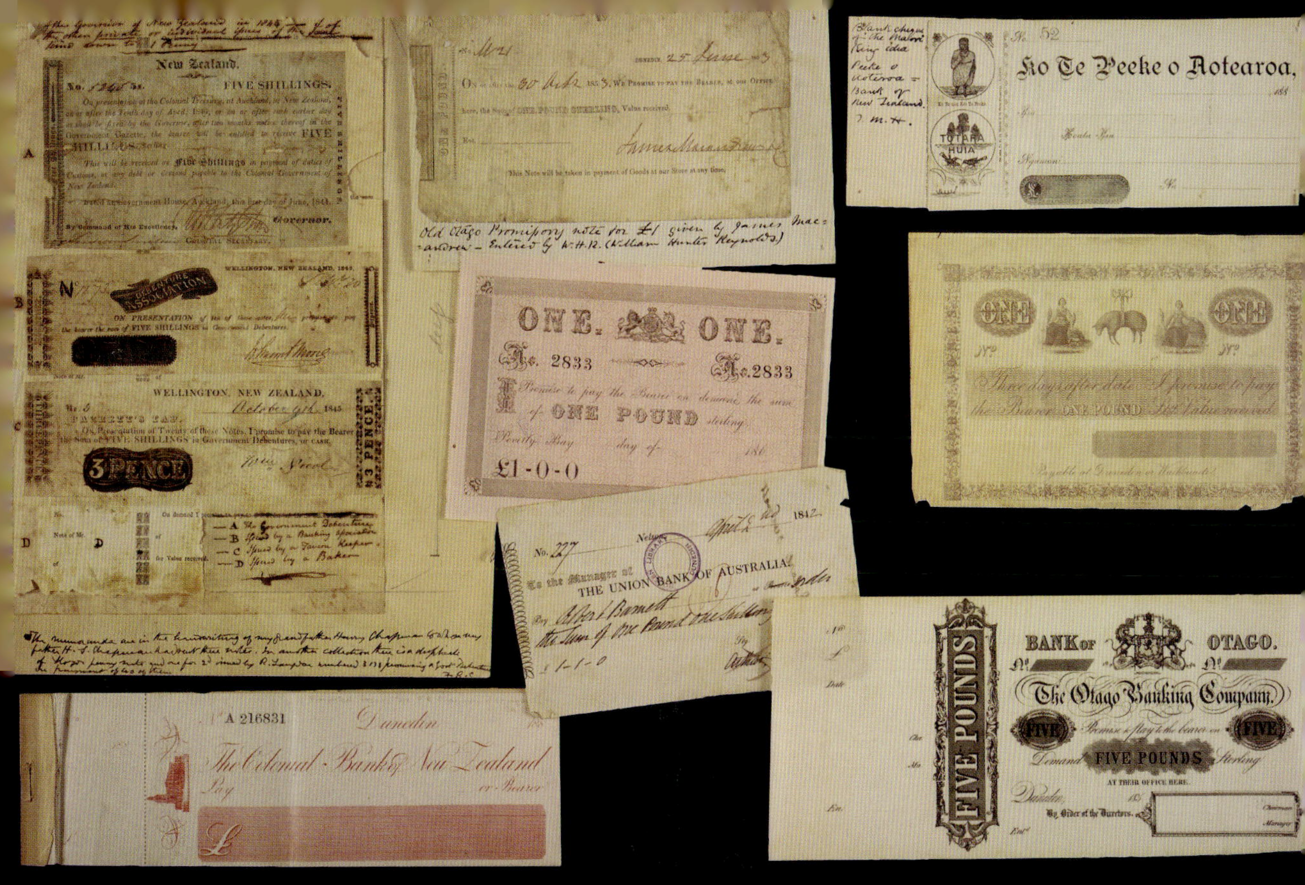

Early currency notes • 1840s–1860s

Promissory Notes, 1840s–1860s. Misc MS-1535/1–3. Various provenances.

Establishing an adequate currency in New Zealand took time and makeshift arrangements were resorted to, as these locally developed notes show.

Governor Robert FitzRoy's ill-fated debentures were first issued in 1844 on behalf of an impoverished colonial government in 5/-, 10/-, £1, and £5 denominations, redeemable on presentation to the Colonial Treasury from 10 April 1846. Not well accepted, they nevertheless saved the government from bankruptcy, with £36,000 in circulation. Trading firms, even small concerns, also circulated promissory notes for amounts as small as one penny (1d.). During the 1850s Otago business rivals, James Macandrew and Johnny Jones, each issued one pound (£1) notes which circulated into the 1860s. Macandrew claimed in August 1853 that almost one third of the paper currency then circulating in Otago was his privately issued notes.

The first successful bank to issue its own notes, the Union Bank of Australia, opened branches in Wellington and Nelson in 1840 and 1842 respectively. Shown here is a one guinea (£1-1-0) cheque redeemable at the bank, signed in April 1842 by Arthur Wakefield, leader of the Nelson settlement. The problem of sufficient currency was not resolved until the goldrushes of the 1860s, when other private banks – all issuing their own redeemable-on-demand banknotes – entered the field. SRS

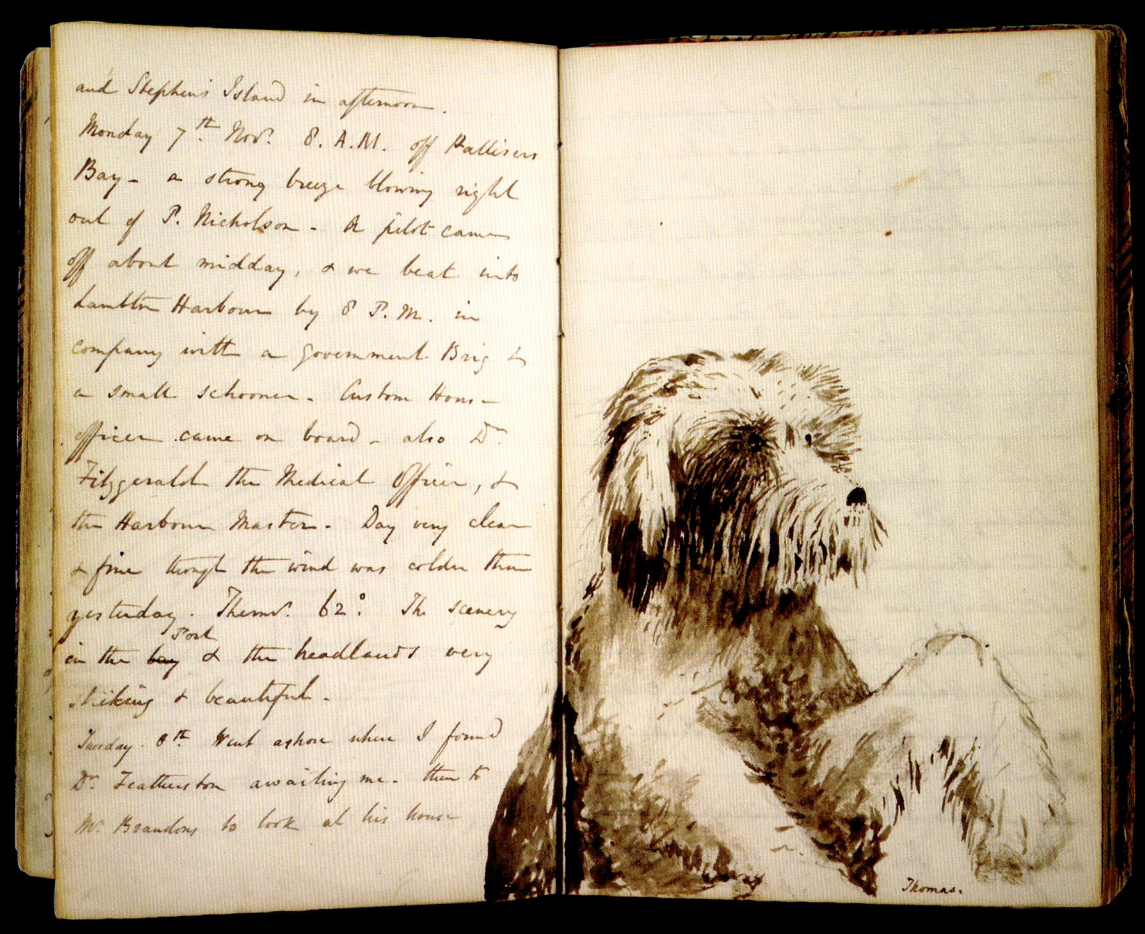
and Stephen's Island in afternoon.
Monday 7th Novr. 8. A.M. off Pallisers Bay – a strong breeze blowing right out of P. Nicholson – A pilot came off about midday, & we beat into Lambton Harbour by 8 P.M. in company with a Government Brig & a small schooner. Custom House officer came on board – also Dr. Fitzgerald the Medical Officer, & the Harbour Master – Day very clear & fine though the wind was colder than yesterday. Thermr. 62°. The scenery in the ~~bay~~ Port & the headlands very striking & beautiful –
Tuesday 8th Went ashore where I found Dr. Featherston awaiting me – then to Mr. Brandon's to look at his house –

A first-class journal • 1842–43

Sir William Fox. *Journal, 1842–43*. MS-0042. Original Collection.

Keeping a diary helped while away the tedium of the long sea voyage from Europe to New Zealand. Future premier William Fox (1812–1893) migrated with his wife Sarah aboard the *George Fyfe* in 1842, leaving Portsmouth on 21 June and finally stepping ashore in Wellington on 8 November. Fox was a lawyer and a gentleman: he and Sarah sailed first class. This did not, however, guarantee comfort. Once they slept under an umbrella, the decks leaking during bad weather. Fox described passengers' amusements, such as backgammon, shooting contests, and dancing 'Irish reels to a guitar by the light of a lantern', and had the usual preoccupation with food, weather and distance travelled.

Fox described the voyage with pictures as well as words. He included sketches of passengers, crew, ships, and creatures ranging from cockroaches and sea birds to this delightful portrait of one of four dogs on board. They demonstrate the skill that later produced some of colonial New Zealand's better watercolour landscapes.

The journal ends soon after arrival, but covers an expedition to find land that Fox made with several other gentlemen, guided by Māori, to the Wairarapa. He believed much of the district 'might at once be occupied without the expense of either clearing or draining. The only thing wanted is a road'. AJC

Early Malay account of Singapore • c. 1843

Gifted by the family of New Zealand's first Surveyor-General, John Turnbull Thompson, the life story of Abdullah bin Abdul Kadir or Munshi Abdullah (1879–1854), friend and admirer of Sir Stamford Raffles, is regarded as a turning point in Malay literature and an important account of life in early Singapore. Written in Malay using Arabic-derived Jawi script between 1840 and 1843, and published in 1849, it is an important record of Singapore's early history and the most accurate of Raffles' arrival. Abdullah wrote about political and cultural events during his early life in Singapore, which was slowly changing under British rule from a sleepy fishing village into a major centre of world trade.

Abdullah was also the first Malay writer to depart from traditional Malay literary style, by writing in colloquial language. Unlike courtly writing, his style was realistic and lively, incorporating many Malay idioms and proverbs. His knowledge of languages and reputation as a teacher earned him the nickname '*Munshi*', meaning 'tutor'.

Only three copies of 'Hikayat Abdullah' survive, the other two being in the Library of Congress and at Harvard University. The left-hand page shown here has Abdullah's drawing of Sultan Hussein Syah's hearse, the 'Usungan Raja di Raja'. LT/SRS

Munshi Abdullah. *Hikayat Abdullah*. c. 1843. AG 726/5.
Donated by Hall-Jones family, 1999.

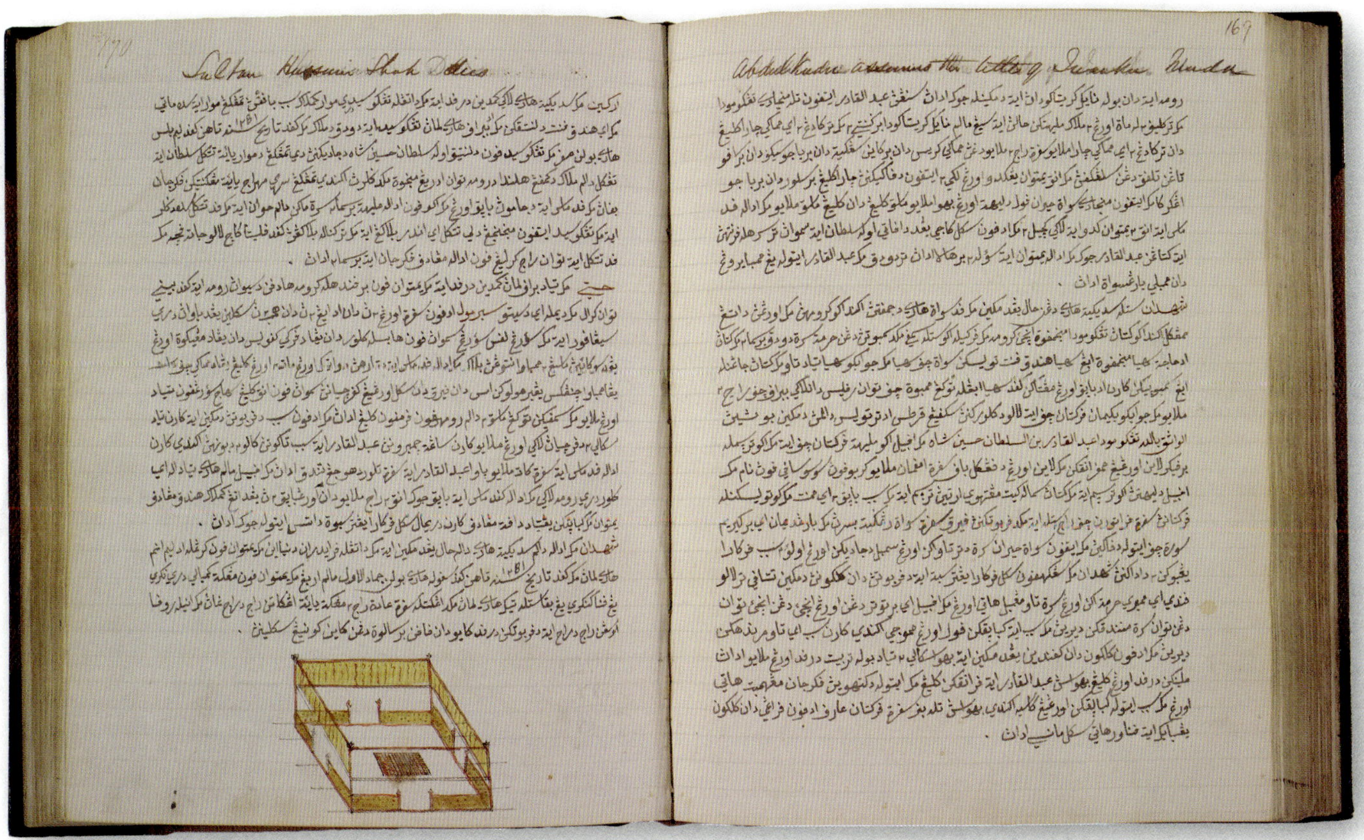

Kai Tahu hāpu • 1848

Following the Otago Purchase in 1848, W.B.D. Mantell compiled these ten bundles of cards recording, phonetically, the names of the hapū of Otago, seemingly according to their common ownership of land blocks purchased by Mantell. The ten bundles involve one hundred and six hapū names, many of which are no longer used.

The cards provide valuable insight into early nineteenth century, Ngāi Tahu perceptions, as hapū names were quoted as the primary indicators of from whom land, and more particularly resource rights, were inherited. Presumably, the groupings are of related sellers, who through these hapū names show a relationship between groups of hapū on the one hand, and blocks of territory on the other. The lists should not themselves be regarded as whakapapa, but in conjunction with whakapapa they reveal how hapū can cohere in groups. Of secondary interest are the phonetic spellings, which give some insights into the southern dialect. These fragile artefacts were given by Mantell to Sir Frederick Chapman, who in turn presented them to his friend Dr Hocken. JW

W.B.D. Mantell. *Names of hapu of Kaitahu, 1848.* MS-0402. Original Collection.

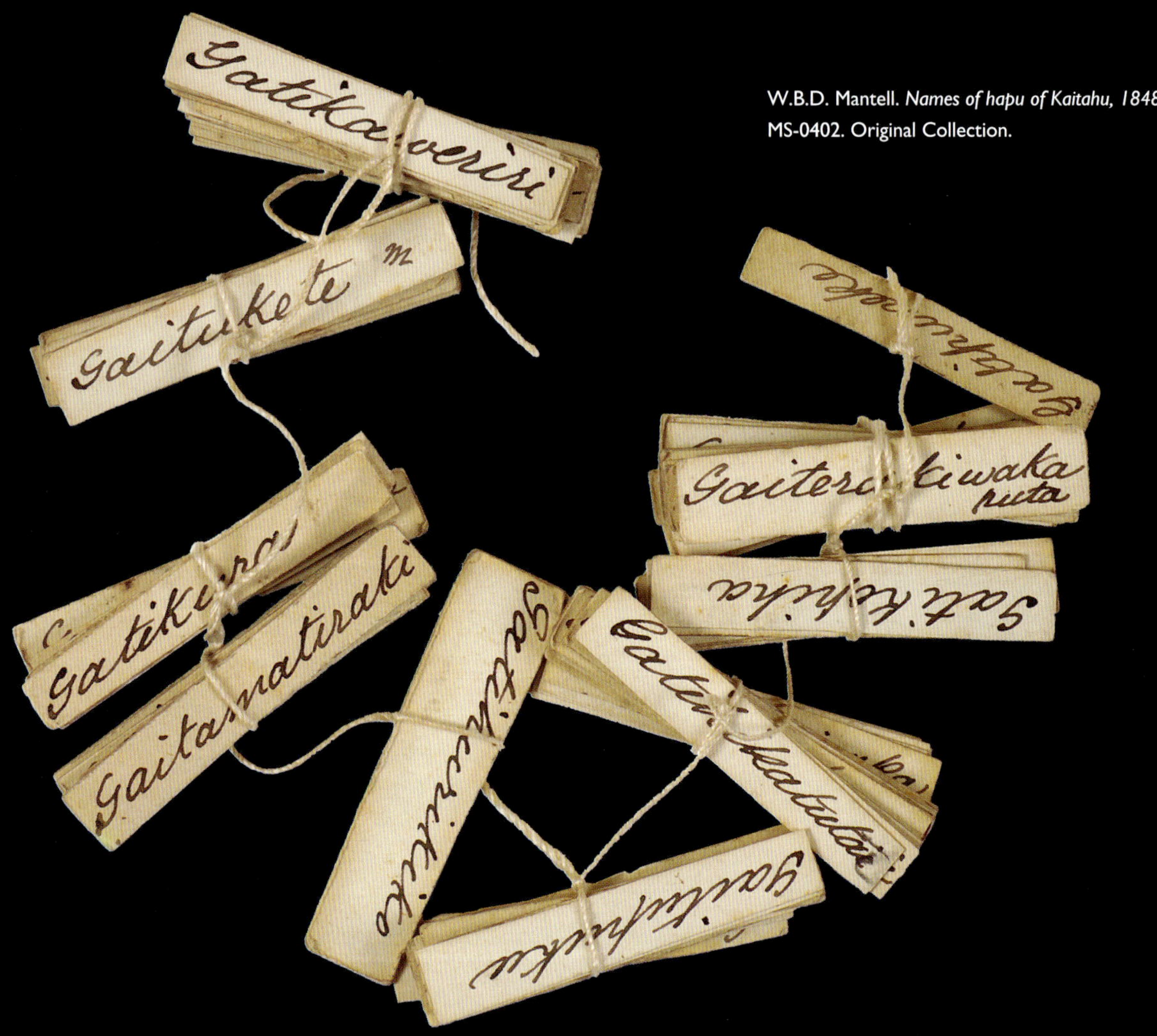

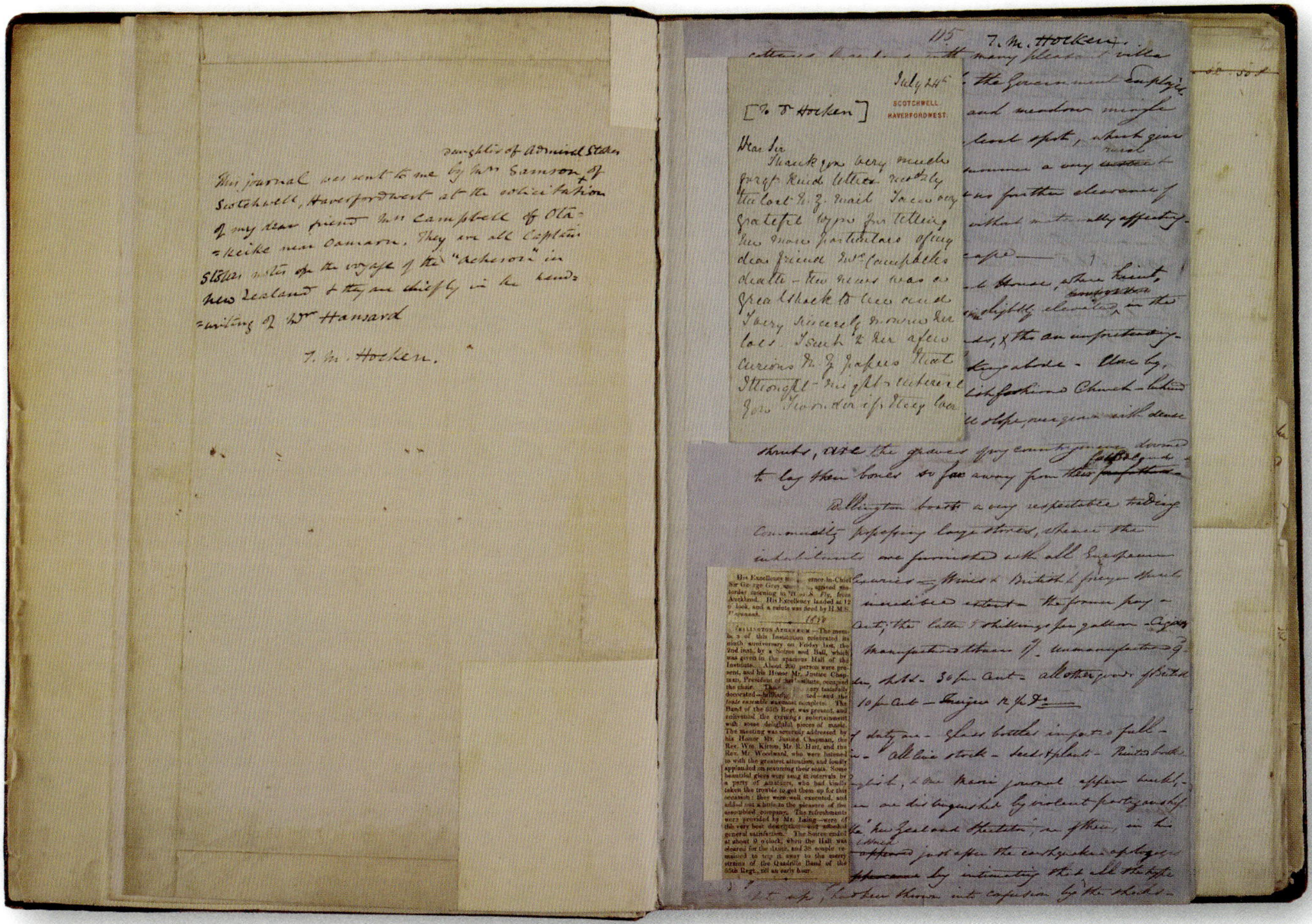

The voyage of the Acheron • 1849–51

George Albert Hansard. *'Voyage of the "Acheron", Part 3rd', 1849–51.* MS-0157. Original Collection.

Captained by John Lort Stokes, HMS *Acheron*, a paddle steamer, was sent from England in 1848 to carry out the first complete hydrographical survey of the New Zealand coast. As a result of their extensive coastal surveys, Stokes and his crew produced many new charts (including the first survey of Foveaux Strait), corrected existing charts, made several inland explorations, and recorded observations of New Zealand's flora, fauna and existing human inhabitants. It was the most important and thorough survey of its kind since that of Captain Cook in the late eighteenth century.

Some mystery has surrounded the voyage's journal. For long thought to be the work of the captain, it is now presumed that the colourful and informative journal was compiled, not just written down, by George Albert Hansard, a supernumerary clerk on board. The Hocken Collections holds only the third part, that concerning New Zealand, from page 115 – the first two parts are in the National Maritime Museum at Greenwich. Dr Hocken received the manuscript from Mrs Samson, daughter of Captain Stokes, who was on board the *Acheron* as a young girl, until she was handed over to relatives in Sydney after her mother's death on the voyage out. ACC

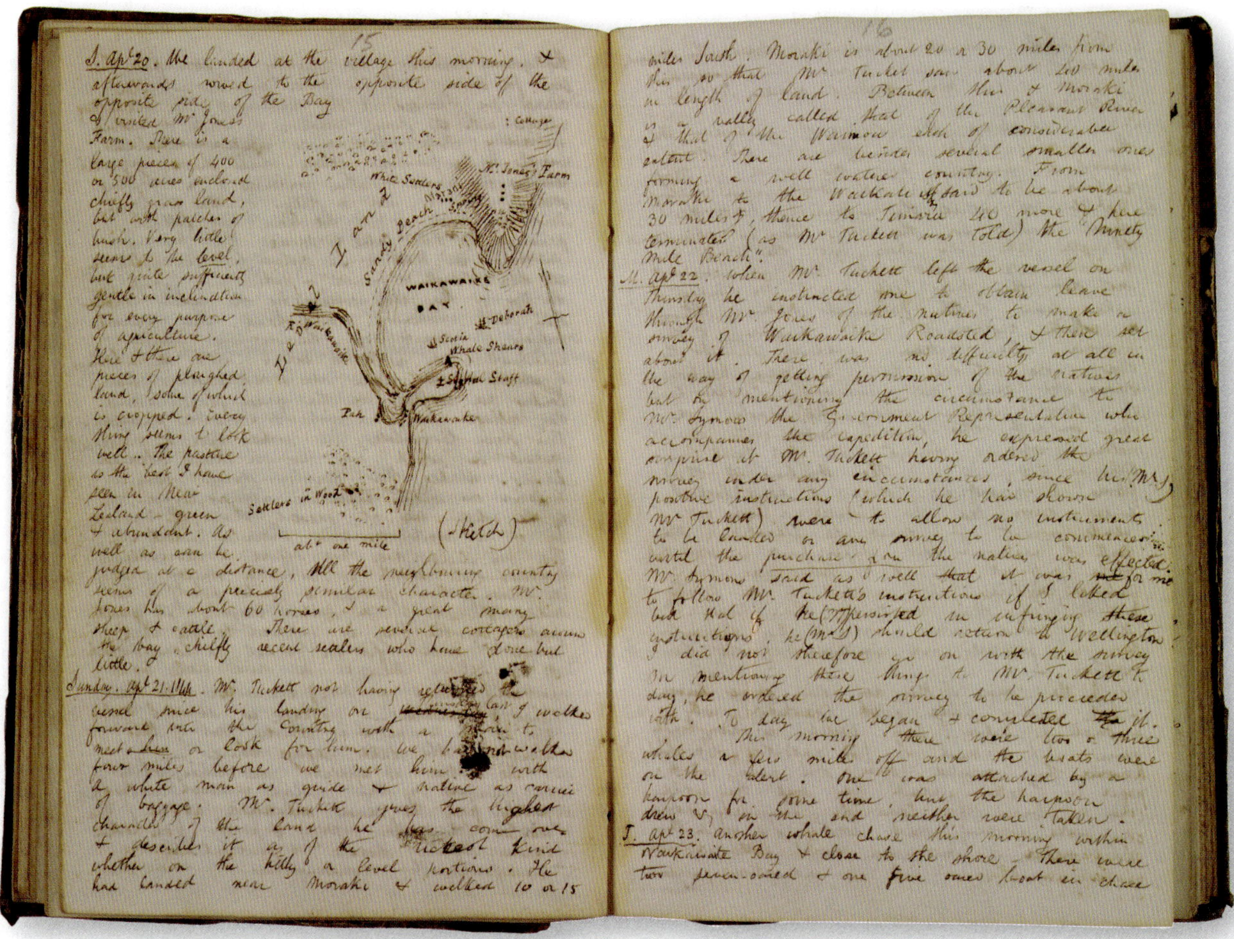

A surveyor's diary • 1843–44

John Wallis Barnicoat. *Journal, 1843–44*. Misc MS-1451-3. Purchased, 1994.

John Wallis Barnicoat, New Zealand Company surveyor and settler at Nelson, kept a detailed diary from September 1841 to October 1844. The first two volumes cover the voyage out to New Zealand in the *Lord Auckland* and his early survey work in Nelson.

The third volume, June 1843 to October 1844, is notable for its detailed account of the fatal confrontation with Te Rauparaha and Rangihaeata at Tuamarina in the Wairau on 14 June, from which Barnicoat and Frederick Tuckett, Chief Surveyor, barely escaped with their lives but left twenty-two settlers and four Māori dead. From April to June 1844, Tuckett and Barnicoat explored the east coast of the South Island to select a suitable site for the New Edinburgh settlement. With the lessons of Wairau well in mind, the Otago Block of 216,000 hectares stretching south from the Otago harbour to beyond the Clutha was selected and purchased from the local Kai Tahu led by Tuhawaiki, Taiaroa and Karetai for £2400.

The diary entry shown is for Saturday 22 April 1844, when Barnicoat landed at Waikouaiti from the *Deborah*, seen here at anchor in the bay. He describes the farming settlement established by Johnny Jones four years earlier.

SRS

The naming of Canterbury • 1848

This handsome, green minute book records the Canterbury Association's first meeting to forward a scheme for a Church of England settlement in New Zealand on 27 March 1848 in its rooms at 41 Charing Cross, London. One resolution was that the name of the settlement be 'Canterbury'; another that the name of the chief town be 'Christchurch', at the suggestion of John Robert Godley after his Oxford college. The book also shows that the Wairarapa district was the site first considered. However, attention soon turned to the 'Middle' Island, and the area around Port Cooper (now Lyttelton) was chosen instead.

Land acquired from the New Zealand Company was to be sold to settlers for a sufficient price, with a large part of the profits being used for educational and ecclesiastical purposes. To achieve a 'proper' social balance, both landowners and labourers were encouraged to emigrate, though only those of good character and Church of England beliefs were considered acceptable.

The Canterbury Association records were acquired by Dr Hocken from Sir William Lucius Selfe, son of Henry Selfe Selfe, London agent of the Canterbury Association, during a visit to England in 1902–03. ACC

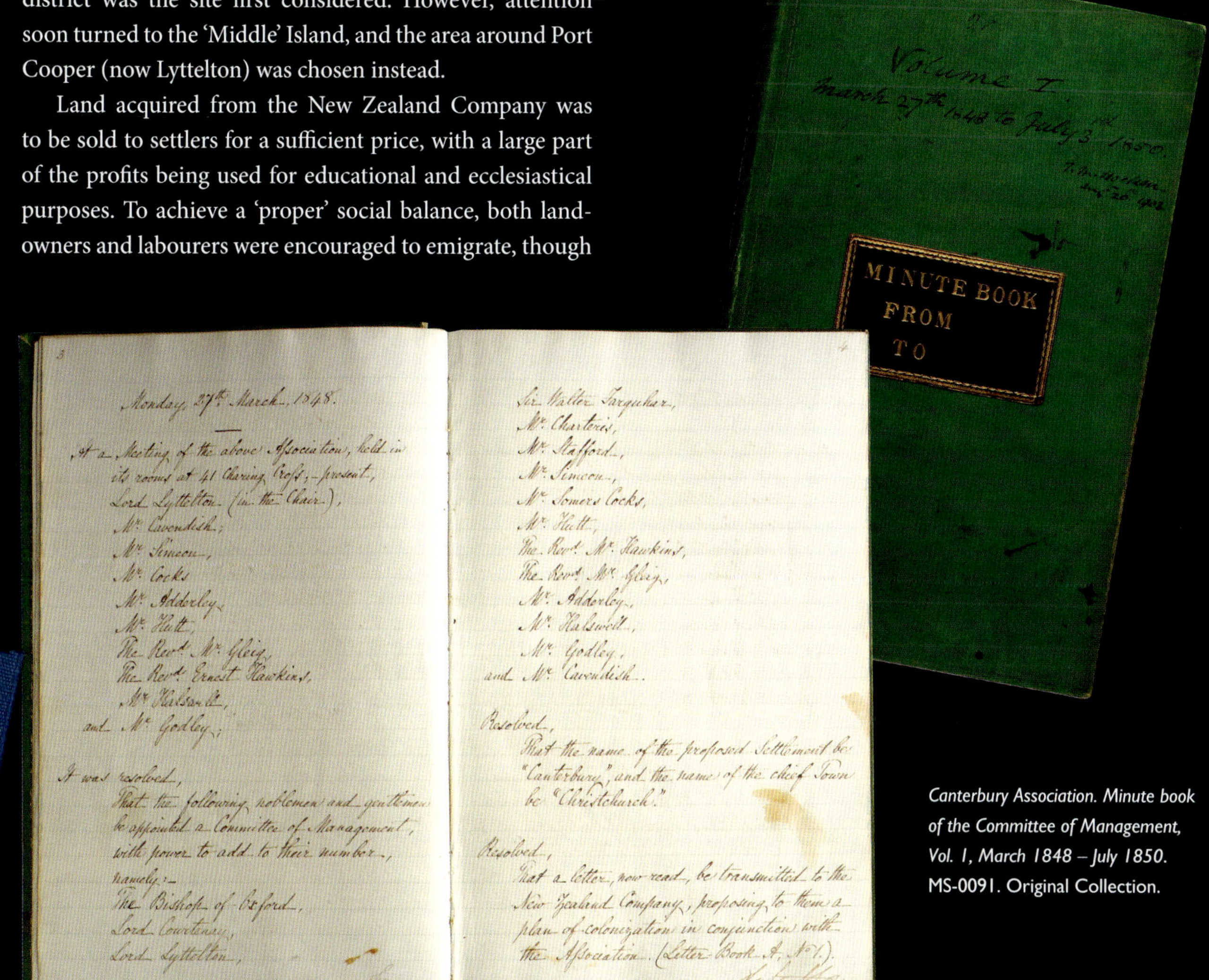

3

Monday, 27th March, 1848.

At a Meeting of the above Association, held in its rooms at 41 Charing Cross, – present,
Lord Lyttelton (in the Chair),
Mr Cavendish,
Mr Simeon,
Mr Cocks
Mr Adderley,
Mr Hutt,
The Revd Mr Gleig,
The Revd Ernest Hawkins,
Mr Halswell,
and Mr Godley;

It was resolved,
That the following noblemen and gentlemen be appointed a Committee of Management, with power to add to their number, namely:–
The Bishop of Oxford,
Lord Courtenay,
Lord Lyttelton,

4

Sir Walter Farquhar,
Mr Charteris,
Mr Stafford,
Mr Simeon,
Mr Somers Cocks,
Mr Hutt,
The Revd Mr Hawkins,
The Revd Mr Gleig,
Mr Adderley,
Mr Halswell,
Mr Godley,
and Mr Cavendish.

Resolved,
That the name of the proposed Settlement be "Canterbury", and the name of the chief Town be "Christchurch."

Resolved,
That a letter, now read, be transmitted to the New Zealand Company, proposing to them a plan of colonization in conjunction with the Association. (Letter Book A, No 1).

Lyttelton

Canterbury Association. Minute book of the Committee of Management, Vol. 1, March 1848 – July 1850. MS-0091. Original Collection.

2

1851 This prison, I find is used both
Sept 3 as a Lock-up and a Gaol.

To day 2 p.m. William Willcocks is brought into the Lock up for being drunk and disorderly, and for Assaulting John Adams of Dunedin (Tailor). The person is a Carpenter and residing in Dunedin; his conduct is most offensive; he perhaps without intending it is constantly assailing the Gaoler, with rude complaints.

Finished writing the Gaol, Rules and Regulations, they are as follows.

DUNEDIN GAOL

Rules and Regulations for the Criminal side of Prison.

General Rules.

1. Each Prisoner on entering this Prison and before being locked up, is to be searched in the presence of not less than two officers; and his name, age, country, religion, height and general description, to be entered in the Register kept for that purpose: such prisoner to be reported to the Sheriff, in the evening of the day of his entry.

2. All money, property, instruments, &c, to be taken from such Prisoner, a minute whereof specifying particulars and signed by the Gaoler is to be entered in a book for that purpose, — duplicate copies of which minute are to be made and signed by the said Gaoler, one to be handed to the Prisoner the

3

other to the Sheriff, such money, property, &c, to remain in the custody of Gaoler; (unless otherwise directed,) untill such time as the Prisoner shall be discharged, or otherwise entitled to it, or other disposition shall be ordered.

3. Every cell to be opened at 6 in the morning, between the 1st September and the 10th April, and at day light during the remainder of the year.

4. Fifteen minutes to be allowed for dressing.

5. The next fifteen minutes to be spent in sweeping, cleaning and dusting the Cell; during which time the Bedding is to be suspended in the Airing Yard, and then folded in the least possible compass.

6. The next thirty minutes, Prisoners to wash themselves as clean as possible, to wash themselves thoroughly. The officer on duty is to see especially to the observance of this rule

7. At 7, the Prisoners are to be assembled and called over, and a portion of Scripture and prayers to be read by the Gaoler or such other person as the Sheriff shall select

8. After Prayers and until a quarter before 8 "Breakfast".

9. At 10 minutes before 8, the Hard-labor men are to muster, and to be called over by the Overseer; at which time each man is to produce the implement with which he is to work or labor during the day.

Henry Monson. *Journal of Henry Monson, Gaoler, Dunedin. 1851–61.* MS-0088. Original Collection.

A gaoler's journal • 1851–61

Henry Monson's journal provides a unique insight into daily conditions at Dunedin's first gaol. Born in Yorkshire, Monson arrived in Dunedin aboard the *John Wickliffe* in 1848. He was appointed gaoler in 1851, and held the position until November 1861. During this time he kept a detailed journal of the comings and goings of the gaol, the behaviour of the prisoners and his battles with authorities over the atrocious conditions. Monson was an unorthodox gaoler in his concern for the moral plight of his prisoners and his objection to harsh physical punishment. The Dunedin gaol lacked security – the gate had no lock to speak of when Monson arrived – and although he records the many escapes with matter-of-fact acceptance, he was generally able to rely on the goodwill of his prisoners to stay put.

Monson's most renowned prisoner was James Macandrew, Superintendent of the Otago Province. After he was imprisoned for debt in 1861, Macandrew famously declared his house at Carisbrook a gaol, and was confined in the comfort of his own home. Monson's disgust and frustration at this are clearly evident. ACC

Allan Houston's Otago goldfields • 1860s

Houston is a mystery. Little about him is known except what is in this manuscript. He was a Scot who visited and travelled through Otago in the 1860s, when the gold fields were full of activity, although yields were declining in some areas.

The manuscript is a charming miscellany of observation and description. He describes the professional diggers and the various townships and settlements, provides a 'diggers phraseology', and explains the processes of digging and extracting the gold. Houston has also written up 'Mr B's Narrative' of the first rush to Gabriel's Gully, also titled 'An Adventure in Going to and Returning from the Otago Gold Fields'. There are descriptions of Taiaroa Head and Otago Harbour, Port Chalmers and Dunedin 'City', and comments on life in Dunedin. Houston also provides a dictionary of colonial phrases and remarks on transport around the province.

Written in a fine spidery hand, Houston's manuscript contains photographs, newspaper cuttings, maps and other illustrations and samples of the local vegetation and the local gold. Houston returned to Scotland with his manuscript still unpublished. AB

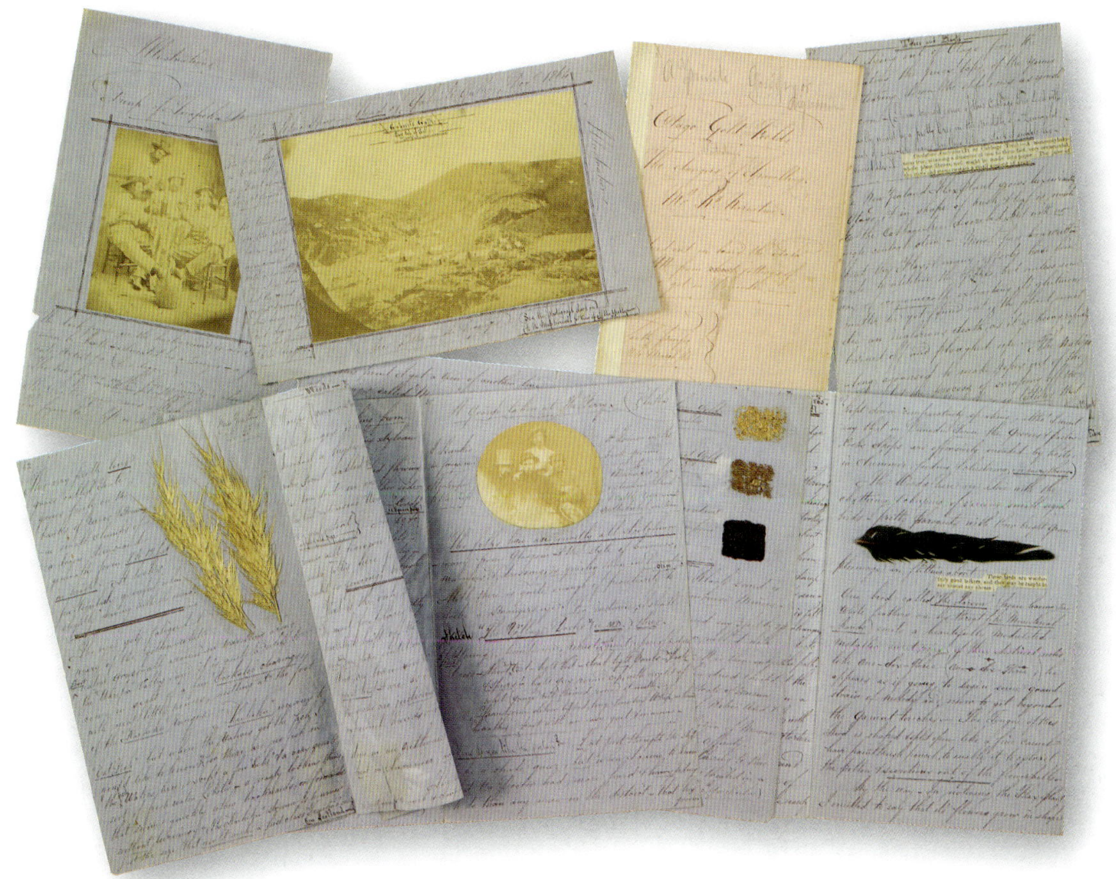

Allan Houston. *'The Gold fields of Otago, A.H.'s Jottings 1865 with Lithographic Illustrations. Memoranda of Otago Gold diggings and of Gold Diggers, from personal inspection and reliable information written in March 1865'.* 1864–66. Misc-MS-1413. Purchased, 1995.

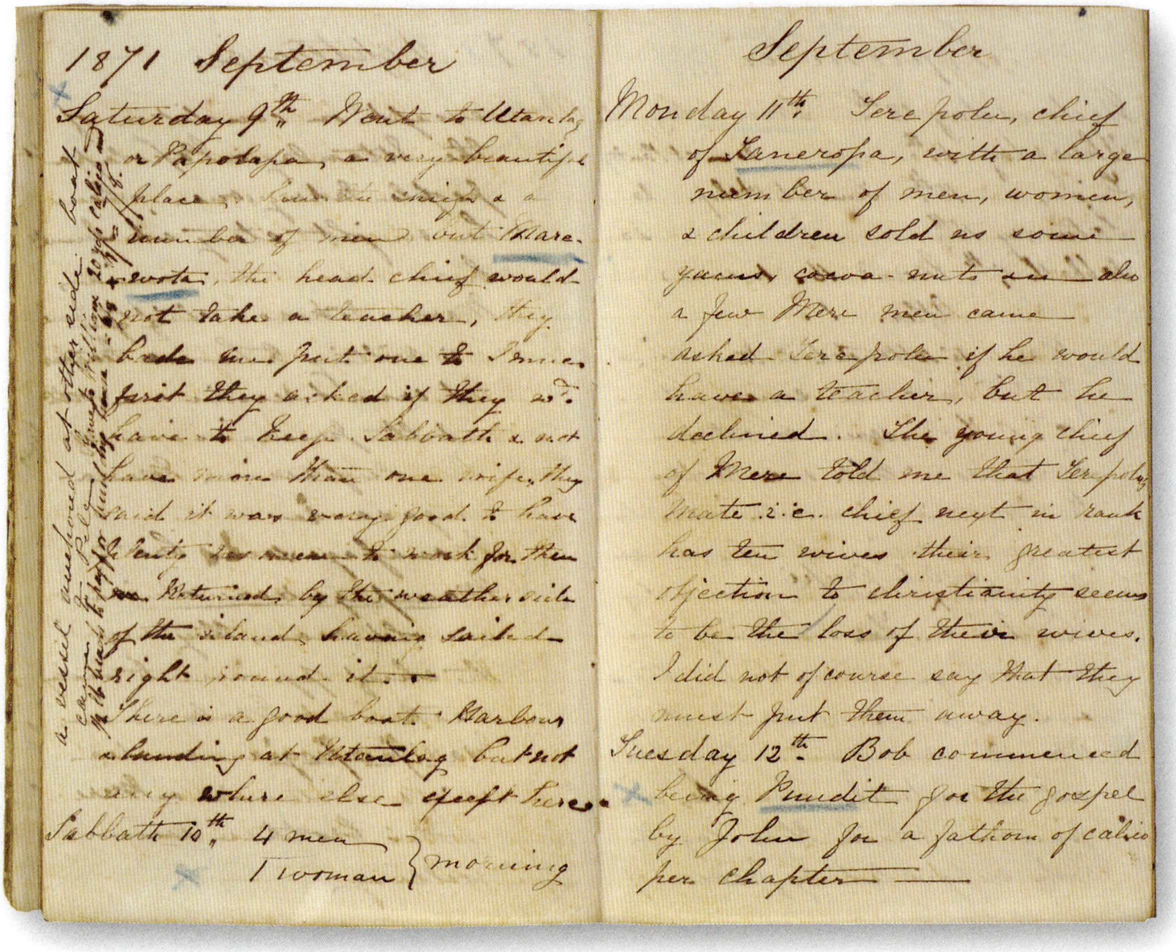

New Hebrides mission diary • 1870–72

Rev. Peter Milne, Nguna Island. *New Hebrides Mission Diary, 1870–72.* MS-0432. Donated by Dr P. Milne, 1956.

Interest in supporting a Christian mission to the New Hebrides was stirred as early as 1852, when the Rev. John Inglis of the Reformed Presbyterian Church of Scotland Mission toured New Zealand prior to leaving for the Islands as a missionary.

At this time the Presbyterian Church in New Zealand was divided into the 'Northern Church' and the 'Southern Church'. The latter, represented by the Presbyterian Synod of Otago and Southland, was based on Free Church of Scotland ideals, which influenced its choice of missionaries for many years. It was not until 1901 that the two churches became joined, so the missions were independent of each other.

The Northern Church enthusiastically agreed to support a missionary to Tanna Island in 1862. Not far behind and equally keen, the southern Synod agreed in 1867 to send the Rev. Peter Milne, a young Free Church of Scotland Licentiate, to Nguna Island. He arrived with his wife Mary Jane in 1870, and was to spend an extraordinary fifty-five years there. During this time he kept a remarkable journal in twelve volumes, vividly recording island and mission life, that has become a prime source for ni-Vanuatu history. The first volume is illustrated. LT

Otago has a singular place in the history of the dairy industry, now New Zealand's most important export earner. The foundation of the co-operative factory system, which characterised the early industry, is witnessed by the minute book of the pioneering Otago Peninsula Cheese Factory Co. Ltd. On 22 August 1871 eight men met at John Mathieson's Springfield farm on the Otago Peninsula, to discuss establishing a business 'for the Purpose of Cheese Making on the Cooperative Principal [sic] with Limited Liability. Shares to Be £1.~.~. Each Share to Represent 10 quartz of Milk.' John Laidlaw McGregor was elected manager at the next meeting on 4 September when he agreed to 'Make Cheese to the Best of His ability'. The first co-operative dairy commenced operations in September, producing Scottish-style 'Dunlop' cheese, in a building provided by Mathieson. In its first year the Company produced 9919 lb. of cheese, making over £246 in profit.

The departure of Mathieson led on 16 June 1875 to a new venture called the Peninsula Cheese Making Company. The new company, managed by George Farquhar, moved the factory a short distance to Pukekihi. It continued cheese production, with some success, until the mid-1880s when the company moved into butter manufacture. The venture finally ceased about 1892. SI

Otago Peninsula Cheese Factory Co. Ltd. Minute book, 1871–84. MS-0186-A. Donated by T.H.R. Fleming, 1951.

1875
June 16
A Meeting of the Projectors of the new Peninsula Cheese Making Company was held in the house of Mr John McGregor for the Purpose of selling shares & makeing arrangments for a site for a Building to Carrey on their Busness of Makeng Chees when Mr. Adam Stewart was Chosen to take the Cheir
After some preliminary Busness the folowin Agreement was drawn up and signed

We The undersigned do hereby agree to Join together for the purpose of makeing Cheese for the term of fourteen years Commencing from the first week of October 1875 and that we will well and truly bring all our Mornings Milk unto this Company Premises, to the amount of 10 quarts for every share held by us. The price of such share to be one Pound sterling bareing Interest at the rate of five Pounds Sterling per Centum, per anum, and that we will abide by and act according to the decision of the Majority of the Share-holders

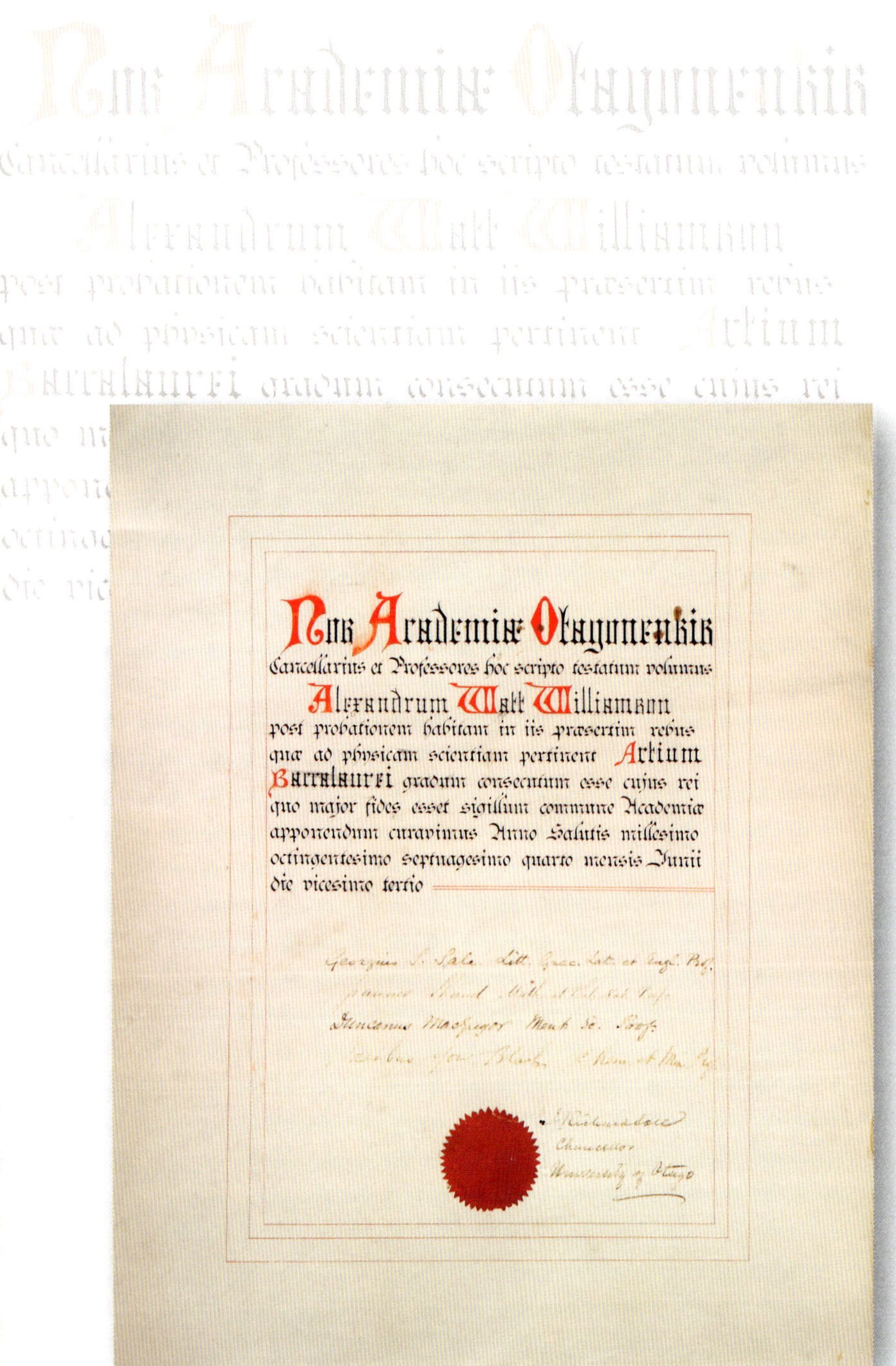

Nos Academiae Otagonensis
Cancellarius et Professores hoc scripto testatum volumus
Alexandrum Watt Williamson
post probationem habitam in iis praesertim rebus
quae ad physicam scientiam pertinent Artium
Baccalaurei gradum consecutum esse cujus rei
quo major fides esset sigillum commune Academiae
apponendum curavimus Anno Salutis millesimo
octingentesimo septuagesimo quarto mensis Junii
die vicesimo tertio

Duncanus MacGregor Ment. Sc. Prof.

Chancellor
University of Otago

Alexander Watt Williamson holds the honour of being the first and only student to be awarded a degree by the University of Otago before amalgamation with the University of New Zealand in 1874. He was, therefore, also New Zealand's first graduate.

Williamson was born in Warwickshire in 1849, and two years later left for New Zealand with his family, which settled in the Wanganui region. After a short time teaching, he went to Dunedin in 1871 to be part of the first intake of students at the University of Otago. Although he took all subjects, including three languages, his diploma notes (in Latin) an emphasis on the physical sciences. According to reminiscences he wrote for the University's 1919 jubilee celebrations, Williamson particularly enjoyed Professor Black's geological tramps around Dunedin. Soon after he received his Bachelor of Arts diploma in June 1874, University of Otago lost the power to award degrees in its own name. After payment of two guineas, Williamson was also awarded a Bachelor of Arts degree from the University of New Zealand in 1876.

Following graduation, Williamson resumed his teaching career. He was headmaster at a number of schools throughout the North Island, before retiring in 1914.

ACC

Alexander Watt Williamson. *Graduation diploma for the degree of Bachelor of Arts, University of Otago, June 1874.* MS-0543. Deposited by the University Council, 1959.

First woman medical student • 1891

On 10 March 1891 Emily Siedeberg wrote to the Chancellor of the University of Otago, requesting admission to the Medical School, as she had already passed the preliminary examinations. Though women had in principle been admitted to the University from its first classes in 1871, the University Council and hospital trustees' eventual acceptance of Siedeberg's applications made her the University's first woman medical student. Its success caused considerable, not always favourable, comment in the press, as in the June 1891 issue of the *Otago University Review*:

> … can a woman who pries into the intricacies of the human frame, with all the ghastly proceedings attendant on the acquisition of such knowledge, remain the delicate and refined creature whom we compare to, and from w take our definition of an angel?

In her second year she was joined by her friend Margar Cruickshank. Emily Siedeberg completed her training 1896 and became the first woman medical graduate in Ne Zealand. After a period of postgraduate study at Dublin an Berlin, specialising in gynaecology, obstetrics, and children diseases, she returned to Dunedin, where she practised fo thirty years and became the first superintendent of the S Helen's Women's Hospital, 1905–38. ACC

Emily Siedeberg. *Letter to Chancellor, Universit of Otago, 10 March 1891*. MS-1689/001. Transferred from Medical Library, 2001.

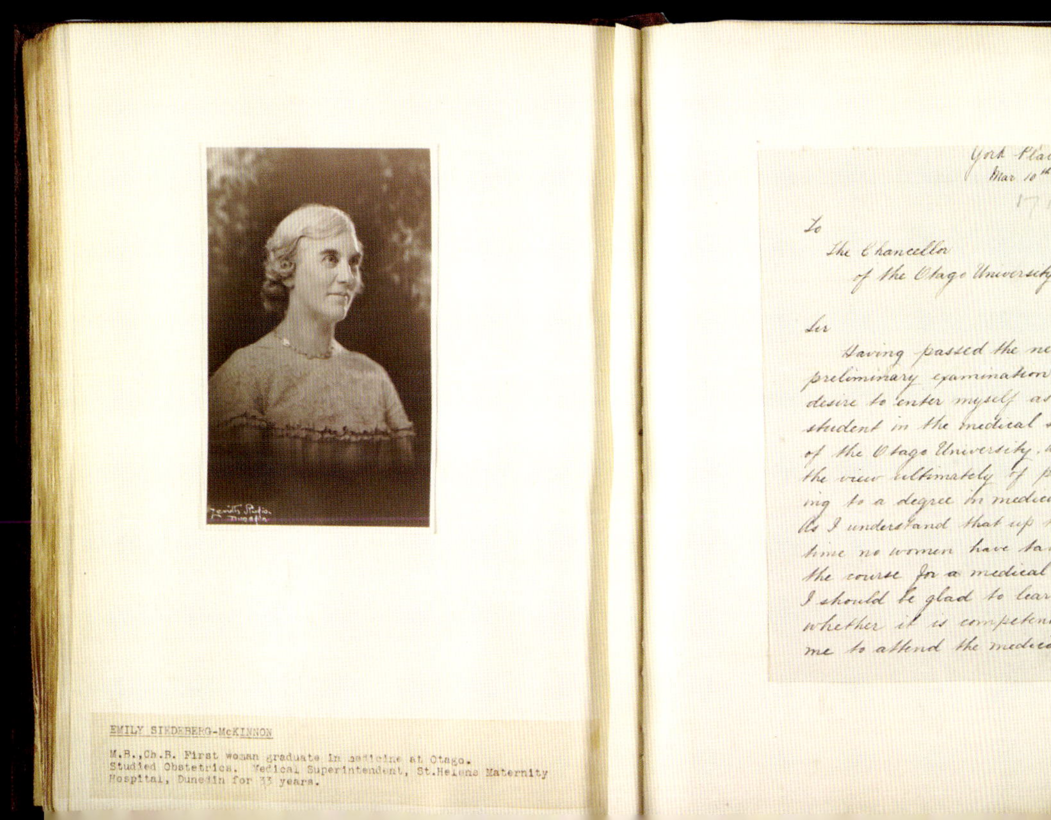

EMILY SIEDEBERG-McKINNON

M.B.,Ch.B. First woman graduate in medicine at Otago. Studied Obstetrics. Medical Superintendent, St.Helens Maternity Hospital, Dunedin for 33 years.

York Place
Mar 10th 1891

17B

To
The Chancellor
of the Otago University

Sir
Having passed the necessary preliminary examination, I desire to enter myself as a student in the medical school of the Otago University, with the view ultimately of proceeding to a degree in medicine. As I understand that up to this time no women have taken the course for a medical degree, I should be glad to learn whether it is competent for me to attend the medical

he set up as an engineer and land agent. By 1859 he had designed the Nelson Provincial Government buildings and the Masonic Hall. In 1866 the family returned to England, but by1870 Bury had returned, alone, to resume his architectural career in Nelson.

In 1877 Bury won a competition to design the new University of Otago building to be erected on the site of the former Botanic Gardens. His winning entry, signed 'To B or not to B', was evidently classical in style, but was changed to this Gothic design seemingly at the University's request. in April 1879. Bury patterned the adjacent geology block and the four professorial houses to a similar Gothic design. Additions by later architects copied his original style.

Architectural work in Dunedin was scarce, and in 1885 Bury returned to Nelson. Sometime after 1890 he moved to Sydney, finally returning to England, where he died in 1912. His clocktower and surrounding buildings, however, remain as great masterpieces of nineteenth-century New Zealand architecture. SI

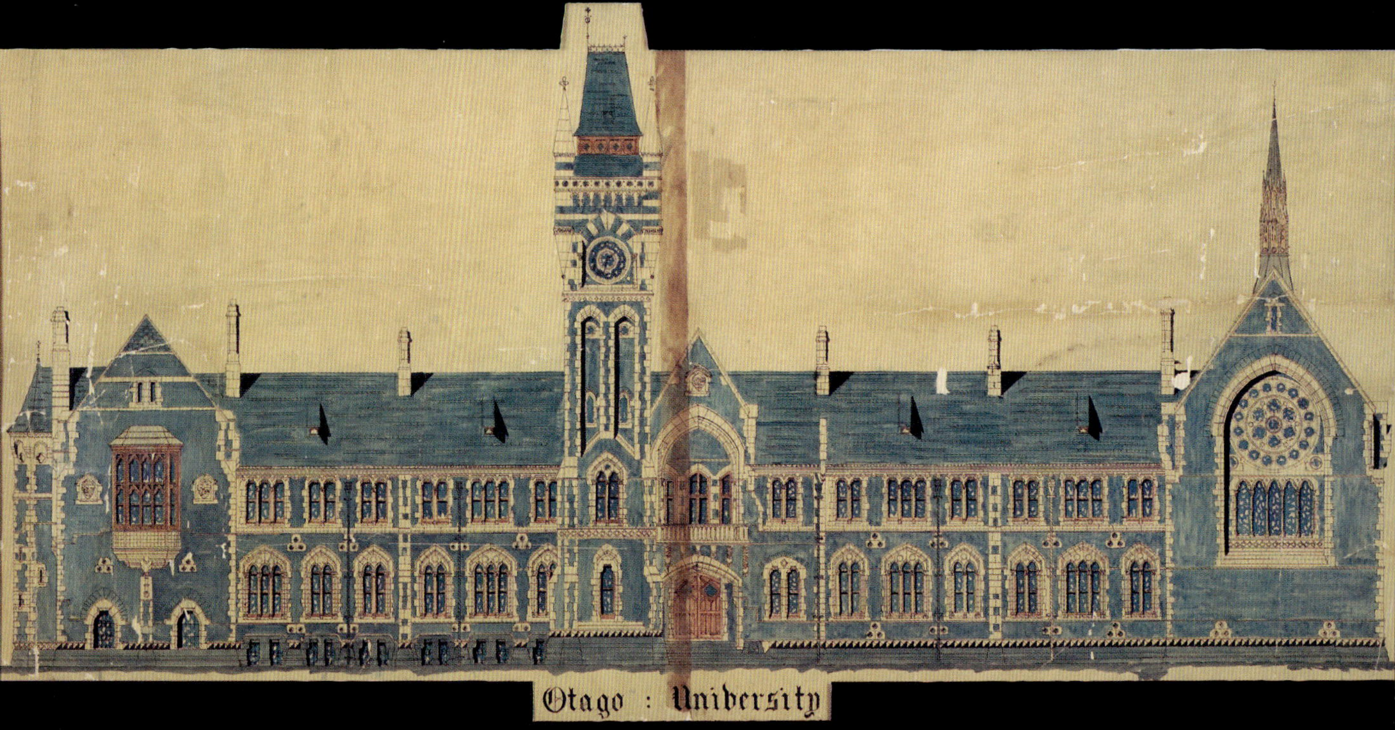

Maxwell Bury, *University of Otago elevation*, 1877, Ink and watercolour, 97-085. Deposited by Dalziel Architects Ltd, 1997.

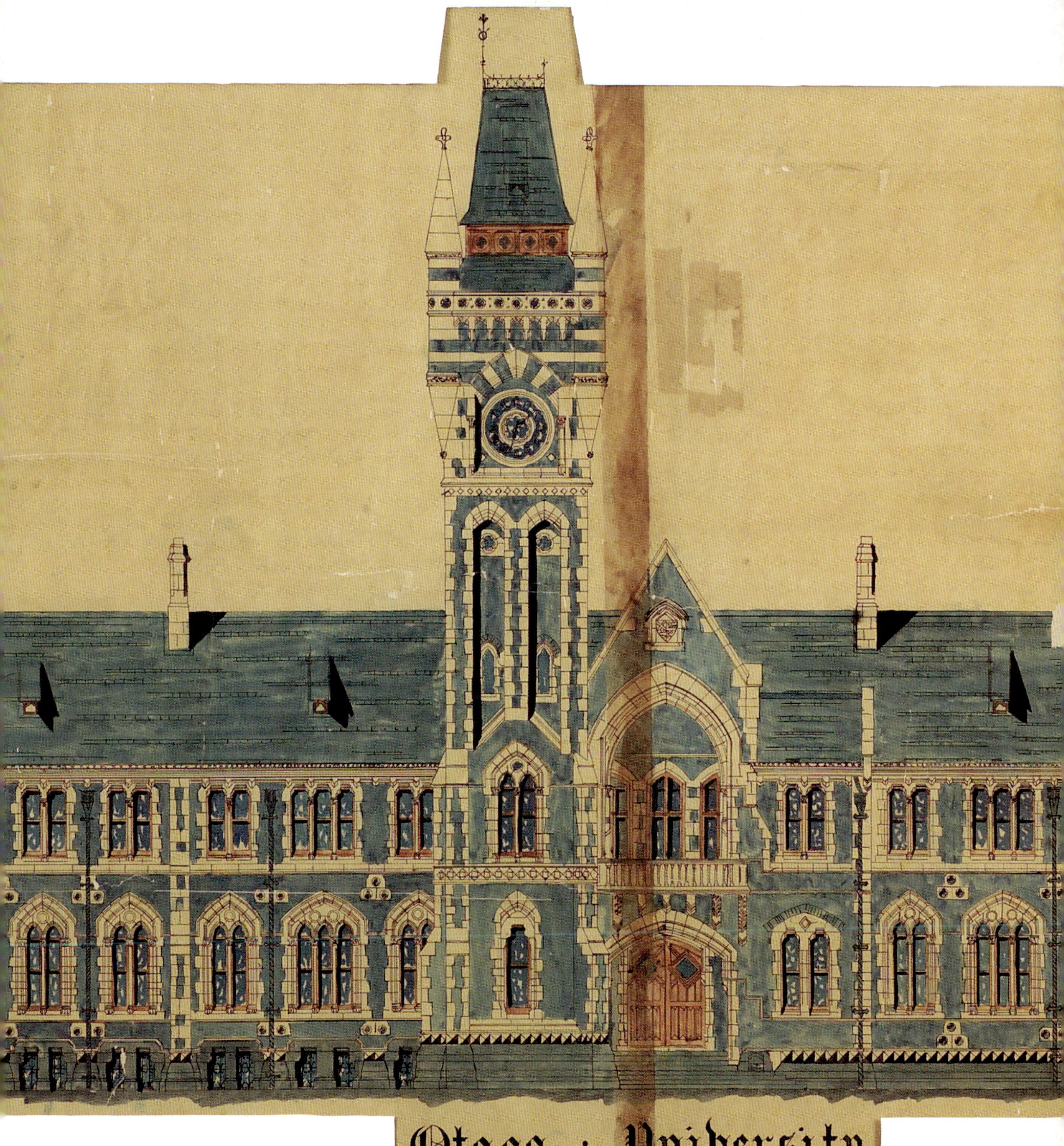
Otago : University

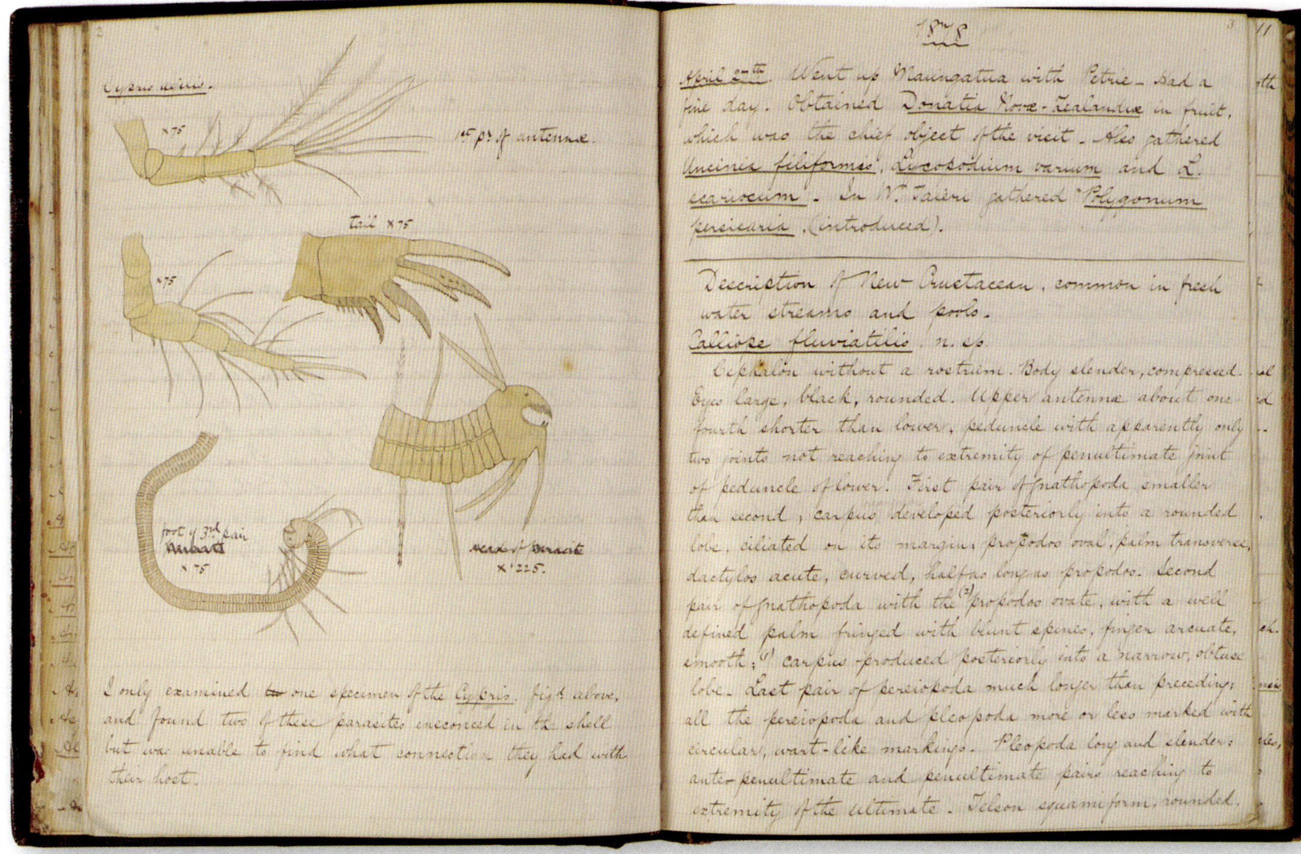

1st pr. of antennae
tail × 75
× 75
× 225.

I only examined one specimen of the Cypris, fig. above, and found two of these parasites ensconced in the shell but was unable to find what connection they had with their host.

1878

April 27th. Went up Maungatua with Petrie. Had a fine day. Obtained Dorsatia Novæ-Zealandiæ in fruit, which was the chief object of the visit. Also gathered Uncinia filiformis, Lycopodium varium and L. scariosum. In N. Taieri gathered Polygonum persicaria (introduced).

Description of New Crustacean, common in fresh water streams and pools.

Calliope fluviatilis, n. sp.

Cephalon without a rostrum. Body slender, compressed. Eyes large, black, rounded. Upper antennæ about one fourth shorter than lower, peduncle with apparently only two joints not reaching to extremity of penultimate joint of peduncle of lower. First pair of gnathopoda smaller than second, carpus developed posteriorly into a rounded lobe, ciliated on its margin, propodos oval, palm transverse, dactylos acute, curved, half as long as propodos. Second pair of gnathopoda with the propodos ovate, with a well defined palm fringed with blunt spines, finger arcuate, smooth; carpus produced posteriorly into a narrow, obtuse lobe. Last pair of pereiopoda much longer than preceding; all the pereiopoda and pleopoda more or less marked with circular, wart-like markings. Pleopoda long and slender: ante-penultimate and penultimate pairs reaching to extremity of the ultimate. Telson squamiform, rounded.

G.M. Thomson. *Scientific Notebook, 1878–82*. MS-1090.
Donated by J.G. Thomson, 1976.

Notes of a naturalist • 1878–82

The papers of Dunedin teacher, naturalist and politician George Malcolm Thomson (1848–1933) include his immaculately kept scientific notebooks. Thomson studied chemistry and botany at Edinburgh, but had been unable to complete a degree as he was needed in his family's business. After migrating to New Zealand in 1868, in the 1870s he began his long career as science master at the Otago Boys' and Otago Girls' High Schools. Thomson had great energy, and, when he could spare time from teaching, family and many community responsibilities, he enjoyed nothing more than an outdoor ramble. During these outings Thomson made careful observations of flora and fauna, and collected specimens which he later examined by microscope, recording his findings with meticulous care in his notebooks.

Some of Thomson's most important work was in marine biology. F.W. Hutton encouraged him to take up the study of small crustaceans, a field not yet explored in detail. He identified and described many species previously unknown to Western science, including a new order of crustaceans. Lack of academic qualifications limited Thomson's career prospects as a scientist, but he published widely, took a leading role in various scientific organisations and, in his latter years as a politician, lobbied effectively for the reform of New Zealand science. AJC

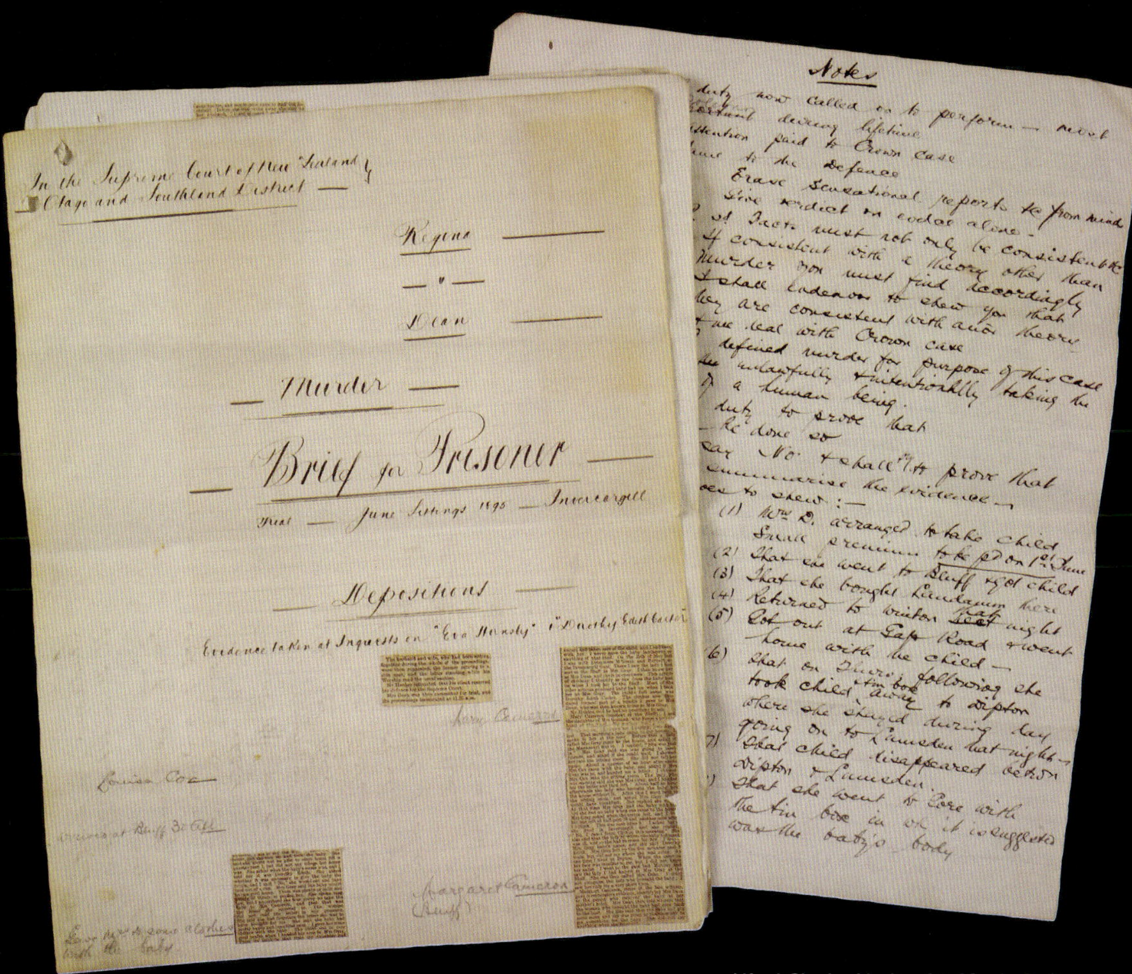

Alfred Charles Hanlon. *Brief for the Defence of Minnie Dean, 1895*. MS-0687. Donated, 1967.

A passionate appeal • 1895

Alfred Charles Hanlon, New Zealand's most famous criminal lawyer, will forever be remembered for his defence of Minnie Dean, the Winton baby farmer, in 1895.

Alf Hanlon's brief for the defence contains newspaper reports on the Dunedin trial, which he annotated, and handwritten notes for his final address to the jury, which on this occasion lasted ninety minutes. Drawing on his great love of Shakespearean drama and the eloquence for which he was renowned, Hanlon skilfully and with great passion argued that Minnie Dean should not be convicted of the murder of Dorothy Edith Carter, as intent to kill the baby had not been proved. Any ounce of doubt had to result in a conviction of manslaughter only, or in total acquittal. Hanlon's address was greeted with applause by the dazzled public gallery. Judge J.S. Williams adjourned until the next day to allow the jury time for calm deliberation. In his summing up, Williams then told the jury that a verdict of manslaughter would be a 'weak-kneed compromise'; it was a question only of guilt or innocence. In what is, even today, a contentious verdict, Minnie Dean was subsequently convicted and sentenced to death. She remains the only woman to be hanged for murder in New Zealand. ACC

Like many other educated Europeans of their generation, Major-General Robley and Dr Hocken were both fascinated by Māori culture. Robley (1840–1930), who was artistically gifted, had fought in the New Zealand Wars as a lieutenant in the 83rd Regiment, but took every opportunity to observe and sketch aspects of Māori life. On retirement in 1887 he built up a collection of thirty-five Māori heads, which he used as the basis for his book *Moko, or, Maori Tatooing*, which was published in 1896. In 1908 the heads were offered to the New Zealand government, who refused the opportunity, and they went to the Natural History Museum in New York.

A second edition of *Moko* was not completed by Robley, and he gave his notes to Hocken, who determined to take up the task instead. As written by hand above the Preface, 'The genius of the Maori artists has hitherto hardly received the attention at the hands of the art historian that is his due….' Other commitments intervened and Hocken failed to complete also, but the interleaved first edition with many additional notes, comments, sketches, and photographs has survived in the Original Collection, where it continues to be an invaluable source of information for Māori scholars about a very significant and distinctive aspect of their culture. SRS

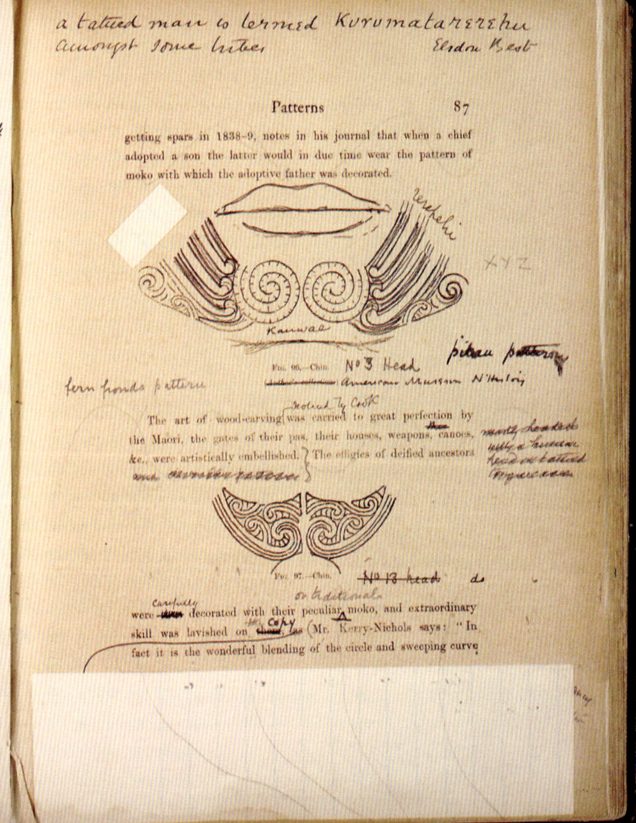
Patterns 87

getting spars in 1838–9, notes in his journal that when a chief adopted a son the latter would in due time wear the pattern of moko with which the adoptive father was decorated.

Fig. 96.—Chin.

The art of wood-carving was carried to great perfection by the Maori, the gates of their pas, their houses, weapons, canoes, &c., were artistically embellished. The effigies of deified ancestors

Fig. 97.—Chin.

were decorated with their peculiar moko, and extraordinary skill was lavished on these. (Mr. Kerry-Nichols says: "In fact it is the wonderful blending of the circle and sweeping curve

Moko, or, Maori Tatooing, by Major-General Horatio Robley. First edition. Interleaved and annotated. 1896–1902. MS-0488-001. Original Collection.

a tatued man is termed Kurumatarerehu amongst some tribes

Elsdon Best

getting spars in 1838–9, notes in his journal that when a chief adopted a son the latter would in due time wear the pattern of moko with which the adoptive father was decorated.

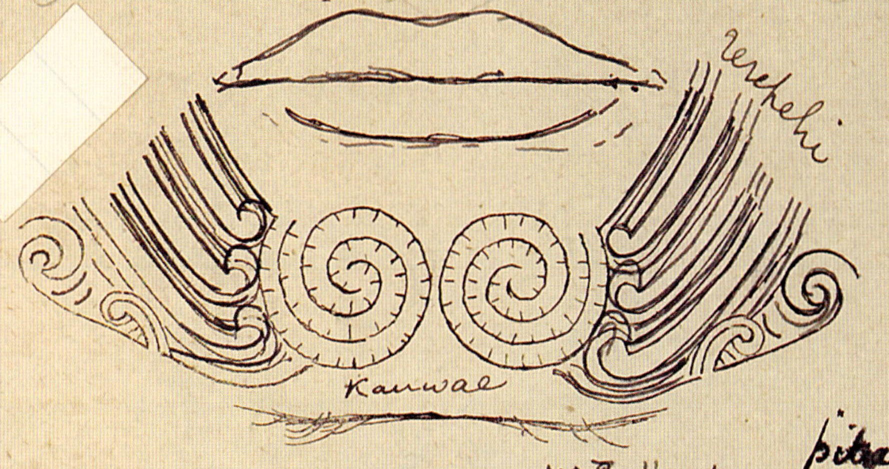

Fig. 96.—Chin. No 3 Head

~~(Author's collection)~~ American Museum N. History

fern fronds pattern

The art of wood-carving (noticed by Cook) was carried to great perfection by the Maori, the gates of their pas, their houses, weapons, canoes, &c., were artistically embellished. The effigies of deified ancestors

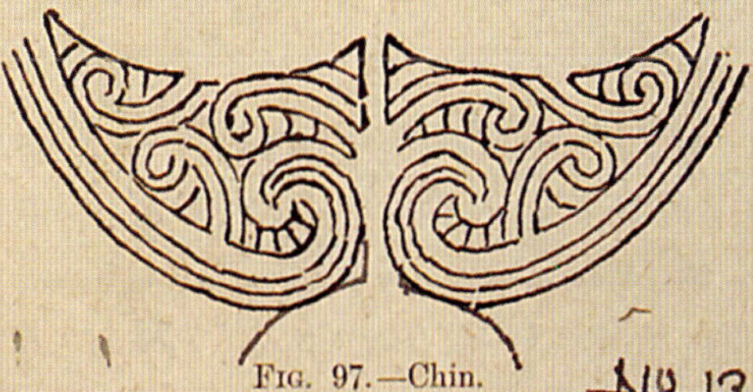

Fig. 97.—Chin. ~~No 13 head~~ do

were decorated with their peculiar moko, and extraordinary skill was lavished on them, as Mr. Kerry-Nichols says: "In fact it is the wonderful blending of the circle and sweeping curve

Women's suffrage • 1909–12

New Zealand feminist Anna Paterson Stout (1858–1931) collected these badges during her three years' involvement in the British campaign for women's suffrage. With her husband, lawyer and politician Robert Stout, she had fought for the women's franchise in New Zealand. The Stouts travelled to England in 1909 and Anna stayed until 1912. She joined the militant Women's Social and Political Union (WSPU), spoke at meetings throughout Britain, and wrote pamphlets and letters to the editor in support of women's suffrage. As a woman of standing – wife of New Zealand's Chief Justice and sometime Premier – her views carried weight. Furthermore, she had herself been enfranchised for seventeen years without loss of sanity, as some predicted for women voters.

The badges are from a variety of British organisations. Among them are Catholic, Anglican and Jewish suffrage societies, Men's League for Women's Suffrage, Women's Tax Resistance League ('No Vote No Tax'), Women Writer's Suffrage League, and Actresses' Franchise League. The purple, white and green badges (purple for dignity, white for purity, green for hope) are from the Women's Social and Political Union, one of them (bearing a woman released from prison) designed by Sylvia Pankhurst. Stout's collection also includes one badge from the other side – the National League for Opposing Woman Suffrage. AJC

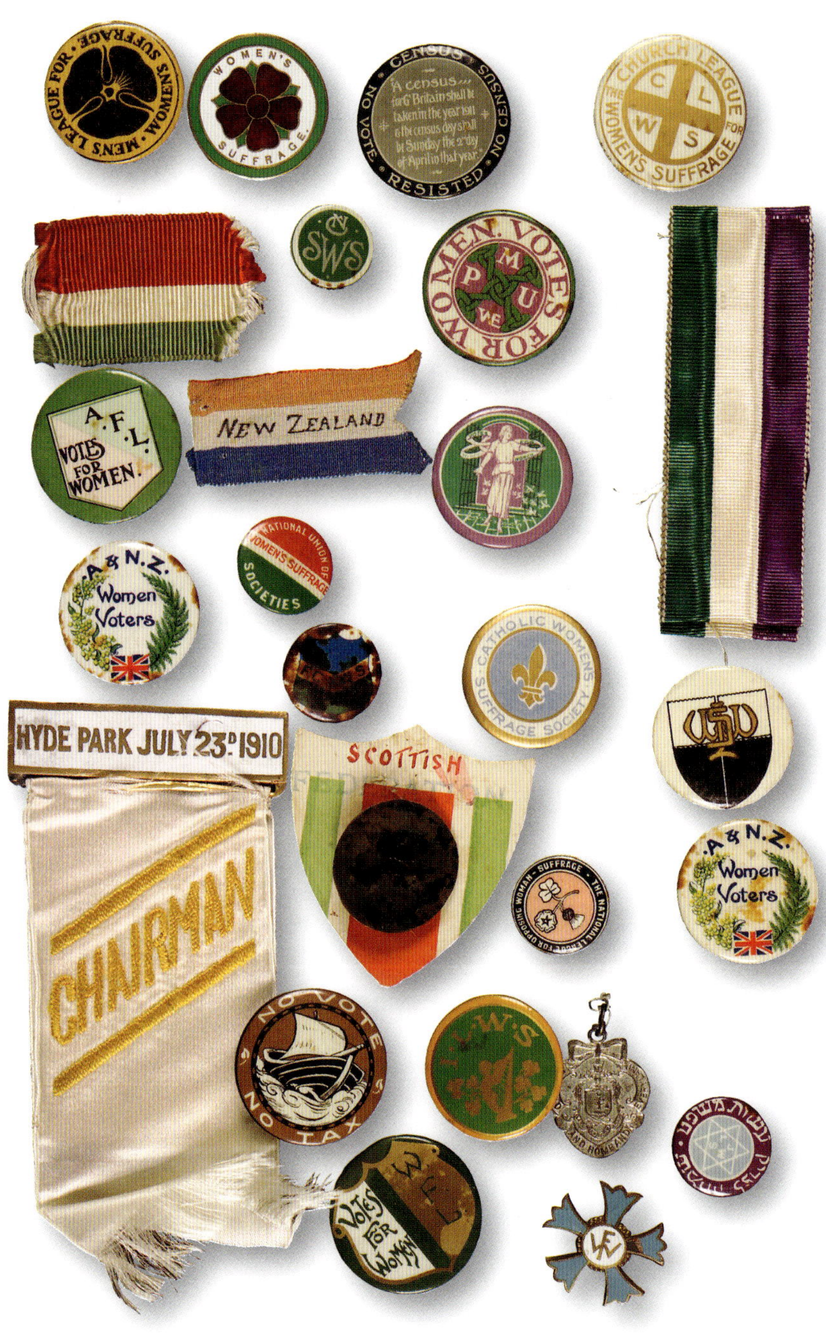

Anna, Lady Stout. *Collection of Suffragette Badges, 1909–12.* MS–0253. Stout Bequest, 1948.

Mediation at the mill • 1911

In July 1911 thirty women from the worsted spinning department of the Roslyn Woollen Mill, Dunedin, walked off the job, starting the first strike in the woollen mills of Otago. It was not, however, harsh working conditions which provoked this unprecedented action. The women objected to the foreman favouring two fellow workers for additional work, creating resentment as payment was by piecework. The recently formed Dunedin and Mosgiel Woollen Mills Employees' Union did not back the strike – it was no radical organisation – but forming a union may have given some of the mill women a new industrial awareness. Jessie Dougherty, first to sign this address, was an early member.

As workers and management could not agree, they called in two arbitrators, the Mayor of Dunedin, William Burnett, and J.T. Paul (1874–1964), Legislative Councillor, journalist, trade unionist and important player in the labour movement. After a day-long hearing, Paul and Burnett found that there had indeed been favouritism, but no evidence of personal misconduct, despite rumours of 'immorality'. To restore harmony, they suggested the two women transfer to another department. This pragmatic and moderate approach was typical of Paul, and brought him wide popularity. It certainly found favour with the mill 'girls', who praised his 'Masterly Tact and excellent Conciliatory Methods'. AJC

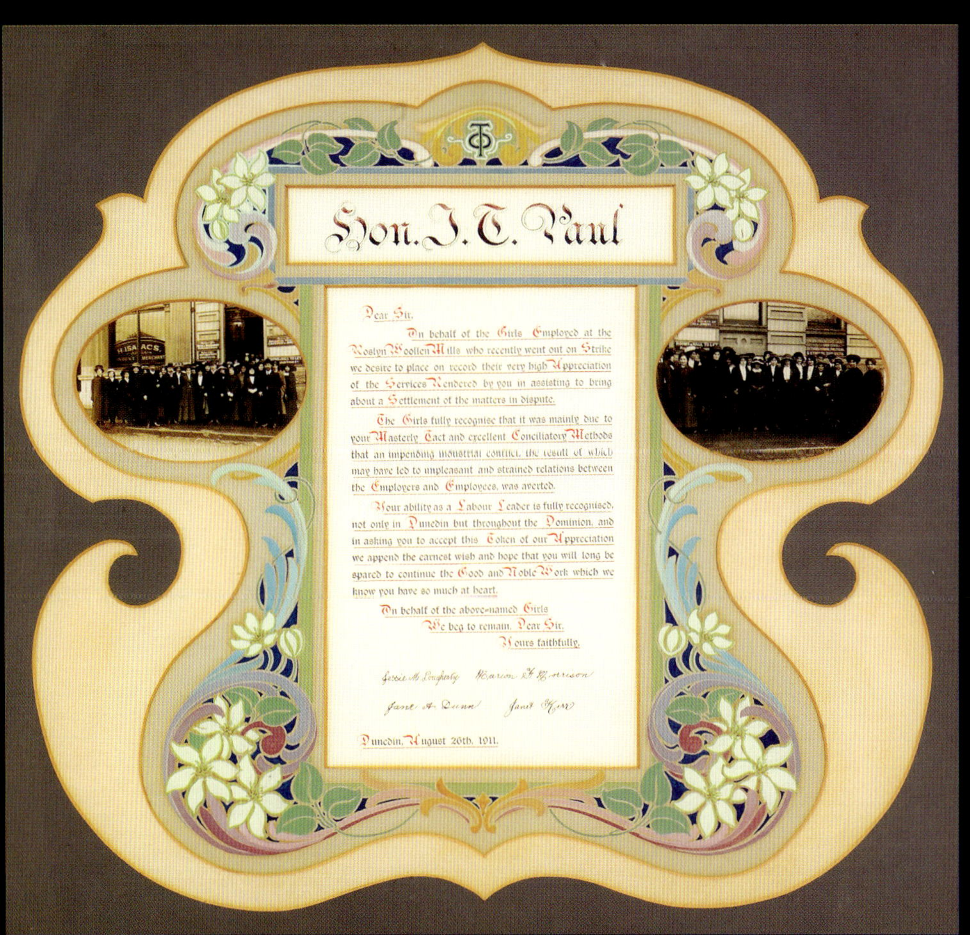

Hon. J. T. Paul

Dear Sir,

On behalf of the Girls Employed at the Roslyn Woollen Mills who recently went out on Strike we desire to place on record their very high Appreciation of the Services Rendered by you in assisting to bring about a Settlement of the matters in dispute.

The Girls fully recognise that it was mainly due to your Masterly Tact and excellent Conciliatory Methods that an impending industrial conflict, the result of which may have led to unpleasant and strained relations between the Employers and Employees, was averted.

Your ability as a Labour Leader is fully recognised, not only in Dunedin but throughout the Dominion, and in asking you to accept this Token of our Appreciation we append the earnest wish and hope that you will long be spared to continue the Good and Noble Work which we know you have so much at heart.

On behalf of the above-named Girls
We beg to remain, Dear Sir,
Yours faithfully,

Jessie M. Dougherty Marion H. Morrison
Jane A. Dunn Janet Kerr

Dunedin, August 26th, 1911.

Illuminated letter of appreciation to J.T. Paul from the 'girls' employed at the Roslyn Woollen Mills, 26 August 1911. MS-0982/796. Donated by the Otago and Southland Clothing and Related Trades Union of Workers, 1979.

A doctor's war • 1913–19

Born in Dunedin, Charles Mackie Begg (1879–1919) studied medicine at the Otago Medical School and Edinburgh, graduating MB ChB in 1903. Following the declaration of war in August 1914, Begg was placed in command of the New Zealand Field Ambulance. After spending some months in Egypt, the Ambulance embarked for Gallipoli in April 1915.

Begg's leather satchel contains letters, military orders and pamphlets, including *Notes for the use of the troops in dealing with the Turkish inhabitants*. He documented his early experiences with photographs. Seen here are the kitchen and hospital at the Zeitoun training base in Egypt. Also shown are fellow Anzacs, landscapes and natives: a soldier's tourist album. Begg was soon responsible for the treatment of over 15,000 wounded Anzacs, becoming Assistant Director of Medical Services. In 1916 the New Zealand forces moved to the western front, where, as Deputy Director of Medical Services for the ANZAC Corps, Begg worked to improve the general health of the troops through better food, accommodation, health education, immunisation, sanitation and counselling. In November 1918 he was promoted to Director of Medical Services in London, but died of influenza on 2 February 1919, just thirty-nine years of age. SI

Charles Mackie Begg. *Papers relating to Begg's medical service during World War I, 1913–19.* AG-497. Donated by Sir Neil Begg, 1994.

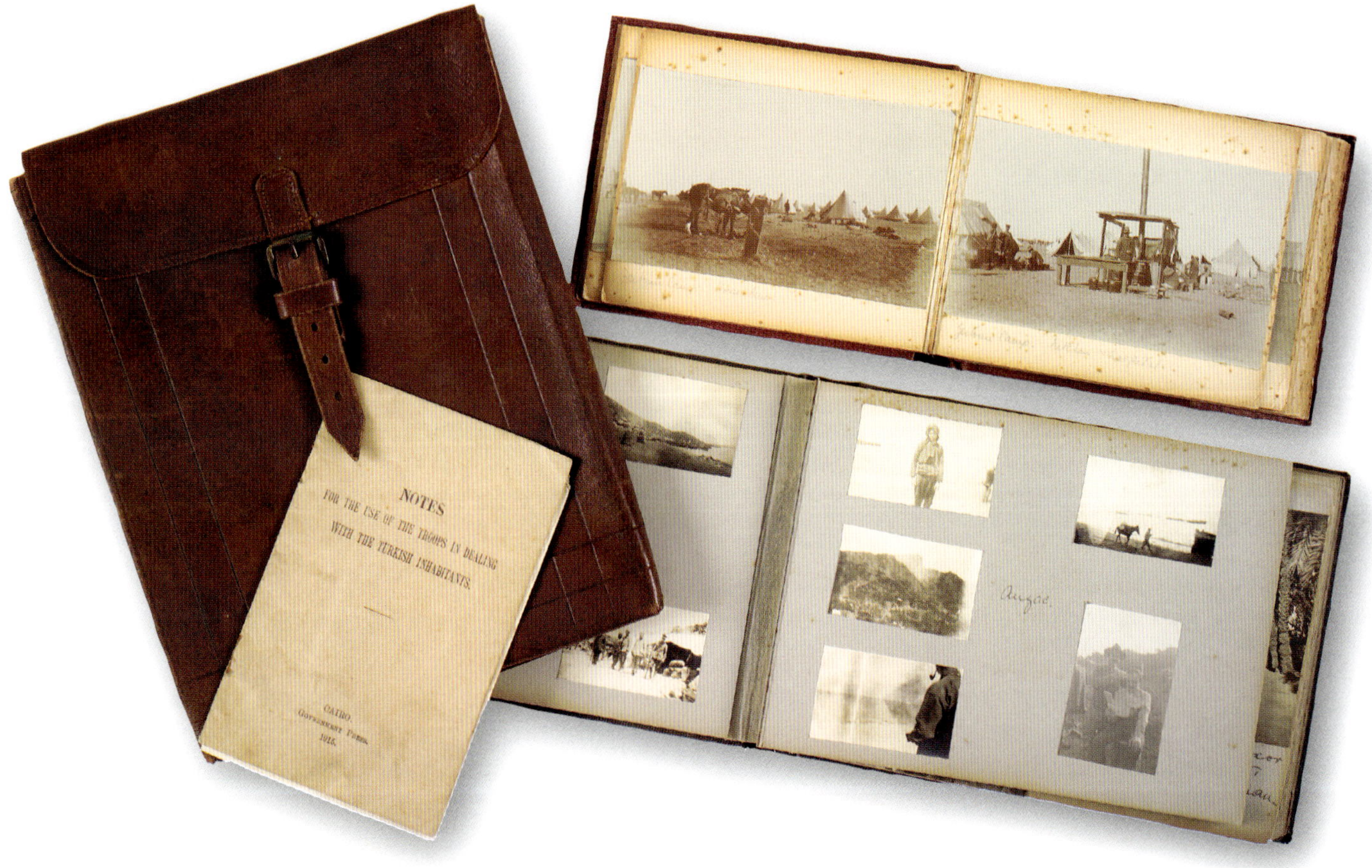

The adventures of Kipper, Jester, Twinkler and the Philosopher • 1914

This album tells the story of a delightful holiday expedition through the Southern Alps and West Coast undertaken by Dorothy Theomin (Kipper) and her friends Eleanor Joachim (Jester), Dorothy Wimperis (Twinkler) and guide Alec Graham (Philosopher) in 1914.

Dorothy Theomin (1889–1966) was the only daughter of a successful Dunedin merchant whose grand house 'Olveston' was built in 1904–6. An independent and capable woman, she enjoyed climbing extensively in the Southern Alps between 1914 and 1933, becoming a member of the New Zealand Alpine Club. Eleanor Joachim was an accomplished bookbinder, and her cousin Dorothy Wimperis came from the same artistically talented family. Alec Graham, a pioneer of tourism in South Westland, helped to establish the Franz Josef Hotel and worked as a guide at Mt Cook.

Dorothy and her friends appear attired in the style pioneered by Freda du Faur a few years previously, with a knee-length, slightly flared skirt, blouse and tie, puttees and boots, accessorised by broad brimmed hat and climbing axe. The album evokes a different age, when these young wealthy women relished a newly found freedom to explore the outdoors in ways unlikely to have been possible for their mothers, unless accompanied by a husband or other suitable chaperon. AB

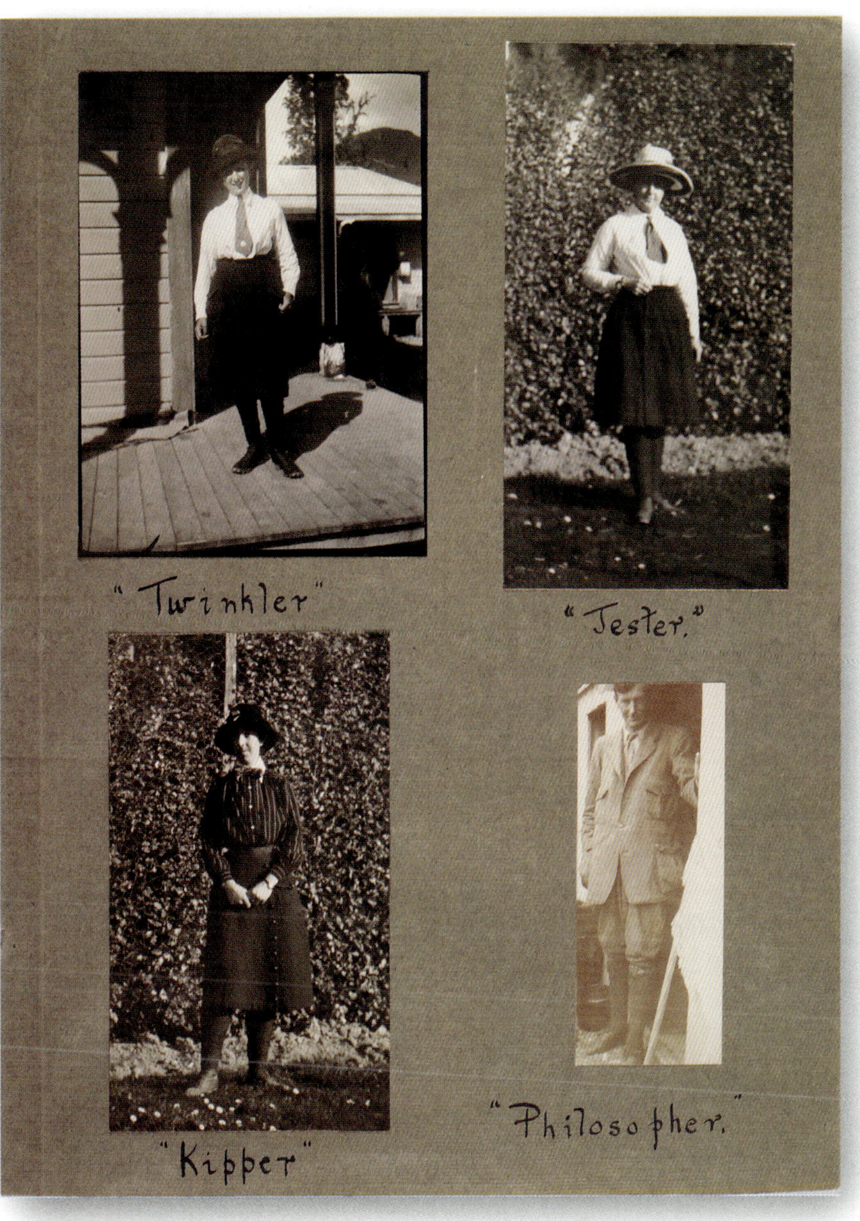

Dorothy Theomin. *'Log of Joyful Days', 1914*. MS-1164-2/77/17. Deposited by the New Zealand Alpine Club, 1980.

Letters from an anthropologist • 1913–17

Wellington-born Diamond Jenness (1886–1969) is regarded today as the foremost Canadian anthropologist to have worked with the Inuit of the Arctic north. Professor George von Zedlitz (1871–1949) was first professor of modern languages at Victoria College, and these letters tell of Jenness's part in the Canadian Arctic Expedition 1913–16, the prejudices that the First World War inspired in New Zealanders, and Jenness's own part in the war.

The first three letters, written from the Arctic coast, describe the progress of the expedition and what Jenness had gathered. The expedition was marred by leadership conflicts and tragedy; one of the ships early became ice-bound and eventually sank. Jenness, although suffering from malaria, was lucky enough to be hunting caribou at the time. Over the course of the expedition seventeen of the original thirty members died.

Delivery of mail was infrequent: news of the war did not reach the expedition until November 1915. Later letters express Jenness's abhorrence at von Zedlitz's treatment in New Zealand, which forced him to resign his university post. Two letters are from the Victoria Memorial Museum in Ottawa, where Jenness continued to write up his work. The final letter is from 'Somewhere in France', where Jenness served as a gun observer with the Canadian Siege and Heavy Artillery. AB

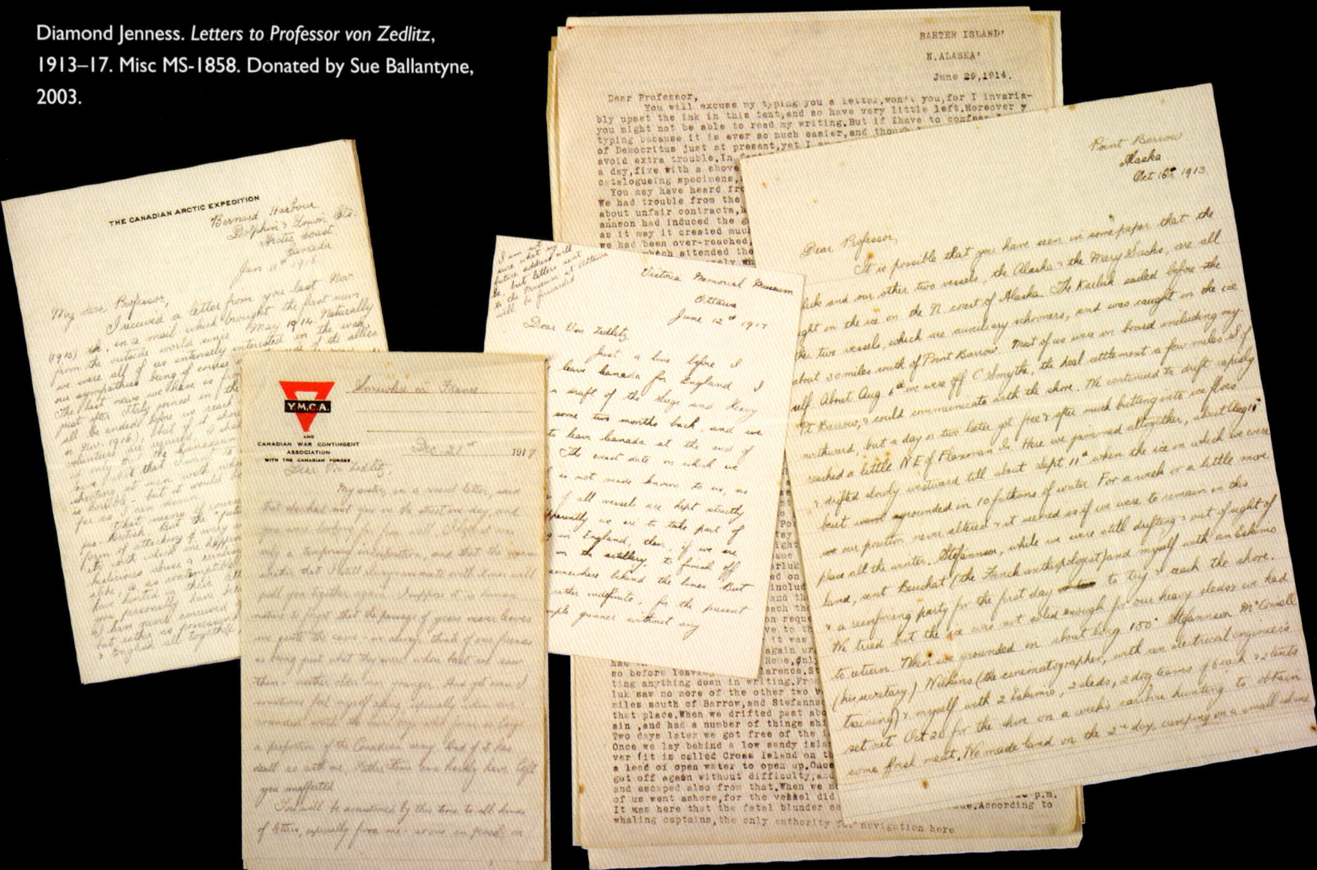

Diamond Jenness. *Letters to Professor von Zedlitz*, 1913–17. Misc MS-1858. Donated by Sue Ballantyne, 2003.

Stranded in Antarctica • 1914–17

James Paton. *Antarctic diaries, 1914–17. Entry for 24th January 1917.* Misc MS-0231 and 1424. Purchased, 1997.

> 'We came to the Antarctic to look for adventure, we are getting it, so why complain?'

James 'Scotty' Paton was boatswain aboard the *Aurora*, the 'other' ship of Ernest Shackleton's 1914 Imperial Trans-Antarctic Expedition. While Shackleton and his team set out on the *Endurance* to cross the Antarctic from the Weddell Sea, the *Aurora* headed for the Ross Sea to lay down food and fuel supplies for those making the crossing.

Paton kept a series of diaries detailing his experiences of what became much more than an adventure. As drama unfolded around Shackleton's unsuccessful mission, the Ross Sea party faced its own battle for survival. The *Aurora* broke free of her moorings in a gale, leaving ten men stranded on shore. With a damaged ship, Paton and the remaining crew were forced to drift in pack ice, with little hope of rescue from a world preoccupied with war. After many months, the *Aurora* broke free of the ice, eventually reaching Port Chalmers in April 1916.

Paton was among those who left for Antarctica once again in December, to rescue the seven surviving men who, despite being stranded, had managed to complete their mission and leave supplies for Shackleton's party. ACC

This is an archetypal Herries Beattie notebook, part of thirty-four boxes and twenty-two volumes in the Beattie collection. The stories and other information it contains were collected from European and Māori inhabitants of the south, beginning in the late 1890s. Neatly transcribed from his field book, Beattie's own observations are clearly identified and recorded separately from material he collected from his informants.

Whilst many of the stories in this notebook are also well known in the North Island, Beattie highlights what he calls 'some little South Island touches not found in the usual narrations'. Other stories are particular to the south. This is a feature of Beattie's life work: a focus on the south that consistently emphasises local peculiarities. Beattie published twenty-seven books, yet this notebook does contain material unpublished in this form, or published in journals but not included in any of his books.

He subsequently organised his collection and mailed it to the Hocken Library in parcels between 1955 and 1972, the year of his death. In his collecting and meticulous recording, Beattie (born 1881) has preserved many valuable recollections. JW

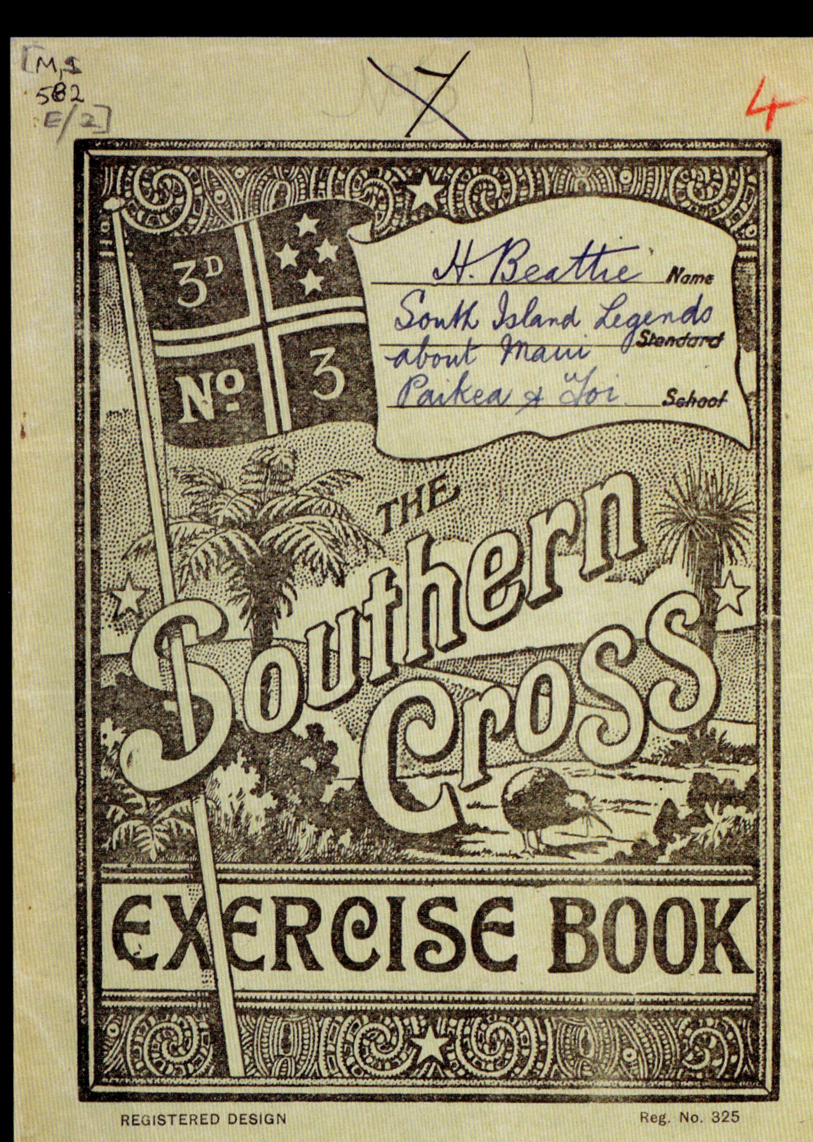

J. Herries Beattie. *South Island Legends about Maui Paikea & Toi*. MS-0582 E/2. Donated by Herries Beattie.

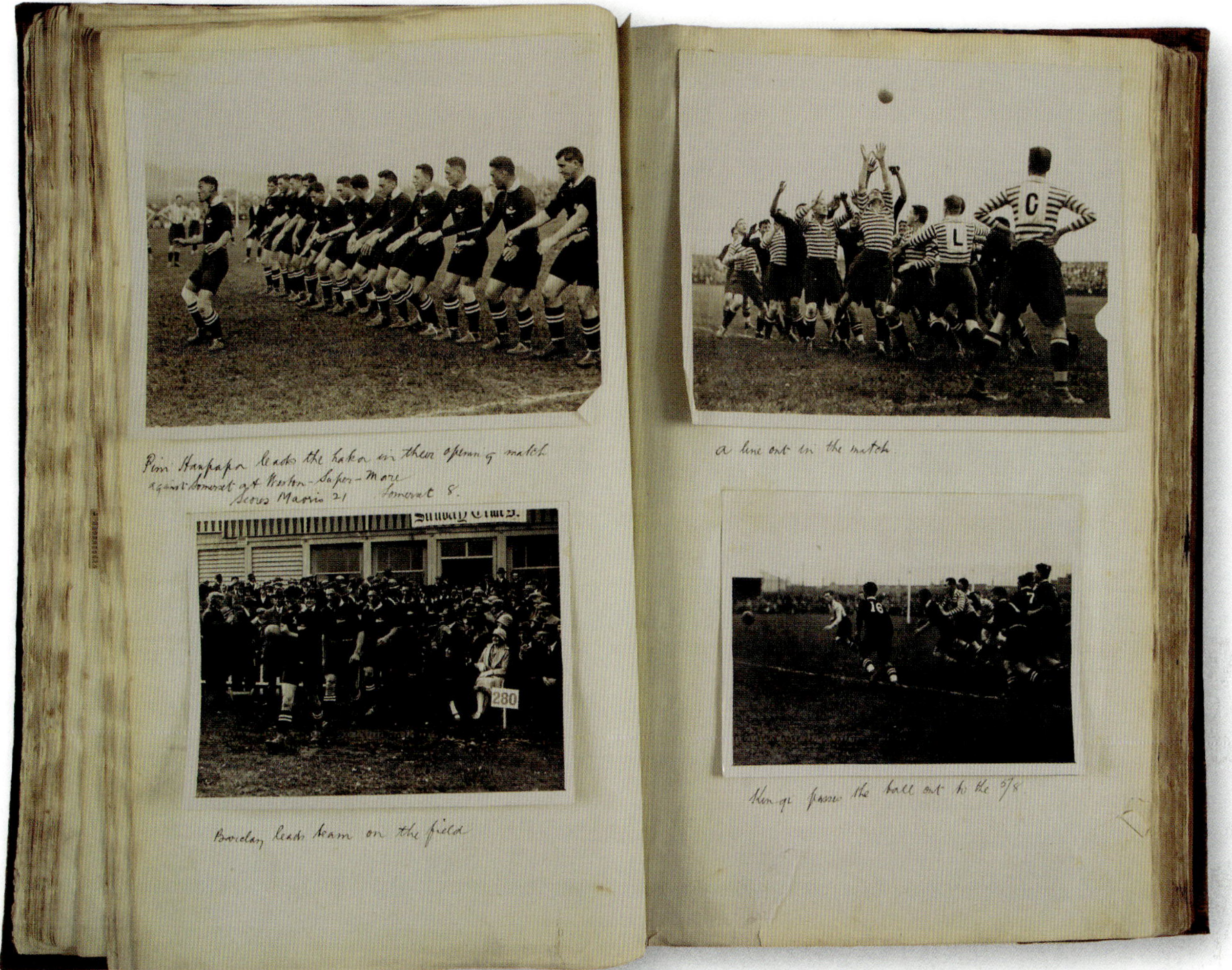

Māori rugby on tour • 1926–27

W.T. Parata. *Album of Maori Rugby Football Team Overseas Tour, 1926–27*. MS-1262. Deposited by Mrs M.D. Preddy, 1986.

Wiremu Teihoka (Ned) Parata (c. 1879–1949), the son of Tame Parata MHR, was born in Puketeraki and came to be regarded as the father of Māori rugby. Under his leadership a New Zealand Māori rugby team toured Australia in 1910. He was team manager for Australian tours in 1913, 1922 and 1923 and joint manager of the 1926–27 tour of Britain, France, Canada, Ceylon and Australia. He lived for many years in Rotorua, where he was the founder and first president of the Bay of Plenty Rugby Union 1911–25, and first chairman of the Māori Advisory Rugby Board of the New Zealand Rugby Football Union, being made a life member in 1943. He was awarded the MBE in 1948.

Throughout the 1926–27 international rugby tour, Ned Parata kept a scrapbook of photographs and newspaper reports detailing the Māori team's games and activities. Forty games were played, and the final tally stood at thirty wins, two draws and only eight losses. These pages are photographs of the opening match against Somerset, which the Māori team won, 21:8. JB

Exeter College
Oxford
6 · VII · 32.

Dear Ibby.

This is one of a series of desperate efforts to catch up on a hopeless correspondence & I'm afraid it will be rather rudely short. Many thanks for yr letter which I shall answer. Yes I'm afraid the life over here is very different from N.Z. but oh boy its a grand life. You meet some grand fellows among the lads up here & there seems to be no way like sport for getting to know them. The Lords etc seem to worry you & you ask what sort of a man David Burghley is. He's one of the nicest fellows I've ever met & a splendid man to go on a tour with. He is captaining England at the Olympics this year. How's Cricket been going Ibby – but that will be all over now & you will be well into Rugger. Over here Cricket is on top at present. How is Doris – still faithful? My love to her, if so! Good old capping & J.H Ainge – no more for you boys this year.

Life here is just hectic, Ibby – no time to do anything. Spend the time tearing round the countryside for some reason or other – with a little work sandwiched in between. Have taken an odd exam or two & seem to be doing sufficient to please my tutors & people but honestly I haven't done much for a whole year. However I have got to know a hell of a lot of people one way &

Jack Lovelock. *Letter to A.K. Ibbotson, 6 July 1932*. MS-94-092. Donated by A.K. Ibbotson, 1994.

Lovelock at Oxford • 1932

The year 1932, his first as a Rhodes scholar at Oxford University studying medicine, was significant for Jack Lovelock. It was then that his running career really took flight: he set British and world records, and proceeded on to the Los Angeles Olympic Games. In this letter written to his old Otago University friend Arthur Ibbotson, or 'Ibby', on 6 of July 1932, Lovelock charts some recent milestones.

Rather modestly he described improvements in his mile times – from four minutes and 26 seconds to the ground-breaking four minutes 12, which he achieved 'as if it were no effort at all' in the company of some of the world's best middle-distance runners, so breaking the British mile record.

Lovelock continued: 'Since then things have not been going quite as well in spite of doing a 3.2 1/5 for ¾ mile'. This world record set on 11 June during the Civil Service Sports at Stamford Bridge made his last-minute inclusion in the New Zealand team for Los Angeles Olympics inevitable. His Timaru home community raised funds for the boat passage. Lovelock ran seventh, and it was another four years until his gold medal run in Berlin. PH

Frame to Baxter • 1947

This letter from Janet Frame, New Zealand's most gifted author, to its most eloquent poet, records a crucial moment in her literary journey. In 1946 she had bought a book of poems, *Beyond the Palisade*, by eighteen-year-old James Keir Baxter. She found the poems 'intimidating', but they helped give her 'hope for my own writing while wakening in me an awareness of New Zealand as a place …'.

Moving to Christchurch in 1947, Frame took a position as housemaid at the Occidental Hotel. Alone and lonely, and despite having silently ignored Baxter at a meeting arranged by a mutual friend the previous year, Frame was now moved to write to him: '… the more I read of your work the more I feel that you are remembering the real way … you are walking up and down there from end to beginning and beginning to end, making …. I am so happy that you have such a true way of making.'

Alarmed 'at having been so paper-bold', Frame asked Baxter to burn this letter at once. Baxter replied – a reply unanswered – but did not burn the letter. It stands as a treasured testament from 'an orphan who discovers that her parents are alive and living in the most desirable home …'. SI

Occidental Hotel,
Ch-Ch.

Dear Mr. Baxter,

You will forgive me, I hope, if I seem to presume in writing to you but I will say to hell with so-called presumption for the world is so sudden there is really no care, war and no war, no war and war.

I do not want to say, fan-mailishly, " I appreciate your poems very much and hope you will be spared many more writing years." No not that, not I Am Illuminated With Thanks.

How can I express myself except by saying that poetry is in memory and to my mind there are two ways of remembering. You can walk a hundred years in time picking and pressing and saving the daffodils and buttercups and daisies that you find there till you have a mind full, and then you can yawn and sit down to fondle your treasure. Look I am remembering, you say. I am making poetry. But what a dead smell your flowers have and the daisies have all fallen to pieces, petal by petal.

But you can remember another and true way. You can annihilate time if you have enough power in you, th ough you suffer terribly, it is like having your feet cut off because you want so much to dance. And then you can walk- or dance up and down for ever and ever from beginning to end and end to beginning. And then look how wet and cool the flowers are for they are still growing and having summers and knowing what the rain is like, for ever.

I am sorry, I do not say it right. But the more I read of your work the more I feel that you are remembering the real way, you are back with the first snows and the first spring, you are walking up and down there from end to beginning and beginning to end, making. It is nice to make. I am so happy that you have such a true way of making.

I am scared to have been so bold. Forgive me, and burn this letter at once after you have read it. I had to write it. How much clear world you have got, while we are bruised with water and looking.

Yours, a bit scared at having been so
paper-bold,

Janet Frame.

Letter from Janet Frame to James Keir Baxter, c. 1947. MS-0975/177. Donated by the Baxter family.

Stewart Island leaf letters • 1950

These two leaves were addressed and sent to Miss E.P. Brown of Oamaru from Stewart Island. The smaller leaf appears to have been collected from remote Mason Bay, the other from Halfmoon Bay. They are postmarked 27 January 1950 at the Halfmoon Bay Post Office. Miss Brown sent them to herself as a keepsake.

These letter leaves are relicts of a popular practice by tourists to Stewart Island, which was apparently started in the early twentieth century by the postmaster at the old Ulva Island Post Office. This office was generally (but not correctly) believed to be the most southerly in the world. Tourists making day trips to Ulva Island delighted in sending letters from the postbox and frequently used the leaves of the muttonbird scrub (*Brachyglottis rotundifolia*) to do so. The leaves are tough and have a smooth soft tomentum on the underside, perfect for writing a short note.

The Post and Telegraph Department banned the practice as early as 1912 to prevent damage to other mail, but the ban was rarely observed. After the Ulva Island office closed in 1923, the Halfmoon Bay office continued to accept the leaves until after the Second World War, and even up to the late 1970s. Susequently, they had to be packaged in envelopes. AB

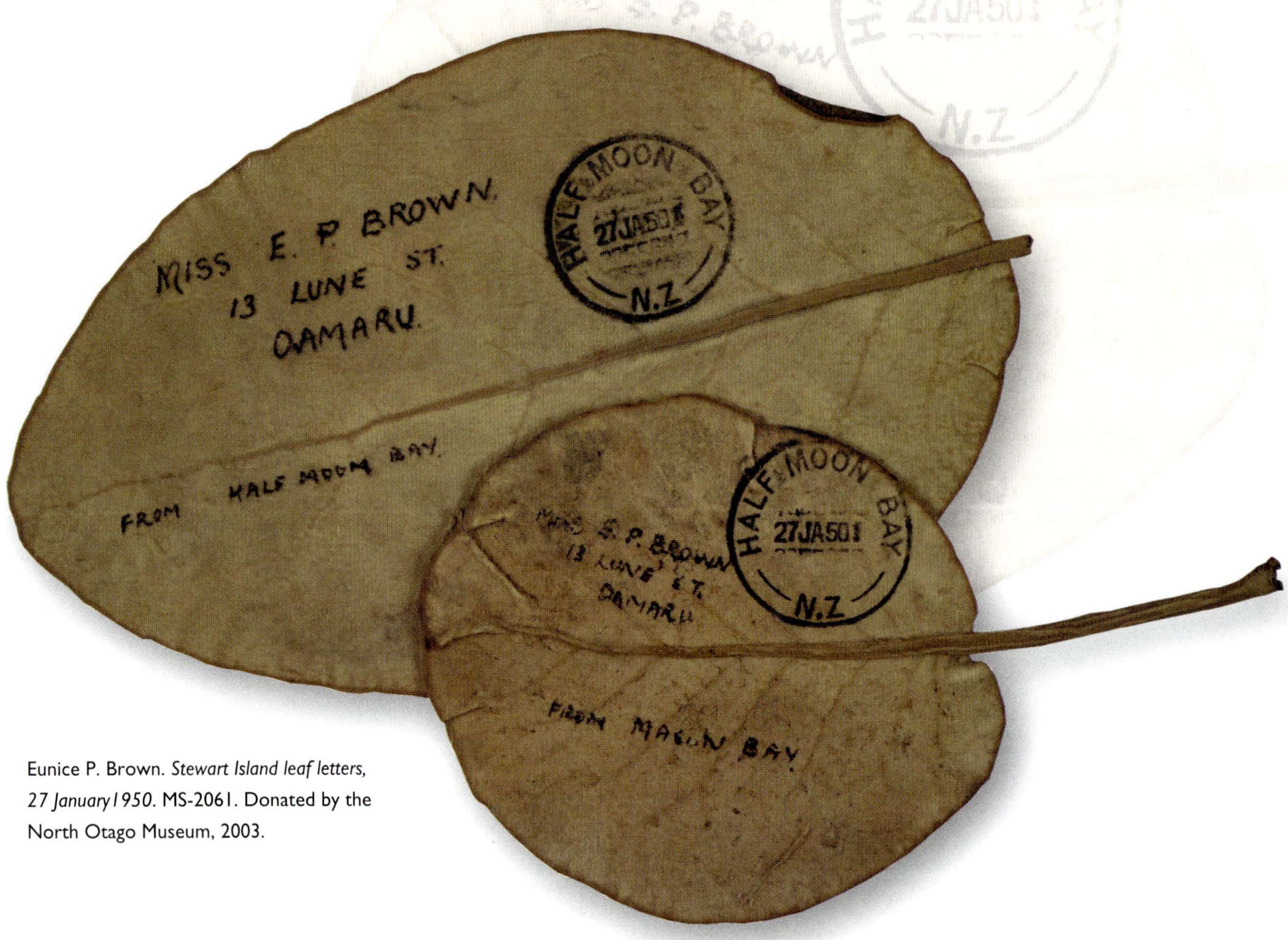

Eunice P. Brown. *Stewart Island leaf letters, 27 January1950*. MS-2061. Donated by the North Otago Museum, 2003.

Charles Brasch diary • 1950–51

Charles Brasch. *Journal, November 1950–December 1951*. MS-996-9/18. Charles Brasch Bequest, 1973.

So far Charles Brasch has chiefly been known as a poet, literary editor, and generous patron of the arts. More obscure has been Brasch the diarist.

With the recent removal of the embargo on his papers, only now is the extent of Brasch's journal-keeping coming to light. His much-loved grandfather, Willi Fels, and father, Hyam Brash, both kept diaries, but it was his sister, Lesley, who presented him with his first diary in 1927. Continuous in thirty-four volumes from 1940 until his death in May 1973, Brasch furnishes first-hand reports and ruminations about figures and events in New Zealand literature, arts and culture. In this example, Brasch describes, 25 May 1951, his impressions of novelist Frank Sargeson, whose 'mind is so quick' that he admits to finding it 'hard to follow his argument or train of thought; & he darts from subject to subject like a bird in search of honey.'

Although the journals contain many such perceptive and delightful descriptions, the portrait of Brasch's own inner life is darker and more searching. It is often assumed that writers intend their journals to be read, in time, yet Brasch appears to hold little back from his eventual audience. Only one journal shows signs of pages removed. SJ

Amazonian apparel • c. 1978

These two homemade skirts (evening and day wear) are embroidered with a pictorial story of Louise Sutherland's travels through the Amazon. She wore them when giving lectures and addresses about her adventures to raise funds for the mobile medical clinic that she helped establish at Humaitá in Brazil.

Louise Juliet Sutherland was born in Dunedin in 1926, the eldest of five girls. After completing her nursing training at Oamaru Hospital, she left New Zealand for a cycling tour of England in 1949. Subsequent years saw her undertake long cycling trips through Europe, parts of Asia and North America. Her first book, *I Follow the Wind* (1960), recounted some of her adventures. A trip in Peru in 1973 led to her working at a mission hospital, until ill-health forced her return. Back in New Zealand, she raised $25,000 for the hospital.

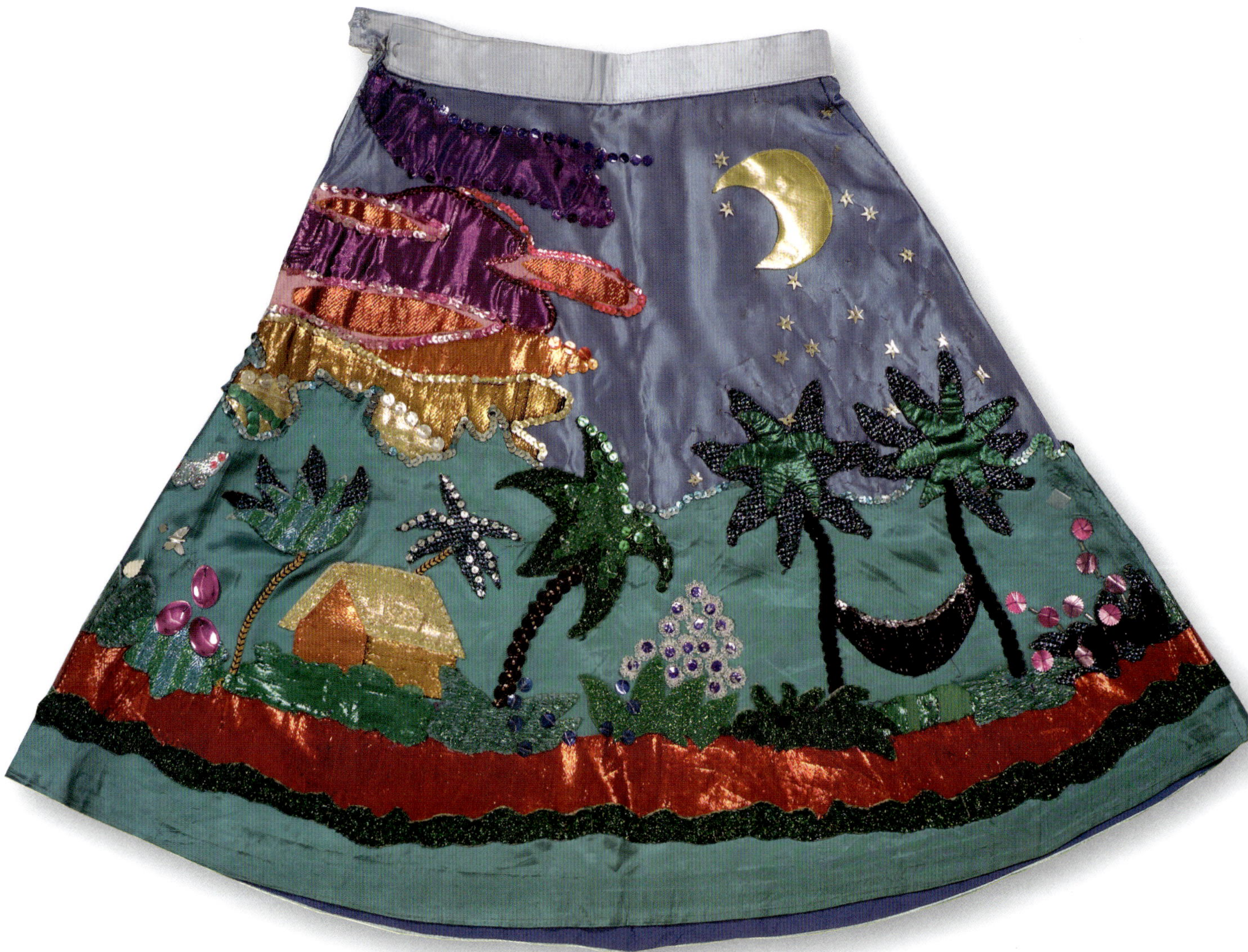

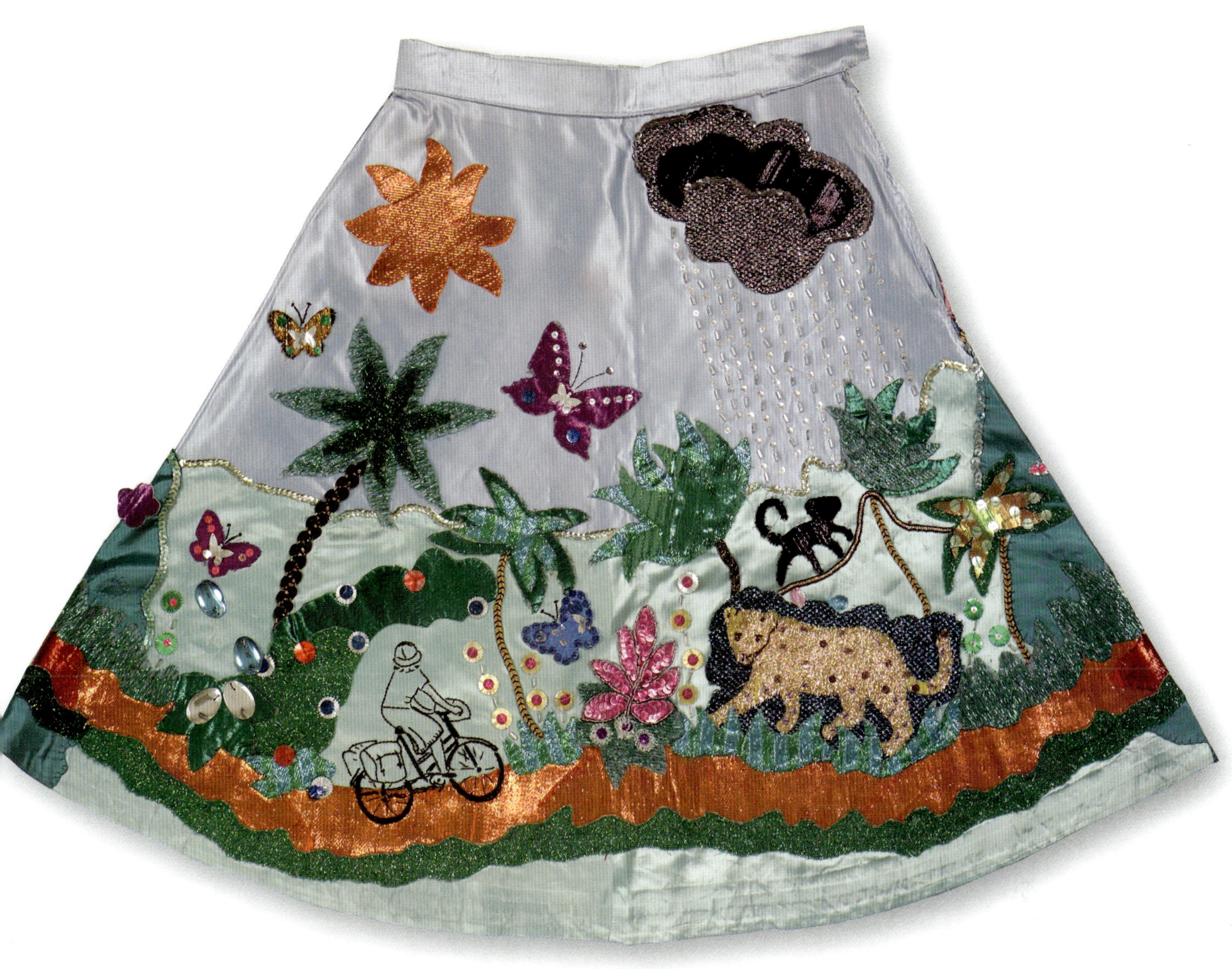

Louise Sutherland. *Embroidered skirts*. c. 1978. 95-008. Donated by Rosemary Hall, 1995.

In 1978 Sutherland became the first person to bicycle through the Amazon jungle. She saw the need for better health care and returned determined to help fund a mobile health clinic for the Indians, using proceeds from lectures and her second book, *The Impossible Ride* (1982). She also became New Zealand organiser for the Amazon Trust, dedicated to helping protect the rainforest, for which she raised $80,000.

Sutherland semi-retired to Waihola near Dunedin, and died in 1994. AB

Publications

Stuart Strachan

Many qualities can make treasures: rarity, intrinsic importance, significance by association, beauty, and even value of materials, singly and in combination. Although not exactly jewel-encrusted, examples of all are to be found in the published collections. Books, in particular, may be distinguished by their illustrations, typography, bindings, and dust jackets.

Dr Hocken's original collection totalled some 6000 books and pamphlets gathered to support his historical and bibliographical interests. The topics ranged far and wide, from *The Anatomy of the Common Mussels* (1887) to *The Egyptian Book of the Dead* (1904). His earliest book, *I Discorsi di M. Pietro Andrea Matthioli Sanese, medico Cesareoi,* dated 1621, testifies to an early and longstanding interest in medicine and botany. An abiding interest in Japan is reflected in his owning Montanus's *Atlas Japannensis: Being Remarkable Addresses by way of Embassy from the East-India Company of the United Provinces, to The Emperor of Japan* (1670), purchased in Yokohama in 1904. Both of these volumes are beautifully illustrated.

The original collection's great strengths, however, were New Zealand and the Pacific, primarily Māori ethnology and language, Pacific exploration and voyaging, missions, European settlement, and natural history. On Samuel Marsden, the New Zealand Company, and the Otago Settlement, Hocken achieved virtual completeness. The collection contains all thirty-five annual reports of the New Zealand Company 1840–58, for instance, including the only known copy of the final one. Abel Tasman, James Cook, and the French and Spanish voyagers of the eighteenth and nineteenth centuries are all well represented, as individual accounts and as part of larger collections of travels, such as those of Thévenot, Dalrymple, Harris and Pinkerton.

Hocken took particular pride in the remarkable runs of missionary magazines he had accumulated, including the *Missionary Register* 1803–55, the *Methodist Magazine* 1778–1859, and the *Annales de la Propagation de la Foi* 1822–77. He acquired newspapers for the earliest years of each major European settlement: the Bay of Islands, Auckland, Wellington, Nelson, New Plymouth, Dunedin, Christchurch and Napier. Some of these are the most complete sets available. Hocken keenly sought Māori-language newspapers and met with some success, amassing important runs of *Te Karere Maori* 1849–61, *Te Waka Maori o Ahuriri* 1863–71 and *Te Hokioi* 1862–63. From Australia he also acquired an extensive run of the *Sydney Morning Herald* and predecessors 1851–83, and a remarkable clutch of early Tasmanian papers. Hocken's collection of pamphlets, in 213 bound volumes, contains over 3000 items, including many rarities, on every aspect of New Zealand life up to his death in 1910.

Since Hocken's time, the holdings of publications have grown forty-fold to almost 240,000 items, reinforcing and filling gaps in the original collection and bringing it up to the present day. The published collections are now overwhelmingly twentieth century in character. Only 15,000 items, about eight per cent, predate 1914, and just 350, chiefly relating to voyaging and natural history, were published before 1801, mostly in London. In the field of exploration, Hocken's subscribing membership of the Hakluyt Society has been continued, and publications of the Linschoten Society, the Dutch equivalent, purchased to 1972. The sequence of expedition reports has been well maintained with the addition of those of the 1873–76 Challenger expedition, of Haddon's Cambridge Anthropological Expedition to Torres Straits 1899, and Thilenius's German South Seas Expedition 1908–10. These are now complemented by complete sets of Bishop P. Bernice Museum bulletins and memoirs.

Gifts of supplementary collections have greatly enriched the original benefaction. They include the pamphlet collections of Hocken's friend and bibliophile Judge H.S. Chapman (1653 items), of the Hon J.T. Paul on trade unionism and labour (658), and of E. Hunter on socialism and communism (1467). Other notable additions have been the Pat Lawlor poetry collection (938), a Whitcombe Story Books collection (704), the Bruce Godward New Zealand and Pacific collection (1410), and the R.P. Hargreaves collection of nineteenth-century periodical articles. From the estate of another collector, William Downie Stewart, came many items relating to the 1920s and 1930s. The deposited library of the Chinese Church in Dunedin contains a remarkable set of Chinese language overseas mission publications: few have survived elsewhere. Of particular research value is the comprehensive collection of almanacs and directories for the whole country, including the annotated archives set from Stone's of Dunedin 1888–1954, and for shipping historians there is a complete set of *Lloyd's Register of Ships,* 1764–2000.

Areas not favoured by Hocken – he was reputed to dislike Seddon, racing, and sport generally, and creative writing was never a particular interest – are now well covered, including verse and popular fiction, children's literature, the environment, fine arts and design, and sport and recreation. Recently, a small collection of New Zealand fine printing has been developed. The Hocken Collections has the signed first copy of Alan Loney's *Squeezing the Bones* (1983).

Amongst older periodicals, not always unique but extremely scarce, may be mentioned: *Typo* the leading design publication of its day 1887–97, the *New Zealand Tablet* the premier Catholic organ published in Dunedin from 1873, *Triad* edited by Charles Baeyertz from 1892, and the *New Zealand Railways Magazine* 1926–40. Recent titles received now number over 2500, and include many relating to popular culture. Their variety can only be hinted at: *New Zealand Woman's Weekly, Charlie, Rip It Up, Mushroom, New Zealand Rugby News,* and even comic books – *Footrot Flats* and *The Adventures of Captain Sunshine.*

Newspapers continue to have large place. There is an extensive holding of Dunedin newspapers, including such forgotten names as *Southern Mercury* and *Otago Workman.* Otago provincial papers – *Lake Wakatip Mail, Cromwell Argus,* and the *Bruce Herald,* for example – give strong coverage of the goldfields in the nineteenth and early twentieth centuries.

Posters have been less prominent but are increasingly appreciated. There is a wide, if eclectic, range, beginning with New Zealand Company emigration posters collected by Hocken himself. In the twentieth century they vary from popular band music and theatre to tourism, health and transport. Many are superbly designed. Even the large collection of *New Zealand Truth* billboards, 1970–97, form a valuable, if unexpected, source of social information.

Dr Hocken's oldest book • 1621

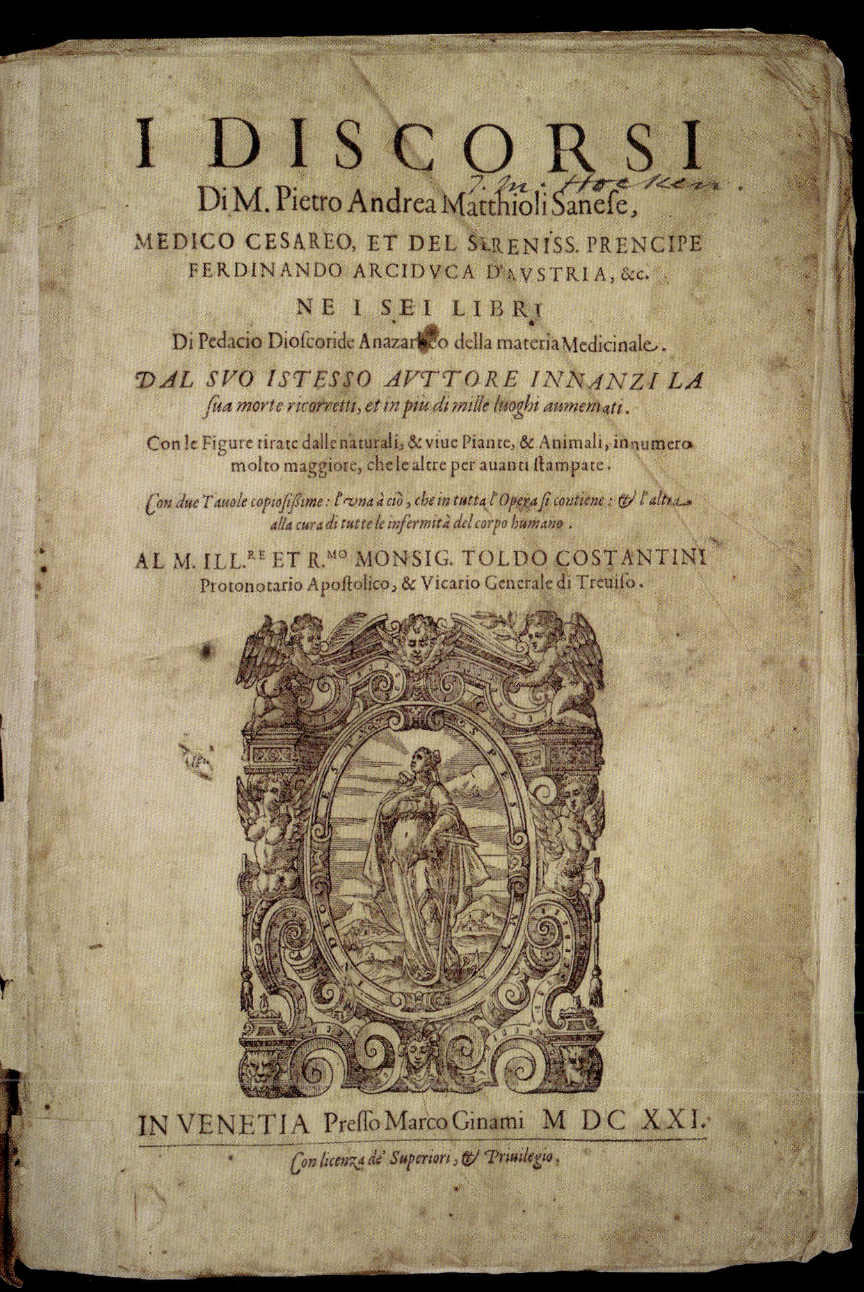

I DISCORSI

Di M. Pietro Andrea Matthioli Saneſe,

MEDICO CESAREO, ET DEL SERENISS. PRENCIPE FERDINANDO ARCIDVCA D'AVSTRIA, &c.

NE I SEI LIBRI

Di Pedacio Dioſcoride Anazarbeo della materia Medicinale.

DAL SVO ISTESSO AVTTORE INNANZI LA ſua morte ricorretti, et in piu di mille luoghi aumentati.

Con le Figure tirate dalle naturali, & viue Piante, & Animali, in numero molto maggiore, che le altre per auanti ſtampate.

Con due Tauole copioſiſſime: l'una à ciò, che in tutta l'Opera ſi contiene: & l'altra alla cura di tutte le infermità del corpo humano.

AL M. ILL.RE ET R.MO MONSIG. TOLDO COSTANTINI

Protonotario Apoſtolico, & Vicario Generale di Treuiſo.

IN VENETIA Preſſo Marco Ginami M DC XXI.

Con licenza de' Superiori, & Priuilegio.

Pietro Andrea Mattioli. *I Discorsi*… Venetia [Venice]: Presso Marco Ginami, MDCXXI (1621). Original Collection.

Pietro Andrea Mattioli's *I Discorsi* is the oldest book in Dr Hocken's collection. Printed in Venice in 1621 by Marco Ginami, this Italian language volume is an encyclopedia of Renaissance pharmacology written by Mattioli, based largely on the work of Pedanius Dioscorides (first century A.D.), who was an army physician. He felt that the nutritional and medical properties of plants were of uppermost importance. Consequently, the lists of many plants he compiled were based on their therapeutic value, rather than morphology. He also included many minerals and animal products.

Originally from Siena, Mattioli (1500–77) studied medicine at Padua where he graduated in 1523. In the course of his career as a physician, he studied hundreds of plants, examining and describing them fully. He added many new species to the original work by Dioscorides, and introduced European readers to plants such as the horse chestnut, lilac and tulip, as well as new plants from the Americas. Woodcut illustrations based on work of Wolfgang Meyerspeck or Giorgio Liberale enhance the text.

First published in 1554, *I Discorsi* was exceedingly popular and was used by physicians, herbalists, and others. It ran through many editions, was periodically revised and corrected, not only in Latin but in other vernaculars. Dr Hocken himself had a life-long interest in botany and the medicinal use of plants. DJK

A remarkable book on Japan • 1670

Between 1630 and 1830 Japan's borders were virtually closed to Western visitors. The only Europeans allowed into Japan were the Dutch. Arnoldus Montanus (1625–83), a Dutch minister, compiled his work on China and Japan using travel accounts by merchants and traders. In 1670, a year after the Dutch edition was published, *Atlas Japannensis: being remarkable addresses by way of embassy from the East-India Company of the United Provinces to the Emperor of Japan* appeared, 'English'd', and 'Adorn'd' by the seventeenth-century map publisher John Ogilby (1600–67). Even though the content is ground in biblical and theological preoccupations, this large folio book remained a major early work written on Japan. There are over sixty engravings, including a large cityscape of Yedo or Edo (now Tokyo). The subject matter covered is various, including murder in Japan, Japanese baths, Japanese tortures, wines and whaling.

Dr Hocken visited Japan twice during his world tour of 1902–4. While in Tokyo in February 1904, he obtained *Iconographie des essences forestières du Japon* (1889), a publication by the noted Japanese dendrologist Dr Homi Shirasawa. A month later, at Yokohama, he acquired this English version of Montanus. The title-page has the dated inscription: 'T.M. Hocken, Yokohama, March 1904.' DJK

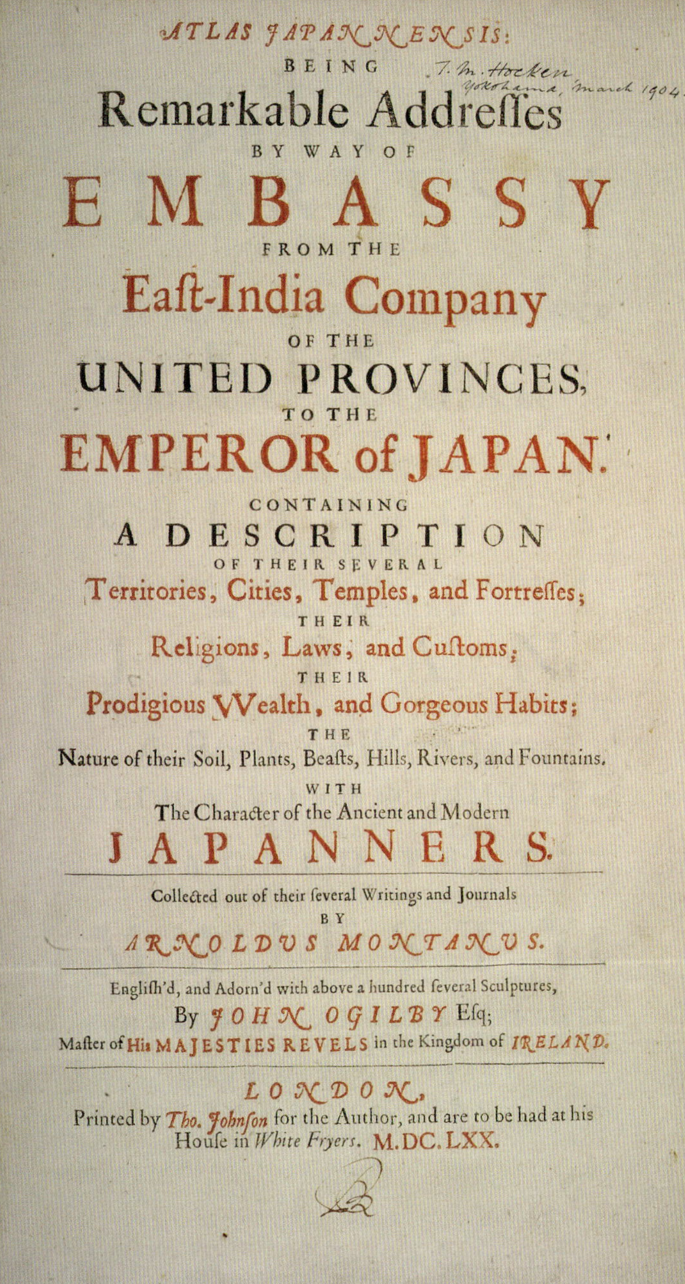

ATLAS JAPANNENSIS:

BEING

T. M. Hocken
Yokohama, March 1904.

Remarkable Addreſſes

BY WAY OF

EMBASSY

FROM THE

Eaſt-India Company

OF THE

UNITED PROVINCES,

TO THE

EMPEROR of JAPAN.

CONTAINING

A DESCRIPTION

OF THEIR SEVERAL

Territories, Cities, Temples, and Fortreſſes;

THEIR

Religions, Laws, and Cuſtoms;

THEIR

Prodigious Wealth, and Gorgeous Habits;

THE

Nature of their Soil, Plants, Beaſts, Hills, Rivers, and Fountains.

WITH

The Character of the Ancient and Modern

JAPANNERS.

Collected out of their ſeveral Writings and Journals

BY

ARNOLDUS MONTANUS.

Engliſh'd, and Adorn'd with above a hundred ſeveral Sculptures,

By JOHN OGILBY Eſq;

Maſter of His MAJESTIES REVELS in the Kingdom of IRELAND.

LONDON,

Printed by Tho. Johnſon for the Author, and are to be had at his Houſe in White Fryers. M.DC.LXX.

Arnoldus Montanus, *Atlas Japannensis*. London: Printed by Thos. Johnson for the author, 1670. Original Collection.

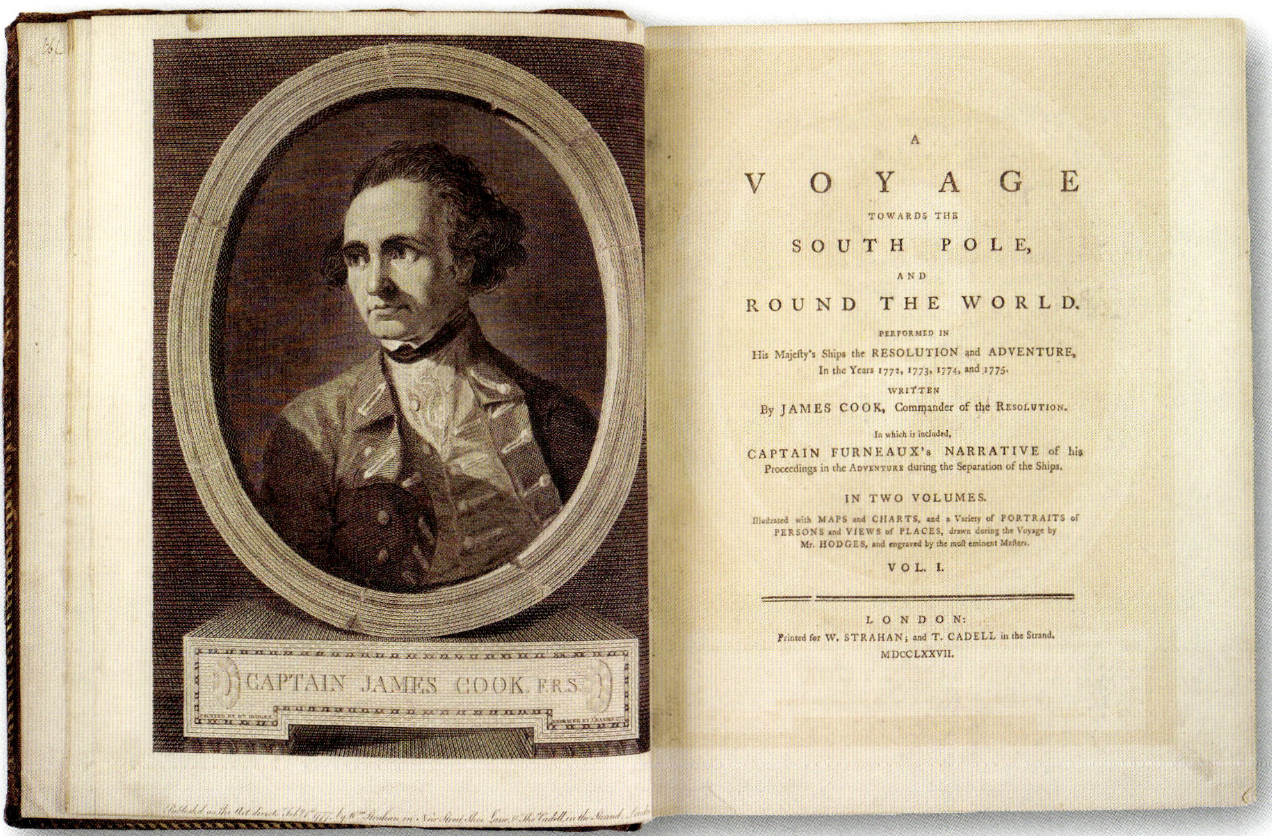

A

VOYAGE

TOWARDS THE

SOUTH POLE,

AND

ROUND THE WORLD.

PERFORMED IN

His Majesty's Ships the RESOLUTION and ADVENTURE,
In the Years 1772, 1773, 1774, and 1775.

WRITTEN

By JAMES COOK, Commander of the RESOLUTION.

In which is included,

CAPTAIN FURNEAUX's NARRATIVE of his
Proceedings in the ADVENTURE during the Separation of the Ships.

IN TWO VOLUMES.

Illustrated with MAPS and CHARTS, and a Variety of PORTRAITS of PERSONS and VIEWS of PLACES, drawn during the Voyage by Mr. HODGES, and engraved by the most eminent Masters.

VOL. I.

LONDON:
Printed for W. STRAHAN; and T. CADELL in the Strand.
MDCCLXXVII.

Cook's own account • 1777

James Cook, *A Voyage towards the South Pole and round the World*. London: W. Strahan, and T. Cadell, MDCCLXXVII [1777]. Original Collection.

A Voyage towards the South Pole covers Captain James Cook's second of three expeditions to New Zealand and the Pacific during the years 1772 to 1775. Crucially, it was written by Cook himself about his most important voyage. Also on board the *Resolution* were botanists Johann Reinhold Forster and his son George, landscape painter William Hodges, and Dr Anders Sparrman, an energetic pupil of Linnaeus. The chief aim of the voyage was to determine the existence of the much-talked-about *Terra Australis Incognita*. In proving that there was no such land, Cook travelled south across the Antarctic Circle, the 'first and only Ship that ever cross'd that line.' There were discoveries and rediscoveries: New Zealand, Tahiti, Tonga, Easter Island, the Marquesas, New Hebrides, New Caledonia, Norfolk Island, and, in the Atlantic, South Georgia. There was also scientific experimentation: testing of chronometers for finding longitude, and how best to combat scurvy.

Dr Hocken enthusiastically collected works by and about James Cook. He owned most seminal works in English, including John Hawkesworth's *An Account of the Voyages … in the Southern Hemisphere* (1773), Cook and James King's third and final *A Voyage to the Pacific Ocean* (1784), Sydney Parkinson's *A Journal of a Voyage to the South Seas* (1773), George Forster's *A Voyage round the World* (1777), John Reinhold Forster's *Observations …* (1778), and James Magra's unauthorised account of the first voyage (1771). Hocken recognised the importance of Cook's own narrative, heartily recommending it to Otago Institute members and *Otago Daily Times* readers as 'Well worth reading!' DJK

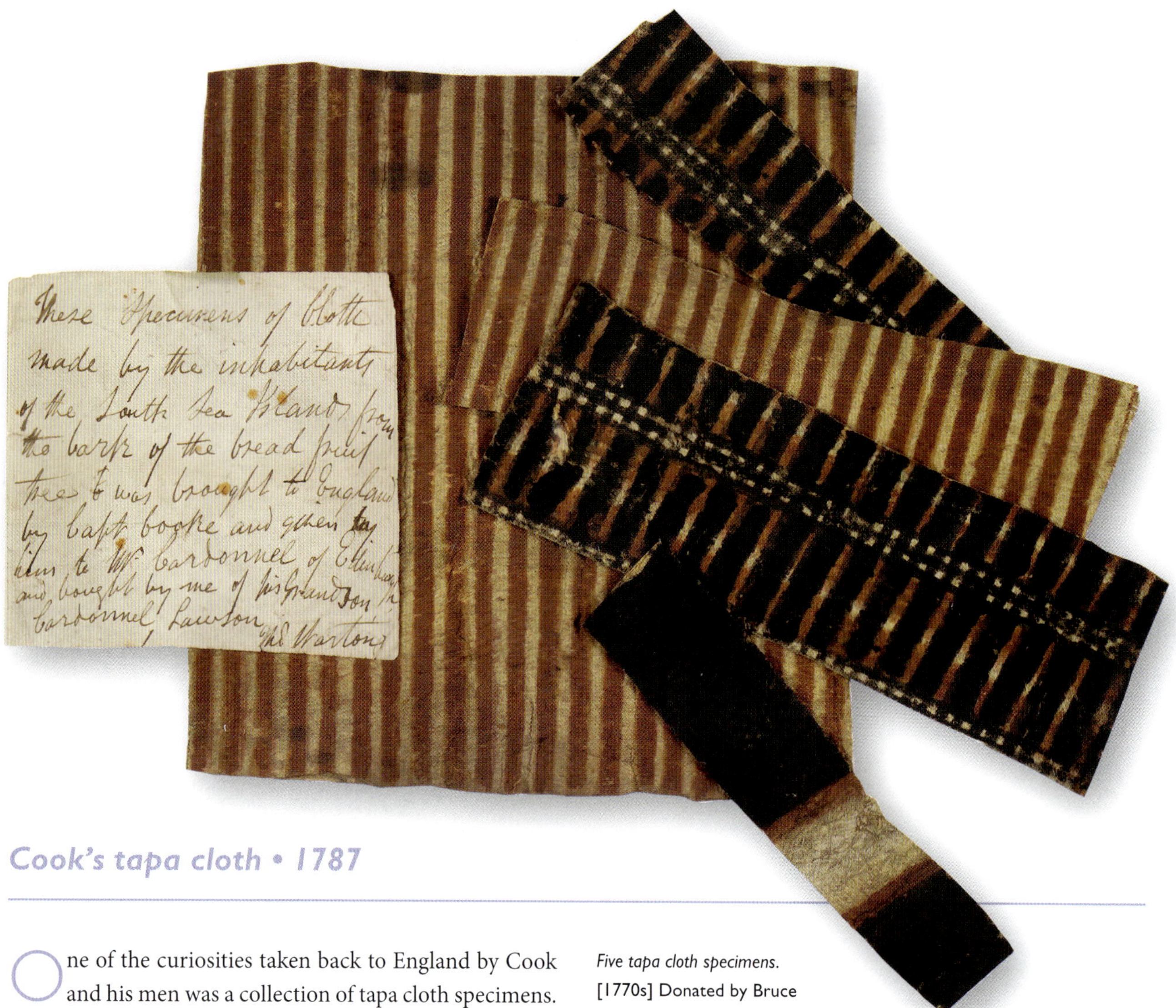

Cook's tapa cloth • 1787

Five tapa cloth specimens.
[1770s] Donated by Bruce Godward, 1991.

One of the curiosities taken back to England by Cook and his men was a collection of tapa cloth specimens. Tapa was an extremely important commodity in the Pacific, used for clothing, bed covers, as a medium for exchange, and for ceremonial purposes. In England, these colourful bark cloth pieces became collectible. The London bookseller Alexander Shaw capitalised on this market interest. In 1787 he assembled small samples from the Hawaiian, Tahitian and Tongan islands and compiled *A catalogue of the different specimens of cloth collected in the three voyages of Captain Cooks to the Southern Hemisphere.*

Bruce Godward (1916–92) gave his extensive book collection on New Zealand and Pacific history to the Hocken Library in 1991. It included these five tapa specimens, which with their decorative linear ornamentation are probably Hawaiian. Although verification is difficult, the accompanying note offers brief provenance details: 'These Specimens of Cloth made by the inhabitants of the South Sea Islands from the bark of the bread fruit tree was brought to England by Capt Cooke and given by him to W. Cardonnel of Edinburgh and bought by me of his Grandson Cardonnel-Lawson. Tho. Warton.' Godward was a young man when he received them from Lilian Unsworth, a nurse living in York, England. DJK

A

T. M. Hocken.

GRAMMAR

AND

VOCABULARY

OF THE

LANGUAGE OF NEW ZEALAND.

PUBLISHED BY THE

CHURCH MISSIONARY SOCIETY.

LONDON:

PRINTED BY R. WATTS,

AND SOLD BY L. B. SEELEY, FLEET STREET; AND

JOHN HATCHARD & SON, PICCADILLY.

1820.

"Part of the impression has been taken off on very strong paper for the use of the N.Z. children." v Miss. Reg. 1820. p 500.

'The greatest gift England gave Maori was literacy' (Pat Hohepa). Two versions of this first major grammar and vocabulary of New Zealand Māori were issued – one on 'superior paper' for general circulation, and the other on strong coarse paper for use in mission schools. It was compiled by the CMS missionary, Thomas Kendall, under the direction of the noted linguist, Samuel Lee, Professor of Arabic, in 1820 at Cambridge, and in the company of the two chiefs, Hongi Hika and Waikato. The grammar was based on material collected by Kendall over five years as a missionary at Rangihoua and on a vocabulary given to Lee by northern chiefs, Tuai and Titeri, in 1818. Kendall had been responsible for the publication of the first New Zealand primer in 1815.

The grammar includes an alphabet with five vowels (short and long forms) and twenty consonants, giving *ng* as a separate consonant; parts of speech and verb forms; dialogues and phrase lists; waiata and prayers; and a vocabulary of approximately 2000 words. It was largely based on Ngāpuhi dialect. This version, of which only four copies are known to survive in New Zealand, was not superseded until 1843. Then another CMS missionary, Robert Maunsell, issued a new grammar based on Waikato dialect followed a year later by William Williams's *First Maori Dictionary*, which with 5380 words became the standard work. SRS

Thomas Kendall and Samuel Lee. *A Grammar and Vocabulary of the Language of New Zealand.* London: Printed by R. Watts, 1820. Coarse paper version. Williams 3. Original Collection.

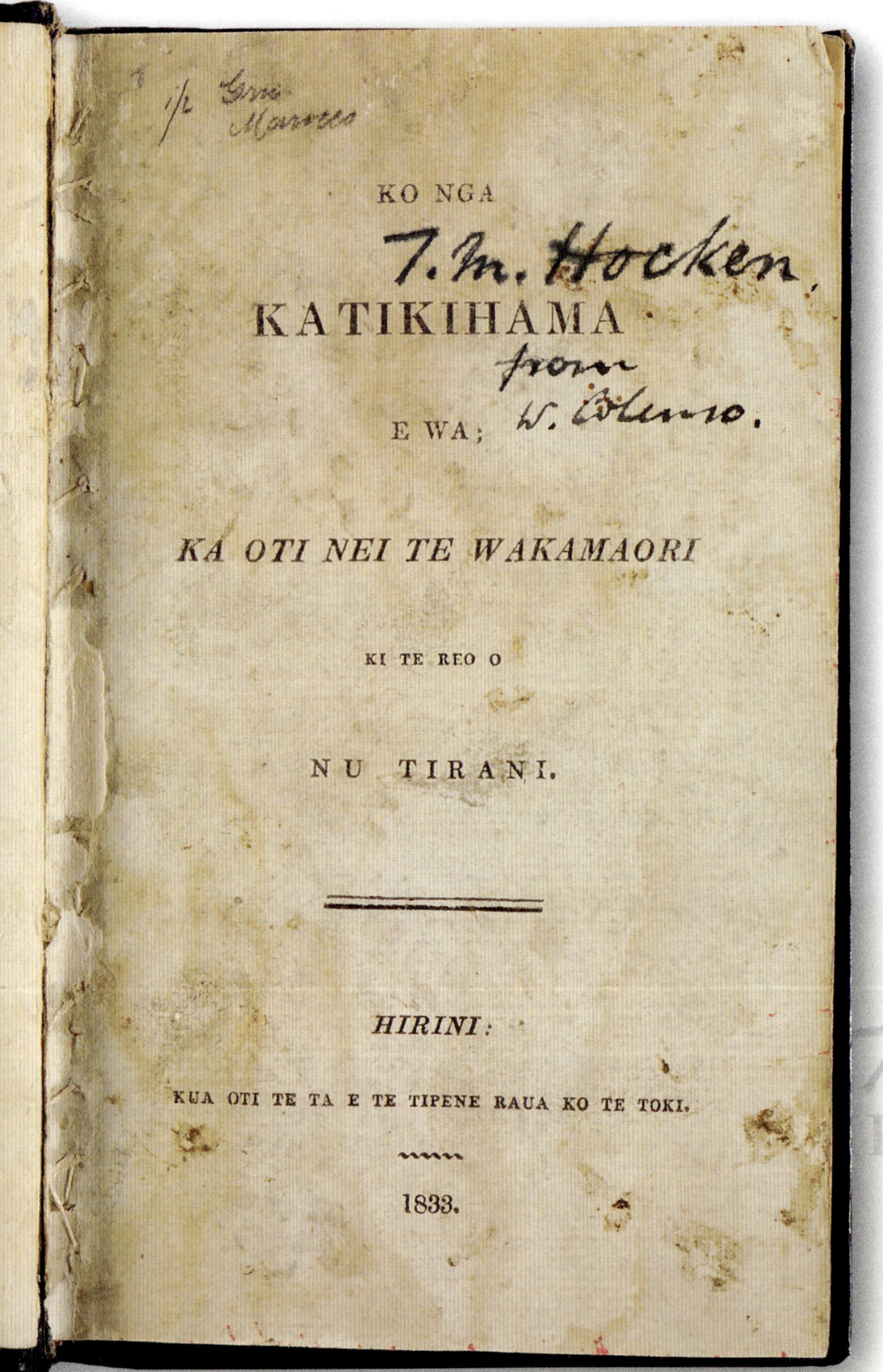

KO NGA

T. M. Hocken.

KATIKIHAMA

from

E WA; W. Colenso.

KA OTI NEI TE WAKAMAORI

KI TE REO O

NU TIRANI.

HIRINI:

KUA OTI TE TA E TE TIPENE RAUA KO TE TOKI.

1833.

Seven hundred and fifty copies of these four catechisms were produced in Sydney, printed by Stephens and Stokes on heavy bluish laid paper, under the supervision of the Rev. William Yate. According to the handwritten note inside the front cover, the copy in the Hocken Collections was given to Dr Hocken by missionary and pioneer printer William Colenso in 1897. Colenso noted its rarity on a preliminary page: 'Interleaved by me, for use in visiting, and in schools – perhaps the only copy existing! – always for 60 years, very scarce.'

As a series of questions and answers teaching key aspects of Christian faith, Catechisms I and II were first translated from the Anglican Church Catechism in the Book of Common Prayer by Yate in Kerikeri c. 1830, with the assistance of fellow missionaries George Clarke and James Kemp. Numbers III and IV are translations of Isaac Watt's *First Catechism containing the Principles of Religion* and his *Catechism of Scripture Names*, first published in English for children in London in 1826. AJ

Church of England. *Ko nga Katikihama e wa…* Hirini: Kua oti te ta e Te Tipene raua ko Te Toki, 1833. Williams 10. Original Collection.

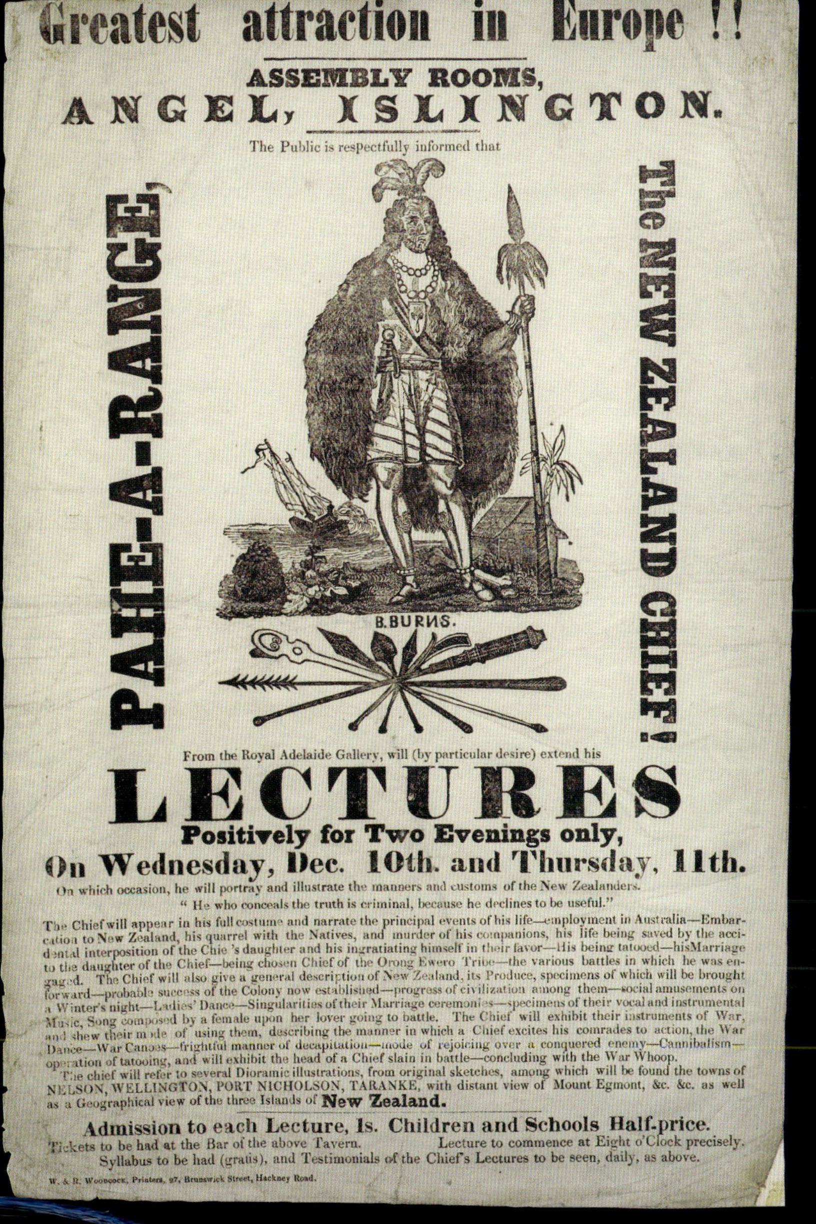

Poster. *Greatest attraction in Europe!! Assembly Rooms, Angel, Islington. The public is respectfully informed that Pahe-A-Range, The New Zealand Chief! From the Royal Adelaide Gallery, will (by particular desire) extend his Lectures positively for Two Evenings only, On Wednesday, Dec. 10th and Thursday, 11th.* [1840s]. Letterpress. Bruce Godward Bequest, 1992.

Representative of the group known as 'Pākehā-Māori', Barnet Burns traded on his years in New Zealand living with Māori, returning to England and giving a series of public lectures where he depicted himself as Pahe-A-Range, a New Zealand Chief. Central to his performance was the description of life among the Māori, displaying his tattoos, wearing Māori costume, and relating his adventures in, as some describe, 'one incongruous jumble of impudence, of ignorance, of low wit, and bare-faced presumption'. Accompanying these lectures was a pamphlet:

> A brief narrative of a New Zealand chief, being the remarkable history of ***Barnet Burns***, an English sailor, with a faithful account of the way in which he became a chief of one of the tribes of New Zealand; together with a few remarks on the manners and customs of the people, and other interesting matter, written by himself.

Various editions have remained, dated between 1835 and 1859, their titles and places of publication differing slightly, reflecting the itinerary of lecture venues.

It is believed that Burns intended to return to New Zealand, where his Māori wife and their three children still resided. Nothing is known of him after 1859, when the Shrewsbury edition appeared, and his date and place of death are unknown. AJ

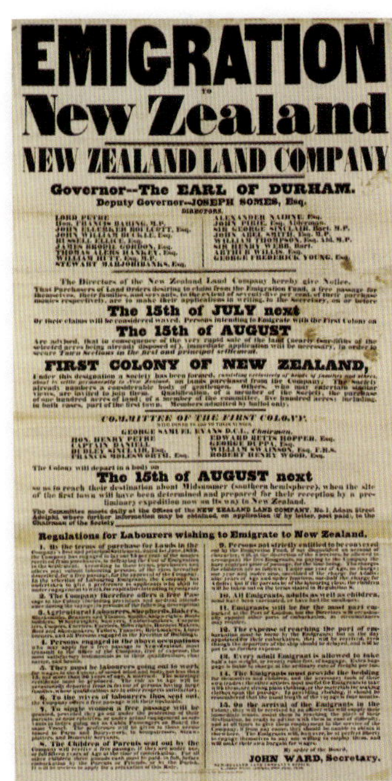

The New Zealand Land Company used this large 1500 by 800 mm poster to catch the attention of prospective emigrants to New Zealand in June 1839. Formed 1838 in London, the Land Company was based on the innovative colonisation theories of Edward Gibbon Wakefield. His name, however, does not appear on the poster, most likely because of his public disgrace for criminally deceiving a young girl into marriage, a gross infraction for which he was never fully forgiven. Prominently listed, instead, are a number of reputable gentlemen whose names have been perpetuated in Wellington street and place names.

The Company set a number of criteria for prospective emigrants who would leave London on 15 August 1839 and land in the southern hemisphere's midsummer – they had to be skilled labourers or engaged in a trade useful for building a settlement, aged between fifteen and thirty years, of sound mind and body and married (certificate to be produced), and able to show testimonials to their qualifications, character and health. The ship *Tory,* under the charge of Colonel William Wakefield, had been dispatched in May 1839 to determine the site of the first town and prepare for the arrival of emigrants. On 22 January 1840 *Aurora,* the Company's first of four emigrant ships, arrived at Port Nicholson with 148 emigrants and twenty-one cabin passengers, and so the settlement of Wellington began. KM

Poster. *Emigration to New Zealand / New Zealand Land Company.* 1839. Letterpress. Original Collection.

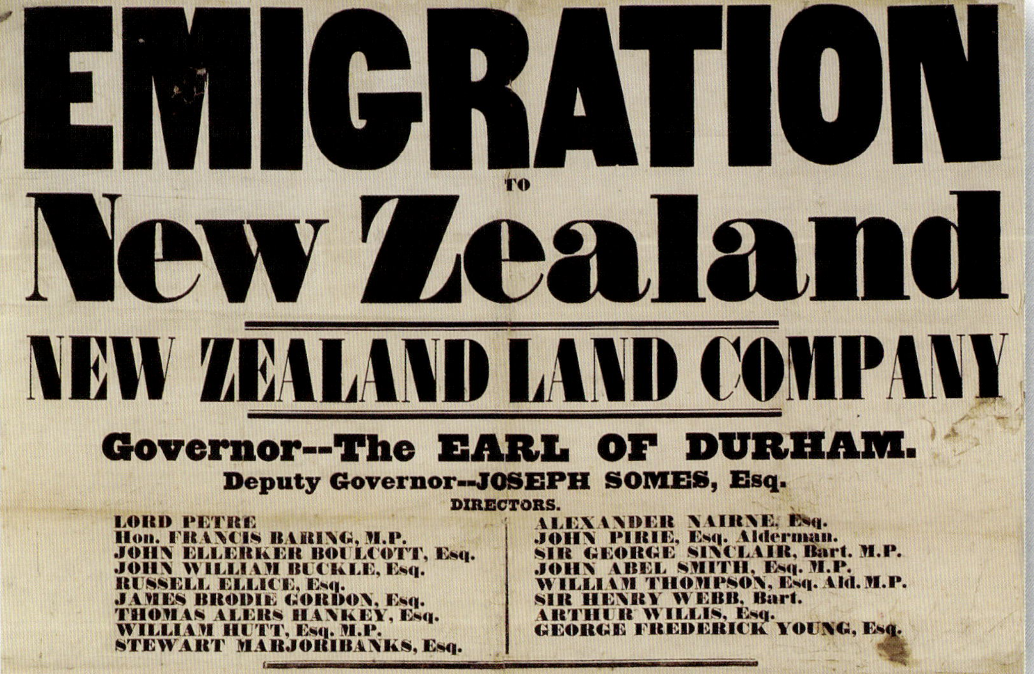
EMIGRATION
TO
New Zealand

NEW ZEALAND LAND COMPANY

Governor--The EARL OF DURHAM.
Deputy Governor--JOSEPH SOMES, Esq.
DIRECTORS.

LORD PETRE	ALEXANDER NAIRNE, Esq.
Hon. FRANCIS BARING, M.P.	JOHN PIRIE, Esq. Alderman.
JOHN ELLERKER BOULCOTT, Esq.	SIR GEORGE SINCLAIR, Bart. M.P.
JOHN WILLIAM BUCKLE, Esq.	JOHN ABEL SMITH, Esq. M.P.
RUSSELL ELLICE, Esq.	WILLIAM THOMPSON, Esq. Ald. M.P.
JAMES BRODIE GORDON, Esq.	SIR HENRY WEBB, Bart.
THOMAS ALERS HANKEY, Esq.	ARTHUR WILLIS, Esq.
WILLIAM HUTT, Esq. M.P.	GEORGE FREDERICK YOUNG, Esq.
STEWART MARJORIBANKS, Esq.	

The Directors of the New Zealand Land Company hereby give Notice,

That Purchasers of Land Orders desiring to claim from the Emigration Fund, a free passage for themselves, their families, and servants, to the extent of seventy-five per cent. of their purchase monies respectively, are to make their applications in writing, to the Secretary, on or before

The 15th of JULY next

Or their claims will be considered waved. Persons intending to Emigrate with the First Colony on

The 15th of AUGUST

Are advised, that in consequence of the very rapid sale of the land (nearly four-fifths of the selected acres being already disposed of), immediate application will be necessary, in order to secure *Town Sections in the first and principal settlement.*

FIRST COLONY OF NEW ZEALAND,

Under this designation a Society has been formed, *consisting exclusively of heads of families and others, about to settle permanently in New Zealand,* on lands purchased from the Company. The Society already numbers a considerable body of gentlemen. Others, who may entertain similar views, are invited to join them. Qualification, of a member of the Society, the purchase of one hundred acres of land; of a member of the committee, five hundred acres; including, in both cases, part of the first town. Members admitted by ballot only.

COMMITTEE OF THE FIRST COLONY,

WITH POWER TO ADD TO THEIR NUMBER.

GEORGE SAMUEL EVANS D.C.L., *Chairman.*

HON. HENRY PETRE	**EDWARD BETTS HOPPER, Esq.**
CAPTAIN DANIELL	**GEORGE DUPPA, Esq.**
DUDLEY SINCLAIR, Esq.	**WILLIAM SWAINSON, Esq. F.R.S.**
FRANCIS MOLESWORTH, Esq.	**ROBERT HENRY WOOD, Esq.**

The Colony will depart in a body on

The 15th of AUGUST next

so as to reach their destination about Midsummer (southern hemisphere), when the site of the first town will have been determined and prepared for their reception by a preliminary expedition now on its way to New Zealand.

The Committee meets daily at the Offices of the NEW ZEALAND LAND COMPANY, No. 1, Adam Street Adelphi, where further information may be obtained, on application (if by letter, post paid), to the Chairman of the Society

Regulations for Labourers wishing to Emigrate to New Zealand.

1. By the terms of purchase for Lands in the Company's first and principal Settlement, dated 1st June, 1839, the Company has engaged to lay out 75 per cent. of the monies received from purchasers, in defraying the Cost of Emigration to the Settlement. According to those terms, purchasers and others may submit labouring persons, of the class hereafter described, for a free passage, for the approval of the Company. In the selection of Labouring Emigrants, the Company has undertaken to give a preference to applicants who shall be under engagement to work for capitalists intending to emigrate

2. The Company therefore offers a free Passage to the Colony (including provisions and medical attendance during the voyage) to persons of the following description:

3. Agricultural Labourers, Shepherds, Bakers, Blacksmiths, Braziers and Tinmen, Smiths, Shipwrights, Boatbuilders, Wheelwrights, Sawyers, Cabinet-makers, Carpenters, Coopers, Curriers, Farriers, Millwrights, Harness Makers, Boot and Shoe-makers, Tailors, Tanners, Brickmakers, Limeburners, and all Persons engaged in the Erection of Buildings.

4. Persons engaged in the above occupations who may apply for a free passage to New-Zealand, must transmit to the Office of the Company, free of expense, the most satisfactory testimonials as to their qualifications, character, and health.

5. They must be labourers going out to work for wages in the Colony, of sound mind and body, not less than 15, nor more than 30 years of age, & married. The marriage certificate must be produced. The rule as to Age will be occasionally departed from in favour of persons having large families, whose qualifications are in other respects satisfactory.

6. To the wives of labourers thus sent out, the Company offers a free passage with their husbands.

7. To single women a free passage will be granted, provided they go out under the protection of their parents, or near relatives, or under actual engagement as servants to ladies going out as Cabin Passengers on Board the same Vessel. The preference will be given to those accustomed to Farm and Dairy-work, to Sempstresses, Straw-platters, and Domestic Servants.

8. The Children of Parents sent out by the Company will receive a free passage, if they are under one, or full fifteen years of Age at the time of embarkation. For all other children three pounds each must be paid, in full, before embarkation by the Parents or Friends, or by the Parish. It will be useless to apply for a relaxation of this Rule.

9. Persons not strictly entitled to be conveyed out by the Emigration Fund, if not disqualified on account of character, will, in the discretion of the Directors, be allowed to accompany the free Emigrants, on paying to the Company the bare contract price of passage, for the time being. The charges for children are as follows: Under one year of Age, no charge; one year and under nine, one-third of the charge for Adults; nine years of Age and under fourteen, one-half the charge for Adults; but if the parents be of the labouring class, the children will be taken out on the terms stated in Regulation 8.

10. All Emigrants, adults as well as children, must have been vaccinated, or have had the small-pox.

11. Emigrants will be for the most part embarked at the Port of London, but the Directors will occasionally appoint other ports of embarkation, as circumstances may require.

12. The expense of reaching the port of embarkation must be borne by the Emigrants; but on the day appointed for their embarkation, they will be received, even though the departure of the ship should be delayed, and will be put to no further expense.

13. Every adult Emigrant is allowed to take half a ton weight, or twenty cubic feet, of baggage. Extra baggage is liable to charge at the ordinary rate of freight per ton.

14. The Emigrants must provide the bedding for themselves and children, and the necessary tools of their own trades; the other articles most useful for Emigrants to take with them, are strong plain clothing, or the materials for making clothes upon the passage. In providing clothing, it should be remembered that the usual length of the voyage is four months.

15. On the arrival of the Emigrants in the Colony, they will be received by an officer who will supply their immediate wants, assist them in reaching the place of their destination, be ready to advise with them in case of difficulty, and at all times to give them employment in the service of the Company, if from any cause, they should be unable to obtain it elsewhere. The Emigrants will, however, be at perfect liberty to engage themselves to any one willing to employ them, and will make their own bargain for wages.

By order of the Board,

JOHN WARD, Secretary.

NEW-ZEALAND LAND COMPANY'S OFFICE,
1, *Adam Street, Adelphi, 29th June, 1839.*

London: Printed by James Truscott, 166, Blackfriars Road

Bay of Islands newspaper • 1840

The short-lived *New Zealand Advertiser and Bay of Islands Gazette* is as notable for highlighting the career of its editor, the Rev. Barzillai Quaife, church minister and early land rights activist, as it is for being New Zealand's second newspaper.

Arising out of the government's need to publish its official decrees, the paper was first published 15 June 1840 at Kororareka. Quaife asserted in his editorial that 'we shall exert ourselves to promote the interests of the community by every possible means …. We wish to do good as far as our power extends, *to the whole Population*.'

A nonconformist at heart, Quaife was unable to quell his outspoken criticisms of the government. His editorials soon focused on Māori interests, particularly land and criminal justice. This earned the displeasure of the Colonial Secretary, Willoughby Shortland, who, recalling an old New South Wales ordinance, ordered Quaife to post several hundred pounds surety and face a fine or transportation should he publish 'expressions tending to bring the Government into hatred or contempt.'

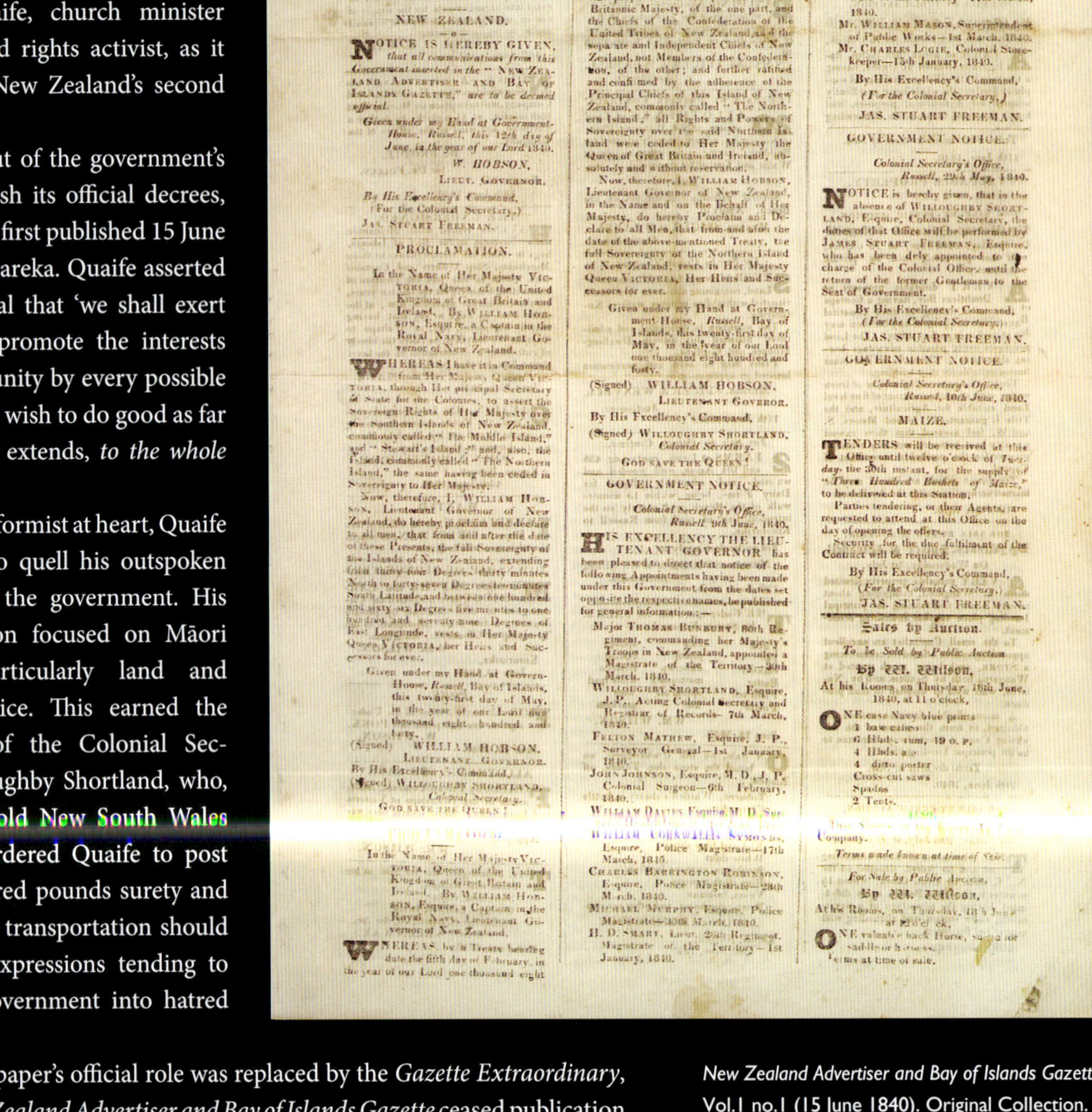

THE
NEW ZEALAND ADVERTISER,
AND
Bay of Islands Gazette.

No. 1.] KORORARIKA, JUNE 15, 1840. [Vol. I.

THE GAZETTE.

NEW ZEALAND.

NOTICE IS HEREBY GIVEN, *that all communications from this Government inserted in the "* NEW ZEALAND ADVERTISER AND BAY OF ISLANDS GAZETTE," *are to be deemed official.*

Given under my Hand at Government-House, Russell, this 12th day of June, in the year of our Lord 1840.

W. HOBSON,
LIEUT. GOVERNOR.

By His Excellency's Command,
(For the Colonial Secretary,)
JAS. STUART FREEMAN.

PROCLAMATION.

In the Name of Her Majesty VICTORIA, Queen of the United Kingdom of Great Britain and Ireland. By WILLIAM HOBSON, Esquire, a Captain in the Royal Navy, Lieutenant Governor of New Zealand.

WHEREAS I have it in Command from Her Majesty, Queen VICTORIA, through Her principal Secretary of State for the Colonies, to assert the Sovereign Rights of Her Majesty over the Southern Islands of New Zealand, commonly called "The Middle Island," and "Stewart's Island;" and, also, the Island commonly called "The Northern Island," the same having been ceded in Sovereignty to Her Majesty.

Now, therefore, I, WILLIAM HOBSON, Lieutenant Governor of New Zealand, do hereby proclaim and declare to all men, that from and after the date of these Presents, the full Sovereignty of the Islands of New Zealand, extending from thirty-four Degrees thirty minutes North to forty-seven Degrees ten minutes South Latitude, and between one hundred and sixty-six Degrees five minutes to one hundred and seventy-nine Degrees of East Longitude, vests in Her Majesty Queen VICTORIA, her Heirs and Successors for ever.

Given under my Hand at Govern-House, *Russell*, Bay of Islands, this twenty-first day of May, in the year of our Lord one thousand eight hundred and forty.

(Signed) WILLIAM HOBSON,
LIEUTENANT GOVERNOR.

By His Excellency's Command,
(Signed) WILLOUGHBY SHORTLAND,
Colonial Secretary.

GOD SAVE THE QUEEN!

[illegible]

In the Name of Her Majesty VICTORIA, Queen of the United Kingdom of Great Britain and Ireland. By WILLIAM HOBSON, Esquire, a Captain in the Royal Navy, Lieutenant Governor of New Zealand.

WHEREAS by a Treaty bearing date the fifth day of February, in the year of our Lord one thousand eight hundred and forty, made and executed by me, WILLIAM HOBSON, a Captain in the Royal Navy, Consul, and Lieutenant-Governor in New Zealand, vested for this purpose with full powers by Her Britannic Majesty, of the one part, and the Chiefs of the Confederation of the United Tribes of New Zealand, and the separate and Independent Chiefs of New Zealand, not Members of the Confederation, of the other; and further ratified and confirmed by the adherence of the Principal Chiefs of this Island of New Zealand, commonly called "The Northern Island;" all Rights and Powers of Sovereignty over the said Northern Island were ceded to Her Majesty the Queen of Great Britain and Ireland, absolutely and without reservation.

Now, therefore, I, WILLIAM HOBSON, Lieutenant Governor of New Zealand, in the Name and on the Behalf of Her Majesty, do hereby Proclaim and Declare to all Men, that from and after the date of the above-mentioned Treaty, the full Sovereignty of the Northern Island of New Zealand, vests in Her Majesty Queen VICTORIA, Her Heirs and Successors for ever.

Given under my Hand at Government House, *Russell*, Bay of Islands, this twenty-first day of May, in the year of our Lord one thousand eight hundred and forty.

(Signed) WILLIAM HOBSON,
LIEUTENANT GOVERNOR.

By His Excellency's Command,
(Signed) WILLOUGHBY SHORTLAND,
Colonial Secretary.

GOD SAVE THE QUEEN!

GOVERNMENT NOTICE.

Colonial Secretary's Office,
Russell 9th June, 1840.

HIS EXCELLENCY THE LIEUTENANT GOVERNOR has been pleased to direct that notice of the following Appointments having been made under this Government from the dates set opposite the respective names, be published for general information:—

Major THOMAS BUNBURY, 80th Regiment, commanding her Majesty's Troops in New Zealand, appointed a Magistrate of the Territory—30th March, 1840.

WILLOUGHBY SHORTLAND, Esquire, J. P., Acting Colonial Secretary and Registrar of Records—7th March, 1840.

FELTON MATHEW, Esquire, J. P., Surveyor General—1st January, 1840.

JOHN JOHNSON, Esquire, M. D., J. P., Colonial Surgeon—6th February, 1840.

WILLIAM DAVIES, Esquire, M. D., Sur[illegible]

WILLIAM CORNWALLIS SYMONDS, Esquire, Police Magistrate—17th March, 1840.

CHARLES BARRINGTON ROBINSON, Esquire, Police Magistrate—28th March, 1840.

MICHAEL MURPHY, Esquire, Police Magistrate—30th March, 1840.

H. D. SMART, Lieut. 28th Regiment, Magistrate of the Territory—1st January, 1840.

JAMES READY CLENDON, Esquire, Magistrate of the Territory—21st February, 1840.

THOMAS BECKHAM, Esquire, Magistrate of the Territory—17th March, 1840.

Mr. WILLIAM MASON, Superintendent of Public Works—1st March, 1840.

Mr. CHARLES LOGIE, Colonial Store-Keeper—15th January, 1840.

By His Excellency's Command,
(For the Colonial Secretary,)
JAS. STUART FREEMAN.

GOVERNMENT NOTICE.

Colonial Secretary's Office,
Russell, 29th May, 1840.

NOTICE is hereby given, that in the absence of WILLOUGHBY SHORTLAND, Esquire, Colonial Secretary, the duties of that Office will be performed by JAMES STUART FREEMAN, Esquire, who has been duly appointed to the charge of the Colonial Office, until the return of the former Gentleman to the Seat of Government.

By His Excellency's Command,
(For the Colonial Secretary,)
JAS. STUART FREEMAN.

GOVERNMENT NOTICE.

Colonial Secretary's Office,
Russell, 10th June, 1840.

MAIZE.

TENDERS will be received at this Office until twelve o'clock of *Tuesday* the 30th instant, for the supply of *"Three Hundred Bushels of Maize,"* to be delivered at this Station.

Parties tendering, or their Agents, are requested to attend at this Office on the day of opening the offers.

Security for the due fulfilment of the Contract will be required.

By His Excellency's Command,
(For the Colonial Secretary,)
JAS. STUART FREEMAN.

Sales by Auction.

To be Sold by Public Auction
By W. Wilson,
At his Rooms on Thursday, 18th June, 1840, at 11 o'clock,

ONE case Navy blue prints
1 bale calico
6 Hhds. rum, 19 o. p.
4 Hhds. ale
4 ditto porter
Cross-cut saws
Spades
2 Tents.

[illegible] Company.

Terms made known at time of Sale.

For Sale by Public Auction,
By W. Wilson,
At his Rooms, on Thursday, 18th June, at 12 o'clock,

ONE valuable back Horse, saddle and bridle[illegible]

Terms at time of sale.

New Zealand Advertiser and Bay of Islands Gazette. Vol.1 no.1 (15 June 1840). Original Collection.

The newspaper's official role was replaced by the *Gazette Extraordinary*, and the *New Zealand Advertiser and Bay of Islands Gazette* ceased publication with the 10 December 1840 issue. Quaife's work at Kororareka continued with the formation of the first Congregational church in New Zealand. AJ

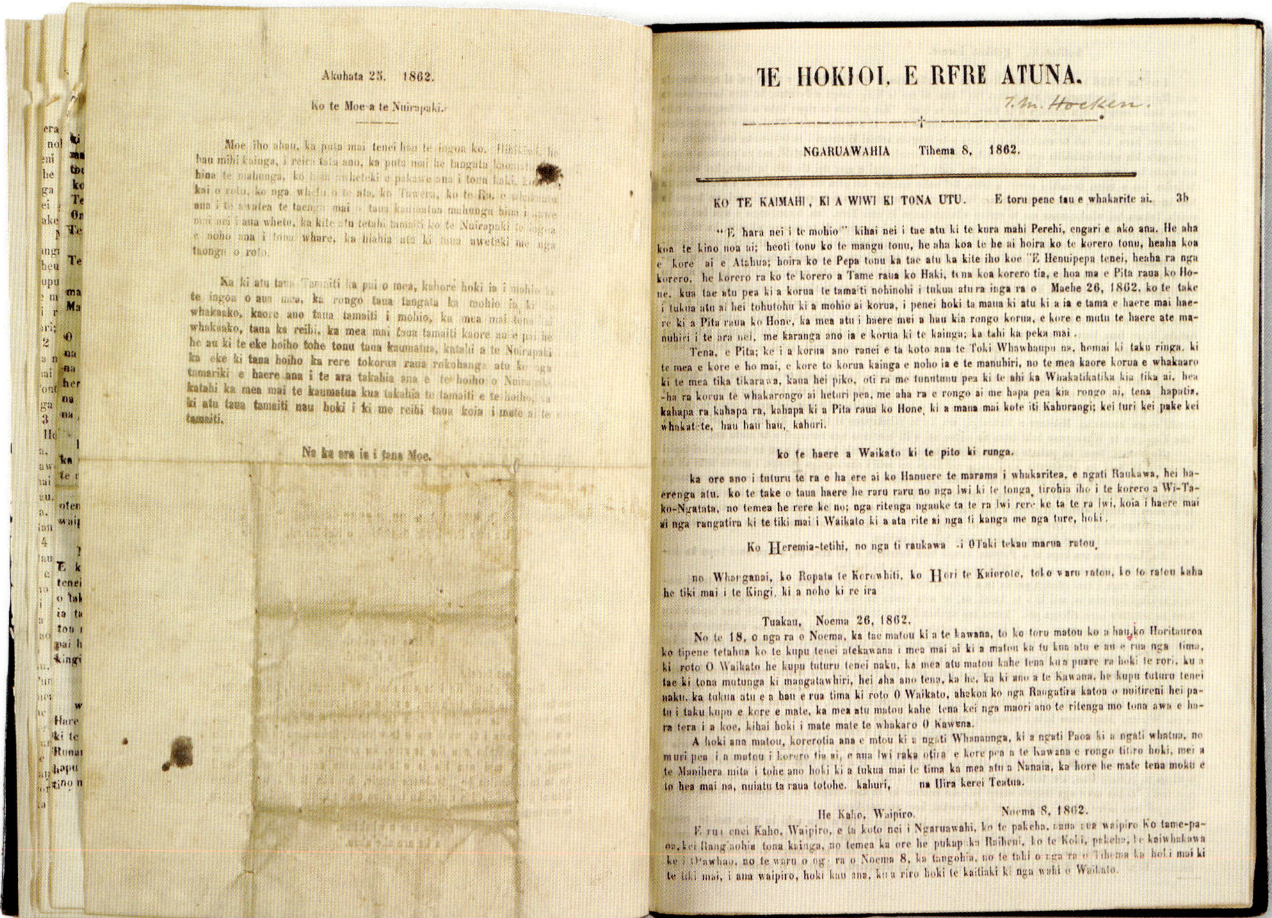

Akuhata 25. 1862.

Ko te Moe-a te Nuirapaki.

Na ka ara ia i taua Moe.

TE HOKIOI. E RERE ATUNA.

T. M. Hocken.

NGARUAWAHIA Tihema 8, 1862.

KO TE KAIMAHI, KI A WIWI KI TONA UTU. E toru pene tau e whakarite ai. 3b

"E hara nei i te mohio" kihai nei i tae atu ki te kura mahi Perehi, engari e ako ana. He aha koa te kino noa ai; heoti tonu ko te mangu tonu, he aha koa te he ai hoira ko te korero tonu, heaha koa e kore ai e Atahua; hoira ko te Pepa tonu ka tae atu ka kite iho koe "E Henuipepa tenei, heaha ra nga korero, he korero ra ko te korero a Tame raua ko Haki, tena koa korero tia, e hoa ma e Pita raua ko Hone. kua tae atu pea ki a korua te tamaiti nohinohi i tukua atu ra inga ra o Maehe 26, 1862, ko te take i tukua atu ai hei tohutohu ki a mohio ai korua, i penei hoki ta maua ki atu ki a ia e tama e haere mai haere ki a Pita raua ko Hone, ka mea atu i haere mai a hau kia rongo korua, e kore e mutu te haere ate manuhiri i te ara nei, me karanga ano ia e korua ki te kainga; ka tahi ka peka mai.

Tena, e Pita; ke i a korua ano ranei e ta koto ana te Toki Whawhaupu na, homai ki taku ringa, ki te mea e kore e ho mai, e kore to korua kainga e noho ia e te manuhiri, no te mea kaore korua e whakaaro ki te mea tika tikarawa, kaua hei piko, oti ra me tunutunu pea ki te ahi ka Whakatikatika kia tika ai, hea-ha ra korua te whakarongo ai heturi pea, me aha ra e rongo ai me hapa pea kia rongo ai, tena hapatia, kahapa ra kahapa ra, kahapa ki a Pita raua ko Hone, ki a mana mai kote iti Kahurangi; kei turi kei pake kei whakatete, hau hau hau, kahori.

ko te haere a Waikato ki te pito ki runga.

ka ore ano i tuturu te ra e ha ere ai ko Hanuere te marama i whakaritea, e ngati Raukawa, hei haerenga atu. ko te take o taua haere he raru raru no nga Iwi ki te tonga, tirohia iho i te korero a Wi-Tako-Ngatata, no temea he rere ke no; nga ritenga ngauke ta te ra Iwi rere ke ta te ra Iwi, koia i haere mai ai nga rangatira ki te tiki mai i Waikato ki a ata rite ai nga ti kanga me nga ture, hoki.

Ko Heremia-tetihi, no nga ti raukawa i OTaki tekau marua ratou.

no Wharganai, ko Ropata te Korowhiti, ko Hori te Kaioroto, tokowaru ratou, ko to ratou kaha he tiki mai i te Kingi, ki a noho ki re ira

Tuakau, Noema 26, 1862.

No te 18, o nga ra o Noema, ka tae matou ki a te kawana, to ko toru matou ko a hau, ko Horitauroa ko tipene tetahua ko te kupu tenei a te kawana i mea mai ai ki a matou ka tu kua atu e au e rua nga tima, ki roto O Waikato he kupu tuturu tenei naku, ka mea atu matou kahe tena ku a puare ra hoki te rori, ku a tae ki tona mutunga ki mangatawhiri, hei aha ano tena, ka he, ka ki ano a te Kawana, he kupu tuturu tenei naku. ka tukua atu e a hau e rua tima ki roto O Waikato, ahakoa ko nga Rangatira katoa o nuitireni hei patu i taku kupu e kore e mate, ka mea atu matou kahe tena kei nga maori ano te ritenga mo tona awa e hara tera i a koe, kihai hoki i mate mate te whakaro O Kawana.

A hoki ana matou, korerotia ana e mtou ki a ngati Whanaunga, ki a ngati Paoa ki a ngati whatua, no muri pea i a matou i korero tia ai, e ana Iwi raka otira e kore pea a te kawana e rongo titiro hoki, mei a te Manihera mita i tohe ano hoki ki a tukua mai te tima ka mea atu a Nanaia, ka hore he mate tena moku e to hea mai na, nuiatu ta raua totohe. kahuri, na Hira kerei Teatua.

He Kaho, Waipiro. Noema 8, 1862.

E rua enei Kaho, Waipiro, e ta koto nei i Ngaruawahi, ko te pakeha, nana i ua waipiro Ko tame-paoa, kei Rang'aohia tona kainga, no temea ka ore he pukapuka Raiheni, ko te Koli, pakeha, te kaiwhakawa ke i Rawhao, no te waru o nga ra o Noema 8, ka tangohia, no te tahi o nga ra o Tihema ka hoki mai ki te tiki mai, i ana waipiro, hoki kau ana, ku a riro hoki te kaitiaki ki nga wahi o Waikato.

Pro-Māori newspaper • 1862–63

Te Hokioi, E Rere Atuna. 8 Tihema 1862. Ngaruawhahia. Williams 337. Original Collection.

Te Hokioi E Rere Atuna ('The war bird in flight to you') was the first Māori-language newspaper to reflect Māori rather than Pakeha concerns. It was produced at Ngaruawahia by the Kīngitanga on a press donated by the Emperor of Austria to Hemara Te Rerehau Te Whanonga and Wiremu Toetoe at the end of their stay in Vienna in 1859. Governor Grey regarded the paper as anti-government, and countered by instructing Gorst, Native Commissioner for the Upper Waikato, to establish a rival publication *Te Pihoihoi Mokemoke i Runga i te Tuanui* ('The lone sparrow on the roof top') at the government's school in Te Awamutu.

The Kīngitanga paper took its name from 'the mythical bird that shrieked as an omen of war or misfortune', and under the editorship of Wiremu Pātara Te Tuhi, a relative of Tāwhiao, who had helped Pōtatau become the first Māori King, the two 'birds engaged in a contest which culminated in a raid on the 'sparrow' by the Ngāti Maniapoto, who shut it down.

Te Hokioi numbered only nine issues, 15 June 1862 to 21 May 1863, continuing briefly after the demise of its rival. The press was sent to Te Kopua for safekeeping when hostilities between the Crown and the Kīngitanga threatened, and was eventually abandoned. AJ

Otago's first newspaper sprang into life with the arrival of Henry Graham on the *Blundell* in 1848. A sixpenny fortnightly, the *News* was conducted with 'unwise energy', its Anglican proprietor resenting the dominance of the Presbyterians. Graham allied himself with the 'Little Enemy' in opposition to the policies of Captain William Cargill and the Otago Association.

Although the first editorial promised that 'our columns will embrace every topic of interest connected with the colony, discussed and commented upon with fairness and impartiality', by the fourth issue Graham was openly attacking the settlement's established leaders, following with criticisms of the Association's emigration policy, and claiming Otago needed labourers not the ill-suited artisans the Otago Association had selected. The paper became the mouthpiece for opposition to the Scottish, religious scheme for the Otago settlement and its promoters.

Cargill withdrew the forty-copy subscription of the Trustees for Religious and Educational Uses, placing the endeavour in jeopardy. Partly due to oppositions to its views and partly to Graham's ill health, *The Otago News* ceased publication with its ninety-first number on 21 December 1850. The Hocken Collections holds the only full run, the copy of its first issue in manuscript. AJ

THE OTAGO NEWS.

PUBLISHED EVERY ALTERNATE WEDNESDAY AFTERNOON AT THREE O'CLOCK.

"THERE'S PIPPINS AND CHEESE TO COME."

No. 1.] DUNEDIN, WEDNESDAY, DECEMBER 13, 1848. [PRICE 6d.

TO ADVERTISERS.

ADVERTISEMENTS inserted in the "OTAGO NEWS" on the following terms:—

Six lines and under ......, 2s. } for the first
All above Six lines, 4d. per line } insertion.
Half price for every subsequent insertion.

All communications, advertisements, and orders to be addressed to H. B. GRAHAM, at the "*Otago News*" Office, Dunedin.

PRINTING.

PAMPHLETS, TRACTS, BILL HEADS, CARDS, CUSTOM-HOUSE FORMS, &c., Printed with neatness, punctuality, and despatch, at the Office of the "*Otago News.*" A considerable reduction made to Missionaries and Religious Societies.

A well assorted stock of STATIONERY always on hand.

Orders received for English Periodicals and Newspapers, to be forwarded by way of Sydney each month, per packet ship.

FOR SALE, at the Store of the undersigned, a large assortment of DRAPERY AND HARDWARE GOODS, consisting of:

Boilers, Saucepans, Tea-kettles, Garden Hoes, American Axes, Nails, &c.
Jams and dried Apples.
Flour, Sugar, Tea, Soap, Pips, Window Glass, Bath Bricks, and Men's Boots.
Port and Sherry Wine in wood and bottle.
Claret, ditto.
Two quarter casks real Scotch Whiskey.
Thirty casks finest India Ale, in 3 dozen casks.
Two Bales of Blankets.
Seasoned Timber in Boards and Scantling.

A. ANDERSON,
Commission Agent.

Corner of Princes and Rattray Streets.

WANTED TO PURCHASE a Suburban Property, unchosen.

Apply to A. ANDERSON,
Commission Agent.

Corner of Princes and Rattray Streets.

CHALLENGE!

THE CRICKET Players of Dunedin hereby publickly Challenge the Cricket Club at Wellington to a trial of skill, at any place equi-distant between the Port of Otago and Port Nicholson: due notice of the acceptation of this Challenge to appear in the "*Wellington Independent*," or by letter, addressed to Mr. WATSON, the Commercial Inn, [illegible]

High Street, Dunedin, Dec. 9, 1848.

NOTICE IS HEREBY GIVEN.

THE COURT OF DIRECTORS of the New Zealand Company, by a despatch dated the 22nd of June, 1848, have determined that the appellation of this Settlement is henceforth to be "OTAGO," as originally advertized.

W. CARGILL,
Resident Agent.

Dunedin, Otago,
December 7, 1848.

STRAW BONNETS.

THE undersigned has just received a large and varied assortment of Dunstable and Coloured Fancy Straw Bonnets, which she can offer to the public at moderate prices.

M. J. GRAHAM.

Rattray Street.

N.B.—Straw Hats and Bonnets made, cleaned, & altered.

JOHN DE LA CONDAMINE CARNEGIE,

GENERAL MERCHANT AND COMMISSION AGENT,

IN returning thanks to the Public in general for the patronage which he has hitherto received, begs to inform them that he has always on hand, at his Store, in High Street, Dunedin, Otago, a well selected stock of GROCERIES, SLOP CLOTHING, &c., and of which he requests their inspection.

N.B.—Orders from round the Coast promptly attended to.

Dunedin, 12th Dec., 1848.

EX "BLUNDELL."

THE undersigned has on hand a small quantity of very superior West of England Pilot Cloth, wool dyed, and which he is now offering at a low figure.

J. DE LA CONDAMINE CARNEGIE.

Dunedin, 12th Dec., 1848.

INDEPENDENT ORDER OF ODD-FELLOWS.

THE HAND-AND-HEART LODGE of the Independent Order of Odd-Fellows, Manchester Unity, formed the 5th of December, 18[illegible], will hold their weekly meetings every Tuesday Evening, at half past Seven o'Clock, at the house of Mr. Watson, Commercial Inn, Dunedin. All parties desirous of joining this Society, and participating in its benefits, are requested to apply immediately to Mr. WATSON, Commercial Inn, who will give them every information.

COMMERCIAL INN, DUNEDIN.

T. S. WATSON begs to return his thanks to the Inhabitants of Dunedin and its vicinity for the very liberal support and encouragement he has received since opening the above establishment, and hopes by a strict attention to business, together with moderate charges, to continue to share their patronage and support. Having made considerable alterations and additions to his house, he is now capable of making up a number of beds for the convenience of people coming from the country.

N.B.—Wines and Spirits of the best qualities.

An Ordinary daily at half past One, p.m.; and at half-past Two, p.m., on Sundays.

NOTICE.

THE attention of the Community, and especially of parents, is requested to the following letter from Dr. RAMSAY, cautioning against the eating of the "Tutu" berry, now approaching to maturity.

[Signed] W. CARGILL,
Resident Agent.

Dunedin, Dec. 11th, 1848.

Dunedin, 9th Dec., 1848.

[illegible] to you the propriety of warning those people who have lately arrived and settled down here against the indiscriminate use of certain plants, growing so luxuriantly amongst us, I mean, more especially, the "Tutu," or, as it is called in more common language, the "Toot."

Of this plant, or shrub, the leaves and fruit contain, as you are already aware, properties highly injurious to sheep and cattle on their being first landed in the country; but not only so, symptoms also of the most alarming kind have been reported occasionally to develope themselves in the human subject after using the fruit. No such case has, as yet, fallen under my own personal observation, nor could this likely have happened at this early period of the season; but that properties adequate to produce the effects described do exist, I have not the least hesitation in believing. For these reasons, therefore, I think it right and proper that the younger members of the community should be strictly warned against eating any part of this well known shrub. I remain,

Yours faithfully,
ROBERT RAMSAY, M.D.

Captain Cargill, Resident Agent.

FOR SALE,

A QUANTITY OF BRICKS, at £2 ℔ thousand; also, Vandikes and Brick Pavement at a moderate price.

Apply to WILLIAMSON & Co.,
or, with orders, on the premises, to
ROSS & MERCER.

Dunedin, 12th December, 1848.

TO LET.

THE TRUSTEES for Religious and Educational Uses have still to Let several TOWN ALLOTMENTS, both at Dunedin and Port Chalmers; also, a large number of Suburban and Rural Allotments.

Dunedin, December 9th, 1848.

DUNEDIN MARKET.

Retail Prices Current, Dec. 8, 1848.

Beef	Fresh, per lb.	0	0	7	0	0	7½
Bread	Per 4 lb. loaf	0	0	10			
Butter	Fresh, per lb.	0	1	8	0	2	0
	Salt, do.	0	1	0	0	1	6
Cheese	Bathurst do.	0	1	0	0	[illegible]	6
Eggs	Per dozen	0	1	6	0	2	0
Flour	First, per 100 lbs.	0	16	0	1	1	0
Fire Wood	Per cord	0	18	0	1	4	0
Ham & Bacon	Per lb.	0	0	6	0	0	8
Iron	Per lb.	0	0	1½	0	0	4½
Lime	Per bushel	0	3	0			
Milk	Per quart	0	0	4			
Mutton	Per lb.	0	0	7	0	0	7½
Pork	Fresh, per lb.	0	0	6			
Potatoes	Per ton	4	0	0	5	10	0
Poultry	Fowls, per pair	0	4	0			
	Ducks "	0	4	0			
	Geese "	0	14	0			
	Ducks, wild, per pair	0	3	0			
Sugar	Loaf, per lb.	0	0	7½	0	0	8
	Raw, "	0	0	4	0	0	6
Cows	Milch, each	12	10	0	15	0	0
Mares	Each	20	0	0	30	0	0
Sheep	Wethers, each	1	0	0	1	8	0
Bullocks	Working, per pair	30	0	0	40	0	0
Wages	Mechanics, per day	0	5	0	0	7	0
	Labourers "	0	3	0	0	4	0

IMPORT DUTIES.

British and *Foreign Spirits*	5s. per gallon.
Tobacco.. Manufactured	1s. per lb.
Unmanufactured	9d. "
Cigars and *Snuff*	2s. "
Wines	20 per cent.
Malt Liquors	15 "
Munitions of War	30 "
[illegible]	10 "
Foreign Goods and *Produce*	12½ "
Glass Bottles (full), Specie, Bulbs and Plants, Live Animals, Printed Books	Duty free.

RATES OF POSTAGE.

Ship letters, weighing ¼ oz. and under,	4d.	To all parts out of N. Z.
Do. do. ½ oz. and under,	8d.	
Do. do. 1 oz. and under,	1s. 4d.	

Letters for any part of New Zealand need not be prepaid.

RULES FOR LITERARY INSTITUTES.—First, the supplying refining amusement freely and ungrudgingly, alike from the shelves of its library, the platform of its lecture hall, and the table of its reading-room. Next, the resolute assertion of the equality of all within its walls, irrespective of their differing social positions beyond them, combined with the determined recognition of usefulness and zeal as the highest titles to office and respect amongst its members. And lastly, the earnestness and silent unobtrusive working of its managers—men who, ever possessed with the all-important nature of the work to be done, have found in its completion, not in public thanks and plaudits, their pleasure and reward.

Otago News. No. 1. 13 December 1848. Original Collection.

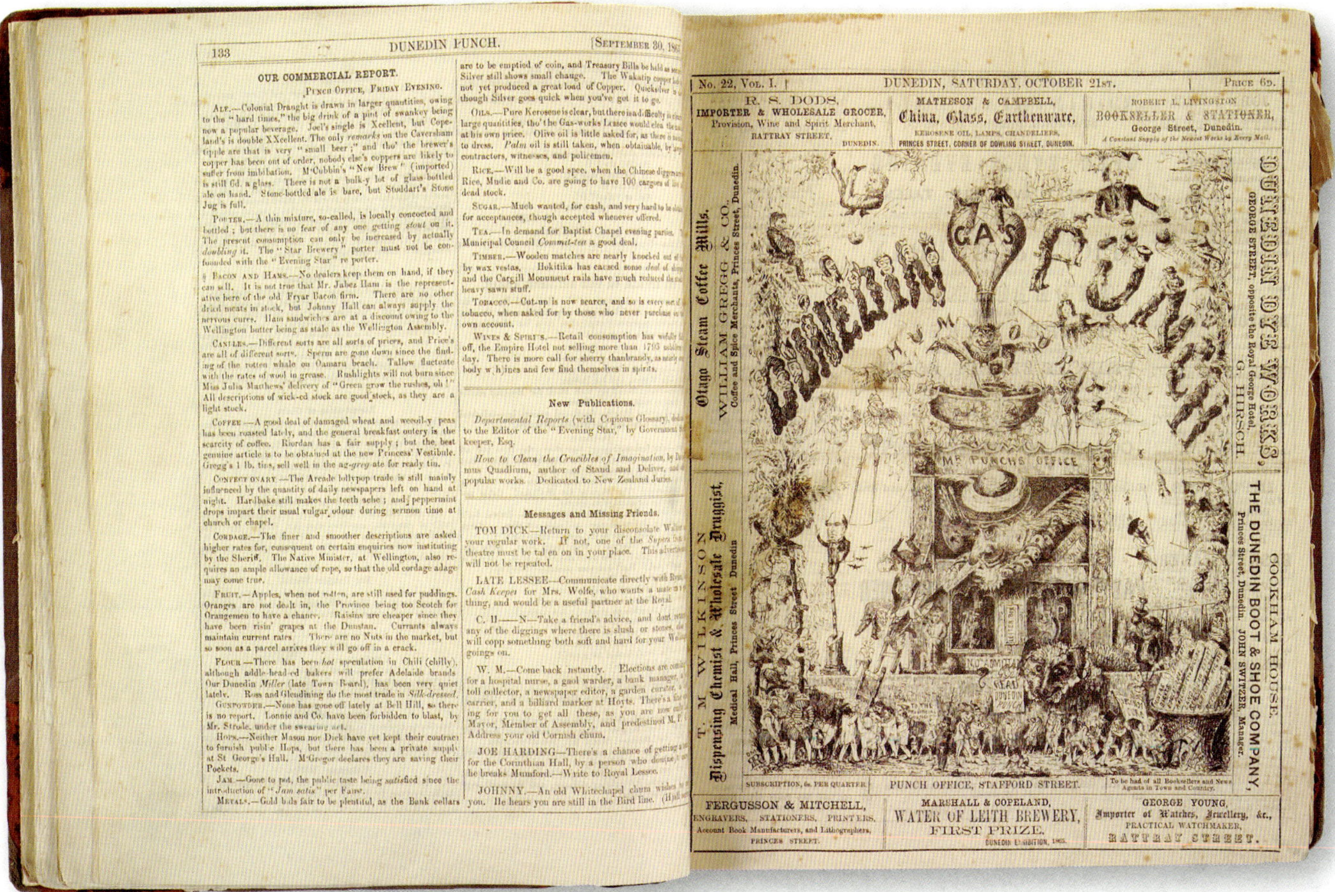

133 DUNEDIN PUNCH. [SEPTEMBER 30, 18

OUR COMMERCIAL REPORT.

PUNCH OFFICE, FRIDAY EVENING.

ALE.—Colonial Draught is drawn in larger quantities, owing to the "hard times," the big drink of a pint of swankey being now a popular beverage. Joel's single is Xcellent, but Copeland's is double XXcellent. The only *remarks* on the Caversham tipple are that is very "small beer;" and tho' the brewer's copper has been out of order, nobody else's coppers are likely to suffer from imbibation. M'Cubbin's "New Brew" (imported) is still 6d. a glass. There is not a bulk-y lot of glass-bottled ale on hand. Stone-bottled ale is bare, but Stoddart's Stone Jug is full.

PORTER.—A thin mixture, so-called, is locally concocted and bottled; but there is no fear of any one getting *stout* on it. The present consumption can only be increased by actually *doubling* it. The "Star Brewery" porter must not be confounded with the "Evening Star" re porter.

BACON AND HAMS.—No dealers keep them on hand, if they can sell. It is not true that Mr. Jabez Ham is the representative here of the old Fryar Bacon firm. There are no other dried meats in stock, but Johnny Hall can always supply the nervous cures. Ham sandwiches are at a discount owing to the Wellington butter being as stale as the Wellington Assembly.

CANDLES.—Different sorts are all sorts of prices, and Price's are all of different sorts. Sperm are gone down since the finding of the rotten whale on Oamaru beach. Tallow fluctuate with the rates of wool in grease. Rushlights will not burn since Miss Julia Mathews' delivery of "Green grow the rushes, oh!" All descriptions of wick-ed stock are good stock, as they are a light stock.

COFFEE.—A good deal of damaged wheat and weevil-y peas has been roasted lately, and the general breakfast outcry is the scarcity of coffee. Riordan has a fair supply; but the best genuine article is to be obtained at the new Princess' Vestibule. Gregg's 1 lb. tins, sell well in the ag-*grey*-ate for ready tin.

CONFECTIONARY.—The Arcade lollypop trade is still mainly influenced by the quantity of daily newspapers left on hand at night. Hardbake still makes the teeth ache; and peppermint drops impart their usual vulgar odour during sermon time at church or chapel.

CORDAGE.—The finer and smoother descriptions are asked higher rates for, consequent on certain enquiries now instituting by the Sheriff. The Native Minister, at Wellington, also requires an ample allowance of rope, so that the old cordage adage may come true.

FRUIT.—Apples, when not rotten, are still used for puddings. Oranges are not dealt in, the Province being too Scotch for Orangemen to have a chance. Raisins are cheaper since they have been risin' grapes at the Dunstan. Currants always maintain current rates. There are no Nuts in the market, but so soon as a parcel arrives they will go off in a crack.

FLOUR.—There has been *hot* speculation in Chili (chilly), although addle-head-ed bakers will prefer Adelaide brands. Our Dunedin *Miller* (late Town Board), has been very quiet lately. Ross and Glendining do the most trade in *Silk-dressed.*

GUNPOWDER.—None has gone off lately at Bell Hill, so there is no report. Lonnie and Co. have been forbidden to blast, by Mr. Strode, under the swearing act.

HOPS.—Neither Mason nor Dick have yet kept their contract to furnish public Hops, but there has been a private supply at St George's Hall. M'Gregor declares they are saving their Pockets.

JAM.—Gone to pot, the public taste being *satis*fied since the introduction of "*Jam satis*" per Faust.

METALS.—Gold bids fair to be plentiful, as the Bank cellars are to be emptied of coin, and Treasury Bills be held as se Silver still shows small change. The Wakatip copper h not yet produced a great load of Copper. Quicksilver is though Silver goes quick when you've got it to go.

OILS.—Pure Kerosene is clear, but there is a difficulty in large quantities, tho' the Gas-works Lessee would clea the at his own price. Olive oil is little asked for, as there is to dress. *Palm* oil is still taken, when obtainable, by contractors, witnesses, and policemen.

RICE.—Will be a good spec. when the Chinese diggers Rice, Mudie and Co. are going to have 100 cargoes of dead stock.

SUGAR.—Much wanted, for cash, and very hard to be for acceptances, though accepted whenever offered.

TEA.—In demand for Baptist Chapel evening parties. Municipal Council *Commit-tea* a good deal.

TIMBER.—Wooden matches are nearly knocked out by wax vestas. Hokitika has caused some *deal* of and the Cargill Monument rails have much reduced the heavy sawn stuff.

TOBACCO.—Cut-up is now scarce, and so is every sort of tobacco, when asked for by those who never purchase own account.

WINES & SPIRITS.—Retail consumption has off, the Empire Hotel not selling more than 1795 day. There is more call for sherry than brandy, as body w(h)ines and few find themselves in spirits.

New Publications.

Departmental Reports (with Copious Glossary), to the Editor of the "Evening Star," by Government keeper, Esq.

How to Clean the Crucibles of Imagination, by mus Quadlium, author of Stand and Deliver, popular works. Dedicated to New Zealand Juries.

Messages and Missing Friends.

TOM DICK—Return to your disconsolate W your regular work. If not, one of the *Supers* theatre must be taken on in your place. This will not be repeated.

LATE LESSEE—Communicate directly with *Cash Keeper* for Mrs. Wolfe, who wants a thing, and would be a useful partner at the Royal.

C. H——N—Take a friend's advice, and dont any of the diggings where there is slush or stones, will copp something both soft and hard for your goings on.

W. M.—Come back instantly. Elections are for a hospital nurse, a gaol warder, a bank manager, toll collector, a newspaper editor, a garden curator, carrier, and a billiard marker at Hoyts. There's a ing for you to get all these, as you are Mayor, Member of Assembly, and predestined M. Address your old Cornish chum.

JOE HARDING—There's a chance of getting for the Corinthian Hall, by a person who he breaks Mumford.—Write to Royal Lessee.

JOHNNY.—An old Whitechapel chum wishes you. He hears you are still in the Bird line. (H

No. 22, VOL. I. | DUNEDIN, SATURDAY, OCTOBER 21ST. | PRICE 6D.

R. S. DODS, IMPORTER & WHOLESALE GROCER, Provision, Wine and Spirit Merchant, RATTRAY STREET, DUNEDIN.

MATHESON & CAMPBELL, China, Glass, Earthenware, KEROSENE OIL, LAMPS, CHANDELIERS, PRINCES STREET, CORNER OF DOWLING STREET, DUNEDIN.

ROBERT L. LIVINGSTON BOOKSELLER & STATIONER, George Street, Dunedin. A Constant Supply of the Newest Works by Every Mail.

Otago Steam Coffee Mills. WILLIAM GREGG & CO. Coffee and Spice Merchants, Princes Street, Dunedin.

T. M. WILKINSON Dispensing Chemist & Wholesale Druggist, Medical Hall, Princes Street Dunedin

DUNEDIN DYE WORKS, GEORGE STREET, opposite the Royal George Hotel, G. HIRSCH.

COOKHAM HOUSE, THE DUNEDIN BOOT & SHOE COMPANY, Princes Street, Dunedin. JOHN SWITZER, Manager.

SUBSCRIPTION, 6s. PER QUARTER. | PUNCH OFFICE, STAFFORD STREET. | To be had of all Booksellers and News Agents in Town and Country.

FERGUSSON & MITCHELL, ENGRAVERS, STATIONERS, PRINTERS, Account Book Manufacturers, and Lithographers, PRINCES STREET.

MARSHALL & COPELAND, WATER OF LEITH BREWERY, FIRST PRIZE. DUNEDIN EXHIBITION, 1865.

GEORGE YOUNG, Importer of Watches, Jewellery, &c., PRACTICAL WATCHMAKER, RATTRAY STREET.

Dunedin Punch: gas, humour. Vol I. No. 22. 21 October 1865. Original Collection.

Colonial satire • 1865

One of several short-lived imitations of *Punch* that proliferated in New Zealand until the 1880s, *Dunedin Punch* was a distinguished publication second only to Canterbury's in sophistication. Published by the Redmayne brothers, Robert and Thomas, the first issue appeared on 27 May 1865.

Thomas Redmaynes's own copy of the first number has the original drawing for the cover, adapted from the London *Punch*. Punch in his office and his dog Toby below are surrounded by an intricate pattern of tiny figures with the faces of local politicians. The whole is surrounded by a gas balloon and in the background are sketches of a belfry and bats. No acid was spared in the skits on local affairs and personalities. *Dunedin Punch* published its own version of the latest overseas news which, to save delays in the mail, was received by telegraphy through Mr Punch's 'medium' in Melbourne, using the 'Patent Double distilled Atmospheric Telegraph'.

Although well regarded, *Dunedin Punch* lasted only forty-one issues before financial difficulties led to its sale in January 1866, when it ceased. The final issue, 6 January, announced that *Punch* had 'passed into other hands …. The show has now commenced with an entire change of performance. Charge of admission only sixpence. Walk up! Ladies and Gentleman. Walk up!' AJ

No. 3.

AN APPEAL

T. M. Hocken.

TO THE

MEN OF NEW ZEALAND.

BY

FÉMMINA.

(Mrs Moeller, wife of Dr M. for long the R. M. of Blenheim.)

The double m in Femmina is the Italian form.

NELSON:
PUBLISHED BY J. HOUNSELL, BOOKSELLER AND STATIONER.
1869.

Fémmina. *An Appeal to the Men of New Zealand.* Nelson: J. Hounsell, 1869. Original Collection.

Written by Mary Ann Müller as 'Fémmina', *An Appeal to the Men of New Zealand* was the first pamphlet to advocate New Zealand women's right to vote, arguing persuasively that they would become *truly* feminine only when able to participate in public affairs and appealing to parliamentarians for support.

Born Mary Ann Wilson in London about 1819, the author emigrated to Nelson with her two children in 1850 after an unhappy marriage. She remarried late 1851, to Dr Stephen Müller, and, while caring for their six children, maintained a long activism for women's rights. She was forced to act clandestinely, since her husband was 'bitterly opposed' to women's suffrage, yet it was his connections that gave her access to key political figures.

Influential in the passing of the Married Women's Property Acts of 1870 and 1884, Müller was supported by Charles Elliot – friend, cousin-by-marriage, and editor-proprietor of the *Nelson Examiner* – who published and disseminated her articles, and guarded her anonymity. She also maintained a close interest in the English struggle, sending a copy of her pamphlet to John Stuart Mill, who reciprocated with a copy of *On the Subjection of Women* published the same year.

Müller's identity was finally revealed in 1898 after her husband's death. She died in 1901, having lived to witness New Zealand strike 'the spark to the train now laid in most civilised countries.' AR

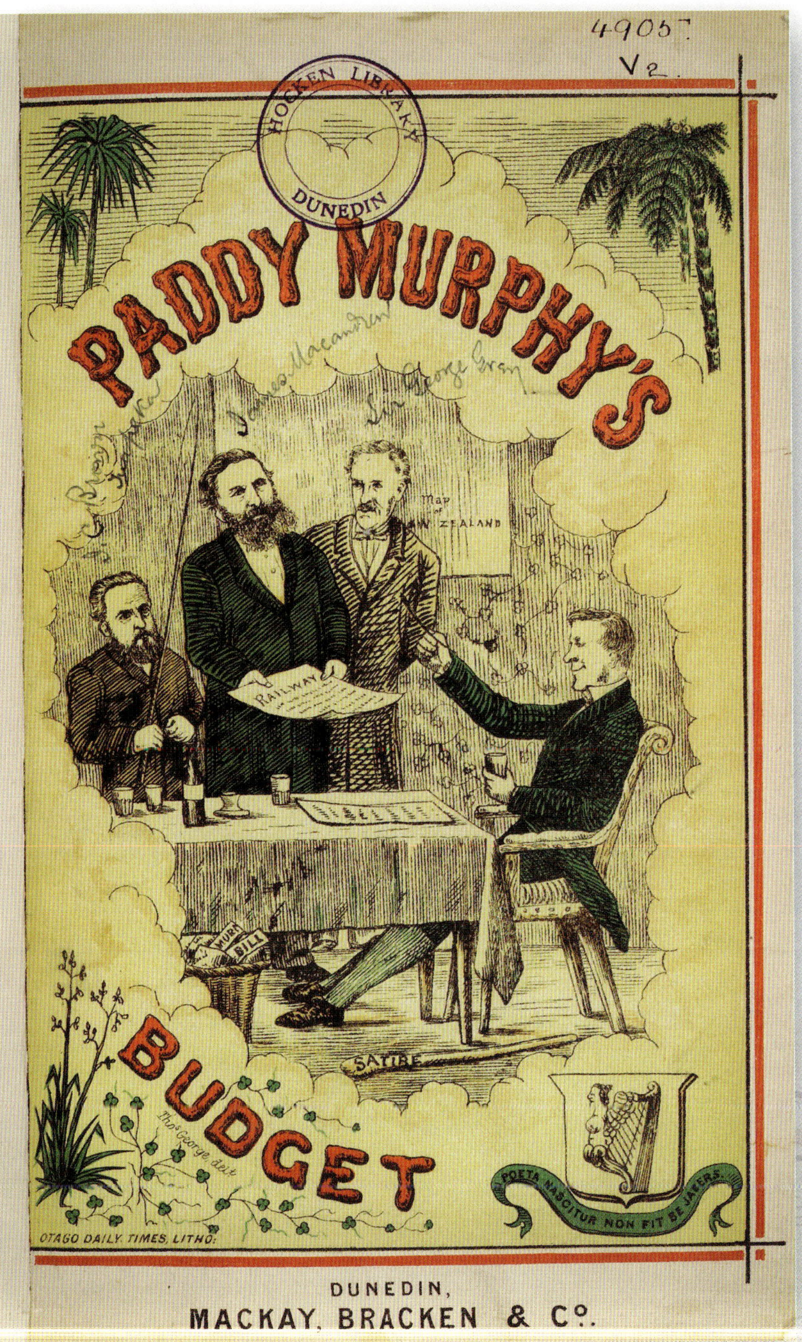

Thomas Bracken. *Paddy Murphy's Budget: a collection of humorous 'poems tiligrams, an' ipistols', by Paddy Murphy* [pseud.] Dunedin: Mackay, Bracken, 1880. Purchased, 1918.

The humour of Thomas Bracken • 1880

Under the pseudonym 'Paddy Murphy,' ostensibly writing from 'Lambton Key' in the capital city, Wellington, Thomas Bracken unleashed his light-hearted and witty observations of colonial political life. They were published over several years in the *Saturday Advertiser*, a newspaper originally owned by Bracken and Alexander Bathgate, and established with the aim of fostering a national spirit and encouraging colonial literature.

Patrick Galvin, of Coulls & Culling (the paper's publisher) and Bracken's friend, remarked on the popularity of these writings and the attribution of their authorship to various prominent public men. Bracken himself wrote the preface, without explaining his relationship to the author, and claimed that Murphy's intention was 'to let the general public into the secrets in connection with the working of our political machinery at Wellington.' He defended Murphy's use of the Irish brogue, claiming its 'idiomatic drollery' was 'proverbial, and observations which would fall pointless if expressed in plain English, become mirth-provoking when infused with the quaint phraseology of the Green Isle.' Some have observed that these writings of Tom Bracken, journalist and politician, may be of greater merit than those of Thomas Bracken, the poet. AJ

Theophilus Daniel, mayor of Riverton, invited inhabitants to a meeting on 4 June 1881 'to consider how to check the influx of the Chinese'. Ironically, the invitation was issued on a red and yellow poster, colours that to the Chinese symbolise luck, happiness and authority. The main complaints aired were that they would introduce smallpox and leprosy; they made no attempt to assimilate – 'a woolly-headed nigger from Africa … would amalgamate … but a Chinaman never'; they took their income back to China; their cheap labour threatened European workers; recent Australian legislation might cause hordes of Chinese to come to New Zealand instead; and they were inferior to Europeans. 'If they were to have Chinese amongst them, they would soon see nothing but a population of monkeys in Riverton.'

These prejudices had long been building, spreading from mining areas, where contact was closest. Previous attempts to legislate against the Chinese had failed, but the 1880s depression helped to force the issue, and some politicians used it to win popularity. The meeting resolved to petition the government to poll tax all Chinese £20. Five days later, the Chinese Immigration Bill was introduced into parliament. By the year's end it had passed and Daniel was the member for Wallace. In 2002, the New Zealand government apologised to the Chinese for earlier discriminatory policies. KM

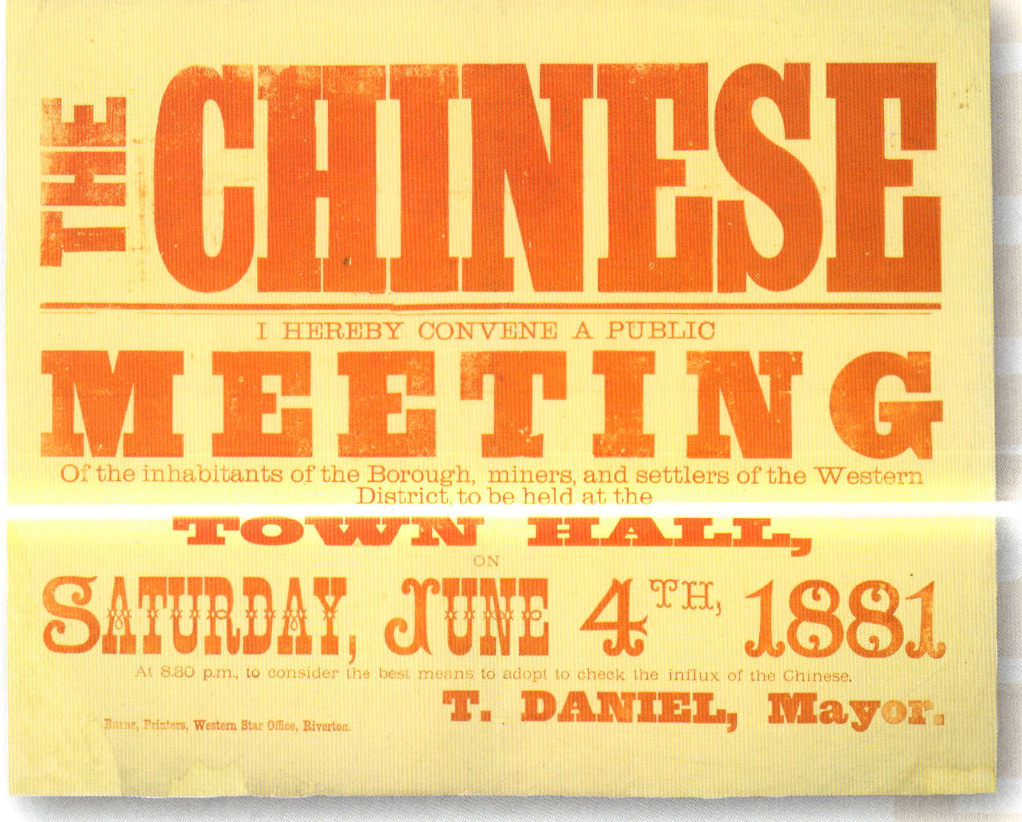

Poster. *The Chinese. Riverton, 1881*. Letterpress. Original Collection.

The judgement of C.N. Baeyertz • 1893–1927

Styled a 'magazine of music, science, and art', *The Triad* was established in Dunedin in 1893 by the Melbourne-born journalist C.N. Baeyertz (1866–1943). Cultured, witty and opinionated (often to the point of rudeness), Baeyertz included subjects as diverse as local concert performances, European literature, Māori culture, philosophy, humour, and scientific discovery. In 1897 he claimed a circulation of around 10,000, an astounding achievement for a cultural journal in a small colony.

The magazine was dominated by Baeyertz's own writing but included contributions from other local writers and overseas journals. The 'Answers to Readers' column encapsulated Baeyertz's acerbic style. To one he wrote: 'Your hymn tune is unspeakably dreadful. I might print it in the TRIAD as a prize puzzle, and offer a prize to the one who could say why you wrote it …. You write music much as Dogberry spoke English, except that many of his words were correct'.

The journal shifted with Baeyertz to Wellington in 1912 and again to Sydney in 1914. Later, it was edited by the equally outspoken Frank Morton, and finally by Leslie Woolacott. Publication ceased in 1927. No comprehensive run of the journal survives, but the Hocken Collections holds most New Zealand issues, some of which are the only copies extant.

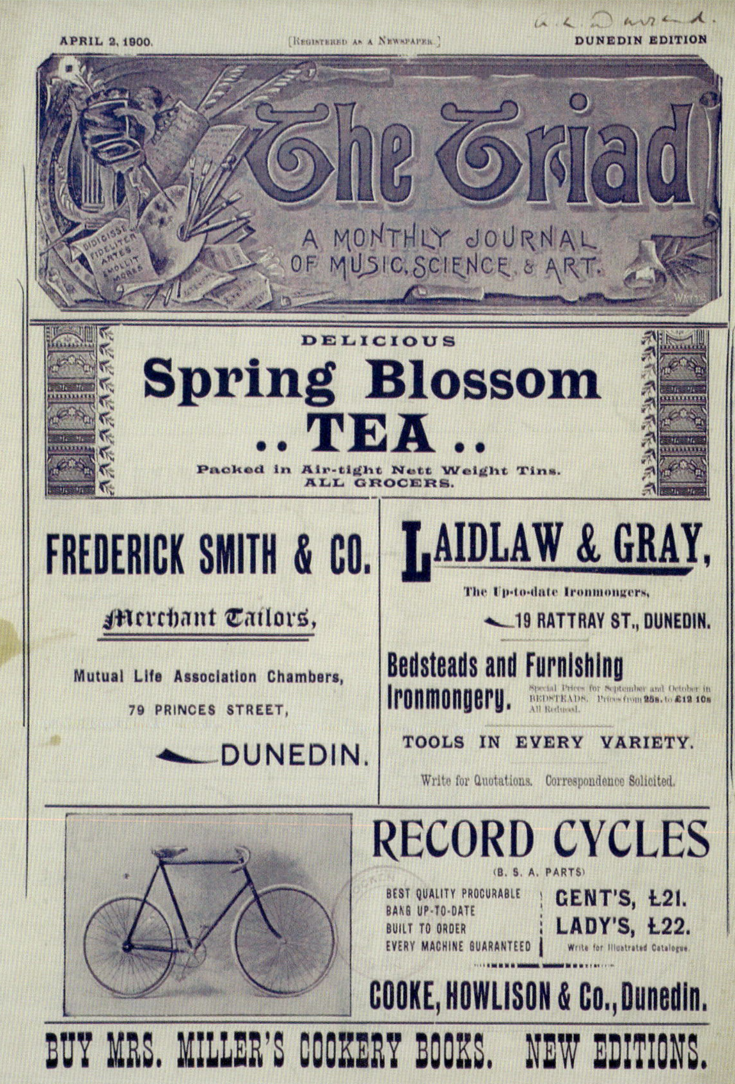

APRIL 2, 1900. [REGISTERED AS A NEWSPAPER.] DUNEDIN EDITION

The Triad

A MONTHLY JOURNAL OF MUSIC, SCIENCE, & ART.

DELICIOUS
Spring Blossom .. TEA ..
Packed in Air-tight Nett Weight Tins.
ALL GROCERS.

FREDERICK SMITH & CO.
Merchant Tailors,
Mutual Life Association Chambers,
79 PRINCES STREET,
DUNEDIN.

LAIDLAW & GRAY,
The Up-to-date Ironmongers,
19 RATTRAY ST., DUNEDIN.
Bedsteads and Furnishing Ironmongery.
Special Prices for September and October in BEDSTEADS. Prices from 25s. to £12 10s All Reduced.
TOOLS IN EVERY VARIETY.
Write for Quotations. Correspondence Solicited.

RECORD CYCLES
(B. S. A. PARTS)
BEST QUALITY PROCURABLE
BANG UP-TO-DATE
BUILT TO ORDER
EVERY MACHINE GUARANTEED
GENT'S, £21.
LADY'S, £22.
Write for Illustrated Catalogue.
COOKE, HOWLISON & Co., Dunedin.

BUY MRS. MILLER'S COOKERY BOOKS. NEW EDITIONS.

The Triad: a monthly journal of music, science, & art. 2 April 1900. Dunedin. Original Collection.

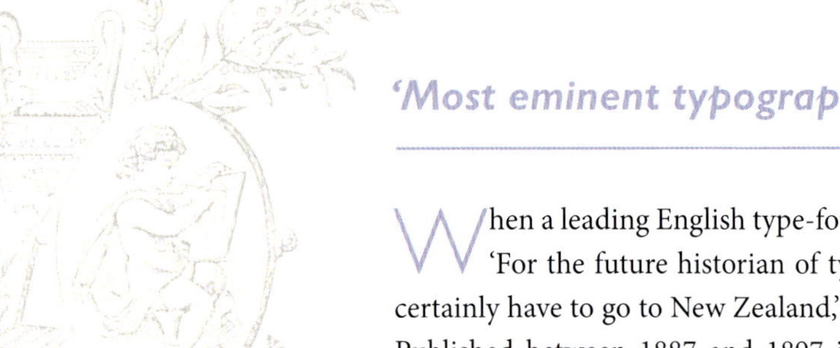

'Most eminent typographer' • 1887

When a leading English type-founder of the late nineteenth century claimed that 'For the future historian of type-founding of the present generation we shall certainly have to go to New Zealand,' he was referring specifically to the journal *Typo.* Published between 1887 and 1897 in Napier, it established exchanges with almost seventy similar journals around the world. It was written, designed and printed by Robert Coupland Harding, who according to one historian of print 'has a strong claim to be considered New Zealand's first and most eminent typographer'.

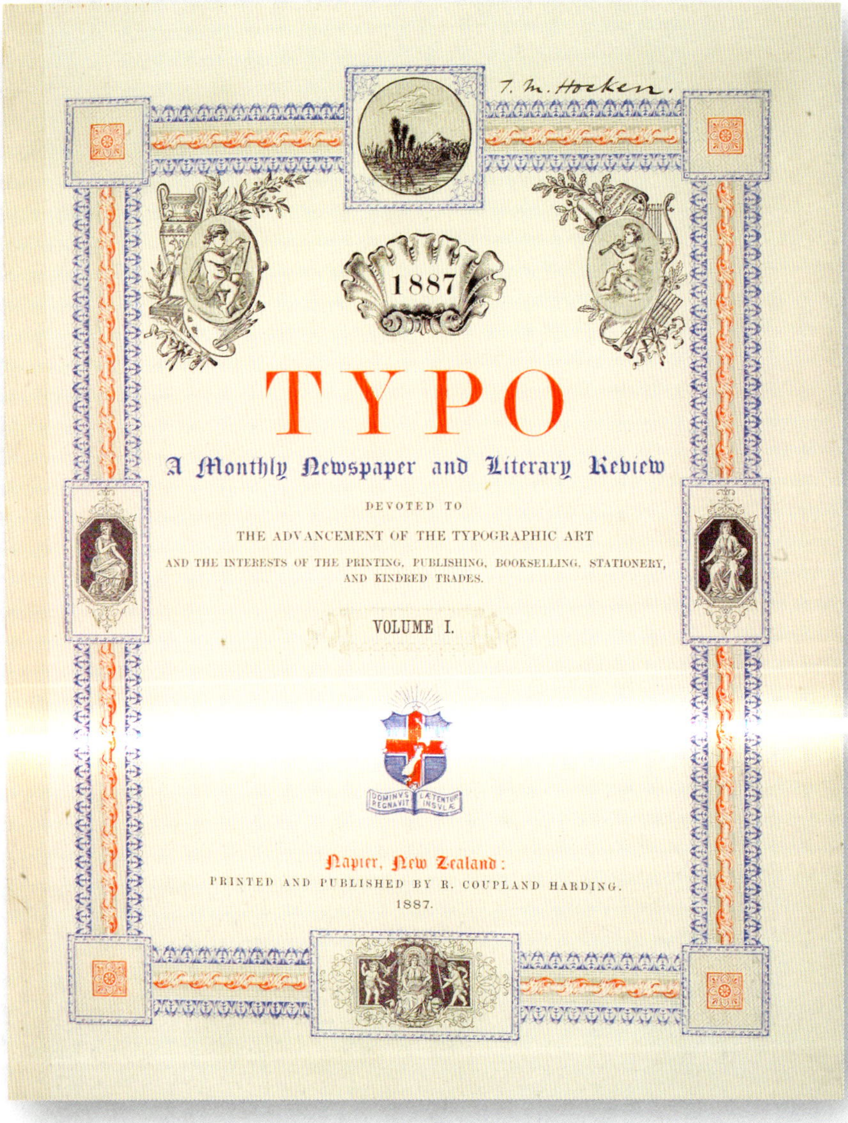

In the late 1870s Harding had imported the first parcels of American and German type into New Zealand and was a successful designer of borders. His critiques of new typefaces were internationally syndicated and very influential. *Typo* is an important resource for nineteenth-century typographic design, in particular Harding's series of articles 'Design and Typography'. These predate a general perception about the emergence of design in New Zealand, and undermine linear colonial models of design influence.

Typo is also critical for understanding the evolution of print culture in New Zealand and how ideas about competition, labour relations and design changed in response to politics and economic conditions. NW

Typo: a monthly newspaper and literary review devoted to the advancement of the typographic art. Jan. 1887 to Feb. 1897. Napier. Original Collection.

Colourful flora in New Zealand • 1889

Although Mr and Mrs. E.H. Featon are noted on the title-page, this impressive colour book is commonly known as 'Mrs Featon's Art Album', after Sarah Featon (1848–1927), an accomplished watercolourist, who painted the originals. Originally appearing in parts (the prospectus is bound in at the back), the *Art Album* was the first fully chromolithographic book to be printed in New Zealand. This collaborative work by the Featons was published by the Wellington-based firm of William Rose Bock (1847–1932) and Alfred Cousins with Nicholas Trübner, the London-based foreign language publisher, undertaking distribution in Britain. Bock and Cousins specialised in map printing, music printing, and detailed chromolithographic work. Personally supervising production, Bock saw through the presses forty coloured plates, each involving some fourteen or more separate colour press passes. It was a complex and courageous undertaking. Unfortunately, the project bankrupted the firm, and two further planned volumes never eventuated.

Dr Hocken's copy is in pristine condition. The title on the maroon cover is in foliage lettering, similar to Walt Whitman's *Leaves of Grass* published in 1855. The *Album's* references to New Zealand flora from early narratives of discovery would have interested Hocken. The frontispiece illustration, 'Wild flowers and berries', is typical of the fine work Bock and Cousins achieved. DJK

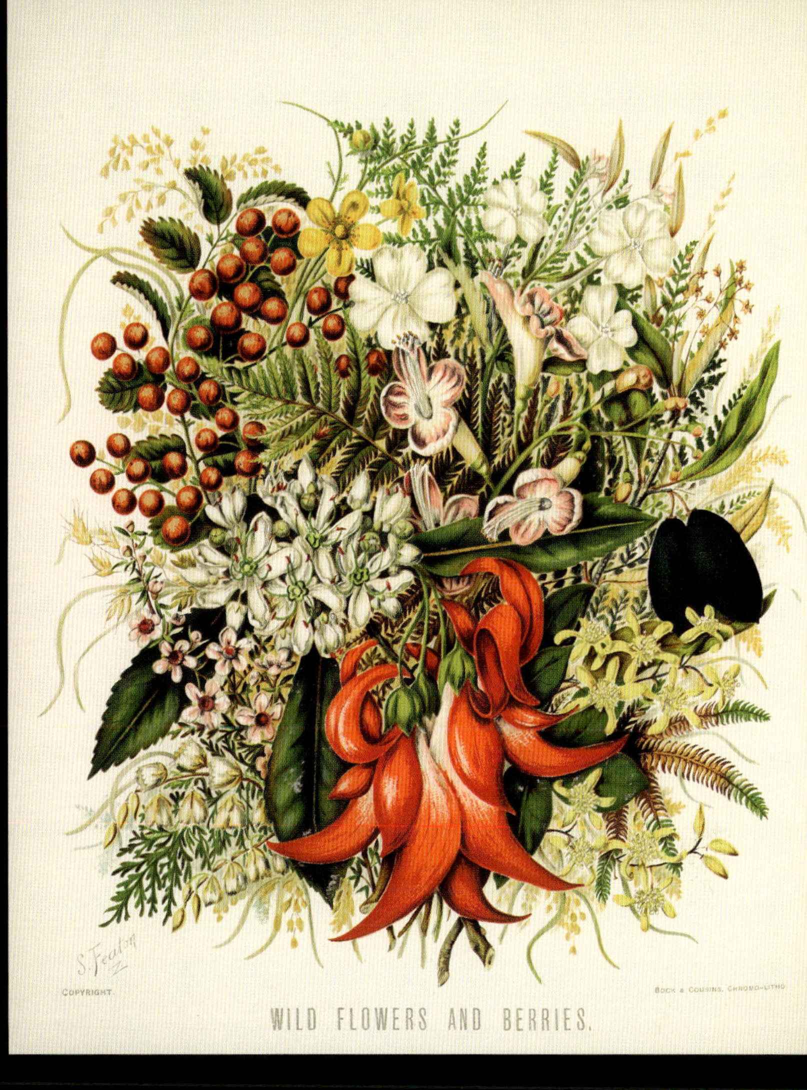

Edward Henry Featon. *The Art Album of New Zealand Flora: being a systematic and popular description of the native flowering plants of New Zealand and the adjacent islands: volume 1*. Wellington: Messrs. Bock & Cousins, [and] Trübner and Co., 1889. Original Collection.

A visionary novel • 1889

Few prime ministers have published novels. Benjamin Disraeli and Sir Julius Vogel, premier of New Zealand, 1873–76, are exceptions. In *Anno Domini 2000* Vogel, in his retirement, visualised a future ideal world in the year 2000 when the United States, defeated at war, would come back into the fold of the British Empire as part of an imperial federation that is ruled by women with its capital at Melbourne. 'It has come to be accepted that the bodily power is greater in man, and the mental power larger in woman.' New Zealand is represented at the imperial parliament by the clever and lovely Hilda Richmond Fitzherbert, who is first fascinated by the wicked Australian republican Sir Reginald Paramatta, but eventually becomes Empress.

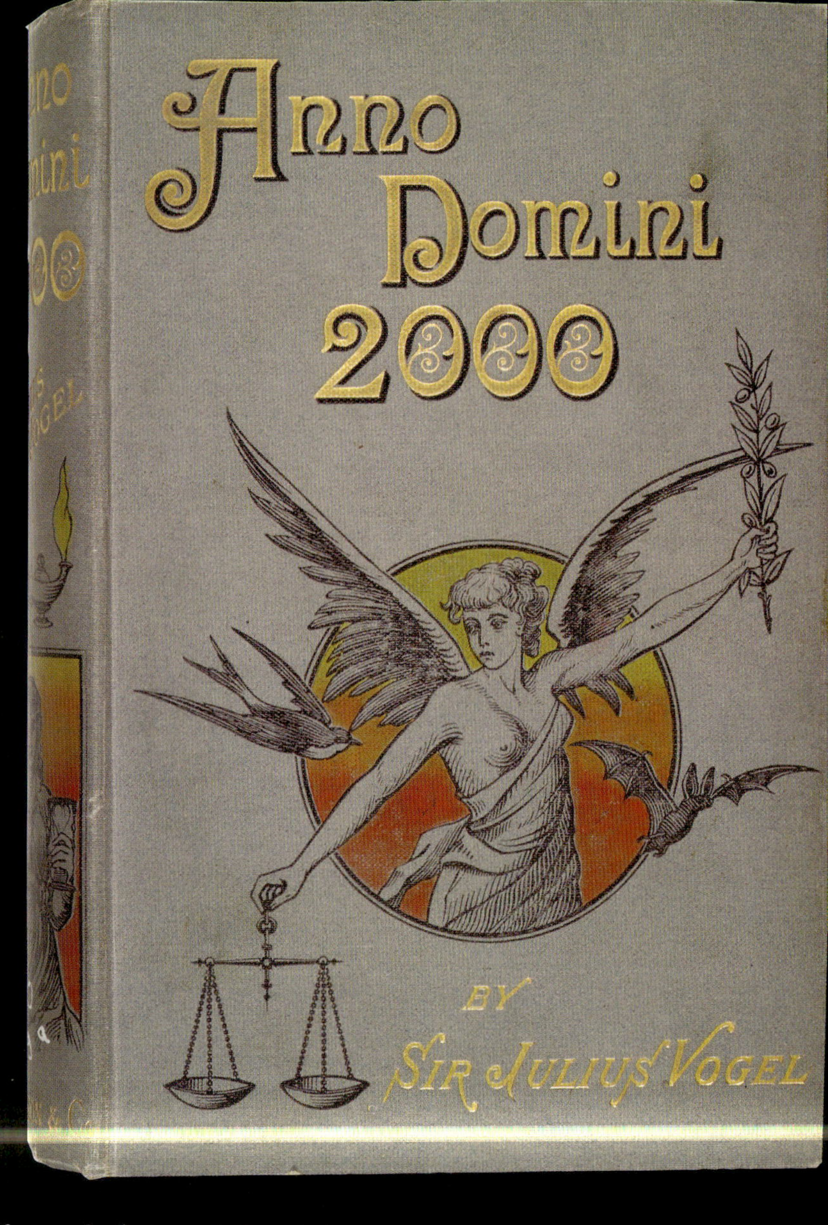

Sir Julius Vogel. *Anno Domini 2000*; or, *Woman's Destiny*. Colonial edition. London: Hutchinson & Co., 1889. Original Collection.

Thought by some to be New Zealand's first work of science fiction, the best parts of this finely produced book, on gender equality and related political tensions, have been said to owe something to Trollope. Generally its reception was lukewarm, only half of the 2000 colonial edition copies and 1000 of the home edition being sold in the first twelve months. More recently, *Anno Domini* has gained wider recognition as anticipating female political, judicial and corporate prominence in New Zealand at the millennium. SRS

A journal for ladies • 1894–96

Published monthly from 1894 by Christchurch-based Charles E. Turner, *Southern Queen* followed a trend to shadow successful English publications. Like Samuel Beeton's *Queen*, published in London from 1861, *Southern Queen* was designed for the distraction and edification of socially elite ladies. Regular features included fiction, music and drama reviews, as well as items about the new hobbies of photography and golf, and detailed accounts of fashion. 'The Business of Pleasure' detailed who was doing what with whom, and what they were wearing at the time. Unlike its London model, *Southern Queen* also included practical domestic advice, such as dress-making instructions, recipes, and pointers for keeping clean, as well as keeping husbands. These perhaps acknowledged that *Southern Queen*'s readers were as likely to be salting hams and starching curtains as attending society weddings and nights at the opera.

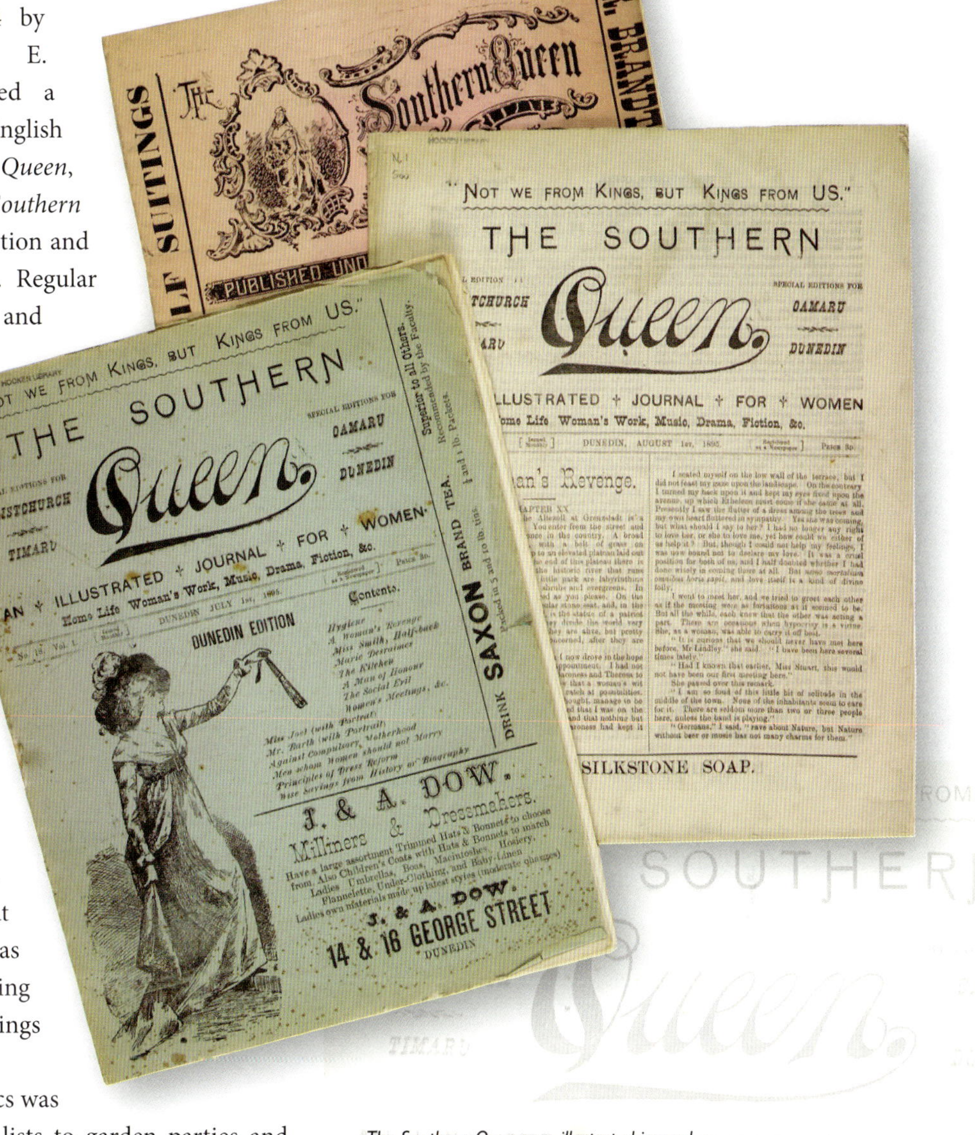

The Southern Queen: an illustrated journal for women. Christchurch, c. 1894–c.1896.
Donated, 1987.

Discussion of society and politics was not entirely defined by invitation lists to garden parties and strategies for successful marriage. At a time when womanhood was being widely debated, *Southern Queen* could be surprisingly liberal. It supported women's 'equal rights with men in property, and self', and called for dress reform. It is impossible to know if such views represented its readership, but they do suggest that the society lady in 1890s New Zealand was ready to consider that she might have influence beyond her own garden gates. JH

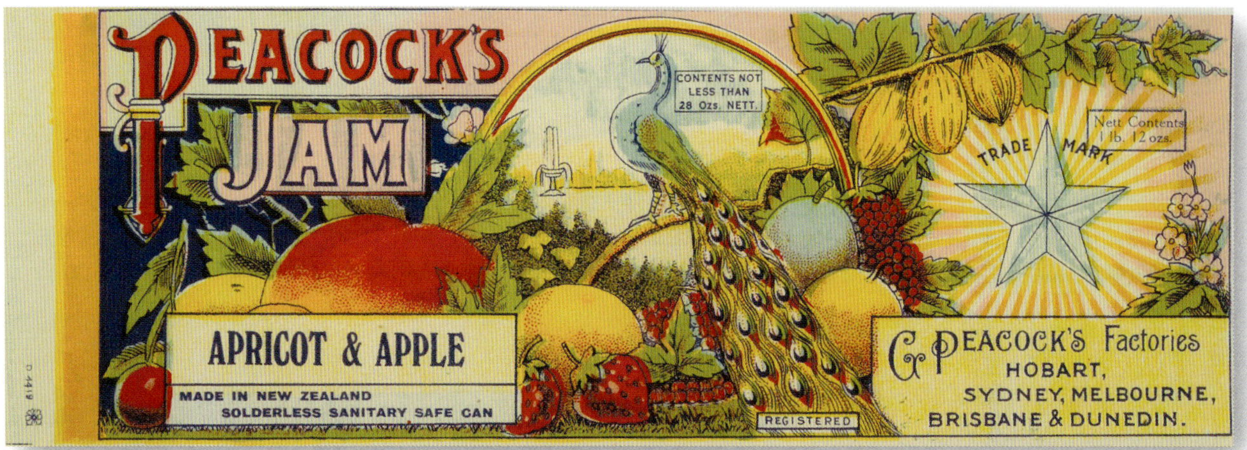

Colourful tinned food labels • c. 1900

Irvine and Stevenson's St George Co. Ltd. *Food product labels.* Dunedin, c. 1900. Chromolithographs. Misc MS 1748. Donated by R.D.J. Collins, 2001.

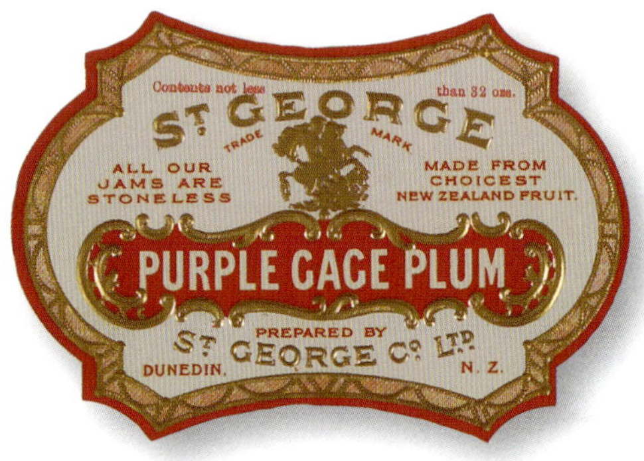

When Otago bibliographer Keith Maslen described a printing office as 'an index of civilisation', he was referring to its ability to record all the various transactions – commercial and cultural – that occur in a society over a particular period. Graphically striking if colonially conventional, these colourful tinned food labels are a rich index of social history. Not only do they record the entrepreneurial efforts of an emergent Dunedin industry to brand its export products, but they also represent the professional application of chromolithography in New Zealand's leading printing and publishing centre.

James Irvine and his son-in-law William Stevenson went into partnership in 1882, building on Irvine's established storekeeping business. In 1885 they registered their distinctive St George and the Dragon trademark, and by 1891 had bought the Dunedin stock and canning plant of the Australian-based G. Peacock.

Colour lithography was a skilled art that entailed the visualisation and careful registration of, in this case, at least six differently inked stones. The labels are printed by Mills, Dick & Co., one of the two major lithographers in Dunedin at that time, and Whitcombe & Tombs, a Christchurch firm that later merged with Dunedin firm Coulls Somerville Wilkie to become Whitcoulls. NW

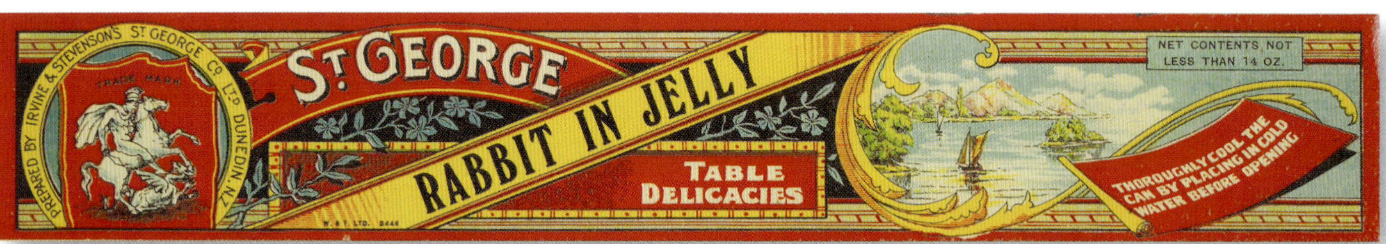

Cautionary temperance novel • 1903

The *Hills of Hauraki* is a temperance novel that makes its point through the tragic story of Christina Bailey. Her husband, Edward, although at first keen to be worthy of his bride, soon reverts to his old bachelor drinking habits. When he takes over his father's pub he begins drinking heavily and is frequently abusive.

Far from being a restraining influence, Christina soon breaks her vow never to touch alcohol. A small dose, 'just as medicine', soon becomes a regular indulgence. Visiting evangelists make Christina aware of her downward spiral, but she fails to confess her sins. The opportunity for salvation passes and Christina continues to drink, eventually dying in agony when she mistakenly quaffs a bottle of ammonia.

Susie Seaman, the author, was born in 1854 and came to New Zealand when she was eleven. Involved in community affairs as a teacher, she also founded the Takapuna Public Library, where she ran a non-denominational Sunday School with her sister Annie. She married Anthony Mactier in 1886 and became an active member of the Auckland YMCA. With her sister she organised the Flower Mission, visiting workrooms, singing hymns and handing out religious tracts. LT

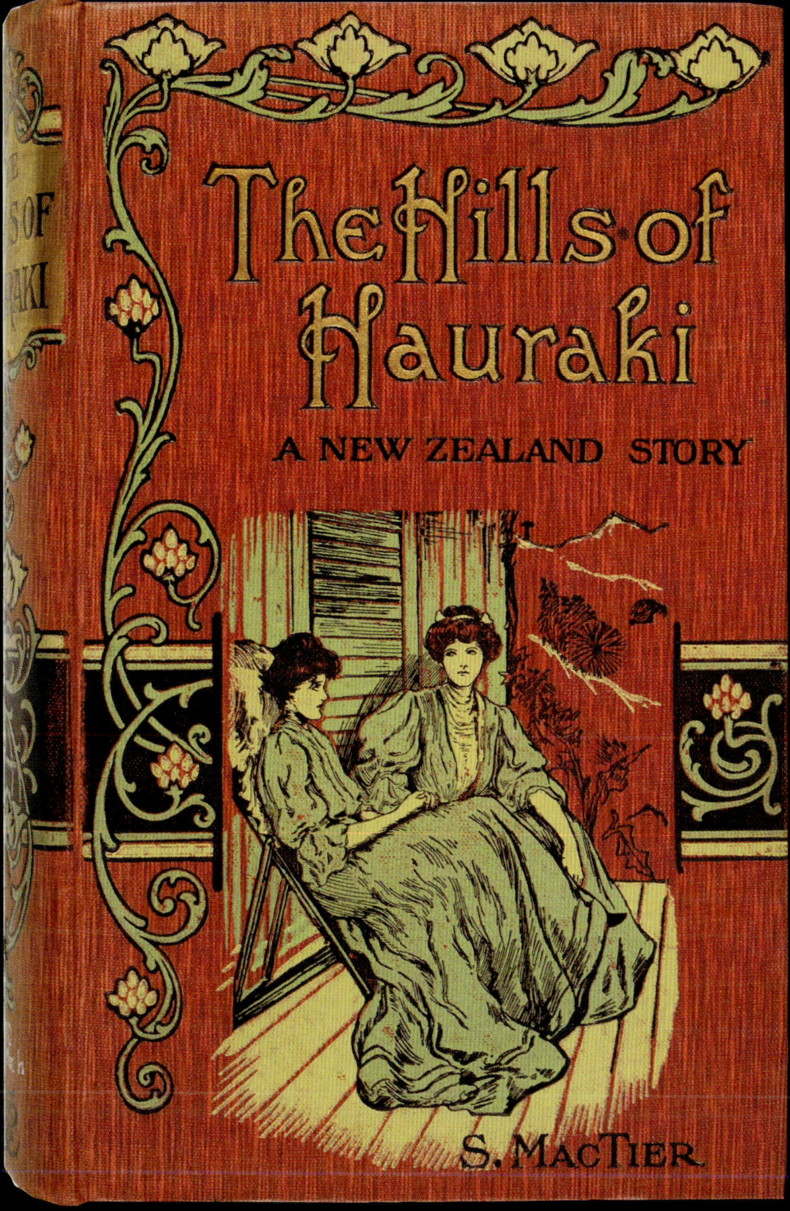

The Hills of Hauraki
A NEW ZEALAND STORY
S. MACTIER

Susie Mactier. *The Hills of Hauraki or the Unequal Yoke: a story of New Zealand life*. London: Sunday School Union, 1903. Purchased 1940.

HKF
E

The Art of Rugby Football

By . .
T. R. Ellison.

T.R. Ellison. *The Art of Rugby Football. With hints and instructions on every point of the game.* Wellington: Geddis and Blomfield, 1902. Purchased, 1974.

One of the earliest rugby coaching manuals published in New Zealand, Thomas Rangiwahia Ellison's *The Art of Rugby Football* was published in 1902, just two years before his untimely death at the age of 36. Ellison was introduced to rugby by his cousins, the Taiaroa family, at the Kaik, Otakou, around 1881, and remained fascinated by the game. He was a prominent member of the New Zealand Native Football Team, which embarked on an arduous fourteen-month tour of Great Britain and Australia in 1888. He would later captain the 1893 New Zealand team on their tour of Australia. He successfully proposed that the New Zealand team be dressed in black jerseys with silver ferns (in the manner of the Native uniform), but was unsuccessful in his bid to have players on tour recompensed for lost wages.

The Art of Rugby Football illustrates why Ellison was known as one of the game's great innovators. It explains the wing forward position and the 2-3-2 scrum formation that he developed for his Poneke club team in Wellington and which became the dominant style of All Black play until the 1930s. The book also reminisces about tours and teams, their tactics, innovations, criticisms and the standard of refereeing, and provides suggestions for the future of the game. ACC

The "Sure to Rise" cookery book: is especially compiled and contains useful everyday recipes, also cooking hints. Christchurch: T.J. Edmonds, 1908. Donated by J.T. Paul Estate, 1968.

Edmonds' cookery book • 1908

Thomas J. Edmonds started his business in Lyttelton in 1879 with the development of his own baking powder, telling customers that cooking with this raising agent was sure to rise. In time the business became a Christchurch landmark, housed in a three-storey, purpose-built factory with a distinctive 'Sure to Rise' symbol on its façade. The building was eventually demolished in 1990.

The early editions of the Edmonds' cookbooks were 'post free to any address, on receipt of one penny stamp'. It is unclear if the 1908 publication is the first edition; anecdotal evidence suggests that the original was published in 1907. The copy shown here is the earliest and only one known to have survived. It contained almost 100 simple recipes, including scones, bread, rolls, puddings, soups, buns, pikelets, cakes and pastry, and omelettes, almost all requiring the use of 'Edmonds' Prize Baking Powder', which sold in great quantity, over half a million tins in 1907.

Edmonds' cookbooks continue to be hugely popular, most homes having one. A fifty-third edition was published as recently as 2004, and recipes have been adapted for modern microwave technology. AJ

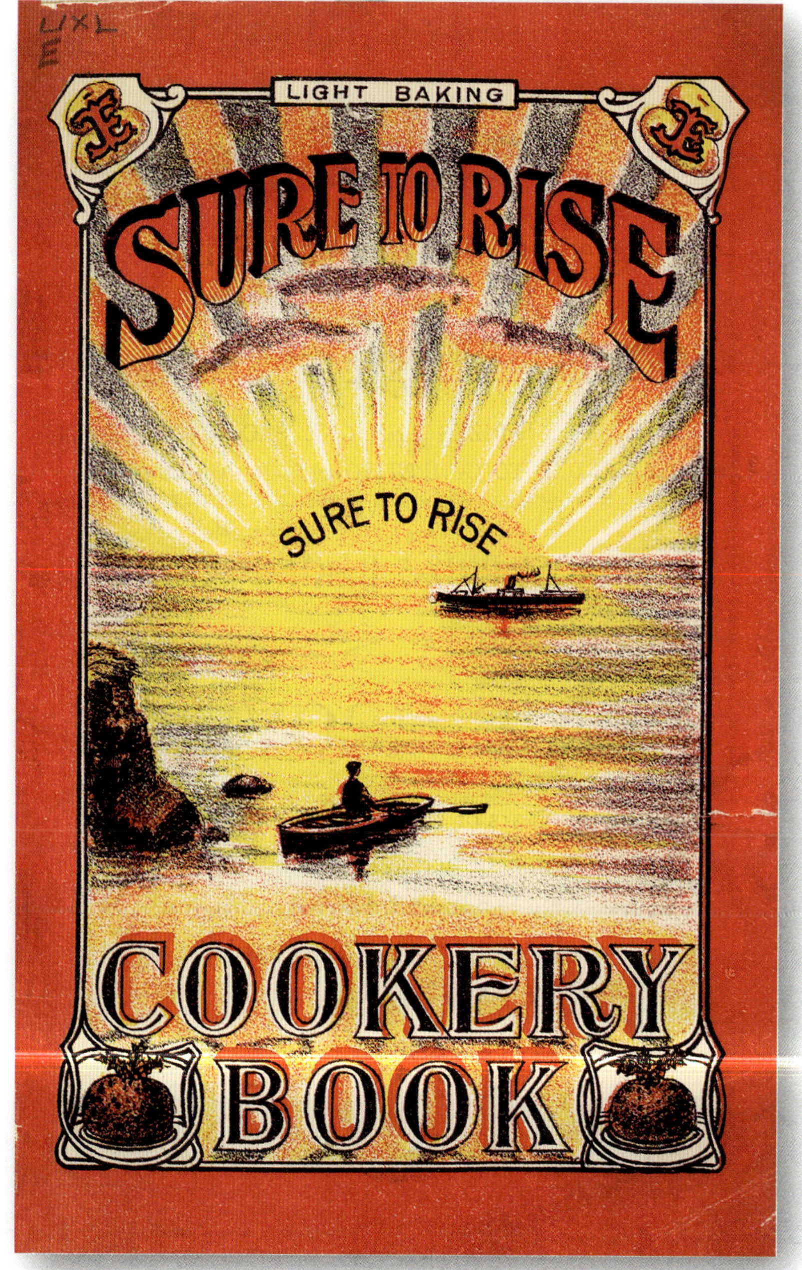

Horse racing was very popular in nineteenth-century New Zealand, and present as a form of entertainment on the Otago goldfields as early as the 1860s.

This dramatic depiction of an 'anxious moment' for horses and jockeys was used as a drawcard for the twenty-fifth annual meeting of the Tuapeka County Jockey Club in 1908. It was promised to be 'more than usually interesting' with large fields of good horses, a course in capital order, abundant seating for ladies, and entertainment between races by the Tuapeka Brass Band.

Good weather on the first day drew a large crowd from as far afield as Dunedin and Invercargill, ensuring healthy takings for the refreshment booths and bookmakers. Sever races were held on the first day – the most exciting being a dead heat between *Sonia* and *Speculate* in the Handicap Mile. Heavy showers on the second day resulted in a smaller attendance for the eight races, but betting was still good and £2206 was taken over the two days. The *Otago Witness* reported that overall the meeting 'was the best that has been witnessed at Lawrence for some time, and it required one or two riders to have been straightened up a bit, together with an improvement in the starting to have silenced adverse criticism.' The two-day meetings continued at Lawrence until 1911. KM

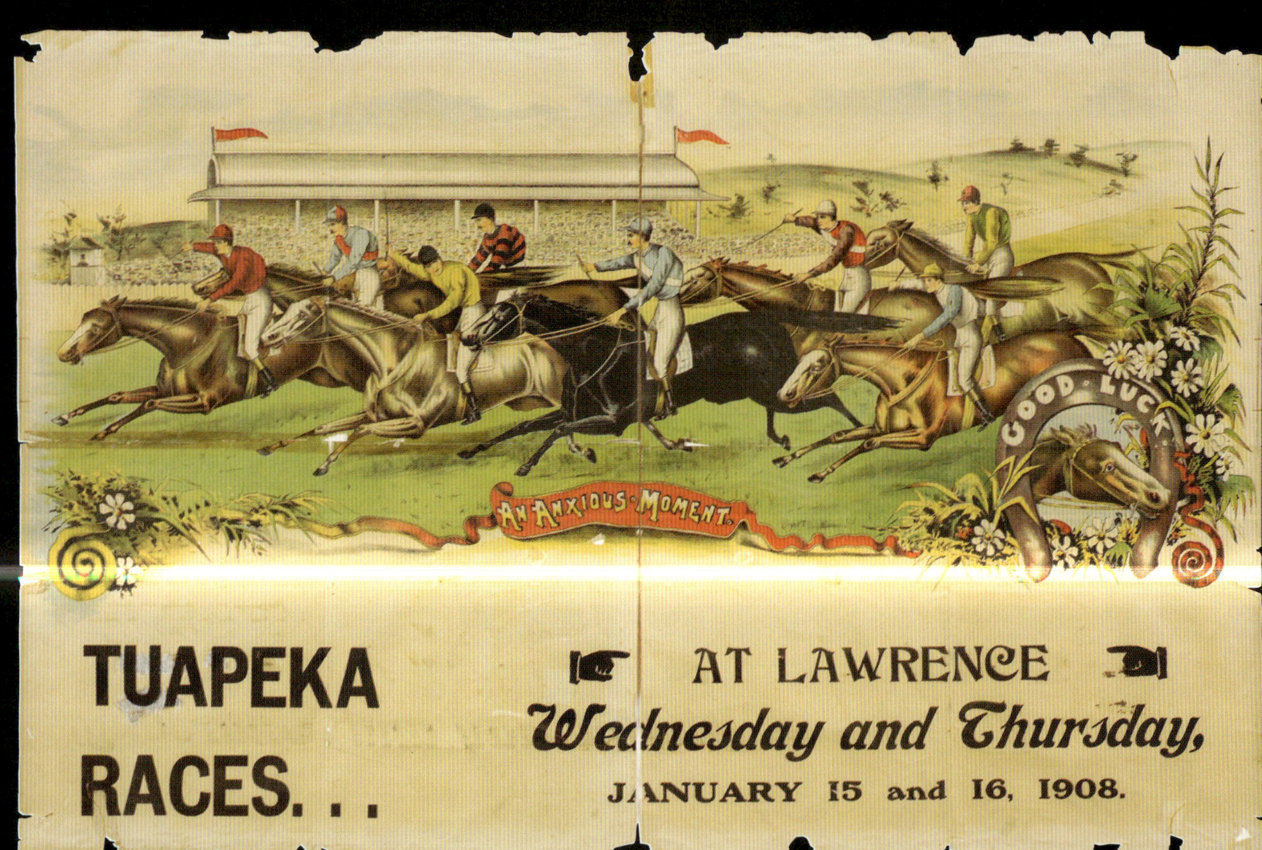

Poster. *Tuapeka Races .... At Lawrence Wednesday and Thursday, January 15 and 16, 1908.* Lithograph overprinted with letterpress. Unknown provenance.

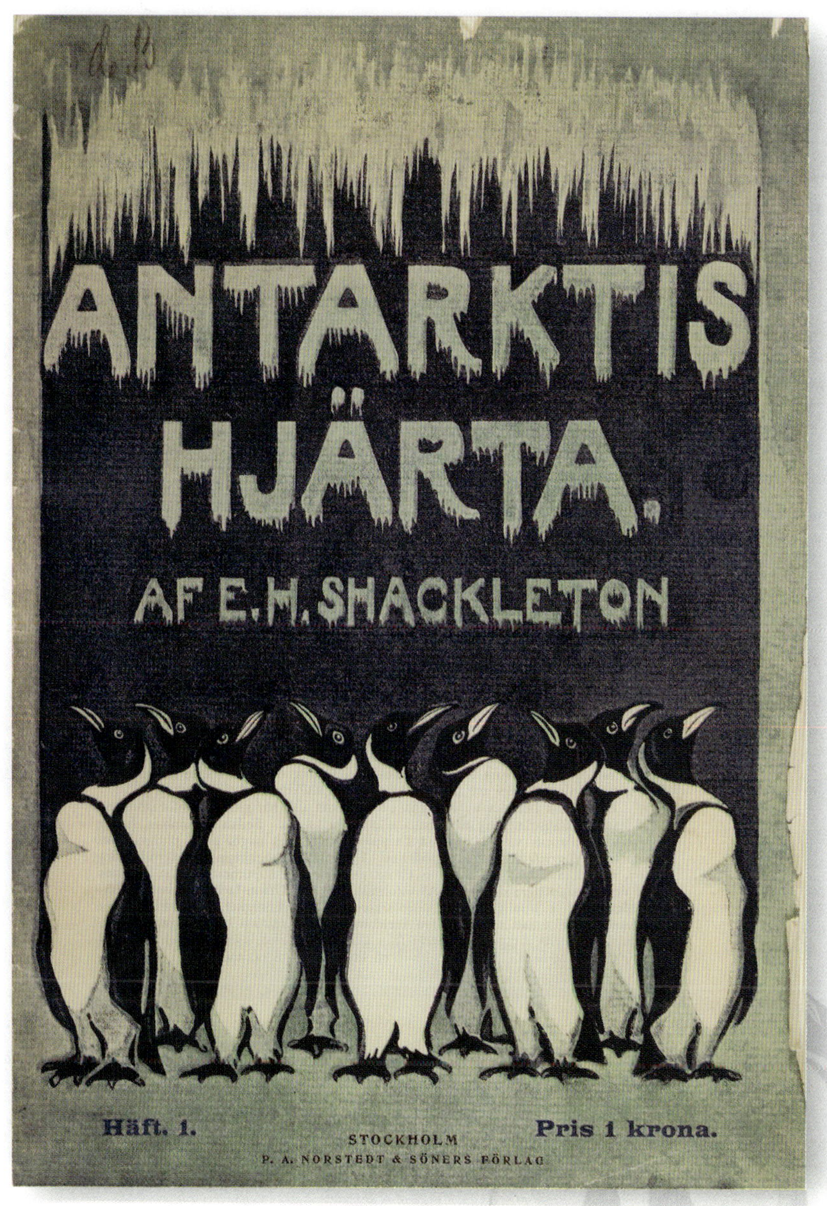

E.H. Shackleton. *Antarktis Hjärta [The Heart of the Antarctic] Berättelsen om den Engelska Sydpolsexpeditionen [Being the Story of the British Antarctic Expedition] 1907–1909.* Translated into Swedish by Carl Forsstrand] – Stockholm: P.A. Norstedt & Söners, 1909–10. First Edition, Vol. 1. Purchased, 1997.

Amongst the many volumes in the Hocken Collections on Antarctic exploration is this very uncommon first Swedish edition of Ernest Shackleton's highly important narrative, still in its original eleven component parts. The cover of each part, priced at one Swedish crown, is identical, with a delightful illustration of a group of Emperor Penguins at the entrance of a stylised ice cave. The numerous illustrations found inside the work are the same as those in the first British edition, also held at the Hocken along with several later editions.

Antarktis Hjärta records the first polar expedition Shackleton led in his unremitting quest to reach the South Pole in 1906. He describes the origin of the expedition, its departure from Lyttelton, New Zealand, sailing to the Antarctic, wintering over, and his trek across the frozen continent as he and his men faced the challenges of the land and the weather, ultimately coming to within ninety-seven miles of his goal. MH

The noble art • 1911

Boxing had a large following in New Zealand cities before the First World War and during the 1920s and 1930s. The date of this stylish poster is not definite, but the advertised event most probably took place in 1911, when there was just such a tournament on 15 and 16 May at Her Majesty's Theatre under the auspices of the Otago Amateur Boxing Association. Six regular weights – Bantam (8st. 6lb), Feather (9st.), Light (10st.), Welter (10st. 7lb), Middle (11st. 4lb), and Heavy (14st. 4lb) – and two novice classes were contested over two evenings by a record number of competitors from Dunedin, all parts of Otago, and Southland. The contests were of three rounds, each lasting three minutes. New rules had come into force: the requirement to avoid persistent clinching; and 'hammering a man over the kidneys when held' (the kidney punch). Dave Smith gave exhibitions of 'sparring and training methods adopted by professional boxers', before leaving 'in a few months for London and America, where he will meet the world's best at his weight.'

The *Otago Daily Times* reported excellent attendances on both occasions. Seating prices were 3/- for the dress circle and reserved stalls, 2/- for the stalls, and 1/- for the pits. However, 'During the last bout several occupants of the circle lit their pipes and indulged in a smoke – a practice so dangerous that it wants at once to be suppressed.' SRS

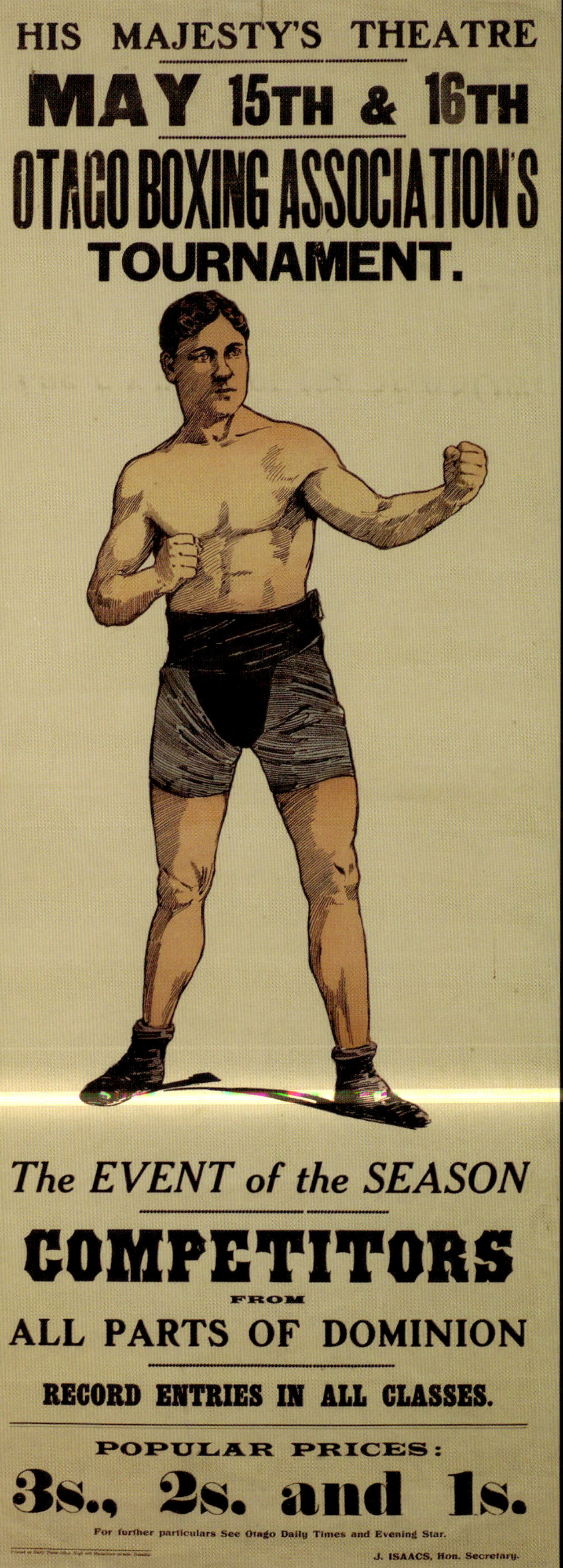

Poster. *Otago Boxing Association's Tournament.* [1911?]. Colour lithograph. Unknown provenance.

Railways poster art • 1927

In the first half of the twentieth century, when new rail and road networks made for easier travel, illustrated poster campaigns encouraged New Zealanders to explore their own country. The railways were then the major means of long-distance transportation for passengers, though the growing availability of motor vehicles did pose a threat to trains. Rather than attempting to compete, the Railways Department instead encouraged co-operation between the various forms of transportation.

Poster. New Zealand Railways. *The Height of Happiness.* 1927. Colour lithograph. Unknown provenance.

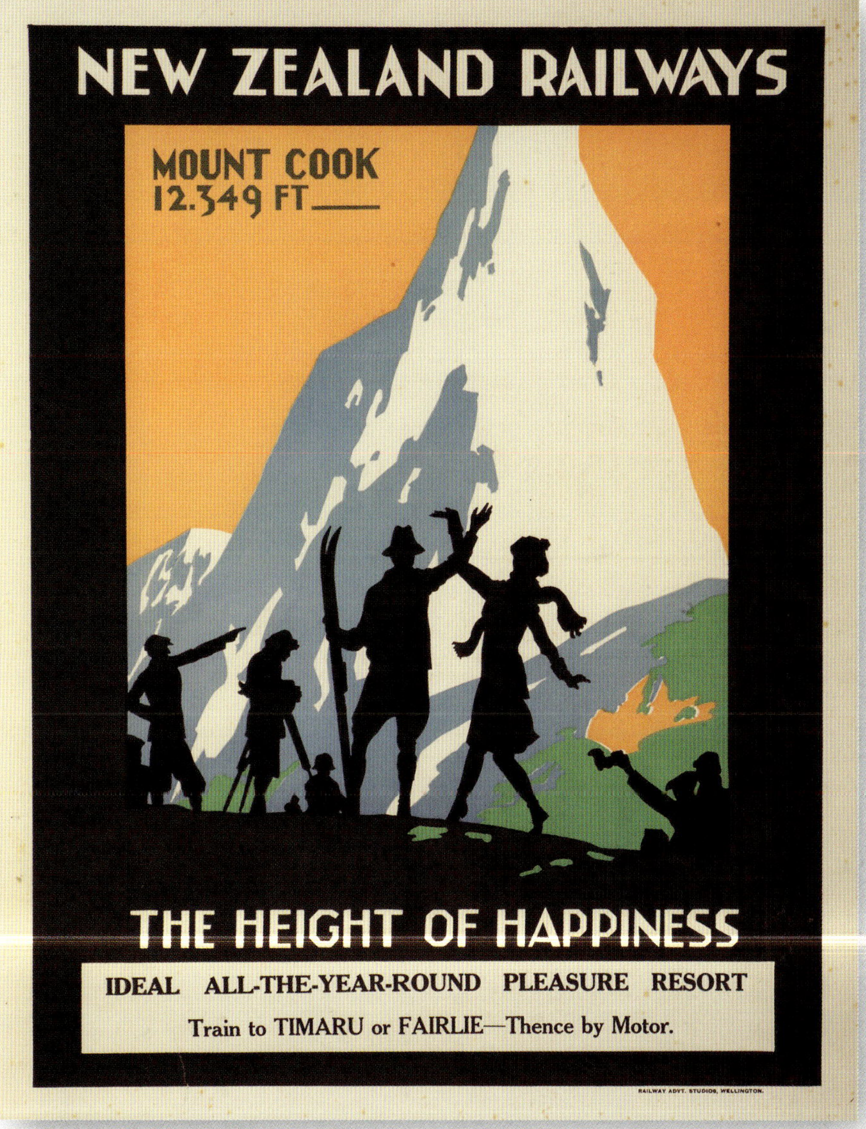

To encourage the use of trains, the New Zealand Railways Department's Outdoor Advertising Branch was founded in 1920. Its studios became one of the most prolific producers of poster art in the country, providing major commissions to artists looking for work during the inter-war period. Promoting not just the railway destinations, but also the businesses which advertised in trains and at stations, the colourful, persuasive posters were displayed in New Zealand, America, Canada, Hawaii, and England.

This Railways Studios poster, dating from 1927, captures perfectly the pleasure-seeking spirit of the twenties. At the time, the Hermitage was strongly promoting winter tourism at Mount Cook. The claim to be 'thousands of feet above worry level' is expressed in the joyful movements of the silhouetted figures, although the pictured skis are slightly misleading as ski conditions were primitive and technique almost unknown. An excursion to this mountain resort included motor as well as rail travel. LE

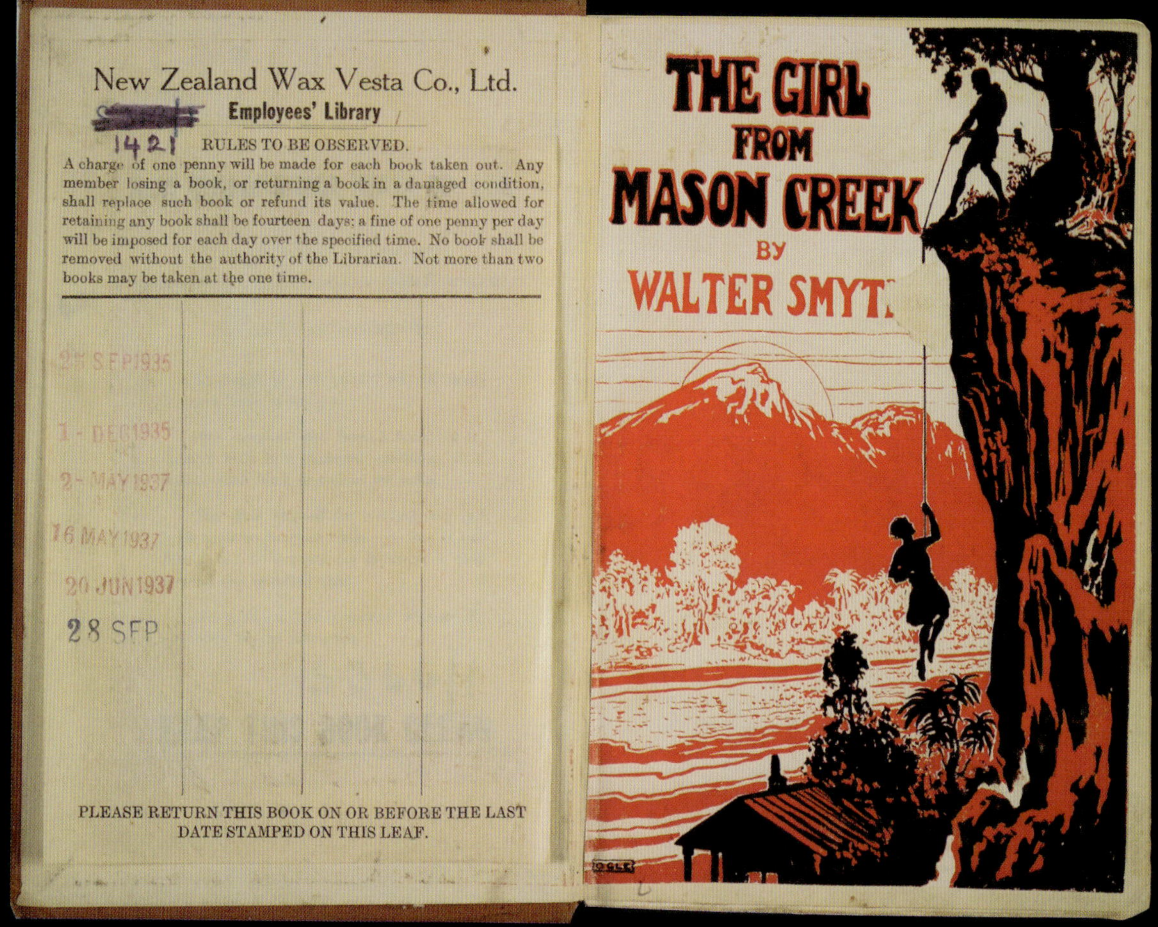

A fine romance • 1929

Walter Smyth. *The Girl from Mason Creek*. London: Mills & Boon, 1929. Unknown provenance.

The first Mills & Boon romances with a New Zealand flavour were written by Walter Smyth who may not have been a man but was the author of *Jean of the Tussock Country* (1928), *The Girl from Mason Creek* (1929), *Bonzer Jones* (1929), and *Wooden Rails* (1930). Set in a hypothetical locality, Te Kauri, *The Girl from Mason Creek* has all the hallmarks of a rollicking good tale – moonshine whiskey, a highway robbery, and a daring rescue from raging floodwaters, as the heroine struggles to solve the mystery of the handsome stranger. All, of course, ends well.

This particular copy is from the Employees' Library of the New Zealand Wax Vesta Co. Ltd., Caversham, Dunedin, one of several workplace libraries in Dunedin. The library catered to a largely feminine workforce, and comprised mainly novels. Perhaps its role was to encourage reading as a leisure pursuit amongst the workers, commonly known as 'matchy tarts', and to support the employer's desire they 'be punctual … clean and tidy … and conduct [themselves] in a manner that would bring credit to the factory'.

This title was issued five times between 1935 and 1937 at a charge of one penny. Warned to 'KEEP THIS BOOK CLEAN' the usual library constraints such as fines for late return are clearly indicated inside the front cover. AJ

A popular arts annual • 1931–1933

Rata was a short-lived arts annual, published in Wellington by Harry H. Tombs and marketed as a Christmas gift for family and friends living overseas. Conservative in style, and uncomplicated in tone, *Rata* featured articles about New Zealand's history and scenery, reproductions of New Zealand landscape paintings and photographs, and poems and stories by local writers. From its masthead and iconic cover imagery to its content, *Rata* demonstrated a pride in New Zealand's natural bounty and a strengthening sense of national identity.

Many of *Rata*'s contributors were among New Zealand's most well-known and respected artists and writers. J.C. Beaglehole, historian, university lecturer and later professor, went 'On Foot Through the Urewera', internationally recognised photographer George Chance gave a glimpse of 'Otago's natural beauty of bush and sealine', and journalist, novelist and poet Robin Hyde paid homage to 'Our Lady of the Snows', Tongariro.

Robin Hyde contributed to all three issues of *Rata*, one of a number of women writers whose work featured in the magazine. Founder and editor Charles Marris was well-known for his support of women with literary aspirations. At the same time he was also much mocked for his editorial conservatism, and it would be the Caxton Press that came to represent the increasingly significant avant-garde of New Zealand literature. JH

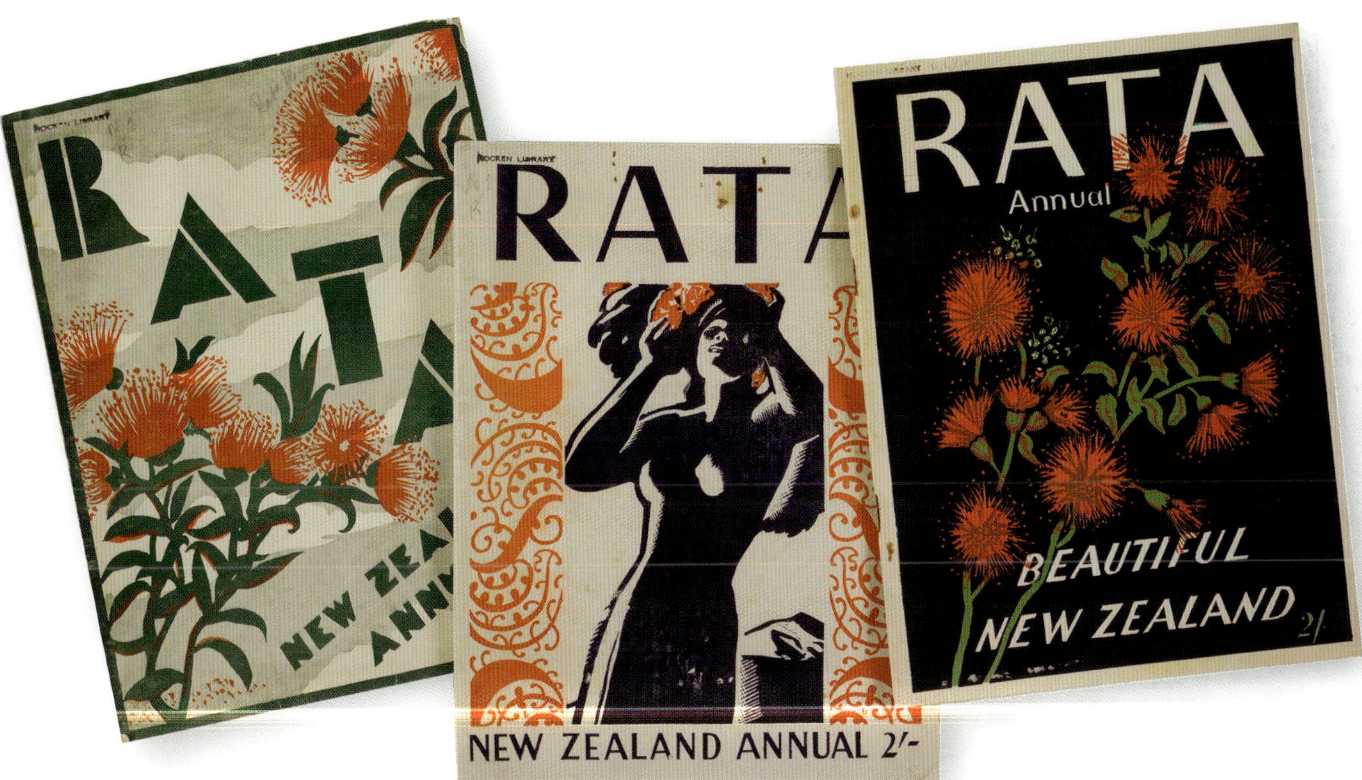

Rata: New Zealand Annual. 1931–33. Wellington: H.H. Tombs. Unknown provenance.

The great social novel • 1934

The remarkable career of John A. Lee (1891–1982) has been summarised as 'criminal, swagger, soldier, politician, hotel-keeper, writer, bookseller'. *Children of the Poor* was his first novel, written during the misery of the 1930s depression while he was a Member of Parliament for Grey Lynn. Lee's introduction to socialism had come through the fiction of popular American authors Upton Sinclair and Jack London, and he followed in their steps with his own realist writing. *Children of the Poor* first appeared in 1934. Its London publisher, T. Werner Laurie, had been alerted to the manuscript by Sinclair.

The book, although fictional, is closely based upon Lee's own experiences as son of a poor Dunedin solo mother. Its stance on petty crime, prostitution and illegitimacy created a sensation and the book was widely banned. Lee had perhaps expected this reaction, for the first edition was published anonymously. However, the book received positive acclaim from those whom Lee admired, including George Bernard Shaw, who advised him to reveal himself as author. The book sold well and was reprinted in 1935 and 1936 proudly bearing the authorship of 'John A. Lee, Labour Member of Parliament in the New Zealand Government'.

His mother, however, was not so pleased by this depiction of her family and wrote a response, *The Not So Poor*, which was published in 1992. AJC

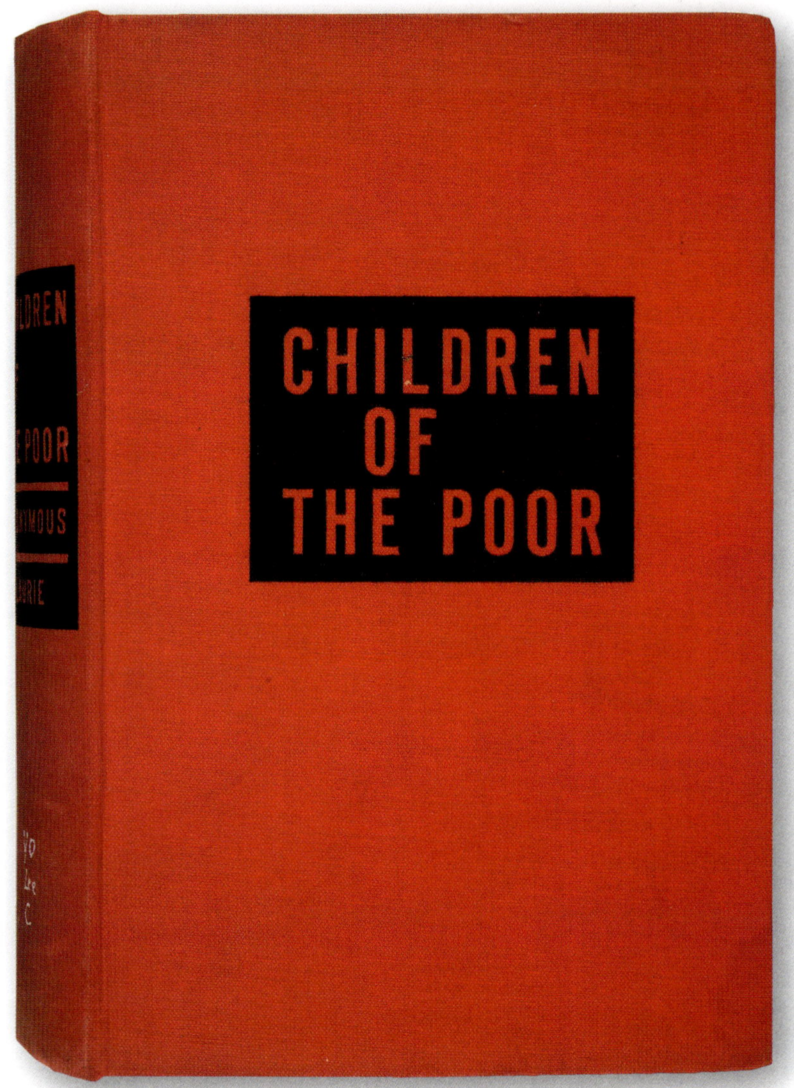

Anonymous (John A. Lee). *Children of the Poor*. London: T. Werner Laurie, 1934. Anonymous donation, 1966.

This starkly utilitarian, four-page document laid down the basis of the class compromise that was to define New Zealand politics for the next fifty years. The result of a two-day discussion at the Labour Party's April 1935 conference, the first draft was written by Walter Nash, who then revised it with Joseph Savage, Peter Fraser, Mark Fagan and David Wilson.

The Manifesto contains the blueprint for legislation that ameliorated the worst consequences of the worldwide economic depression, whilst creating a paternalistic welfare state. Labour promised a statutory minimum wage, restoration of wage cuts, universal healthcare, and a comprehensive pensions system, bringing real gains to the working class but at the expense of the party's stated commitment to 'socialism', which was pushed into the distant future. Compulsory arbitration and compulsory unionism, introduced in Labour's first term, further blunted the challenge of revolutionary unionism to the capitalist system.

The ensuing election on 27 November was a watershed in New Zealand politics. Successive wage cuts, mass unemployment (12 per cent of the workforce in 1933), and collapsing markets for primary produce had made the electorate open to radical change in direction. Huge crowds assembled in the main centres on election night to hear the results. Labour scored a remarkable victory, increasing its Members of Parliament from 24 to 53,

LABOUR'S ELECTION MANIFESTO

SECURITY and PROSPERITY For All

Higher Wages, Guaranteed Prices, Credit Control

On November 27th, the electors of the Dominion will be faced with the responsibility of making one of the most momentous decisions in the history of the country.

Following four years of unprecedented hardship and worry, accompanied by poverty and deprivation in tens of thousands of homes, the electors will have the opportunity of recording their opinion of the acts of the Government, whose followers are now offering themselves as "Nationalist" Candidates, and also of the policy of the Labour Party, whose members in Parliament during the past four years have endeavoured to prevent the passing of reactionary legislation, and to ease the burden of those who have suffered, and are suffering, from the effects of the legislative and administrative actions of the Government.

LABOUR ONLY ORIGINAL PARTY LEFT.

It is well to remember that the Labour Party is the only political party to retain its original name. The Reform and United Parties have merged into the Nationalist Party—and the one-time organiser of the Reform Party, and subsequent founder of the United Party, has now formed another group, styled "Democrats."

It is, however, accepted by all students of Dominion politics that the responsibility of forming the next Government can only rest on either the Labour Party or the Nationalist Party. The electors must either approve of the acts of the Government during the past five years or support the policy and candidates of the Labour Party.

DEMOCRATS ARE ANTI-LABOUR.

The correctness of the interpretation as to the choice of the electors is confirmed by the statement of the Leader of the Democrat Party, in which he says that he will not give a vote that would mean the placing of the Labour Party in power, which means that the Democrats in Parliament would vote for the continuance of the present Government.

THE LABOUR PARTY'S OBJECTIVE.

The Objective of the Labour Party is to utilise to the maximum degree the wonderful resources of the Dominion.

First: For the purpose of restoring a decent living standard to those who have been deprived of essentials for the past five years.

Second: To organise an internal economy that will distribute the production and services in a way that will guarantee to every person able and willing to work an income sufficient to provide him and his dependents with everything necessary to make a "home" and "home life" in the best sense of the meaning of those terms.

The quickest route to the Objective is:—

(a) **Guaranteed Prices** to farmers for the supply of primary products sufficient to satisfy the internal and external requirements of the Dominion.

(b) **A Statutory Minimum Wage or Salary** based on the sum required to provide everything necessary to an adequate standard of living. This minimum will be graded upwards according to the value of the extra skill, knowledge or experience of the worker.

(c) **A National Health and Superannuation Scheme** to provide:—

1. Full medical, nursing, and hospital attention for invalids, together with maintenance for themselves and their dependents during ill-health. This covers the blind, victims of miners' disease, and those suffering from all accidents or diseases which prevent or restrict any person from working.

2. A payment to widows to enable them to maintain themselves and their children, until the children are able to earn their own living.

3. Superannuation to all persons at the age of sixty years.

(d) **The reorganisation of our School, College and University System** to provide the maximum facilities for all children through kindergartens to the University.

The attainment of these objectives is dependent only on the organisation of the Dominion's resources to provide the necessary goods and to organise the required services.

The Labour Party believes that in and out of our Public Service the men and women are available with the capacity and experience to carry out the organising and administrative work necessary to achieve these objectives.

New Zealand Labour Party. *Labour's Election Manifesto: Security and Prosperity For All.* Wellington: The Labour Party, 1935. Donated by E.W. Hunter, 1961.

At the time it appeared, *Passport To Hell* was described by John A. Lee as the most important New Zealand war book yet published. It tells in documentary novel form the extraordinary story of 'Starkie', a real-life Invercargill-born borstal boy of mixed Spanish and Delaware Indian descent, who, expelled from five different schools, enlisted in the Otago Regiment at the age of sixteen and saw service at both Gallipoli and on the western front in northern France. Renowned for his bravery (he was recommended for the Victoria Cross) and wounded in thirty-seven places on his body, he was equally known for his lack of respect for authority, being court-martialled no less than nine times. The author Iris Wilkinson, who wrote as Robin Hyde, was instantly attracted to his story and assigned half the proceeds from the book to Stark. A sequel, *Nor the Years Condemn* (1938), told of his continuing unruly life in Australia and New Zealand after the war. Stark died in 1942, just three years after Wilkinson took her own life.

The Hocken Collections' copy belonged to W. Downie Stewart, who was in Stark's battalion for part of the war and later supported both Wilkinson and Stark financially. It is inscribed 'W. Downie Stewart, with grateful appreciation of the author, who liked Dunedin. Robin Hyde (Iris G. Wilkinson) 23.11.36'. SRS

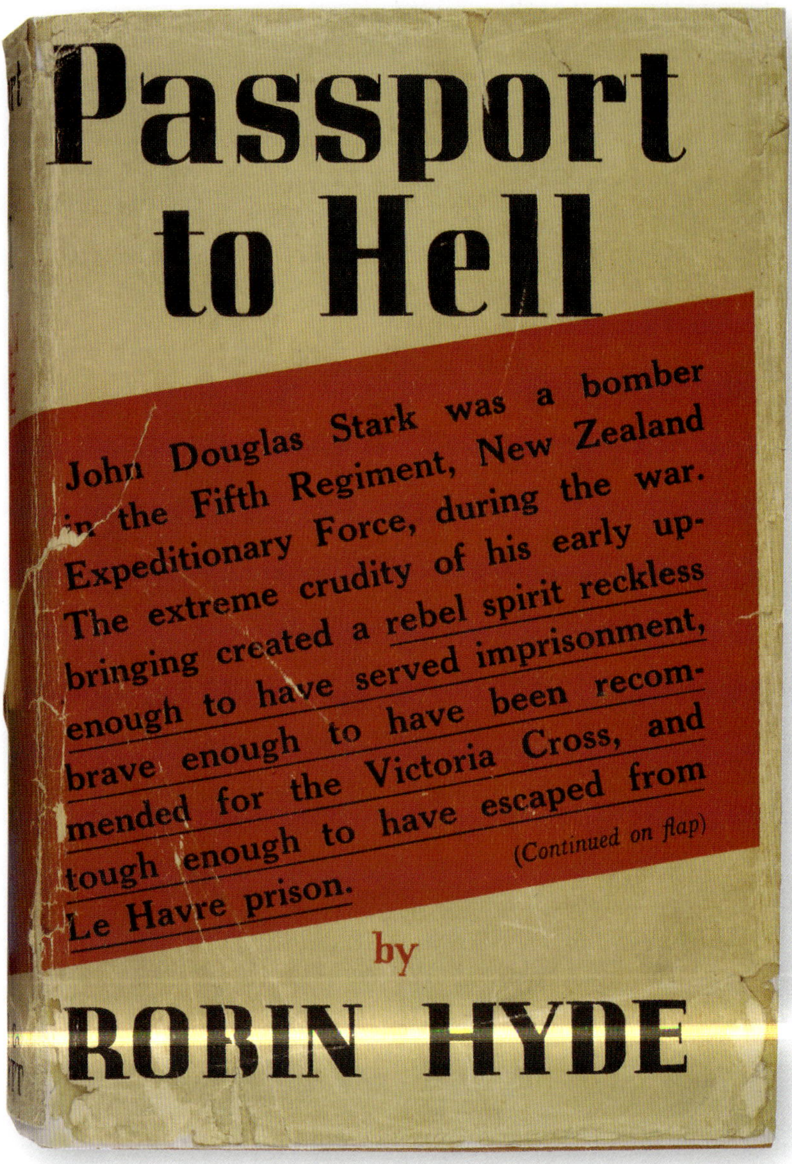

Robin Hyde (pseud.). *Passport to Hell: the Story of James Douglas Stark, Bomber, Fifth Regiment, New Zealand Expeditionary Forces*. London: Hurst & Blackett [1936]. Donated by the W. Downie Stewart Estate, 1965.

A great pacifist memoir • 1939

We Will Not Cease is perhaps New Zealand's most remarkable war memoir. Archibald Baxter (1881–1970), an Otago farm labourer of Highland Scottish descent, became a convinced pacifist during the South African War. *We Will Not Cease* tells, in understated yet moving prose, of his experiences as a prisoner, including the notorious 'Field Punishment Number 1' he received at the frontline in France.

The book was published in January 1939 by Victor Gollancz, the left-wing London publisher. Baxter received a £30 advance for the work, which sold at 7/6 a copy. By the end of March, British sales stood at 321, with a further eighty-six sold overseas. Ironically, the book itself became a victim of war. The author's wife, Millicent, felt that Gollancz, a Jew who supported the war against Hitler, did not promote the book well. War then affected its shipping beyond Britain, and in 1941 most remaining copies were destroyed during the London blitz.

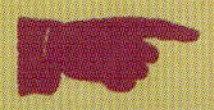

Archibald Baxter. *We Will Not Cease: the autobiography of a conscientious objector*. London: Gollancz, 1939. Donated by Muriel Bell, c. 1971.

The first edition is, therefore, fairly rare. Gollancz was unwilling to publish the book again, but in 1968 the Caxton Press brought out a new edition, with further printings in 1980, 1987 and in 2003. It became available electronically through the New Zealand Electronic Text Centre in 2005 – another indication of

O fons Bandusiae
The green hill-orchard where
My great granduncle lived
Is overgrown: no cache and no reprieve

With this first verse of the first poem in his first book of verse, complete with reference to Horace, James K. Baxter, born in Dunedin 1926, demonstrated the qualities of eloquence and inventiveness that made him the most natural of New Zealand poets.

The thirty-two poems of *Beyond the Palisade*, published when he was just eighteen and mostly written from fifteen to seventeen, established Baxter's reputation. They were received with acclaim by Allen Curnow, who included six in his forthcoming anthology of New Zealand verse, 1923–45, and were highly complimented by Basil Dowling and Charles Brasch, who became a loyal patron. It was the beginning of a remarkable life as poet and visionary that ended only with his death in 1972.

Five hundred copies were designed and printed by the Caxton Press to its customarily high standard. SRS

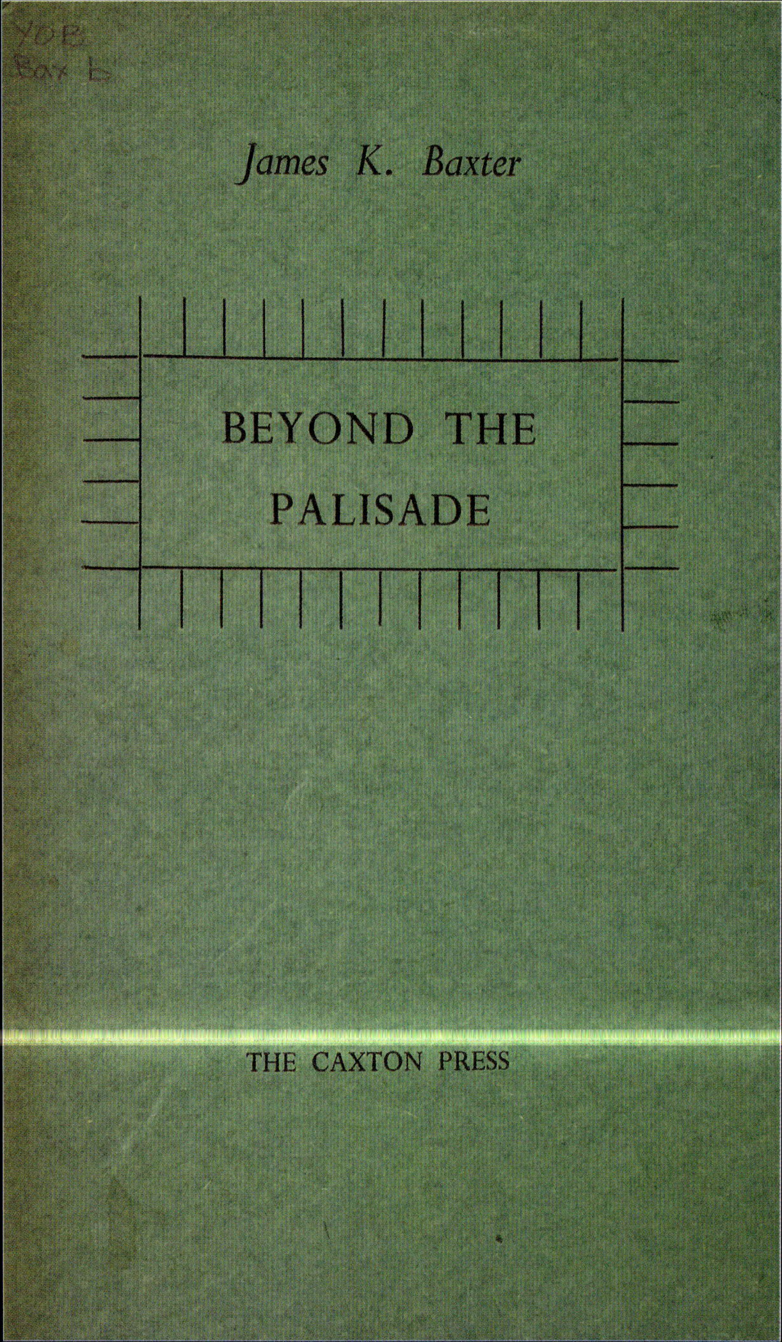

James K. Baxter. *Beyond the Palisade: poems.* Christchurch: Caxton Press, 1944. Donated by Charles Brasch, 1968.

James K. Baxter

BEYOND THE PALISADE

THE CAXTON PRESS

Janet Frame's first book • 1952

Denis Glover's last job at the Caxton Press was to print a collection of short stories by Janet Frame, now recognised as New Zealand's most important novelist. It was her first book, collected by her friend John Money, and consisted of twenty-four short stories written when in and out of hospital, mistakenly diagnosed as a schizophrenic. The stories are somewhat reminiscent of Mansfield's childhood stories. Told from the perspective of children or of outcasts with imaginary worlds barred to ordinary adults, they also 'foreshadow many of the unique preoccupations and imagery of the novels that followed'.

After a first, devastatingly unfavourable review in the Christchurch *Press*, the collection was noticed and championed by her friend Frank Sargeson and Dunedin librarian Dorothy Neal White. On 26 December 1952 it was announced that Janet Frame of Oamaru had won the Hubert Church memorial award for prose, worth £25, then the country's major literary award. By a matter of days it also saved her from a potentially crippling prefrontal leucotomy operation, when the hospital superintendent, Dr Geoffrey Blake-Palmer, recognised its inappropriateness, declaring 'I've decided that you should stay as you are. I don't want you changed'. SRS

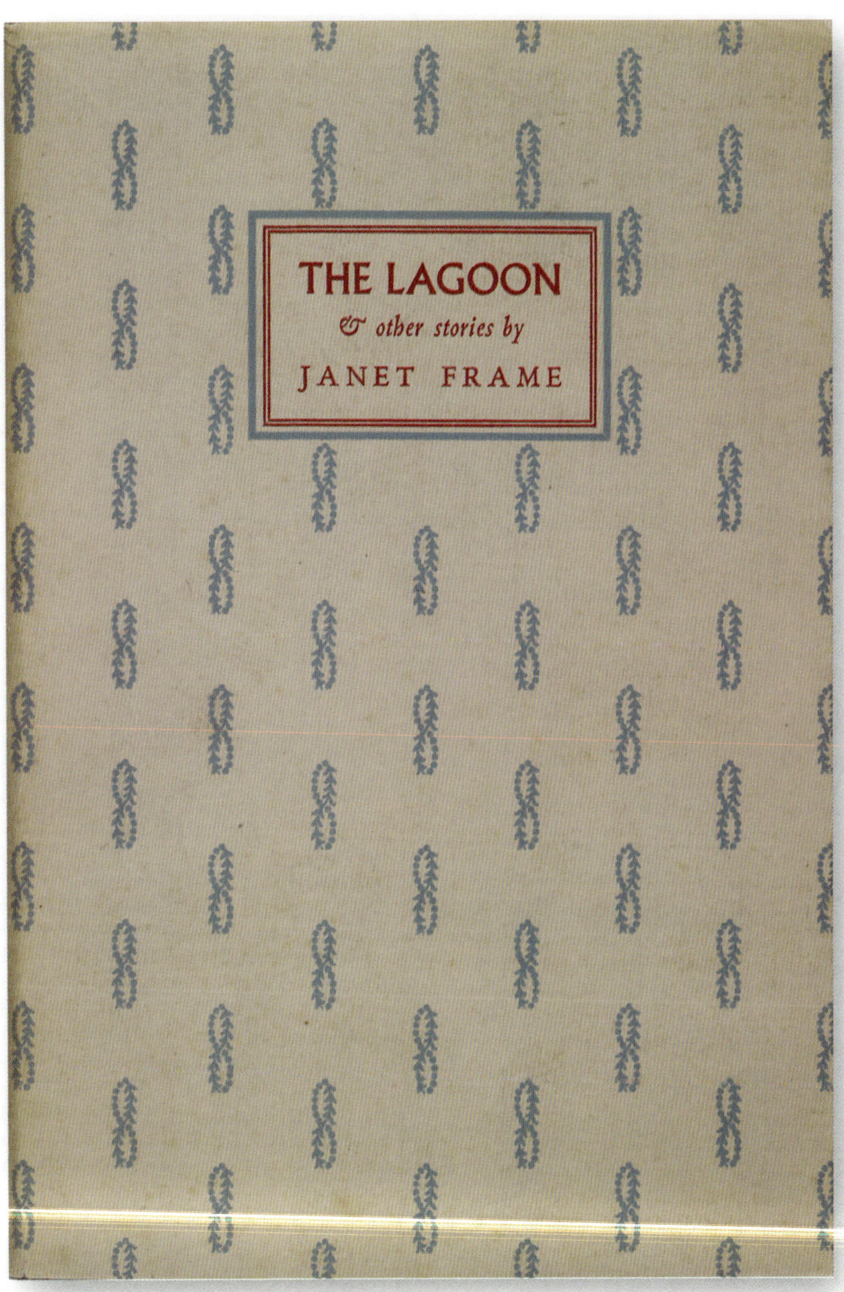

Janet Frame. *The Lagoon & other stories*. Christchurch: The Caxton Press, 1951 [1952]. Purchased, 1965.

A most popular book • 1960

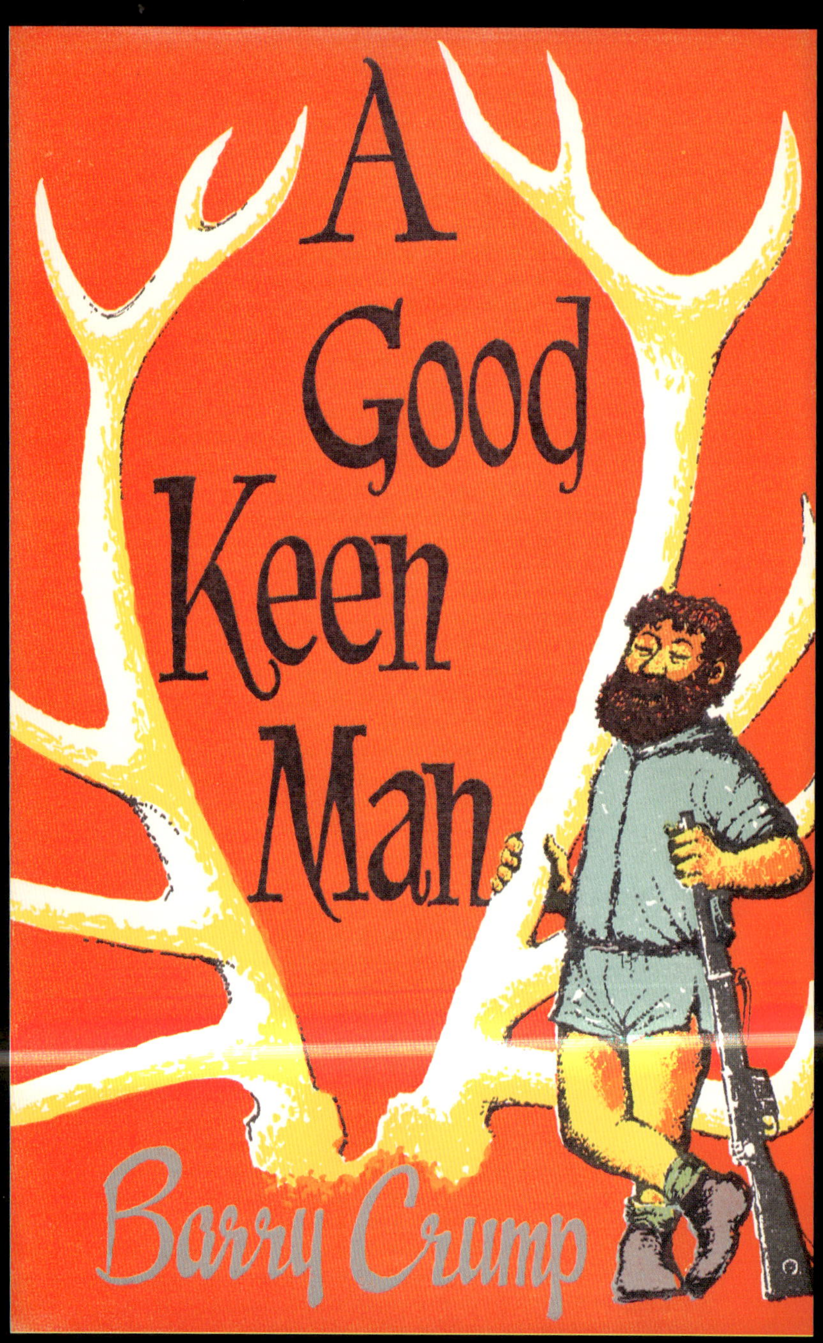

Barry Crump. *A Good Keen Man*. Wellington: Reed, 1960. Donated by Ruth Dallas, 1965.

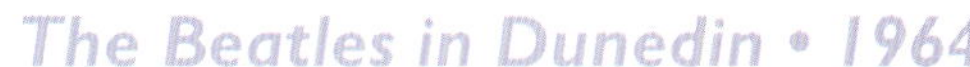

The Beatles in Dunedin • 1964

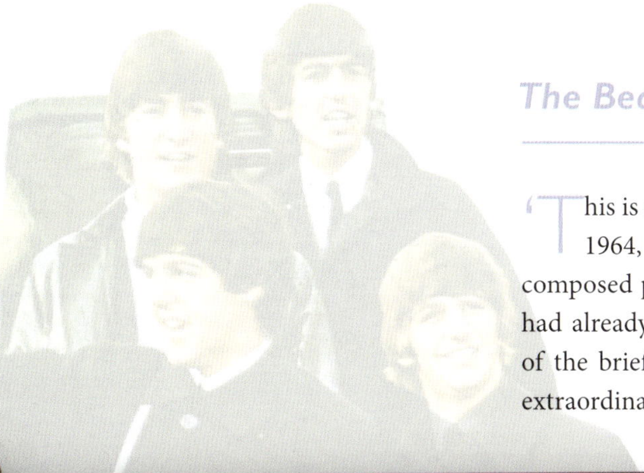

'This is normally a quiet place,' commented a bewildered bystander in June 1964, when four English musicians arrived in Dunedin and the usually composed population was swept up in a wave of mass hysteria. 'Beatlemania' had already seized Wellington and Auckland during the band's northern leg of the brief eight-day tour and the South proved equally susceptible to the extraordinary effect of the Beatles. Cheers, screams and fainting fans greeted the young men at Momona Airport and the chaos continued until their departure the next day.

A seven-page spread in the Dunedin *Photo Review* captured such moments when the Beatles' motorcade arrived outside the City Hotel and approximately two thousand people surged forward. Security took no chances later in the day and a decoy band provided a distraction as John Lennon, Paul McCartney, George Harrison and Ringo Starr left for their performance through the back door. They were greeted at the Town Hall with equal appreciation, and their voices struggled to be heard over those of the audience. A line of twenty policemen formed a barricade between the stage and the fans, keeping people at a safe distance as they left their seats to dance in the aisles. LE

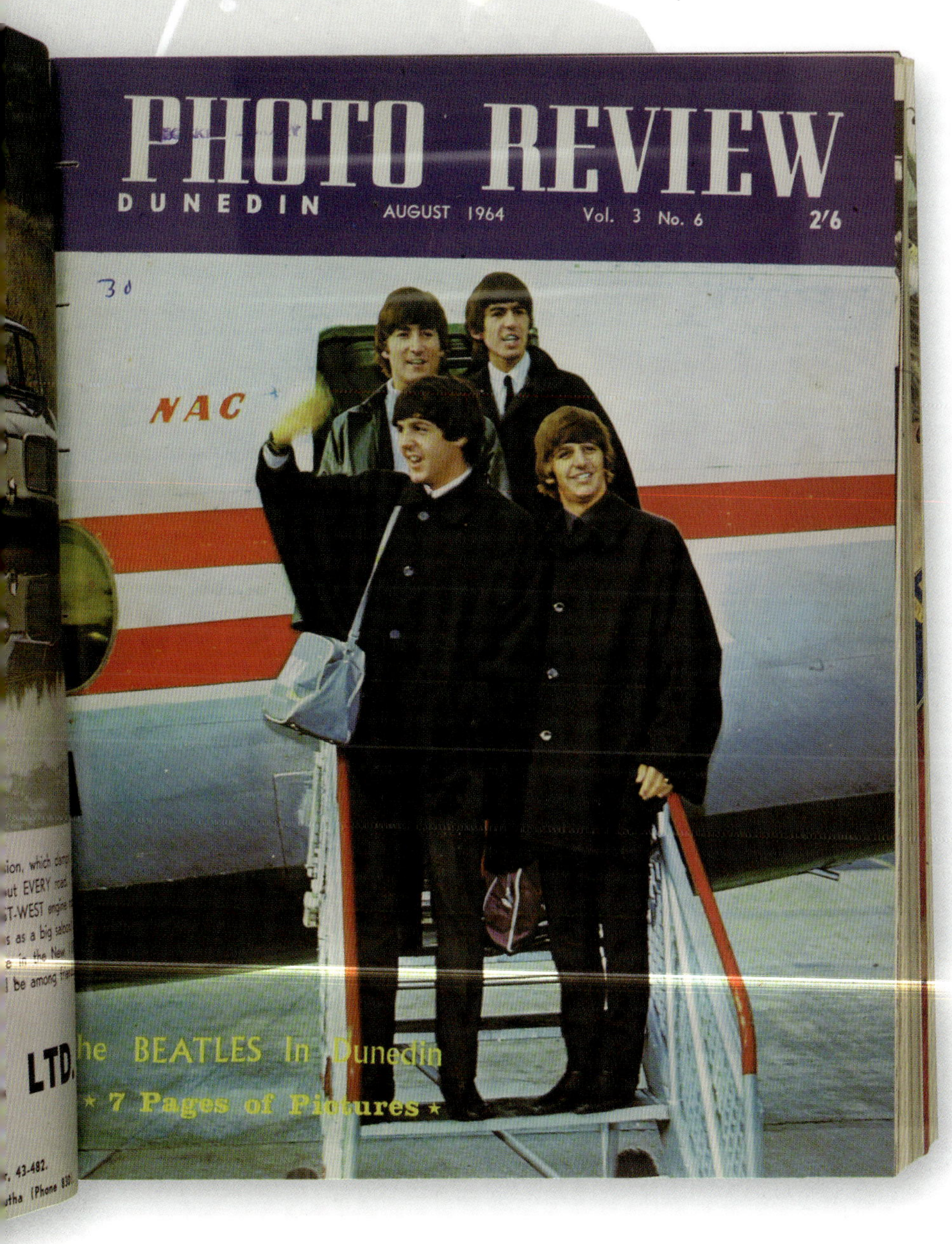

Photo Review. Vol. 3 No. 6. August 1964. Dunedin. Unknown provenance.

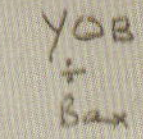

James K. Baxter

A SMALL ODE ON MIXED FLATTING

Elicited by the decision of the
Otago University authorities
to forbid this practice
among students.

*

Dunedin nights are often cold
(I notice it as I grow old);
The south wind scourging from the Pole
Drives every rat to his own hole,
Lashing the drunks who wear thin shirts
And little girls in mini-skirts.
Leander, that Greek lad, was bold
To swim the Hellespont raging cold
To visit Hero in her tower
Just for an amorous half-hour,
And lay his wet brine-tangled head
Upon her pillow—Hush! The dead
Can get good housing—Thomas Bracken,
Smellie, McLeod, McColl, McCracken,
A thousand founding fathers lie
Well roofed against the howling sky
In mixed accommodation—Hush!
It is the living make us blush
Because the young have wicked hearts

In 1967, a male student at the University of Otago in need of accommodation moved into the Union Street flat of three female students. His entirely practical actions inadvertently propelled the campus into a state of uproar. Mixed flats were uncommon and viewed by the public with suspicion and disapproval. The University believed in its duty to act *in loco parentis* and took steps to ensure the propriety and safety of its students. 'The existence of this type of living,' Vice-Chancellor Robin Williams claimed, after ordering the male student to find housing elsewhere, 'brings the university into discredit.'

Although a flurry of letters to the *Otago Daily Times* indicated strong support for Williams, many students were less impressed, believing that they deserved the freedom of the general public regarding their private lives. On 4 July 1967, approximately 1000 protestors staged a 'sleep-in' in the Union building. The embarrassed student at the centre of the debate did not attend and eventually, on legal advice, moved out of the flat. The affair provoked the publication of *A Small Ode on Mixed Flatting* by James Baxter, then in the second year of his Robert Burns Fellowship. Sold for 15 cents, this slightly bawdy poem, gently mocking of older attitudes, was widely circulated and immensely popular. LE

James K. Baxter. *A Small Ode on Mixed Flatting*. [Christchurch]: Caxton Press, 1967. Purchased, 1967.

Published weekly from 1905 and still going, *New Zealand Truth* has long been New Zealand's only genuinely populist tabloid newspaper. Its heyday was in the 1950s and 1960s when, styling itself 'the champion of the little person and the scourge of corruption and scandal in high place', it had a mass circulation. It did engage in genuine investigative journalism, its no-holds-barred, abrasive approach resulting in numerous libel allegations and court cases, most famously in 1959 for falsely accusing Phil Holloway, Minister of Industries and Commerce, of 'fixing' import licences.

Its stock in trade, however, was scandal, particularly of a sexual nature. This was most evident in its very distinctive billboard posters, which shocked, titillated and entertained generations of New Zealanders, and by a well understood convention usually promised more than they delivered. This particular example, one of scores in the Hocken Collections, refers to the shenanigans that took place at a Henderson Squash Club party one evening in October 1969, resulting in charges of indecency. An all-male jury found the two female strippers guilty, but recommended leniency on the grounds that the performance was below standard because of audience participation. SRS

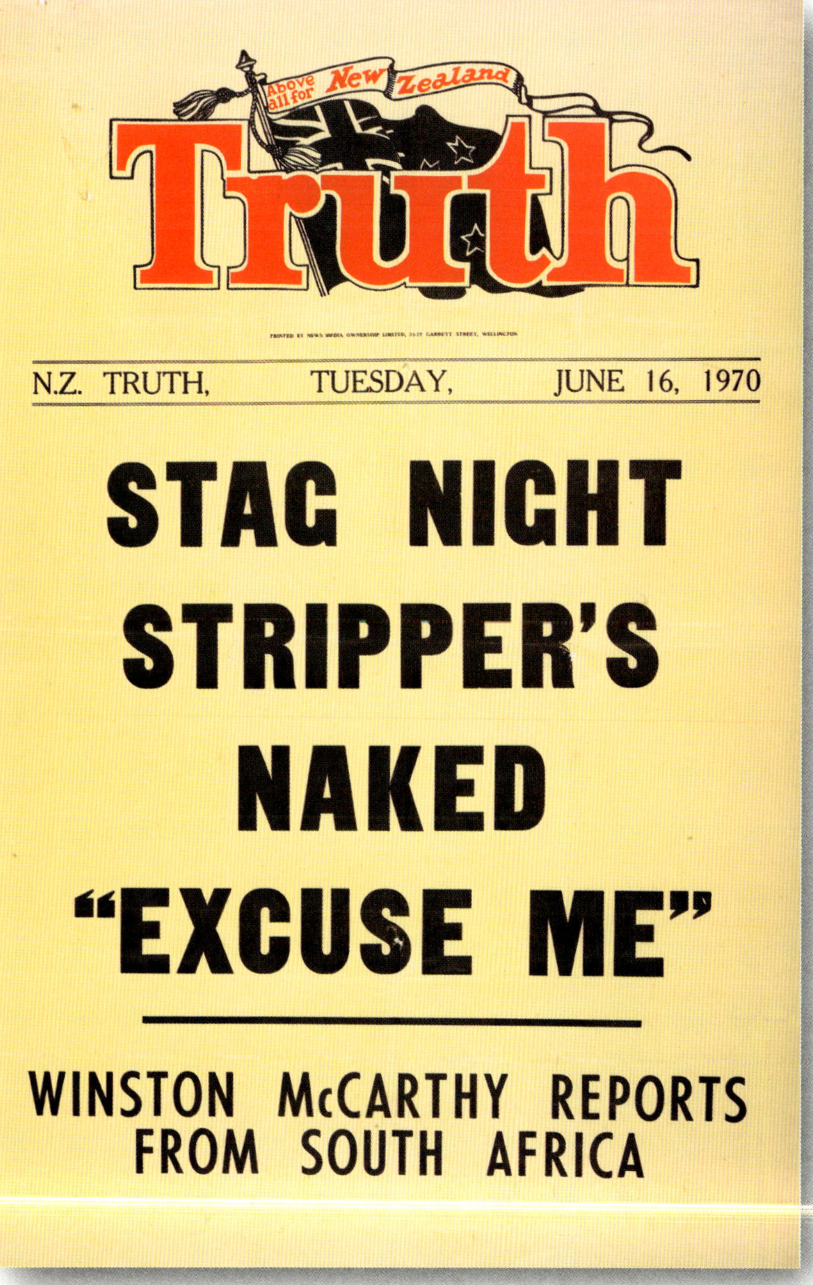

New Zealand Truth billboard poster, 16 June 1970. Donated by a Dunedin news agent, 1970.

World famous from Waitati • 1974–85

Part of the counter movement embracing 'hippy culture' and alternative living, *Mushroom* was an information source for alternative lifestylers all over the world. Beginning in Christchurch in 1974, by its second issue the magazine's editorial group was firmly based in Waitati, a rural community twenty kilometres north of Dunedin, which provided a haven for those 'drawn from wide socio-economic backgrounds, from graduates to the unemployed, all imbued with a fundamental dissatisfaction with what they saw as an increasing diminution in reverence for life, and a drift away from the fundamental activities of life.'

Mushroom's content ranged from guidelines for setting up an ohu (commune) under a government scheme for kibbutz-type communities on leased crown land, to how to utilise natural energy sources, grow herbs, cook vegetarian food, construct a composting toilet, and run a food co-op. Gradually its scope widened, and by the mid 1980s it was also discussing gay rights, men's liberation and nuclear war.

Compiled by volunteers, each issue had a plea for those living the life to help with the magazine. *Mushroom* survived until 1985. AJ

Mushroom: a magazine for alternative life styles. Vol. 2. 1975.
Waitati. Purchased, 1974–85.

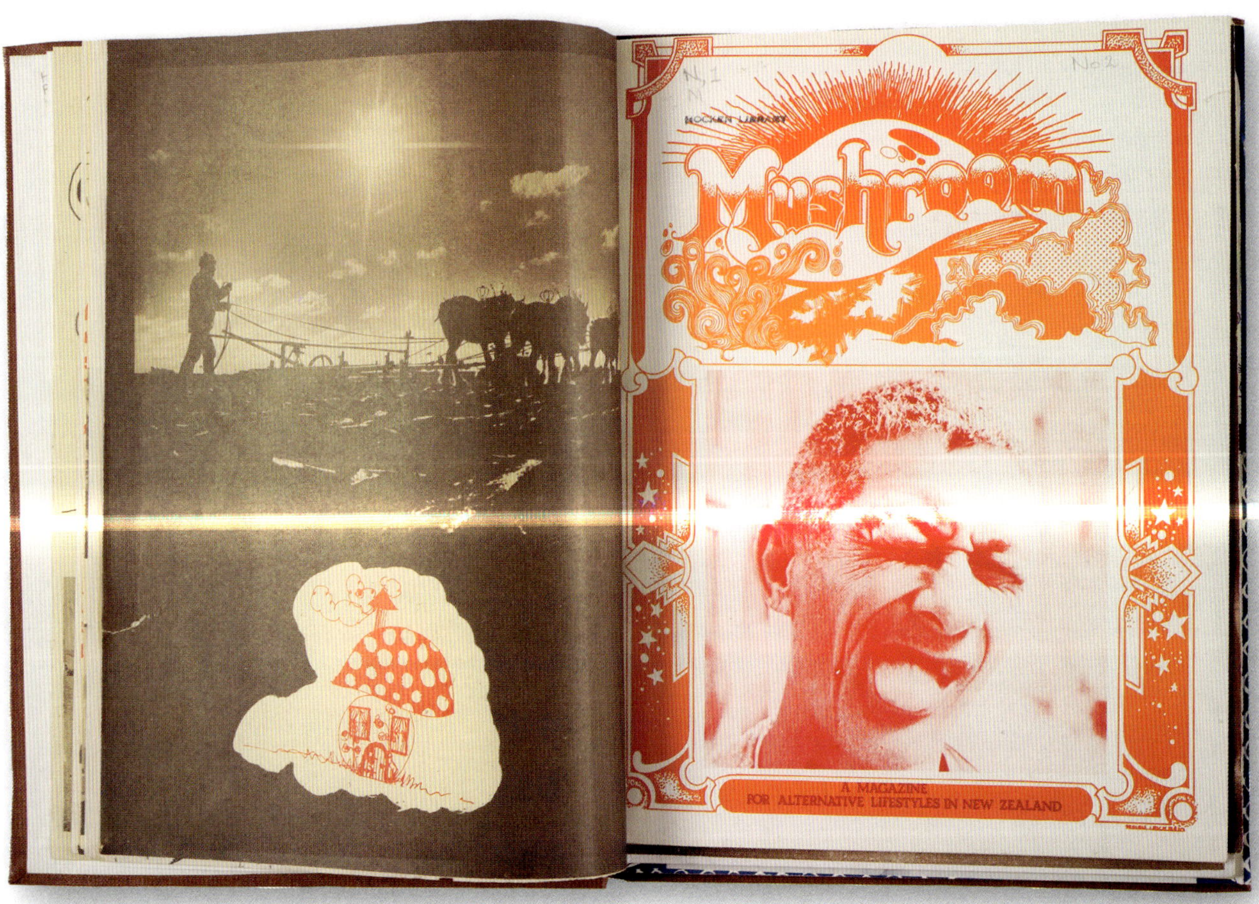

First full-colour comic • 1979

Published late 1979 to promote the Suntracker – a plastic sundial watch marketed by the Sunshine Watch Co. – *The Adventures of Captain Sunshine* was the first full colour comic produced in New Zealand. Only two copies are known to be held in public collections.

The character of Captain Sunshine, dubbed Australasia's first eco-superhero, had appeared once previously, in an Australian eco-living magazine, *Simply Living*. A group of local businessmen together with the character's originator, Peter Farrell, initiated the project by engaging Colin Wilson, co-editor of the successful Auckland-based comic, *Strips*, to produce a complete local superhero comic for a New Zealand audience. Wilson drew most of the artwork, assisted by Jean-Luc Rizzoli, Joe Wylie and Helen Cross. He also co-wrote the story with Farrell, Reuben Sandler and Roy Middleton.

Printed using an offset colour-printing process that was more expensive than the one usually favoured by United States comic publishing houses, *Captain Sunshine* was the most visually impressive comic yet produced in New Zealand. The comic sold well and enthusiasm was such that another issue was prepared. The watch, however, was a commercial failure and the whole project was pulled. The artwork subsequently disappeared, its fate still unknown. AR

Colin Wilson et al. *The Adventures of Captain Sunshine*. Auckland: Sunshine Watch Co., 1979. Donated by Tony Renouf, 2004.

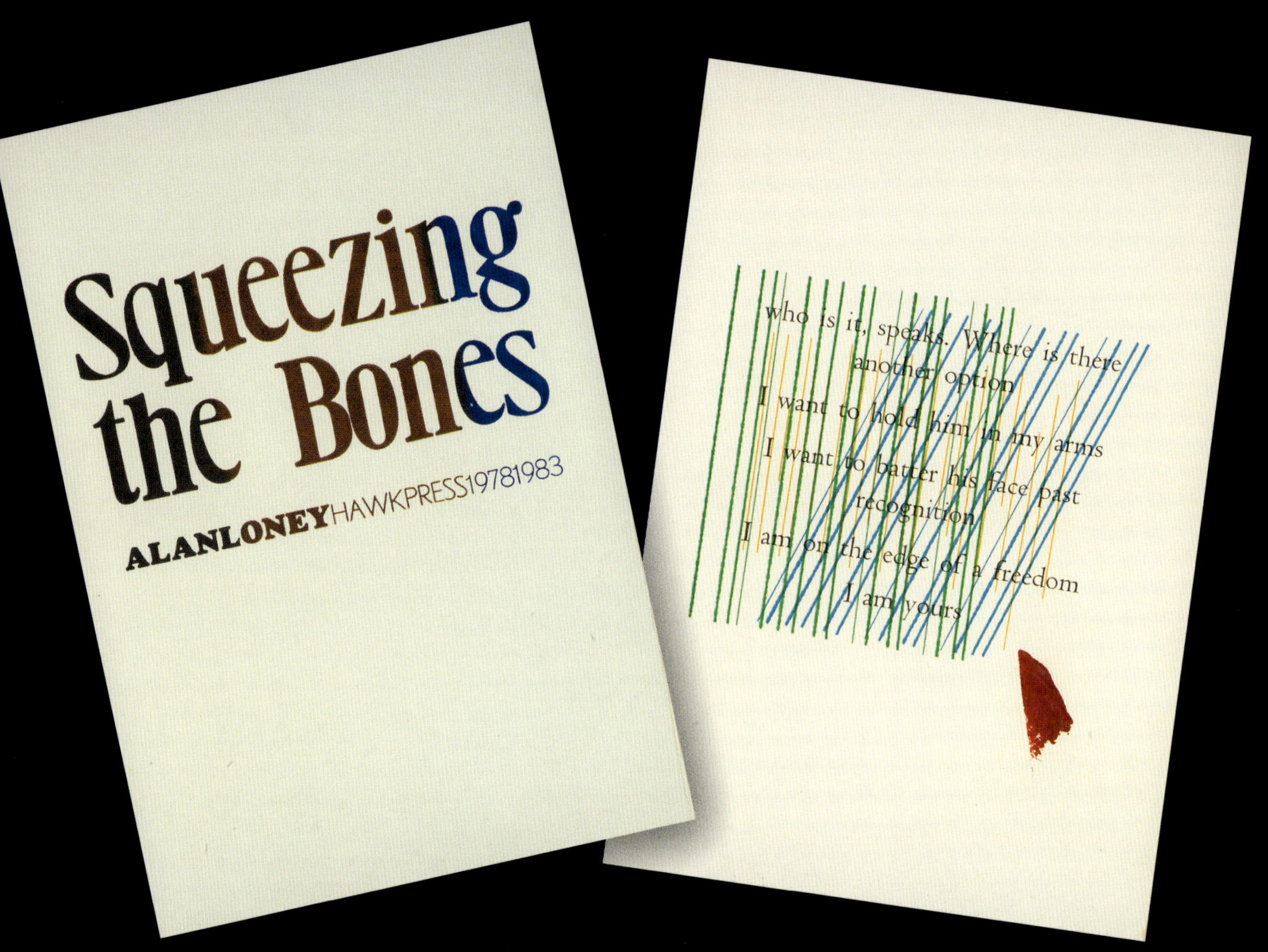

Superb handmade book • 1983

Alan Loney. *Squeezing the Bones*. [Wellington]: Hawk Press, 1983. Purchased, 1999.

Alan Loney is regarded as New Zealand's best private press bookmaker. In the course of a long career of private press production, Loney has operated Hawk Press (Christchurch), Black Light Press (Wellington), the Holloway Press (in conjunction with the University of Auckland), and more recently Electio Editions (Melbourne). In 1983 Loney created *Squeezing the Bones* in response to his father's battle with cancer and death in 1978. This rather personal poem was hand-printed on thick paper from the Richard de Bas mill in France in a limited edition of fifteen copies only, eleven of which were for sale. The text is enhanced by multi-coloured images, each a superb example of typographical skills. The colophon states that the Hocken copy is No. 1, signed.

Under copyright law as it was then, Loney was required to submit three copies for legal deposit at the National Library. As this would have reduced the number of copies for sale by one fifth, he sent one copy only. The authorities were not amused. His point was eventually taken, however, as in 2004 the requirement was reduced to one where the cost exceeded $1000 a copy or the number of copies published was fewer than 100. DJK

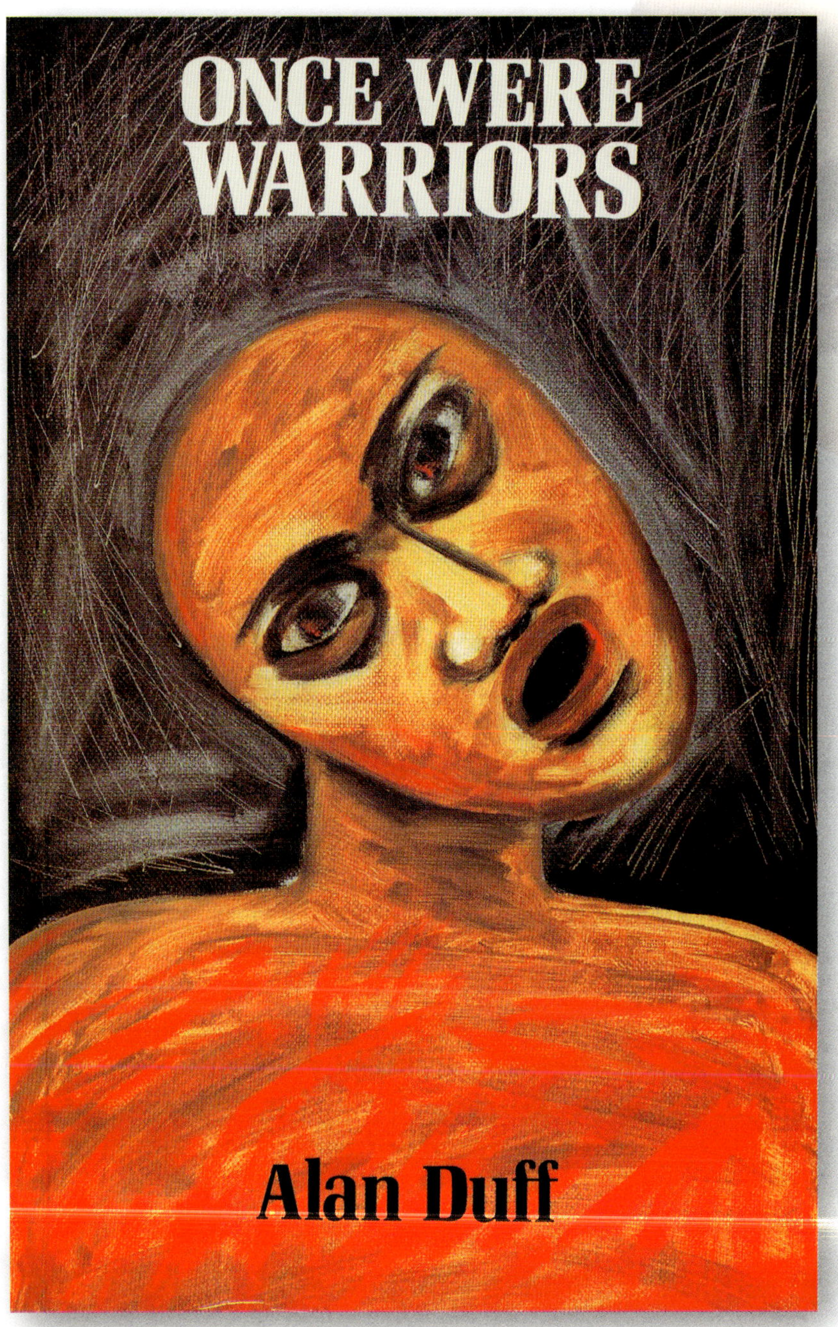

Alan Duff. *Once Were Warriors*. Auckland: Tandem Press, 1990. Purchased 1990.

No other contemporary New Zealand novel has had quite the explosive force of Alan Duff's *Once Were Warriors*. Duff, of Ngati Rangitihi and Tuwharetoa descent, tells the story of the Heke family, who live in a state housing area, Pine Block, in a town not unlike Rotorua. Jake, unemployed, is given to drinking with his mates and to violence, including beating his wife. A 'fist-happy bastard', she says. Beth is apathetic, addicted to television, and fond of alcohol herself. Their children are neglected, and two, estranged, die tragically. The sense of alienation is complete. In the end, Beth achieves partial redemption, but Jake is left 'a broken man.' The clear message is that the traditional warrior code of violence will no longer serve.

The book's great power comes from authenticity of language and strong narrative in its unflinching representation of the realities of urban life for many Māori. Its impact was immediate: 80,000 copies were sold, and it has not since been out of print. A screen version, equally searing, gained wide overseas recognition, making *Once Were Warriors* the best-known New Zealand novel internationally. Enhanced by Robyn Kahukiwa's striking cover painting, *Once Were Warriors* is well on the way to becoming a modern treasure. SRS

Maps and Plans

Karen Craw

Maps are essential to historical enquiry, so it may seem surprising that there were fewer than 100 in the original 1910 collection and that there should still have been only 150 by 1936. Since then, however, their number has grown through steady accumulation to a very respectable 12,000 – maps, charts, plans and atlases – offering strong coverage of early world representation, New Zealand, the Pacific, and Antarctica.

Those maps that Dr Hocken did collect were important and instructive. Always interested in showing social interaction with geography, he concentrated on acquiring early maps of settlement in New Zealand – the Hokianga River in 1827, Wellington's proposed harbour reclamation in 1851, and planned layouts for the New Zealand Company settlements of Wellington, New Plymouth, Nelson, and Otago, often annotating them to elucidate content. Hand-drawn manuscript maps appealed to him, too, and he drew or had drawn for him, often by his wife Bessie, maps based on information he collected. He interpreted written and oral information supplied by Māori on topics such as iwi boundaries and routes to find pounamu, with additional information supplied by early explorers and settlers such as Edward Shortland. He also collected Māori pā plans, such as that of Kawiti's pā at Ruapekapeka in 1846. Several of these maps were included in the twenty-nine displayed at the New Zealand and South Seas Exhibition in Dunedin 1889–90. Notable among them were Bessie Hocken's copy of Tuki's 1793 map of New Zealand made when held captive on Norfolk Island, and the only known copy of the first map printed in New Zealand, E.M. Chaffers's chart of Port Nicholson issued in 1841.

Subsequent additions were mostly by gift and occasional purchase until 1960, when systematic collection began. In part, this may have been brought about by the gift from the Portuguese government of the magnificent *Portugaliae Monumenta Cartographica* published that same year in six volumes. More prosaically, full sets of topographic and cadastral series maps produced by the Department of Lands and Survey, first published in 1939, began to be acquired. Out of print charts and plans were also purchased when they came up at auction or in antiquarian sale rooms. In this way the *Complete East India Pilot* (fifth edition 1827 with additions to 1829), the only known copy of this version and one of the first editions to include a separate chart of New Zealand, was acquired.

The small collection of eighteenth and nineteenth century maps also benefited, in 1992, from Bruce Godward's bequest of 120 maps, mainly of New Zealand and the Pacific. There are now many rare and important maps in this part of the collection, including: *Isles de Salomon* (Paris, D. Thierry, 1683?), one of the earliest maps in the collection; *A Complete Map of the Southern Continent: Survey'd by Capt. Abel Tasman & depicted by order of the East India Company in Holland* (London, 1744); *Mapemonde Planisphere* (1706?); *Ins kleine gebrachte karte von den Sud-Laendern zur Historie dr Reisen* (Bellin, Leipzig? 1753); and *Océanique. Écrit par Giraldon; gravé par J.B. Chamouin* (Paris, 1812?). A further boost came in 1998 from the deposit of the Lowe collection of over 100 seventeenth- and eighteenth-century maps.

Maps from this early period show New Zealand as part of a larger geographic area, some derived from the first outlines drawn by Abel Tasman on his 1642 visit, but most based on James Cook's first visit in 1769: they provide an insight into the history of mapmaking itself. Included here is Antonio Zatta's Italian version of Cook's chart, *La Nuova Zelanda,* published in Venice in 1778 with Cook's tracks marked, and showing vegetation and relief through hachures and bathymetric soundings. French and English versions of this map are held.

The map collection also contains all twenty-five charts of the New Zealand coastline resulting from detailed surveys made by Dumont d'Urville on his visit in 1826 and the twenty British charts, mainly of the coast north of Auckland, that appeared in the same period up to 1840. The Admiralty charting of New Zealand's coastline 1848–55 produced over fifty-five charts, forming the basis of most subsequent charts over the next 100 years.

Large-scale land settlement maps issued from the 1880s until the late 1930s for the Otago and Southland land districts are a major part of the collection, and show areas offered for pastoral lease. Plans of estates subdivided under the Lands for Settlement Acts and Land Act 1908 and lands for sale and lease to discharged soldiers after the First World War are also part of the collection. These are rich with land information – the existence of swamp, bush, pasture, ploughed land, water races, hedges, fences, buildings and whether the neighbours were owners or occupiers. Handwritten notes on a number of these maps show the names of the successful applicants for leases and of purchasers. Individual pastoral station plans, usually only in manuscript, are much less common, but a magnificent example is that of Teviot Station in Central Otago, over one metre square and dated about 1910, showing similar information.

Nineteenth-century town plans published by the survey departments of the provincial and central governments, and street maps published by individual municipalities, were followed by privately published town plans produced for directories such as Harnett's in the 1860s, and Stone's and Wise's from the 1880s onwards. The Dunedin map of 1869 published by B. Riemann gives the location of all business premises in the central Dunedin area at the time. Fire insurance plans issued between 1880 and 1920 are even more detailed. Cadastral sheet maps of Dunedin published in the early twentieth century are still used to locate abolished boroughs, suburbs, streets and sections.

As Dunedin and other towns spread out between 1870 and 1930, sale plans were issued by land agents and auctioneers promoting property subdivision in Dunedin and Otago. Many are ornate and enticing, often with illustrations and, occasionally, photographs. They show buildings, land owners, land use and services, sometimes with later annotations on price paid and purchaser.

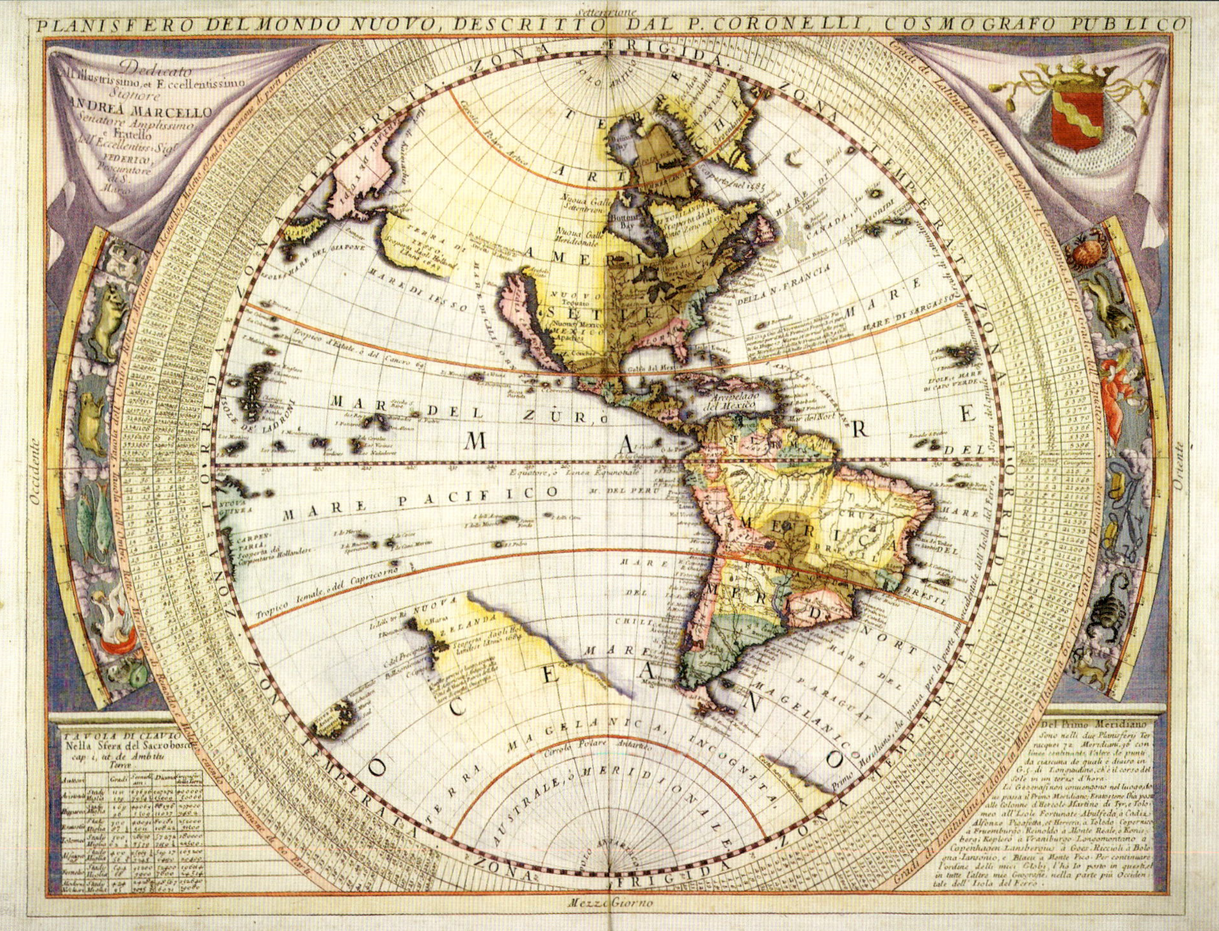

Coronelli's new world map • 1696

V.M. Coronelli. *Planisfero del Mondo Nuovo descritto dal P. Coronelli.* Venice: 1696. Copper-engraved hemispheres, hand-coloured in outline. Purchased, 1979.

Vincenzo Maria Coronelli (1650–1718) was an Italian theologian, mathematician and cartographer, and founder of the first geographical society, the Academia Cosmographica degli Argonauti in 1680. His first major work was a large atlas, *Atlante Veneto*, which he published in 1690–1, followed by *Isolario dell' Atlante Veneto* in 1696–7. Coronelli maps are distinctive for their skilfully engraved outlines and for their decoration. Coronelli drew and engraved over five hundred maps, and also constructed many terrestrial and celestial globes.

In his delineation of the Pacific, Coronelli has omitted the Solomon Isles and the Terre de Quir. A note near New Zealand says, incorrectly, that it was discovered by the Dutch in 1684. South of New Zealand the Antipodean position of Venice is given. He also shows New Zealand as forming part of a southern continent. Using the 1649 discovery of Tasman for part of the west coast, he inserts an assumed east coast running southeast almost to Terra del Fuego. Here he makes a break, and further east continues a coastline to the edge of the map marked 'Costa non conosciute'. The theory of a large southern landmass was not dispelled until Cook's voyages over seventy years later. KC

Zatta's map of New Zealand • 1778

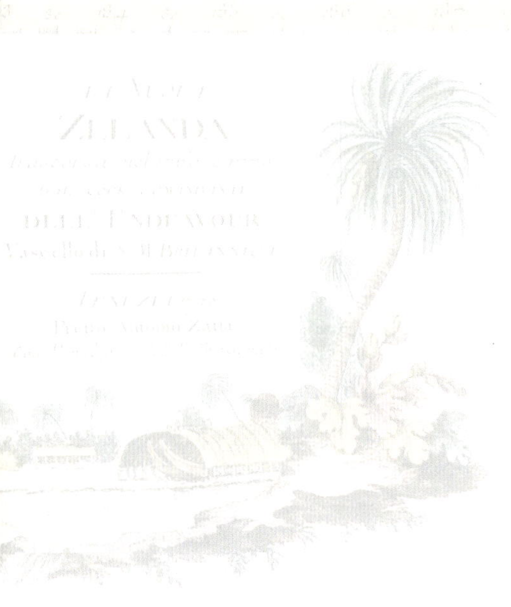

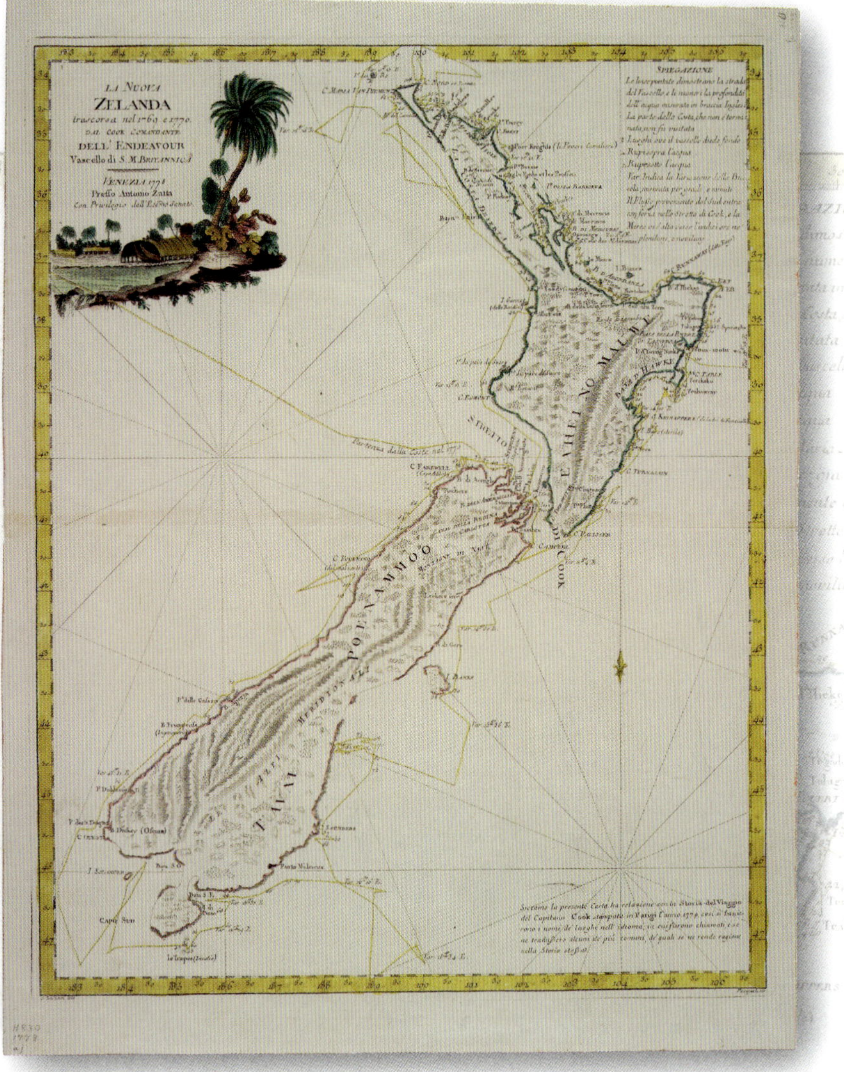

Antonio Zatta. *La Nuova Zelanda: trascorsa nel 1769, e 1770 dal Cook Comandante dell' Endeavour vascello di S.M. Britannica.* Venice: Presso Antonio Zatta, 1778. Purchased, 1959.

A Venetian cartographer, printer, publisher and bookseller, Antonio Zatta (fl.1750–1804) produced *Atlante Novissimo* in four volumes with maps from 1775 to 1799, including this map of New Zealand dated 1778.

One of the first and more attractive of the maps of New Zealand to show the results of Cook's voyages, Zatta's map traces the *Endeavour's* path around the two islands in 1769 and 1770. It also records inland topography, astronomical observations, and marine soundings; and provides careful surmise where facts were not at hand. Stewart Island is attached to the mainland and Banks Peninsula is an island, but by this time an error on the 'Mare del Sud' 1776 map in the same volume, which shows Cook's *Endeavour* track passing between the mainland and Banks Island, has been corrected. A mix of native and European placenames line the coast. Many are still in use today. The decorative cartouche shows a fanciful tropical native village scene that little represents New Zealand.

Cook's careful observations dispelled the myth of the Great Southern Continent, and his survey results remained unchallenged for forty years, forming the basis for the first British Admiralty hydrographic charts of New Zealand.

KC

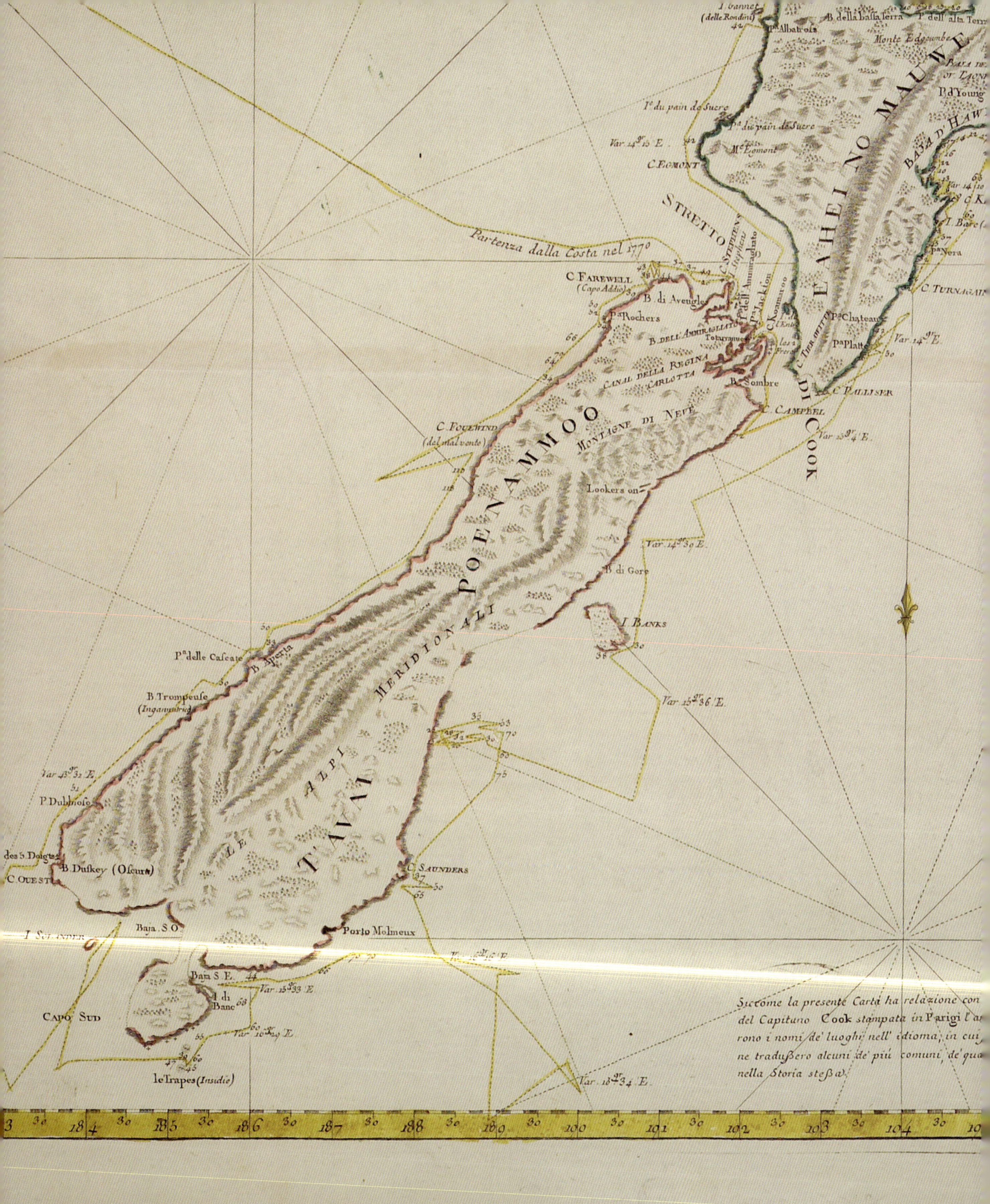

B. della bassa terra
Pta Albatrois
Monte Edgcumbe
P. d'Young
Pa du pain de Sucre
Pta du pain de Sucre
Mte Egmont
C. Egmont
Var. 14gr 15 E.
Stretto
Partenza dalla Costa nel 1770
C. Stephens
Pta dell' Ammiragliato
E AHEI NO MAUWE
C. Turnagain
Pta Nera
C. Farewell
(Capo Addio)
B. di Aveugle
Pta Rochers
B. dell' Ammiragliato
Totaranue
Canal della Regina Carlotta
C. Koamaroo
Pta Chateau
Pta Platte
Var. 14gr E.
C. Palliser
B. Sombre
C. Campbel
Di Cook
Var. 13gr 4 E.
C. Foulwind
(del mal vento)
Montagne di Neve
Poenammoo
Lookers on
Var. 14gr 30 E.
B. di Gore
I. Banks
Meridionali
Pta delle Cascate
B. Aperta
Var. 15gr 36 E.
B. Trompeuse
Var. 13gr 32 E.
P. Dubbioso
Le Alpi
T'avai
B. Duskey (Oscura)
C. Ouest
C. Saunders
Baja S.O.
Porto Molineux
Baja S.E.
I. di Banc
Var. 15gr 33 E.
Var. 16gr 29 E.
Capo Sud
le Trapes (Insidie)
Var. 18gr 34 E.
Siccome la presente Carta ha relazione con
del Capitano Cook stampata in Parigi
rono i nomi de' luoghi nell' idioma, in cui
ne tradussero alcuni de' più comuni, de'
nella Storia stessa.
184
185
186
187
188
189
190
191
192
193
194

In May 1793, Tuki Tahua and Ngahuruhuru, two young Northland Māori chiefs, were forcibly taken to Norfolk Island to teach convicts flax rope-making. Treated as guests by Lieutenant-Governor King, they stayed at Government House, ate at his table, and were excused manual labour. The plan did not succeed due to the poor quality of Norfolk Island flax and because within Māori society working with flax was traditionally a skill of women only. In November the two chiefs were returned by King to New Zealand.

The most remarkable outcome of the kidnapping was Tuki's map of New Zealand. Originally drawn in chalk on the floor in Government House, the map is a unique record of Māori cartographic thought. Emphasising the northernmost part of New Zealand, known then and now as Muriwhenua, it included geo-political and mythical information provided by Tuki and Ngahuruhuru.

This copy, made by Dr Hocken from the printed version in Collins's 1793 *Account of … New South Wales*, is extensively annotated by him with the help of S. Percy Smith, a former Surveyor-General of New Zealand. Two significant features are the spirits' pathway (AAAA) leading to 'Terry-inga' (Te Reinga), where they leapt off into the underworld, and 'Poenammoo' (Te Wai Pounamu/the South Island), including the 'Lake where stones for hatchets are got', presumed by Hocken to be Lake Wakatipu. SRS

Reproduced Map of New Zealand originally drawn by two Maori Chiefs, Tuki Tahua and Ngahuruhuru, at Norfolk Island, 1793.
Manuscript. Original Collection.

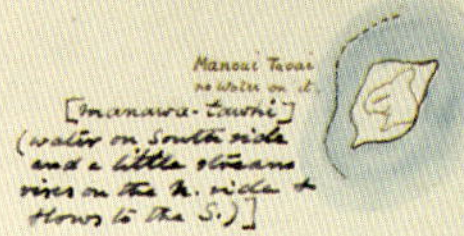

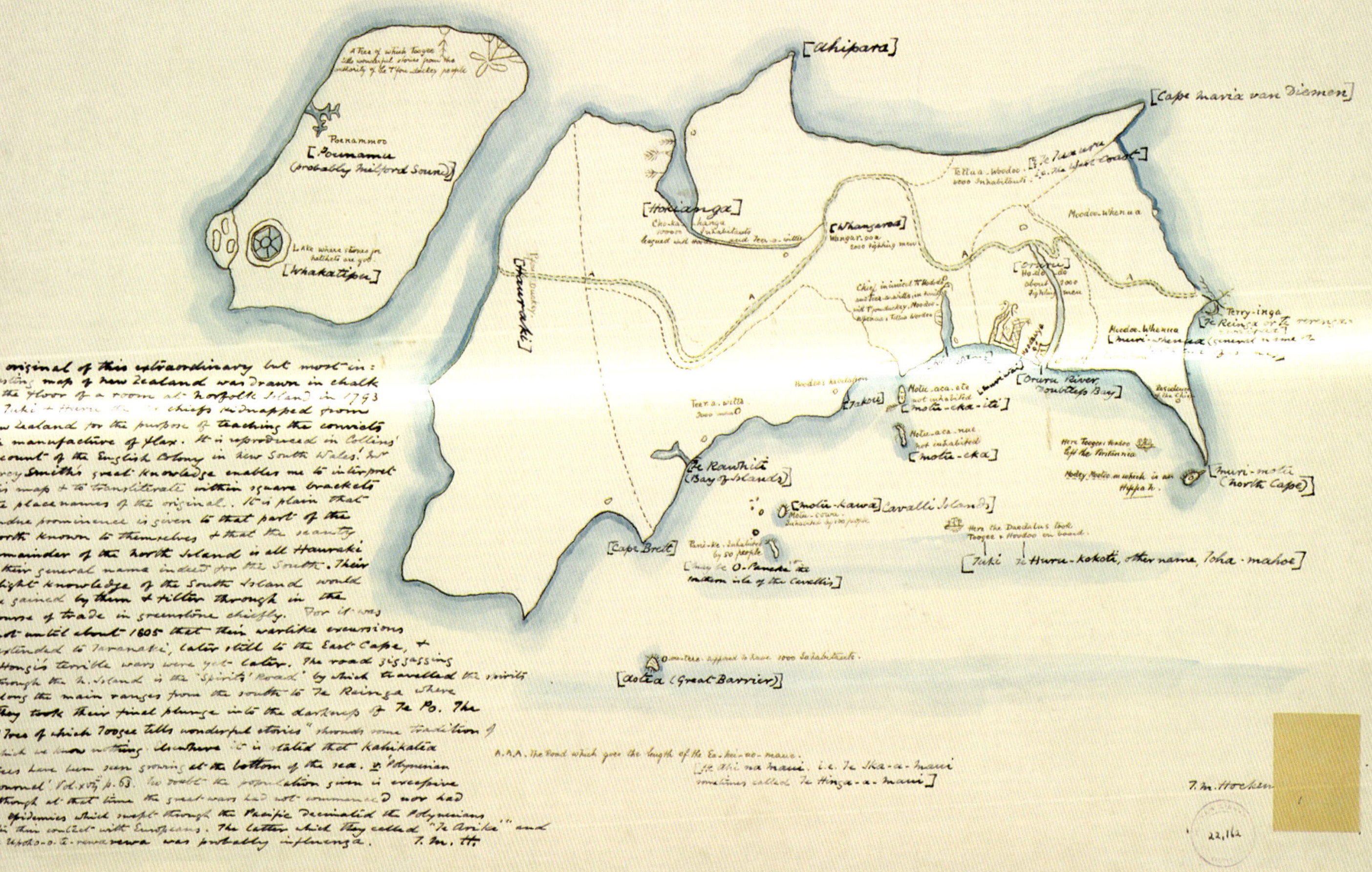

The original of this extraordinary but most interesting map of New Zealand was drawn in chalk on the floor of a room at Norfolk Island in 1793 by Tuki & Huru the two chiefs kidnapped from New Zealand for the purpose of teaching the convicts the manufacture of flax. It is reproduced in Collins' 'Account of the English Colony in New South Wales'. Mr Percy Smith's great knowledge enables me to interpret this map & to transliterate within square brackets the place names of the original. It is plain that undue prominence is given to that part of the North known to themselves & that the scanty remainder of the North Island is all Hauraki – their general name indeed for the South. Their slight knowledge of the South Island would be gained by them & filter through in the course of trade in greenstone chiefly. For it was not until about 1805 that their warlike excursions extended to Taranaki, later still to the East Cape, & Hongi's terrible wars were yet later. The road zigzagging through the N. Island is the 'Spirits' Road' by which travelled the spirits along the main ranges from the south to Te Reinga where they took their final plunge into the darkness of Te Po. The "Tree of which Toogee tells wonderful stories" shrouds some tradition of which we know nothing. Elsewhere it is stated that kahikatea trees have been seen growing at the bottom of the sea. v. 'Polynesian Journal' Vol. xvii p. 63. No doubt the population given is excessive although at that time the great wars had not commenced nor had the epidemics which swept through the Pacific decimated the Polynesians after their contact with Europeans. The latter which they called "Te Ariki" and "Te Upoko-o-te-rewarewa was probably influenza. T. M. H.

THE COMPLETE

EAST INDIA PILOT,

FROM

London to any Part of the Indian & China Seas,

AUSTRALIA, VAN DIEMEN'S LAND, & NEW ZEALAND,

COMPREHENDING

A SET OF NEW AND ACCURATE CHARTS,

Both General and Particular,

EXHIBITING ALL THE PASSAGES OUT AND HOME;

PARTICULARLY DESIGNED FOR

Ships bound to the Cape of Good Hope, Isle of France, Red Sea, Persian Gulf, Bombay, Ceylon, Madras, Bengal, Prince of Wales's Island, Malacca, Singapore, Siam, Bencoolen, Batavia, Canton, Manilla, Amboyna, Melville Island and Port Jackson in Australia, Hobart Town in Tasmania, or Van Diemen's Land, New Zealand, &c.

THE WHOLE DRAWN FROM THE MOST RECENT SURVEYS,

AND IMPROVED BY

The Remarks of several experienced Officers in the Royal Navy, and the Honourable East India Company's Service.

TO WHICH IS ADDED

A CHART OF THE VARIATION OF THE MAGNETIC NEEDLE, BETWEEN THE LATITUDE OF 60° NORTH AND SOUTH.

FIFTH EDITION,

SELECTED AND ARRANGED BY

J. W. NORIE, HYDROGRAPHER,

Author of a new and complete Epitome of Navigation, Linear Tables, Celestial Maps, &c. &c.

London:

PRINTED FOR, AND PUBLISHED BY J. W. NORIE & Co.

Chartsellers to the Admiralty and the Honourable East India Company, and Agents to the Board of Admiralty for the Sale of their Office Charts;

AT THE NAVIGATION WAREHOUSE AND NAVAL ACADEMY, No. 157, LEADENHALL STREET, NEAR THE ROYAL EXCHANGE:

Where may be had all the Charts and Nautical Publications of STEEL & Co. late of No. 70, Cornhill.

[Price Ten Pounds].

1827. *Additions to 1829.*

The Complete East India Pilot, from London to any Part of the Indian & China Seas, Australia, Van Diemen's Land & New Zealand, comprehending a set of new and accurate charts, both general and particular … Fifth edition, selected and arranged by J.W. Norie, Hydrographer. London: J.W. Norie & Co., 1827 [additions to 1829]. Purchased, 1957.

Prior to the 1750s, nautical charts were published in a folio atlas which included sailing directions and were known as 'Pilots'. Later pilots contained charts, title and contents pages, with the sailing directions published in a separate directory or navigator. These were used on merchant ships before Admiralty charts became available to them. Many would have found a watery grave, split into individual sheets or sets for specific voyages and disintegrated with use, or discarded when superseded.

Originally published in Paris in 1693, the first English edition appeared in 1799. The 1820 edition of the *Complete East India Pilot,* containing thirty charts, is thought to be the first with the additional chart of New Zealand but no copies are known to exist. This copy of the amended fifth edition, which underwent extensive conservation in 1994, is the only known copy in a public institution.

Chart 30 has an additional complementary chart of the entrance to Macquarie Harbour Van Diemen's Land, William Stewart's chart of Stewart Island, Capt. J. Herd's chart of the entrance to Jokeehangar [Hokianga] River, surveyed in 1827, and a sketch of the Bay of Islands, 1828. KC

First New Zealand published map • 1841

Widely considered to be the first map or chart to be printed and published in New Zealand, Chaffers's chart of the harbour at Wellington went on sale in late May 1841 for 2s 6d. This copy is the only one known to survive.

Compiled from surveys over five days in September 1839 by Edward Main Chaffers, attached to the New Zealand Company advanced survey ship *Tory,* the chart features harbour soundings and coastal features, with bays and points as named by Colonel William Wakefield. Topographic features are defined by hachuring and North is placed at the bottom.

This was the third version of Chaffers's chart, two earlier ones being published in 1840 in England and Australia. The Hocken copy has added the site of Wellington and shows a slightly different stream pattern at the Hutt end. A later version of this chart was published in 1842 by the British Admiralty as Chart 1423 with North at the top. KC

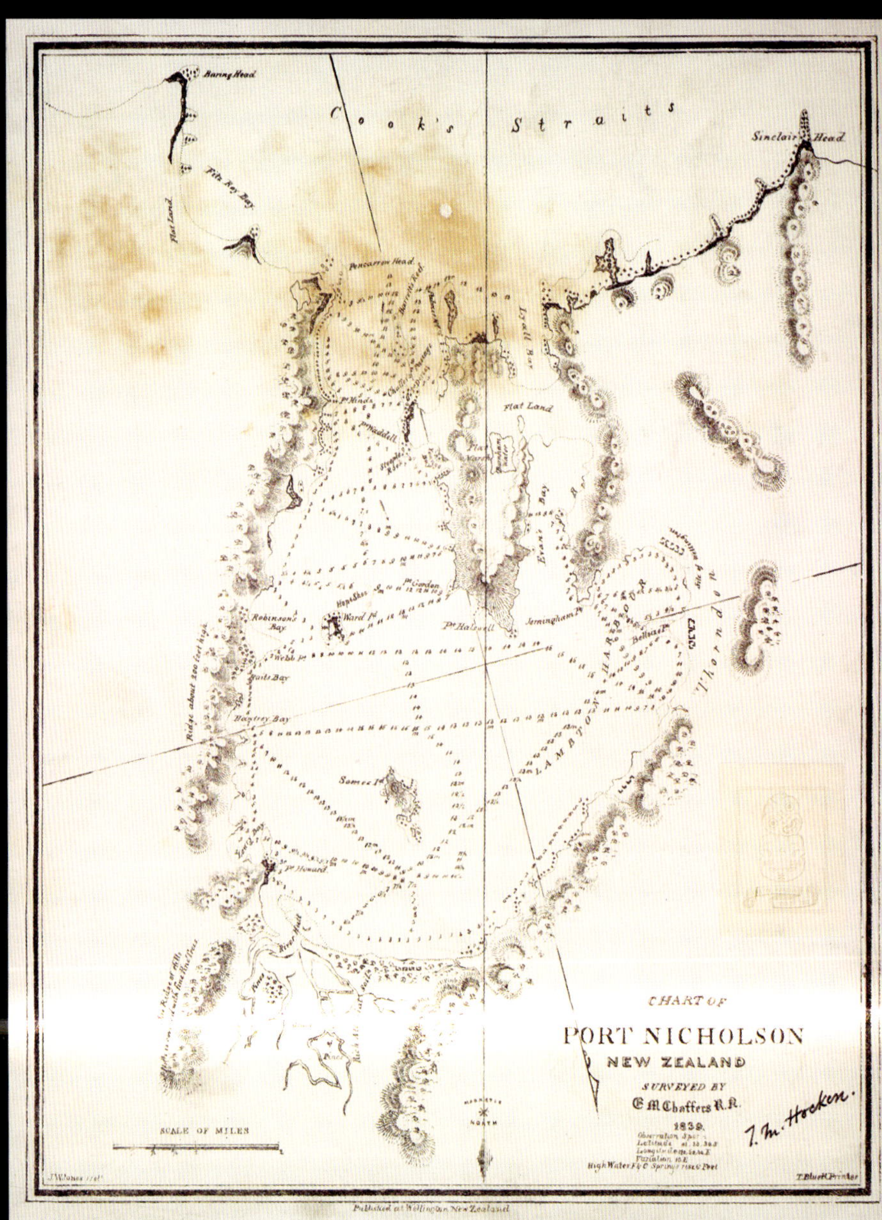

Chart of Port Nicholson, New Zealand, surveyed by E.M. Chaffers, R.N., 1839. Wellington: T. Bluett Printer, 1841. Original Collection.

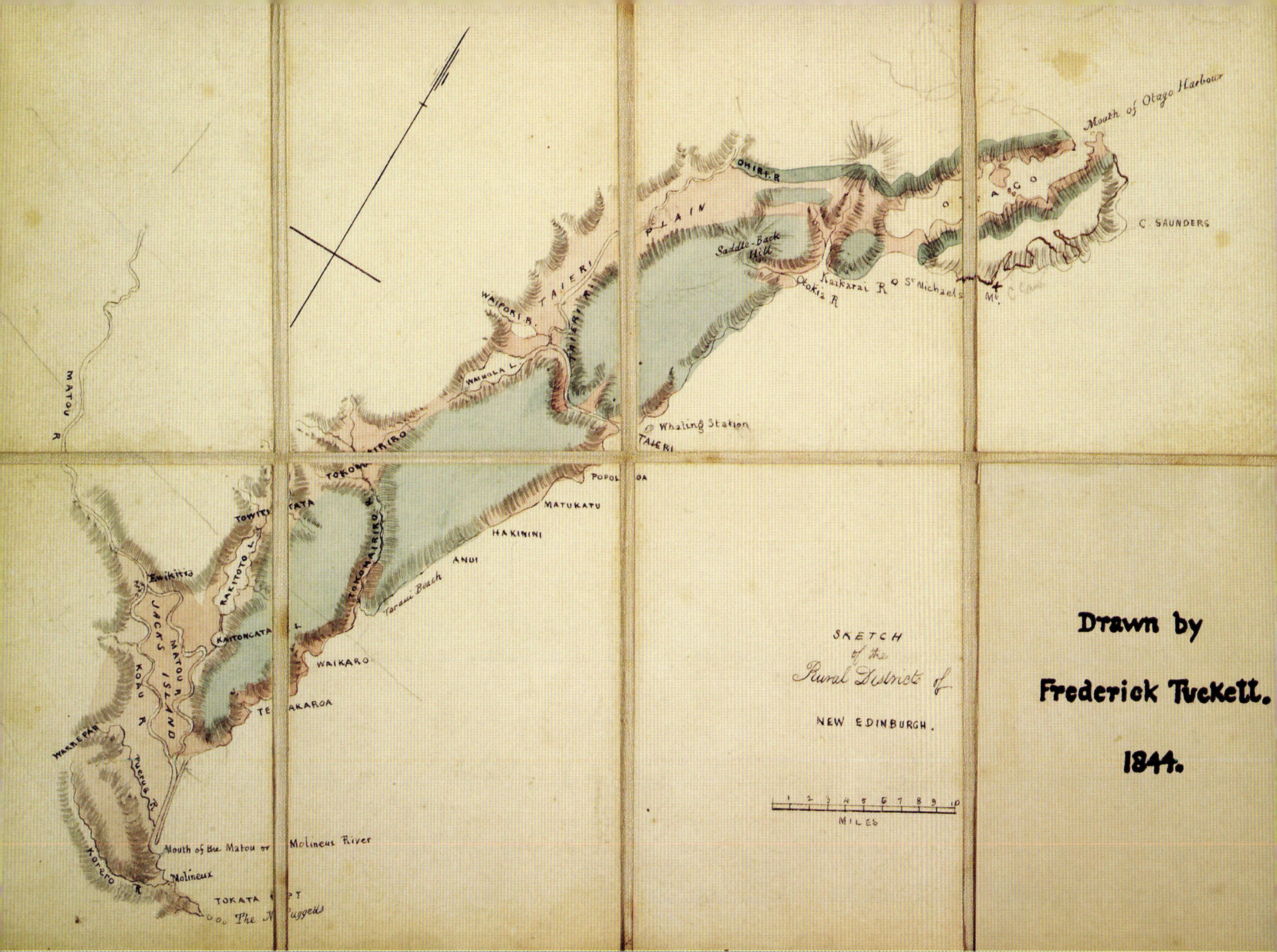

Tuckett's Otago Block map • 1844

Sketch of the rural district of New Edinburgh drawn by Frederick Tuckett, 1844. Manuscript map. Original Collection.

In 1844 Frederick Tuckett was appointed by the New Zealand Company to choose a site for the 'New Edinburgh' settlement in the South Island. Assisted by surveyors J.W. Barnicoat and W.E. Davison, he headed south from Nelson on the schooner *Deborah*.

Having rejected the Port Cooper (Lyttelton), Tuckett and his party disembarked at Waikouaiti and journeyed overland, meeting the *Deborah* in the Otago Harbour. Continuing on land to the mouth of the Matau (Clutha) River, they rejoined the *Deborah* for the journey south to Rakiura (Stewart Island). Returning, they disembarked at the Clutha River for the arduous journey back to the Otago Harbour. Tuckett presumably then drew this sketch, showing the area between Tokata in the south and Otakou in the north as the area desired for the New Edinburgh settlement.

On 31 July 1844, after negotiating with local Kai Tahu, the deed of purchase for the Otago Block was signed at Koputai (Port Chalmers). The choice of site for New Edinburgh proved wise, as shown by the later success of the Dunedin settlement. It was further surveyed by Charles Kettle in 1846–47, with the first settlers arriving in 1848.

KC

Plan of Kawiti's Pā at Ruapekapeka • 1846

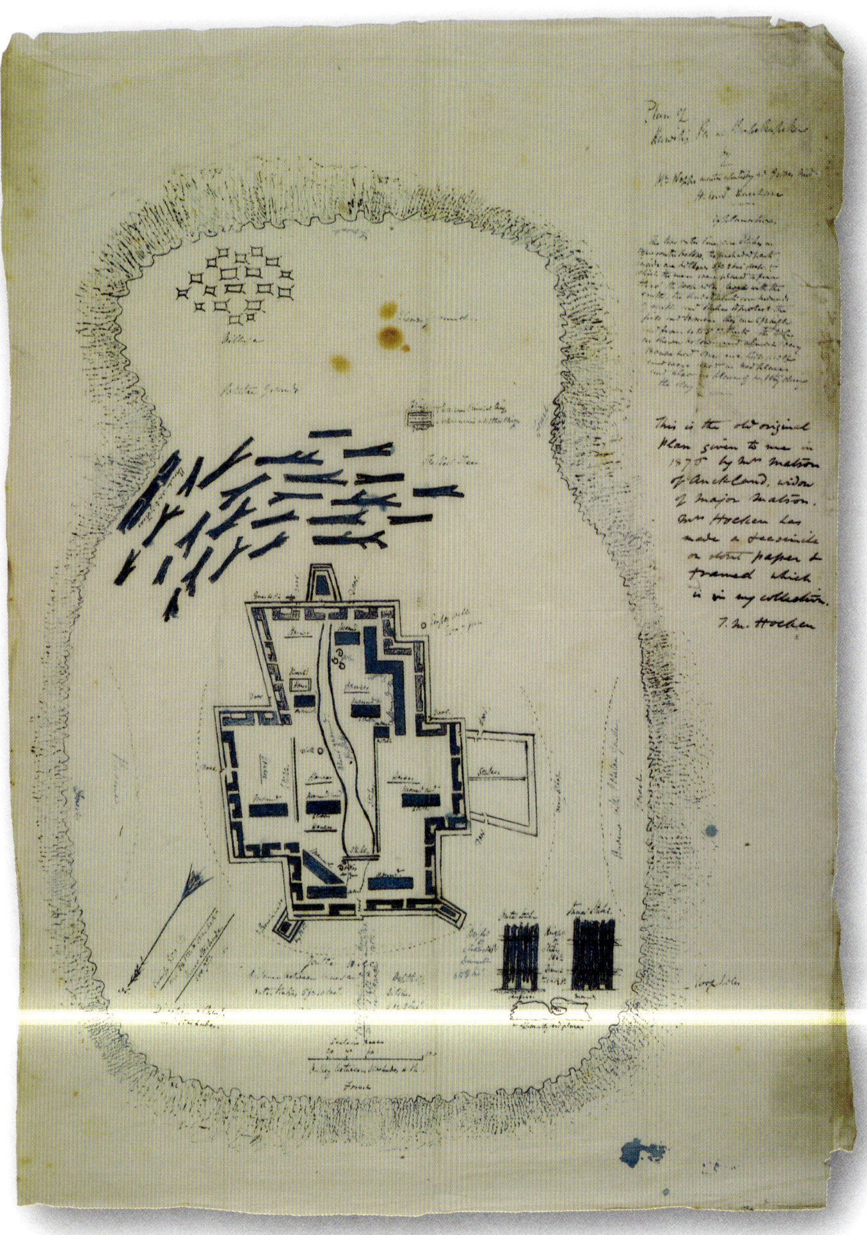

Plan of Kawiti's Pa at Ruapekapeka by Mr Mopps, Master … H.M.S. Racehorse. 1846. Manuscript. Original Collection.

The capture of Ruapekapeka Pā by British forces was the final engagement of the northern war, which had been sparked by Hone Heke's successive fellings of the flagstaff at Kororareka in the Bay of Islands. On 10 January 1846, after an arduous march, 1100 soldiers, marines and seamen, and 450 allied Māori, armed with cannon, mortars and rockets, attacked the last major centre of resistance, the new pā at Ruapekapeka. Opposing were approximately 500 Ngāpuhi commanded by Te Ruha Kawiti and Hone Heke. Over two days the defenders were subjected to continuous artillery bombardment, ultimately breaching the defences and forcing the defenders to make a tactical retreat. Twenty were killed and twelve of their attackers. Though the war was ultimately lost, Heke had carried his point and the flagstaff was not re-erected.

The ingenious fortifications of the pā, approximately 110 by 85 metres and specially designed to counter European warfare, aroused general admiration. This plan, one of several made, records the internal layout of the pā, with houses, defensive mounds and palisades, and bombproof shelters clearly marked. Also shown are the well, the flagstaff, the breastwork of felled trees, and potato grounds. The surrounding stockade was 15 feet high, with. firing positions through ground-level loopholes. Dr Hocken collected a number of such pā plans, of which this is an excellent example.

SRS

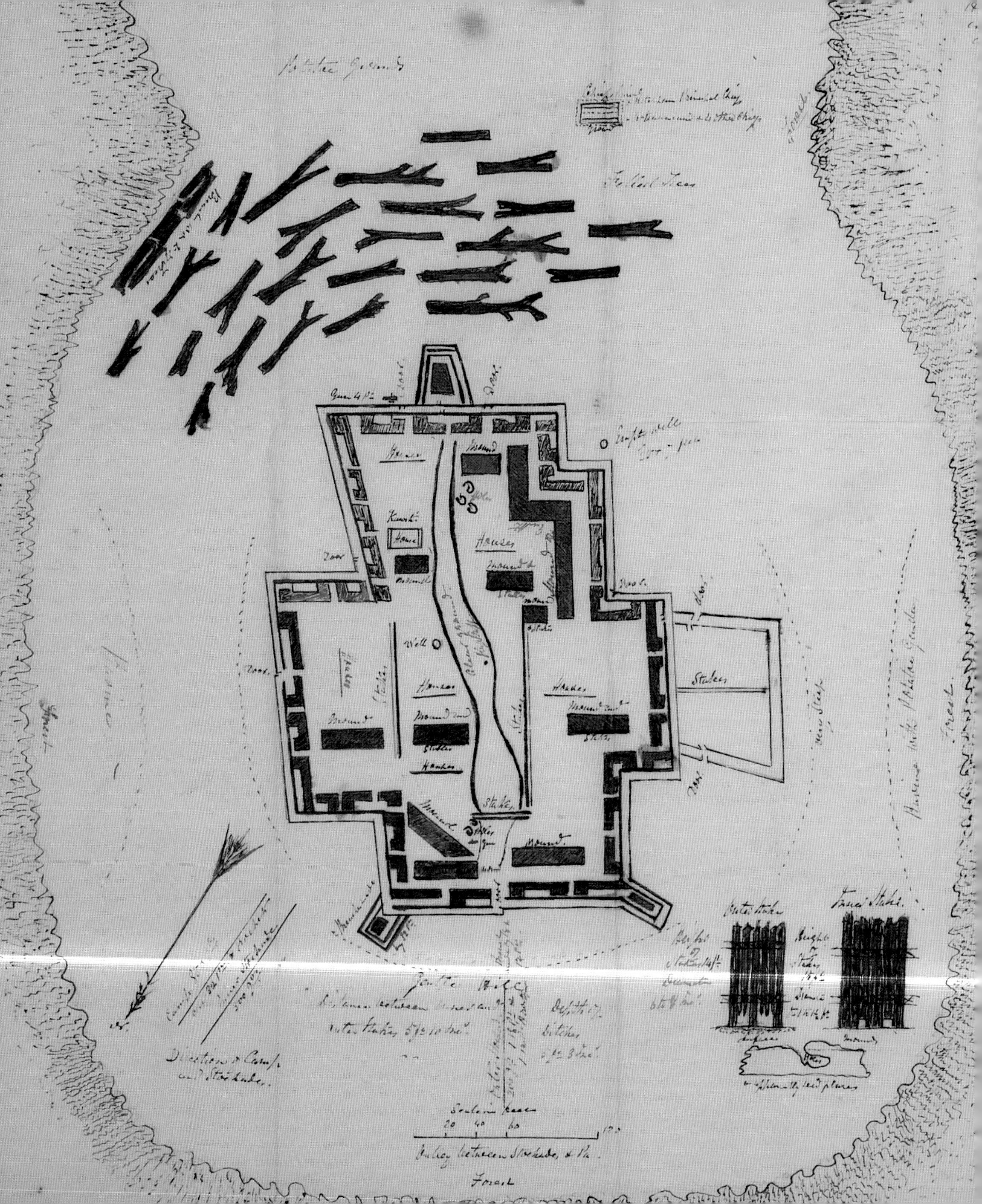

Potatoe Ground
Felled Trees
Forest
Gun 4 Pr
Door
Mound
House
Houses
Well
Stakes
Gentle Hill
Distance between inner and outer Stakes 5 ft 10 in
Depth of Ditches 5 ft 3 in
Outer Stake
Inner Stake
Scale in feet
20
40
60
120
Valley between Stockade, & Pa
Forest

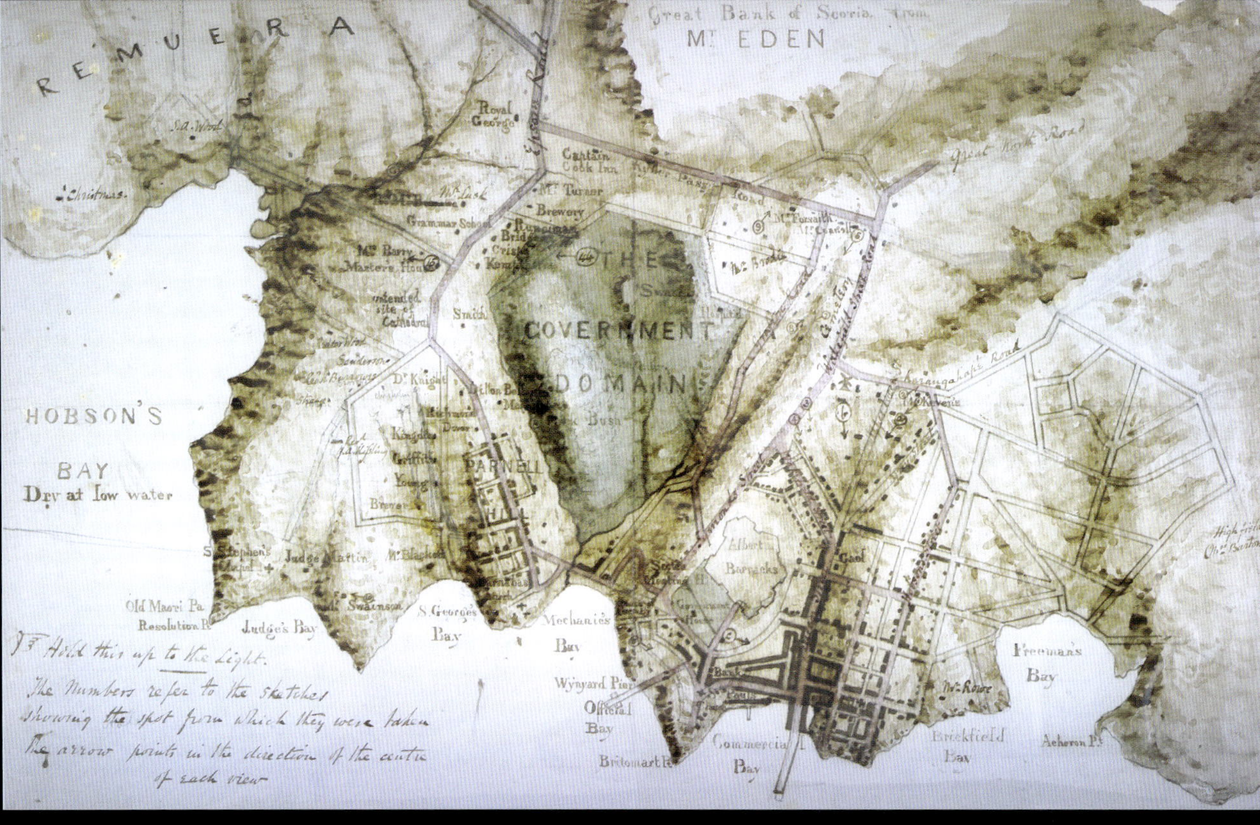

John Kinder. *Plan of Auckland. 1856*. Watercolour, pen, ink and pencil on paper. Donated by Mrs W.D. McCurdie, 1922.

Relief plan of Auckland • 1855

Better known for his watercolours and photography, the Rev. John Kinder drew this remarkable relief plan of Auckland soon after arriving in Auckland in 1855. Initially not at all impressed with the settlement, finding its wooden buildings to be of 'the poorest and shabbiest description, mere shanties in fact', he nevertheless set about recording his surroundings systematically in a series of sepia wash drawings. The location and direction of each are marked in numbered sequence on the plan, no.1 being at Mr Keven's house, where Kinder first lived, near the corner of Hobson Street and Karangahape Road.

The plan clearly shows the most significant areas of settlement to be around lower Queen Street and the suburb of Parnell, the dominating feature being the massively walled Albert Barracks immediately adjacent to Government House. The Government Domain is covered with 'thick bush'. Many individual residences are shown, particularly of important people, such as Judge Martin, William Swainson, Reader Wood, Dillon Bell, and especially of Anglican notables, such as the Rev. Vicesimus Lush and the Rev. George Kissling. St Stephen's Chapel, the Grammar School and the Master's House, and the 'intended site of Cathedral' are also marked. The Presbyterian church is dismissively recorded as the 'Scotch Meeting H[ouse]', reflecting Kinder's stern Anglicanism. SRS

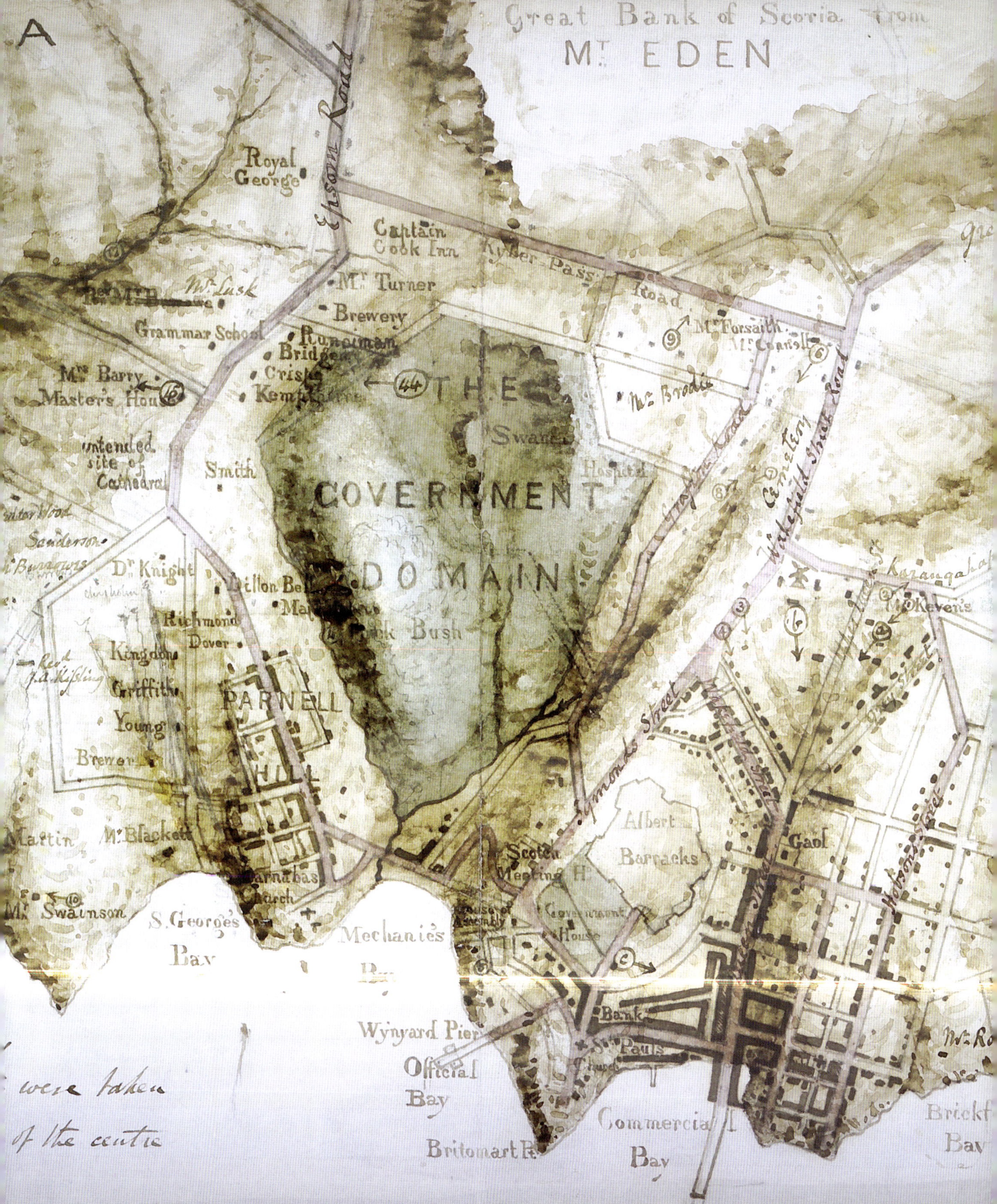

A
Great Bank of Scoria from
Mt. EDEN
Epsom Road
Royal George
Captain Cook Inn
Kyber Pass Road
Mr. Turner
Brewery
Mr. Lusk
Grammar School
Runciman
Bridge
Mrs Barry
Master's House
intended site of Cathedral
Smith
THE GOVERNMENT DOMAIN
Swamp
Hospital
Mr. Forsaith
Mr. Connell
Mr. Brodie
Grafton Road
Cemetery
Wakefield Street Road
Karangahape
McKeven's
Sanderson
Dr. Knight
Dillon Bell
Bush
Richmond
Dover
Kingdon
Griffiths
Young
Brewer
PARNELL
HILL
Martin
Mr. Blackett
Barnabas Church
Mr. Swainson
S. George's Bay
Mechanics Bay
Symonds Street
Albert Barracks
Gaol
Queen Street
Hobson Street
Scotch Meeting H.
House of Assembly
Government House
Bank
St. Pauls Church
Wynyard Pier
Official Bay
Britomart Pt.
Commercial Bay
Brickfield Bay
Mr. Ro
were taken
of the centre

Reconnaissance Survey of part of Otago Province executed during the months of Jan., Feb. and Mar. 1857. J.T. Thomson, Chief Surveyor. C.W. Mountfort delt. Manuscript. Original Collection.

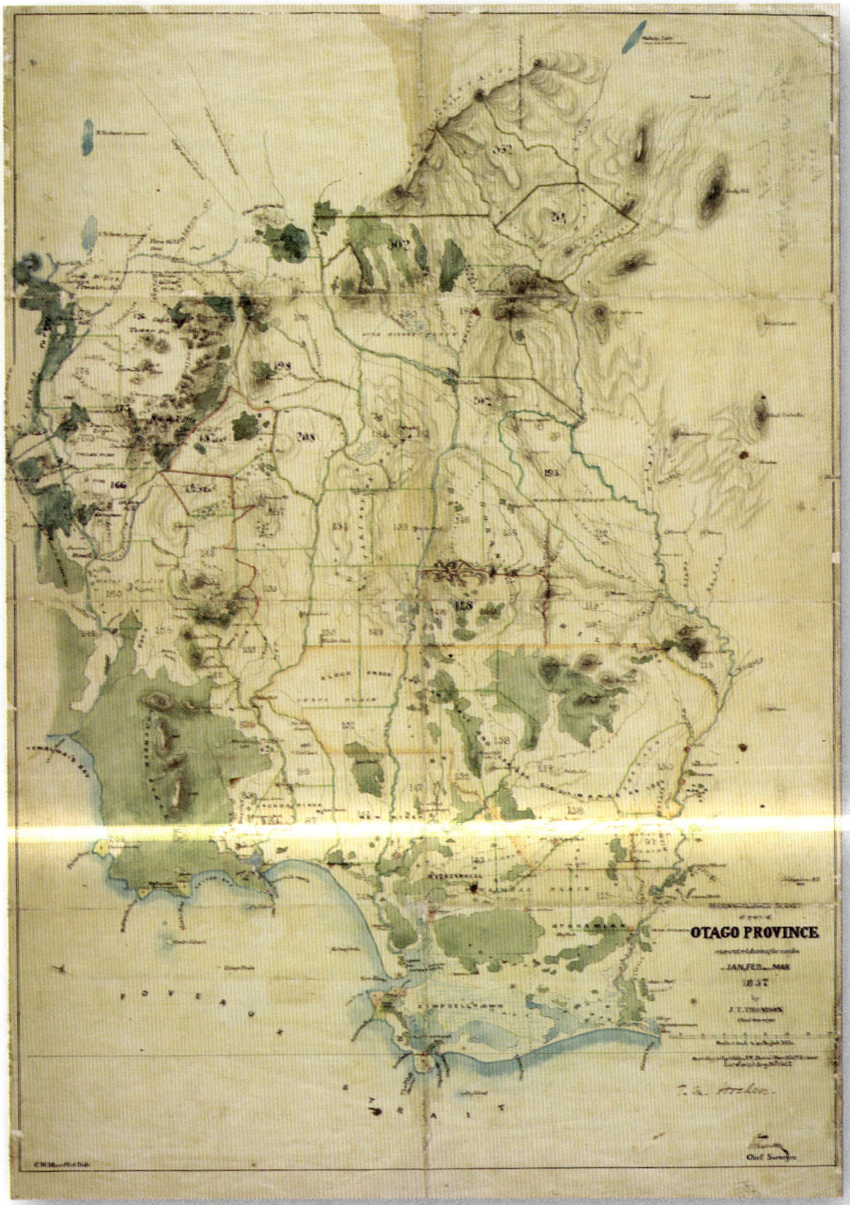

John Turnbull Thomson (1821–84) was appointed Chief Surveyor for the province of Otago in May 1856, when the only map of Otago was a coastal chart with large interior areas designated 'unexplored'. A map was needed to register pastoral runs being taken up and to locate clusters of European settlement.

From January to March 1857 Thomson covered the southern part of Otago, as Southland was then called, with his assistant Lindsay, travelling west to the Waiau River and north to the Takitimu range. A triangulation survey was carried out, using Bluff Hill as the southern station and Mid Dome, 115 kilometres distant, as the northern one. He surveyed the length of the south coast, swimming his horses over three major estuaries. Altogether, 2400 square kilometres of difficult country were surveyed. This wonderful detailed map, incorporating place names chosen by Thomson and drawn by C.W. Mountfort, is the result.

Thomson was the first surveyor to see Lakes Te Anau and Manapouri, which he named South Te Anau, from Centre Hill. As the map states, he did not sight Lake Wakatipu but received information from local Māori. In 1876, Thomson became first Surveyor-General of New Zealand and established the national survey system based on triangulation. KC

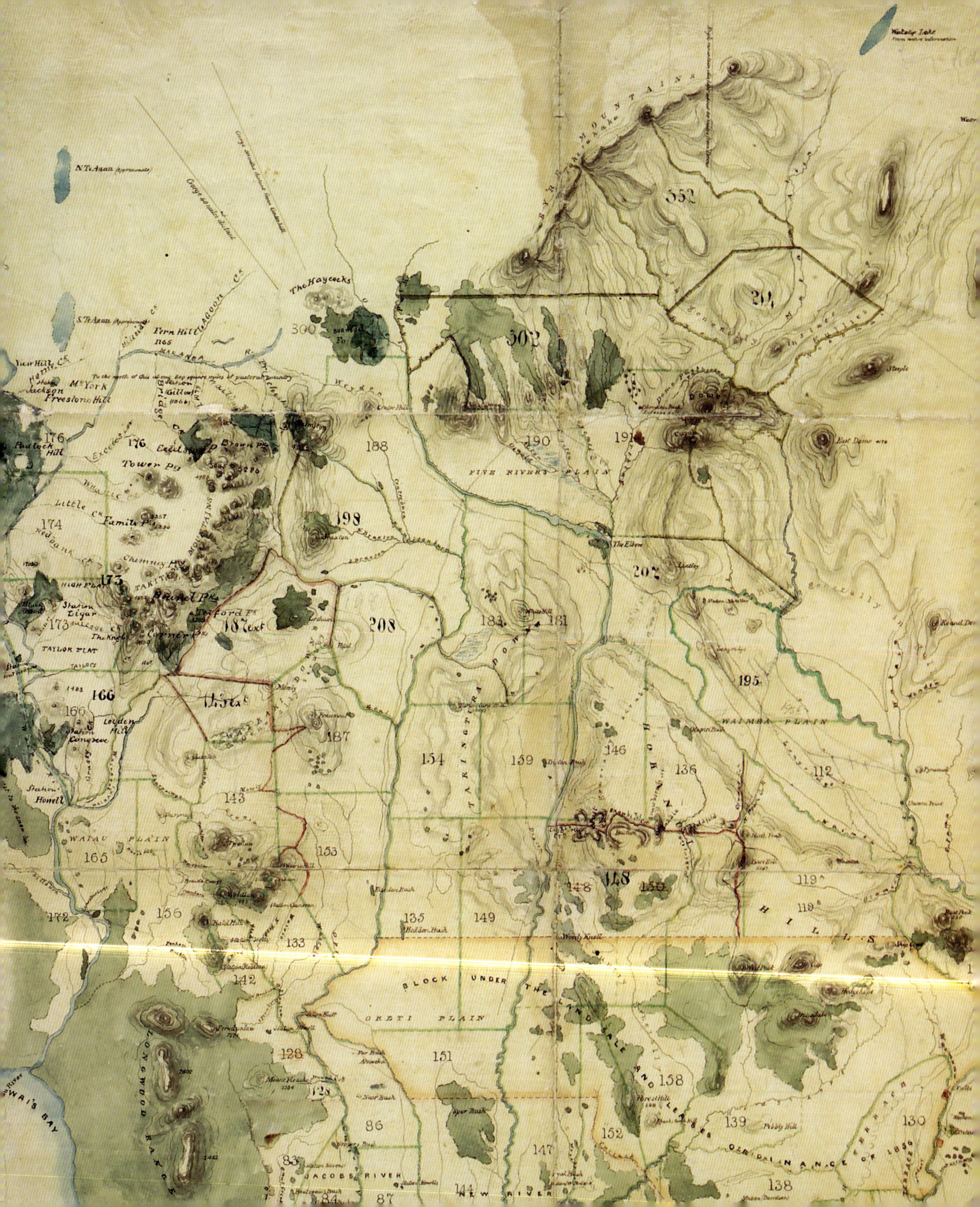

The Haycocks
Fern Hill
300
552
204
302
FIVE RIVERS PLAIN
188
190
191
198
208
The Elbow
202
195
WAIMEA PLAIN
176
Padlock Hill
Tower Pk
174
173
TAYLOR FLAT
166
187
154
159
146
136
112
143
WAIAU PLAIN
165
153
156
172
135
149
148
150
133
142
BLOCK UNDER
ORETI PLAIN
151
128
158
139
130
86
152
147
JACOBS RIVER
NEW RIVER
144
138
87
LONGWOOD RANGE

Before the 1860s, maps of Dunedin were either cadastral surveys or charts of the harbour. The town was first surveyed by Charles Kettle in 1846, and the outline of his original plan was the basis of Riemann's large-scale map of 1869.

One of the first Dunedin street maps to be produced by a commercial publisher, Riemann's map is an attractive and ambitious attempt to combine street map and business directory on one sheet. Street and business directories of Dunedin were produced from this time by companies, including Joseph MacKay, Harnett & Co, and Henry Wise & Co., but they did not consistently include street maps until the 1880s. Riemann has provided a time capsule of the Dunedin business area as it was in 1869. Reclamation, which began in the 1870s and continued through to 1924, considerably altered the shoreline from that shown here.

The index of business by trade includes Riemann himself listed under 'Artists', along with lithographers David Henderson and S. Lister & Co. From this index and Wise's 1868 directory it can be seen that he had premises in Stuart St and later at York Place. Little else is known about Riemann, except that he appears also to have been a Dunedin photographer, publishing photographs as R.B. Riemann in 1867. KC

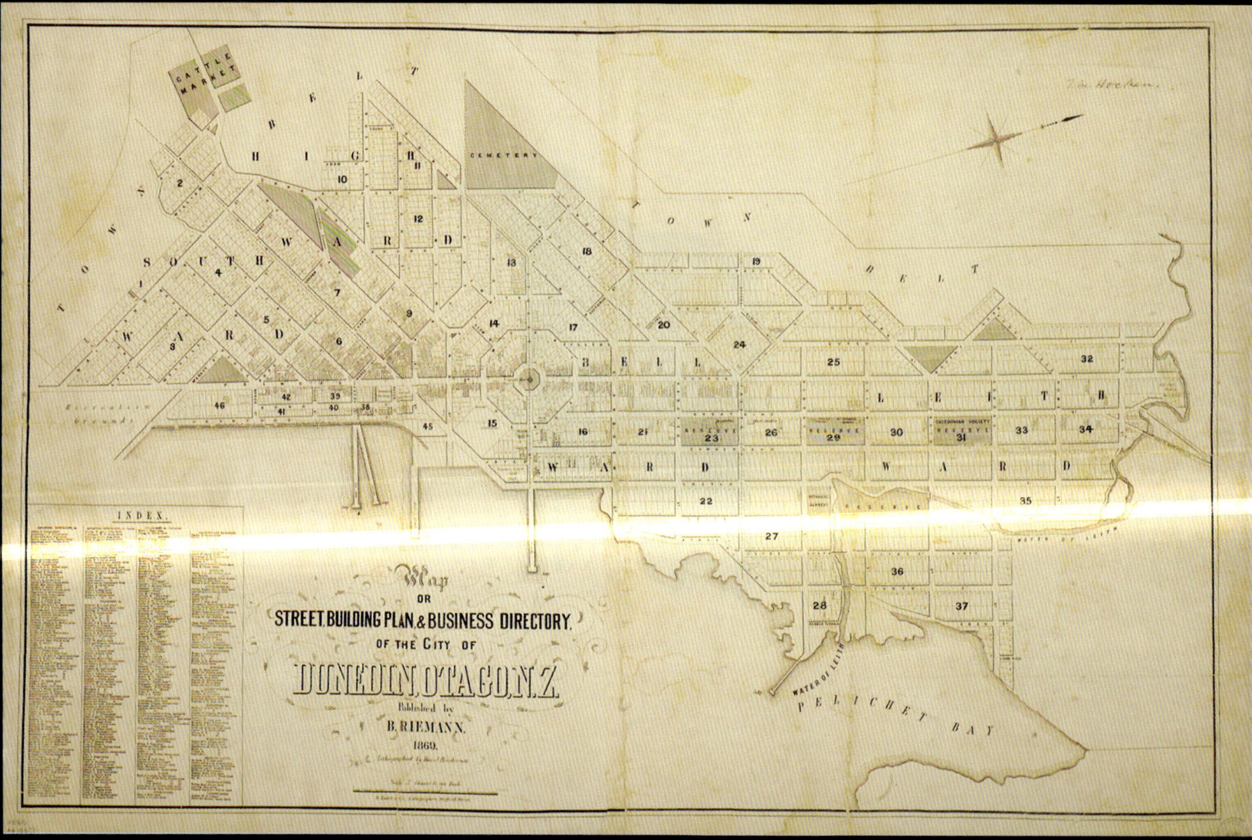

Map or street building plan, & business directory, of the City of Dunedin, Otago, N.Z. Dunedin: B. Riemann, *1869*. Lithographed by David Henderson,

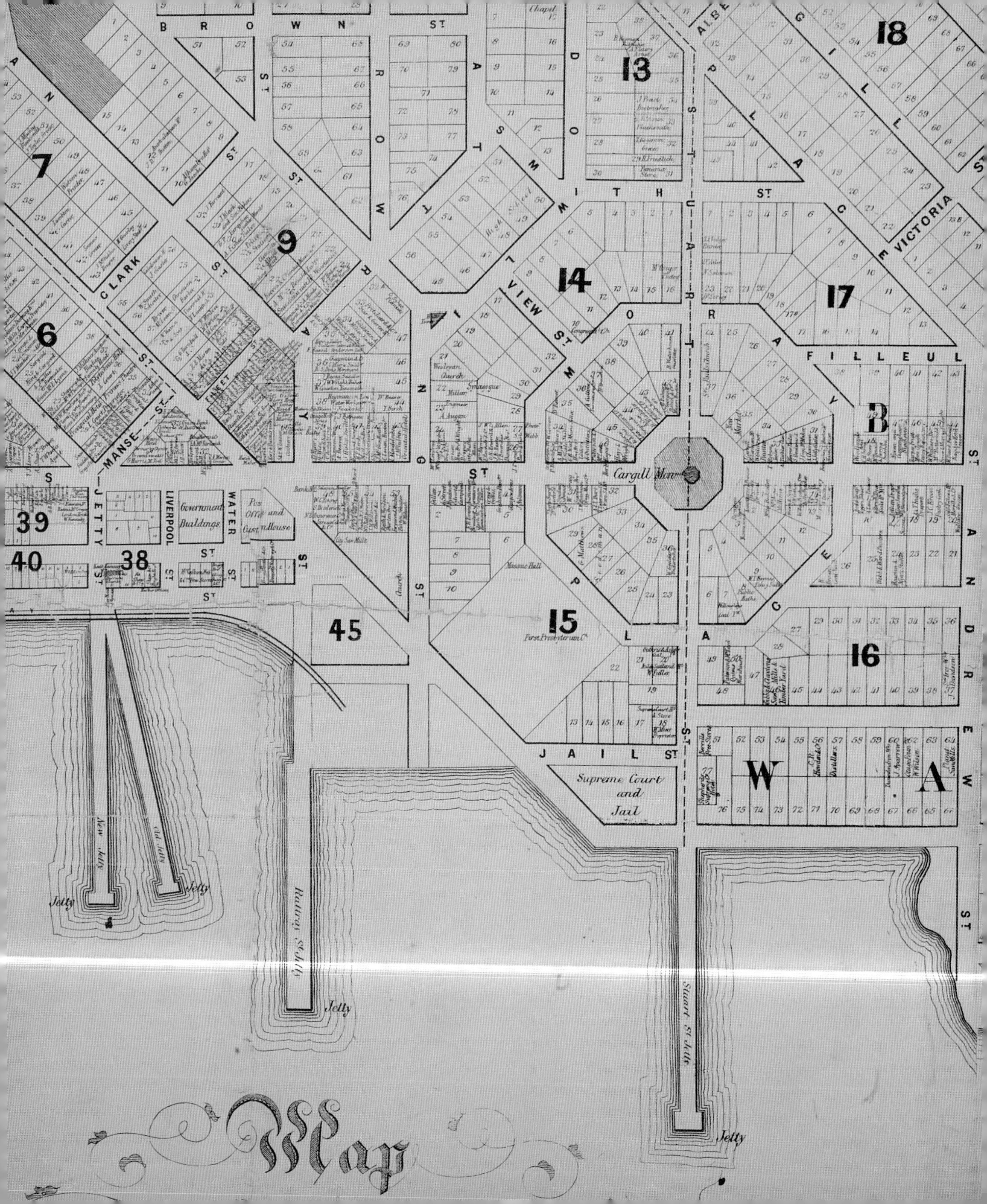

BROWN ST
CLARK ST
MANSE ST
JETTY
LIVERPOOL
WATER
ST
SMITH ST
VIEW ST
MORAY PLACE
STUART ST
FILLEUL ST
VICTORIA
ANDREW ST
JAIL ST
Wesleyan Church
Synagogue
Cargill Mont
New Market
Public Baths
Masonic Hall
First Presbyterian Ch
Government Buildings
Post Office and Custom House
Supreme Court and Jail
New Jetty
Old Jetty
Rattray St Jetty
Stuart St Jetty
Jetty
7
6
9
13
14
15
16
17
18
39
40
38
45
B
W
A
Map

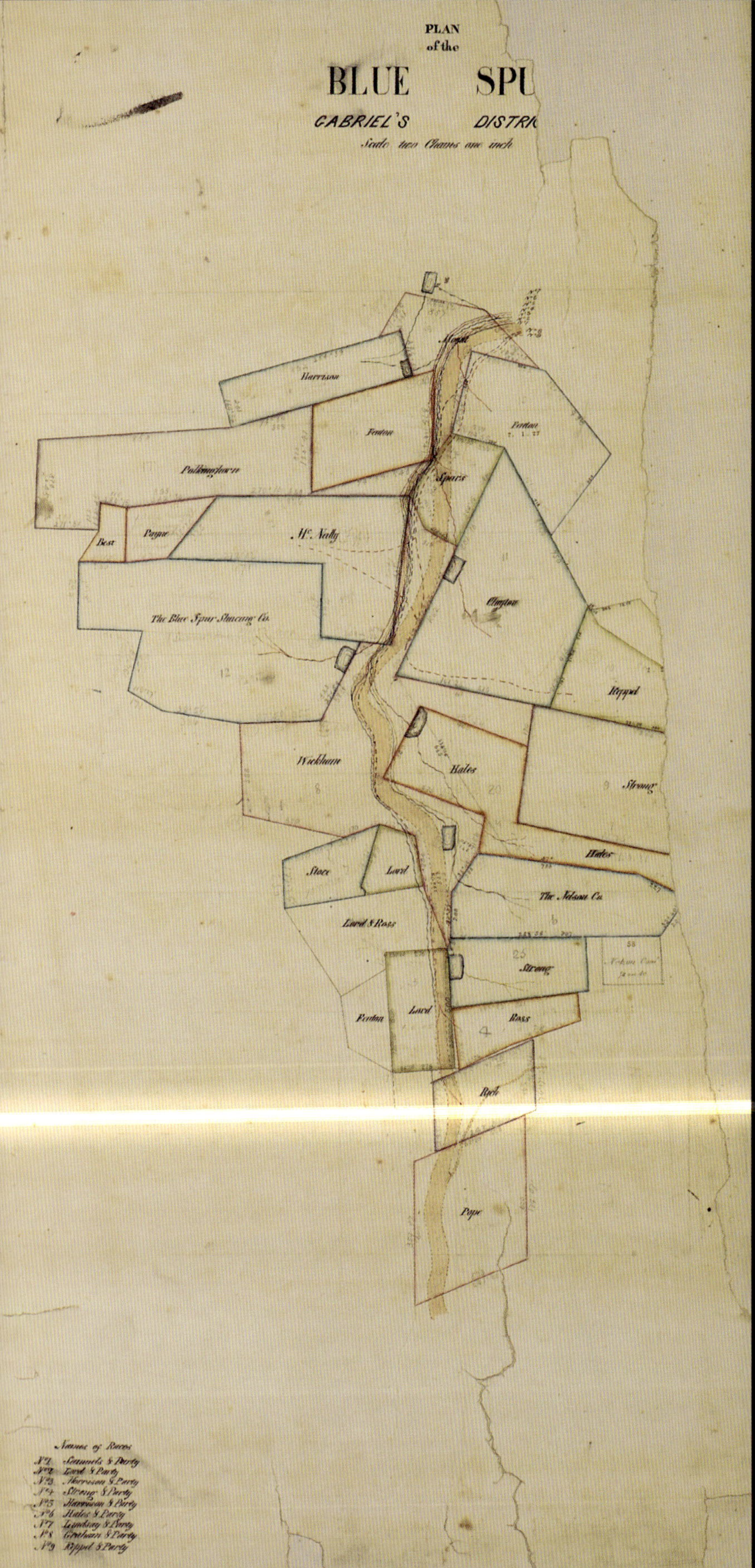

Goldmining claims plan • c. 1880s

This map portrays an industry and a landscape near Lawrence in Otago, which as early as 1862 had begun to change significantly through efforts to mine less accessible deposits of gold, including those of Blue Spur, a hill of bluish-grey conglomerate lying between Gabriel's and Munro's Gullies. It was the source of rich alluvial gold in both gullies. The changes were apparent in the large size of the claims, and the appearance of mining and specialised water supply partnerships and companies.

Of nine sluicing companies registered in Otago by the end of 1866, five held Blue Spur claims: the Blue Spur Sluicing, Great Extended Sluicing, Perseverance, Polkinghorns Gold Claim, and Richs Gold Claim companies. They invested heavily in crushing and sluicing machinery, introduced external capital, employed large numbers of miners on wages, and displaced the once important water carriers. At Gabriels Gully and Blue Spur there was also conflict between hill or ground sluicers and gully miners. The former washed material down the hillsides into tail races, depriving the latter of water and inundating claims.

As elsewhere on the Otago goldfields (notably Tinkers), the changes culminated in the formation in 1888 of one very large mining company, the Blue Spur and Gabriel's Gully Consolidated Gold Company, registered in London with a nominal capital of £130,000. TH

Plan of the Blue Spur: Gabriel's District.
Manuscript. c. 1880s. Unknown provenance.

Suburban sale plan, Dunedin • 1881

Between 1870 and 1930 there was extensive property subdivision in Dunedin, as in all cities, with much business for speculators, auctioneers, surveyors and printers. In the Hocken Collections are many suburban sales plans from this period, including this attractive example of Waverley Township on the opposite side of the harbour. It is coloured, and has inset photographs of a ferry and of the view across to entice prospective purchasers.

W.J. Larnach and his partner James Smith, the vendors, hoped to dispel any sense of isolation from Dunedin by providing a free ferry service to purchasers of sections. They commissioned Dennys of Dumbarton, Scotland, to design and build a paddle-wheel ferry steamer to be assembled by R.S. Sparrow & Co., engineers of Dunedin. Named *Colleen*, it was to ply regularly between Dunedin and the new jetty at Burns Point. Although the ferry service was guaranteed to run until January 1883, when it was hoped a railway or tramway would be built, sections sold so slowly that the service was removed in January 1882.

Several sections of about one acre in Block I, close to the harbour, road and jetty, have sale prices ranging from £35 to £70 added in pencil. KC

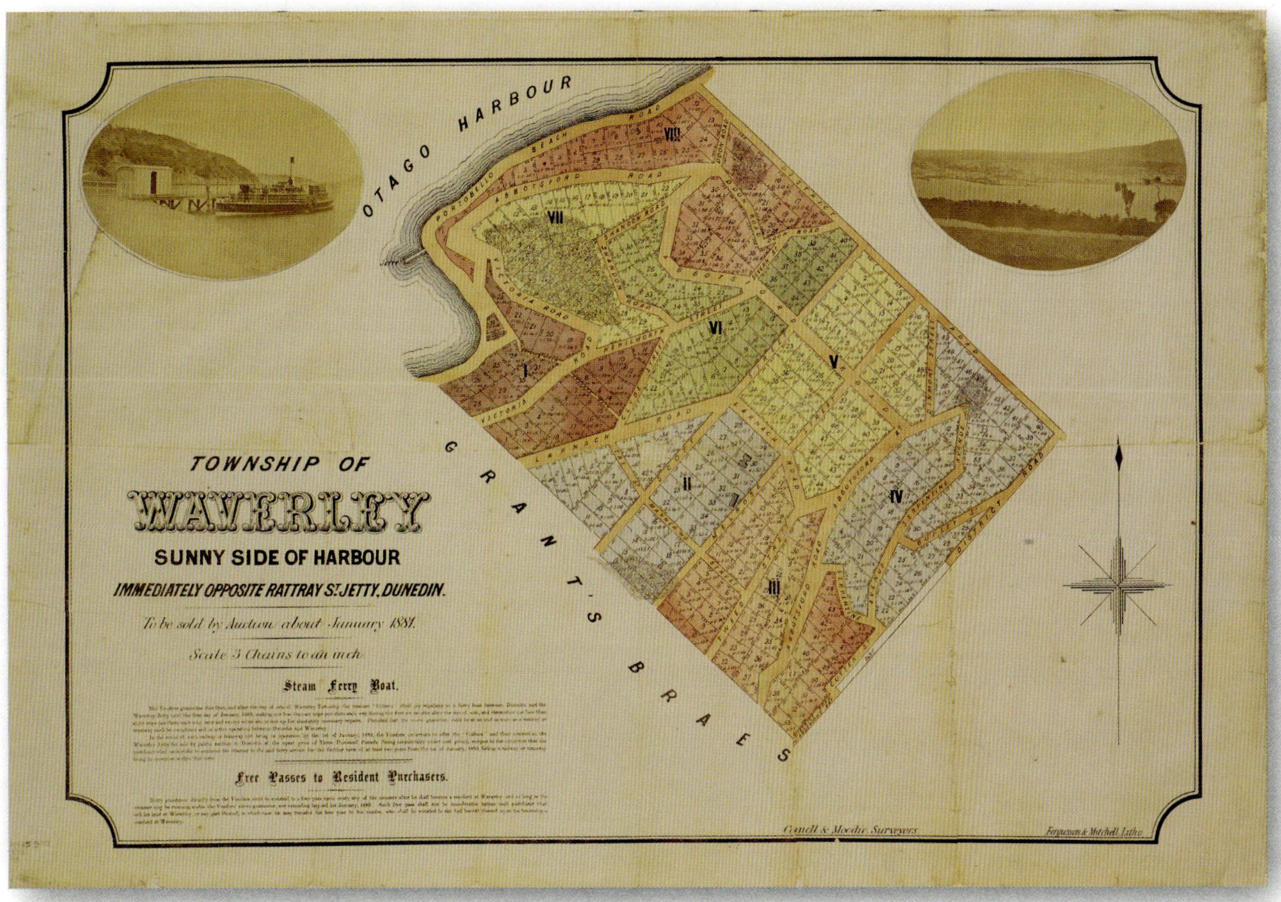

Township of Waverley, sunny side of harbour, immediately opposite Rattray St. Jetty, Dunedin. To be sold by auction about January 1881. Connell & Moodie, surveyors. Dunedin: Fergusson & Mitchell, Litho. 1881. Unknown provenance.

Portable terrestrial globe • 1880s

In 1850 John Betts produced a small, 12.5 cm diameter, paper globe consisting of eight hand-lithographed gores. Cotton cords held between gores and backing paper extended through the poles and when pulled together and secured with a glass bead formed an inflated globe. Subsequent versions put out by Betts and later George Philip, of which this is an example, were made of silk with a metal framework which inflated like an umbrella. Originally patented by Betts, Philips took over production around 1880. Examples appeared as late as 1932.

Wear and tear of the silk has meant such globes are now relatively rare. Intended as a cheap portable educational device, the inflatable globe comes in a sturdy wooden box ideal for safe transportation and loaning to schools. KC

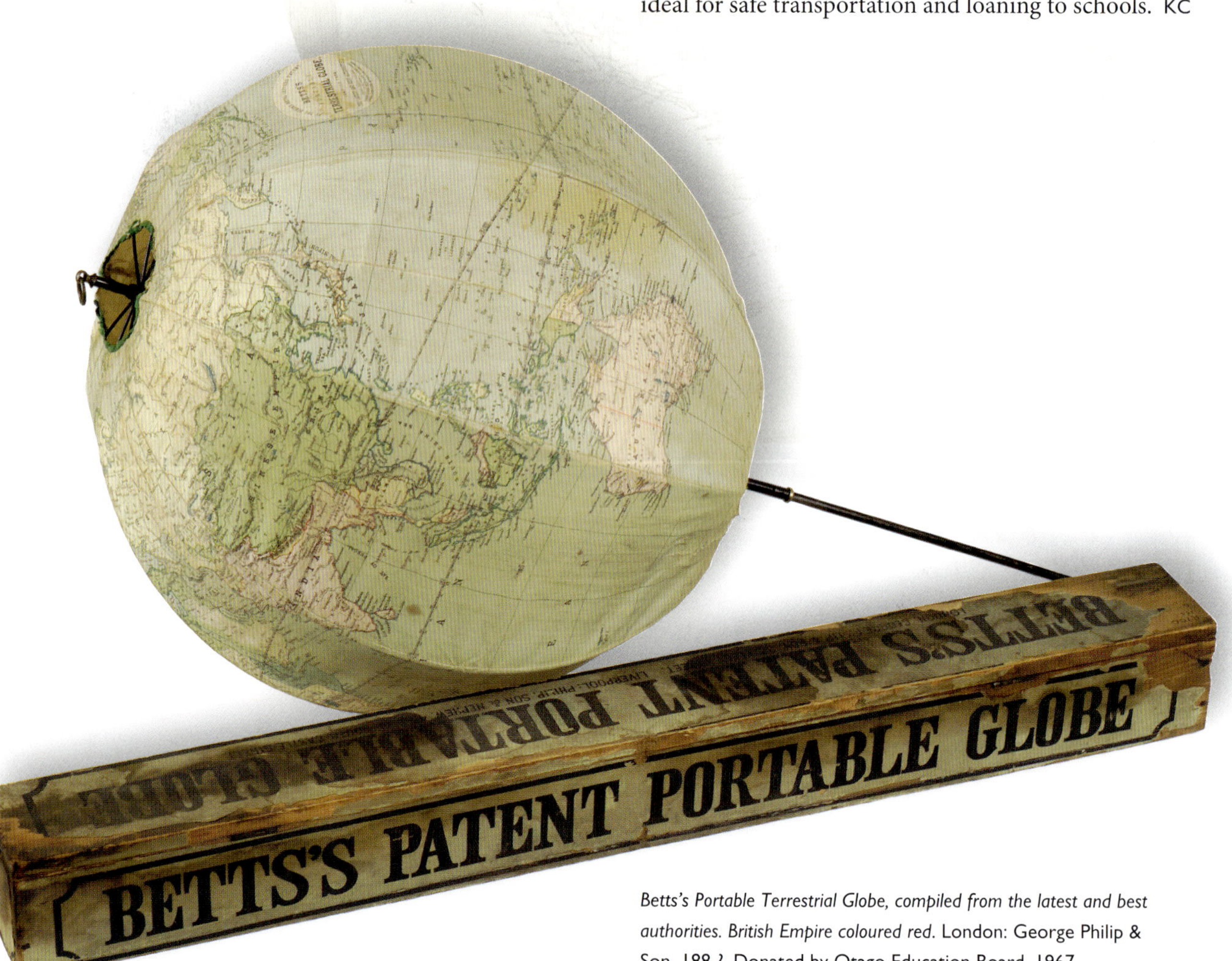

Betts's Portable Terrestrial Globe, compiled from the latest and best authorities. British Empire coloured red. London: George Philip & Son, 188-?. Donated by Otago Education Board, 1967.

Europe in pieces • c. 1940

> *The Nazis have battered their crooked sign into the face of Europe, shattering nearly all of it – except Britain. The task that lies before us is that, whatever the cost, we must – PUT EUROPE TOGETHER AGAIN!*

This 256-piece jigsaw puzzle depicts a map of Europe, the Near East and North Africa during the Second World War. The political situation is neatly conveyed through the shape of the pieces. Germany, its allies and conquests have swastika pieces, while Great Britain and the neutrals do not.

The map depicted dates the puzzle to some point in 1940, probably shortly after the surrender of France. Poland has been divided; France has been overrun but not partitioned into Vichy and Occupied France; and the USSR has not occupied the Baltic States and parts of Rumania.

The message on the box lid is Churchillian in tone, evoking his epic speeches. As such, it was probably felt that the puzzle would go some way towards steeling the peoples of Great Britain, the Dominions and the British Empire for continued resistance against Germany.

Manufactured under the Mere logo, the puzzle proudly claims to be 'devised, drawn, printed and cut in New Zealand, using cardboard and printing inks made in New Zealand.' DJM

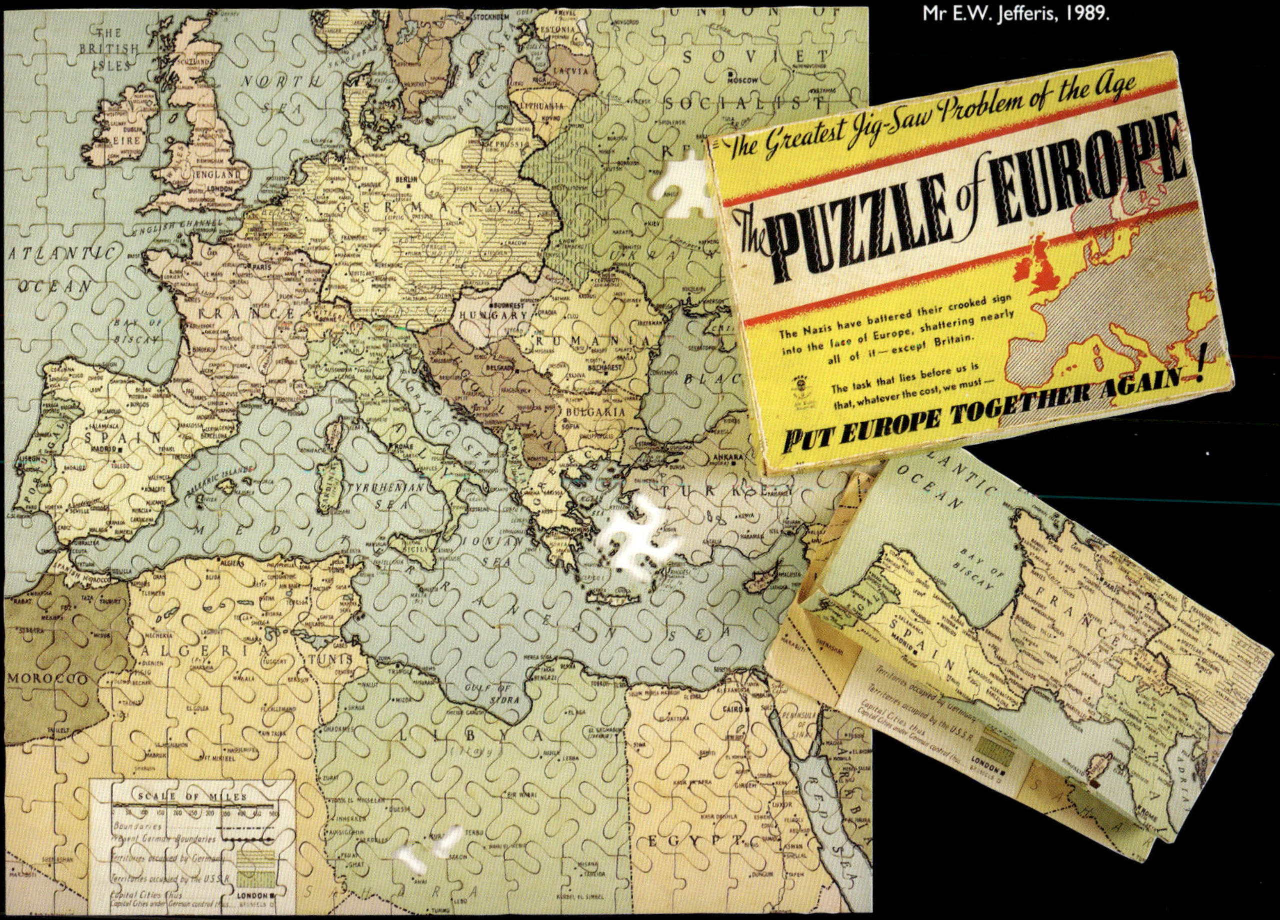

The Puzzle of Europe. Jigsaw puzzle in box. 256 pieces. c. 1940. Donated by Mr E.W. Jefferis, 1989.

Music and Sound

Paulette Milnes

Music is the most recently established of the major Hocken collections, and many would say the liveliest. Dr Hocken's original gift contained very few items of a predominantly musical nature. Certainly no music is listed as such in the 1912 published catalogue. This is unsurprising as Hocken was not himself notably musical, and the sound recording industry was still in its infancy. In ensuing years some musical items did appear in the Hocken collections, but this was by accident rather than design. The majority were either part of wider ethnological studies or isolated examples of high culture.

By the early 1970s it had become apparent that there were significant deficiencies in the preserving and accessing of popular culture by Hocken and other heritage libraries in New Zealand. These shortfalls included sport, light fiction, women's magazines, and popular music. At this time the best collections of New Zealand music were held privately, or at radio stations, where access was difficult and preservation was not a consideration. To improve the situation the Hocken Library decided in 1977 to establish a separate collection of musical recordings performed or composed by New Zealanders.

From the outset it was determined that the collection should consist of commercially produced records, embracing all styles of music, and be comprehensive to fully reflect New Zealand culture. The collection received an initial boost when in 1978 the Australasian Performing Right Association (APRA) gave a significant donation of recordings nominated for the Silver Scroll Award since its inception in 1965. Still running, the award is for the best local popular music composition commercially recorded over a twelve-month period. Subsequent nominated works have also been added to the collection, including works by Dave Dobbyn, Neil Finn, Shona Laing, Bic Runga, Don McGlashan, and Billy Urale (King Kapisi).

By the mid-1980s it was estimated that the Hocken was collecting eighty per cent of current recordings. A concerted effort was also made to acquire older recordings through advertisements asking for donations on local radio stations and in music stores; a second-hand recording in imperfect condition was better than not preserving one at all. At the same time, other music-related material was collected: sheet music, scores, posters, music periodicals, concert programmes, and music archives.

The earliest 'New Zealand' recording held at the Hocken is that of Wellington-born John Prouse, a notable baritone, who cut 'The Maid of Morven' in June 1905 for the Gramophone and Typewriter Company, forerunner of HMV, in London. Other undoubted early treasures are the recordings by Ana Hato and Deane Waretini of Māori music in 1927 on the Australian branch of the Columbia label, and those of Lex Macdonald, the 'boy soprano', also released through an Australian branch of an international label, Regal Records, in 1932. The Hocken also holds the first record entirely produced in New Zealand from 1949, Ruru Karaitiana's *Blue Smoke*, from the TANZA label.

Since the mid-1980s, assisted by advances in technology, there has been an exponential growth in the number of recordings, range of styles, and formats so that it is no longer feasible for Hocken to comprehensively collect New

Zealand music, and the emphasis is now on obtaining a representative and richly diverse collection of styles: punk, death metal, pop avant garde, jazz, classical, brass band, choral, gospel, country, Māori, and Pacific. The expansion of the New Zealand music industry has been fostered by government support and voluntary radio quotas, as well as by technological advances that have made recording easily accessible to individuals. The collection continues to grow and now comprises 13,500 items: records (78s, 33 1/3s, 45s), tapes, compact discs, and digital video discs.

The sheet music collection, totalling 2500 items, includes many priceless pieces. Before widespread broadcasting lessened the need for home-made entertainment, many families had their own pianos and there was a flourishing market for sheet music. The Hocken's earliest sheet music dates from the 1850s: *The Whalers of the Deep Deep Sea* with music composed by Te Heu Heu. Other rarities include the first printing, in London, of *God Defend New Zealand*, J.J. Woods's personal copy of a later edition, and the only known copy of *All Hail Zealandia* from 1885. Further examples are *The New Zealand Dreadnought* by R.L. Christie of Gore, *The Old Flag* by L.D. Cox, and *The Flower of the Bush* by David S. Sharp.

Complementing the Music Collection are many archival sources, including an extensive collection of Anthony Ritchie's music scores; scores of Raphael Squarise and Anthony Watson; papers of the noted Ellwood family; those of Walter J. Sinton, general manager of Begg's head office in Dunedin; and local music teacher, Yetti Bell. Organisational records held include the New Edinburgh Folk Club, New Zealand School Music Association, and the Institute of Registered Music Teachers of New Zealand, Otago Branch. Within the Pictorial Collection are many promotional posters of New Zealand musicians and groups, as well as photographs.

One of the earliest pieces of New Zealand-related sheet music, 'Whalers of the Deep, Deep Sea!', was advertised in the *Australian and New Zealand Gazette* as a 'new song' in September 1857. The words were written by Mrs St. George, who also wrote the words to a 'Gold Diggers' Song', and the music is attributed to 'Te Heu Heu'. This may refer to Te Heuheu Tukino, third upoko ariki of Tuwharetoa, but the name is probably a pseudonym.

The song cheerfully and nostalgically narrates the whaler's life to a melody reminiscent of a sea shanty. The second verse reads:

> Tho' coarse our fare,
> Sunburnt our cheek,
> No terrors can our Souls unman
> No lesser prey we deign to seek
> Our prey is the Leviathan!
> Neither for watch, nor toil care we,
> The Whalers of the deep, deep Sea

The song was published in London by Z.T. Purday and printed there by S. Rothenthal. The cover features a striking portrait of an unidentified Māori woman with a fantastical background of waka, whales and rocky outcrops. The original was probably painted by Joseph Jenner Merrett, an artist active in Auckland from the 1840s. Very few copies of this music are known to have survived. DM

THE WHALERS OF THE DEEP DEEP SEA.

COMPOSED BY TE HEU HEU. ARRANGED FOR THE PIANOFORTE BY W. GRANDHAM. London

Whalers of the Deep, Deep Sea! Words by Mrs St. George, Music by Te Heu Heu (arr. W. Grandham). Sheet music. London: Z.T. Purday, 1857. Donated by Guy Morrell, c. 1968.

On 1 July 1876 the Dunedin *Saturday Advertiser,* edited by Thomas Bracken who was keen to foster a national spirit, announced a competition with a prize of ten guineas for 'the 'best national air' to accompany five verses of Bracken's poem 'God Defend New Zealand'. The winning entry, one of twelve judged by a panel of Melbourne musicians, was from a Lawrence schoolteacher, John J. Woods, under the pseudonym 'Orpheus'. *God Defend New Zealand* had its debut on Christmas night 1876 in the Queen's Theatre, Dunedin. Performed by the Lydia Howard Troupe, accompanied by the Artillery Band, it found immediate favour with the public.

The first printing of the new anthem, in London in 1877, caused an upset in Central Otago as the cover had only Bracken's portrait. The second printing, in Lawrence two years later, had portraits of Bracken and Woods and contained a Māori version.

In 1940 the anthem became New Zealand's national hymn. After a petition of 7750 signatures to Parliament and with the consent of Queen Elizabeth II, *God Save the Queen* and *God Defend New Zealand* were accorded equal status in November 1977. New Zealand is the only country in the world to have two official national anthems.

LT/PM

National Anthem, God Defend New Zealand. Words by Thomas Bracken, Composed by John J. Woods. London: Hopwood & Crew, 1877. Sheet music. Donated by C.S. White, 1967.

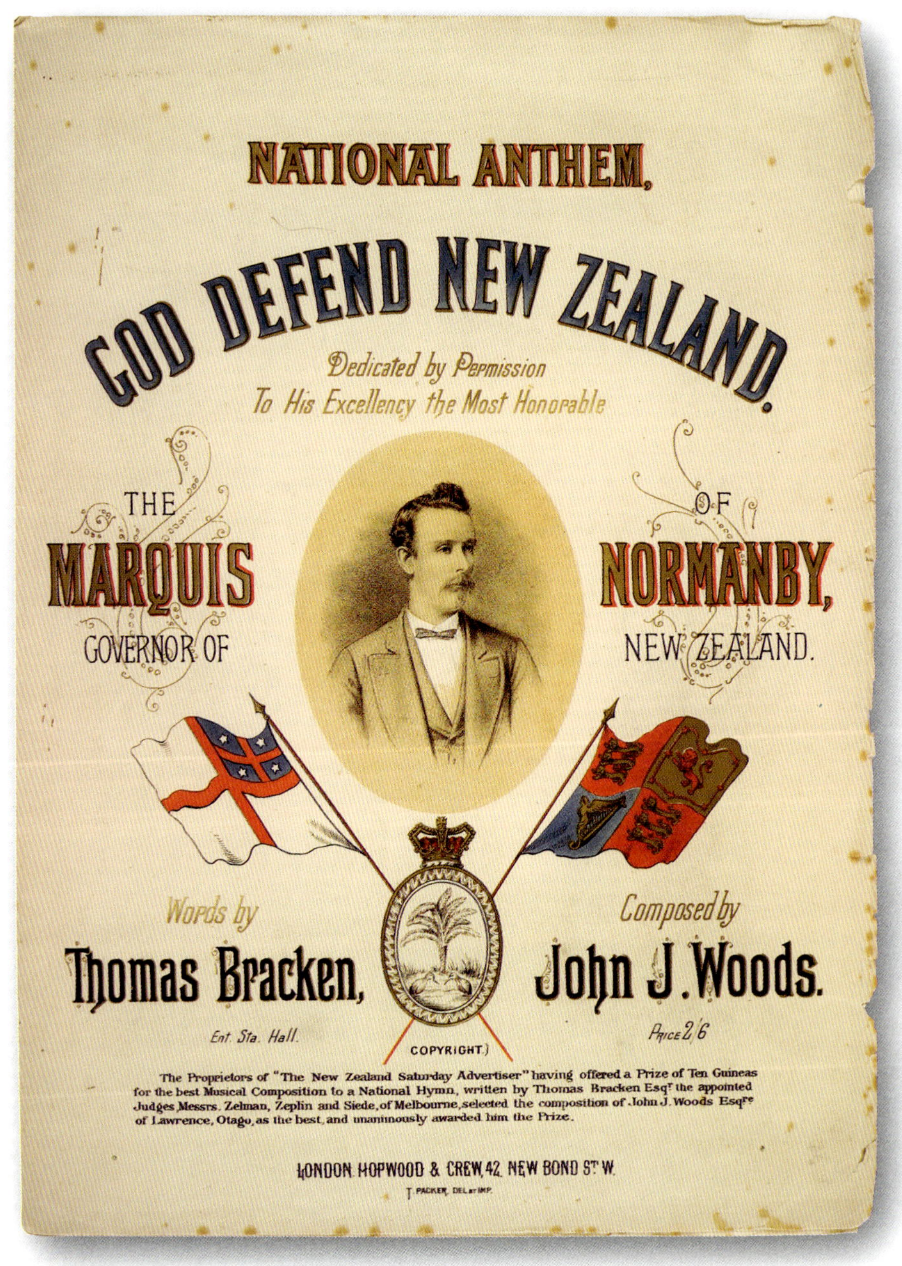

An alternative national anthem • 1885

The maiden 'Zealandia' was very familiar to New Zealanders of the late-nineteenth and early twentieth centuries. Akin to Great Britain's Britannia and America's Columbia, her name and image personified New Zealand in poetry, political cartoons, music, and even household goods. The version depicted on the cover of R.P. Crosbie's song, 'All Hail! Zealandia', emphasised the colony's youth, vigour, and agricultural wealth (which apparently extended to the production of pineapples!). She carries the flag associated from 1834 with the United Tribes of New Zealand but which later gained a wider association.

Styled as a national anthem, the first verse of the song proclaims:

All hail! All hail Zealandia
Queen of Southern Isles
On whose bright destiny
Benignant Nature smiles
Louder than cannons' roar
Echoes from shore to shore
All hail! Zealandia
Zealandia, all hail!

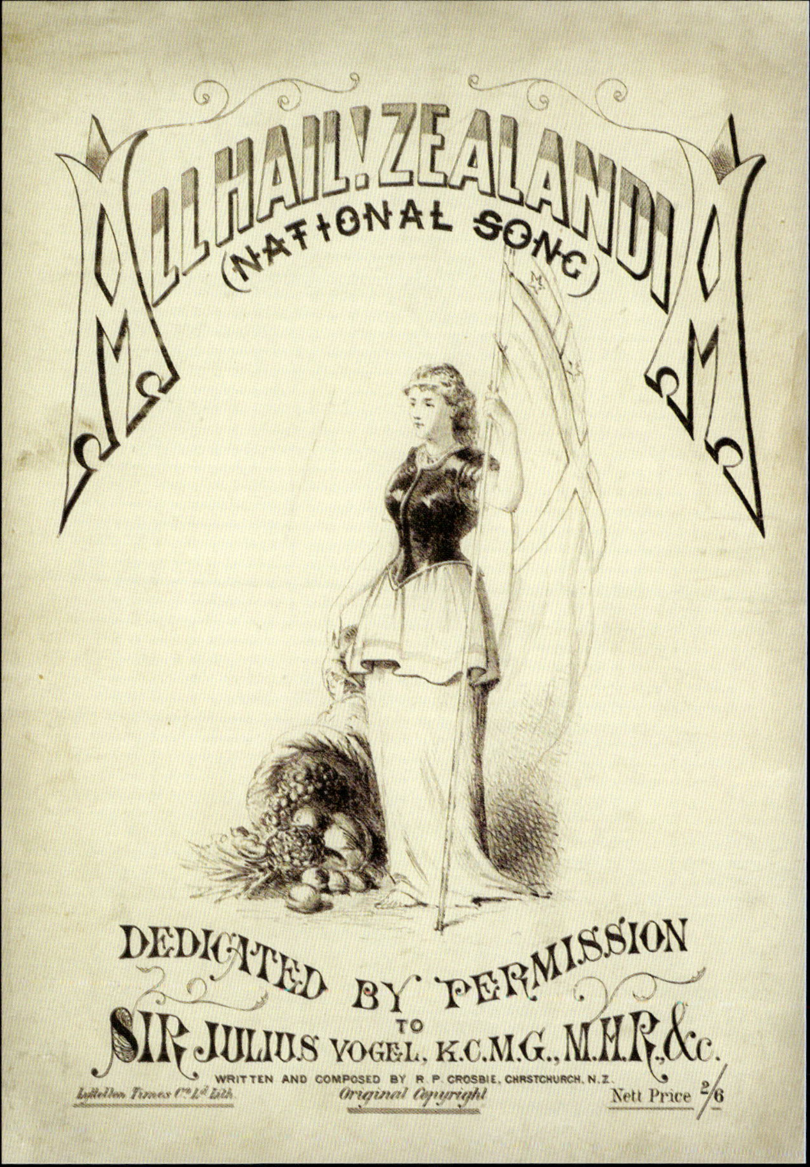

Both words and music were written by Christchurch resident Robert Peel Crosbie, with some assistance from Francis Hopkins Valpy with the text. The first performance took place at Lyttelton, probably in 1871 or 1872, several years before the composition of 'God Defend New Zealand'. The sheet music was eventually published in 1885 with a dedication to former premier Sir Julius Vogel. By this time an alternative setting by Dunedin music teacher Frederick Leech had also been published. DM

All Hail! Zealandia. Words and music by R.P. Crosbie. Sheet music. Christchurch: Lyttelton Times, 1885. Donated by David Murray, 2006.

The 'Tarakoi Waltz' is the earliest known composition of James Henry Brown (1875–1947), an eccentric Dunedin-born composer better known by the pseudonyms Adrian Hope and Raymond Hope. His later compositions included the highly popular 'Silver Fern' and 'Golden Shadows' waltzes, which ran to multiple editions.

'Tarakoi Waltz' was dedicated to the Dunedin Amateur Boating Club, a rowing club established in 1891. With the boat 'Tarakoi' the club won three first prizes and a second prize at the Otago Rowing Association's annual regatta at Port Chalmers on 10 March 1894. Several weeks later, the club hosted a regatta at Lake Waihola. The following month, a positive review of the sheet music appeared in *The Triad*, describing the waltz as 'bright and tuneful'.

Such music was typically produced in very small quantities and the sheet held by the Hocken Collections may be the only copy extant. It is a remarkable example of an entirely local music publication. The music was published by the Dresden Piano Company, a large Dunedin-based firm of music retailers and instrument manufacturers with branches throughout the country. The beautifully elaborate printing work was carried out by J. Wilkie & Co., also of Dunedin. DM

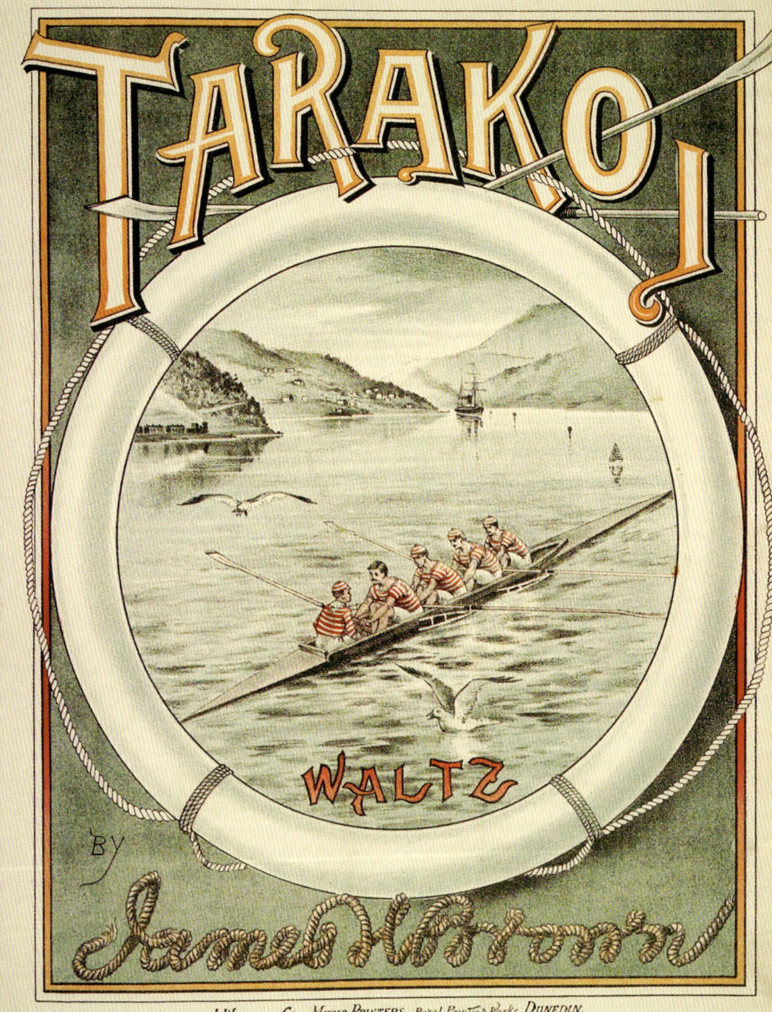

Tarakoi Waltz. Music by James Henry Brown. Sheet music. Dunedin: Dresden Pianoforte Manufacturing & Agency Co., 1894. Donated by Fred Strachan, 2001.

First commercially recorded New Zealander • 1905

The first New Zealander to be recorded commercially on disc appears to have been Wellington-born John Prouse (1856–1930), a noted oratorio and concert baritone in New Zealand and Britain, who had trained at the Guildhall and under Sir Charles Santley. Prouse, when on a visit to Britain in 1905, made a series of twelve test pressings with the Gramophone and Typewriter Company of London (precursor of His Master's Voice). Only half of these were released and very few discs are known to have survived. This is one of 'The Maiden of Morven', an old Scottish song arranged by Malcolm Lawson. Other songs Prouse recorded about the same time included 'Queen of Connemara', Tchaikovsky's 'Pilgrim's Song', and 'Heart of Oak' by Bryce.

The shellac disc is recorded on one side only. The 'Recording Angel' motif of the Gramophone Co. is shown on the label and on the reverse is stated 'Reproduced in Hanover'. The flat recording disc had been invented in 1887 by Emile Berliner in the United States. Ten years later Europe's first pressing plant was established at Hanover, the Berliner family's home town in Germany. By the end of the nineteenth century the plant was making 2400 discs daily for the Gramophone Company, an arrangement which continued until the First World War. SRS

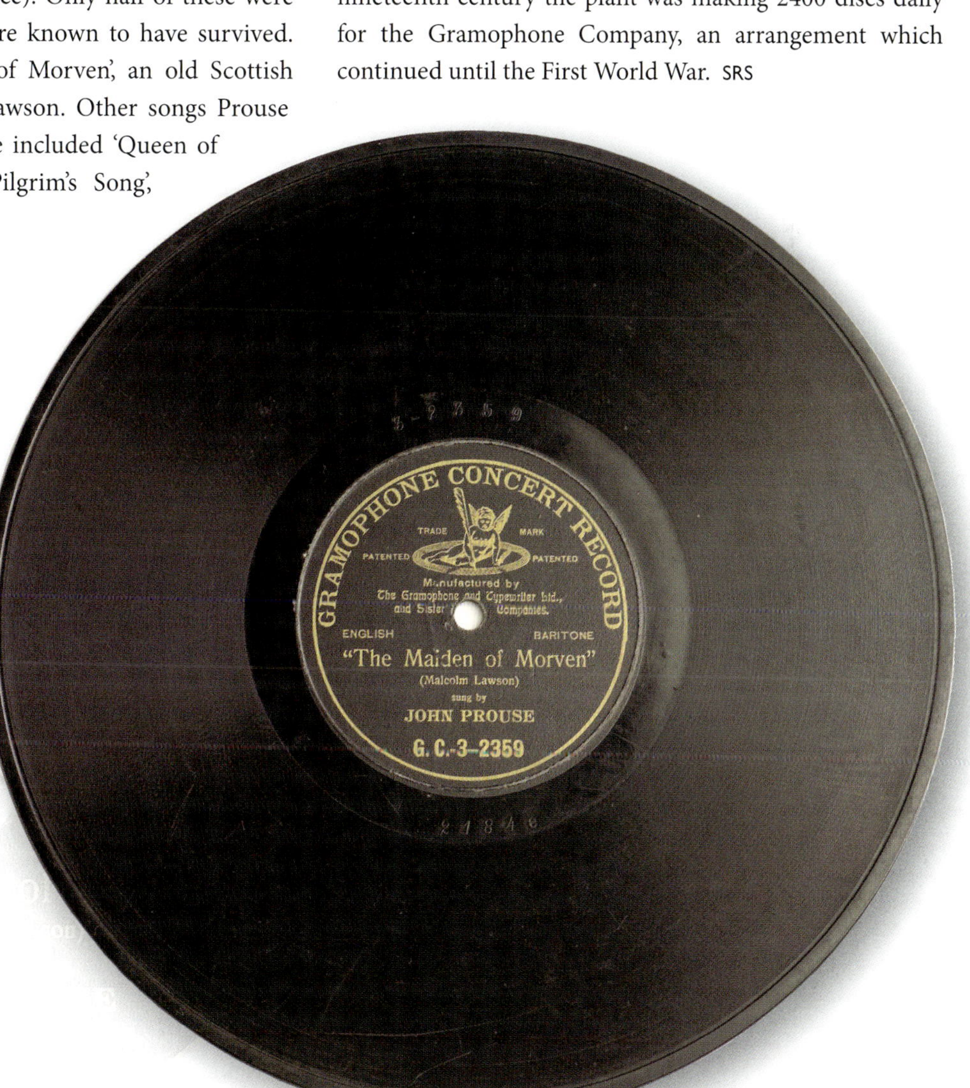

John Prouse (English baritone). *The Maiden of Morven*. Arranged by Malcolm Lawson. Sound recording. 10" 78 rpm. 3-2359. London: Gramophone and Typewriter Company, 1905. Donated by the Rev. P.M. Spencer, 1989.

A patriotic march • 1916

Patriotic marches and songs were published in abundance during the First World War, both in New Zealand and overseas. 'March of the Anzacs' by Alexander F. Lithgow was published by Carl Fischer of New York as both a full brass band arrangement and as the piano solo pictured here. The piece was written in March 1916, less than one year after the Gallipoli landings of April the previous year. The lithographed sheet music cover is a rare and striking example of an early Anzac-related publication. It pictures the landing of troops and supplies at Kabatepe, although the landing in fact took place more than a mile further north, at Ari Burnu: a mistake commonly made at the time, as the original intention had been to land at Kabatepe.

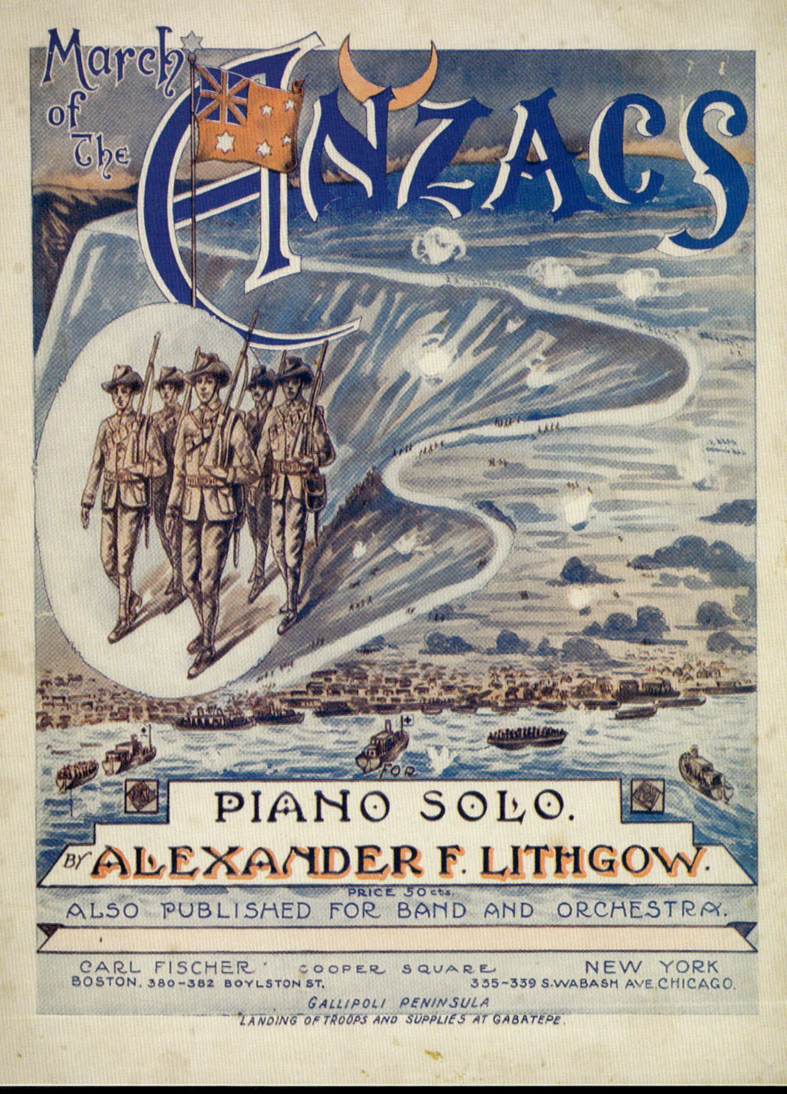

March of the Anzacs. By Alexander F. Lithgow. Sheet music. New York: Carl Fischer, 1916. Purchased, 1991.

Alex Lithgow (1870–1929) was one of the great march composers of the early twentieth century. Born in Scotland, he lived in Invercargill, New Zealand, from the ages of six to twenty-three before moving to Tasmania. His most famous march, 'Invercargill', was fondly dedicated to his former home and is still played regularly by military bands in the United States and

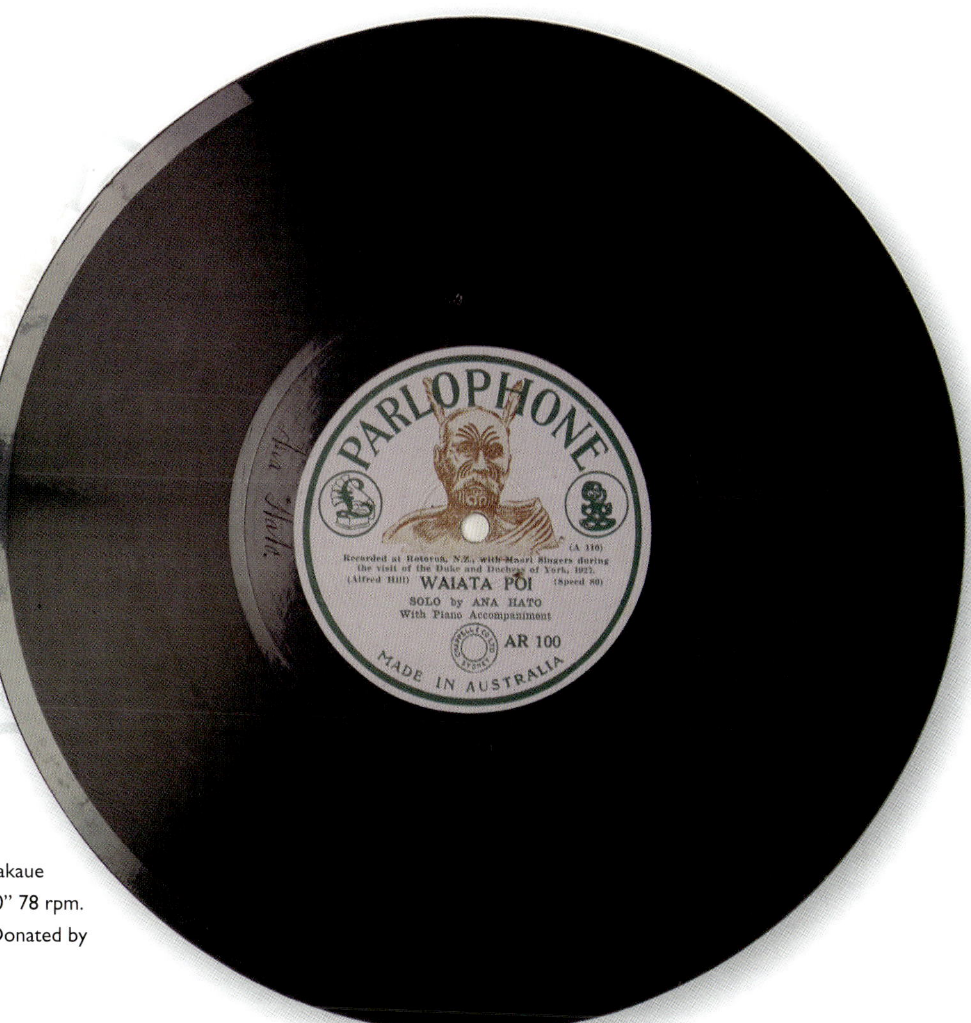

Pioneer Māori recording artist • 1927

Waiata Poi, Te Taniwha and *Haka*.
By Ana Matawhaura Hato (Ngati Whakaue and Tuhourangi). Sound recording. 10" 78 rpm. (AR100) Sydney: Parlophone, 1927. Donated by Rev. P.M. Spencer, 1989.

Ana Hato (c. 1906–53) and her cousin Deane Waretini were amongst New Zealand's first commercial recording artists and possibly the first to be recorded in this country.

Born in Ngāpuna, Rotorua, Ana grew up at the Whakarewarewa pā, where the omnipresence of tourists helped to make performance an integral part of her early life. While she had little formal training and could not read music, Ana's matchless voice – described by her niece Bubbles Mihinui as having a *hotu* in it as in old Māori waiata – and immaculate pitch, saw her acclaimed as *the* voice in Rotorua by the mid-1920s. In 1927, Ana and Deane were invited to perform at Ohinemutu before the Duke and Duchess of York. Parlophone Australia made eight mono acoustic recordings of Ana at this concert of which this disc is one. The 10" shellac disc is engraved with her signature on the lead-out.

The A-side of this recording, 'Waiata Poi', is a good example of Ana's recorded songs setting lyrics in te reo Māori to Pākeha melodies. Composed, or partially composed, by Alfred Hill in c. 1905 after many sessions with kuia and koroua in the painter Goldie's Auckland studio, it became immensely popular. It was adopted as standard repertoire by Māori concert parties and the sheet music was published in some twenty-six editions. AR

The boy soprano • 1932

Brahms: Lullaby / Schubert: Hark, Hark, the Lark. Sung by Lex Macdonald with Gil Dech at the piano. Sound recording. 10" 78 rpm. Sydney: Columbia/Regal, 1932. Donated by G.N. Jeffrey, 1978.

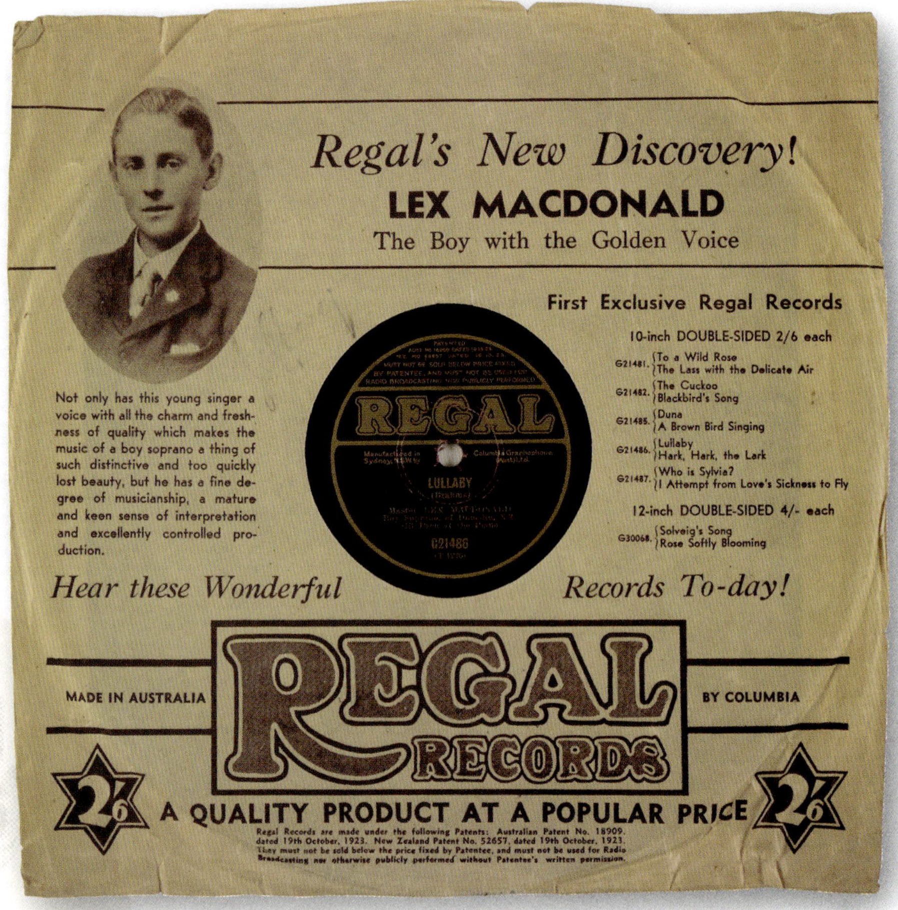

The boy soprano Lex Macdonald (b. 1917) was one of the most popular New Zealand singers of the 1930s. A pupil of the celebrated voice teacher Ernest Drake, Macdonald first came to notice at concerts in his home town of Dunedin between 1930 and 1931 and favourable comparisons were soon made with Ernest Lough, the 'Westminster Wonder Boy' who had recorded HMV's biggest-selling record of 1927.

Macdonald reached the peak of his popularity in August 1932, when over 3000 people gathered to hear him in the Dunedin Town Hall. The concert preceded a trip to Sydney, where he was paid a fee of more than 300 guineas (an Australian record at the time) for a broadcast performance on the 2FC radio station. While in Sydney he recorded six discs for Columbia Records, which were issued on their Regal label. The album pictured here features Brahms' 'Lullaby' and Schubert's 'Hark, Hark, the Lark', with piano accompaniments performed by Gil Dech (1897–1974), who later became a successful broadcaster and recording artist in New Zealand. More than 100,000 of Macdonald's records were sold. A successful tour of New Zealand followed, but within six months his voice began to break, and his retirement was announced in February 1933. DM

To Aid New Zealand Artists • 1949

New Zealand's first record 'wholly processed in New Zealand', *Blue Smoke/Kohu Auwahi*, appeared in 1949 under the TANZA label (To Aid New Zealand Artists). The song was composed by Dannevirke-born Ruru Karaitiana (1909–70), of Rangitāne and Ngāti Kahungunu descent, during World War II. The vocalist was Pixie Williams, who had previously sung at local dances around Wairoa.

Karaitiana had taught himself the trombone, ukulele and guitar. He also played the piano and, before leaving for the Middle East with the 28th Māori Battalion, he had weekly engagements performing at cabarets in Wellington.

Carolina Moon, a dance band favourite, gave him the structure of *Blue Smoke*.

Seeking to recreate the emotions of women left behind as troop trains carrying soldiers chuffed their way out of small town stations, the first verse (in English) is sung by male voices and is followed by a verse in Māori, sung by female voices.

Karaitiana's real inspiration for writing *Blue Smoke*, however, was watching how quickly smoke disappeared. As he later related, 'We were on the troopship *Aquitania* in 1940 off the coast of Africa when a friend drew my attention to some passing smoke. He put the song in my lap'. LT

Ruru Karaitiana Quintette. *Blue Smoke* and *Senorita*. Sound recording. 10" 78 rpm. Wellington: TANZA, 1949. Purchased, 1977.

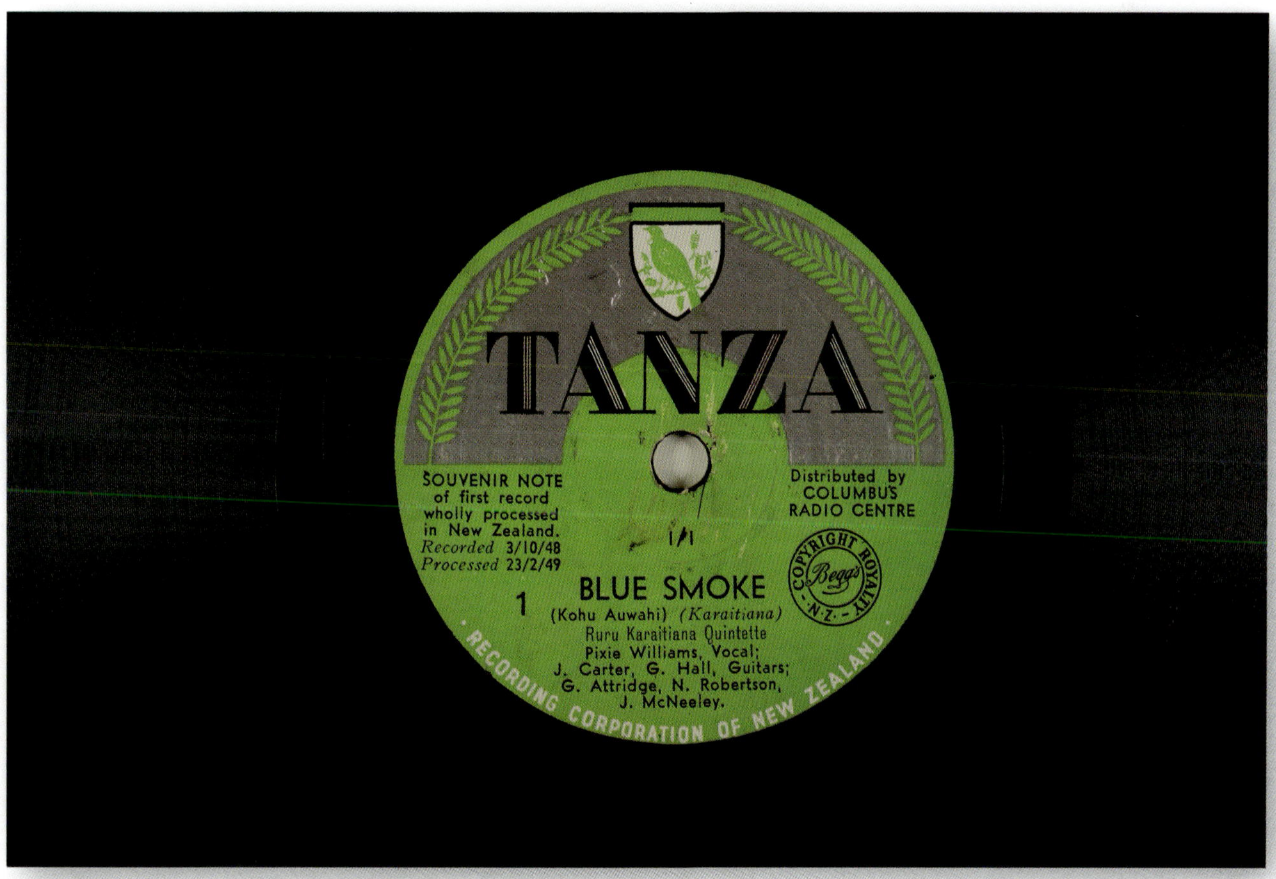

Country music pioneers • 1949

In March 1949 Cole Wilson, Colin McCrorie, Nola Hewitt and Bill Ditchfield came together to form 'Cole Wilson and the Tumbleweeds', a country music band at a time when there were few such performers. Based in Dunedin, the Tumbleweeds took New Zealand by storm. Three months later they were performing regularly on local radio, and in September 1949 had their first recording session in Wellington for TANZA Records, producing six songs on three 78s. One was 'Maple on the Hill / Will You Be Lonesome Too'. Only the tenth album produced by TANZA, it sold over 80,000 copies in New Zealand, making 'Maple on the Hill', until recently, the country's highest selling record.

Part of the Tumbleweeds' appeal was the Pacific influence. Cole Wilson had a keen interest in Pacific music and the group per-formed this under the name of the Kalua Islanders, incorporating it into their Tumbleweeds shows.

The band continued to perform and record for several decades. It won many awards and its pioneering contribution to New Zealand country music has been widely applauded. In 1997 the three remaining band members made concrete imprints to adorn the Hands of Fame statue at Gore. PM

Cole Wilson and the Tumbleweeds. *Maple on the Hill* and *Will You Be Lonesome Too*. Sound recording. 10" 78 rpm. Wellington: TANZA, 1949. Purchased, 1977.

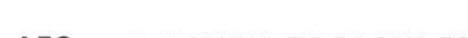

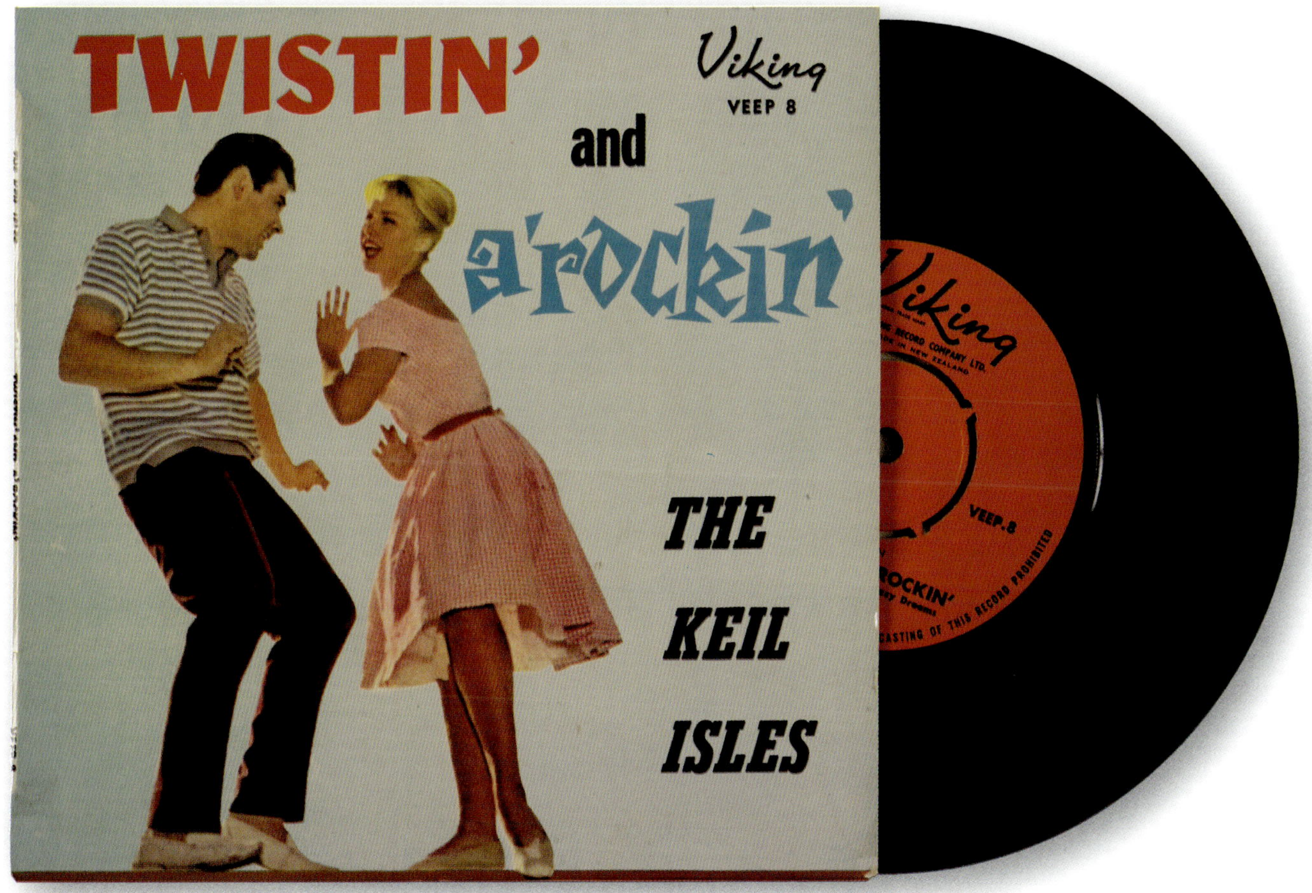

Rock and Roll • 1960

The Keil Isles. *Twistin' and a'Rockin'*. Sound recording. EP 7" 45 rpm. Wellington: Viking, 1960. Purchased, 1980.

Founder of this fifties and sixties covers band was the enterprising Olaf Keil, who emigrated from Samoa to New Zealand in 1952. He taught his brother Herma to play guitar, and together with siblings, Klaus on drums and Rudolph on bass, they formed the first incarnation of The Keil Isles in 1956, playing at their local Mormon church in Auckland. Recruiting pianist Heke Kewene to fill out their sound, they approached the owner of the TANZA record label and released their first single at the end of 1958.

Olaf was a brilliant guitarist who could duplicate the guitar solos he heard on the American records that were then dominating the world market. Sisters Eliza and occasionally Helga sang with the group, but Freddie Keil was the main vocalist.

Through the Mormon Church's American connections The Keil Isles were able to import equipment and stage outfits that added to their dynamic visual act. Every Saturday night, they played at the Jive Centre in Auckland and they recorded twenty-six records there for Viking.

Olaf departed for the United States in 1962 at the urging of a Mormon missionary, but the group continued, becoming the resident band on the New Zealand television show 'C'mon'. LT

Progressive rock • 1970

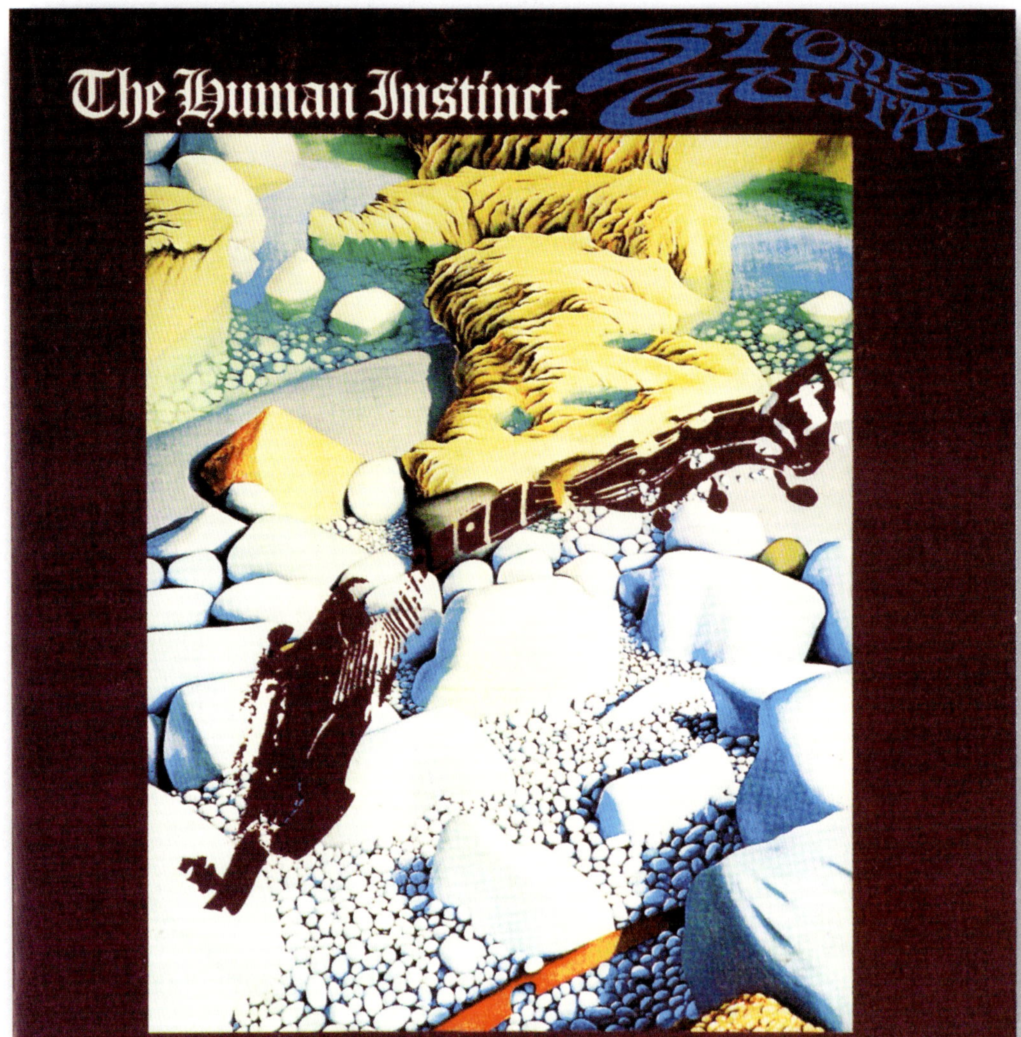

The Human Instinct. *Stoned Guitar*. Sound recording. LP stereo 12" 33 rpm. Auckland: AIR (Allied International Records), 1970. Purchased, 1978.

The Human Instinct's definitive album kicked off the Seventies with a mixture of bluesy hard rock like the classic single 'Black Sally' to the improvised psychedelic freak-out of the title-track 'Stoned Guitar.' *Stoned Guitar* was recorded at Stebbing's studio in Auckland in 1970, the band's follow-up to *Burning Up Years*. The final track 'Railway and Gun' was recorded live at the Bo-Peep Club in Durham Lane, where The Human Instinct had been resident band since the end of 1968.

Initially called The Four Fours, a successful beat group from Tauranga, the band renamed themselves The Human Instinct during a spell in the United Kingdom after experiencing the burgeoning British psychedelic scene. After their first British tour, original guitarist Bill Ward left the band, to be replaced by the great Billy Te Kahika (aka Billy TK). Larry Waide replaced Peter Barton on bass and it is this lineup that joined drummer/vocalist and band-leader, Maurice Greer, to record *Stoned Guitar*.

The album features the iconic cover art of Michael Smither, an electric guitar melting over the super-realist stones of Smither's composition, 'Two Rock Pools', from 1968. MD

Break-out rock band • 1975

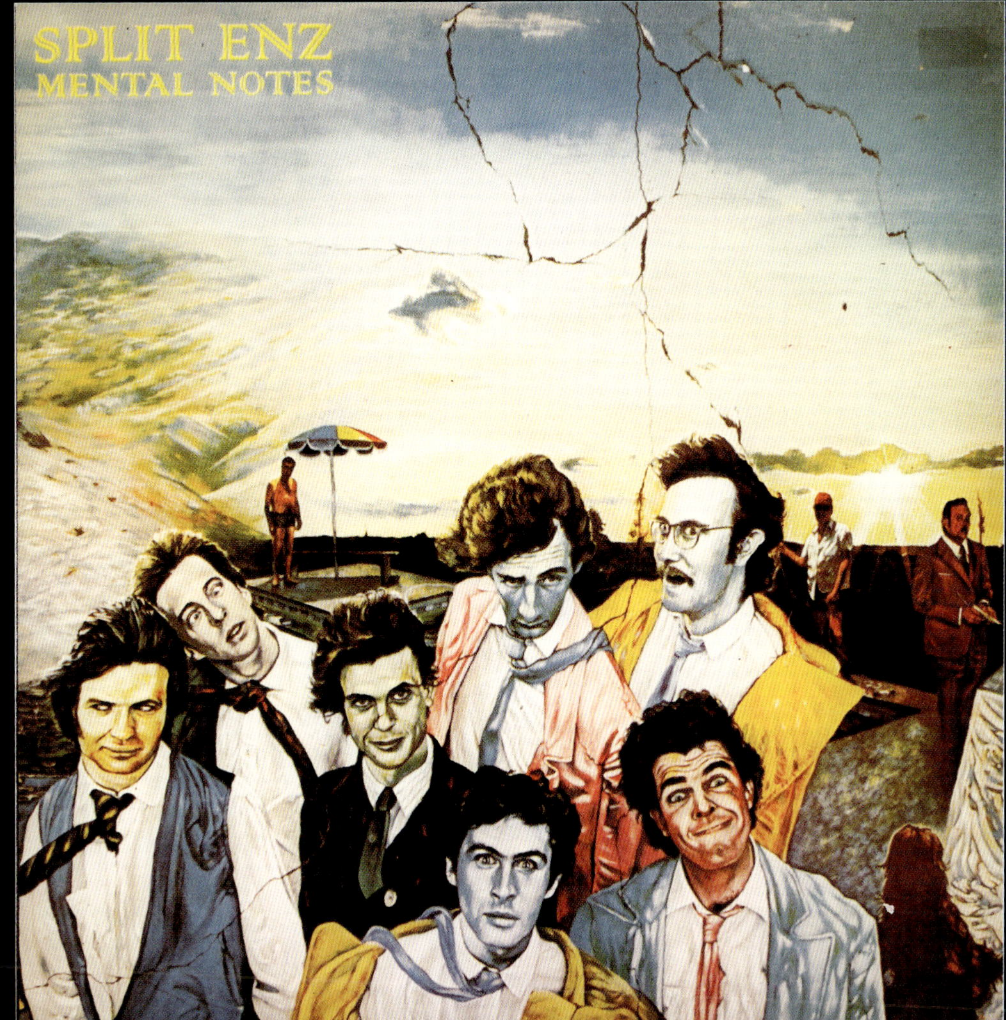

Split Enz. *Mental Notes.* Sound recording. LP 12" 33 rpm. Auckland: White Cloud Records, 1975. Purchased, 1977.

Split Enz (earlier known as Split Ends) has so far been the most significant rock New Zealand band of all time. Formed in 1972 by Tim Finn and Phil Judd it was the first New Zealand group to achieve international success, becoming well known for the eclectic, theatrical presentation of its music. After touring extensively in New Zealand the band decided in 1975 to break into the Australian market. Australian audiences proved apathetic to Split Enz's sound, but they intrigued the head of Mushroom Records, who arranged for their first album, *Mental Notes,* to be recorded. Interest in Split Enz further afield was slight, until 'I Got You', from the band's fifth album, *True Colours*, gained international recognition in 1980.

In 1982, the single *Six Months in a Leaky Boat* caused an outcry in the United Kingdom as it was believed to be a veiled attack against the British war in the Falkland Islands (even though it had been recorded months before the onset of hostilities). Despite breaking up in 1984, Split Enz has continued to be influential in New Zealand, with some members of the band becoming leading figures in the New Zealand music industry, amongst them Tim and Neil Finn, Mike Chunn, and Eddie Raynor. PM

Coming of age • 1980s

From the late 1970s, popular New Zealand music blossomed. The advent of new recording technologies – particularly the CD, reductions in taxes, and the introduction of government grants all helped. Local independent recording companies sprang into being, and the number of New Zealand recordings increased markedly. This was well exemplified by the success of the Flying Nun label, founded in Christchurch by Roger Shepherd in 1980. He made possible the Dunedin Sound, as with The Clean, The Chills, and The Verlaines. In the North Island, Ripper and Propeller were influential, as was Mushroom based in Australia. New Zealand music also gained some international acceptance, particularly in Britain and in the United States, where New Zealand bands found favour on the college radio circuit. More New Zealand records began to be sold overseas than at home.

A large number of music posters in the Hocken Collections, of which these are a sample, capture the excitement of that time. SRS

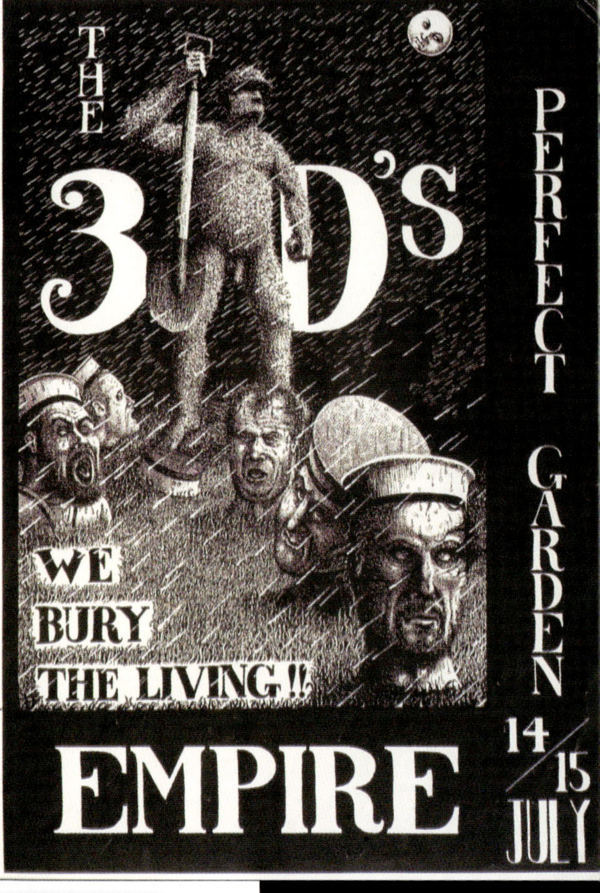

Poster. *The 3D's. Perfect Garden.* 1980s. Donation.

Poster. *The Clean. Great Outdoors Tour* 1984. Donation.

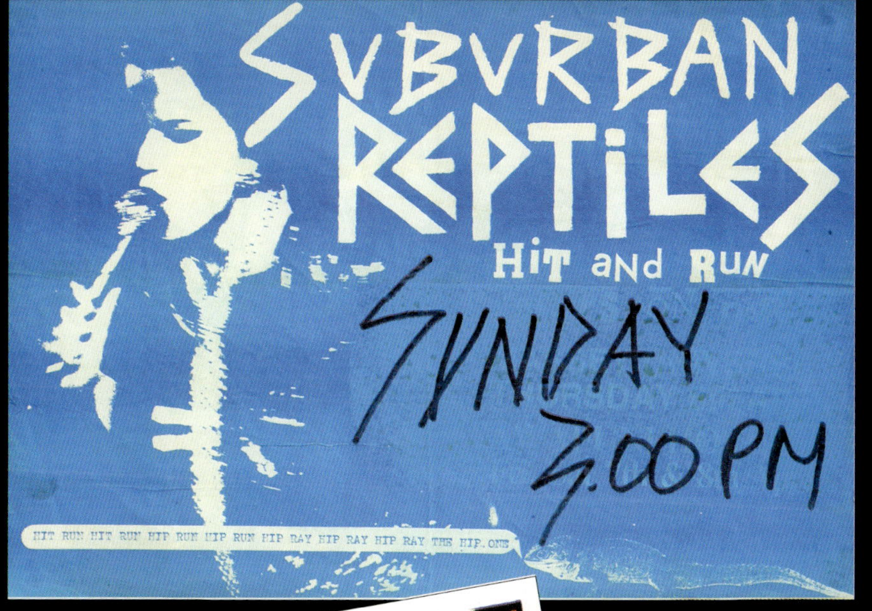

Poster. *Suburban Reptiles. Hit and Run.*
c. 1979. Donation.

Below left:
Poster. *The Kiwi Animal. Wartime.*
c. 1983. Donation.

Below right:
Poster. *The Rip. At the Empire …*
1984. Donation.

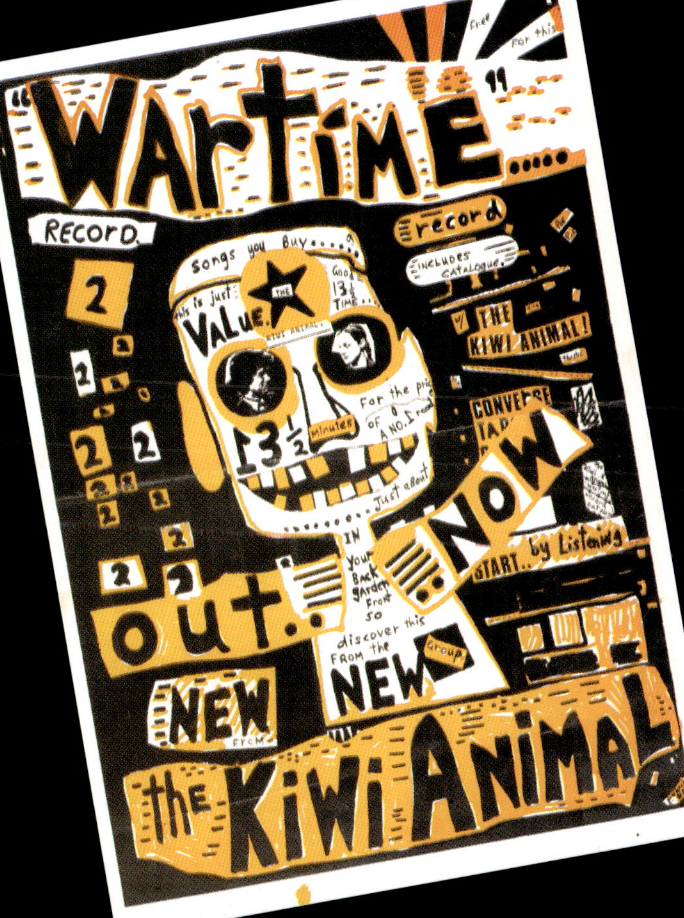

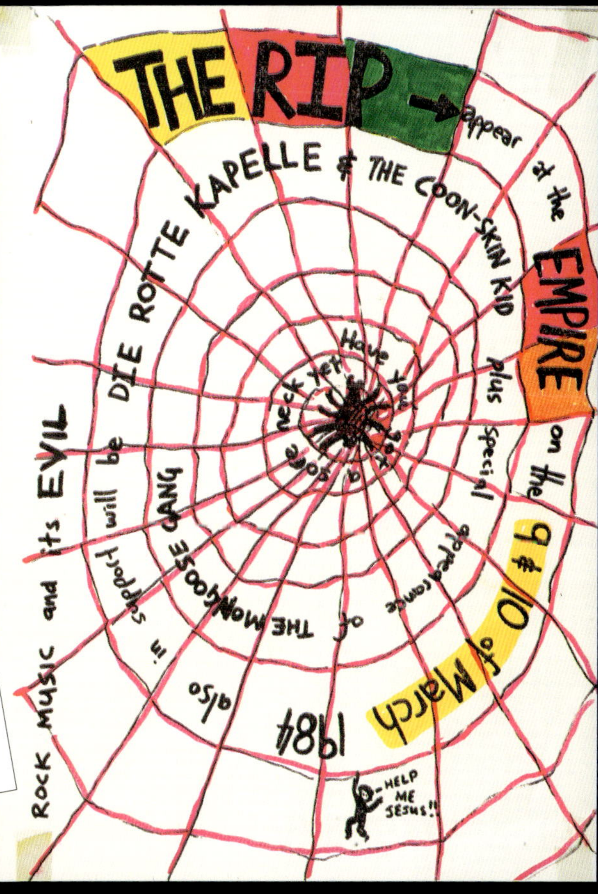

Paintings and Drawings

Linda Tyler

In a letter written for the opening of the library in 1910, Dr Hocken gave his reasons for collecting pictures. Aesthetic merit was not a consideration it seems; he was interested in art's enduring informational value:

> The value of a picture in itself is but little if there is no full description of that to which it refers. With this description, its educational value is vastly increased, and to attain this end I have, as will be noticed, endeavoured to describe the pictures and arrange them so that it will be easy for all, our young folks especially, to secure a good idea of the incidents of early colonisation; and from this basis they will, perhaps, be induced to enter upon a most interesting study for themselves.

Despite a second marriage in 1884 to painter, photographer and Otago Art Society member Elizabeth Mary Buckland (1848–1933), Hocken did not acquire major works by prominent Dunedin painters. William Mathew Hodgkins (1833–98) is represented by a single early watercolour, and his famous daughter Frances does not feature at all in the collection. Tellingly, despite his belief that John Gully (1819–88) was New Zealand's greatest artist, Hocken never acquired his work. His was not to be a collection of art for art's sake based on taste, but a New Zealand history-in-pictures.

To that end, Hocken concentrated his collecting on New Zealand subjects. An essay 'Early Pictorial Illustrations of New Zealand' published in *The New Zealand Educational and Literary Monthly* in June 1884 shows he was governed primarily by an interest in human history. Bessie Hocken's painting of the Takahe, *Notornis mantelli*, from 1898–99 was the only exception – and even that was occasioned by Walter Mantell's rediscovery of the bird.

Hocken made no list of his pictures, and the 1912 catalogue does not include them. Curators have subsequently had to deduce from the affixing of his tiki emblem of ownership that there were 429 in the original collection when the Hocken Library opened in 1910. A quarter were watercolours from the sketchbook bequeathed by William Fox (1812–93). Hocken's humour is evident in the amassing of over fifty topical cartoons, and the documentary nature of his mission is attested by the portraits corresponding to place names.

Amongst the other pictures Hocken acquired, images of Otago, Canterbury and Auckland predominate: Otago features in a total of sixty-six images. Helping her husband, Bessie Hocken drew key plans to some pictures and copied borrowed ones, including some of the forty-five views of Christchurch and Lyttelton. Hocken annotated many of the thirty-six paintings of Auckland subjects to identify landscape features or to give the Māori history of a place. Māori were of particular interest to him, and he corresponded regularly with ethnographers, collecting fifty-six images of Māori subjects ranging from engravings after William Hodges to sixteen works by Joseph Jenner Merrett.

Thirty-six years later, when a catalogue of the pictures was first published (1948), the collection had doubled in size. Hocken endowment funds had assisted with the purchase of sketchbooks by John Alexander Gilfillan (1793–1863), George O'Brien (1821–88), David Con

Hutton (1843–1910), James Crowe Richmond (1822–98) and his daughter Dorothy Kate Richmond (1861–1935). Gifts included the illustrated notebooks of Charles Edward (Mr Explorer) Douglas (1840–1916) and watercolours and lithographs by geological surveyor John Buchanan (1819–98). Journals kept by Colonel E.A. Williams (1824–98) while in command of the Royal Artillery during the mid-1860s directing the Tauranga-Waikato and Taranaki campaigns of the New Zealand Wars were deposited by Dr H.D. Skinner (1886–1978) because of their exquisite depictions of troops and military activity.

The arrival of a Cadbury's truck from Auckland in 1961 changed the historical orientation of the collection irrevocably. Containing 394 modern art works donated by Canadian-born art educator Charlton Edgar (1903–76), this gift would update the Hocken with thirty years worth of modern New Zealand art. It included works such as Rita Angus's oil *At Sea* 1958, which illustrated cubism, and Tony Fomison's *Abstract* 1961, exemplifying expressionism. The Mona Edgar Collection also contained seventy-two of Charlton Edgar's own works, showing regional realism as he taught it at the Dunedin School of Art in the 1930s and his excursions into each of the major twentieth century art movements: cubism, futurism, surrealism, constructivism and expressionism.

Ex-Dunedinite Colin McCahon (1919–87) made the Hocken the major public repository for his work in the 1970s, gifting new paintings and facilitating the bequest of his parents' collection of early works, a total of 99 McCahons in all. Charles Brasch's bequest of 448 paintings and drawings followed in 1973, so that by September 1980 when 'The New Hocken' exhibition opened, there were sufficient masterpieces of the modern period for the collection to have assumed national importance for its twentieth century holdings. Rodney Kennedy's gift of 177 works in 1989 further enhanced this reputation. Sketchbooks and working drawings have also been added since 1967, as the Frances Hodgkins Fellowship has brought the best New Zealand contemporary artists to Otago University. Many of them, including Ralph Hotere (b.1931) and Sarah Munro (b.1970), have donated working drawings recording their year in the university studio.

Donations continued to develop Hocken's historical strengths: the De Beer family donated a major collection of watercolours by John Barr Clark Hoyte (1835–1912), and the Hall Jones family of Invercargill gifted 203 sketches and paintings by surveyor John Turnbull Thomson (1821–84) in 1992. Also in that year, Invercargill's Bruce Godward (1916–92) bequeathed his collection of 1140 eighteenth and nineteenth-century prints. In 2001, a painting of the *SS Dunedin* which carried the first shipment of frozen meat from Port Chalmers to London was bought at auction with assistance from the Community Trust of Otago.

Now totalling over 14,000, works of the Hocken Pictures Collection are frequently exhibited, loaned, and reproduced; and it continues to fulfil the founder's vision that visitors 'will, perhaps, be induced to enter upon a most interesting study for themselves'.

For an expedition to the South Land by the Dutch East India Company in 1642, Abel Tasman was made commander of the flagship, the *Heemskerck*, while Isaac Gilsemans, a skilled draughtsman, commanded the *Zeehaan*. Gilsemans (c. 1606–c. 1646) was instructed to 'perfectly chart and describe all lands, islands, promontories, bights, inlets, bays etc. that you encounter or pass', and he curved his long views, exaggerating the spherical appearance of earth and sea, to retain the true proportional distances between major landmarks. His work was subsequently adapted by eighteenth-century English and French engravers, such as Joseph Collyer (1748–1827), who overlaid their own stylistic conventions, but the accuracy of Gilsemans' original record endured.

After four months at sea, on 18 December 1642, Tasman came around into Taitapu – now Golden Bay. Gilsemans recorded the fateful encounter with Ngati Tumatakokiri, who paddled out in four waka, blowing a conch shell to warn the Europeans off. A 'canoe of rogues' (as Tasman described them) used their taiaha to kill three of the *Zeehaan*'s crew and mortally injure a fourth man. Tasman had been instructed by the expedition's sponsors to 'take due care that no injury be done them in their houses, gardens, vessels, or their property, their wives, etc.', so after firing warning shots, they continued on their way. LT

Joseph Collyer, after Isaac Gilsemans. *View of Murderers Bay on New Zealand in 15 fthm Water, 1770* and *View of Abel Tasman's Bay on New Zealand in 33 fthm Water, 1770*. From Alexander Dalrymple, *An Account of the Discoveries made in the South Pacifick Ocean, previous to 1764*. Part I. .... London: 1767 [1769], p. 144. Hand coloured engraving on paper. 182 x 358 mm. Purchased, 1991.

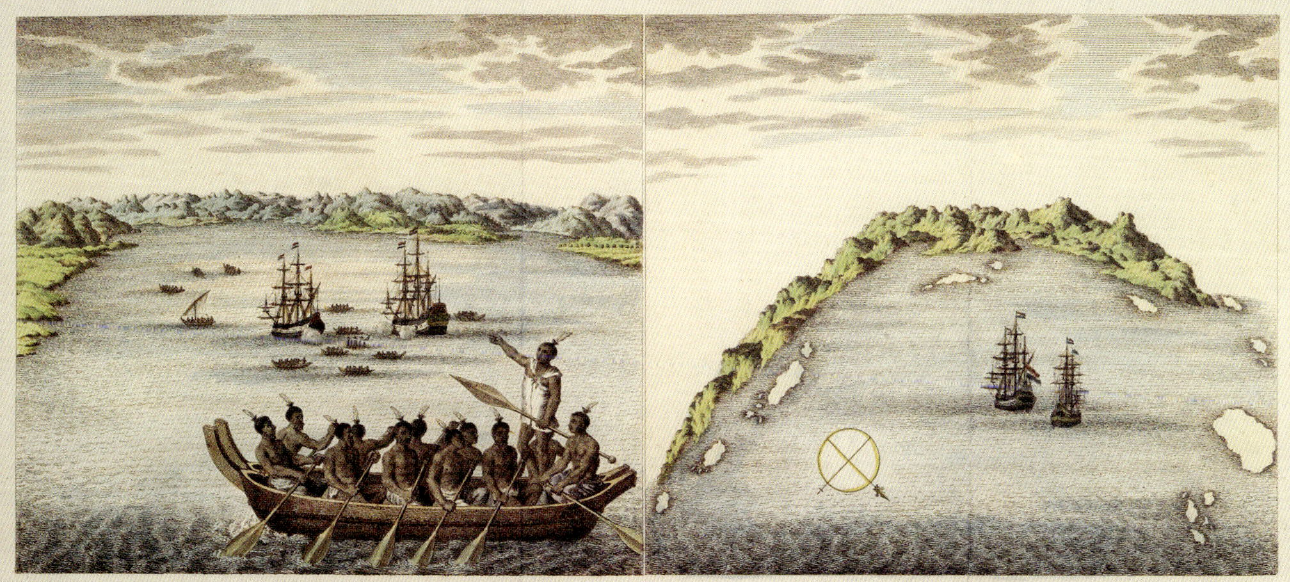

First colour mezzotint • 1776

This print of a tui, drawn from a specimen taken back to England by Captain Cook after his second voyage to New Zealand, was the first ever made using the difficult colour mezzotint process. Only six original copies are known to exist.

Apprenticed to Robert Sayer, a publisher of prints, maps, and charts in Fleet Street from 1770 to 1777, Robert Laurie (1755–1836) was only twenty when he developed a method for colour printing using mezzotint engravings, and was awarded 30 guineas for disclosing how it was done. He demonstrated his process to the Royal Society for the Encouragement of Arts, Manufactures and Commerce, engraving outlines on copper, then applying oil colours with camel-hair stump brushes to a warmed plate, wiping with a coarse gauze cloth, then passing the plate through the press. Technically exacting, his process required the creation of separate plates for each colour, passing the same piece of paper through the press several times to print the colours in exact registration. Called the Poa, or Parson Bird, Laurie's tui was also the first published illustration of a New Zealand bird, appearing in Peter Brown's *New Illustrations of Zoology* in 1776, almost a century before colour lithography opened the way for commercial colour printing. LT

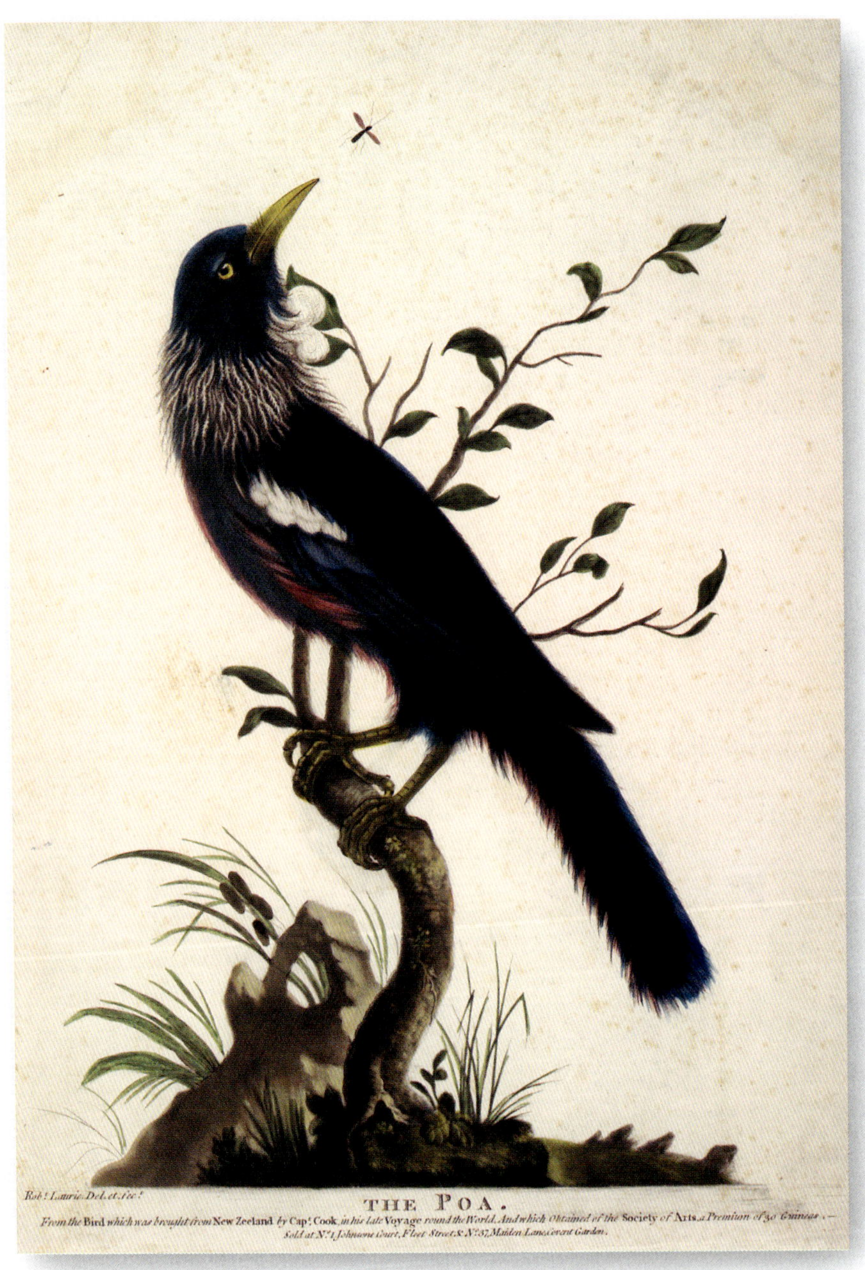

Robert Laurie. *The Poa. From the Bird which was brought from New Zealand by Capt. Cook in his late Voyage round the world. And which Obtained of the Society of Arts, a Premium of 30 Guineas. – Sold at No. 1. Johnsons Court, Fleet Street, & No. 37 Maiden Lane, Covent Garden. Robt. Laurie. Del. et fect.* [1776]. Colour mezzotint, hand finished in colour, on paper. 355 x 250 mm. Purchased, 1916.

Encyclopédie des voyages could just as well have been entitled *Encyclopédie des costumes* since the 432 colour plates – all the author's own work – evidence much imaginative speculation about what the races of the world might wear. Never having seen any of the ethnicities he represented, Grasset de Saint-Sauveur (1757–1810) turned to classical antiquity to create a colourful array of noble savages and savagesses, with just a hint of Parisian fashion in their clothing. His contemporary readership would not have realised that in eighteenth-century New Zealand this Māori woman's fringed tunic, many-feathered headdress and stylised contrapposto stance would have made her rather conspicuous.

Grasset de Saint-Sauveur was fascinated by other cultures. An accomplished linguist born in Montreal, he trained as a diplomat and served first in Hungary and then Cairo. As an etcher, drawer and writer, Grasset de Saint-Sauveur was a prolific polygraph, in keeping with the encyclopedic spirit of the eighteenth century: he wrote exotic novels as well as documentary works on various subjects. One of his biographers diminished his artistic achievement, saying he was 'a draughtsman without genius but a good example of the taste of his time', neglecting to observe his unfettered use of brilliant colours. LT

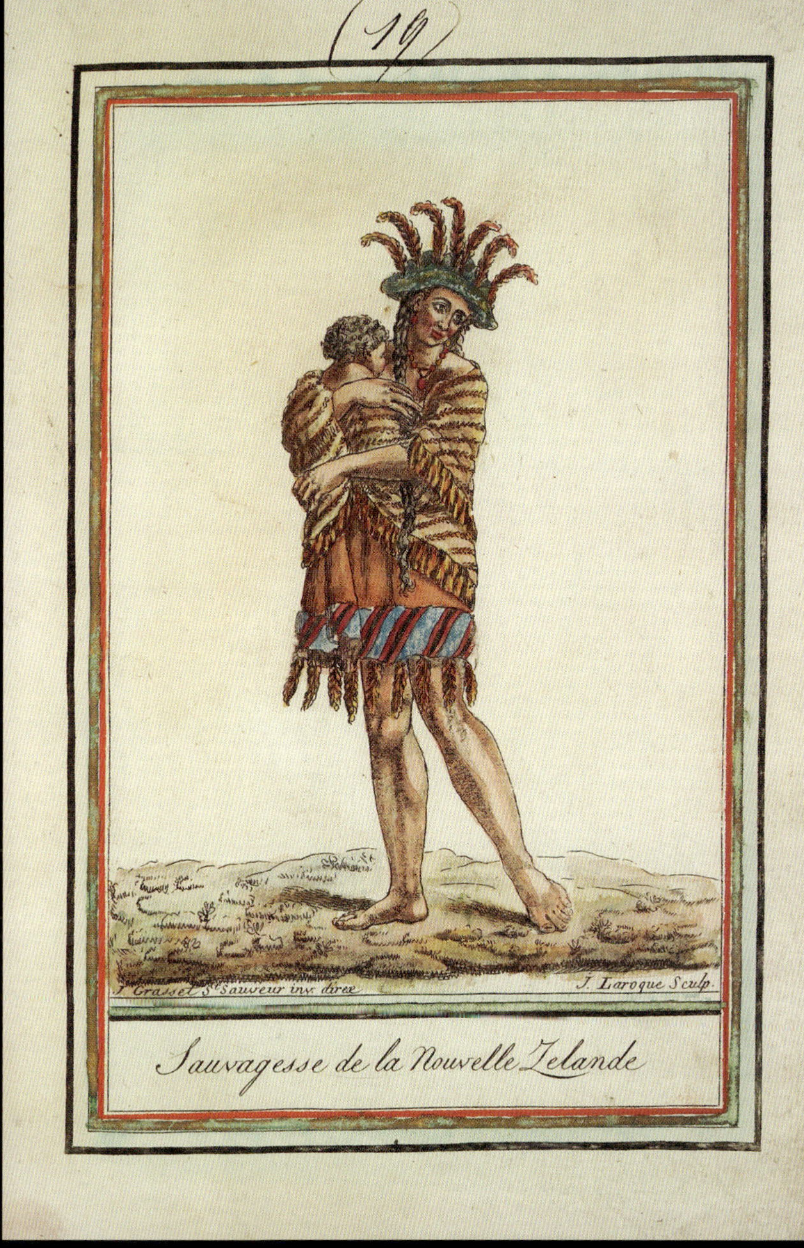

Jacques Grasset de Saint-Sauveur. *Sauvagesse de la Nouvelle Zelande*. 1796. From *Encyclopédie des voyages [...]*. Paris: Deroy: 1795–6. 5 vol. Etching, aquatint and watercolour on paper. 104 x 122 mm. Purchased, 1965.

Portrait of a Scottish Poet • 1829

The settlers who came to nineteenth-century New Zealand brought with them or had sent many family heirlooms, their own treasures, to help remember the best of what they had left behind. The subject of this full-face portrait is James Hogg (1770–1835), later known as the Ettrick Shepherd. Of humble rural origins, Hogg is commonly regarded as Scotland's finest pastoral poet after Robert Burns, rivalling in his time the reputations of Scott and Byron. He published his first book of verse, *Scottish Pastorals,* in Edinburgh in 1801. Later Hogg turned to novel-writing with considerable success, and had a long and profitable association with *Blackwood's Edinburgh Magazine*. Not always fully appreciated, Hogg is now seen as having 'made a distinctive Scottish contribution to European romanticism'.

Painted about 1829, this fine James Scott oil portrays a soberly attired poet complete with checked plaid over the left shoulder as worn by a Lowland shepherd. It closely resembles another oil, that by Sir John Watson-Gordon now in the Scottish National Portrait Gallery. Hogg married Margaret Phillips in 1820. A daughter, Harriet, emigrated with her husband, Robert Gilkison, to New Zealand in 1879. Presumably a brother later sent the portrait to her son, also Robert, as the label on the reverse reads: 'This portrait of my father is now the property of my nephew, Robert Gilkison of Clyde, Otago, New Zealand, 15th August 1895'. SRS

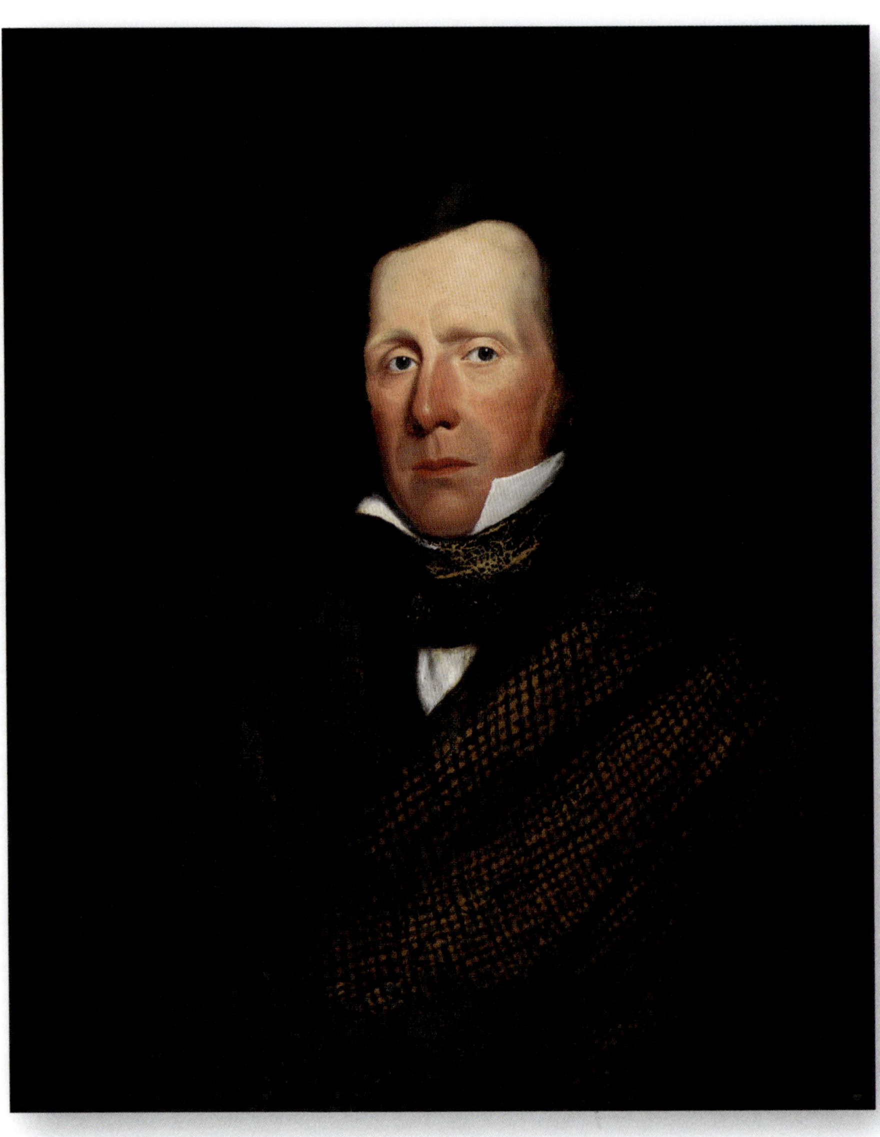

James Scott. *The Ettrick Shepherd (James Hogg).* c. 1829. Oil on canvas. 760 x 640 mm. Donated by Mrs Scott Gilkison, 1978.

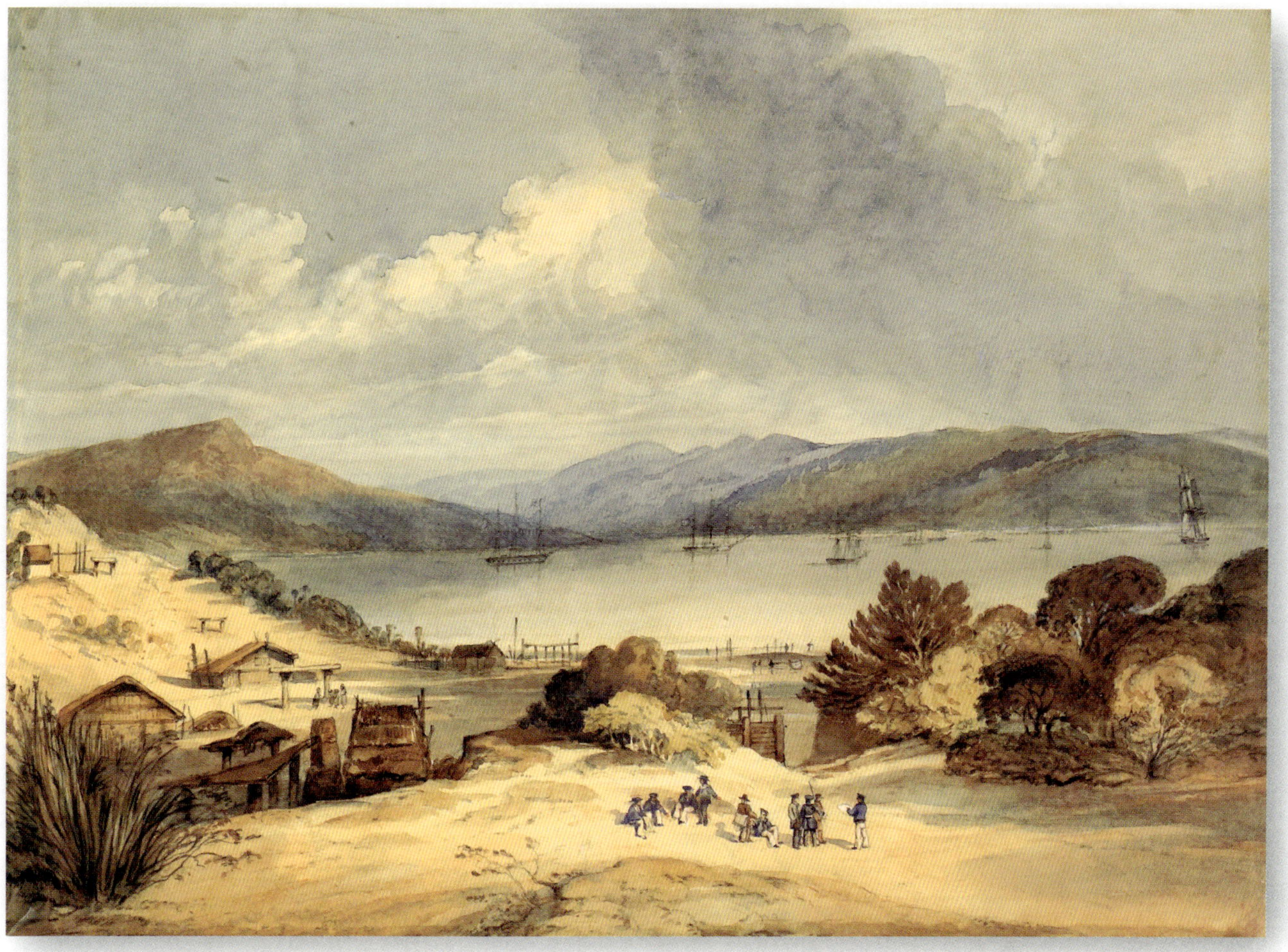

Port Otago • 1840

Louis Le Breton. *Port Otago*. 1840. Watercolour and charcoal on paper. 343 x 479 mm. Donated by James Johnstone, 1925.

Distinctive in their naval uniforms of blue jacket and white trousers, the French sailors centrally grouped to populate this scene have come ashore from Dumont d'Urville's corvettes *Astrolabe* and *Zelée*. These can be seen at anchor in the bay, while another vessel sails in from the right. Le Breton's *Port Otago* is the Weller Brothers onshore whaling station, just inside the Heads, and his view looks up the harbour towards what is later known as Mount Cargill, with Mount Charles on the left. Simple structures with thatched roofs and several storage platforms are visible on the left.

As his name suggests, Louis Le Breton (1818–66) was from Brittany and had studied at the Naval Medical School in Brest in 1836–7 before departing for the South Pole as surgeon on board the *Astrolabe*. By late March 1840, when Otago Harbour was sighted, Le Breton had replaced the official artist to the expedition, Ernest-Auguste Goupil, who had died at Hobart in the summer.

Although twenty-five of the 174 watercolours Le Breton produced were exhibited on his return to Paris in 1841, nearly all have been lost, making this painting rare both as a view of pre-colonisation Otago and as an example of the artist's lucid watercolour technique. LT

Māori tangi • c. 1843

Having trained as an architect and then as a civil engineer in Bristol, Brees (1809/10–65) designed the London to Birmingham railway line, and published three technical works on railway construction. His three-year appointment as principal surveyor with the New Zealand Company brought him to Wellington in 1842. Journeying to Upper Hutt and over the Rimutaka range the following year with his Māori guide, Te Kaeaea, he estimated the cost of building a road at £300. He painted this tangi while preparing plans for subdivision of southern Wairarapa.

During the 1840s, European diseases caused the deaths of many Māori in the Wairarapa, as elsewhere. Pressure for land was increasing, and Te Korou, a Christian convert, and a Rangitāne and Ngāti Kahungunu leader from Kaikokirikiri, near present day Masterton, travelled around the Wairarapa encouraging Māori to facilitate European settlement. Set at Huangarua near Martinborough, Brees's scene shows the chief in front of a whare in a clearing, addressing those gathered for a tangi.

Brees published his *Pictorial Illustrations of New Zealand* on his return to England in 1847. Its engraved illustrations of North Island scenes had an introduction which described the process of 'redemption and occupation of wasteland' through colonisation. LT

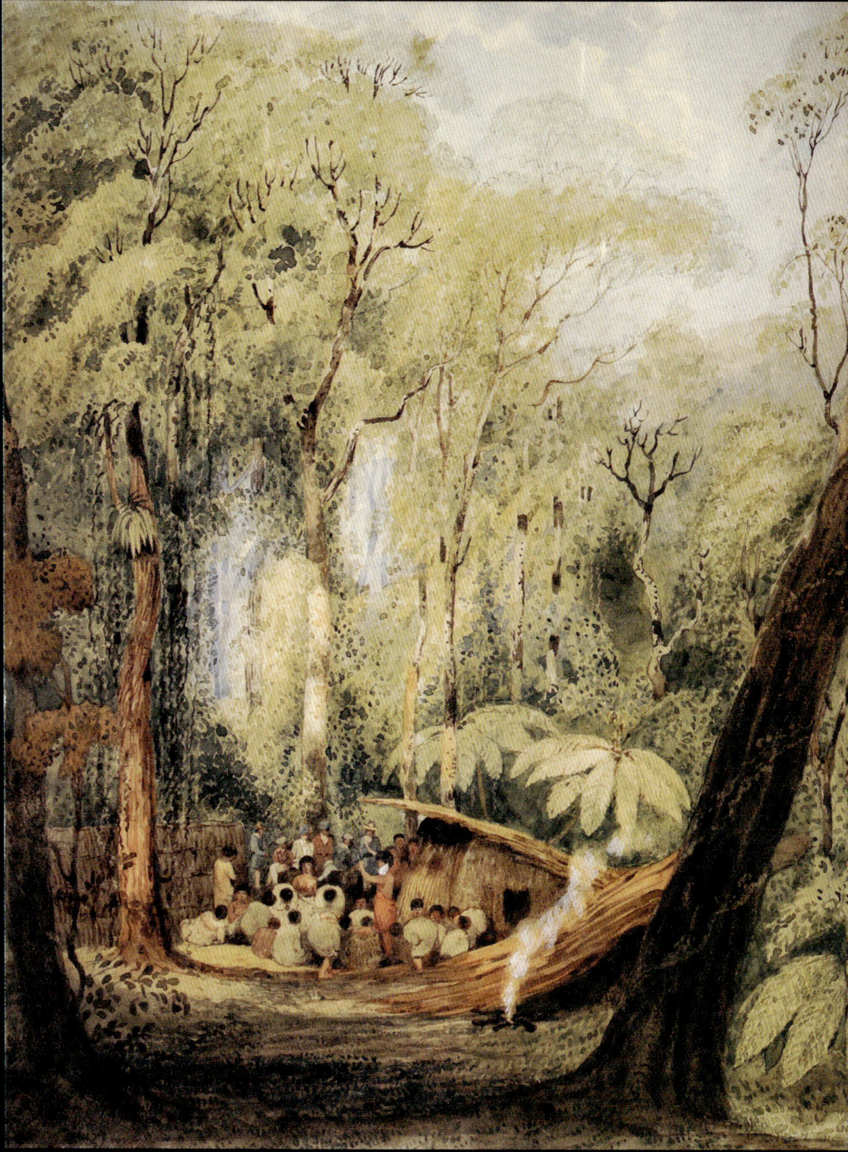

Samuel Charles Brees. *A Tangi at Kopekehinga, Wairarapa. E Koro, the chief of the Kaikokerri, Meeting Some of the Huangaroa Natives.* c. 1843. Watercolour and opaque white on paper. 299 x 228 mm. Purchased, 1920.

Christianity on Taranaki shores • 1844

Despite being known for his many works relating to New Zealand and the South Pacific, printer and inventor George Baxter (1804–67) never left London. In 1836 he patented a method of high quality colour printing incorporating the aquatint method, superimposing the colours using multiple wooden blocks. Although hugely popular and useful, his technique was by the 1860s superseded by less laborious chromo-lithography and he died in poverty.

Baxter's image purports to record an historical event – the landing of the Wesleyan missionary Charles Creed (1812–79) and his wife at Ngamotu beach, the site of modern New Plymouth, on 14 January 1841 – but the artist's lack of familiarity with the area shows. Mount Taranaki is based on Heaphy's conical version, the vegetation is tropical, and New Plymouth has moved south. With feather headdresses and togas, the Māori are noble savages with an American Indian flavour.

It would seem that Christianity is being joyously welcomed on heathen shores. While Creed can be identified in the rowboat, it is his wife who is the centre of attention as she is carried on to the beach by ecstatic Māori women. Even though distracted by a gesticulating Māori, the Rev. Waterhouse still doffs his hat to the approaching Mrs Creed, reminding us that she was the first European woman to set foot in Taranaki. LT

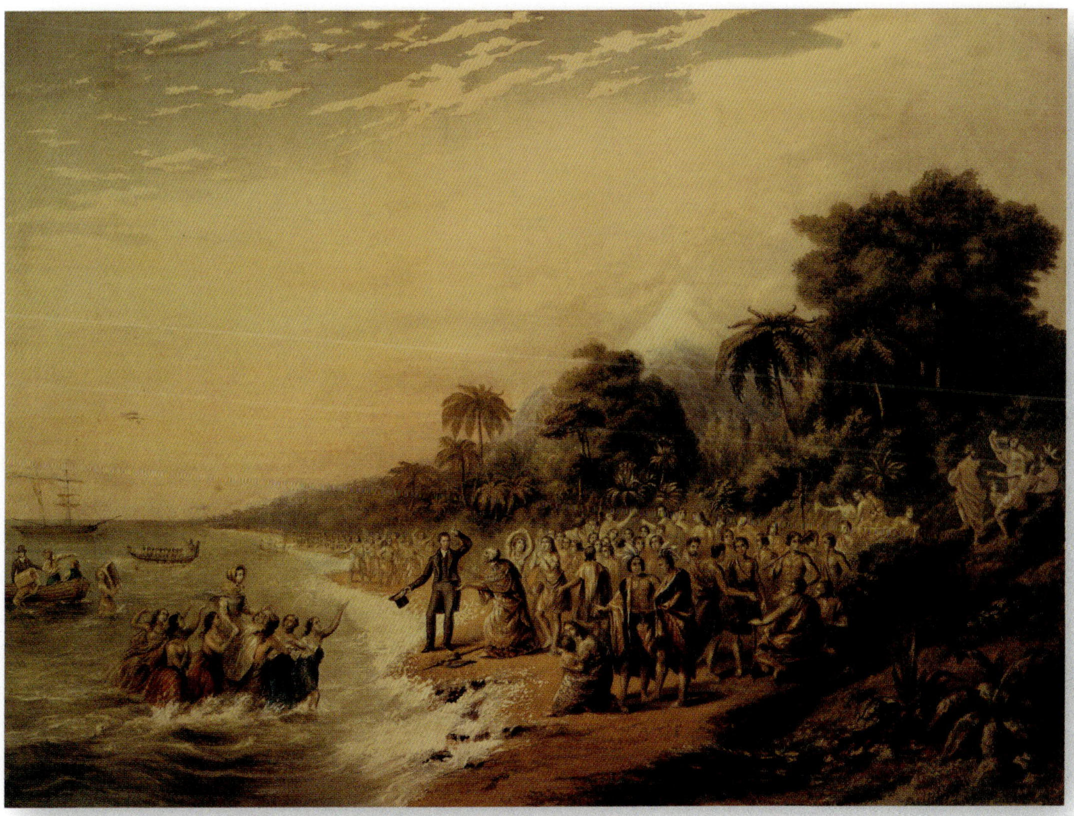

George Baxter. *The REV. J. WATERHOUSE Superintending the Landing of the Missionaries, at Taranaki, New Zealand. Designed, Engraved and Published by G. Baxter, Patentee of Oil Colour Printing, 11, Northampton Square, London, Novr 1, 1844.* Baxter print. 308 x 420 mm. Original Collection.

Conciliation between the races • 1844

Marriage to a 'native female' and the ability to speak te reo gave Joseph Merrett (1816–54) privileged access to Māori subjects in post-Treaty New Zealand. Arriving from New South Wales in 1839, he was described by Hocken as an interpreter, although he had also worked as a land surveyor.

Merrett's surveying skills are evident in this work. Remuera is shown as a vast plain with the volcanoes of Mount Hobson and Mount Eden looming in the distance. While it seems like a battle scene, this image is in fact a carefully constructed demonstration of conciliation between the races. In the centre, flag-bearing Māori perform a haka before Governor FitzRoy, whose horse rears up in fright at the spectacle. Behind him are Alexander Shepherd, the Colonial Treasurer, and William Swainson, the Attorney-General.

The image was widely distributed, reproduced in 1845 as a lithograph with the title *The New Zealand Festival.* Reassuring words below the image explain that order is being maintained by the colonial administration, and that Christianity is on the advance: 'The Maori feast depicted in this picture was one of the largest ever held in New Zealand. It was given by the Waikato chiefs. The site chosen was in the vicinity of Mt Hobson, at Remuera, near Auckland. About four thousand natives were present. A shed 400 yards long had been erected and was covered with blankets;

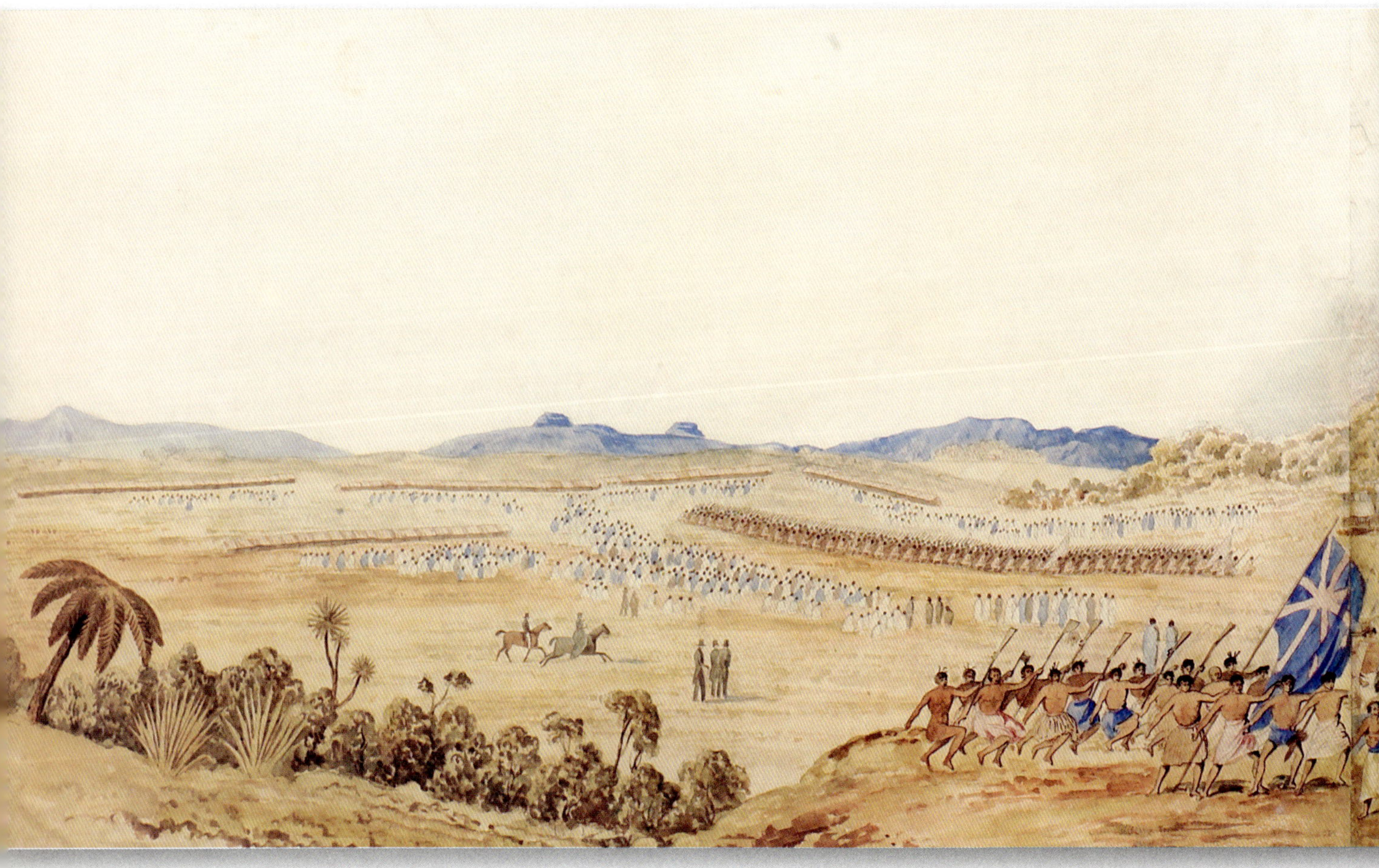

and tents decorated with little flags, dotted the ground. The provisions comprised 11,000 baskets of potatoes, 9,000 sharks, 100 pigs, and large quantities of tea, tobacco, and sugar. A thousand blankets had been provided as presents. Governor Fitzroy, with his suite, visited the meeting on 11 May 1844, when 1600 natives, armed with guns and tomahawks, danced the wardance. The assembling of so large a force near the infant capital caused some uneasiness among the settlers, but admirable order was maintained throughout. The various tribes were accompanied by their missionaries, and religious services were well attended. The feast lasted about a week.' LT

Joseph Jenner Merrett. *Native Feast held at Remuera, Auckland, May 11, 1844*. c. 1844. Watercolour, pen and ink on paper. 284 x 912 mm. Original Collection.

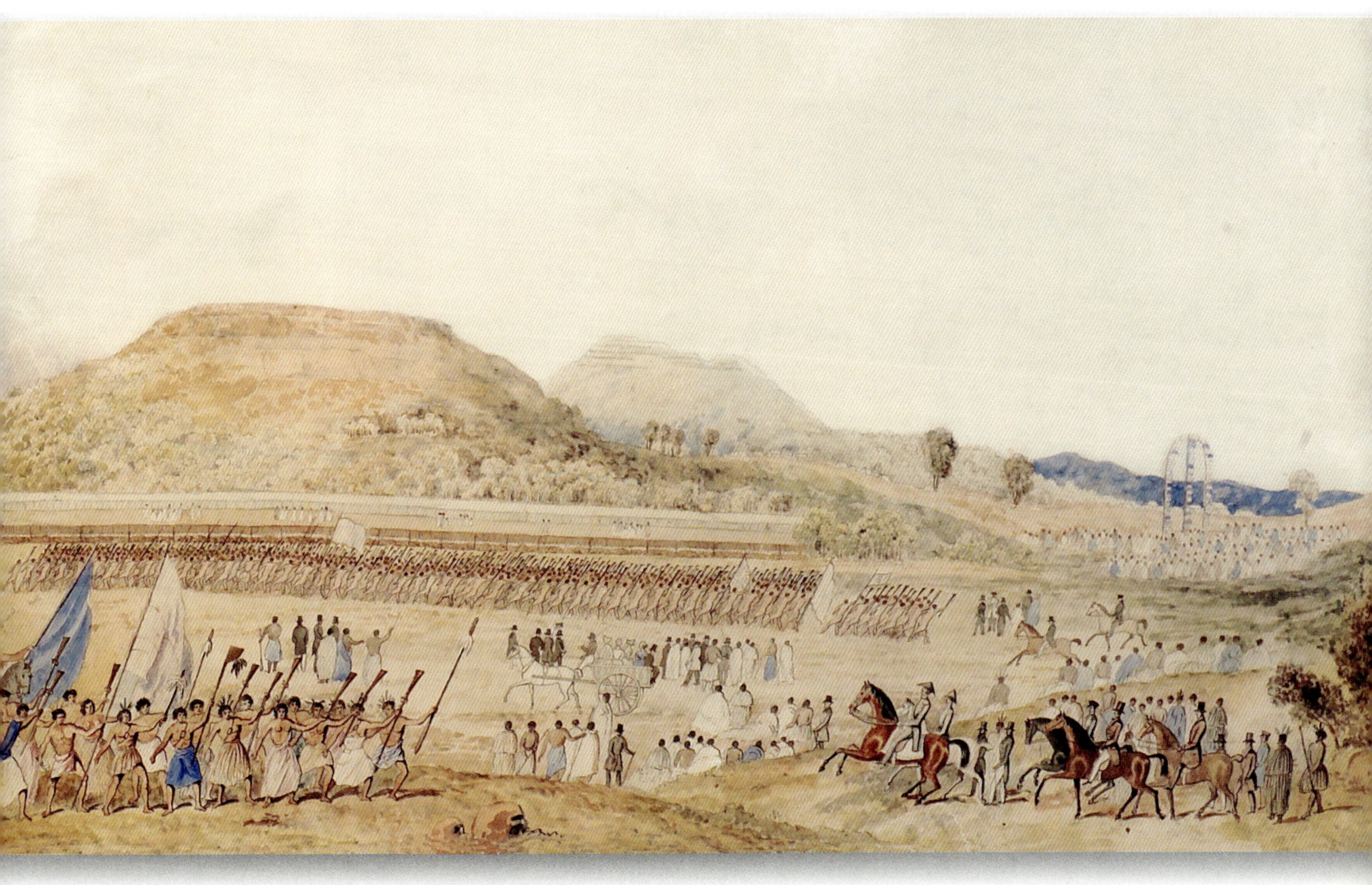

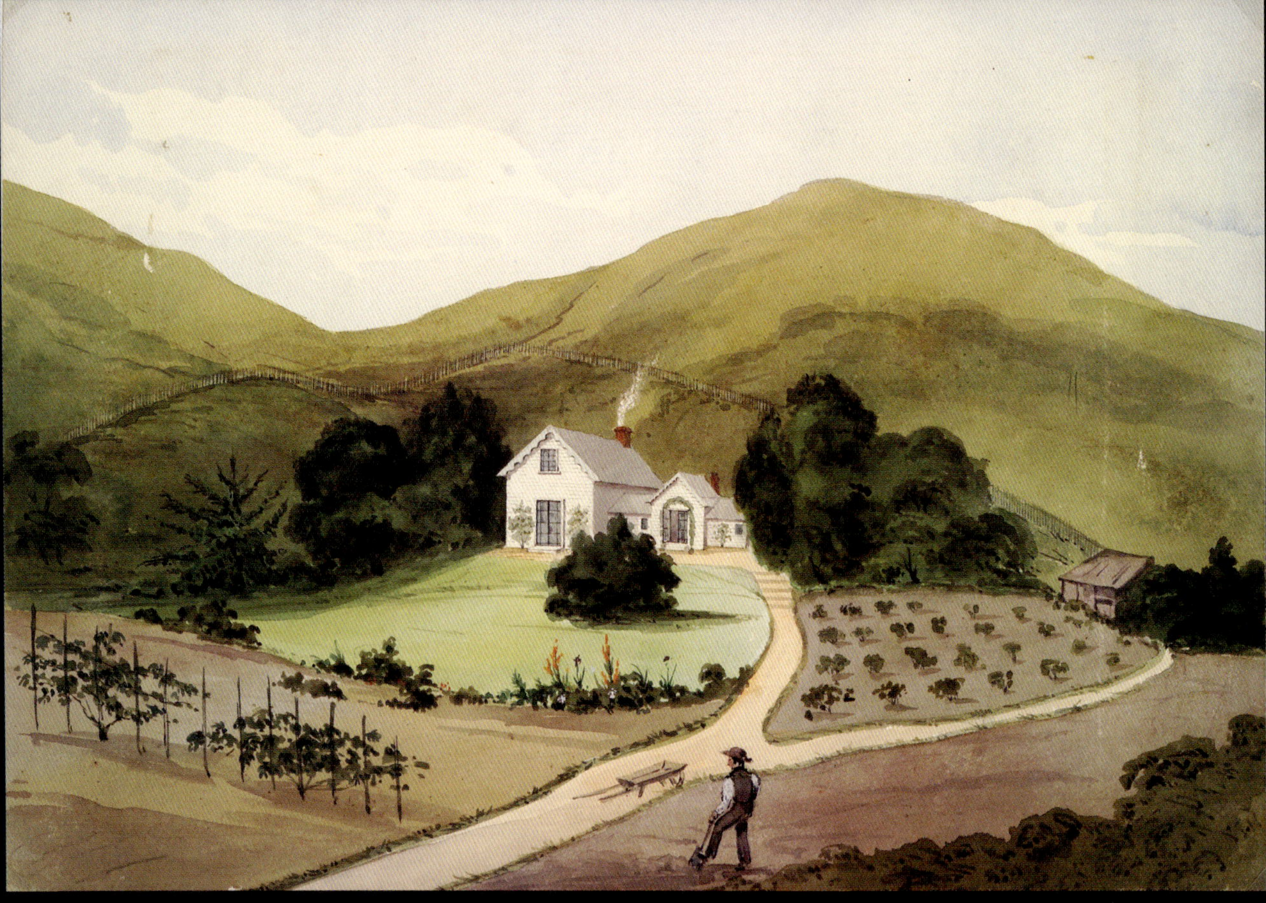

The benefits of cultivation • 1848

William Fox. *W. Fox's House, Nelson*. 1848. Watercolour on paper. 238 x 345 mm. Original Collection.

Dr Hocken's collection of around 300 pictures of historical interest was boosted by the bequest of 118 watercolours by Sir William Fox (1812–93) after the artist's death. Whereas Alexander Turnbull purchased his Fox watercolours in London as part of the New Zealand Company collection, Hocken's inscription proudly records, 'Gifted to Thomas Morland Hocken by Sir William Fox who well knew the interest I took in old New Zealand & was a frequent visitor at my house, and promised to bequeath to me these sketches which he commenced to take from the time of his arrival in 1842.'

Trained as a lawyer, Fox worked first as a newspaper editor, then as the New Zealand Company's agent in Nelson, before becoming a politician and the country's premier during the New Zealand Wars. As this painting helps attest, Fox believed that cultivation of the land resulted not only in its improvement but had a beneficial effect on the moral fibre of the gardener as well. His incipient interest in social reform was manifest first in Nelson, when the New Zealand Company defaulted from its obligations. Employing working class settlers for three days, Fox proceeded to allocate them sections so they could grow vegetables for the remainder of the week. LT

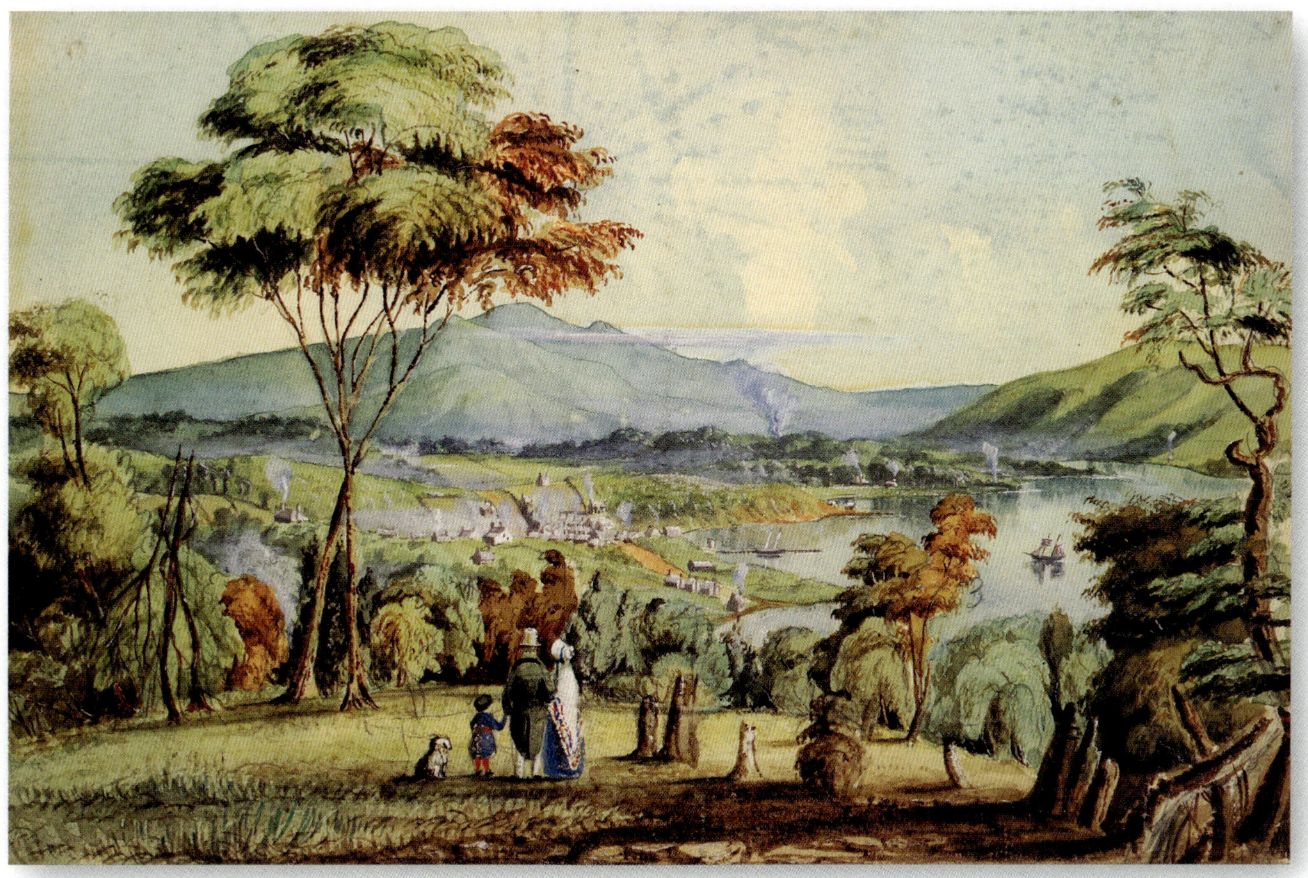

Dunedin • 1849

Edward Immyns Abbot. *Dunedin from Little Paisley*. 1849. Watercolour and opaque white on paper. 177 x 275 mm. Original Collection.

The Otago settlement was founded by the Free Church of Scotland in 1848, but economic rather than religious reasons brought most settlers to Dunedin. Hardy and adaptable, they travelled with everything, gravestones included. John Barr, who arrived as a weaver from Paisley in Scotland in 1848, worked as the gaoler and pound-keeper before becoming sexton of the adjacent Southern Cemetery. He now rests there 'under his old hearthstone', according to Dr Hocken's annotation on this work.

Dr Hocken also recognised the 'superior abilities' that distinguished Abbot (c. 1820–49) as a young New Zealand Company surveyor. This watercolour and a fine pencil portrait of Te Rauparaha from June 1845, also in the Pictures Collection, testify to Abbot's draughting skills. Joining Sydney Scroggs in the preliminary survey of the Otago Settlement and Taieri Plain in 1847, he painted this Paisley weaver family gazing north towards Mount Cargill from their new home two years later. Lithographs based on this sylvan scene were made in Bloomsbury in 1853 and lured many more British immigrants to Dunedin.

Abbot's ten months of employment ended tragically with his death in October 1849. Having once watched Abbot wade across the Kaikorai Stream, chief surveyor Charles Kettle decided to name Abbotsford in the talented young assistant's memory. LT

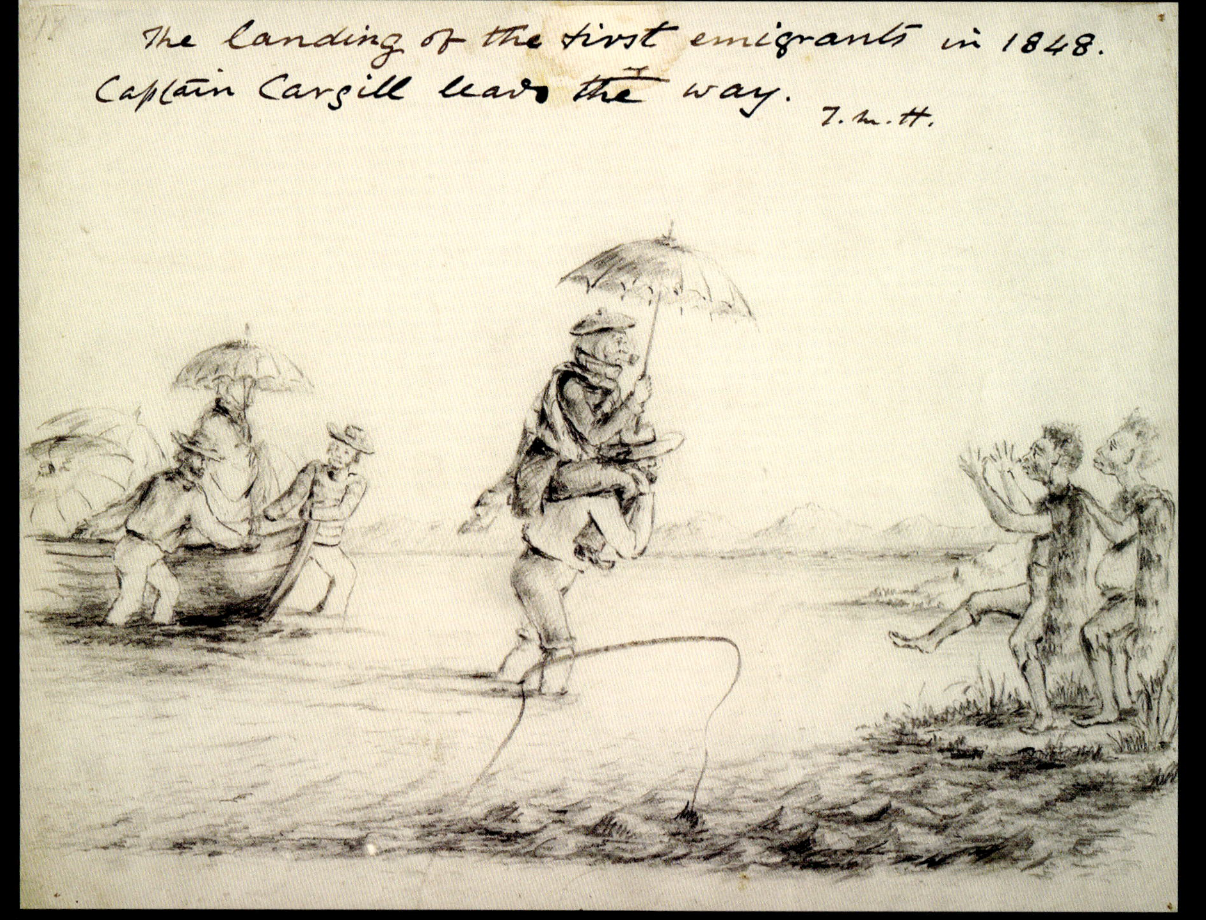

New Zealand's first cartoonist • 1850s

James Brown. *The landing of the first emigrants in 1848*. n.d. Pencil on paper. 195 x 254 mm. Original Collection.

Drawing caricatures lampooning Dunedin's numerous self-important public figures may have satisfied the egalitarian impulses of James Brown (1819–77), but he was not inclined to jeopardise his engraving business by publishing them. Six appeared illustrating James Barr's *Old Identities* in 1879, but that was two years after Brown's death. Dr Hocken subsequently acquired these and another forty-two pencil drawings, and it is on this collection that James Brown's posthumous reputation as New Zealand's first cartoonist rests.

Arriving in 1850, Brown worked for a year with his friend Henry Graham to produce the *Otago News* until Captain William Cargill, Superintendent of Otago, ensured it was subsumed by the *Otago Witness*. Although Brown designed the masthead of the latter paper, he disliked 'cock of the walk' Cargill and was inventive in his ridicule of him, once wickedly depicting him as a performing monkey.

In this example, Cargill is identifiable as the quintessential Scotsman with his tam o'shanter, tartan scarf and attachment to smoking a pipe. Cargill is obviously afraid of getting wet, so must be piggybacked ashore carrying his open umbrella aloft. Even the two Kai Tahu men, who may be performing a welcoming haka, find this astonishing, but, as ever, Captain Cargill is oblivious of being the butt of the joke. LT

Māori policeman • 1850

A hakari food platform built for a feast at Kerikeri in August 1849 was one of the first New Zealand subjects drawn by the Anatolian-born artist John Cuthbert Clarke (1818–68) while accompanying Governor Sir George Grey on a trip north. Impressed by his delicate draughtsmanship in rendering this architectural subject, Grey again engaged Clarke's services in December of that year. This time they travelled down the coast in the *Undine* to the Kaweranga mission station in Thames before heading overland to Taranaki. Finding work for a professional artist scarce thereafter, Clarke became a customs clerk at Auckland in early 1851 before departing for Australia.

This cross-legged Māori constable playing his flute seems whimsical, but the purpose of the drawing was to document one of the governor's many meritorious ideas. As Dr Hocken noted: 'Part of Sir George Grey's Native Policy … was to confer various civil + other appointments upon the natives … with the view of bringing the two races into closer & more friendly contact.' Māori policemen – who had to buy their own uniforms – were valued for their specialist knowledge and mediation skills. In contrast to their significant tribal standing, however, they were resented by many Europeans. LT

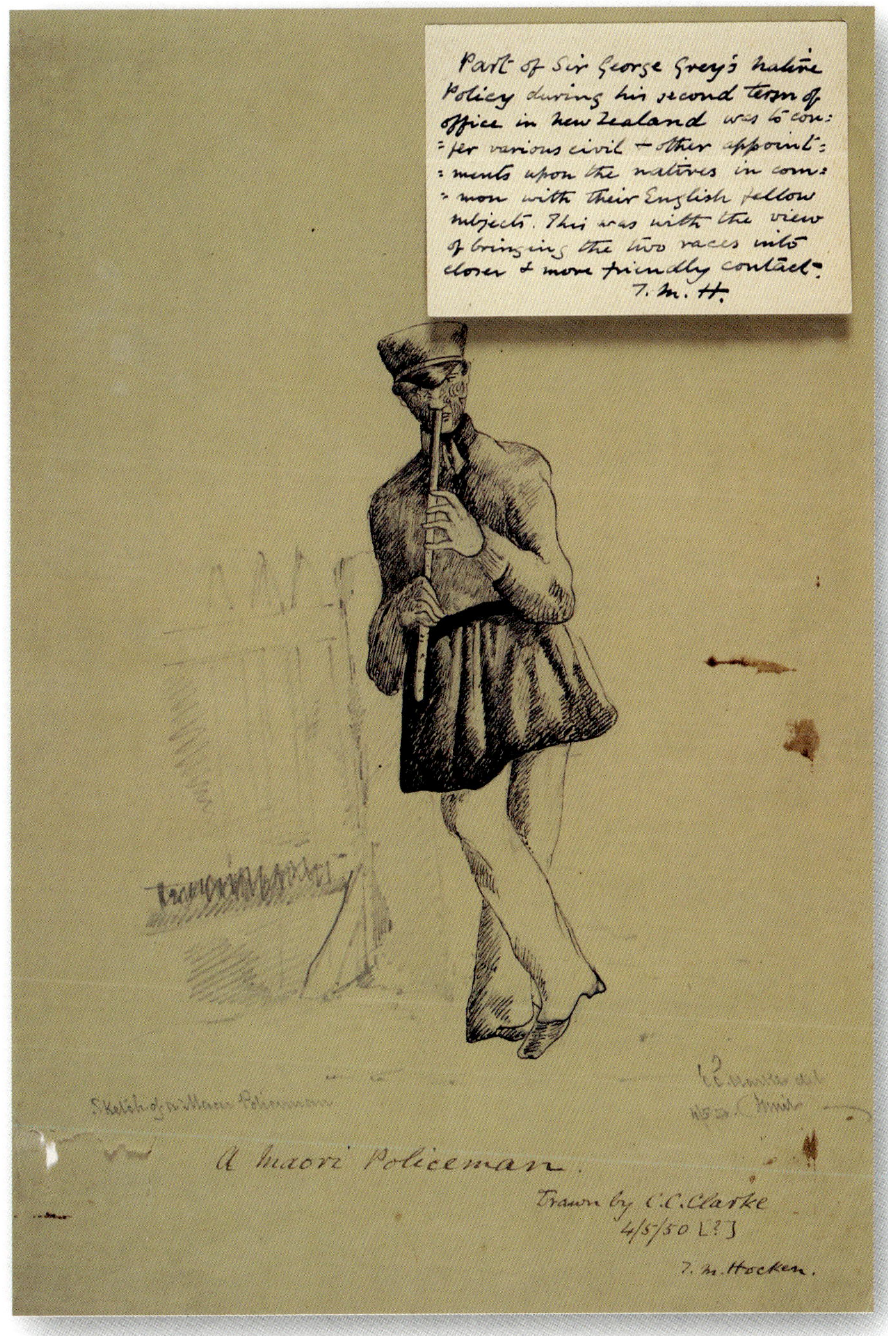

Cuthbert Charles Clarke. *Sketch of a Maori Policeman.* 1850. Pencil, pen and ink on brown paper. 344 x 249 mm. Original Collection.

Māori council of war • 1853

Before emigrating with his family to the New Zealand Company settlement of Wanganui in 1842, Gilfillan (1793–1864) had studied portraiture with Henry Raeburn and worked for fifteen years as painting master at Glasgow's Andersonian College. He farmed for five years in the Matarawa Valley until, on 18 April 1847, a Māori war party raided his farmhouse, killing his wife and three of their children. He fled to Australia with his surviving children, but continued to paint New Zealand subjects using two sketchbooks he took with him as source material. The fifty finely detailed pencil drawings within these books were purchased by Dr Hocken in 1905, while *A Native Council of War* was bought for £105 the following year.

This historical landscape painting, exhibited in 1853 at the Victoria Fine Arts Society, is in the academic tradition, and not intended as a record of an observed event. Descriptions in the catalogue of how 'the Orator while speaking runs backwards and forwards and as he gradually becomes excited throws off his clothes' suggest that Gilfillan wanted his work to have exotic appeal. The reclining half-draped nude in the foreground is one of the many classical conventions and motifs he used in this representation of Māori as a warrior race intent on utu, or revenge. LT

John Alexander Gilfillan. *A Native Council of War*. 1853. Oil on canvas. 955 x 1270 mm. Original Collection.

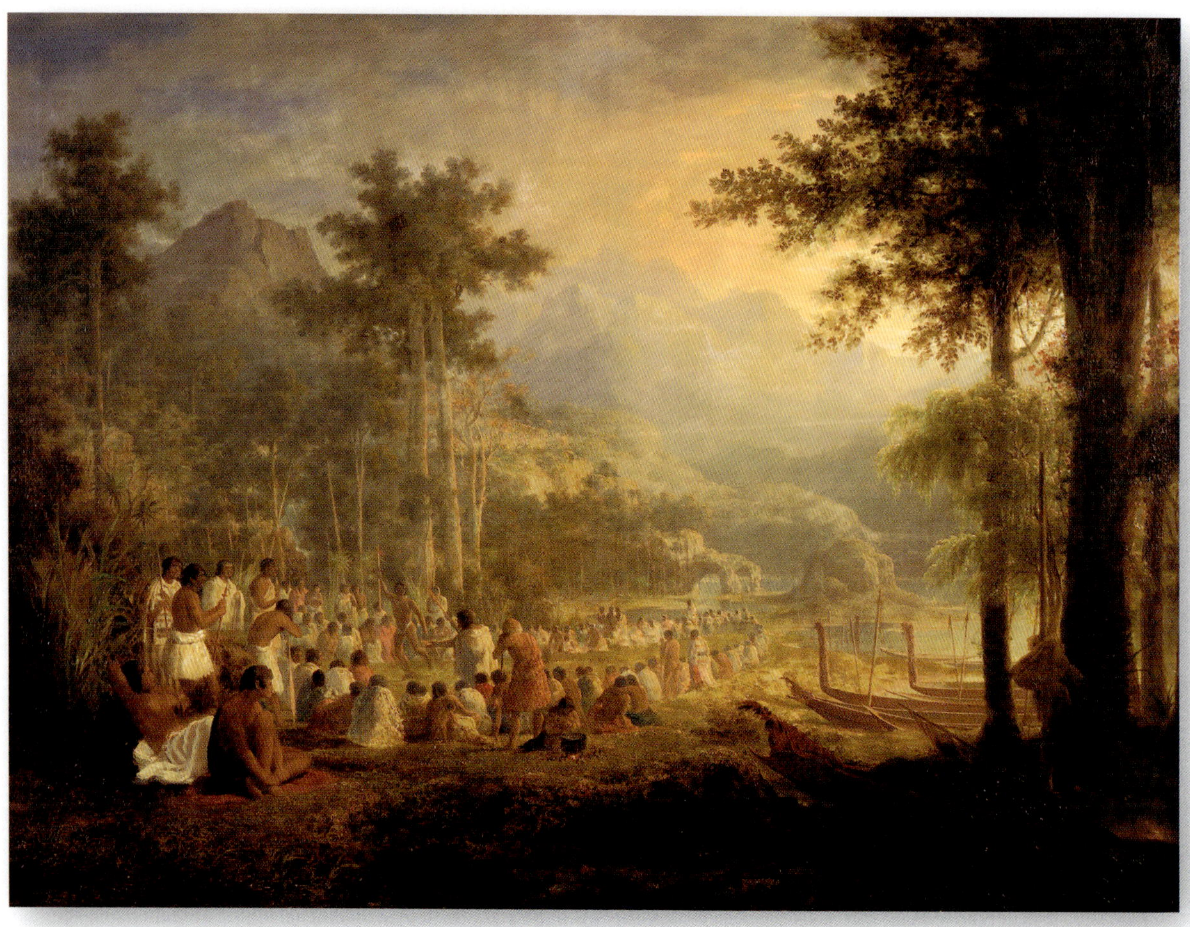

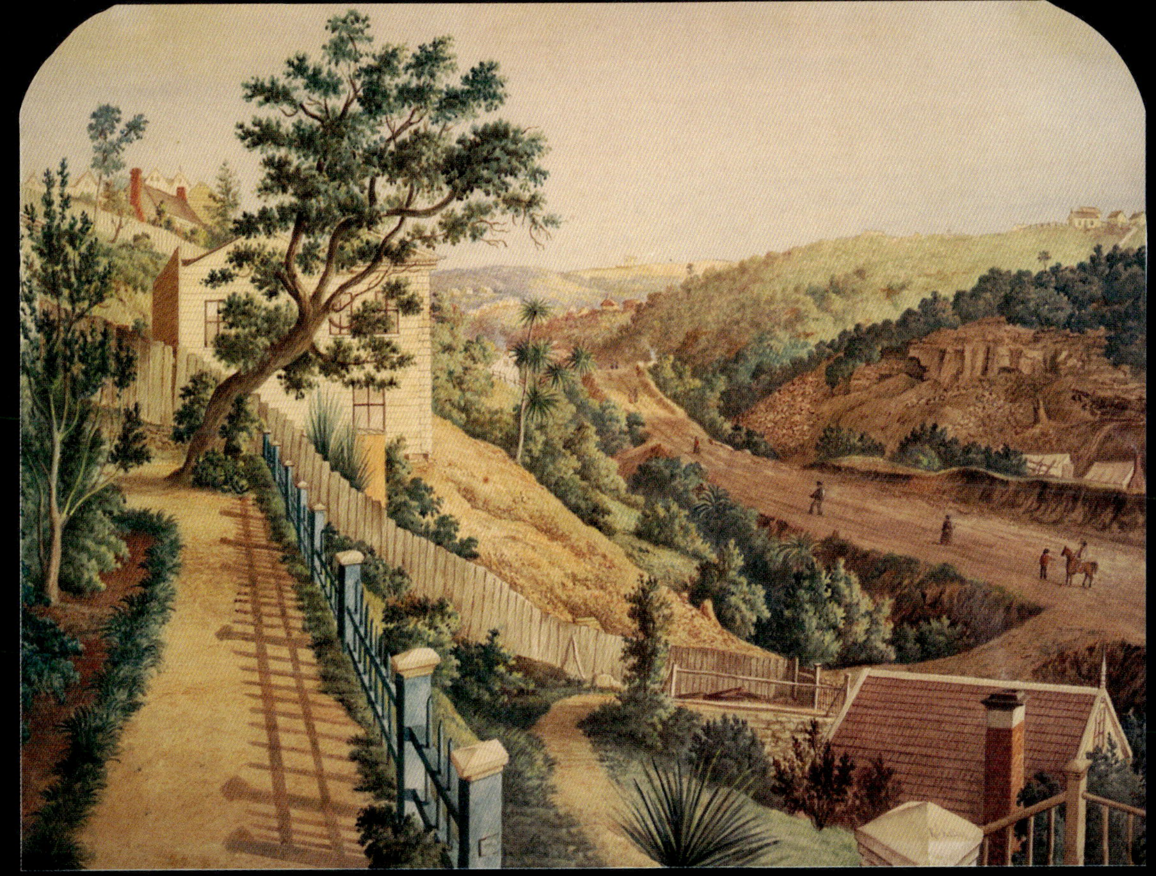

Richard Seymour Kelly. *Dunedin 1862 from the zig-zag of Graham Street, between High and McLaggan Streets.* 1862. Watercolour and gum arabic on paper. 400 x 587 mm. Original Collection.

View to detail • 1862

Irish-born watercolourist Richard Kelly (1820–73) moved with his Cornish wife Elizabeth Nancarrow from Sandridge, Victoria, to Dunedin after gold was discovered in Otago in 1861. Showing the nascent development of the hill suburbs above the town, his view looking west toward Mornington and Belleknowes is remarkable for the botanical precision with which the vegetation is recorded. A young *Cordyline australis* pops its head up by the groomed lawn in the immediate foreground, pointing to the starburst of a mature cabbage tree clinging to a cleared hillside section beyond. Punga flourishes in the steep gully on the near side of McLaggan Street, and an asymmetrically placed rātā leans over the fence from its vantage point in the middle of the path, as if surveying the view.

Kelly shows examples of two prevailing styles for Dunedin's newly built houses: classical neo-Georgian with hipped corrugated iron roof, built in wood but with quoining at the edges to simulate stone, and Victorian Gothic with gable, shingles, dormer window and finial. Below, on the road, a rider has stopped his horse to chat in the morning sunshine, and men and women come and go from town. A quarry opposite offers salvation from the quagmire of 'Mud-edin'. LT

Ignoring Captain William Cargill's advice that, in view of his poor health, he should stay in the office, John Turnbull Thomson (1821–84) struck out for Bluff in January 1857 to begin a reconnaissance survey. Twenty years later, he used his field book sketches to complete albums of watercolour paintings chronicling his adventures as chief surveyor of Otago.

His affection for the 'small hardy mare' that bore him south is evident in this humorous caricature showing him tumbling from her back while negotiating the hazards of Wakari. Battling the sandflies, he determined the latitude of Bluff Hill for the southern end of his baseline and chose Mid Dome about 113 kilometres to the north for the other end. Triangulating from these two points allowed him to fix the position of every notable landscape feature he encountered.

Thomson climbed 1479 metres to the top of Mid Dome with Scotsman Peter Lindsay. In this painting, Thomson is proceeding with his observations, but is 'disturbed by the chatter of Lindsay's teeth'. Discovering that his assistant had left his coat behind – reasoning that it would be warmer up high as it was closer to the sun – Northumbrian Thomson commented drily, 'I mention this incident as a curious example of a Scotchman's idealisation.' LT

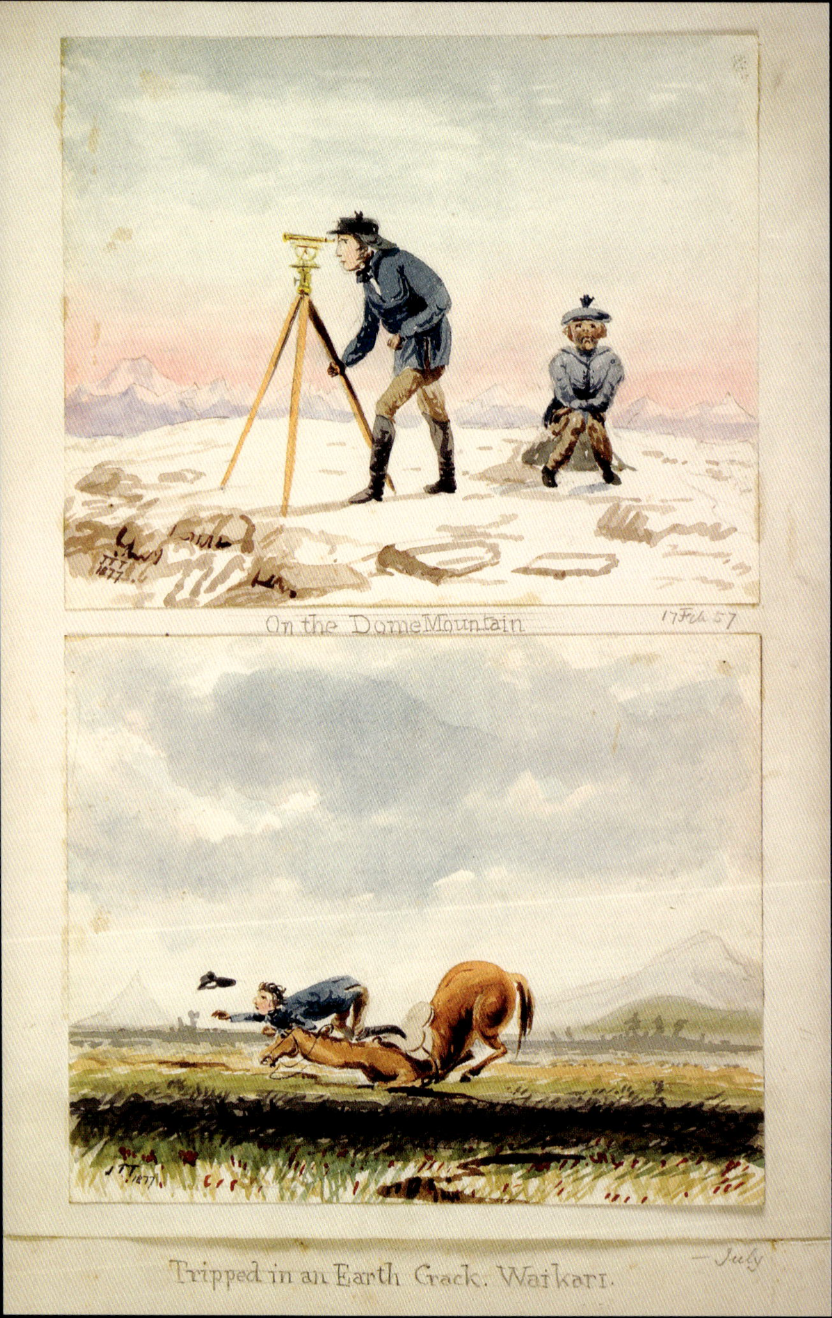

John Turnbull Thomson. *On the Dome Mountain, 17 February 1857* and *Tripped in an Earth Crack. Wakari.* 1877. Watercolour on paper. 130 x 162mm. Donated by the Hall-Jones family, 1992.

Classic Milford Sound • 1863

Though Scottish-born John Buchanan (1819–98) had worked as a textile pattern designer and botanised in his leisure hours before emigrating to Dunedin in 1852, he had no formal training in painting. In Otago he found gold in the Tuapeka and Clutha rivers and then employment as a botanist and draughtsman on Alexander Garvie's reconnaissance surveys and with James Hector's 1863 geological survey.

Milford Sound was first displayed, along with a selection of rocks, to illustrate the work of the Geological Survey of Otago at the 1865 New Zealand Exhibition in Dunedin. It established, in panorama, the sound's classic configuration, with Mitre Peak at centre and Bowen Falls to the right, which became the model for generations of subsequent artists. With its muted tones and heavy reliance on line, it is less a painting than a coloured drawing, and would probably have been regarded by the artist as a technical exercise rather than a work of art. However, by 1940 when the work was selected for the touring National Centennial Exhibition, the treatment of form, stark simplicity and limited colour range had begun to seem strikingly modern, and this modest watercolour is now established as one of the icons of New Zealand art. LT

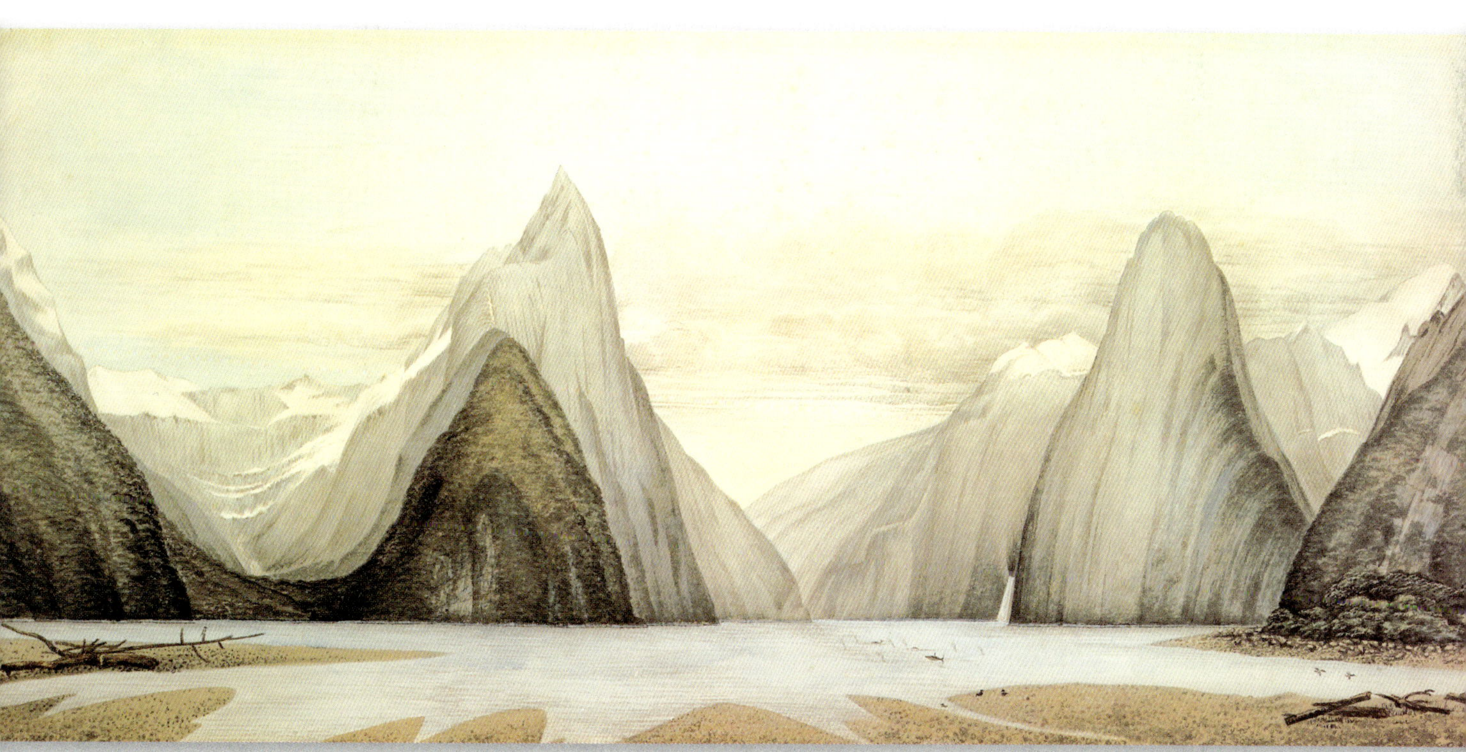

John Buchanan. *Milford Sound, looking north-west from Freshwater Basin*, 1863. Watercolour on paper. 222 x 509 mm. Donated by Peter Buchanan through the Otago Museum, 1920s.

At Wesley's house In London • 1863

Commemorating the 1863 visit to England by a Māori group led by Nelson-based William Jenkins, a defrocked lay preacher, this painting was commissioned for the fortieth anniversary of the Wesleyan mission in New Zealand. Painted by John Smetham (1821–89), a minor Pre-Raphaelite artist, and set in the home of the founder of Methodism, John Wesley, it shows Jenkins centre right, in front of the piano with Wiremu te Wana standing opposite him, pointing to Wesley's portrait above. Dr Hocken divined the didactic purpose of the painting as 'the meeting of the civilised Maori with the Missionary, to whose labours his advancement is due' and researched each identity:

Left-hand group, back row, left to right:
Takarei Ngawaka, grandson of Te Heu Heu; Horomona te Atua, son of Te Anga, one of Hongi's generals; Hare Pomare, son of Pomare who was imprisoned during the Northern War; Hapimana Ngapiro, son of Mokoera, grandson of Rangitawhanga, and great grandson of Te Ra Taunga of Ngāti Awa, Taranaki; Kameriera te Hau-Takiri Wharepapa (1823–1920); Paratene te Manu (1806?–1896), son of Kau te Awa and descendant of Rangitukiwaha of Ngā Puhi.

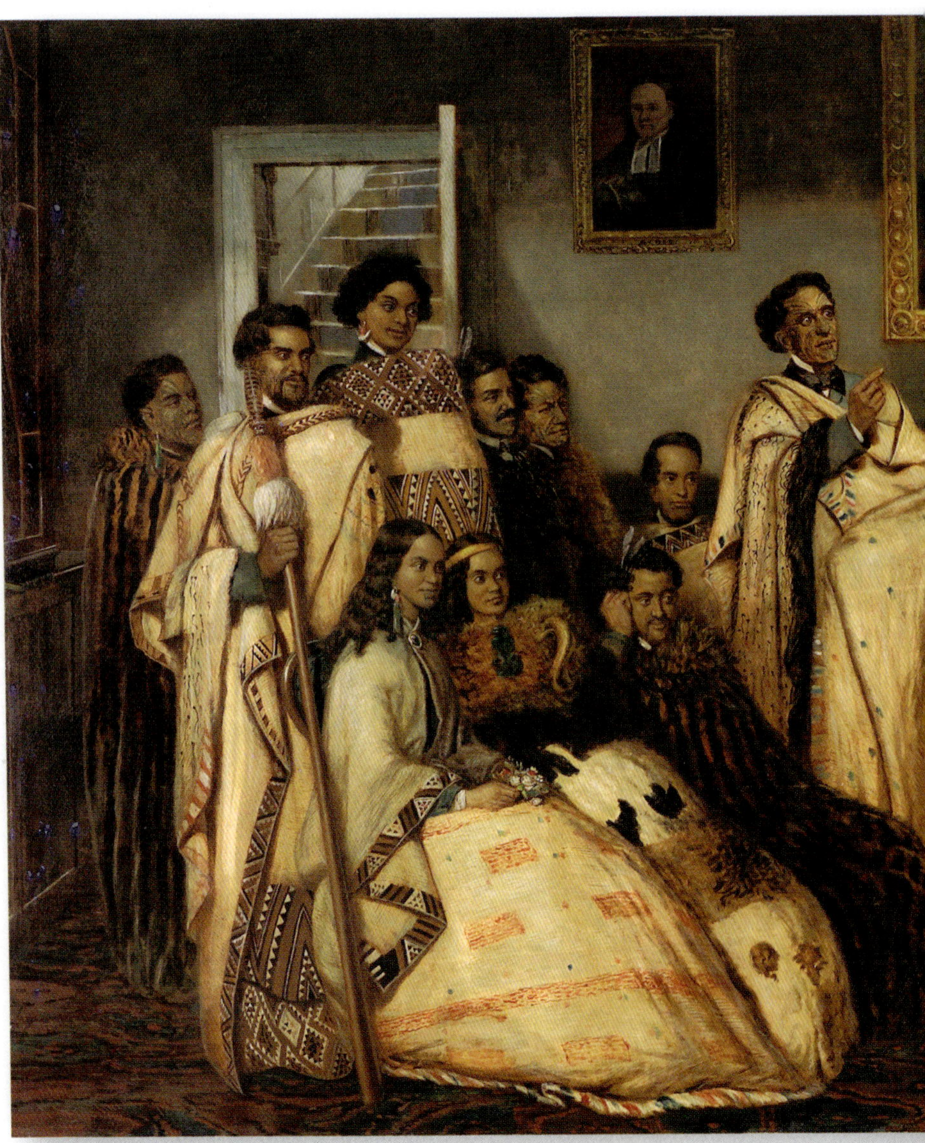

James Smetham. *The New Zealand Chiefs in Wesley's House*. 1863. Oil on canvas. 1025 x 1835 mm. Original Collection.

Left-hand group, front row seated, left to right: Ngahuia, granddaughter of Te Horeta Taniwha of Coromandel; Hariata Tutapuiti, wife of Hare Pomare; Reihana Taukawau, son of Tukarewa of Ngā Puhi.

Standing beneath the portrait of John Wesley: Wiremu te Wana, son of Pou, one of Hongi's generals, and William Jenkins.

Right-hand group, standing, left to right: Kihirini te Tuahu, son of Whareri, grandson of Te Whiu and descendant of Rangitiki of Tarawera; Hirini Pakia, son of Tipene Hare, cousin of Hongi and grandson of Waharaupo, a general of Hongi and Kawiti.

Right-hand group, seated, left to right: Mrs Jobson; Reverend Dr Jobson, Secretary of the Wesleyan Society; Hariata te Iringa, wife of Hirini and grand-daughter of Kawiti; Mrs P. Brames Hall.

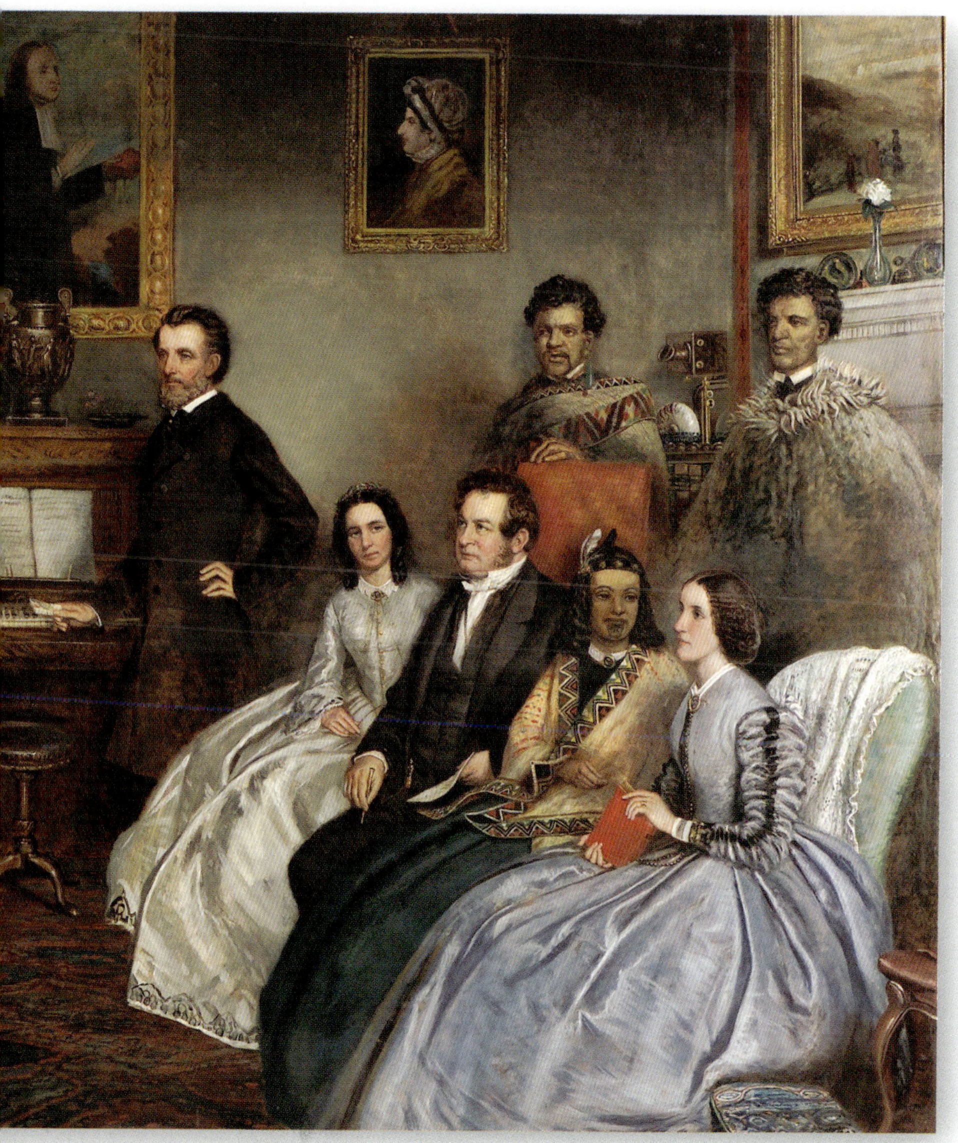

With Governor Grey's support for what the *Wellington Independent* had called 'the exhibition of some fifteen natives in England', Jenkins had departed soon after the outbreak of the first Taranaki land war. Six different iwi were represented in the group of thirteen men and women he took on a lecture tour to educate the English about Māori life.

Crowds turned out to see them, many receptions were held, and they were individually presented to Queen Victoria, who became godmother to the child born in England to Hariata Tutapuiti and Hare Pomare. As money dwindled, however, some of the Māori abandoned Jenkins to join the Alhambra theatre troupe, and the enterprise foundered. LT

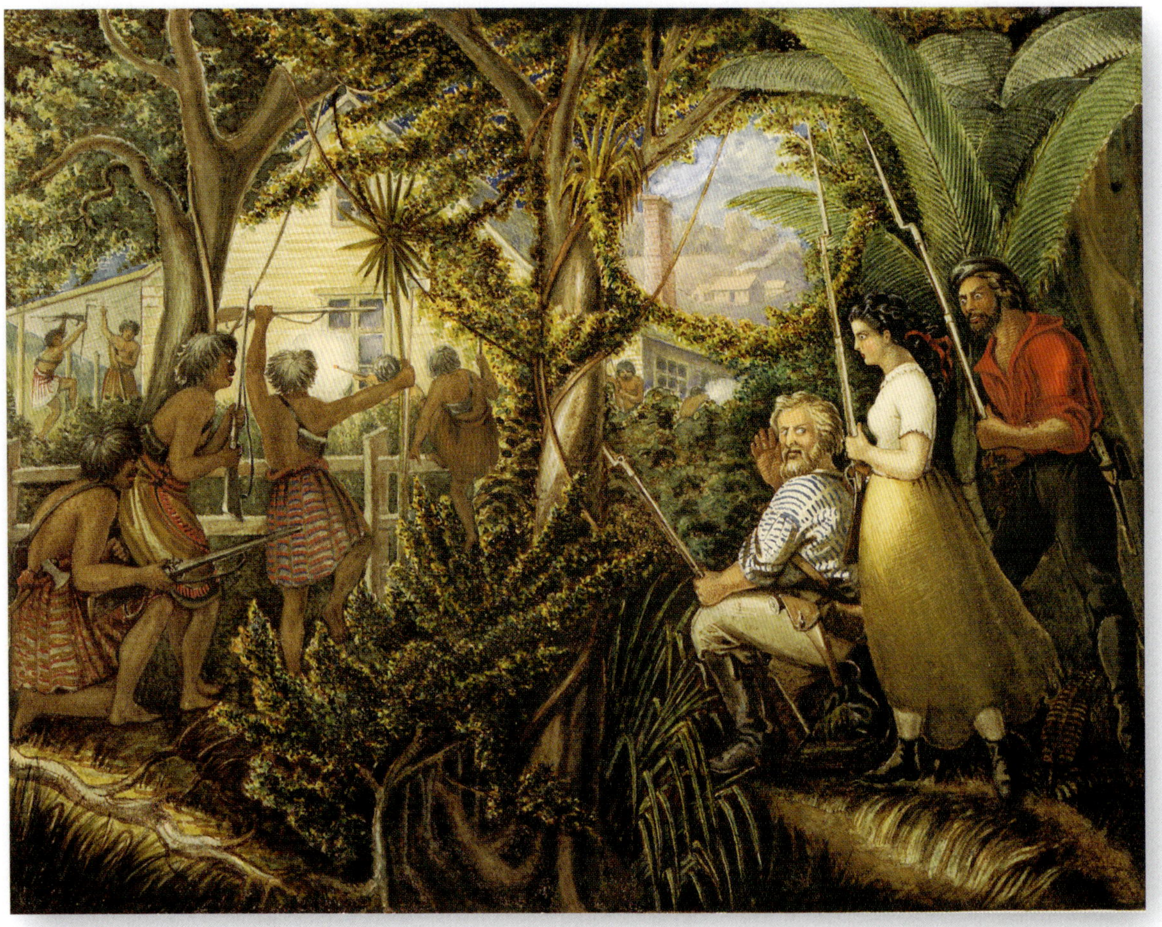

Soldier as artist • 1863

Gustavus Ferdinand von Tempsky. *An Incident during a Hau-hau Raid on a settler's farm.* 1863. Watercolour and gum arabic on paper. 221 x 288 mm. Donated by Mrs N. Kettle (née von Tempsky), 1918.

Coromandel gold drew the Prussian von Tempsky (1828–68) to New Zealand in 1861, but it was as a soldier and artist that he made his name. Known to the Māori as Manurau, 'the bird that flits everywhere', he was a daring irregular ranger force leader, who believed that the Māori had to be subdued. Having risen to the rank of major, he was killed covering a withdrawal in Taranaki at Te Ngutu-o-te-manu on 7 September 1868.

Rather than aiming at naturalism in his watercolours, von Tempsky sought to capture 'the spirit of certain incidents', recreating scenes from stories told to him. Having recently been fighting in Central America, he made a tropical jungle of the pūriri and rātā surrounding Burtt's farmhouse at Paerata, near Pukekohe. Rampaging Māori swarming around the house are all of a type, whereas the depictions of the heroic neighbour, James Hamilton, and his worker, Alexander Goulan, are carefully individualised.

Planning their strategy to fire bullets from all directions to trick the Māori into thinking they are outnumbered, the settlers are wild-eyed with righteous determination. To underscore the extremity of the situation, and the collective bravery, prominence is given to young Miss Watson. It is her mother under attack in the house. LT

With a wife and eleven children to support, necessity made the artist Wilbraham Liardet (1799–1878) an inventive fortune-seeker. Having lost his inheritance before emigrating from London to Melbourne in 1839, he became a publican. In 1842 he was running a coach and mail service and had purchased a run at Mount Macedon, but by 1845 was bankrupt. Undeterred, he fell back on self-taught skills as a watercolourist and produced an engraved view of Melbourne which sold in London for a guinea.

Returning to Liardet's Beach (now Port Melbourne), he became a net fisherman, entertained hotel clientele with his guitar, flute and voice, and organised horse races, regattas and archery. Gold lured him to New Zealand in 1863, and he drew, painted and made lithographs in Dunedin in 1865 and Thames in 1868. Exhibition buildings and the recent construction of the road around Anderson's Bay date this view.

In 1869, when the Royal Dockyard at Deptford was closed, Liardet, now 70, went to England to argue that his ancestor, the diarist John Evelyn, had wanted his heirs to inherit the land if shipbuilding there ever ceased. His claim did not succeed. Back in Melbourne in 1874, he began work on an illustrated history of Victoria, but died with the venture incomplete. LT

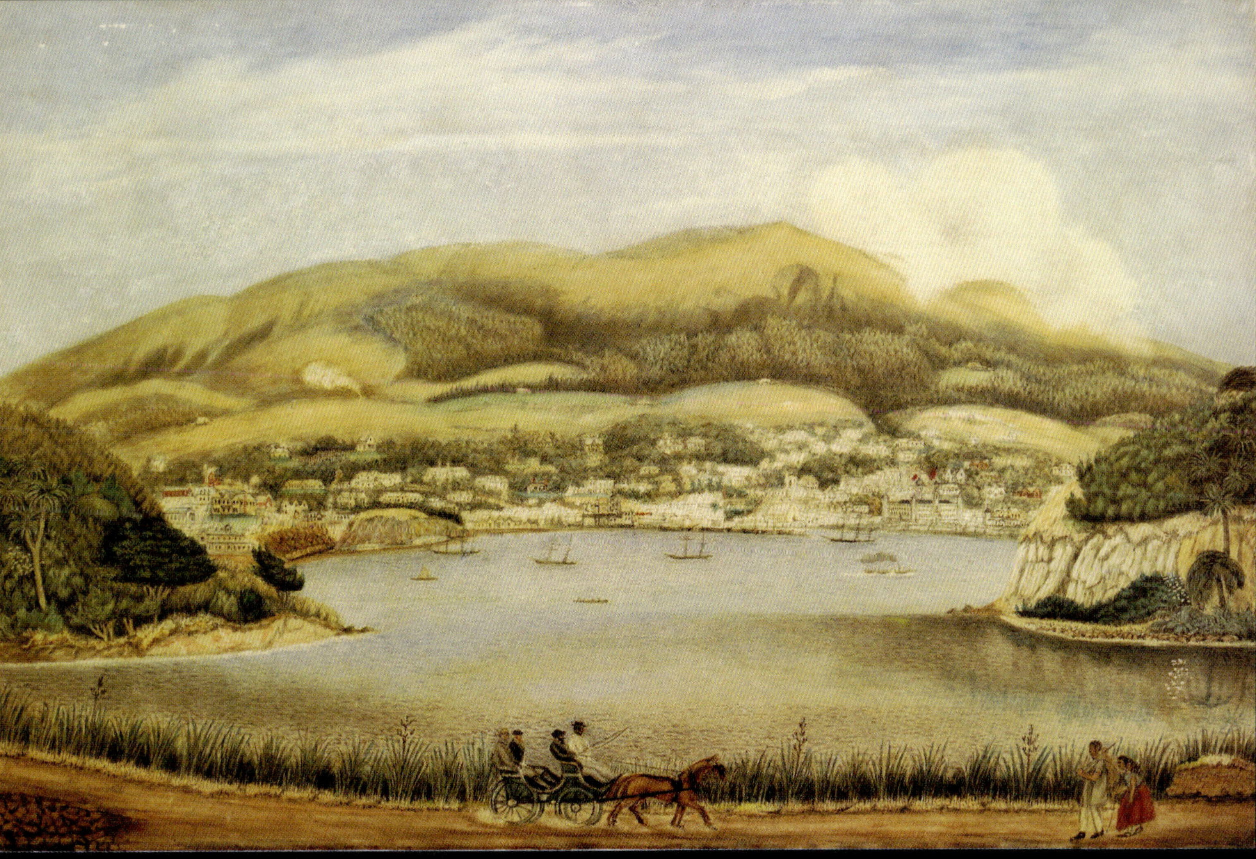

Wilbraham Frederick Evelyn Liardet. *Dunedin from the Portobello Road*. c. 1865. Watercolour, pen and ink on paper. 249 x 375 mm. Purchased, 1986.

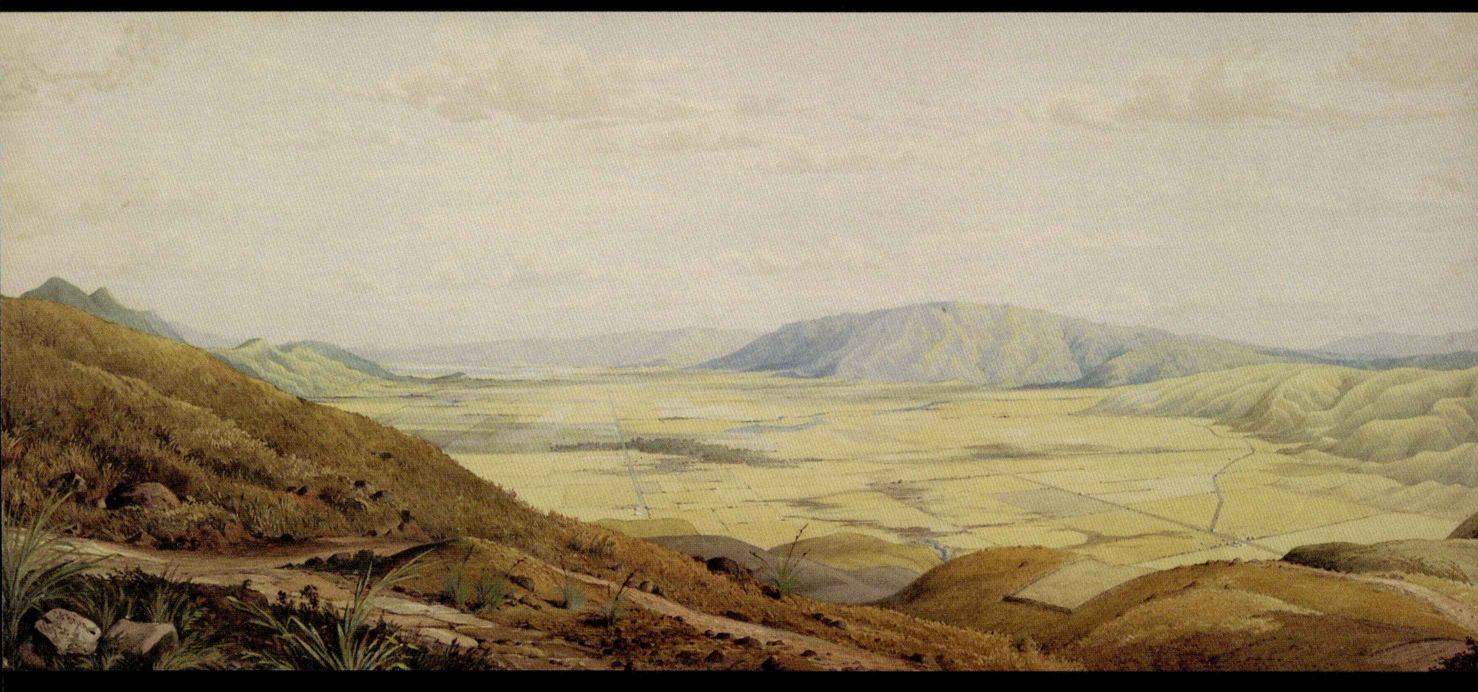

George O'Brien. *The Taieri Plains. Taken from the Upper or Halfway Bush Road leading down to the North Taieri.* 1867. Watercolour and opaque white on paper. 292 x 704 mm. Original Collection.

The Taieri Plains • 1867

Born into Irish aristocracy in County Clare and employed as an engineer and architectural draughtsman in Melbourne, George O'Brien (1821–88) already had a reputation as an accomplished watercolourist before arriving in Dunedin in 1863. Here he worked initially as a perspectivist for leading New Zealand architects of the day, including William Mason, Robert Lawson, Thomas Forrester and William Clayton. He went on to become a founding member of the Otago Art Society in 1876 and dominated their first exhibition with twenty-eight works.

Underneath the mount, Dr Hocken has written his own label, c. 1900, explaining the landscape – a tribute to O'Brien's topographical realism, and showing how for Hocken the countryside around Dunedin was inscribed with its human history:

To the left & below Saddle Hill (so named by Cap. Cook) are Scrogg's Hill, after the surveyor, and the main south road just discernible. Mosgiel is not visible and indeed was hardly in existence. In the distance are the Waipori Hills & Waihola Lake & Maunga-Atua mountain, a shoulder of which shows a piece of the zig-zag road leading to the Tuapeka diggings & where the highwayman Garret seized his prisoners in 1862. Near the foot was Mr James Fulton's property. The entrance to the Taieri Gorge with the Taieri River are visible, the end of the Chain Hills forming a boundary. The West Taieri ferry & Outram are here. To the extreme right is the termination of Flagstaff. The winding road passes the old racecourse & Donald Reid's farm & is in the vicinity of the Otago Central Railway. No vestige remains of the Big Bush. LT

Lake Wanaka • 1866

To Nicholas Chevalier (1828–1902), born in Russia, the South Island seemed like 'the Switzerland of the Southern Hemisphere' when he arrived in Dunedin from Melbourne in late November 1865. The Otago Provincial Government paid him a commission of £200 to paint Otago scenic attractions to 'help attract settlers to the beautiful and fertile land'. The Canterbury Provincial Council followed suit, and he finished his New Zealand stay in June 1866 with a quick tour of the Mount Cook region, visiting Lakes Tekapo, Pukaki, and Ohau, and travelling over the Lindis Pass to Wanaka and Hawea.

Rising to a height of 240 metres and named for its resemblance to a clothes iron, Mount Iron offered the artist a fine vantage point from which to paint the spectacular surroundings of valleys, peaks, rivers and lakes. Although composed in the grand European manner, Chevalier's view is a topographically accurate panorama.

Fidelity to nature in his work was appreciated by viewers of the 200 paintings which Chevalier toured to Christchurch, Wellington and Dunedin before his departure for Melbourne in August 1867. Despite returning to Europe permanently in 1869, he continued to exhibit New Zealand subjects at the Otago Art Society until 1891, maintaining a loyal following amongst the buying and viewing public. LT

Nicholas Chevalier. *View looking north from Mt Iron, Wanaka*. 1866. Oil on canvas. 517 x 1408 mm. Purchased, 1969.

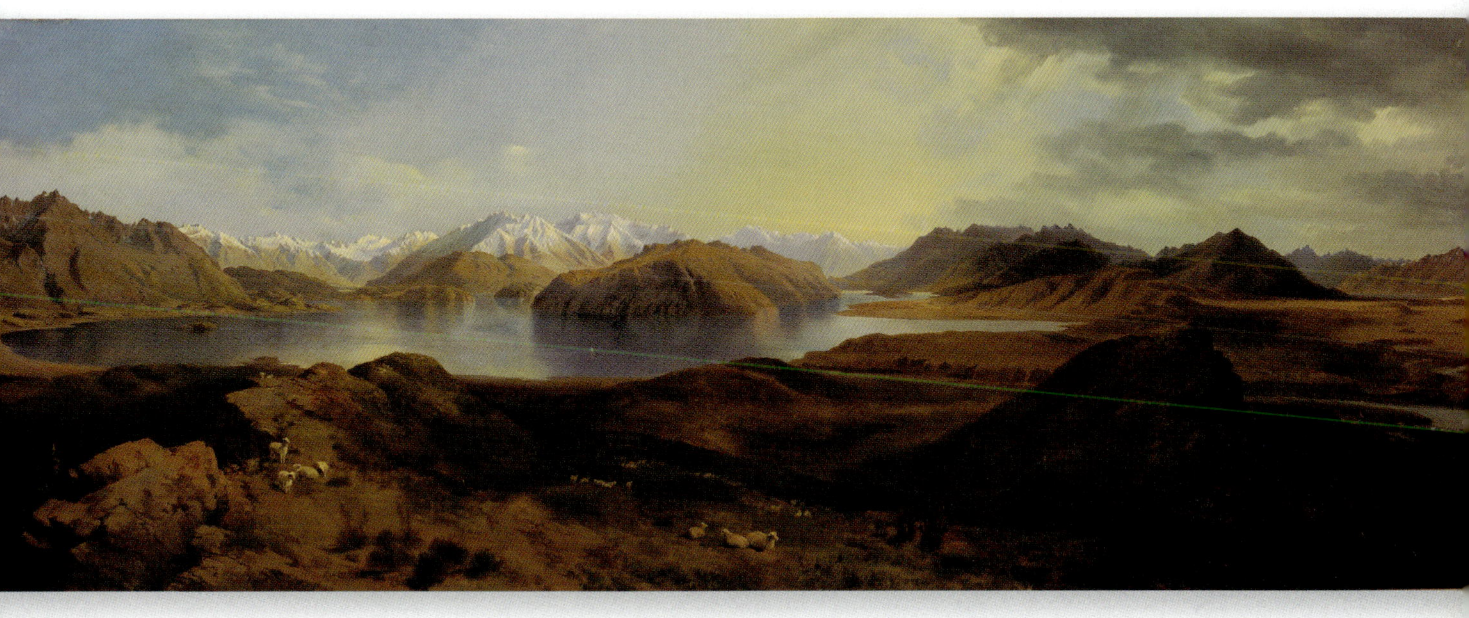

Described as 'exquisite pastelline beauties', the stepped silica formations of the Pink and White Terraces near Rotorua were the eighth wonder of the natural world – and New Zealand's most famous tourist attraction – until they were buried by Mount Tarawera's eruption on 10 June 1886. Images of them, before and after their destruction, were a lucrative source of income for many artists.

Arriving in Auckland in 1860, John Hoyte (1835–1912) taught art at the Church of England Grammar School and helped found the Auckland Society of Arts. Its 1873 exhibition has been described as Mr Hoyte's own show with eighteen of his watercolours of lake scenery, based on drawings made round Lake Rotorua, Lake Rotomahana and Lake Tarawera, on display. Priced between £5 and £12, ten of them had sold by the third day of the exhibition. Topographically accurate, and painted in clear colours, Hoyte's use of lapis blue to indicate shadows made his paintings particularly distinctive.

Dunedin's reputation as a cultural centre drew him south in 1876, and Otago's mountains, lakes and rivers were exemplary of, in his words, 'the fruitful source of subjects which our Provincial scenery offers to the painter's brush'. Art buyers were few, however, and three years later he departed for Australia. LT

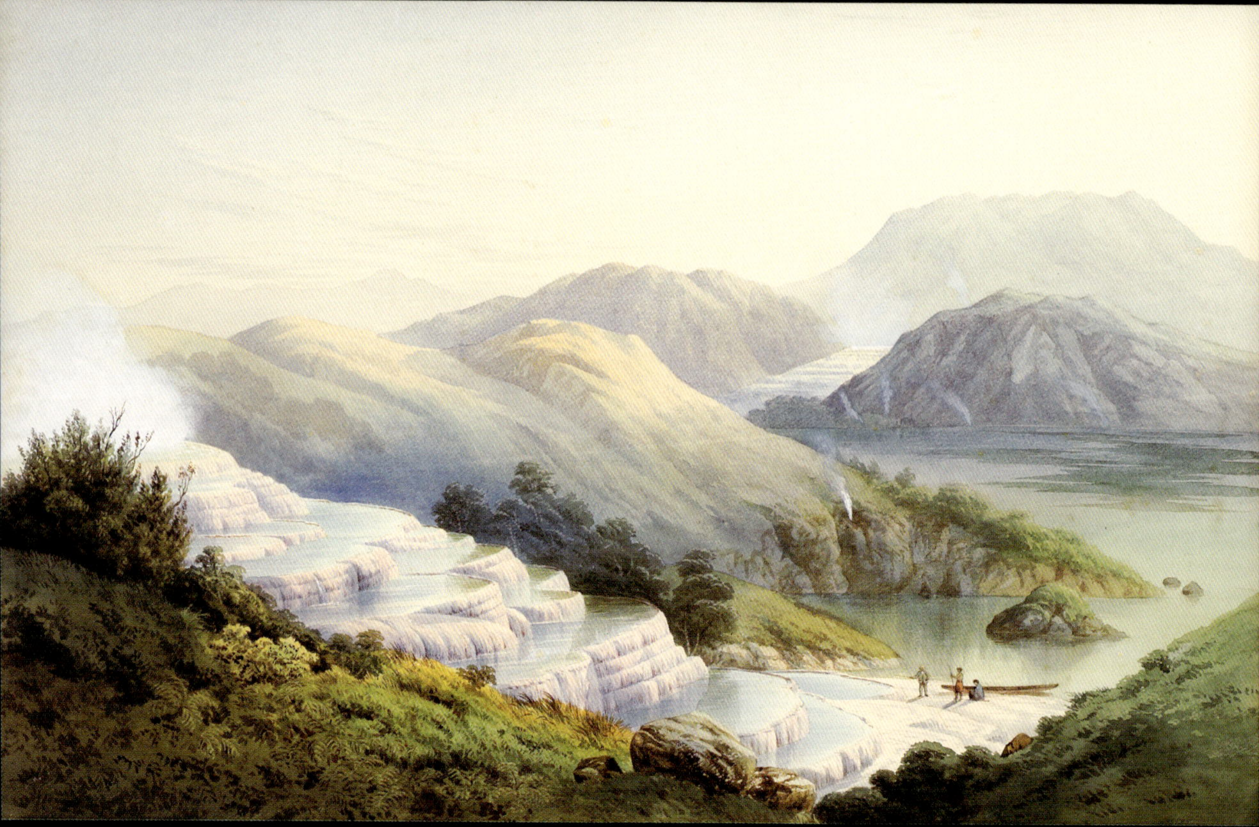

John Barr Clark Hoyte. *Pink and White Terraces, Lake Rotomahana and Mount Tarawera.* c. 1873. Watercolour and gouache on paper. 417 x 654 mm. Donated by Miss D.E. Harrison, 1973.

Romance of Dusky Sound • 1884

Travelling to Fiordland on the *Hawea* in 1878, William Mathew Hodgkins (1833–98) filled a whole sketchbook with his impressions of its majestic beauty. He subsequently exhibited many views of the Dusky Sound landscape, but only this one of its human history. Shown at the Otago Art Society in 1884, it depicts the Māori man recorded in Cook's Journal as startling the European sailors with his shouting: 'The man called to us as we passed by him from the point of a Rock, on which he stood with the staff of destruction in his hand'. In contrast to William Hodges' paintings of the same subject from 1773, Hodgkins anticipated the moment of Māori-European encounter by depicting the man gazing towards Cook's landing party, rather than confronting the viewer.

By profession a lawyer, Hodkgins neglected his career to concentrate on his artistic hobbies. He helped found the Otago Art Society in 1875, and establish the art gallery in 1884, exhibited extensively and also wrote on art. His 1880 lecture, 'A history of landscape art and its study in New Zealand', was influential in developing a landscape tradition here. Hocken collected just one of his paintings, a view of Otokia in 1860, perhaps preferring its topographical style to the Turneresque romanticism of Hodgkins's later work. LT

William Mathew Hodgkins. *Dusky Sound, West Coast of New Zealand: an incident of Captain Cook's second voyage, March 1773.* 1884. Watercolour on paper. 648 x 978 mm. Donated by Mrs E.V. Acland, 1965.

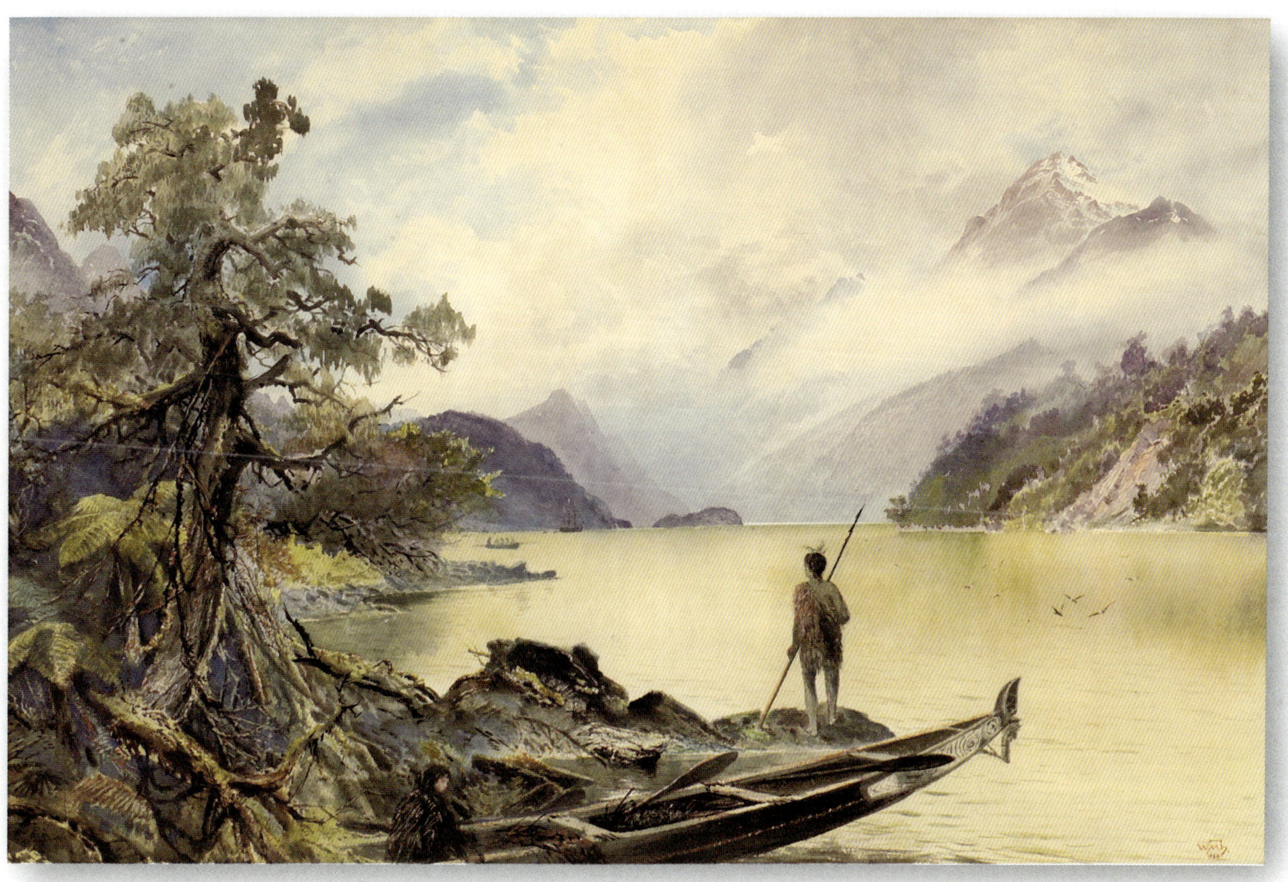

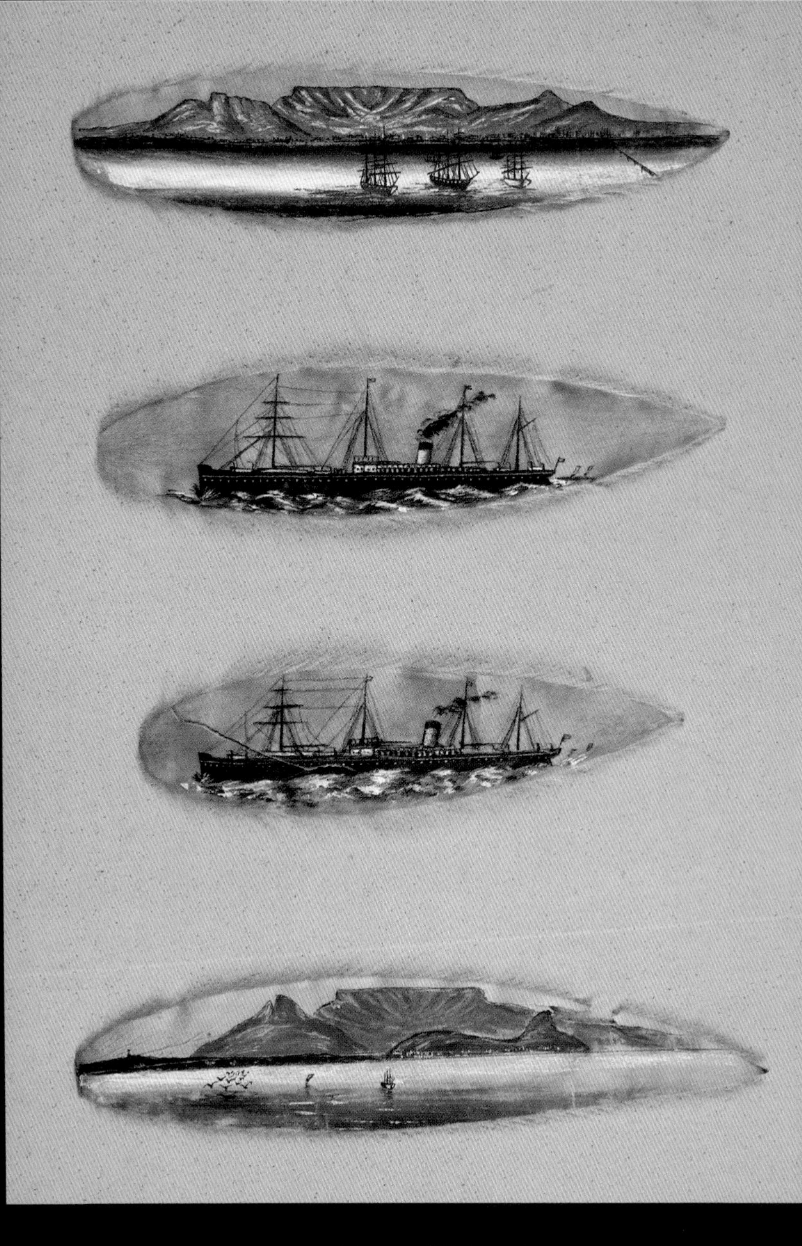

Edmund O'Keeffe. *Set of four paintings of ships*. c. 1880. Ink and china white on leaves. 279 x 208 mm. Donated by Mrs A.C. Coghill, 1969.

Irish goldminer Edmund O'Keeffe (c. 1828–1908) arrived in Dunedin from Australia by 1866, working first as a grocer and carter before settling in to life as a publican at the Liverpool Arms Hotel in Filleul Street. He exhibited paintings of ships annually at the Otago Art Society from its inception in 1876 until 1880, but as well painted charming genre scenes of Dunedin life, such as *School Class* c. 1895, also in the Hocken. As an artist, his reputation has been overshadowed by his son, Alfred Henry O'Keeffe, who developed a bold and colourful style in Paris, and worked as a professional painter for over fifty years.

Miniature painting was Edmund O'Keeffe's speciality, working in watercolour and gouache on shells, waxed paper, and in this case, silken leaves. He used fine squirrel hair brushes on these tiny supports to achieve such minute detailing as the rigging and portholes on the steamships and diminishing size of a flock of seagulls.

After the invention of photography, limning ('pictures in little' as the Elizabethans termed it) became the province of amateurs. The practice continued as a curiosity throughout Victorian and Edwardian times, having its own section in art exhibitions, but did not survive the onslaught of modernism in the later

The 'Dunedin' • 1875

Frederick Tudgay (1841–1921) was an English artist who worked on commission, producing commemorative paintings of new ships under sail and steam. The *Dunedin*, which made its maiden voyage in 1874, was one of six ships with New Zealand names built for P. Henderson and Co. of Glasgow and placed under the Albion Shipping Company in 1877. Between 1874 and 1889, she made a total of seventeen round voyages between Britain and New Zealand, eleven of them to Port Chalmers, before disappearing in 1890, presumed wrecked off Cape Horn.

This oil of the *Dunedin* depicted off the coast of England in 1875 was originally given by the Port Glasgow shipbuilder Robert Duncan to Captain John Whitson, master of the vessel for thirteen of its voyages to New Zealand. It shows the ship in the Albion Line colours of black hull and pink boot topping, and flying the Albion Line flag, as she would have appeared when sailing from Port Chalmers on 15 February 1882 with the first shipment of 4909 frozen sheep carcases bound for London. This breakthrough moment for New Zealand's pastoral economy is commemorated as National Lamb Day, and meat exports now generate $5 billion annually. LT

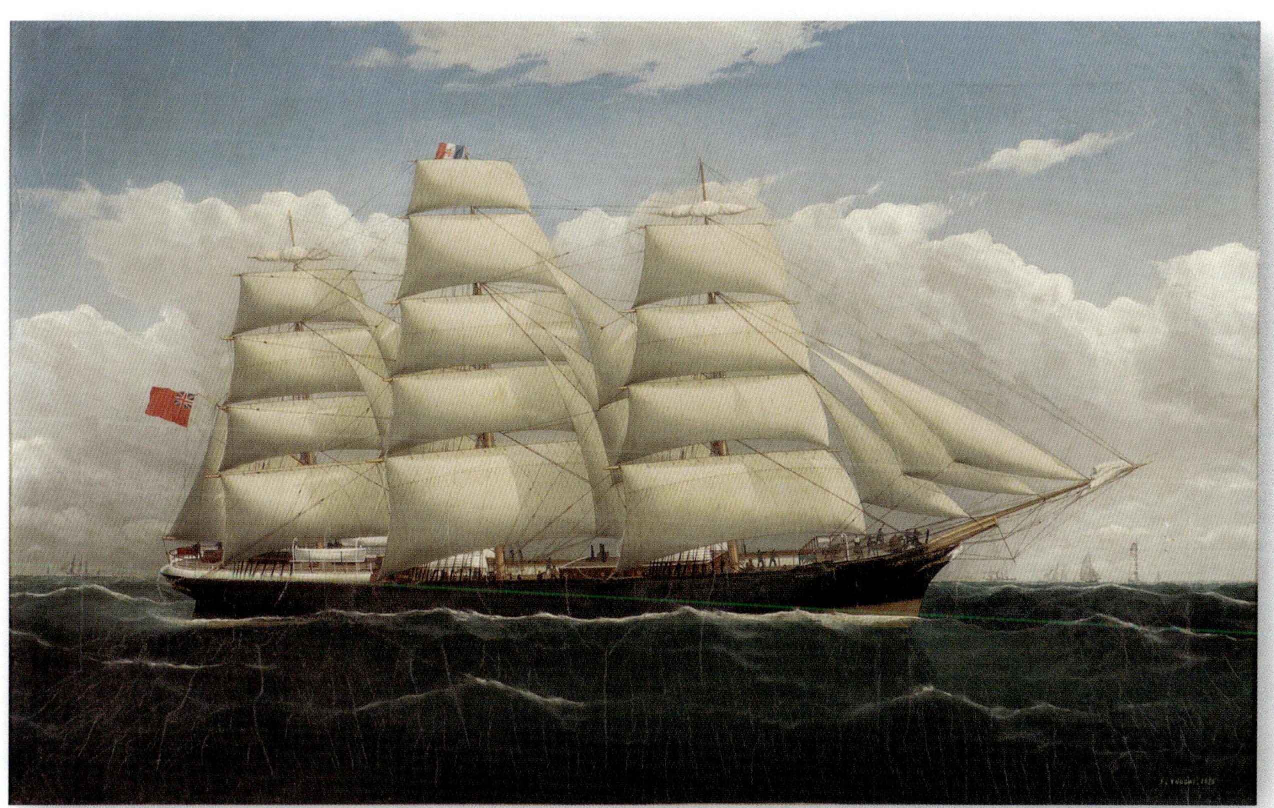

Frederick Tudgay. *The 'Dunedin' off the English coast.* 1875. Oil on canvas. 487 x 790 mm. Purchased, 2001.

Portrait of a boy • 1873

Head of New Zealand's first art school when it opened in Dunedin in 1870, Scotsman David Con Hutton (1843–1910) set up his plaster casts from antique sculpture for pupils to draw in two large rooms in the former Stock Exchange Building. Students were offered courses in the British South Kensington system of National Art Training, with an emphasis on the principles of ornament.

Hutton's own artistic style had a Pre-Raphaelite quality, which relied on many preparatory drawings. Working slowly in watercolour on a bright white ground back in his studio, he carefully recreated the colours and textures seen in nature. Here he emphasised the golden filigree of his son's curls and the soft velvet of his tailored breeches and jacket, while capturing his sense of purpose in striding out with his whip.

David Edward Hutton would have been seven years old when this portrait was made. He went on to become the first New Zealand male to gain a full Art Masters' Certificate from South Kensington, and then travelled to Britain to study architecture under Sir Banister Fletcher. From 1917 to 1931 he worked as an architect in Christchurch, where he designed Opawa and Philipstown schools and Christchurch West District High School (now Hagley Community College). LT

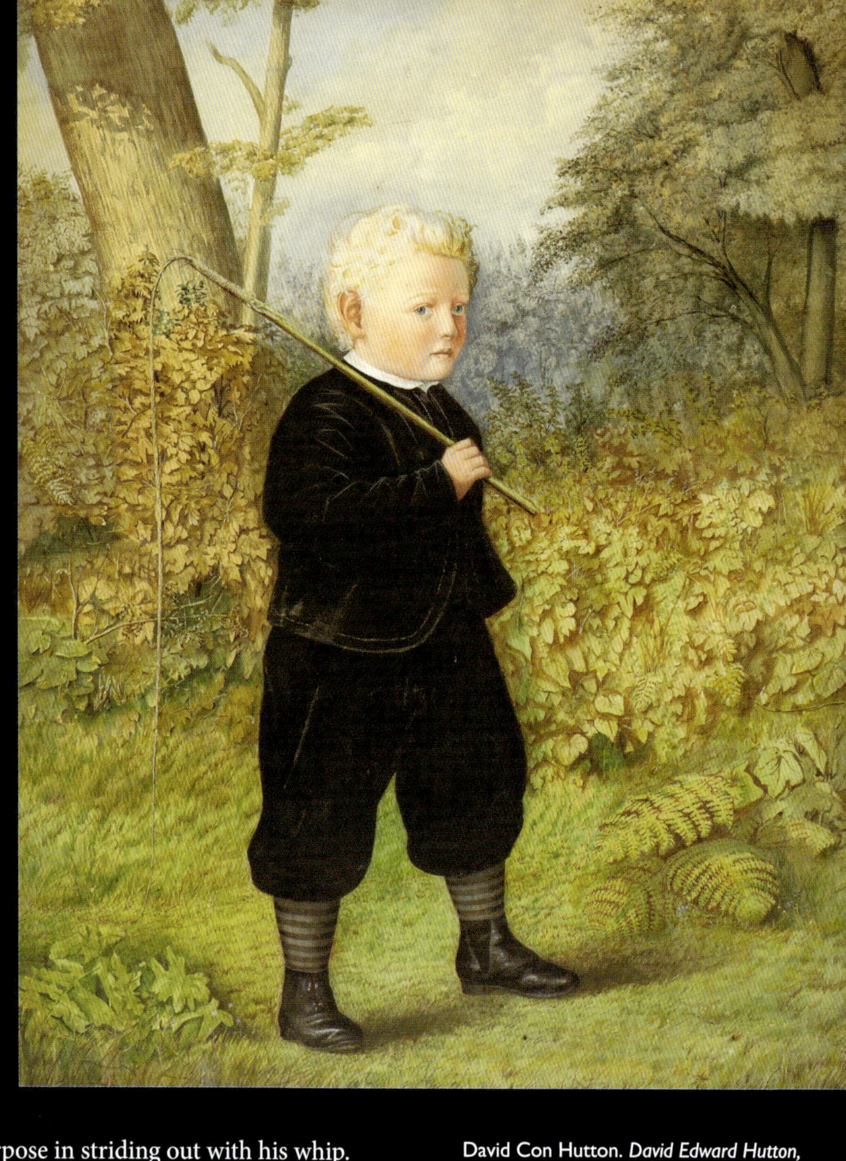

David Con Hutton. *David Edward Hutton, eldest son of the artist.* 1873. Watercolour on paper. 840 x 655 mm. Donated by Sheila and Kathleen, grand-daughters of the artist, 1956.

Chinese mission • 1880

Alexander Don (1857–1934), who was a Presbyterian missionary to Chinese miners working on the Otago goldfields in the later nineteenth century, is shown here seated with Chau Yip Fung, whom the American Presbyterian Mission employed on the island of Shamian in the Pearl River to teach their workers Chinese writing and reading skills. Having initially trained as a school teacher, Don first came to Dunedin in 1879 to study theology but was sent to Canton (Guangzhou) for sixteen months. A companion painting, also in the Hocken, depicts the house he lived in there.

Despite the fact that both subjects are men, and that the painting was made in China, the painting was once used to discuss cross-cultural marital relationships in nineteenth century New Zealand. That Chau Yip Fung is male, and hence nobody's wife, is indicated by his clothing and hairstyle – he wears the standard Manchu cut of tonsure and queue (only just visible) imposed on all Han Chinese after the Manchu conquest of China in the mid-seventeenth century. The display of appendages here is also most unfeminine. The feet of an educated Chinese woman of this period would have been both bound and hidden. LT

Unknown Cantonese artist. *Alexander Don and Chau Yip Fung, Shameen, September 1880.* Oil on canvas. 292 x 408 mm. Deposited by Jean McNeur, c. 1966.

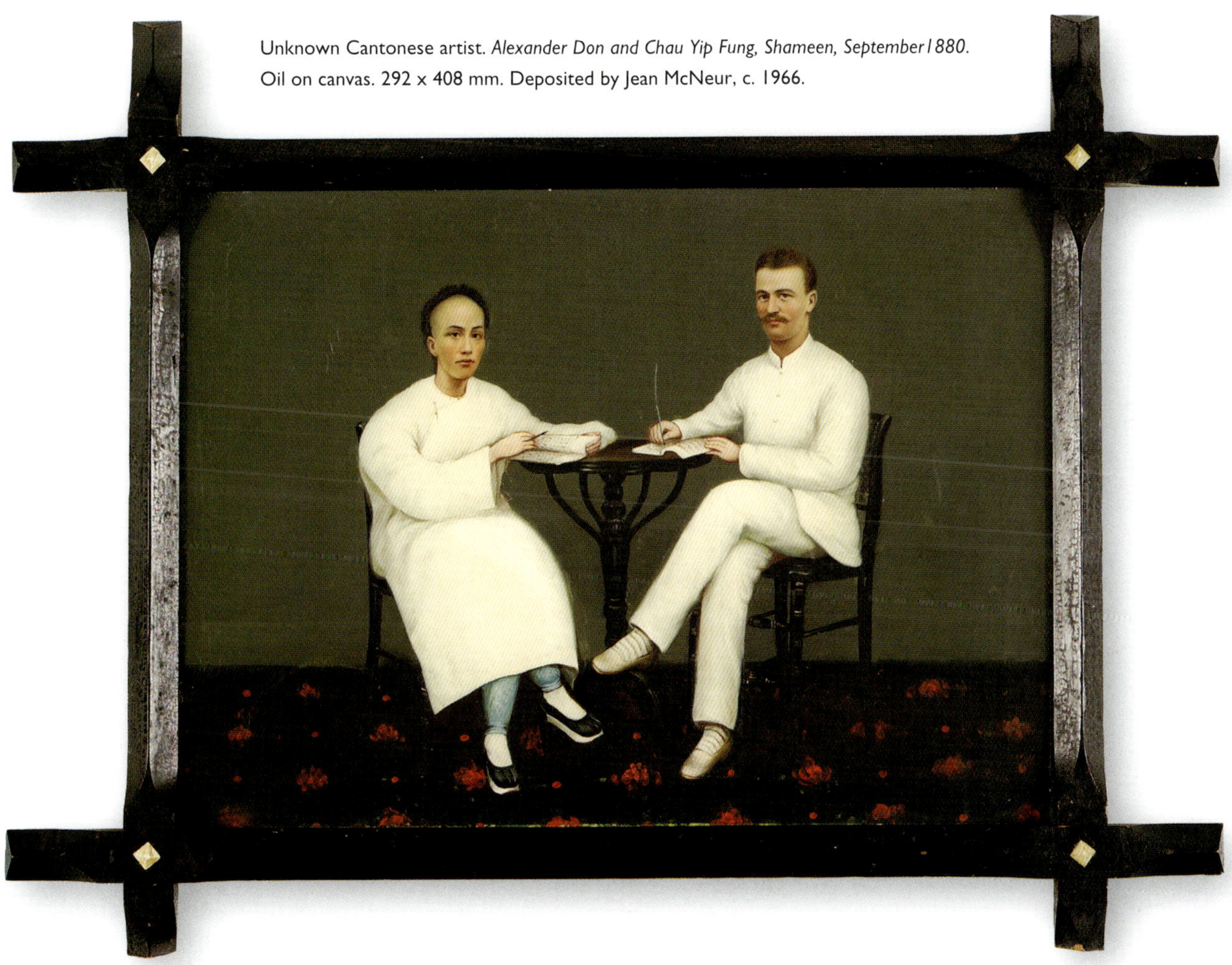

Mysterious woman • c. 1889

Holding her oil palette and brushes like a shield, and wearing an apron to protect her clothing, the subject of this portrait seems proud of the appurtenances of her calling. Surrounded by exotic fabrics, her location is ambiguous. Down at her feet gleams a decorated Polynesian headdress. She belongs to the Antipodes, yet the studio in which she is posed is dressed with the fashionable accessories of Europe's Aesthetic Movement. Oriental lacquer work and brocades glow against the black background. Perhaps a pupil of Nerli's, perhaps a personification of Art itself, her identity remains elusive.

Having emigrated to Australia from Italy in 1885, Nerli (1860–1926) announced his arrival with a few well-placed paintings of bacchanalian orgies. It was not only his subjects that shocked; by comparison to the tame Impressionism of the Heidelberg painters in Melbourne, his style seemed 'dashing, unfinished and bold'. Dunedin had appealed on his brief visit in 1889, and he returned in 1893. He was to stay just three years, starting his own art school before being recruited to the Dunedin School of Art and Design, but the effect he had on art produced in the city – including the painting of Frances Hodgkins – was profound.

LT

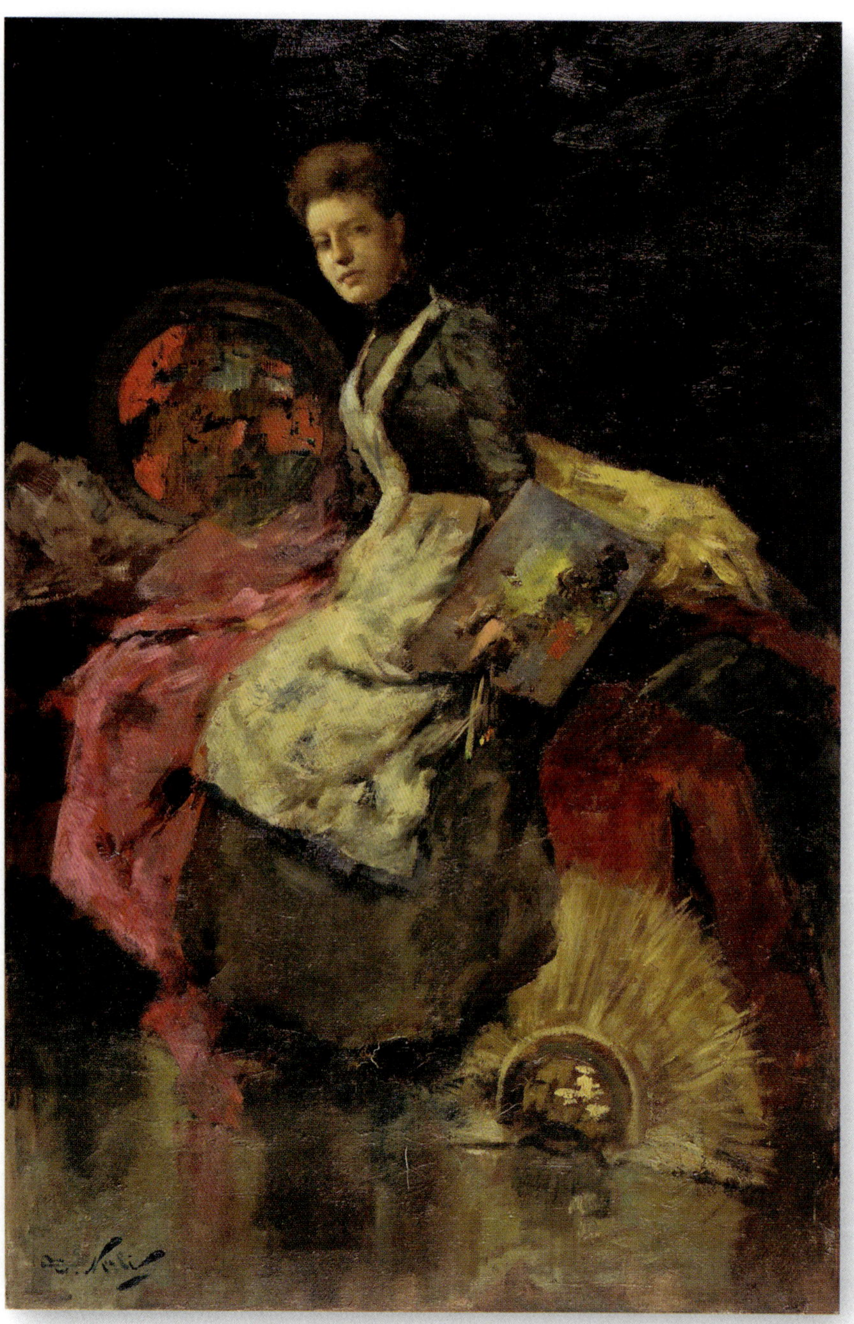

Girolamo Pieri Nerli. *Portrait of a Young Woman Artist*. c. 1889. Oil on canvas. 612 x 406 mm. Purchased, 1959.

Vision in pink • c. 1890

Second cousin to Premier Julius Vogel, Grace Joel (1865–1924) came from an educated and wealthy Dunedin family who were able to send her to study art at the National Gallery School in Melbourne for five years in her twenties. Painting portrait and figure studies with the Italian painter Girolamo Nerli on her return, she concentrated on developing her Impressionist style before leaving for Europe in 1899. Apart from a brief visit home in 1906, she lived in London for the rest of her life, working and exhibiting as a professional painter.

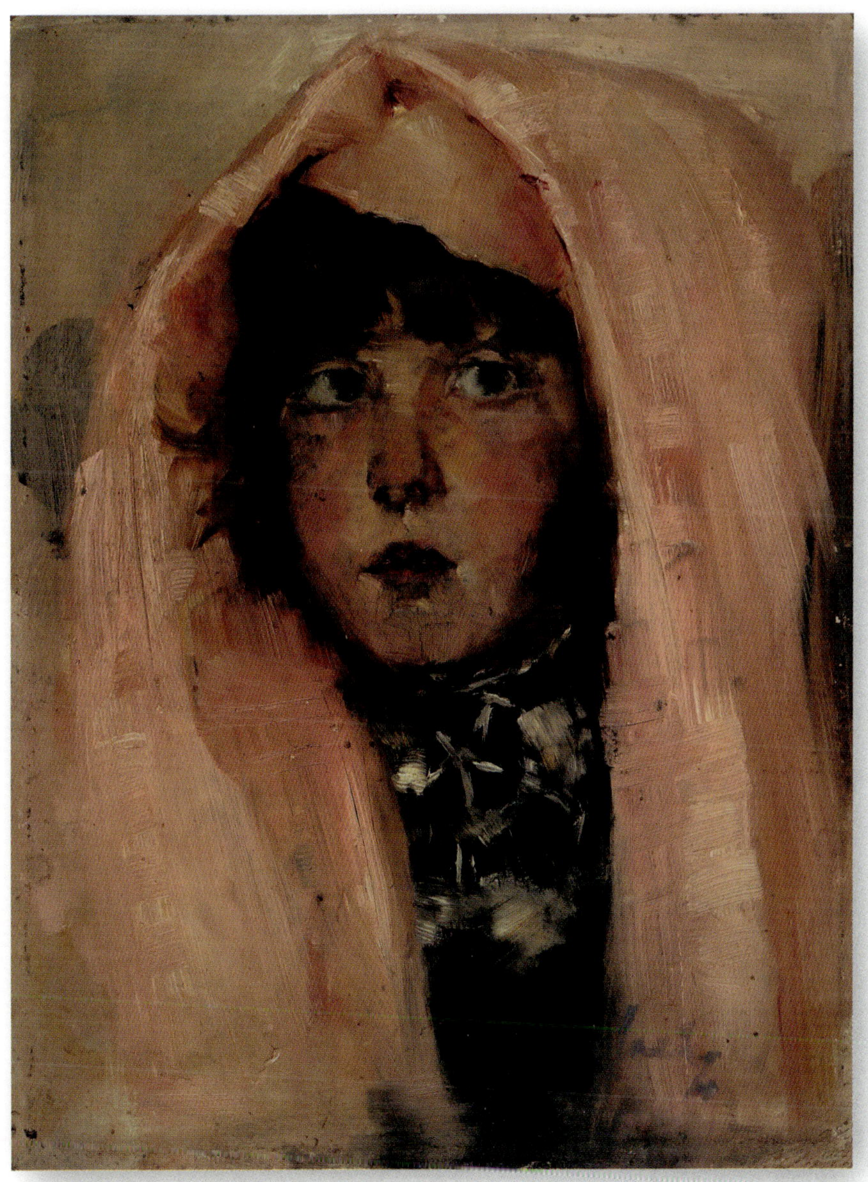

Grace Jane Joel. *Portrait of a Girl in a Pink Shawl.* c. 1890. Oil on prepared board. 310 x 234 mm. Purchased, 1966.

In this painting, a young girl with auburn hair looks solemnly from beneath a swathe of pink material worn somewhat like a cap in traditional Breton peasant dress. Complementing her innocence, this volume of colour frames her face and imparts sweetness to her expression. Touches of pink on her lids, around her mouth and in the suggestion of embroidery at her throat locks visual interest in tightly to the centre of the composition. Retaining the immediacy of a sketch with its visible cross-hatched brushwork, this work is typical of Joel's technique of enlivening the surface with texture and glinting highlights. The girl's identity is a mystery, perhaps suppressed in favour of a generically appealing vision of the hope and innocence of girlhood. LT

Portrait of the artist's wife • c. 1900

One of the Glasgow Boys, a group of rebellious young Scottish artists who rejected academic traditions of classical subjects and grand themes in favour of painting scenes capturing the bustle of modern life, James Nairn (1859–1904) was a fully fledged Impressionist when he arrived in Dunedin in 1890. Although he moved to Wellington later that year, he maintained his presence in the south by exhibiting regularly at the Art Society.

Nairn joined the New Zealand Academy of Fine Arts in Wellington but found the laboured sentimentalism of the prevailing landscape style tedious. In 1892 he formed a splinter group called the Wellington Art Club. His rented rural retreat, Pumpkin Cottage at Silverstream in the Hutt Valley, was where they met to paint out in the countryside *en plein air*. It was in Silverstream that he married nineteen-year-old Ellen Smith in 1898.

Twenty years her senior, Nairn celebrated his wife's youth and vibrant manner in this portrait. Even her smock seems energetic, enlivened with patches of blue and red. Though carefree here, after just six years of marriage Ellen was left by Nairn's early death in poverty with two young daughters to support, and was forced to sell all the works of his that she owned. She was to outlive her husband by over fifty years. LT

James McLauchlan Nairn. *Smiling Woman (Portrait of the artist's wife)*, c. 1900.
Oil on canvas. 576 x 487 mm.
Donated by Charles Brasch, 1972.

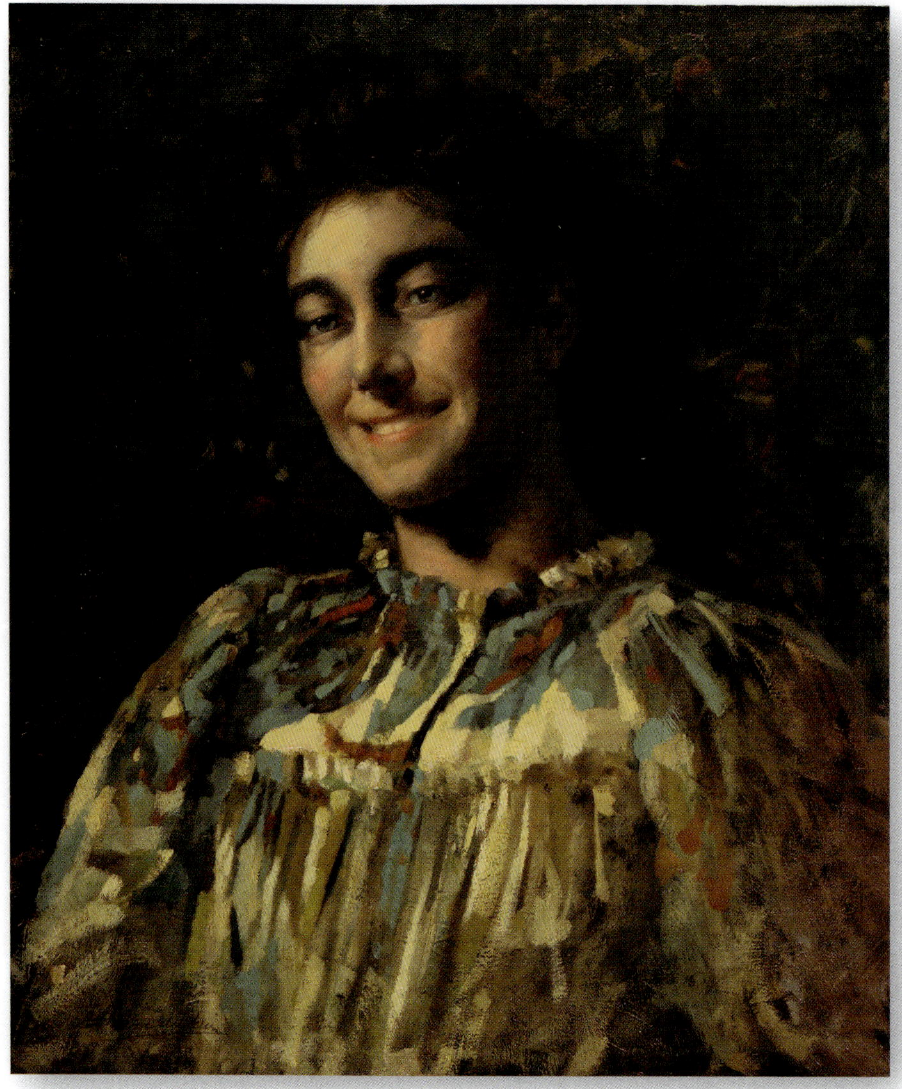

Regarding himself as 'a nuisance dedicated to sanity', Dunedin-born David Low (1891–1963) came to fame with his English political cartoons of the 1930s and 1940s. During the New Zealand International Exhibition of 1906–07, Fred Rayner first hired him to illustrate the Exhibition *Sketcher* for £2 per week. He then became the Liberal-inclined *Spectator*'s political cartoonist, finding time to contribute two half-page cartoons to the *Weekly Herald*, a new Labour paper. This moonlighting – and also his Labour sympathies – forced a move to the *Canterbury Times* in 1910, where he worked briefly before leaving for Sydney.

Low's subject here is the Liberal MP for Eastern Māori, James Carroll, or Timi Kara as he was known by Māori. Knighted in 1911 after eleven years as a Member of the House of Representatives, Carroll had become the first Māori Minister of Native Affairs in 1899, and was acting prime minister in 1909 and 1911. His stature in the Liberal Party is indicated by Low's description of him as Prime Minister Sir Joseph Ward's 'brown right hand'. Drawn as a wooden tekoteko figure with a feather in his hair and smoking his pipe, Low shows Carroll as the staunch protector of Māori land – the M.L. of the caricature's title. LT

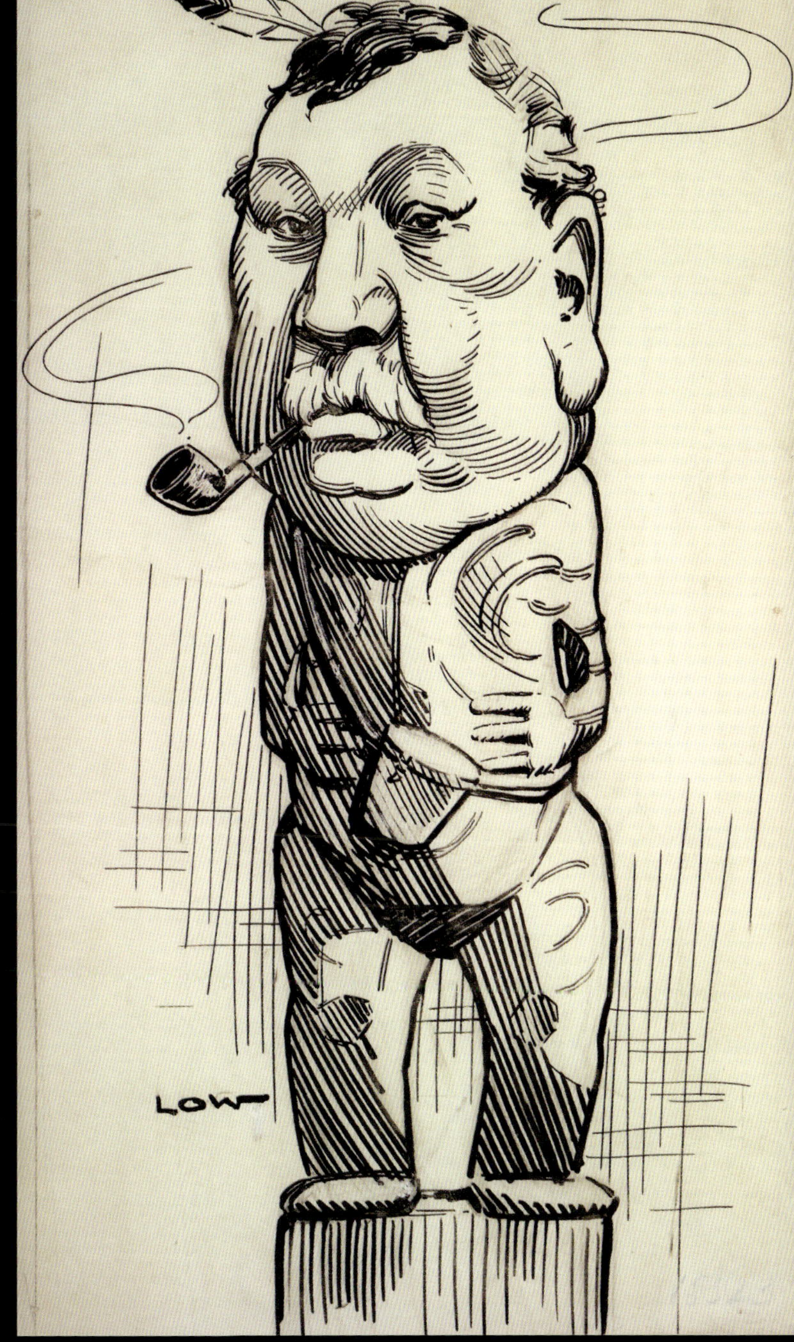

David Alexander Cecil Low. *The Hon. Jimmy Carroll of M.L. Joe Ward's Brown Right Hand.* 1911. Pen and ink on paper. 280 x 163 mm. Provenance unknown.

Modern beauty • c. 1914

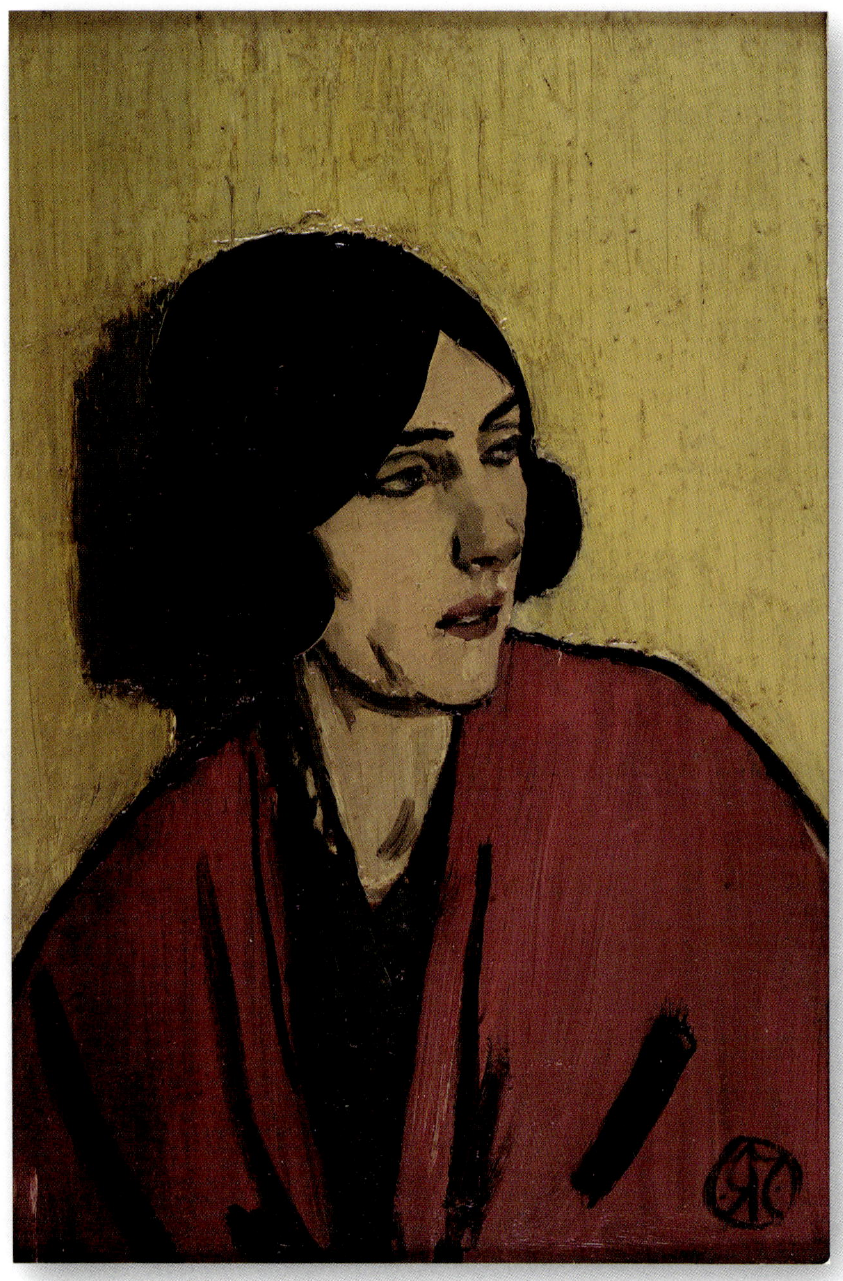

Raymond Francis McIntyre. *Portrait of a Dark-haired Woman*. c. 1914. Oil on panel. 292 x 202 mm. Donated by Charles Brasch, 1959.

Twenty-two-year-old Phyllis Constance Cavendish with her 'very refined interesting pale face' became Christchurch-born Raymond McIntyre's (1879–1933) model in London for four years from 1911. He was completely disinterested in her personality; it was her look that fascinated him, representing an ideal of modern beauty which he wanted to perfect.

Putting formal concerns ahead of representation, McIntyre achieved an Art Nouveau decorative patterning effect in his many images of the actress. With ideas learned from Japanese prints, he contrasted black shapes and lines against lighter tones. Limiting detail and planning colour tonalities to flatten and unify the surface, he used balancing geometries to structure the composition: the angles of the opposing triangles of the apex of her face and neckline are balanced by circular coils of hair. The potential for symmetry in the composition is averted by tilting and turning the head to the side.

Buns over the ears were not Miss Cavendish's choice of hairstyle. In a letter to his photographer brother, McIntyre wrote, 'I always make her do it how I want it – which is in a more severe style. A la Breton or in plaits – or plastered down. I like the shape of the head to show, especially if it is a good shape – and hers is.' LT

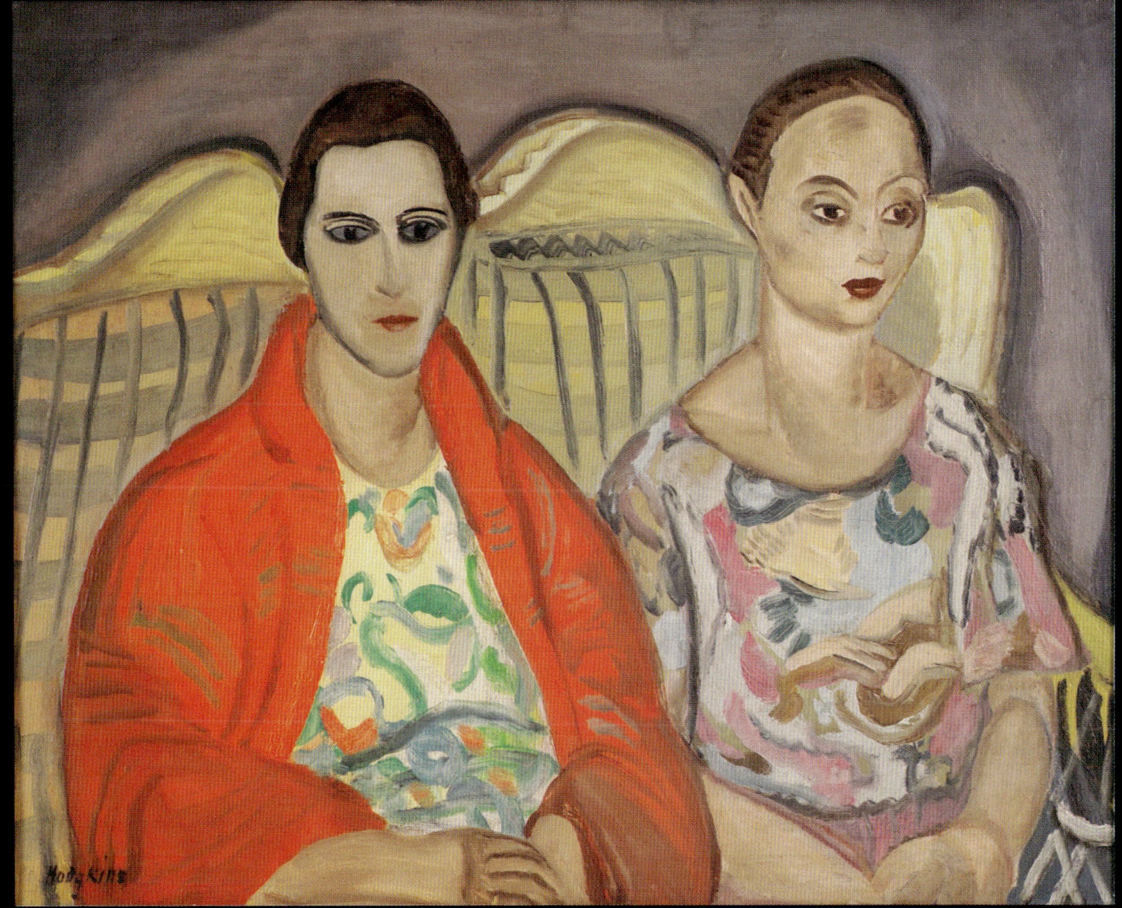

Double portrait • 1922–25

Frances Hodgkins. *Double Portrait.* 1922–25. Oil on canvas. 610 x 770 mm. Charles Brasch Bequest, 1973.

Showing a knowledge of the elongated figures and oval eyes which characterised the work of Amadeo Modigliani, this painting also recalls the flattened forms and bright colour of Henri Matisse, whose retrospective Frances Hodgkins (1869–1947) had seen in 1910. *Double Portrait* brings to the fore Hodgkins's latent interest in abstract pattern-making in the treatment of the fabric of the women's dresses. In 1925 she would work as a textile designer for the Calico Printers' Association in Manchester.

The portrait commemorates a long association. Hannah Ritchie (on the left) had joined Hodgkins's painting class in Montreuil in 1911 and the following year brought her friend Dorothy, later Jane, Saunders (on the right) to St Valery-sur-Somme. The couple attended later classes in England and France, and frequently had Hodgkins to stay when both became art teachers at Manchester High School for Girls. While visiting them, Hodgkins herself studied briefly with the English Post-Impressionist Walter Sickert, known for his paintings of theatrical or music hall subjects often arranged in couples or pairs.

Hannah Ritchie and Jane Saunders separated in 1931, but Hannah kept the painting until 1957, when she sold it through the Leicester Gallery to Charles Brasch. LT

Pure paint • 1928

Robert Field (1899–1987) began teaching art in Dunedin in 1925. Committed to both creativity and Christianity, his integrity encouraged a generation of New Zealand modernists to pursue careers as painters. Colin McCahon felt indebted to him, and wrote 'the painter's life to me was exemplified by the life and work of R.N. Field'. While also skilled as a potter and sculptor, Field believed in the pre-eminence of painting as the art form that nourished the eye, training it to see.

Dominating this painting is Field's own portrait in clay of Robert Lee, a fellow teacher at the King Edward Technical College. Though it is night outside, the blinds are up in the sitting room of his home at Tomahawk Road, with a consequent play of reflections. Beyond the bright confines of the lit room, a shadowy exterior world is suggested, with depth created through darker hues rather than linear perspective. Janus-like, the head seems to face in two directions, while gladioli in a vase on the right signal summer, and a new year.

Influenced by Expressionism, Field worked with pure, bright colours. His bold palette excited pupil Toss Woollaston, who wrote, 'his pictures, brilliant and heady, were painted with jewel like, full-sized brush strokes, or with rainbow-like spots and scales of pure paint shimmering'. LT

Robert Nettleton Field. *Interior*. 1928. Oil on plywood. 355 x 263 mm. Purchased, 1967.

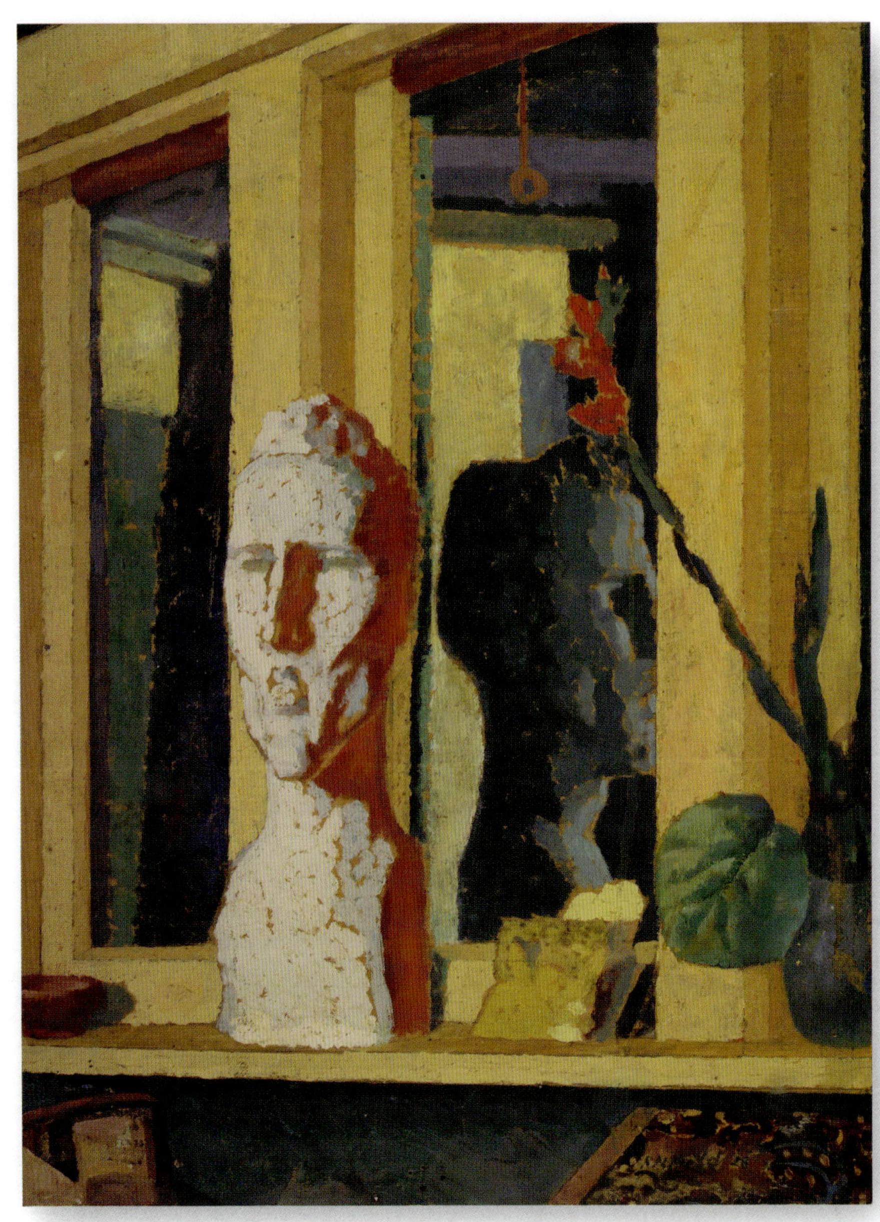

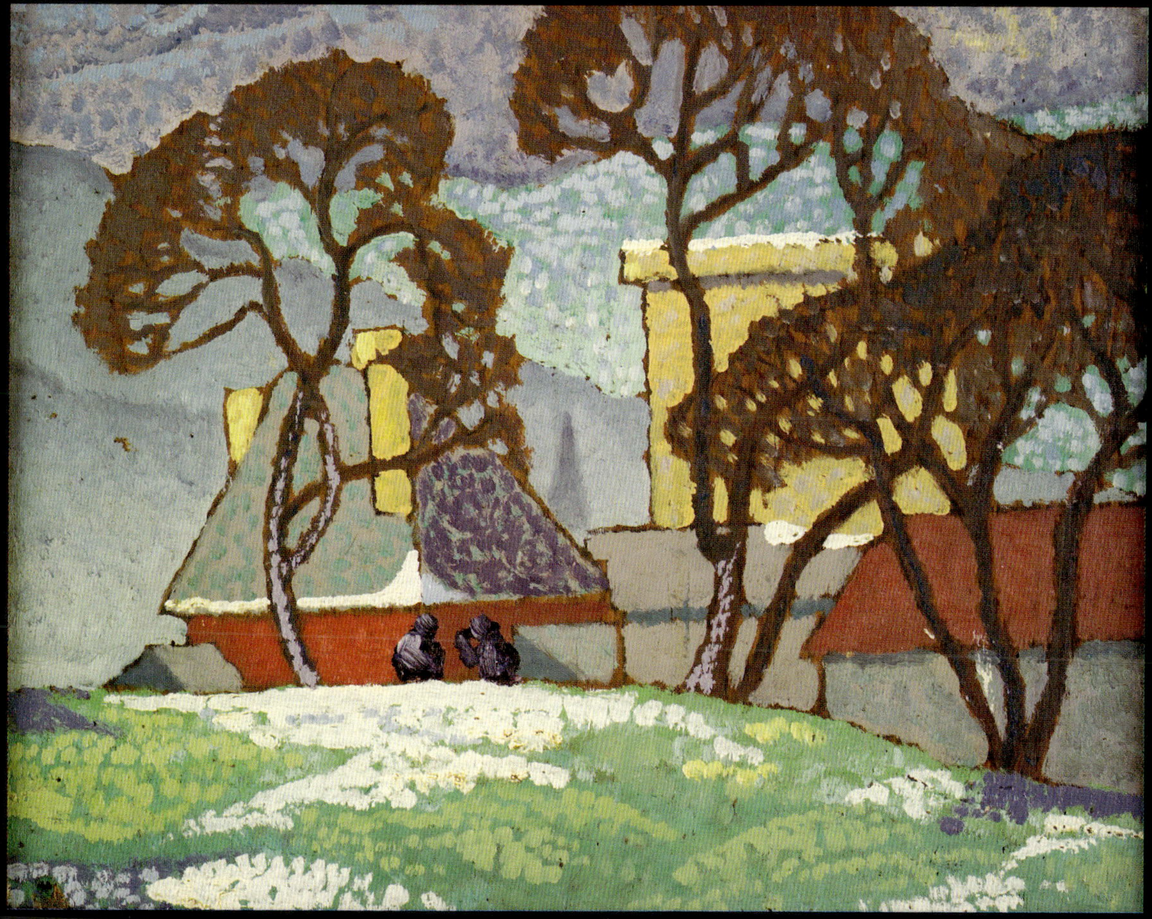

Modern art In Otago • 1930

Harry Vye Miller. *Houses through the Trees*. 1930. Oil on plywood panel. 272 x 376 mm. H.V. Miller Bequest, 1986.

Studying painting under Robert Nettleton Field and William Henry Allen in 1928, H.V. Miller (1907–86) felt part of what he called 'the first cell of modern art in Otago'. Field and his friend, fellow Royal College of Art graduate, Allen, had been recruited under William Sanderson La Trobe's scheme to invigorate art in New Zealand, and proved highly successful revolutionaries. Training first at Dunedin Teachers' College, Miller felt compelled by these charismatic teachers to become an art specialist.

Miller learnt to build his compositions like a mosaic, using jewel-like dabs of bright colour laid side-by-side, and unblended. His complementary matching of mauve accents in the sky and roof areas with acid greens in the foreground knits the composition together and signals his understanding of the decorative patterning of Post-Impressionism. Silhouetted trees act as a decorative orientalising screen in the midground, flattening out the space into a series of planes, and dividing the patched grass of the foreground from the abstracted buildings beyond. The subject in this painting is generic rather than specific, and traditional perspective has been abandoned. With no central focus to the composition, the idea of painting as illusionistic view – a window on the world – is gone. LT

Flower piece • 1933

Better known as an art collector and promoter of theatre than as a painter, Rodney Kennedy's (1909–89) knowledge of modernism was shaped by the years he spent at the Dunedin School of Art. Attending full-time in the late 1920s and part-time in 1930, when Englishmen William Allen and Robert Field were the influential teachers, he learned to deploy colour, directional brushstrokes and simple geometries to create strikingly bold compositions. Painting still-life subjects, Kennedy's starting point was observable reality, but his use of Post-Impressionist strategies pushed naturalism to the brink of abstraction.

Here the space created by the acid green which curtains off the background is ambiguous. Its main role is to activate the other colours, curving around behind the vase of flowers to enhance their complementary orange and contrasting with the purple of the tipped-up tabletop. Boundaries are edged with a bright turquoise suggestive of backlighting. Though almost centrally placed, the chrysanthemums are asymmetrically arranged and cropped at the top to suggest arbitrary framing and artifice.

Meeting Toss Woollaston in 1932, Kennedy organised the artist's first exhibition in 1936 and introduced him to Colin McCahon. Kennedy later abandoned painting for theatre but remained an influential Dunedin identity, with a thorough understanding and commitment to modernism in the arts. LT

Rodney Eric Kennedy. *Flower Piece.* 1933. Oil on canvas. 455 x 410 mm. Donated by R.E. Kennedy, 1988.

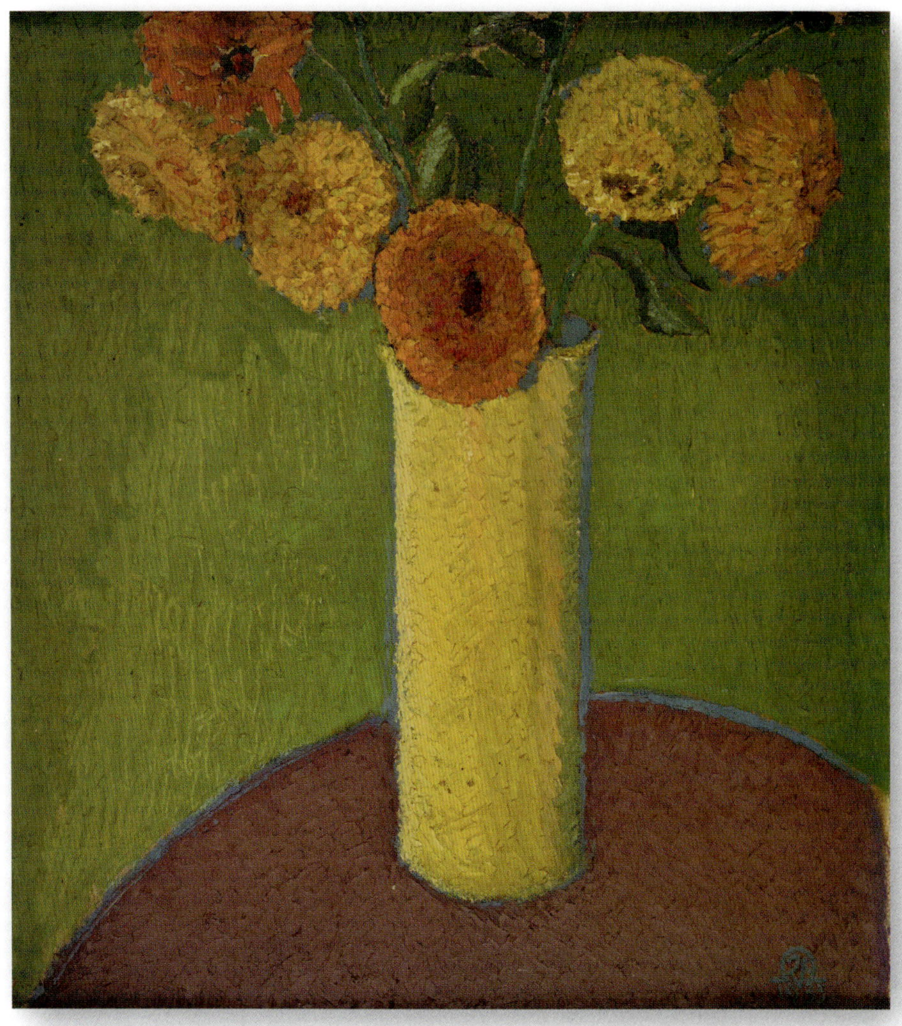

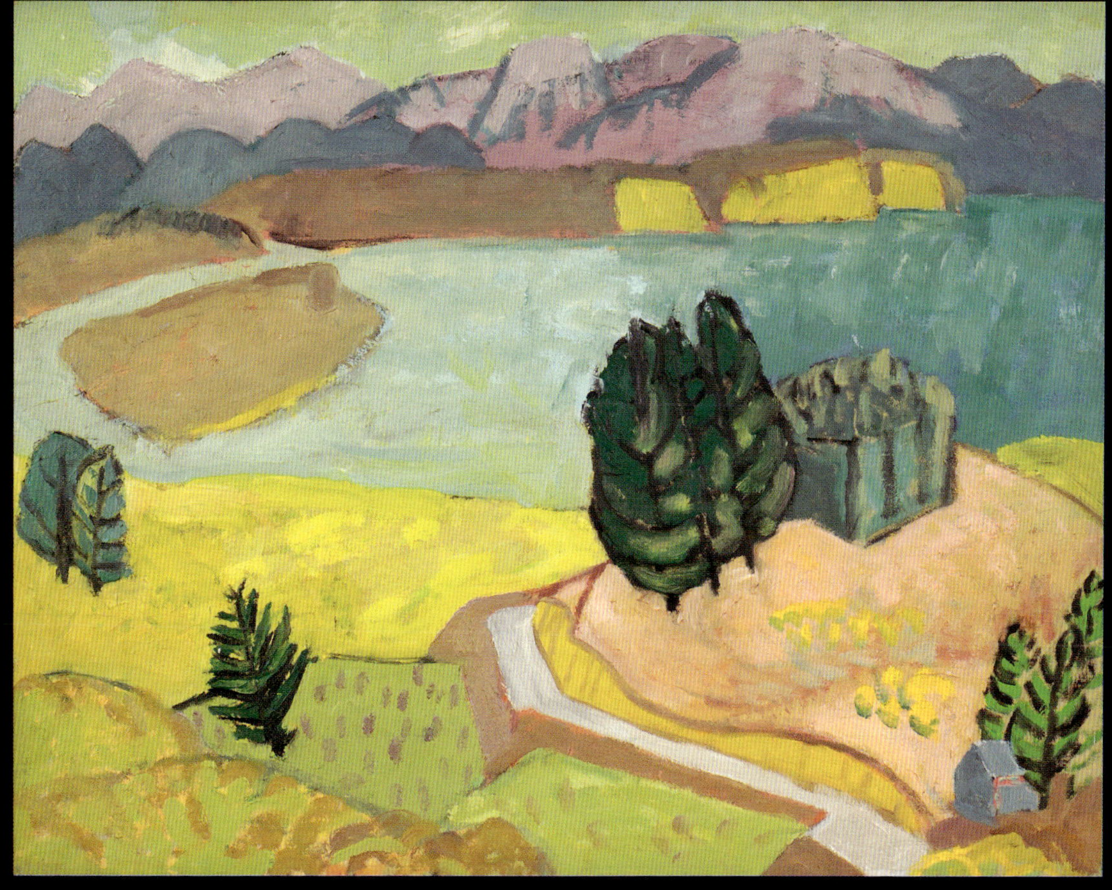

Mountford Tosswill Woollaston. *Landscape, Tahunanui.* 1934. Oil on canvas mounted on board. 483 x 610 mm. Charles Brasch Bequest, 1973.

Breakthrough for Woollaston • 1934

Completing his art schooling with R.N. Field in Dunedin in 1932, Woollaston (1910–98) was settling into his own quiet variant of Post-Impressionism when he met modernist painter Flora Scales (1887–1985) in Nelson in 1934. Scales had studied painting at the Hans Hofmann School of Fine Arts in Munich and Woollaston was eager to analyse the principles of German Expressionism at one remove. He spent the summer copying from Scales's notebooks. What Woollaston learned was to use exaggerated colours and distorted shapes to express an emotional response to his subjects.

Painted under Scales's tutelage, *Landscape, Tahunanui* was a breakthrough for Woollaston. The Nelson landscape was the one he knew best, and he succeeded in expressing its raw energy. A bird's-eye viewpoint flattens perspective, and the brightly painted land forms are abruptly sectioned. As the unlikely hues used clash and clamour, the landscape is suddenly restless rather than relaxed. Patterning shifts from the decorative to the disruptive.

Recognising in his friend's work less a likeness of place than a symbol of his reaction to it, Charles Brasch referred to Woollaston as being 'one of the first to see and paint New Zealand as a New Zealander'. Woollaston continued to develop his painterly response to the experience of landscape for a further sixty years. LT

Accomplished still life • c. 1938

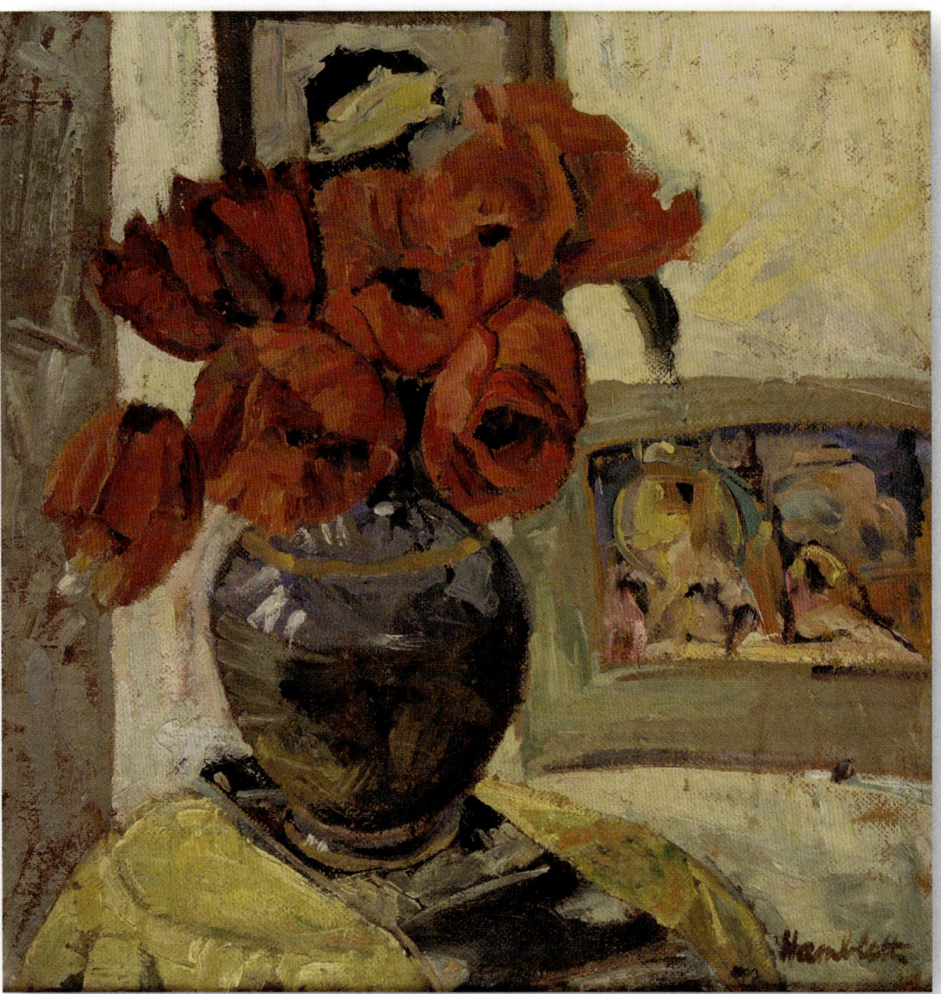

Anne Hamblett. *Poppies*. c. 1938. Oil on composition board. 456 x 452 mm. John and Ethel McCahon Bequest, 1973.

Anne Hamblett's (1915–93) *Poppies* shows the accomplishment of the future Mrs Colin McCahon when only twenty-two years old, and still at art school in Dunedin. Living at home, she relied on sales of work from the annual Otago Art Society exhibition for income.

Still-life painting was Hamblett's strength, and she used flowers and vases as vehicles for the display of her skills in Post-Impressionist brushwork and modern composition. Handling primary colours and geometric forms with a sure touch, she juxtaposed the luscious reds of Oriental poppies with the luminescent blue of a ceramic vase tilted up on a yellow cloth-covered table. She daringly included glimpses of two other paintings in the background, in the manner of Paul Cézanne, whose work bridged the fleeting impressions of forms in light that characterised Impressionist painting and the structural analysis of nature that would eventually be introduced by the Cubists.

Despite such promising beginnings, after marriage in 1942 Anne Hamblett ceased to exhibit her paintings. She did, however, collaborate with her husband on a set of children's murals and work as an illustrator for School Publications. *Poppies* remained unsold and entered the collection of her parents-in-law. It became part of the large bequest of works to the Hocken arranged by Colin McCahon after his mother's death in 1973. LT

Early Lusk • 1940

Determined to become an artist since the age of twelve, Doris Lusk (1916–90) left Otago Girls' High School without matriculating, and enrolled at King Edward Technical College to study art in 1934. Taught by Canadian Charlton Edgar and Englishman R.N. Field, she absorbed theories of modernism, and learned how to construct space in a painting, schematising the forms and using dark outlines to divide the components.

Colin McCahon, Anne Hamblett and Rodney Kennedy were fellow students, as was Toss Woollaston, who described Dunedin in the 1930s as 'the most artistically enlightened place in New Zealand. They were looking at artists unheard of in Christchurch – Matisse, Picasso, Cézanne ….' Leaving art school, Lusk spent January 1939 at the Woollastons' house at Mapua, painting the Nelson region. She had her first solo exhibition back in Dunedin in August 1940, at the Moray Place studio which her young artist friends had rented as a group. She exhibited this painting there for sale for five guineas as *Mixed Flowers*, its tipped-up tabletop and snaking tulips a study in decorative pattern making.

Lusk went on to become one of New Zealand's foremost regionalist artists, developing her specifically localised landscapes from naturalism towards abstraction in a career that spanned over fifty years.

LT

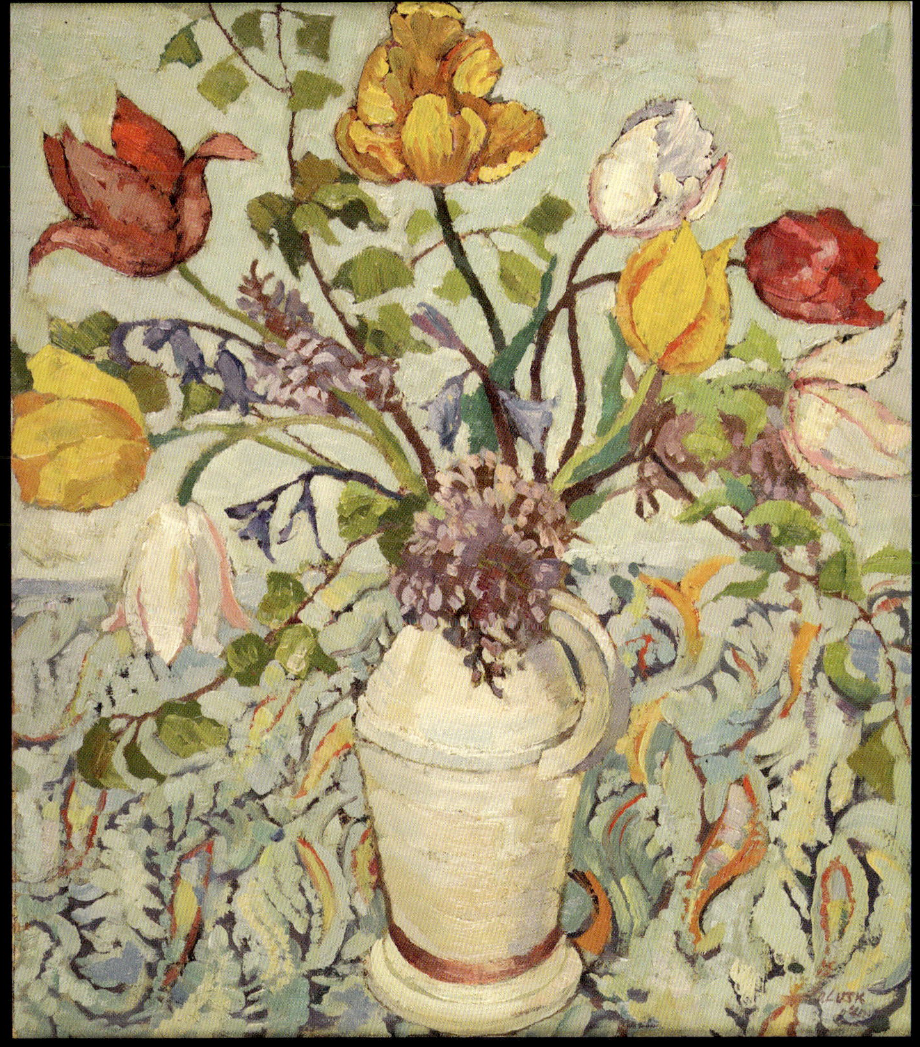

Doris Lusk. *Mixed Flowers*. 1940. Oil on board. 473 x 420mm. Donated by Charlton Edgar for the Mona Edgar Collection, 1963.

Virgin and Child compared • 1948

Married and living with his wife and young son near Nelson in the late forties, Colin McCahon (1919–87) turned from depicting landscapes to Christian imagery. By synthesising disparate elements – portraiture, still life, and words – McCahon emphasised that his works had a message.

The purity and innocence of childhood are memorialised in this post-war work, but it also carries art historical and cinematic references. *The Blessed Virgin Compared*, McCahon revealed, owed its being to the grisly sixteenth-century German painter Grünewald and to 'that cruel and beautiful film, *Open City*'. Director Rossellini explained his aim there as showing that acts of heroism and human kindness obviously spring from faith, and the brutalities of war from cynicism and absence of moral code.

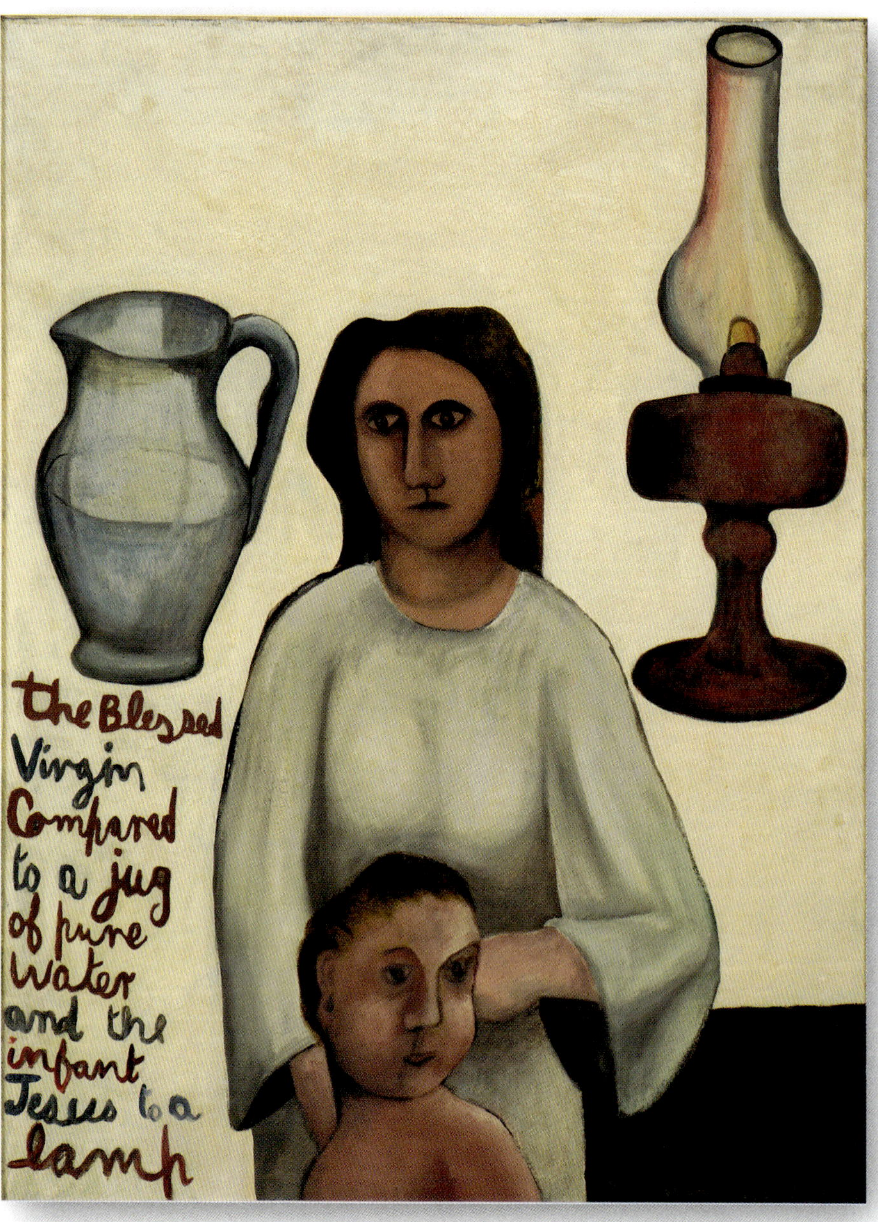

Colin McCahon. *The Blessed Virgin Compared to a jug of pure water and the infant Jesus to a lamp*. 1948. Oil on canvas stretched on board. 1053 x 805 mm. Donated by Charles Brasch, 1963. Courtesy of the Colin McCahon Research and Publication Trust.

McCahon's work was often ridiculed when exhibited and proved difficult to sell. The religious paintings, in particular, attracted derisory comments from critics, such as A.R.D. Fairburn, who described them as being like 'graffiti on the walls of some celestial lavatory'.

Charles Brasch, who had this painting in his own collection, in 1950 reproduced it in *Landfall*, a literary journal which he also used to promote artists. Very few understood McCahon's need to 'map the relationship between man and his God', as John Caselberg described it, but without such support McCahon would not have continued painting. LT

Characterising Wellington • 1967

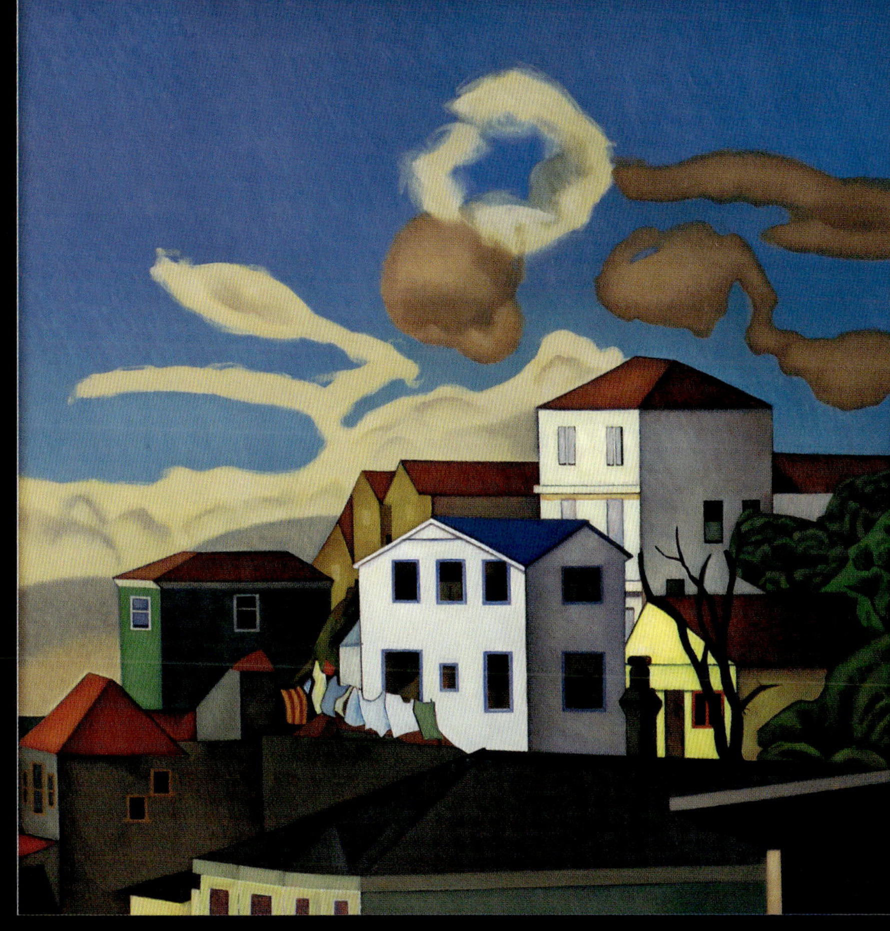

Rita Angus. *View from Tinakori Road.* 1967. Oil on board. 604 x 599 mm. Charles Brasch Bequest, 1973.

Rita Angus (1908–70) was born in Hastings and studied at the Canterbury College School of Art from 1927 to 1933. Leaving Christchurch finally in 1954, she bought 'Fernbank Studio' in Wellington, when she was forty-seven. She was to live there for the last fifteen years of her life, the distinctive Victorian heritage of her Thorndon neighbourhood providing her with abundant imagery for her painting. This view is from the corner of Tinakori Road and Bowen Street, and focuses attention on 'The Wedge' and 'The Moorings', two landmark houses in Glenbervie Terrace.

Simplified into a series of planes, her cubist houses climb up the picture plane like stepped building blocks. Nursery colours differentiate roofs from weatherboards, and the faces of the houses are bathed by a northerly sun. To relieve this angular geometry and the sharp shadows cast by the bright light, amorphous cloud shapes hover in the cerulean blue sky, and on the right, the sinuous branches of a silhouetted winter tree snake up like lightning. And lest her collection of folksy buildings begin to resemble the deserted towns of American realism, she introduced a clothesline in the mid-ground, animating the gaily coloured towels and sheets with a characteristically boisterous Wellington wind. LT

Vive Aramoana • 1982

Most painters begin with a white canvas, but the impact of Ralph Hotere (b. 1931) relies on black. The reflectivity of a window at night becomes a mirror held up for contemplation, with surfaces activated by Leonardo-like reverse writing to convey messages. In this case, a Victorian sash window frame locks in the composition, a square of darkness sectioned into four quadrants with a white cross. Above, letters and numbers are stencilled, and then partially erased, as if human systems for ordering are being undermined.

In the bottom right corner, the calendar month of June has the 24th circled, with the French 'Vive Aramoana' below. Diagonally opposite, in capitals, 'Towards Aramoana' floats backward as if reflected in water. Is Aramoana, 'pathway to the sea', still a landscape under threat and this the view through the scope of a rifle, or is some victory over the proposed smelter scheme being signalled? Could the painting be a blackboard, displaying a chalked-up score in the preservation battle? Typically cryptic, Hotere provides no answers, merely more references. With a nod to McCahon's Necessary Protection series (based on the gannet sanctuary at Muriwai) in the block form at bottom left, he situates himself in an evolving tradition of conservationist painting in New Zealand. LT

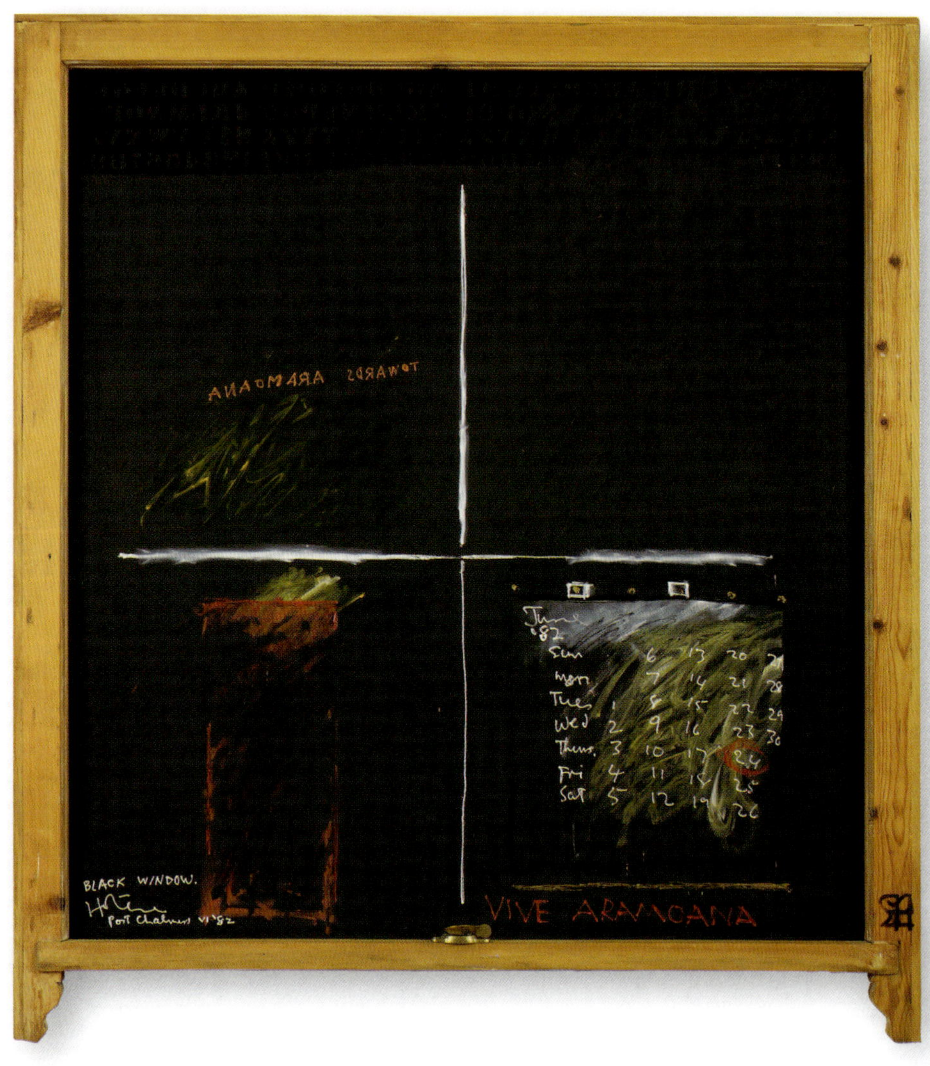

Hone Papita Raukura (Ralph) Hotere. *Black Window, Port Chalmers*. 1982. Synthetic polymer paint on board. 1030 x 970 mm. Purchased, 1982.

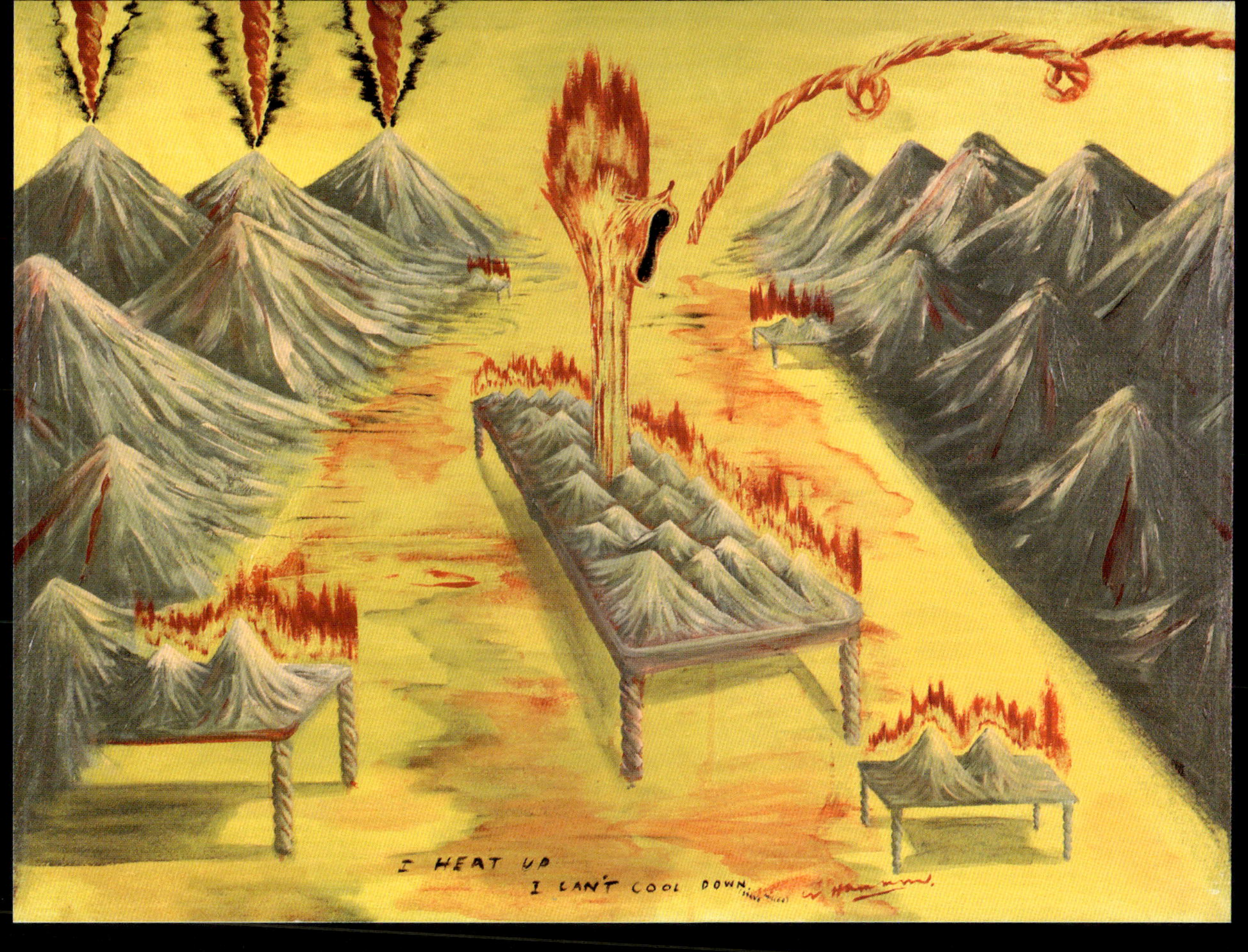

Blistering panorama • 1985

William (Bill) Hammond. *I heat up, I can't cool down (Steve Miller)*. 1985. Synthetic polymer paint on canvas. 560 x 763 mm. Purchased, 1986.

Lyrics from the Steve Miller Band's 1982 hit 'Abracadabra' gave rise to Bill Hammond's blistering panorama *I heat up, I can't cool down*. Here is a painting where popular culture has invaded the realms of high art and the volume is turned up loud.

Hammond (b. 1947) has switched the traditional emphasis in New Zealand landscape painting from nature to culture. In a revisiting of his old teacher Doris Lusk's mid-century painting of the Canterbury plains from high up on the Cashmere Hills, the centre of Hammond's work is emptied by a Red Sea-like parting, perhaps suggesting that the tide has gone out on the painting tradition that Lusk exemplifies. Staccato volcanoes punctuate the landscape in a steeply rising tableau that includes a depiction of what are literally table-top mountains. There is also a suggestion of old master Colin McCahon's interest in geomorphology, with his portentous reverence for the body of the land stripped bare to reveal its bones.

But while these may be the Southern Alps, they are also mountains of the mind. Beneath the surface of polite society with its nicely turned table legs, things are literally coming to a head. A yawping mouth that is part Edvard Munch and part cartoon lets off steam at centre. LT

Interrupting tradition • 1998

Robin White (b. 1946) lost all her printmaking materials when her house and studio in Kiribati burned down in 1996. She began making drawings for mats which could be created from the dried leaves of the pandanus tree, a material used throughout Oceania for weaving. She used watercolours of everyday items made during a residency in Canberra as a basis for the imagery, bearing in mind the colourful and innovative mats produced in Tuvalu, where the substructure of the mat is woven and then coloured elements inserted. This style of weaving is called Te Wanin and is described by textile artists as a warp and weft overlay.

The title of the woven mats is the same as a brand of tinned mackerel, and each image is presented in three stages relating to the intention of the work as a whole to examine issues to do with tradition and belief and how these are subject to change. All the items depicted – fish, bread, milk, tobacco and matches – are either imported or made with imported products on Kiribati.

In the first state, the central image makes its appearance, interrupting the traditional pattern. In the second, it starts to cast a shadow, and words are introduced so that the traditional pattern is dispersed. In the third and final coloured state, the traditional patterns are marginalised and the image has been formalised to have a recognisable setting, paralleling the eclipse of indigenous cultures by Westernisation.
LT

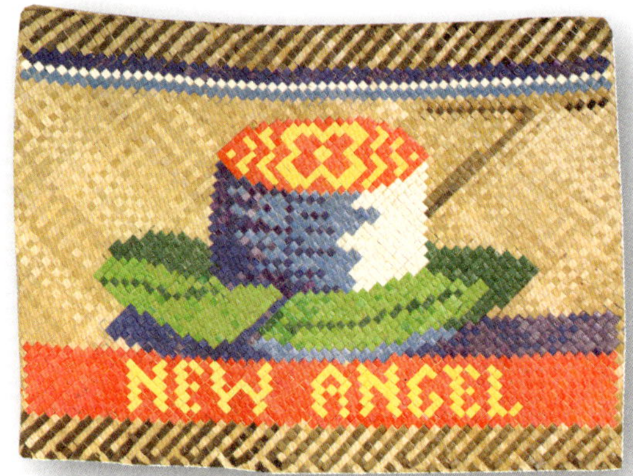

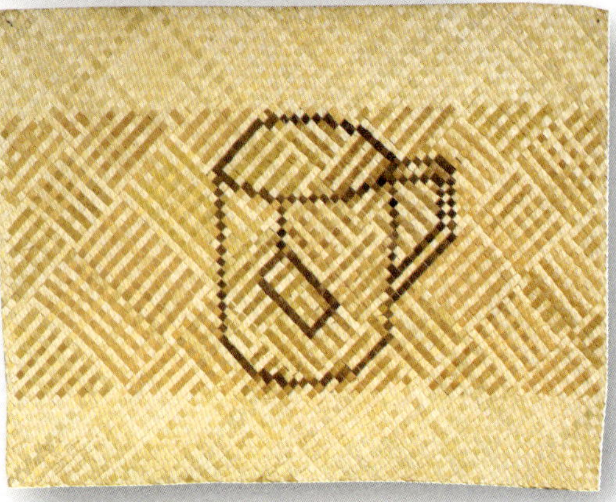

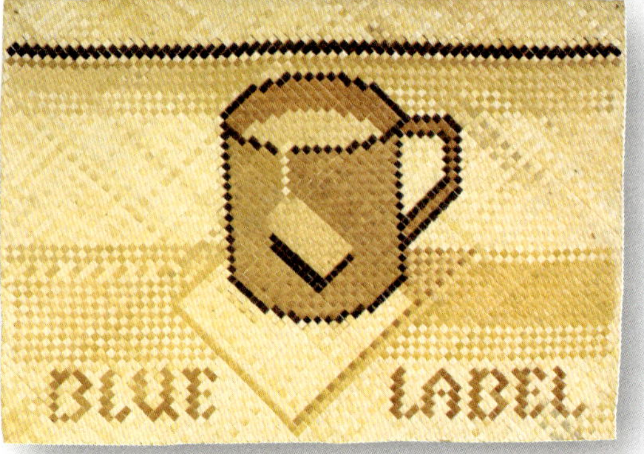

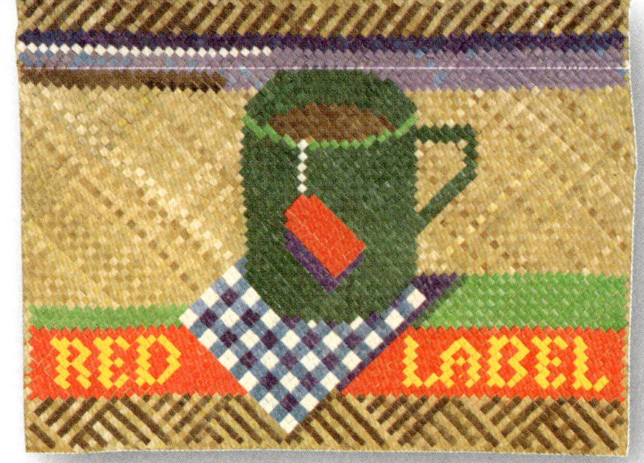

Robin White. *New Angel*. 1998. Pandanus woven by the women of the Itoiningaina ('The Day Star') Catholic Women's Training Centre, Teaoraereke, Kiribati, under the supervision of Nei Katimira. Edition 20. Commercial and traditional dyes on woven pandanus mats, each approx. 315 x 450 mm. Purchased, 2000.

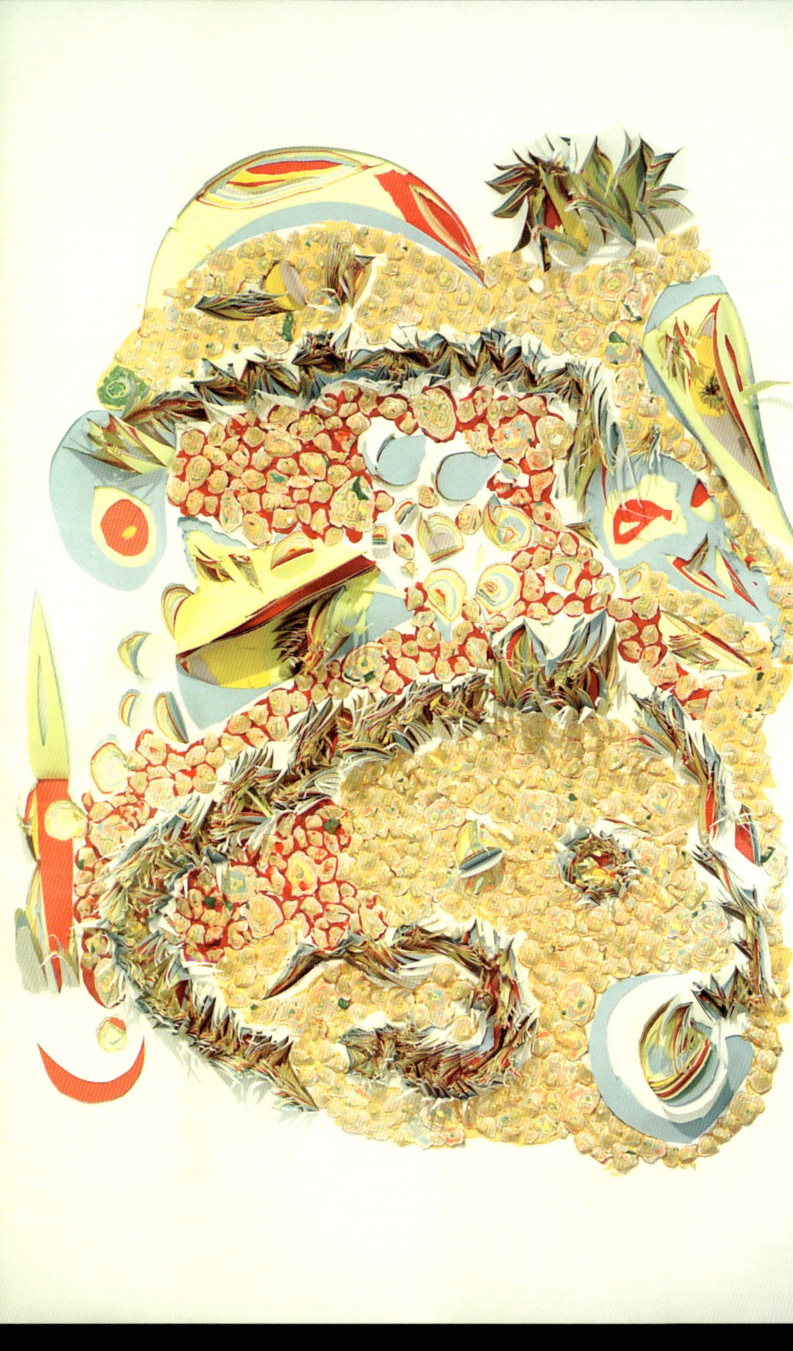

Detoxing at the outset of his year as Frances Hodgkins Fellow in Dunedin, Rohan Wealleans (b. 1977) left his favourite mistints unmolested in the can and invented horrorgami, his version of origami done with scissor hands. Able to quarry his own supply of rainbow-layered pieces of dried acrylic to apply as decoration to the surface of the carved paper, he taught himself how to sculpt with paint. Despite being produced with a technique inspired by slasher movies, the beguiling baby pinks and blues in this *Big Horror* turned out to be too pretty to be frightening.

Blooming with a myriad of hues, shoals of paint pieces eddy around paper fans and fringes. The image seems to be bursting with life, like a coral reef (replete with sea anemones waving their tentacles) surrounded by a sea of calm pastel blue. Despite the appearance of natural growth, there is careful orchestration of shape, colour and composition to harvest maximum visual interest from the decoration. Green shapes float on ponds of complementary blue and orange, and excavations beneath the surface send hot pink paper sinking and swelling strategically. This is artist as landscape architect, pruning and shaping for organic effect to create a fantasy garden rich with imaginative possibilities. LT

Rohan Wealleans. *Big Horror-Gami.* 2005. Acrylic and paper. 1030 x 650 mm. Purchased, 2005.

Photographs

Anna Petersen

From small beginnings, the Hocken Photographs Collection is now estimated to contain well over a million prints and negatives. It includes work by many of New Zealand's most important historical and contemporary photographers, and for some aspects of our past it is definitive. The emphasis is on Otago and Southland, but the Collection ranges over all New Zealand, nineteenth-century Australia, Antarctica, Melanesia and the Pacific generally.

The photographs in the Original Collection reflect Dr Hocken's interest in the early history of New Zealand. Of course, he was limited in that photography was not invented until 1839, but amongst his earliest acquisitions on arriving in Dunedin was a full issue of Joseph Perry's prints of Otago taken c. 1865. These he valued as the first ever taken of the local interior. He also laid the foundation of a useful portraits collection of colonial identities. Equally notable are two scrapbook albums of Māori subjects, important evidence of his interest in the tāngata whenua.

For many years the number of photographs in the collection remained small, but as businesses and private individuals came to recognise the historical value of photographs and the need to preserve them, the volume increased, and the Collection developed its own identity. Some of the largest holdings derive from twentieth-century commercial studios based in Dunedin, namely Campbell Studios, Morris Kershaw, E.A. Phillips, Franz Barta, McRobie and Clark. These include indexed banks of negatives. The work of other, leading nineteenth-century professional photographers in Dunedin, notably the Burton Brothers, F.A. Coxhead, Hart Campbell, Morris, and Muir & Moodie, are also well represented though only in print form.

An interesting feature of the Photographs Collection is the diversity of formats, right up to the present with digital scans on compact disc. It holds examples of all the main early forms of photography. The earliest daguerreotypes, ambrotypes and tintypes reveal how portrait photographers provided mementoes, first for the well-to-do and then for the average family. These photographs on metal and glass supports were later replaced in popularity by paper albumen prints, again presented in a variety of ways – from cartes-de-visite and cabinet cards to stereograms and panoramas.

Although photographic technology developed continuously, the history of photography can also be seen as a succession of temporary enthusiasms. For instance, following advances in photo-mechanic means of reproduction, postcards became all the rage in the early twentieth century, peaking in 1909 when over 14 million were posted in New Zealand. Dunedin was the centre of production, with Muir & Moodie releasing Burton Brothers' images and scenic photographs of their own on thousands of cards printed first in Europe and then in New Zealand once the 'real-photo' format became the vogue. There is a comprehensive selection of most early twentieth-century producers of these cards and a growing number of later names. Muir & Moodie, F.G. Radcliffe, and the Aotearoa Series published by Hugh and G.K. Neill are the best represented.

The Photographs Collection includes over 500 albums, once an essential item on every fashionable drawing-room table. Many of the best were passed on from the Dunedin Public Library in 1990, and date from the 1860s, 1870s and 1880s, when photographers like James Bragge and the Burton Brothers employed glass plate technology to capture the dramatic and varied New Zealand landscape, and to record what evidence they could find of traditional Māori life and building development within the towns. As cameras became more common and easier to use, the nature of albums changed. Those in the Tily collection, for example, are valuable for social history, with informal snapshots of family, friends and holiday tours during the 1920s and 30s.

Transparencies are another format that covers a wide range of subjects. The 156 lantern slides of scenes from the First World War given by the Victoria League served to inform audiences back in New Zealand; and five lantern slides from the Otago Medical School Alumnus Association Museum are clinical studies taken in 1919 of facial injuries sustained by soldiers in action. Colour advertisements for products, such as Regina pineapple chunks and Roslyn Woollen Mill blankets, were used at Amalgamated Picture Theatres in the 1960s; 35mm colour transparencies from the John McGibbon collection help to document the Clutha Valley Development Project between 1977 and 1980; and 35mm colour transparencies of celebrated New Zealanders, including Peter Snell and Kiri Te Kanawa in London, were taken by Geoff Adams when he worked as a correspondent for the *Weekly News* during the 1960s.

As with most public photographic collections, the Hocken's holdings are largely the result of what people have chosen to keep and give. Thanks to the passion and generosity of a few male donors, the Photographs Collection is very strong in the field of shipping and transport. Outstanding in the realm of ships are the I.J. Farquhar, Mallard Estate and P.L. Moore collections. Large railway holdings are located in the R.H. Wilton, J.A. Dangerfield and Joe McNamara collections. The G.C. Ditchfield collection mainly covers trams and cable cars (which often double as a source of little-photographed outer city suburban views), while buses are concentrated in the Peter Bennie, Basil Horwood, Alan Smith and J. Herbert collections.

The main thrust of the Photographs Collection continues to be historical, but there is also a strong current of art photography. The most comprehensive holdings are of George Chance, whose name has been synonymous with pictorial photography in New Zealand since the 1930s, and the Dunedin Photographic Society prints on permanent loan are rich and varied. A modest acquisition budget and association with the Frances Hodgkins Fellows at the University of Otago ensures some currency with modern trends. Laurence Aberhart, Mark Adams, Gary Blackman, Ben Cauchi, Margaret Dawson, Gavin Hipkins, Adrienne Martyn, Peter Peryer, Fiona Pardington, Ava Seymour, Ann Shelton and Christine Webster are all represented in the Collection.

A unique daguerreotype of Captain William Cargill (1784–1860) provides a fine likeness of the tenacious old colonist who was lay leader of the Scottish settlement of Dunedin. The image was used as the basis for several painted portraits that have survived, and an engraving by H. Sadd, also in the Hocken Collections, acknowledges the daguerreotypist as T.A. Hill.

Captain Cargill was sixty-three when he emigrated to New Zealand in 1848 and it is probable that the daguerreotype was commissioned after he became Otago's first Super-intendent in 1853. Newspaper advertisements indicate that daguerreotypes were being made in Dunedin during the 1850s, sometimes by photographers on the road. All that is known of Thomas Adams Hill is that he had studios in Bourke Street East and Collins Street West in Melbourne between 1855 and 1869. It is possible that Hill worked as an itinerant before this date, or Cargill may have made a visit to Australia.

Created from a thin copper plate with a mirror-like coating of silver, daguerreotypes could be easily scratched and so were usually mounted under glass. Thus Cargill's daguerreotype is housed in an elaborate, velvet-lined case.

AP

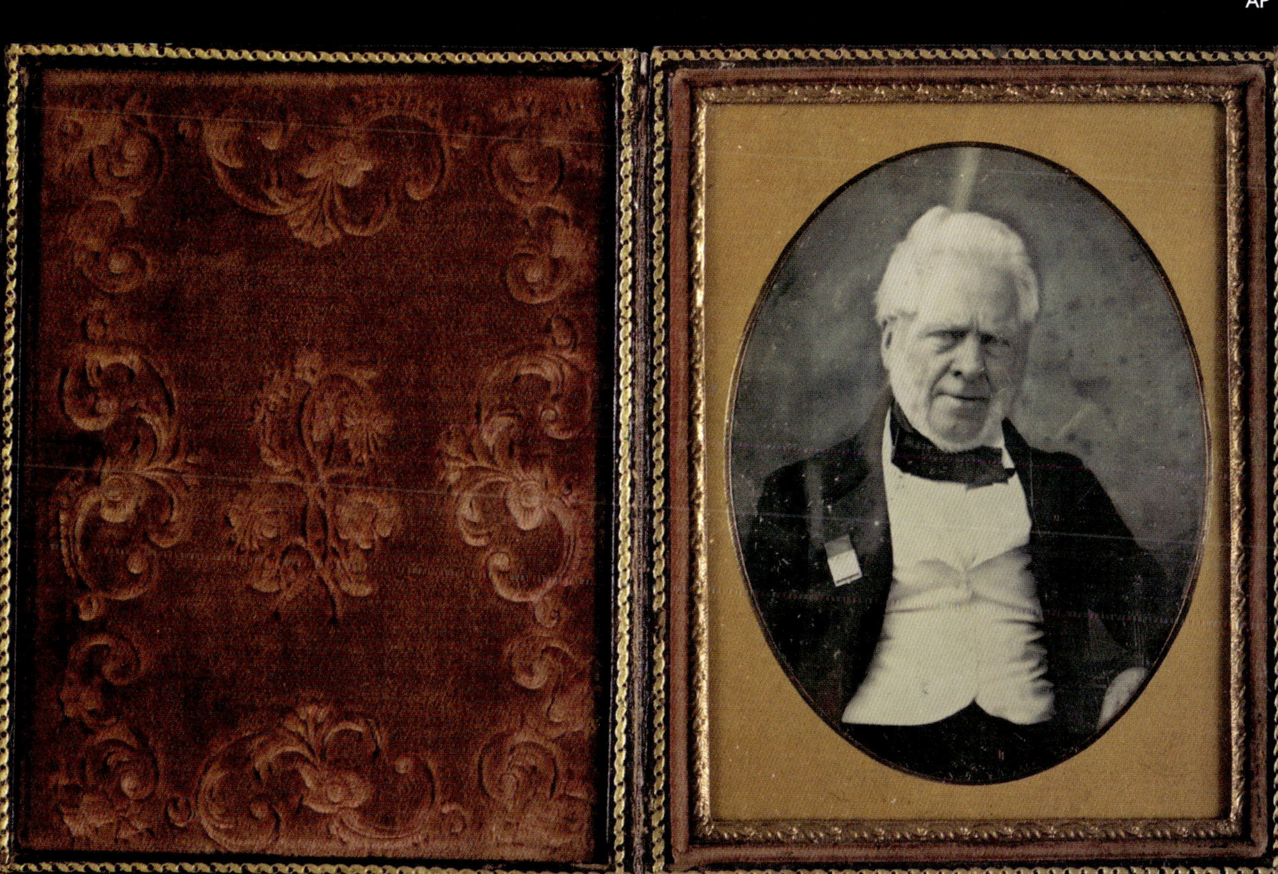

T.A. Hill. *Portrait of Captain William Cargill*. Daguerreotype. Donated by Beta Cass, 1983.

Last of the Tasmanians • c. 1864

Dressed in adopted European clothes and posed like actors in a play – only the tragedy was real – from left, Bessy Clark, William Lanne ('King Billy'), Mary-Ann Arthur and Trucanini (also known as Lalla Rookh) were photographed in Henry Frith's Hobart studio as remnants of the local indigenous population.

William Lanne (c. 1834–69) and Trucanini (1812–76) became widely known as the last full-blooded male and female representatives of their race in Tasmania. Trucanini suffered great personal loss as a girl and worked with white authorities during the 1830s to protect other survivors of The Black Wars. More trauma would follow when William, her third husband, died at a young age and his body was dismembered before burial, in the name of science. Trucanini's own skeleton was used as a museum display for several years and not given the funeral rites she had requested until 1976 on the centenary of her death.

Dr Hocken owned two versions of this print, which must date to 1864 at the latest because Samuel Calvert created a wood engraving from it, published in the *Illustrated Melbourne* in November that year. It is possible that Hocken acquired them from the photographer, as Frith moved to Dunedin in 1867.

AP

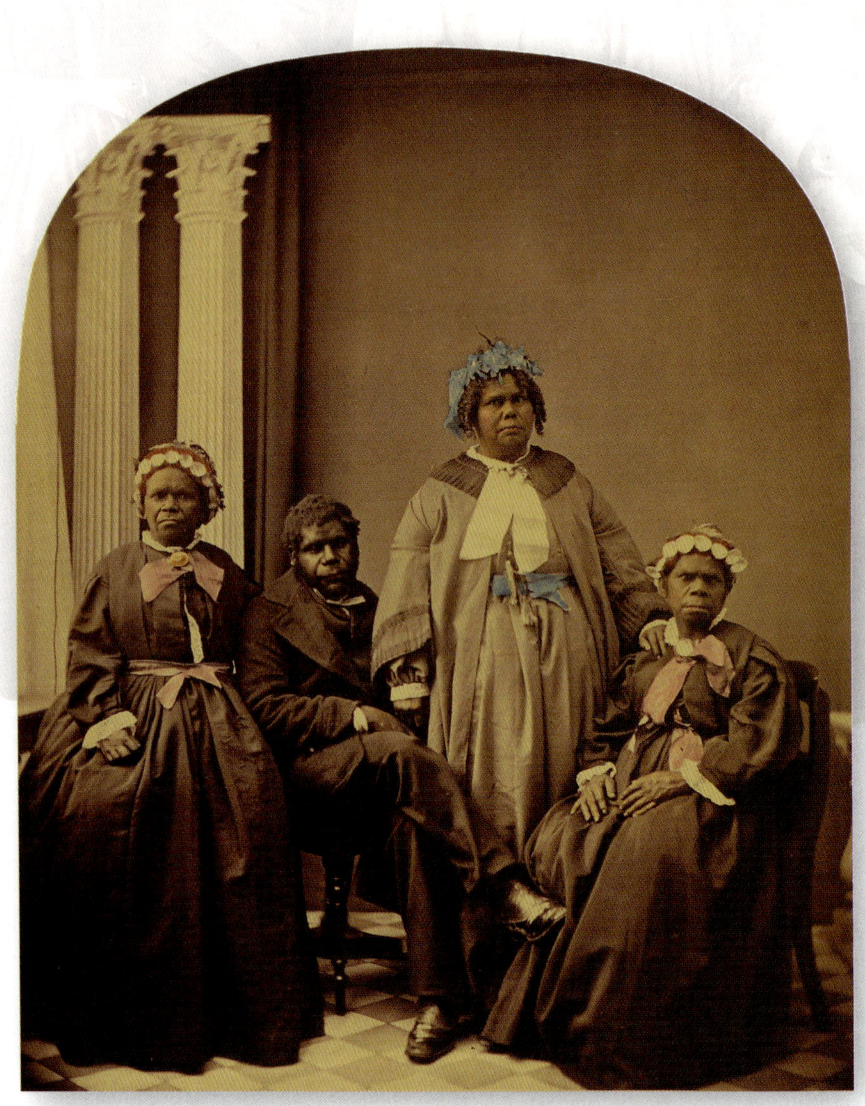

Henry Frith. *The Last of the Tasmanians*. c. 1864. Hand-coloured albumen print. Original Collection.

The Hocken Collections contain the pre-eminent assemblage of Kinder's albumen prints, gifted in 1922 by the artist's niece, Olga McCurdie.

The Rev. John Kinder (1819–1903) took up photography as a hobby c. 1860, not long after he arrived in New Zealand. A holiday at Whangaparaoa in 1868 gave rise to a series of photographs of the rugged coastline, including a study of the monumental 'Kotanui Rock', otherwise known as 'Frenchman's Cap' because of its shape.

The print displays many of the features and qualities for which Kinder's photography is prized. The focus is on recording the dramatic geological formation which almost assumes the look of architecture. The full plate print has a rich, luminous surface and is distinguished for its depth of tone and sense of pattern. Kinder has avoided conventional framing and kept the foreground open. The presence of a figure at the foot of the rock adds to the spectacle.

Kinder's studies of geological features were part of a world-wide trend in topographical photography during the 1860s. *Kotanui Rock, Frenchman's Cap* could almost be mistaken for Louis-Alphonse Davanne's *Needle of Etretat* c. 1864 – the Needle being a celebrated landmark on a stretch of French coastline that Kinder knew well. AP

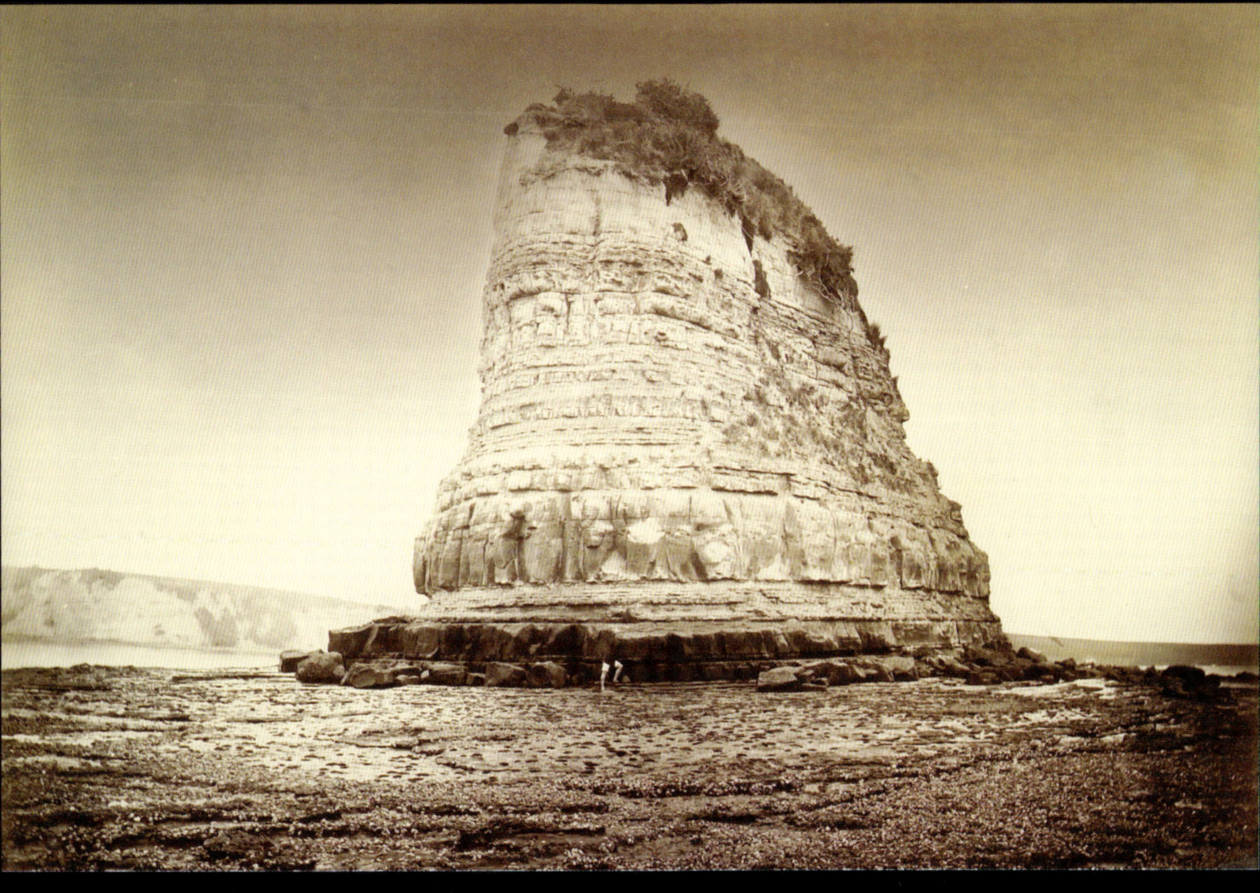

John Kinder. *Kotanui Rock, Frenchman's Cap*. 1868. Albumen print. Donated by Olga McCurdie, 1922.

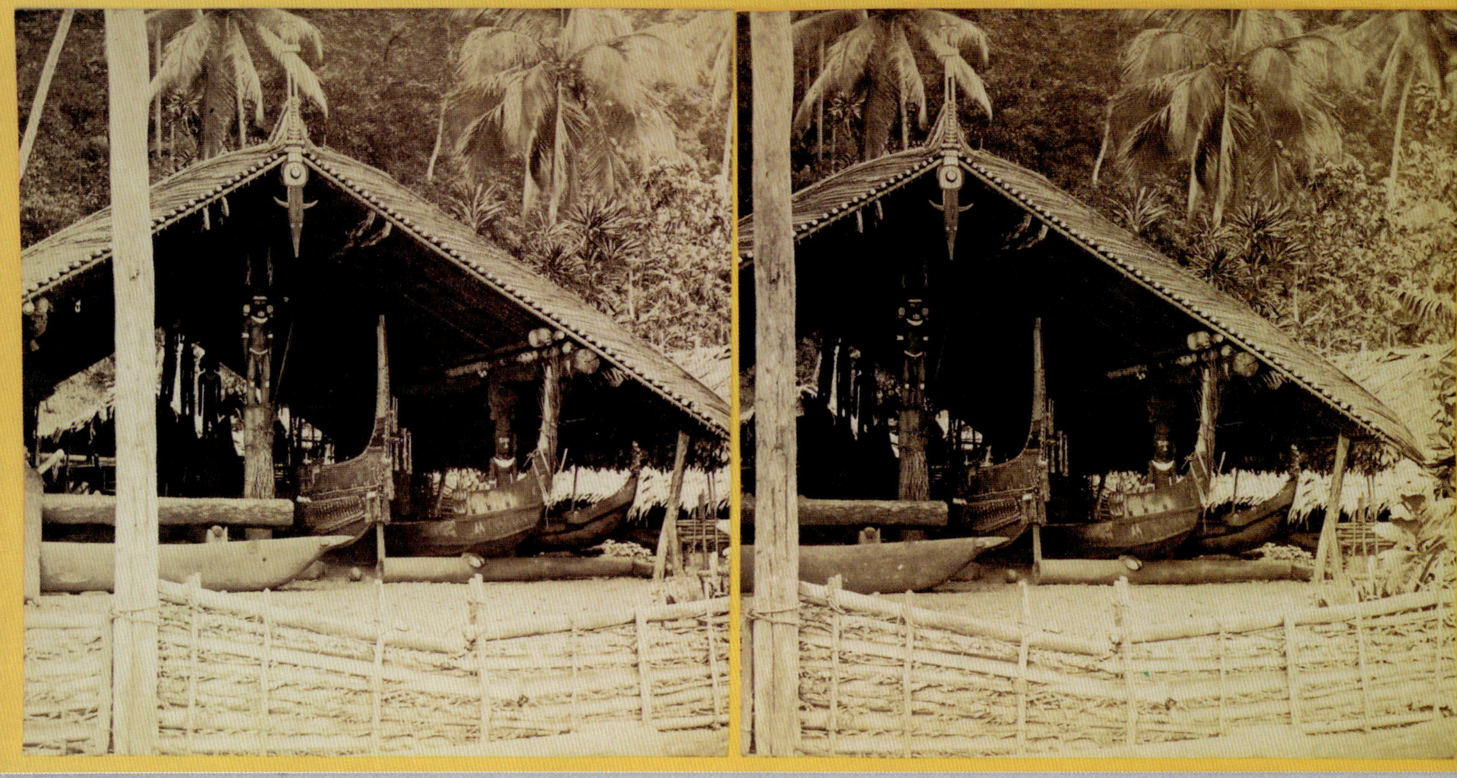

Unique Solomons stereograph • 1873

George Smith. *Canoe Shed at Makira, San Christoval* [sic], *Solomon Group*. [1873]. Stereograph. Mounted albumen prints. Provenance unknown.

Viewed through a stereoscope, these two prints, taken from slightly different points, converge into a three-dimensional image and now provide a rare record of a Solomon Island canoe house on the western end of Makira (then called San Christobal). It is one of a collection of twenty-one stereographs of 'South Sea Islands', which may well have been used at fund-raising meetings for the Presbyterian mission in the New Hebrides (now Vanuatu) or Anglican Church of Melanesia.

A single print of this image appeared as a frontispiece for the illustrated edition of C.F. Wood's book, *A Yachting Cruise in the South Seas* (London, 1875). Wood explained in the preface how the photographer, George Smith, who accompanied him on this voyage, worked to record and collect anything of ethnographic interest.

Wood found the communal sheds to be the focal point of every village. They housed the large, delicately inlaid canoes, which rose to a peak at each end and had no outrigger. The sheds themselves were decorated with elaborately carved figures and doubled as meeting houses. They showed signs of public feasting. Here, a row of skulls is just visible along one of the rafters. AP

Goldmining at Blue Spur • c. 1874

Commissioned by the New Zealand government to make a photographic record of industrial progress around New Zealand for display at the Philadelphia Exhibition in 1876, Herbert Deveril produced several images of the goldmining operations at Blue Spur which helped to make Otago the richest province in the country.

Since 1861 when gold had first been discovered in the area, goldmining at Blue Spur had developed into a corporate concern. Gun powder and water blasting had largely replaced the efforts of individual diggers to remove ore from the ground with water transported by a 29-mile-long race and the rock crushed by several batteries of stampers. The tailings were estimated to have buried the original township of Gabriel's Gully to a depth of around 100 feet.

Nowadays, the fine detail and delicate tones of Deveril's albument prints hold an intrinsic beauty of their own, as well as serving as a valuable historic record. The Hocken holds over a hundred Deveril prints from around the country. AP

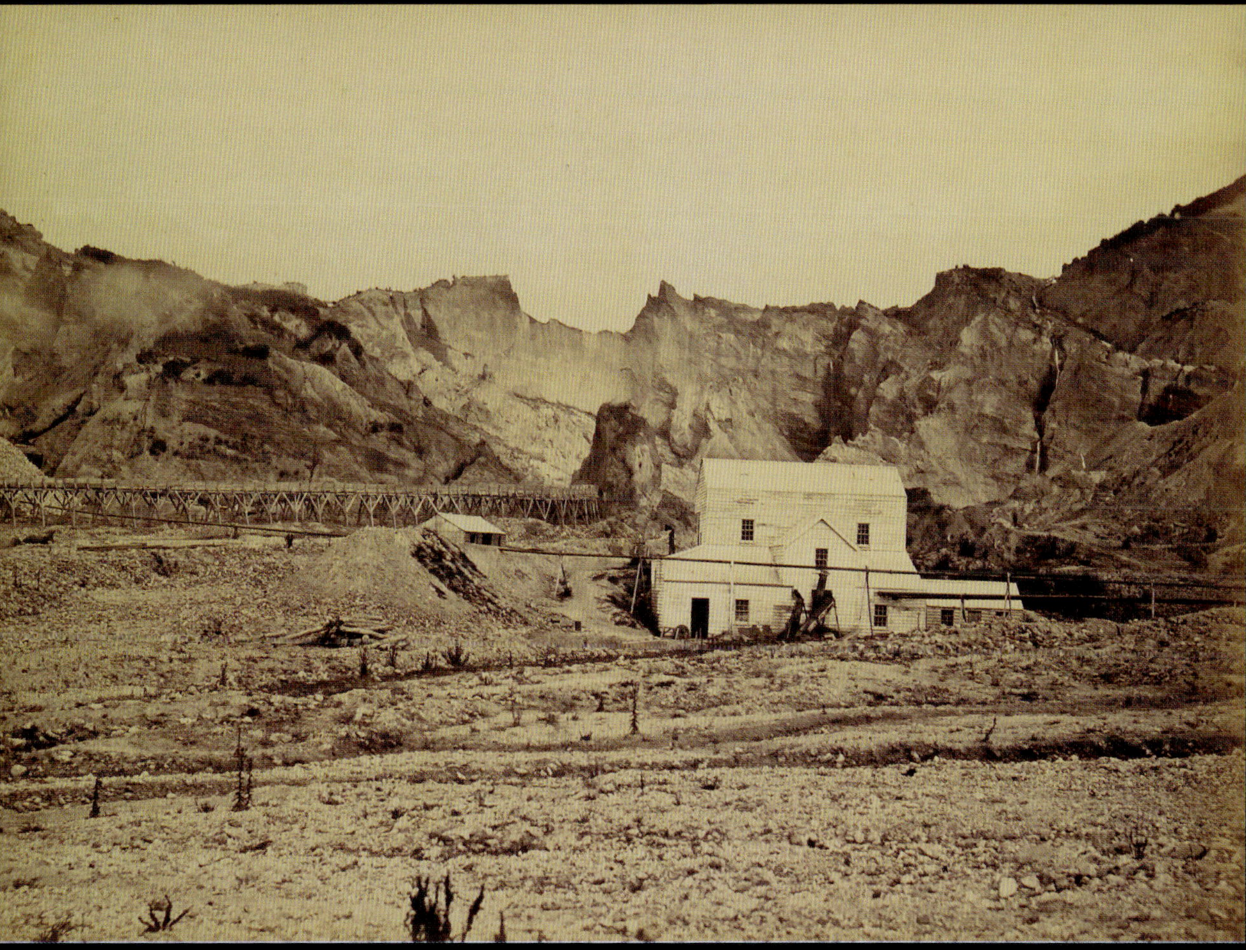

Herbert Deveril. *Gold Workings at the Blue Spur, Gabriel's Gully, Tuapeka, Otago, New Zealand*. c. 1874. Albumen print. Provenance unknown.

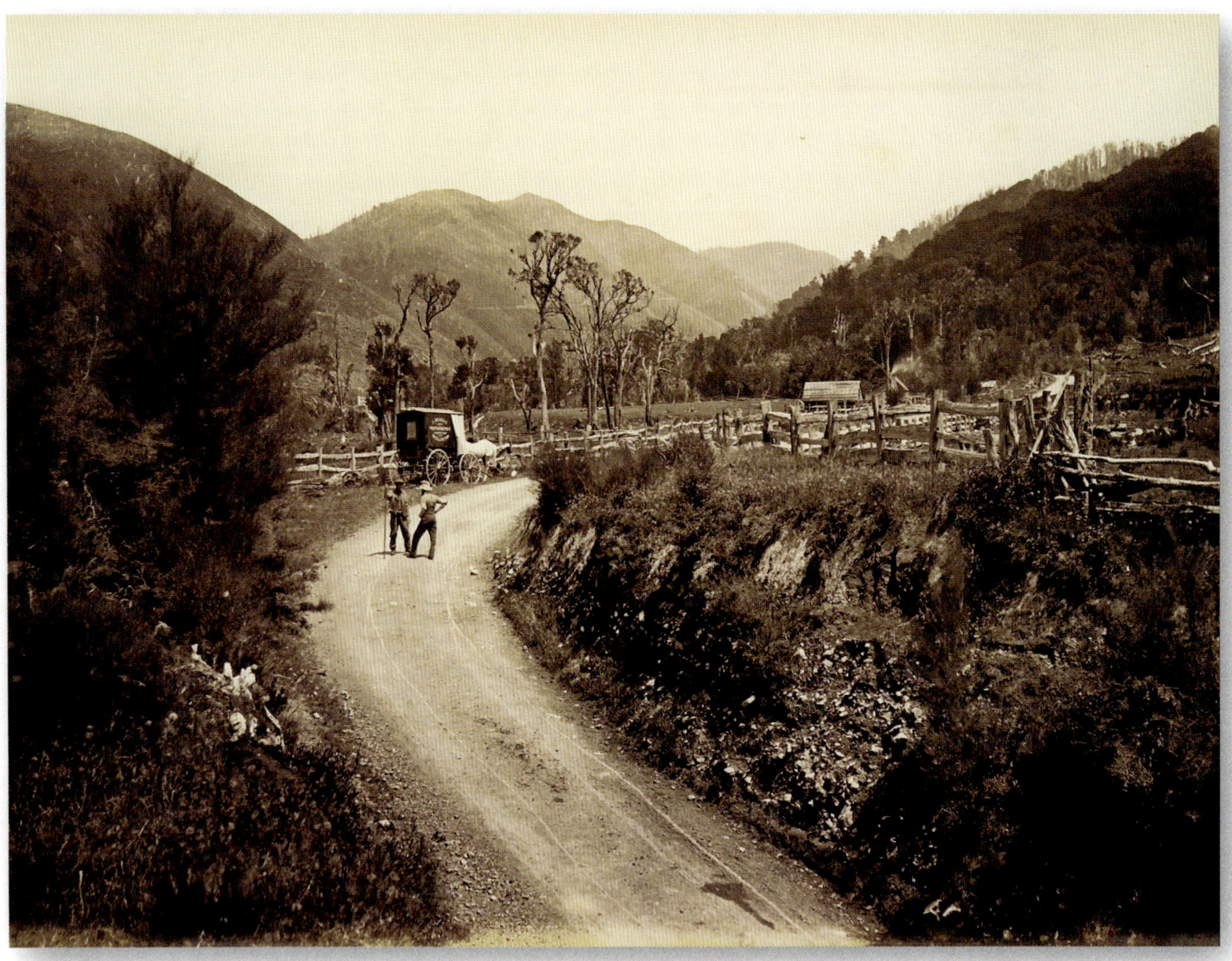

James Bragge. *Featherston Side of the Remutaka* [sic] *Hill From the Cutting at Caves Bridge, NZ* no. 224. c. 1876. Albumen print. Album 336. Donated by Dunedin Public Library, 1990.

Classic Bragge • c. 1876

Only four complete, morocco-bound albums of James Bragge's *New Zealand Scenery Wellington to the Wairarapa* are known to exist. Issued in 1876, each contains a slightly different selection of town and country views that helped to document major developments in the lower North Island region during the Vogel administration. The Hocken volume contains fifty-five prints, ending with an extra photograph of 'Five Mile Avenue' – an area of bush settled by Scandinavian immigrants near Eketahuna.

'Featherston Side of the Remutaka Hill' is a classic Bragge print, showing technical mastery and a number of recurring motifs. Bragge uses the road as a compositional device, includes one or two figures to provide scale and added interest (Bragge himself may be pictured on the right), and parks his own horse-drawn carriage along the way. This carriage contained the equipment and solutions needed for preparing and developing wet-plate collodion negatives. Bragge carried the large 10 x 12 inch glass plate negatives back to Wellington and made the prints at his studio on Lambton Quay. AP

Fijian warriors • c. 1876

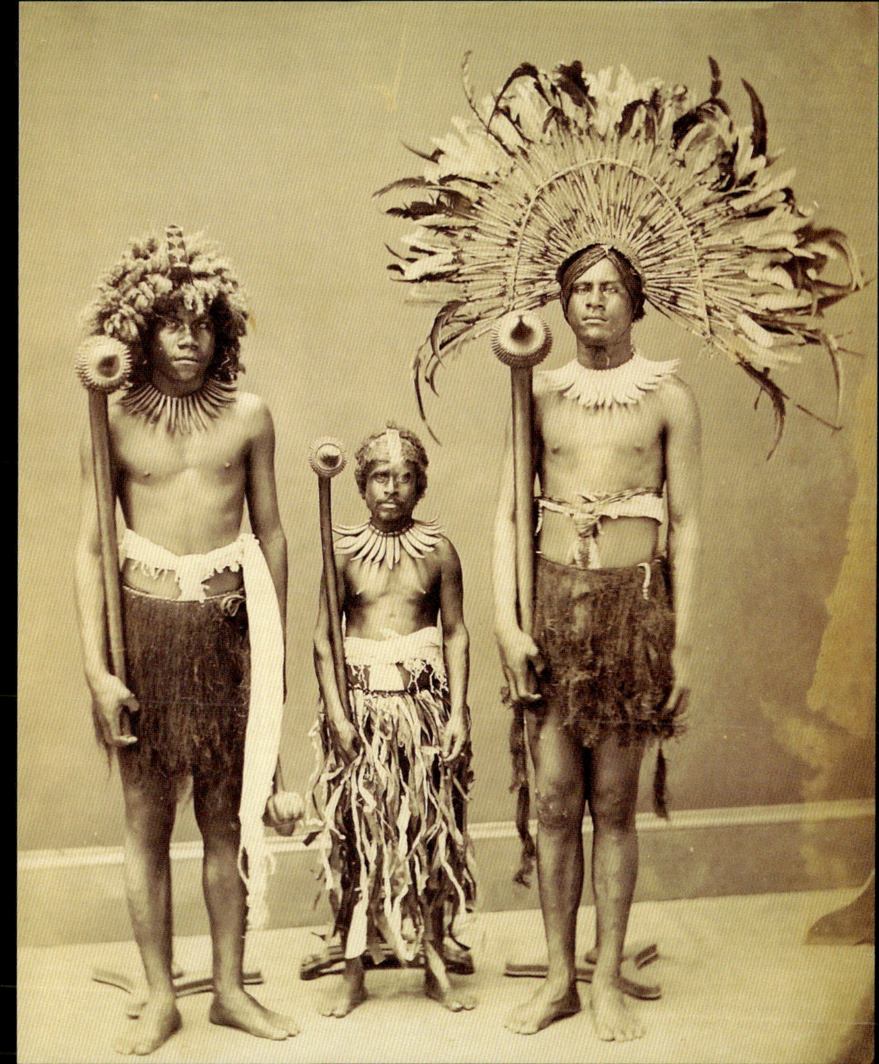

Photographer unknown, *Fiji Soldiers*. c. 1876. Albumen print. Album 43. Original Collection.

Among Hocken's original collection of photographs is this proud portrait of three young Fijian men. Dr Hocken no doubt found it interesting ethnographically, as the men are all holding a type of club known as totokia and wearing wasekaseka (or waseisei) necklaces of boar teeth or whale ivory, and head-dresses of various types. Hocken collected artefacts from the Pacific Islands and published 'An Account of the Fiji Fire Ceremony' in 1898.

The three men have been identified as Kina Bose Yaca, General Ra Biau (centre) and Kora Tumasamora. They featured as 'Fijian Man-eaters' at the Philadelphia Exhibition in 1876, appearing on 'The Midway', a separate area from the official pavilions, along with other attractions like 'The Wild Man from Borneo' which appealed to the Western appetite for the exotic and bizarre.

It is intriguing to consider now what these men were thinking. Rather than active cannibals, they had been raised in a Christian mission on Viti Levu. Living conditions at the exhibition were not good, but presumably the experience did provide an opportunity to travel to America and be part of a fair designed to demonstrate the progress of the developing superpower. AP

Riria Potiki (1808?–1913) was born into Kai Tahu, the daughter of Karetai and his third wife Pitoko. Chief Karetai had been a signatory of the Treaty of Waitangi at Otakou and his senior son, Korako (Riria's full brother), also played a part in major land transactions around Dunedin. Riria married Wi Nera Potiki, another prominent local chief, but had no children of her own.

Riria Potiki was very involved in local Māori affairs and it was possibly in connection with the Māori Court at the New Zealand and South Seas Exhibition held in Dunedin, 1889–90, that she came to have her portrait taken by Elizabeth Hocken. Dr Hocken organised this section of the Exhibition and 'Bessie' generally supported her husband's efforts to collect and record whatever he could relating to Māori.

It is not well known that Elizabeth Hocken was an accomplished amateur photographer. Few of her prints survive but the portraits held in the Hocken Collections reveal great sensitivity. Similar in angle and proportion to some portraits by Samuel Carnell in the same album, the backdrop used here is more in keeping with the subject and one gets a real sense of Riria's enduring physical beauty and inner strength.

AP

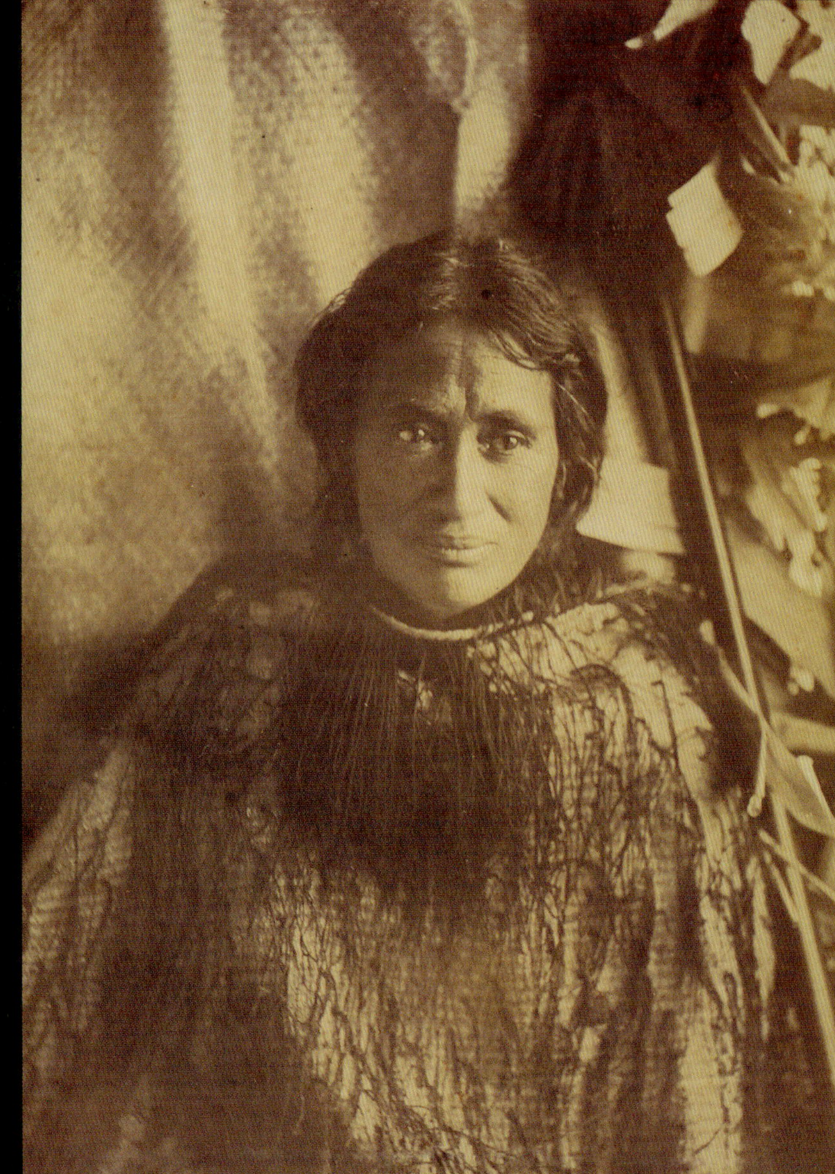

Elizabeth Hocken, *Riria Potiki*. Albumen print, c. 1889. Album 45. Original Collection.

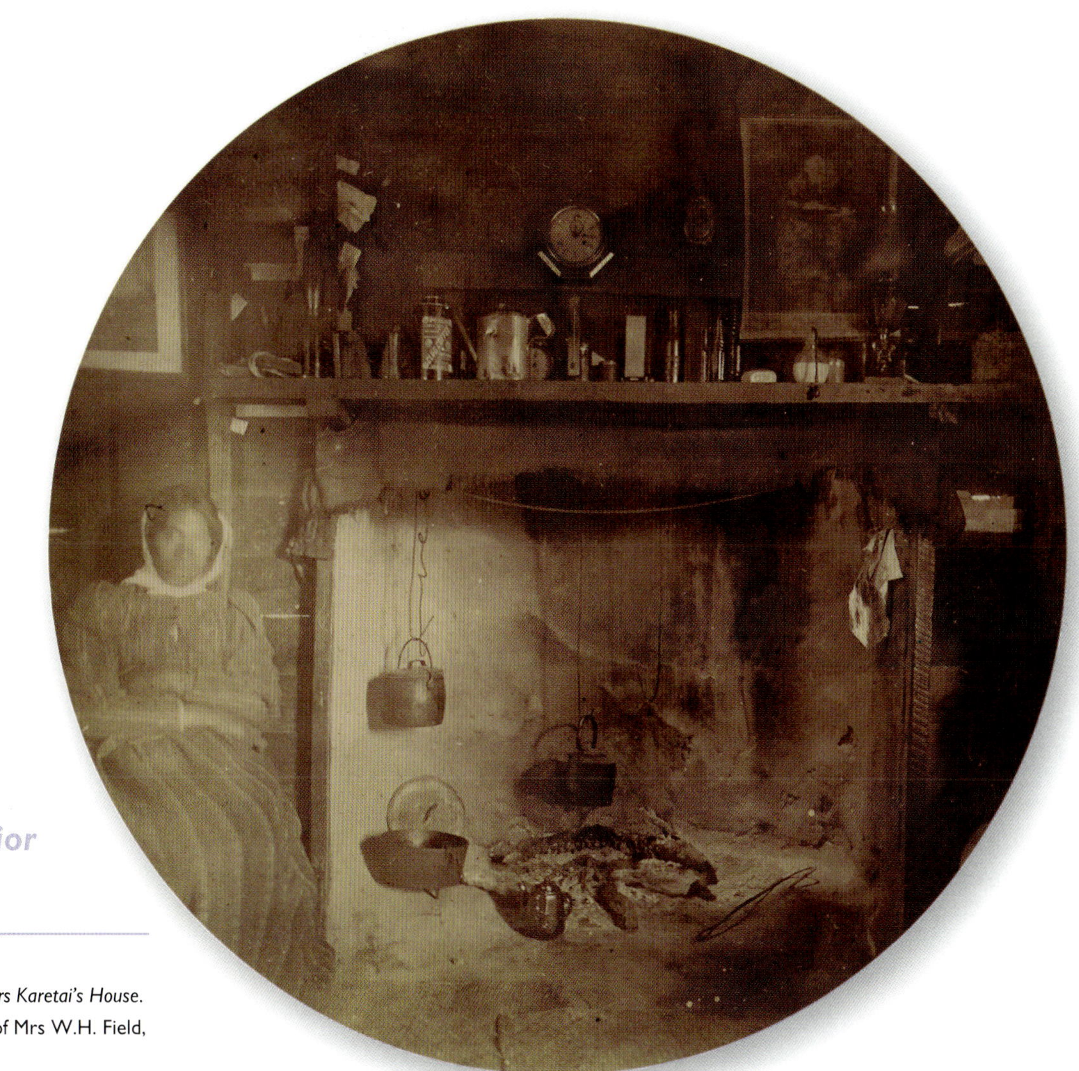

Earliest interior • c. 1893

John Halliday Scott. *In Mrs Karetai's House.* c. 1893. Album 52. Gift of Mrs W.H. Field, Wellington, 1953.

The earliest known photographs of the interior of a Māori family house (as opposed to a whare) were taken by Dr Scott, first Dean of the Otago Medical School. Four photographs of the Karetai dwelling at Pukekura, Otago Heads, are pasted into lawyer and painter William Mathew Hodgkins's album. One photograph shows the exterior of what looks to be a one-room weatherboard house. Two show Mrs Horiwia Karetai seated by the fireplace and one shows her daughter, Mere.

Māori living on Otago Peninsula had been in close proximity to Europeans since the early 1830s and the arrangement of the furniture in the Karetai house, which includes a chair by the fire, plated food on a cloth-covered table and teapot on the hearth, all suggest the adoption of European practices within the home. Visible in each photograph is the clock over the mantelpiece, framed pictures on the wall and a small array of cooking containers. Only the traditional woven floor mats, which could be easily removed for cleaning, remain.

Notable for its absence is the new technology of the late nineteenth century, such as a coal range. Just the lamp on the mantelpiece may have made life a little easier for Mrs Karetai. AP

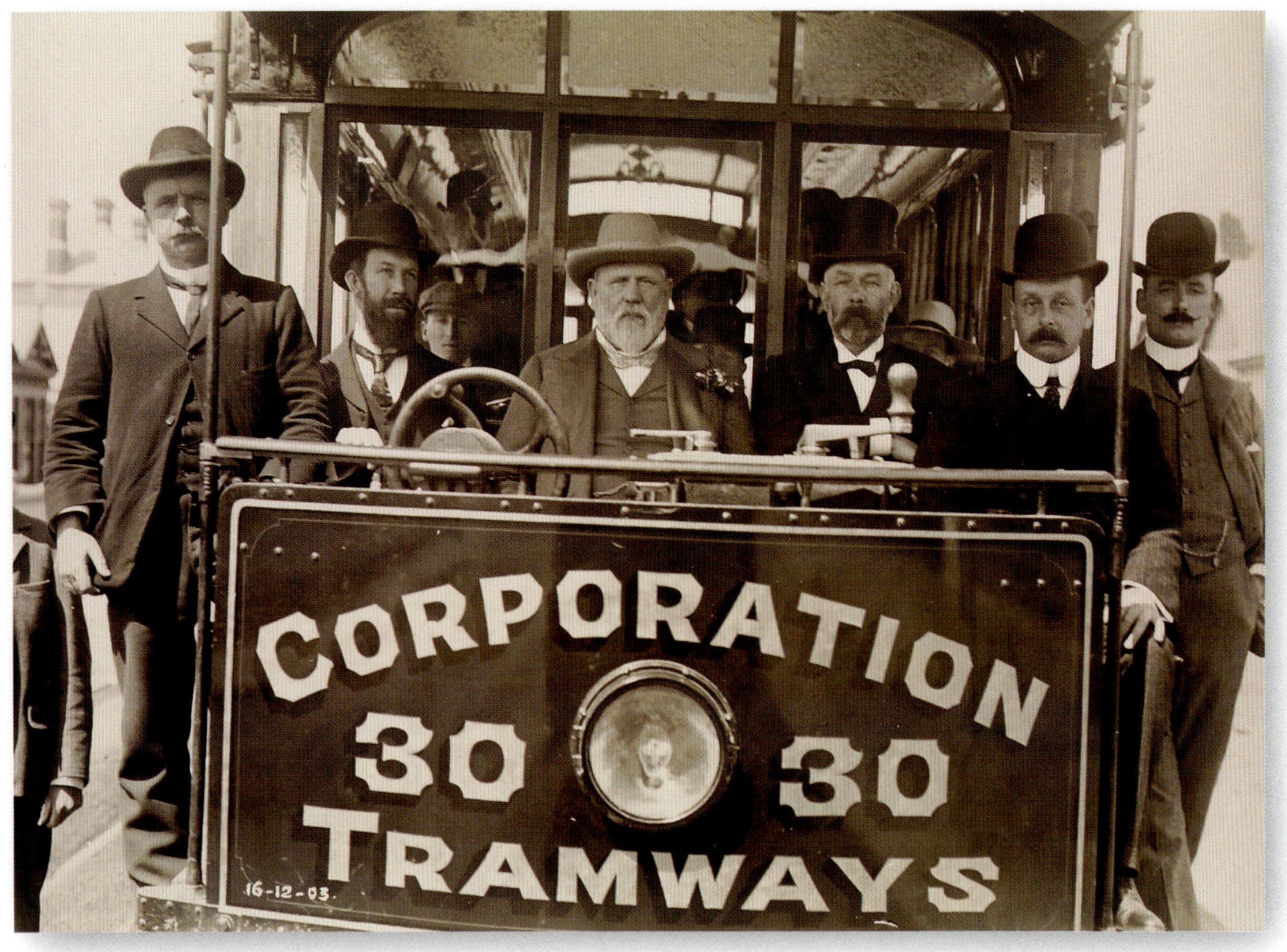

Richard Seddon takes a jaunt • 1904

Guy Morris. *The Premier, while in Dunedin, takes a jaunt on the electric cars.* 1904. Printing out paper. Published in *Otago Witness Illustrated*, 6 January 1904. Bequeathed by Marina Morris Estate, 1999.

Guy Morris (1868–1918), was press photographer for the *Otago Witness* for almost twenty years. His photograph of Richard Seddon, Premier of New Zealand, and accompanying local officials taking a ride on a new electric tram in Dunedin has a particularly intense quality as the power of King Dick's personality and weight of the tram behind him hit the viewer square on.

Newspapers had long included illustrations of one sort or another but the introduction of a weekly supplement of photographs by the *Otago Witness* in December 1899 lent a new immediacy and verification to news reports. Some of the vitality of press photographs was inevitably lost in the photo-mechanical printing process, so it is fortunate that the Hocken holds over two hundred Guy Morris prints in the original, of which this is one.

The introduction of electric trams at the beginning of the twentieth century was regarded as a significant step towards modernisation of New Zealand's towns and cities. Not only did they provider a more efficient, cleaner and safer means of public transport, they also made possible suburban living. AP

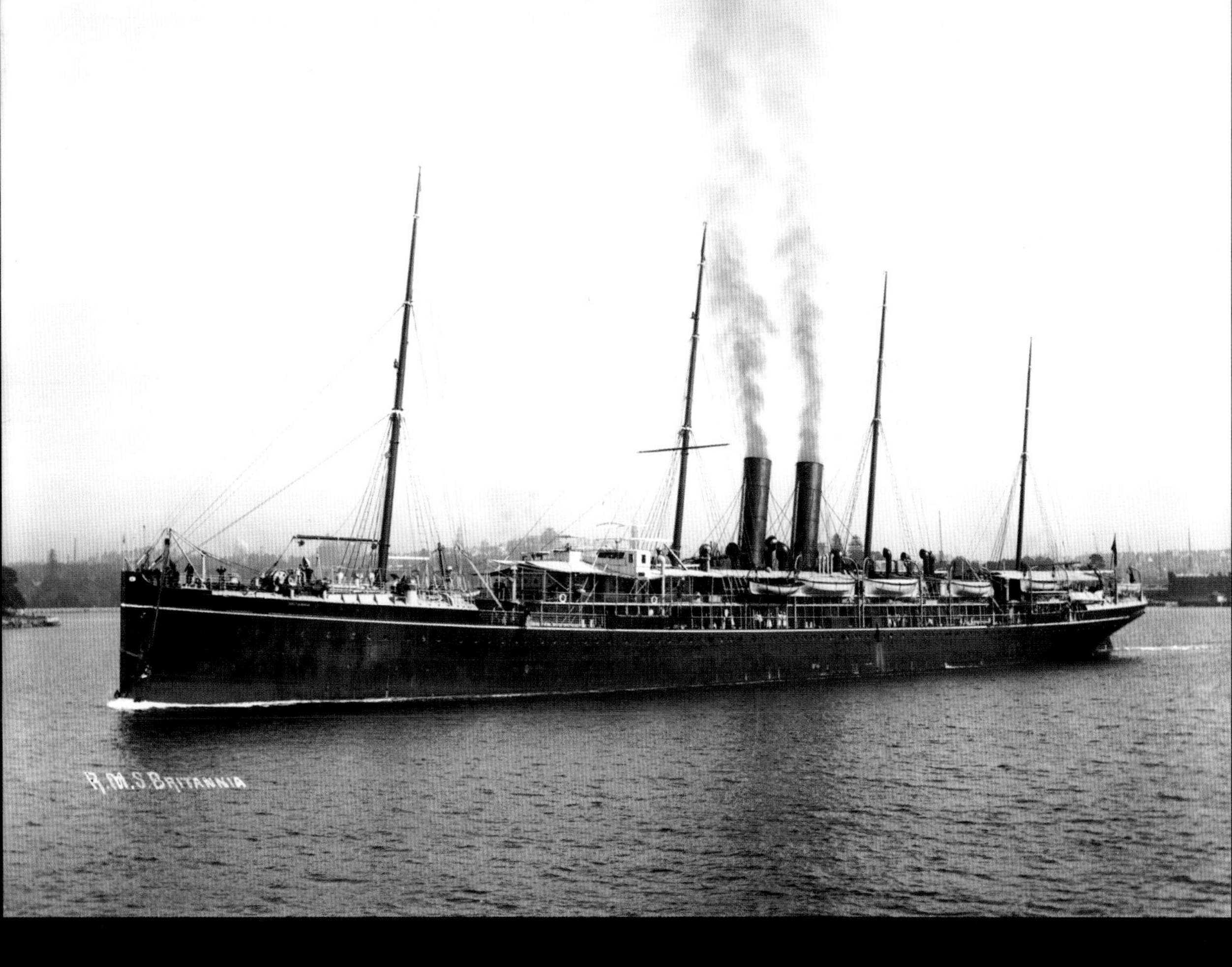

RMS Britannia at Sydney • *1904*

William Livermore. *RMS Britannia, Sydney Harbour, 1904*. Glass plate negative. I.J. Farquhar Collection. Donated by I.J. Farquhar, 2000.

New Zealanders travelling to England in the latter part of the nineteenth century had the option of taking a direct steamer via Cape Horn, but far more popular was to travel by Union Company steamer to Sydney or Melbourne and connect with the P & O steamer to England via the Suez Canal. By the late 1880s, P & O dominated passenger services and the *Britannia* was one of four Jubilee-class vessels built for the Australian trade. She was 6500 tons gross, and could take 230 passengers in first class and 156 in second class. She was on the Australian service from 1887 to 1909.

This photograph of the *Britannia* was taken in Sydney Harbour, June 1904, by William Livermore, a photographer who specialised in shipping. His work, along with that of Gould of Greenwich and of Port Chalmers photographer David de Maus, provides the best record of steamships in the late nineteenth century. His glass plates and prints were sold to a sea captain in the 1920s and were later purchased by Ian Farquhar in 1954. The Hocken Collections holds several hundred Livermore plates amongst the Farquhar Collection, many of them in the same pristine condition as when they were made over a century ago. IF

A most distinguished graduate • c. 1904

From Dunedin boot factory worker to world-leading chemist, Joseph William Mellor (1869–1938) led a remarkable life. Born at Lindley, Yorkshire, he migrated to New Zealand with his family in 1879. Secondary school was not an option for this working-class family, so thirteen-year-old Joseph began work in the boot trade. He continued to better himself, and when twenty attended evening classes at the newly formed Dunedin Technical Classes Association. With a scholarship and leave from his employer he then attended the University of Otago part-time, graduating first class honours in chemistry in 1898; a later Chancellor would describe him as its most distinguished student.

After teaching chemistry briefly at Lincoln College, Mellor sailed for England with his wife, eventually completing a doctorate at Manchester University. He then taught at Newcastle under Lyme, Staffordshire, developing an interest in the local pottery industry and science of ceramics. Mellor published widely; his 16-volume study of inorganic chemistry was hugely influential.

This charming photograph of the teacher at work comes from a family album that belonged to Job Mellor, Joseph's father. The first line of calculus written on the blackboard appears to be Van der Waals equation and relates to the behaviour of gases. AJC

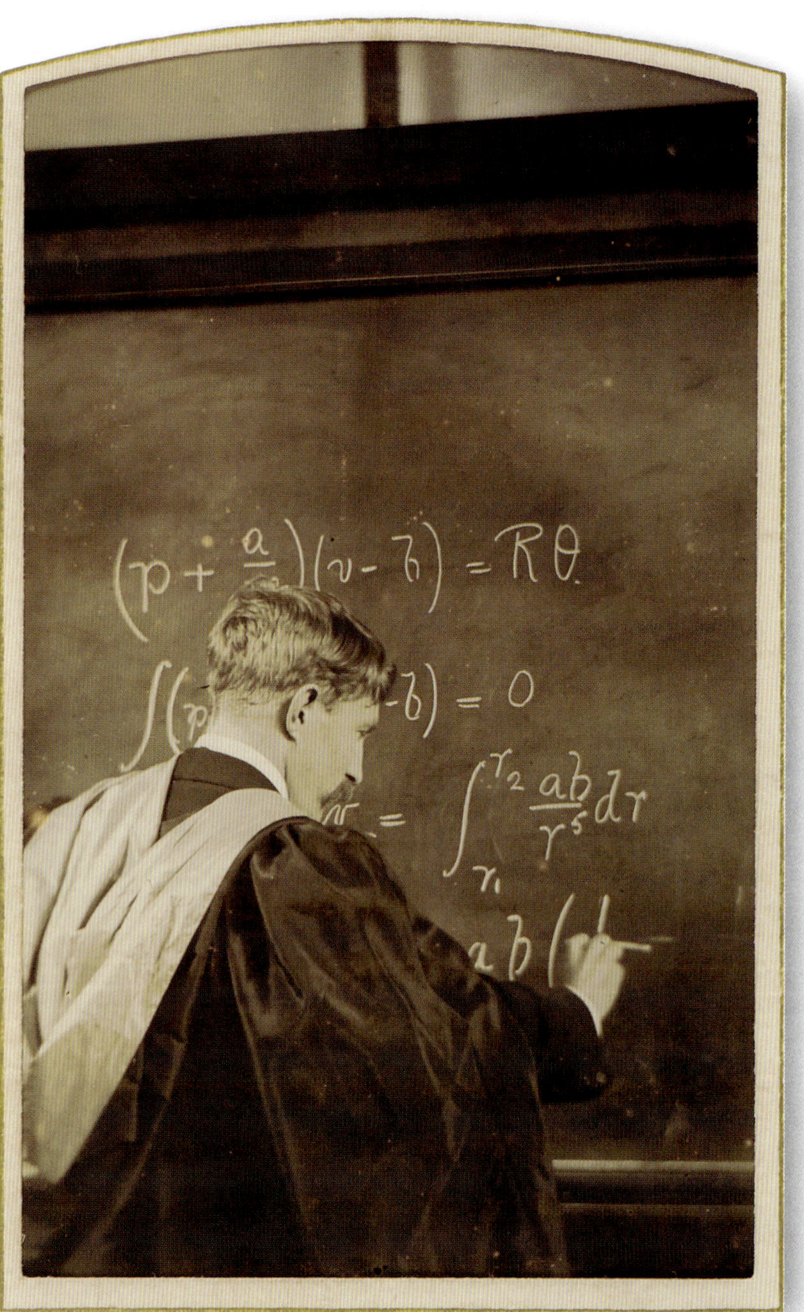

Photographer unknown. *Dr J.W. Mellor*. c. 1904. Album 518. Donated by A.J. Mulder, 2001.

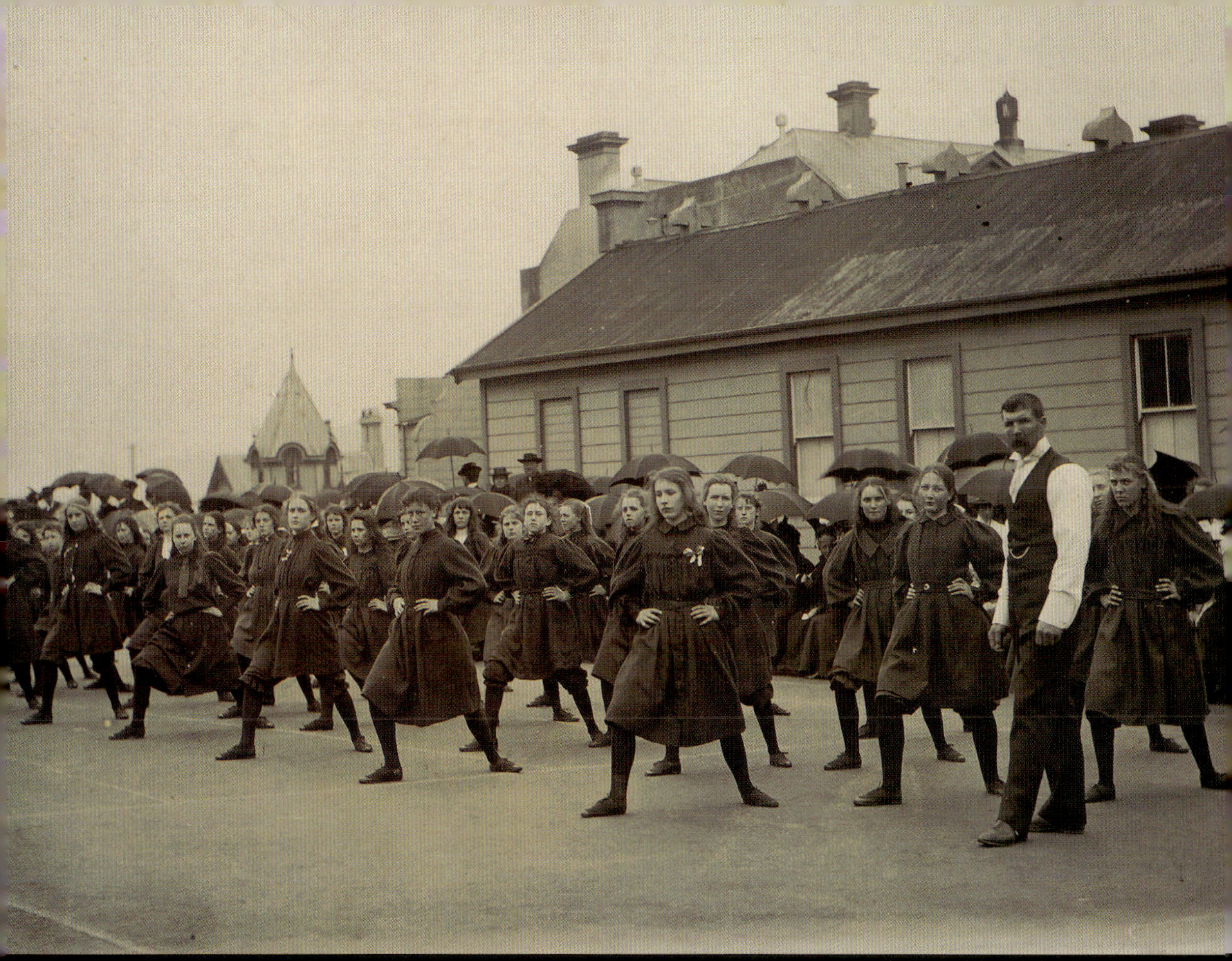

Young womanhood • 1905

Photographer unknown. *Otago Girls' High School Gymnasium Class.* 1905. Gelatin silver print. Donated by G.J. Griffiths.

Established in 1871, Otago Girls' High School in Dunedin was the first public secondary school for girls n New Zealand. Around the turn of the twentieth century, ›hysical education became increasingly important in its :urriculum, and this photograph, one of a number taken n 1905, probably by a photographer for the *Otago Witness*, well conveys the discipline instructor John Hanna instilled n his girls.

John Hanna had a knowledge of the latest methods of ›hysical training being used in Great Britain. In 1902, he ›ad spent five months visiting gymnasiums in Scotland, England and Ireland, and on his return Hanna introducec netball, a game which eventually gathered immense popularity around New Zealand.

The girls exercised in gym frocks which the headmistress Miss Marchant, introduced, also after a period of study leave in England in 1901. Here they appear in the playgrounc outside the old, dilapidated school buildings which frontec on to Tennyson Street. Miss Marchant campaigned anc was successful in gaining government funding for a new architecturally designed building constructed on the same site not long afterwards in 1910. AP

Country childhood • c. 1905

Selected for the cover of Janine Graham's 1991 Hocken Lecture 'My brother and I … ', this photograph says much about family bonds and childhood in New Zealand in the early 1900s. It is one of a collection of over 900 photographs taken by amateur photographer Dr J.E. Fitzgerald, a father of six and surgeon at the small South Otago township of Kaitangata from 1891 to 1912.

The photograph shows eldest daughter Dorothy reading to some of her siblings in a field. Dorothy's mother had died giving birth to Bobby on the left. Their father had since married their mother's sister and the family had grown. The children sit on a rug laid over the prickly grass, leaning against a haystack sheltered by a row of macrocarpa trees behind.

The image forms a picture of love and innocence and a record of days spent close to nature. It combines a Victorian ideal with a New Zealand reality. It also shows the power of a book to capture children's imagination. Both Bobby (Robert) and Walden (in front) went on to become medical doctors. AP

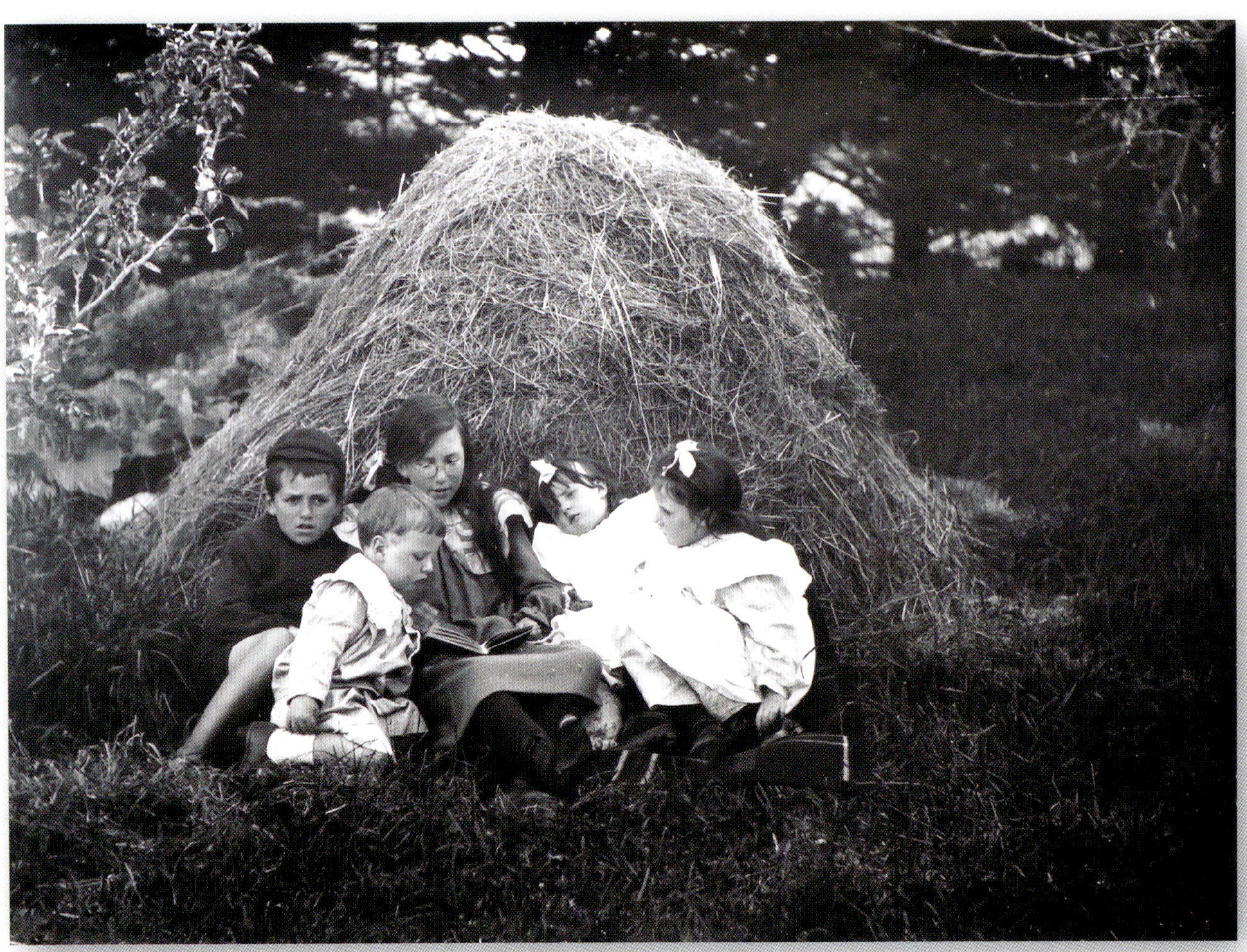

J.E. Fitzgerald. *Dorothy Reading*. c. 1905. Contact print from original glass plate negative. Fitzgerald Collection, no. 786. Donated by the Fitzgerald family.

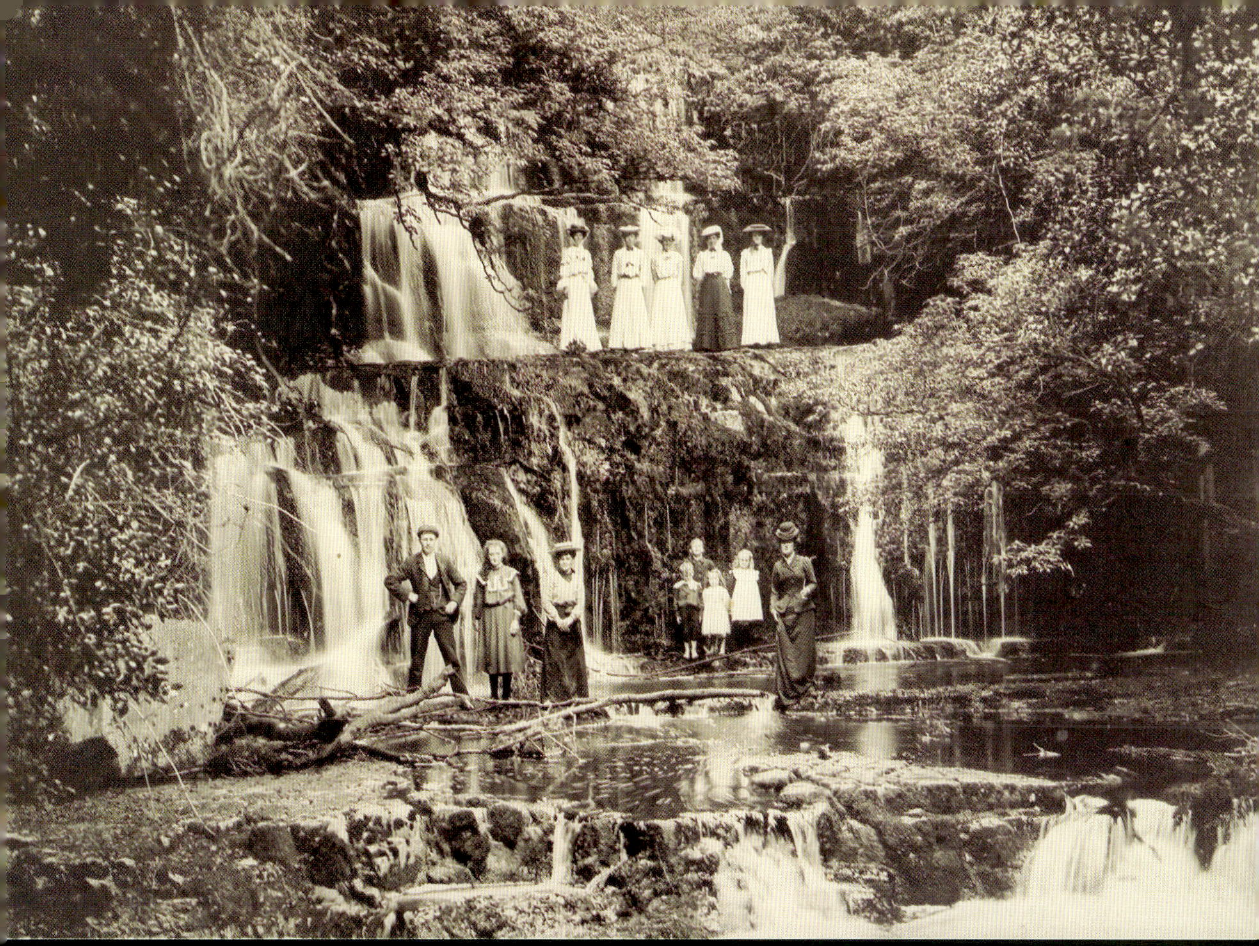

Cecil Pattillo. *Purakaunui Falls*. c. 1907. Silver gelatin print. Geddes collection. Donated by Iona Isaacs, 1997.

Art and Nature • c. 1907

In the two decades before the First World War, European New Zealanders had more time to enjoy the natural beauty of the country in which they were now settled and, increasingly, born. The Scenery Preservation Act 1903 ensured that some areas remained relatively intact.

This print of one such beauty spot, the Purakaunui Falls in the Catlins, constituted something of an enigma for many years until Ian Lochhead identified all of the people as members of the Findlater family from the Catlins area and attributed the photograph to Cecil Pattillo (1875–1968). Evidently Pattillo courted Susan Findlater (in the riding habit at bottom right) while she worked as his studio assistant in Dunedin.

The careful arrangement of figures relative to the falls of water and surrounding trees reveals that Pattillo had an eye for composition and a strong artistic bent. This group portrait in a landscape is unusual within his oeuvre. Pattillo's reputation has always rested on his career as a portrait photographer specialising in bridal photography. However, as was common amongst photographers, Pattillo also painted. He was no doubt aware of the many precedents in European art for placing figures in the landscape. AP

Dunedin from the air • 1910

The Dunedin company of Muir & Moodie was the biggest publisher of postcards in Australasia. It took over the Burton Brothers' business in 1898 and reissued many of their historic prints in postcard form. The top view of the Dunedin Town Hall and Octagon taken from a balloon, however, reveals the lengths the company was ready to go in order to produce new images. It is interesting to compare with a second card of Princes Street, below, which also offered a new bird's-eye view of the city.

Although taken at different times of the day, the two cards illustrate how the Exchange area was more the city centre than the Octagon as it is today. Both also show buildings no longer standing, such as the old St Paul's cathedral and the imposing Exchange Building at the bottom left, which had originally been designed as the Post Office in 1864–8. It served as the University for a few years, then a bank before becoming the Stock Exchange in 1900. This building was demolished in 1969. AP

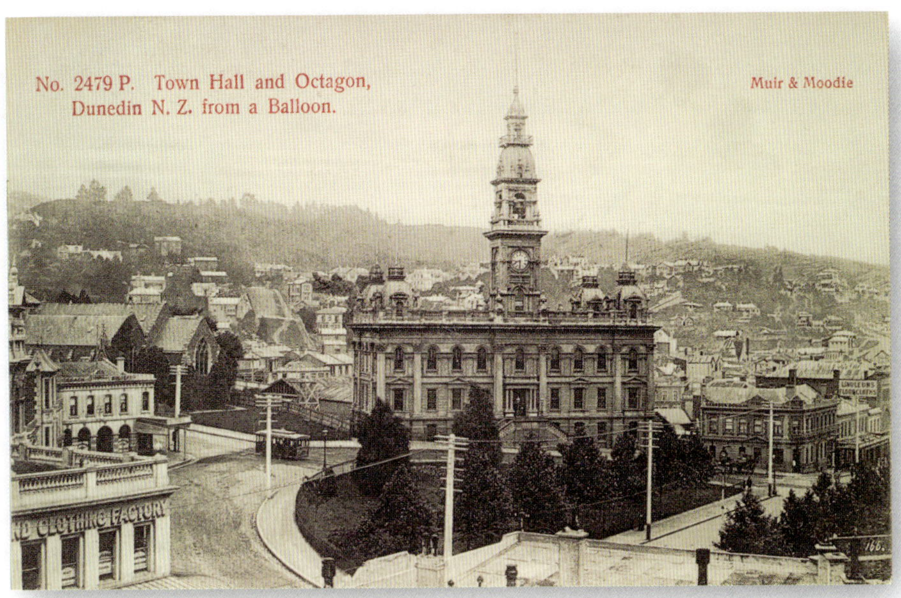

Muir & Moodie, No. 2479 P. *Town Hall and Octagon Dunedin N.Z. from a Balloon.* [1910]. Postcard. Provenance unknown.

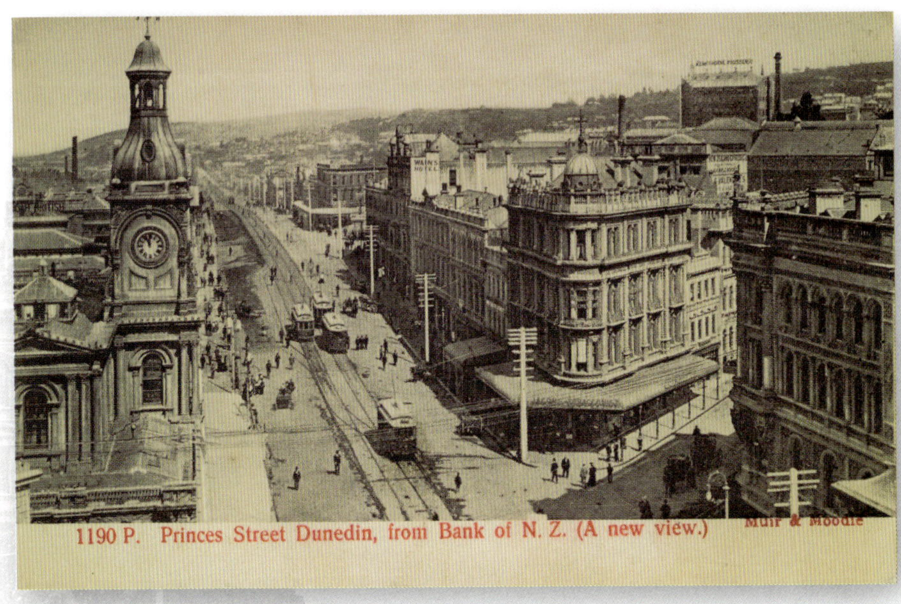

Muir & Moodie, No. 1190 P. *Princes Street Dunedin, from Bank of N.Z. (A new view.)* [1910]. Postcard. Provenance unknown.

The Terra Nova at Cape Evans • 1911

In Herbert Ponting's book, *The Great White South*, the author and photographer described the scene:

> The *Terra Nova* was wonderfully picturesque as she lay berthed alongside the ice; she was of a type nowadays seldom met with on the seas, and her square-rigged masts and rugged hull, mirrored in the water, lent great effect to my pictures. ... One day a small iceberg bore towards her, scraping along the icefoot until its further progress was arrested not a hundred yards away. This berg was all a-hanging with icicles, from the warmth of the sun, and it composed with the ship to add a treasured page to my now rapidly growing album.

Ponting's large-scale prints have a well-recognised place in the history of world photography, not only as a pioneering record of Scott's 1910–12 Antarctic expedition and for their considerable artistic merit, but also as evidence of technical advances at the time. Ponting equipped his laboratory on board the *Terra Nova* with the most rapid plates available, with the idea of capturing the Aurora Australis. He experimented with artificial light, colour filters and orthochromatic plates while in Antarctica, in this case choosing to produce a green-toned carbon print.
AP

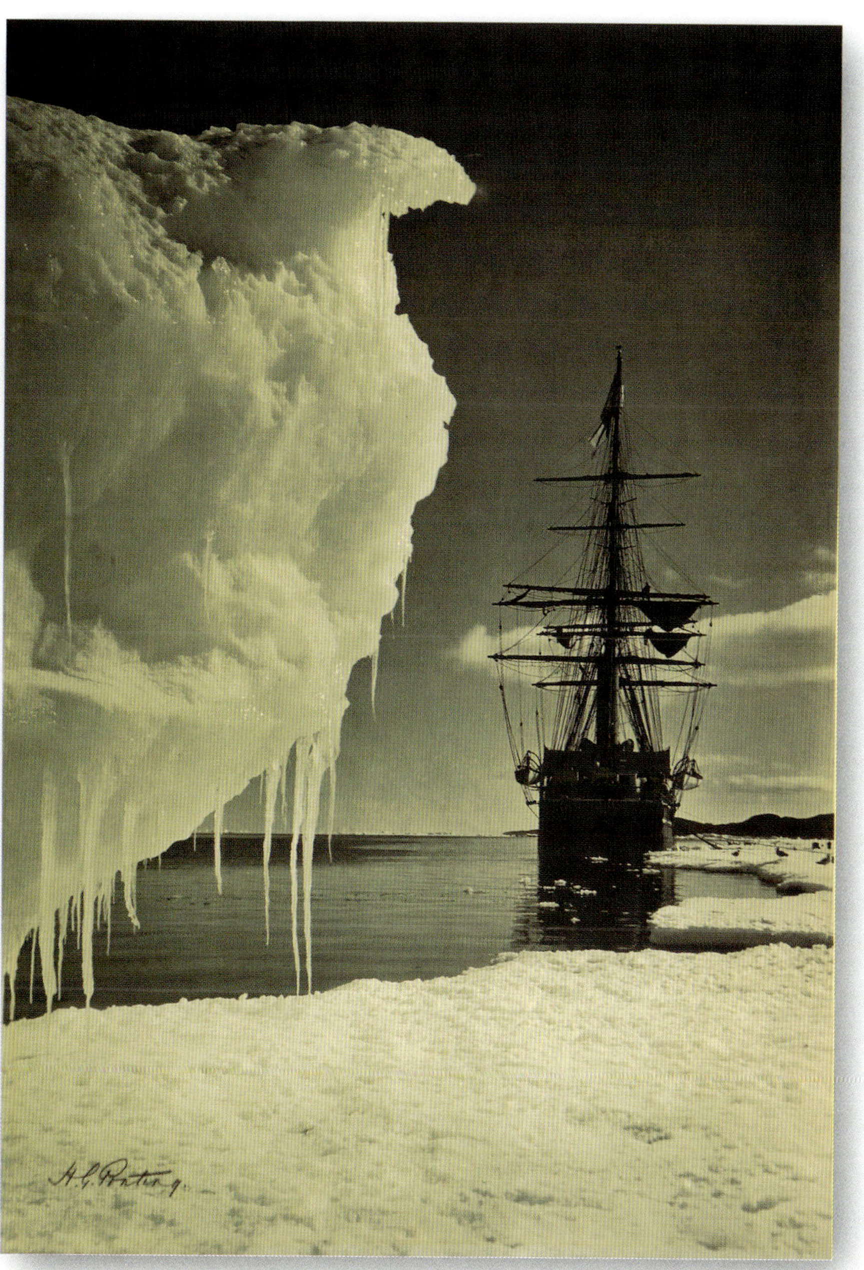

Herbert Ponting. *The Terra Nova at the Ice-foot, Cape Evans*. 1911. Green-toned carbon print. Provenance unknown.

Kauri logging near Hokianga • 1913

Around 1912, Arthur Northwood (1880–1949) decided to document every aspect of kauri logging in the Kohukohu area, near Hokianga, because these magnificent trees were becoming a limited resource. European colonists had quickly realised the ready market for the high-quality, straight-grained timber in the building and furniture trades, and kauri gum was prized in the manufacture of varnish overseas.

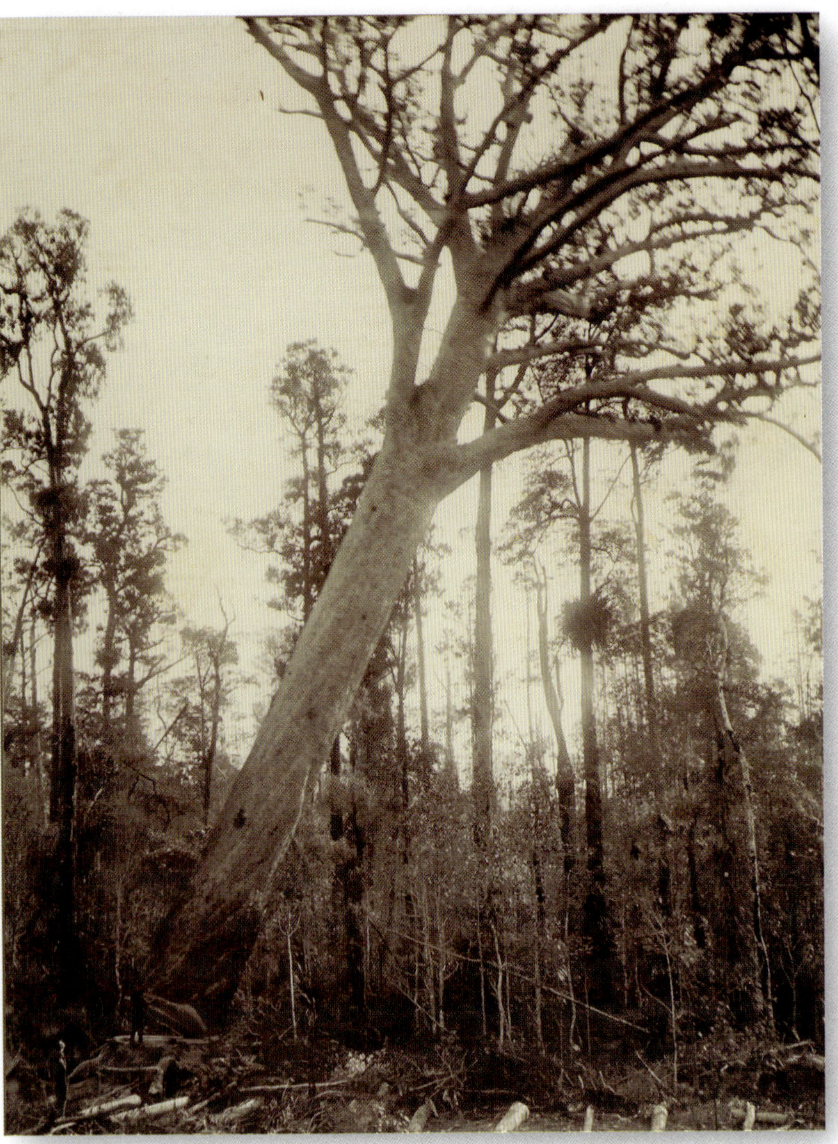

Arthur Northwood. *Falling*. 1913.
Silver gelatin print. Album 97. Purchased, before 1970.

Album 97 contains sixty prints, that on page 24 capturing a kauri in motion as it fell. The printed introduction at the beginning of the album notes, 'You can imagine what a crashing roar the king of the forest gives when he falls, sweeping out of his path all obstacles of whatever description.' Men at the bottom were dwarfed by the height of the tree, which could grow to more than fifty metres high with a girth of up to sixteen metres.

Other photographs in the album reveal the skill and hard work involved with felling and removing the huge logs from the bush. The logs were dragged out by bullock and steam train or else floated down stream to the coast. AP

Ross Sea whaling • 1923–24

The Norwegian Hvalfangerselskap Rosshavet, otherwise known as the Ross Sea Whaling Company, was the first to be granted a whaling licence for the Ross Sea and an album in the Hocken Photographs Collection helps record their pioneering expedition in the summer of 1923–24.

A fleet of six vessels braved the dangerous conditions. They found mostly blue whales, which were harpooned out at sea, winched up, pumped with compressed air and chained to one of the Star catchers as shown here, so that just their bloated underbellies lay above the water. The carcases were then towed to the mother ship at Discovery Inlet for processing.

In *Whaling in the Frozen South* Alan Villiers describes how temperatures of 30°F below zero left decks and rigging encrusted with ice. Noses and ears bled in the wind; faces, mouths and hands became frost bitten daily; and the stench was all-pervading. The four-month season disappointed investors, with only about 200 whales yielding an average of eighty-five barrels of oil each, but they were the biggest and fattest blue whales ever seen and the following season proved more lucrative. AP

Photographer unknown. *Rosshavet Whaling*. 1923–24. Gelatin silver print. Album 54. Provenance unknown.

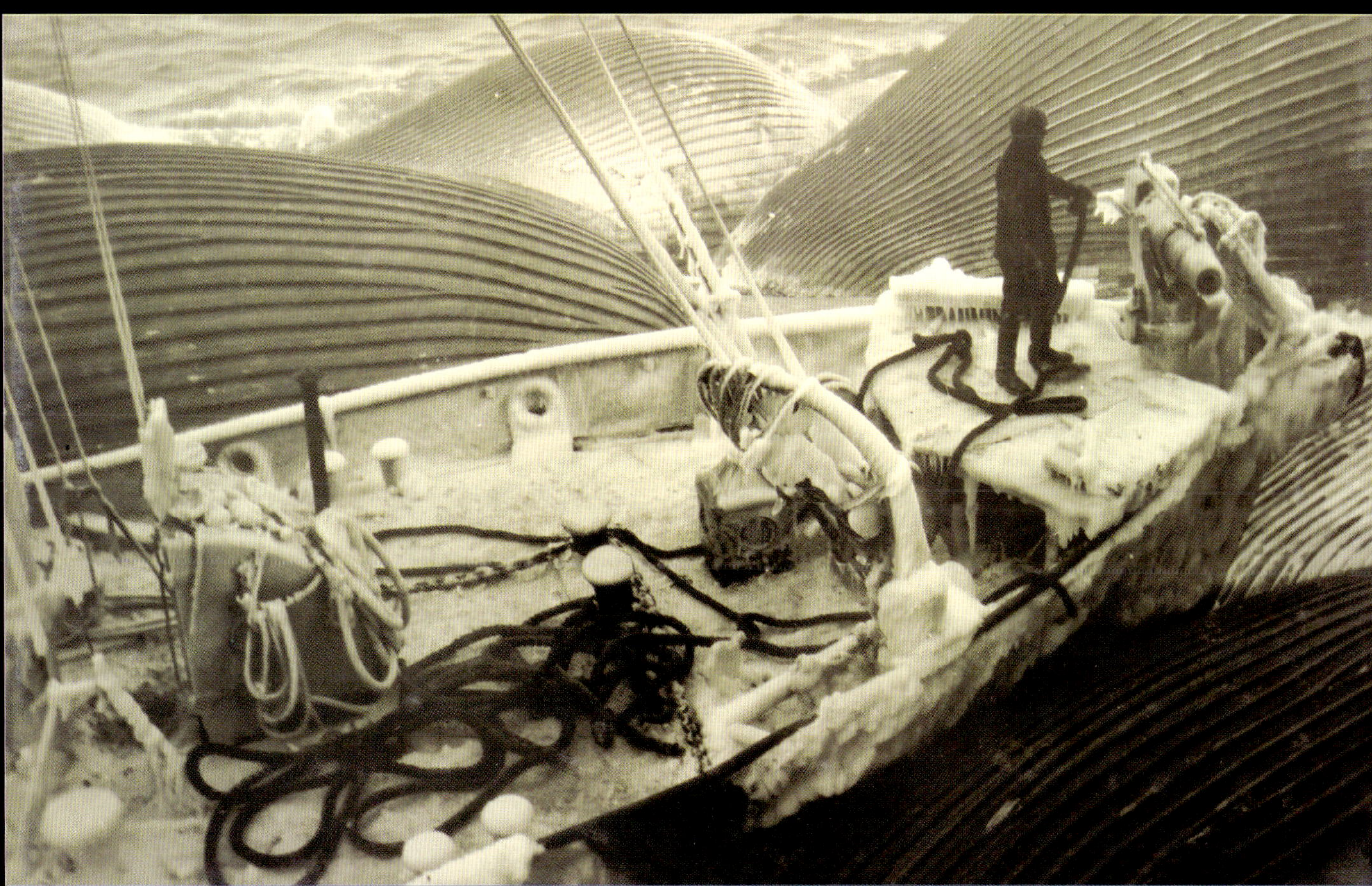

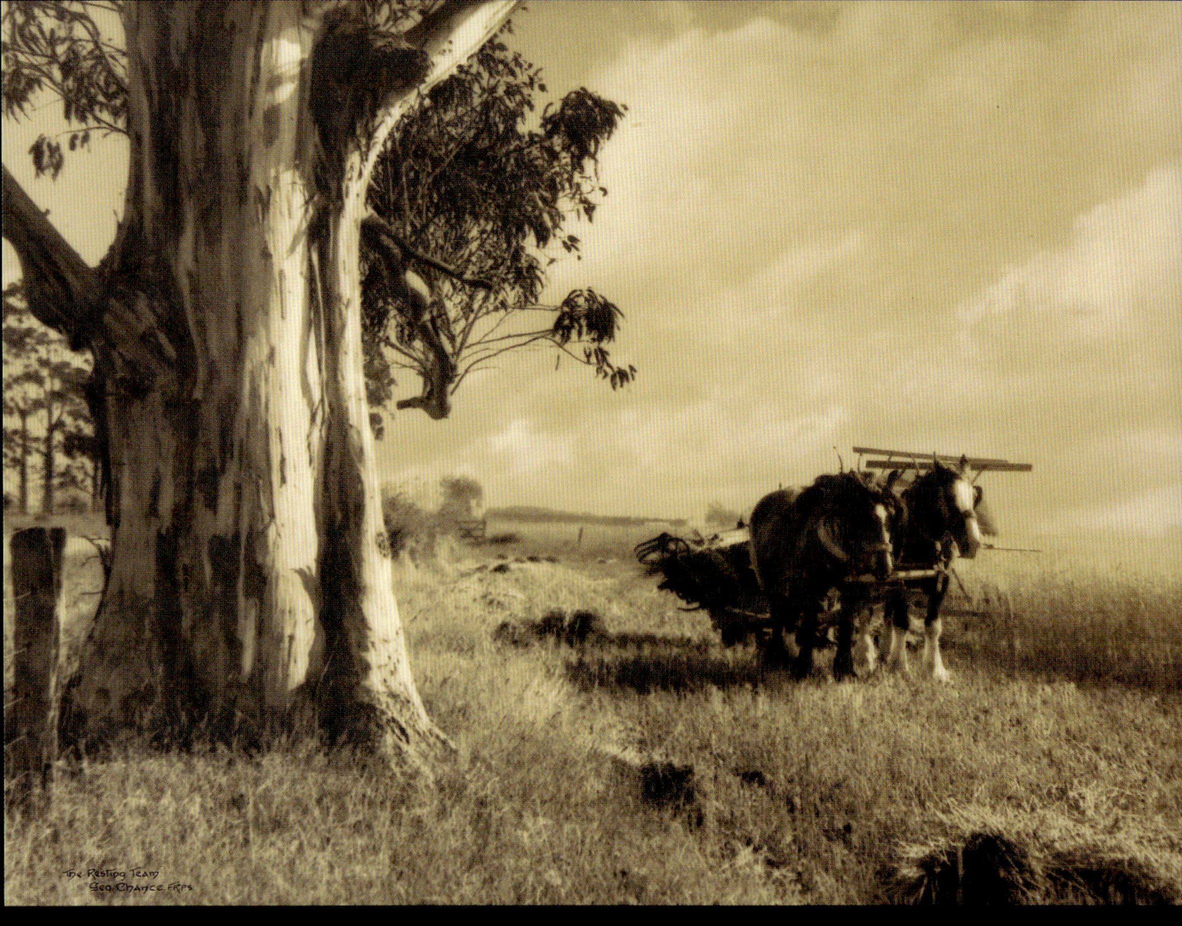

George Chance. *The Resting Team, South Otago*. 1932. Gelatin silver print. Deposited by George Chance jnr, 1991.

Photography as Art • 1932

Working in the pictorial genre, professional Dunedin photographer George Chance (1885–1963) catered to the interwar nostalgia for the peaceful rural lifestyle and successfully promoted photography as an art form in its own right.

An explanation of *The Resting Team*, written by the photographer and contained amongst the extensive Chance archive in the Hocken photographs collection, reveals just how deceptive this photograph is in its naturalistic simplicity. The print was not a single snapshot but a composite work with the clouds painstakingly grafted on, before the days of Photoshop. He used a screen and carefully manipulated the tones so as to resemble the soft-focus and colour of an etching.

The team had to be resting because Chance caught the farmer at a bad moment when the machinery had broken down and he refused to pose for the camera. The photographer balanced himself on top of a fencepost to be at the right height. Finally, Chance focused on the old gum tree which he had long admired. He liked the bark and texture and the fact that it had stood near Milton for years like a 'crusader in armour', planted by some hard-working pioneer. AP

Ready for anything • c. 1942

Some unexpected treasures lie hidden amongst the pages of amateur snapshot albums, such as those of George Hendry, owner of a Dunedin menswear shop and member of a local artillery unit during the Second World War.

This photograph is at once comic and disturbing. The soldier in the middle of the second row looks particularly silly, with his glasses reflecting the light like the paua shell eyes of the row of tiki above. At the same time, the sight of gas masks, protection against a particularly insidious death, conveys a sense of foreboding.

There is the added discomfort that the boys posed outside the entrance of Otakou marae on the Otago Peninsula were perhaps not showing due respect to the carved concrete impressions behind. A second photograph in the album of the group unmasked reveals that most soldiers were of European descent, including George Hendry seated on the right end of the front row. But then, the masks, like the entranceway, acted as a barrier to the outside world and the army was there to protect everyone.... AP

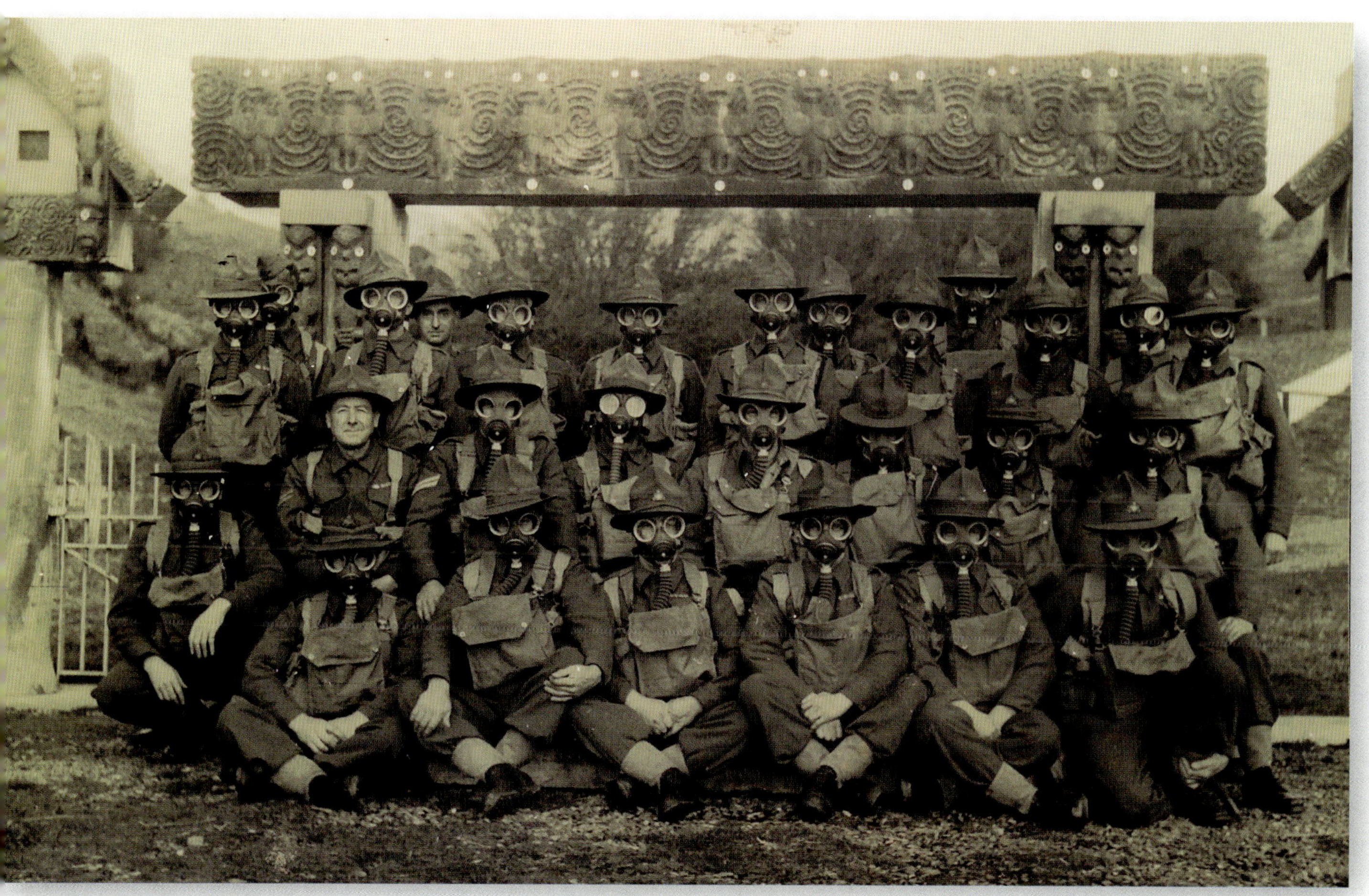

Photographer unknown. *Post 10 in Gas Masks*. c. 1942. Gelatin silver print. Donated by Graham Hendry, 2002.

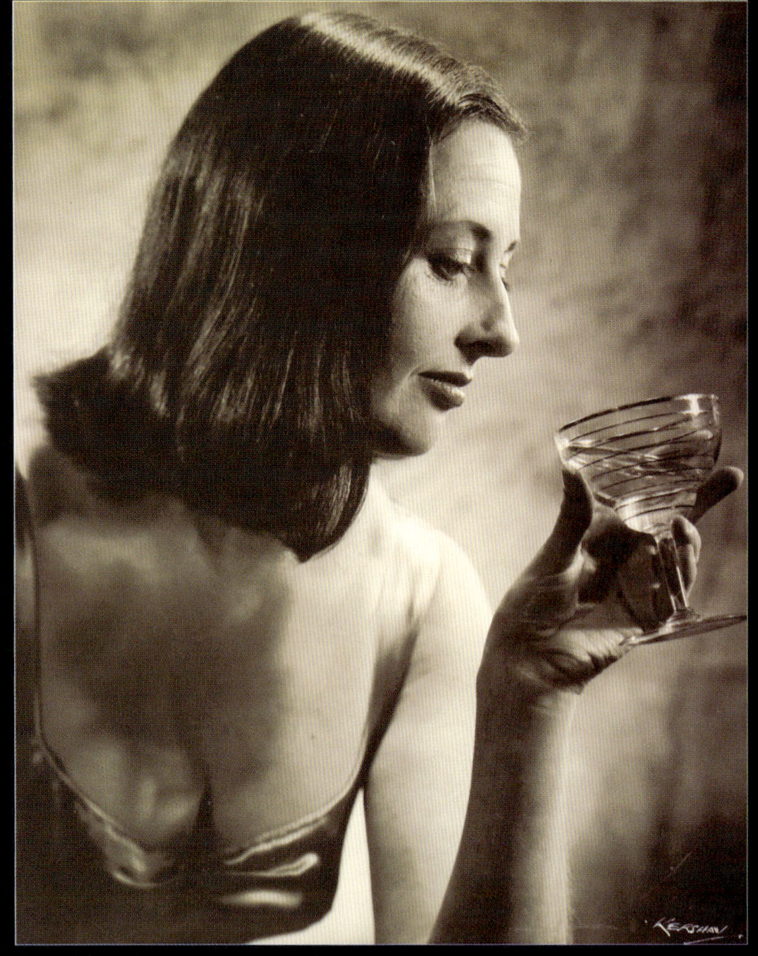

Portrait of Shona McFarlane • 1950s

Morris Kershaw. *The Sophisticate*. Undated. Gelatin silver print.
Donated by Morris Kershaw, 1964.

Morris Kershaw (1912–77) was a leading light in the early days of the association of professional photographers in New Zealand. His portrait of Shona McFarlane is one of a small series of large format prints from a much larger number of his photographs in the Hocken photographs collection.

Titled *The Sophisticate*, the black and white photograph shows the then unknown young art teacher holding a fine glass elegantly in one hand like a connoisseur of good living. She is posed as if considering the quality of the wine, but the viewer does not necessarily share her focus. The view of the model's cleavage and silky, shoulder-length hair suggests something possibly even more alluring. Kershaw's use of dramatic lighting further heightens the tension in this portrait of a woman.

The Sophisticate was a publicity shot for Kershaw's Dunedin studio, which played perfectly to the popular thirst for Hollywood-style glamour in New Zealand in the 1950s. Shona McFarlane CBE (1929–2001) later became a celebrity in her own right as a painter, writer, panellist on the television programme 'Beauty and the Beast', and wife of politician Alan Highet. AP

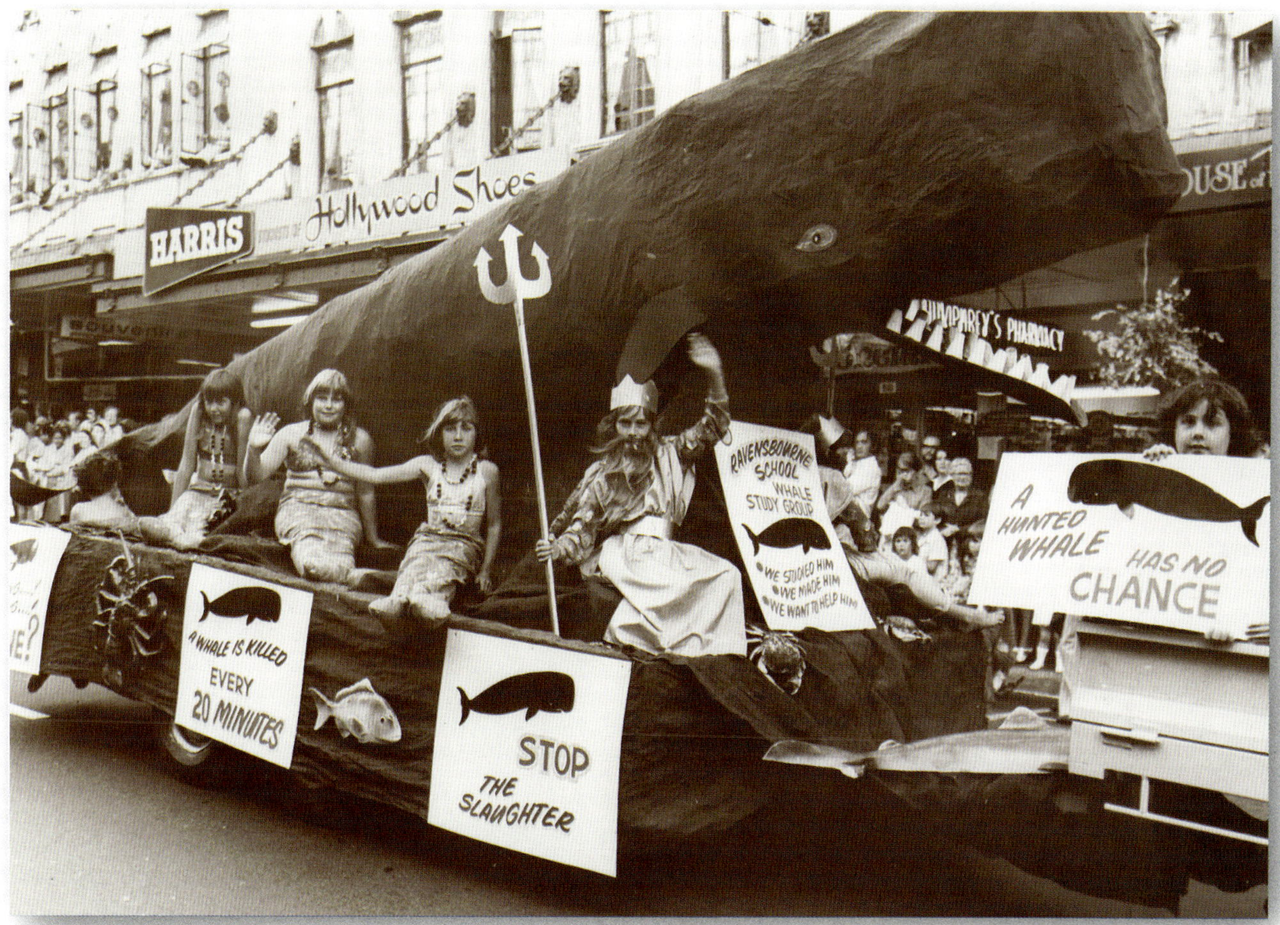

Save The Whales • 1978

Photographer unknown. *Festival Week, 1978*. Gelatin silver print. Donated by the *Otago Daily Times*, 1983.

The Festival Week procession of floats along the main street of Dunedin each February is a combined community effort. Children especially enjoy participating in the spectacle, and judging from this newspaper photograph, the pupils of Ravensbourne School spent hours preparing their protest against the slaughter of whales in 1978.

In 1978, some whale species were on the verge of extinction due to their low reproductive rate and depletion by commercial fishermen from around the world. Three years earlier the international organisation, Greenpeace, had begun direct action at sea against whalers and four years later, in 1982, the International Whaling Commission succeeded in passing a moratorium for whale protection.

Whales are an emotive subject for Pākehā and Māori New Zealanders, partly because these huge mammals regularly visit our waters and sometimes need to be rescued from the beaches. As the children dressed as King Neptune and mermaids suggest, whales are also part of our joint mythological heritage. The extraordinary nature of whales has long appealed to the human imagination and the distinctive shape of the sperm whale, which the children have chosen to construct, is the most archetypal of all. AP

Christine Webster (b. 1958) studied drama before taking up photography in 1979. After photographing people at night under street lighting she recognised the dramatic potential of darkness. Black backgrounds and elements of performance continue to dominate her work and are visible in *Clairvoyant*.

Taken in France, this life-size cibachrome image belongs to Webster's *The Players* series, named after the line in *As You Like It*: 'All the world's a stage and all the men/women merely players.' Revising the allegorical figure-type, the series, which includes *Child, Wanton, Provider, Gambler, Seducer, Rescuer, Rememberer, Judge* and *Soldier*, uses Webster's Parisian landlady Sarah as model. The costumes and highly directed poses allow Webster to reveal how gender roles are constructed and perceived.

In *Clairvoyant* the process of gender construction is hinted at by the model holding two mirrors. An implement for looking at ourselves, the mirror was also central to feminist theorist Simone de Beauvoir's idea that women often see their identity in terms of how they appear to other people. Webster's female subject does not subscribe to the passive role conventionally associated with the artist's model. Her forward-facing pose is assertive yet serene and her powerful eyes deflect the viewer's gaze. NP

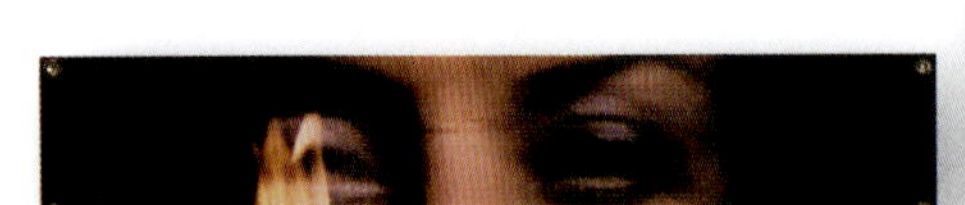

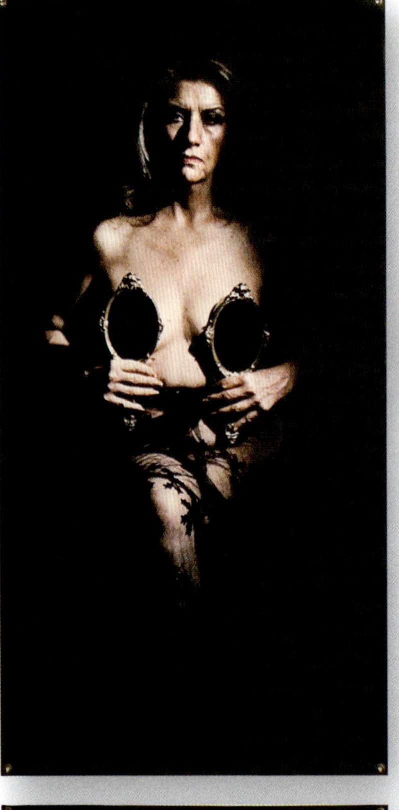

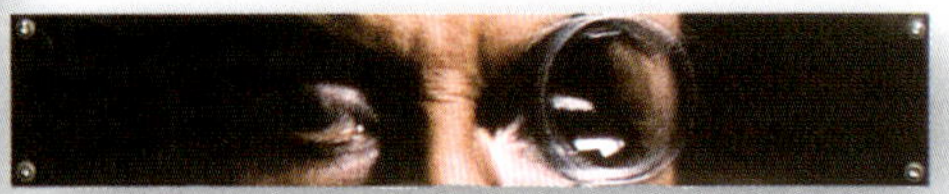

Christine Webster. *Clairvoyant*. 1991. Cibachrome. Purchased, 1992.

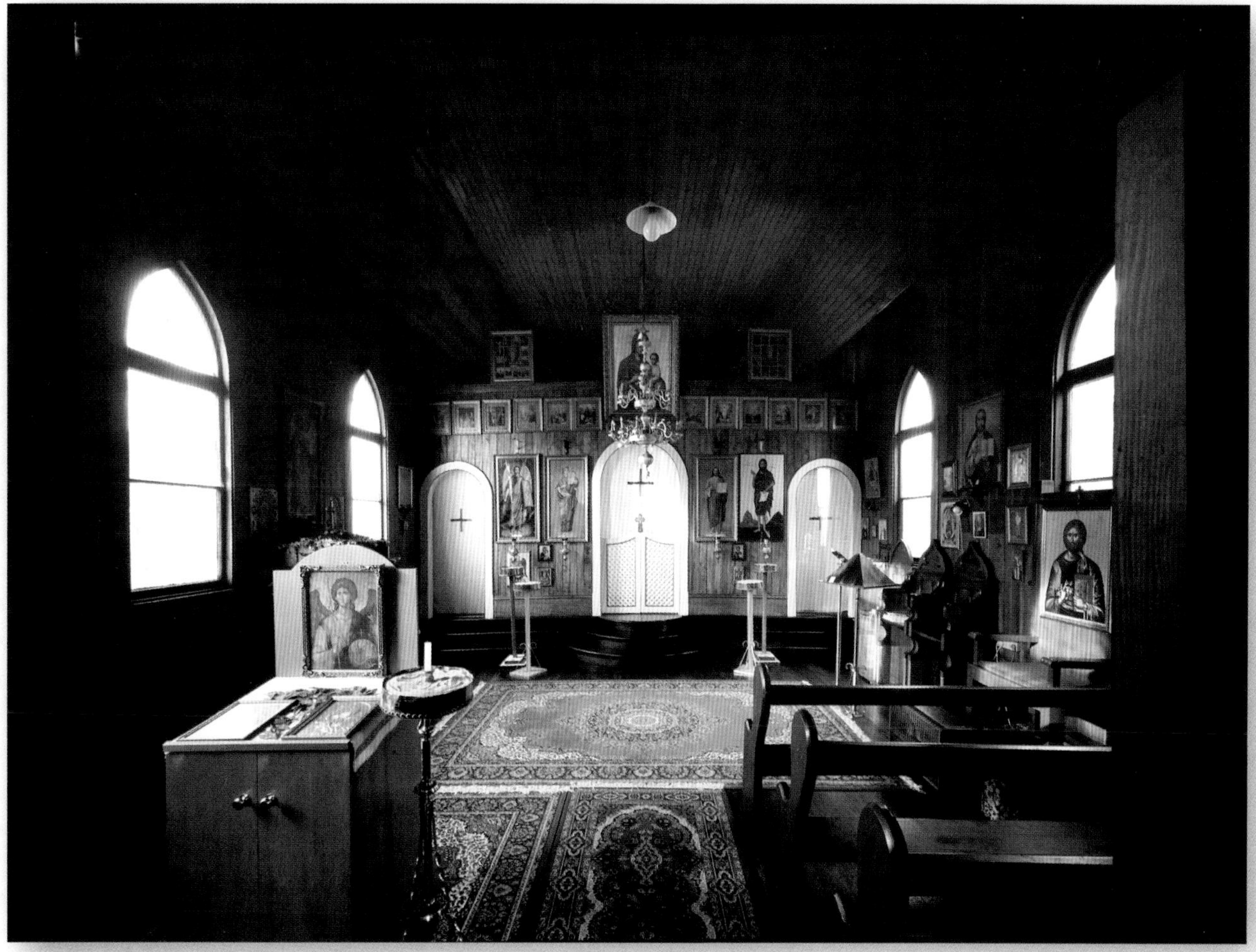

The past as present • 1999

Laurence Aberhart. *Interior #1, St Michael's Orthodox Church, St Kilda, Dunedin, 16 April 1999.* Contact print. Purchased, 2001.

Straddling the gap between past and present, Laurence Aberhart (b. 1949) used a nineteenth century plate camera to photograph the interior of St Michael's Orthodox Church, Dunedin, in 1999. It was New Zealand's first purpose-built Orthodox church, consecrated 14 January 1911, and still stands, an unassuming little building on the outside, in the suburb of St Kilda.

While Aberhart's intention seems, in part, to have been to record this largely unappreciated piece of history, he has also imposed his own vision. Most obvious is Aberhart's decision to render the exotic wealth of gold-painted icons and brass candle sticks in black and white. Their richness is conveyed in detail and tone. The photographer's distortion of space adds another dimension – the converging lines of the wooden ceiling giving width and depth to what, in reality, is a very confined space.

The print belongs to a series of unpopulated, communal spaces Aberhart has taken during the course of his career. The absence of any people accentuates the feeling of stillness and silence in his work, though the presence of light brings life. AP

Principal Benefactors

This list acknowledges the generosity of principal benefactors, who through their gifts of money and additions to the Hocken Collections, often over many years, have helped build them to their present eminence. Many others, too numerous to list here, have also contributed substantially.

1906	Original subscribers
1906	New Zealand Government
1907	Dr T.M. Hocken
1910	Public subscribers
1913–33	Mrs Elizabeth Hocken
1918	A. Moritzson
1919–77	Dr H.D. Skinner
1920–36	Sir Frederick Chapman
1922	Mrs W.D. McCurdie
1928–32	T. Lindsay Buick
1938	T. Lindsay Buick Estate
1955	Sargood Trust
1955	de Beer family
1955–	G.S. Parsonson
1955–72	J. Herries Beattie
1956–88	Rodney Kennedy
1956–72	Charles Brasch
1960–	Dr R.P. Hargreaves
1961	Charlton Edgar
1962	Hon. J.T. Paul
1962	Kenneth Webster
1964–90	Dr Morris N. Watt
1965–2005	Professor F. Fastier
1966	E.W. Hunter
1966–	Dr Roger Collins
1968–79	James K. Baxter
1969	G.W. Armitage
1969–	Dr George Griffiths
1970	Horace Tily
1970–2002	Janet Frame
1971–	Ian Farquhar
1972–	QEII Arts Council/Creative NZ
1972–81	Colin McCahon
1973–96	Charles Brasch Estate
1973	Jack and Ethel McCahon
1974	Frank H. Canaday
1974–83	R.A.K. Mason
1978	Australasian Performing Rights Assn
1980–98	Rev. Warren Green
1984	C.E.R. Webber Estate
1986–	Professor J.S. Ryan
1988–91	George Chance jnr
1991–	Friends of the Hocken Collections
1991	Bruce Godward
1991	Anne McCahon
1992	Hall-Jones family
1993	Peter Bennie Estate
1995	Patricia France Estate
1995	A.J. & L.P. Wilson Estate
1996	Lottery Environment and Heritage
1997–	Community Trust of Otago
1997	Alexander McMillan Trust
1998	Community Trust of Southland
1998–	A.A.W. Jones Charitable Trust
1998	Digital Equipment Corp. (NZ) Ltd
2002–4	N.Z. Lottery Grants Board
2002	Ministry of Foreign Affairs
2005	Frances Alexander Estate

Acknowledgements

Many have helped make this book. Martin Anderson, Director of Information Services, and Michael Wooliscroft, University, Librarian, got the project under way in 2004. The early blessing and practical financial support of Professor David Skegg, Vice-Chancellor, were crucial. Sue Pharo, University Librarian from 2005, has given every assistance throughout. The steering committee, under Professor Lyn Tribble, provided essential guidance. Its other members were Professors Erik Olssen and Tom Brooking, Dr John Broughton, Karin Warnaar followed by Ruth McKenzie-White of the University's Marketing Department, Sue Pharo and Maureen Miller from the University Library, Kathy Young of the University's Development Office, Wendy Harrex of the Otago University Press, and myself as Hocken Librarian and editor.

Especial thanks are reserved for staff of the Hocken Collections. In many ways this is their book. Despite the press of other duties, collectively and individually they made most suggestions for inclusion, contributed almost three-quarters of the individual descriptions, wrote section introductions, and otherwise gave general support. They are: Anna Blackman, Ian Chambers, Lucy Clark, Dr Ali Clarke, Amy Coleman, Karen Craw, Malcolm Deans, Laura Elliott, Judith Holloway, Mark Hughes, Pennie Hunt, Susan Irvine, Anne Jackman, Mary Lewis, Katherine Milburn, Paulette Milnes, Dr David Murray, Dr Anna Petersen, Natalie Poland, Mark Quarrie, Alexander Ritchie and Megan Vaughan, as well as myself. I particularly wish to thank: Anne Jackman, who also shouldered much of my normal work to allow me time for editing; Dr Anna Petersen, who helped with final editing, checking, proofing, and indexing, particularly the photographs, and paintings and drawings sections; and Laura Elliott, who gave essential administrative support. Latterly, Jennifer Black, Hocken Operations Manager, has ensured my full attention to the project.

Of the twenty-six contributors, eight were from outside the Hocken Collections: Dr Donald Kerr, Ian Farquhar, Dr Jim Williams, Dr John Broughton, John Milnes, Linda Tyler, Dr Noel Waite, and Dr Terry Hearn. Grateful thanks are given to these, and also to copyright owners who gave permission to reproduce images.

My co-editor, Linda Tyler, Curator of Pictorial Collections before her departure for Auckland early 2006, developed the initial structure of the book, contributed to its design, and made many of the initial selections. Later, she was responsible for the Paintings and Drawings section.

All photography was commissioned from Bill Nichol, and the design work has been superbly rendered by Jenny Cooper of the Otago University Press. Wendy Harrex, publisher at the Press, managed the finances and steered the book determinedly through publication. Essential fundraising was organised by Kathy Young.

Finally, this project has in part been funded by a number of donors, whose generosity is gratefully acknowledged. They are listed separately.

Stuart Strachan

Hocken Librarian

May 2007

Treasures Index